IN THE SHADOW OF THE TEMPLE

JEWISH INFLUENCES ON EARLY CHRISTIANITY

OSKAR SKARSAUNE

InterVarsity Press
Downers Grove, Illinois

InterVarsity Press
P.O. Box 1400, Downers Grove, IL 60515-1426
World Wide Web: www.ivpress.com
E-mail: mail@ivpress.com

©2002 by Oskar Skarsaune

InterVarsity Press® is the book-publishing division of InterVarsity Christian Fellowship/USA®, a student movement active on campus at hundreds of universities, colleges and schools of nursing in the United States of America, and a member movement of the International Fellowship of Evangelical Students. For information about local and regional activities, write Public Relations Dept., InterVarsity Christian Fellowship/USA, 6400 Schroeder Rd., P.O. Box 7895, Madison, WI 53707-7895, or visit the IVCF website at <www.ivcf.org>.

Cover photograph: Erich Lessing/Art Resource, N.Y.

ISBN 0-8308-2670-X

Printed in the United States of America ∞

Library of Congress Cataloging-in-Publication Data
Skarsaune, Oskar, 1946-
    In the shadow of the temple: Jewish influences on early Christianity/Oskar Skarsaune.
    p. cm.
    Includes bibliographical references.
    ISBN 0-8308-2670-X (cloth: alk. paper)
    1. Church history—Primitive and early church, ca. 30-600. 2. Christianity and other religions—Judaism—History. 3. Judaism—Relations—Christianity—History. 4. Christianity—Origin. 5. Judaism—Influence. I. Title.
BR165 .S59 2002
270.1—dc21   2001051600

CONTENTS

PART 1
THE MOTHER SOIL: JUDAISM FROM THE MACCABEES TO THE RABBIS

PART 2
CHRISTIAN BEGINNINGS: FROM JEWISH PARTY TO GENTILE CHURCH

PART 3

THE PERSISTENCE OF THE JEWISH HERITAGE: FAITH & ORDER IN THE EARLY
CHURCH

PART 4

Epilogue

Introduction

Yet another book on the Jewish roots of Christianity?

Yes, but hopefully with a difference. Most books on this topic are written by scholars for fellow scholars or as textbooks for students. This book is neither. It is intended for the general reader. Through the years, I have felt an increasing fascination with the story of Christian origins. In this book I try to convey some of that fascination.

I decided not to tell the story as a connected, chronological narrative. The approach is rather to focus on some selected themes, then illustrate them with representative episodes, snapshots, anecdotes.

When a scholar writes for the general reader, he or she normally uses quite some space to inform about different theories and points of view. I do that to a certain extent, but I have not been shy to present my own picture. It goes without saying that on many, perhaps all points, it is possible to see things differently. For this reason—and to answer the inquisitive reader's question, "Where can I read more, and something different, about this?"—the book is dotted with footnotes and "Suggestions for Further Reading." Many of the titles in these sections represent other points of view than those argued in the book.

My work on the book began in 1983 in Jerusalem. Since then, a formidable flood of books and articles on the theme has appeared. It has meant much work in trying to keep abreast of all these interesting publications; it has also been great fun. Hopefully some of the fun has spilled over into the book.

Most authors feel the need for serious disclaimers with regard to books as comprehensive as this one: it simply must contain mistakes of fact, judgement and method. It certainly does. But it lies in the very nature of historical inquiry that "results" are always preliminary and open to revision and improvement. I would very much like to think of a book like this as my contribution to an open-ended conversation going on in the enlightened community of readers.

Let me add a few lines about the book's main thesis. Many standard works about Jewish-Christian relations in antiquity more or less presuppose that all real contact and debate between Jews and Christians had already come to its natural end during the first decades of the second century A.D. According to this view, the Jewish matrix of Christianity is something to be treated quite briefly on the very first pages of textbooks on church history. The church historian often assumed that he or she could leave the more thorough treatment of Jewish background and Jewish matters to the New Testament experts, since this was most relevant to the first-century period and not very important with regard to the predominantly Gentile church of the second and later centuries.

In 1971 Robert L. Wilken published a groundbreaking study entitled *Judaism and the Early Christian Mind*. The surprising and refreshing thesis of this book was not revealed in the main title, which might create expectations of yet another book about first-century phenomena, but in the sub-title: *A Study of Cyril of Alexandria's Exegesis and Theology*. Cyril was a *fifth-century* bishop. In other words, he was not the kind of author one would think of as involved in anything like a living dialogue or encounter with real Judaism. According to the conventional wisdom, this encounter had by then been dead for more than three hundred years. But Wilken made a vigorous case for another view of the matter and opened his book with a review of Jewish-Christian relations in the entire period between A.D. 70 and Cyril's time. It emerges from this survey that borrowing from and debating with Jews cannot be written off as something that later Christian authors only excerpted from their Christian predecessors of the early period. The Jewish heritage and the anti-Jewish polemics of later Christian authors testify to an on-going, continuing encounter.

This means that the question of Jewish influences cannot be left behind once we pass, let's say, A.D. 150. It is a question that to some extent accompanies the church for a long period of time—and that later, in different periods of medieval and later church history, comes back as a challenge from contemporary Judaism.

Concerned with the Jewish roots of Christianity, this book begins earlier and with more emphasis on Jewish matters than is usual in church histories. For the same reason the approach chosen does not break off around A.D. 150, but is followed through the pre-Constantinian period.

I dedicate this book to the enthusiastic staff at the Caspari Center for Biblical and Jewish Studies in Jerusalem. Through many years, they have accompanied the birth process of this volume and contributed to it in no small measure. I owe them more than can easily be expressed here. I would also like at this point to greet the Jewish believers in Jesus, in Israel and abroad, for whom the book was originally conceived. If any of you find this book to be a good read, I am more than pleased and richly rewarded.

Temple Square
Most of the chapters contain a text box at the end, with this appearance and heading. Each pursues a theme that emerged more clearly at the end of my quest than it did in the beginning, a theme that stood out as a warp in the weave, as it were. What stands out here is the significance of the fact that Christianity originated within a Judaism that still had a temple. During the first forty years of the Jesus community, the temple in Jerusalem was still up and running. On the other hand, most of Christian literature and all of rabbinic literature come from a time when there was no temple, a time when the Christian and Jewish communities had learned to do without it, and do well without it. We often tend to project the picture given us in these sources back into the pre-70 situation. But then we miss the significance of the temple.

I list here some titles which inspired me to pursue this theme this way (others occur in the general bibliography). They are listed here once and for all, but ideas that emerged from my interaction with them will crop up in many of the "Temple Squares":

Horbury, William, ed. *Templum Amicitiae: Essays on the Second Temple Presented to Ernst Bammel.* Journal for the Study of the New Testament: Supplement Series 48. Sheffield: Sheffield Academic Press, 1991.

McKnight, Scot. "A Parting Within the Way: Jesus and James on Israel and Purity." In *James the Just and Christian Origins.* Edited by Bruce Chilton and Craig A. Evans. Supplements to Novum Testamentum 98. Leiden: Brill, 1999, pp. 83-129.

Schwartz, Daniel R. "Temple and Desert: On Religion and State in Second Temple Period Judaea." In *Studies in the Jewish Background of Christianity.* Wissenschaftliche Untersuchungen zum Neuen Testament 60. Tübingen: J. C. B. Mohr (Paul Siebeck), 1992, pp. 29-43.

Oskar Skarsaune
Oslo/Jerusalem

A Note on Abbreviations and References

The footnotes and the references to literature are not meant as scholarly documentation of my narrative and theses, but rather as pointers for the interested reader to literature for further information. Some books and studies are relevant for more than one chapter of the book; they are listed here below once and for all, under the abbreviated title used in all references to them. After each chapter, more literature relevant for that chapter is listed. Some studies referred to once are listed with full details in the notes only. In references to rabbinic literature, *TB* means the Babylonian Talmud *(Talmud Bavli), TJ* means *Talmud Jerushalmi,* the Jerusalem or so-called Palestinian Talmud. *M* is *Mishnah.* Other abbreviations should be self-explanatory or are explained in the general bibliography.

General Literature

Ådna/Kvalbein, *Mission of the Early Church:* Ådna, Jostein and Hans Kvalbein, eds. *The Mission of the Early Church to Jews and Gentiles.* Wissenschaftliche Untersuchungen zum Neuen Testament 127. Tübingen: Mohr Siebeck, 2000.

Alon, *The Jews 1-2:* Alon, Gedalyahu. *The Jews in Their Land in the Talmudic Age (70-640 C.E.).* 2 vols. Jerusalem: Magnes, 1980, 1984.

Alon, *Studies:* Alon, Gedalyahu. *Jews, Judaism and the Classical World: Studies in Jewish History in the Times of the Second Temple and Talmud.* Jerusalem: Magnes, 1977.

Barclay/Sweet, *Early Christian Thought:* Barclay, John and John Sweet, eds. *Early Christian Thought in Its Jewish Context.* Cambridge: Cambridge University Press, 1996.

Borgen, *Early Christianity:* Borgen, Peder. *Early Christianity and Hellenistic Judaism.* Edinburgh: T & T Clark, 1996.

Cohen, *Jewishness:* Cohen, Shaye J. D. *The Beginnings of Jewishness: Boundaries, Varieties, Uncertainties.* Berkeley/Los Angeles/London: University of California Press, 1999.

Cohen, *Maccabees to Mishnah:* Cohen, Shaye J. D. *From the Maccabees to the Mishnah.* Library of Early Christianity. Philadelphia: Westminster Press, 1987.

Compendia 1:1 etc.:

1:1-2: Safrai, Shmuel and Menachem Stern, eds. *The Jewish People in the First Century.* 2 vols. Compendia Rerum Iudaicarum ad Novum Testamentum Section One, 2 vols. Assen: Van Gorcum/ Philadelphia: Fortress, 1974, 1976.

2:1-3: Safrai, Shmuel, et al., eds. *The Literature of the Jewish People in the Period of the Second Temple and the Talmud.* 3 vols. Compendia Rerum Iudaicarum ad Novum Testamentum Section Two, 3 vols. Assen/Maastricht: Van Gorcum/Philadelphia: Fortress, 1984-1989.

The individual volumes:

Compendia 2:1: Mulder, J. and H. Sysling, eds. *Miqra: Reading, Translation and Interpretation of the Hebrew Bible in Ancient Judaism and Early Christianity.* Assen: Van Gorcum/Philadelphia: Fortress, 1988.

Compendia 2:2: Stone, Michael E., ed. *Jewish Writings of the Second Temple Period: Apocrypha, Pseudepigrapha, Qumran Sectarian Writings, Philo, Josephus.* Assen: Van Gorcum/Philadelphia: Fortress, 1984.

Compendia 2:3.1: Safrai, Shmuel and Peter J. Tomson, eds. *The Literature of the Sages.* Vol. 1: *Oral Torah, Halakha, Mishna, Tosefta, Talmud, External Tractates.* Assen/Maastricht: Van Gorcum/ Philadelphia: Fortress, 1987.

Compendia 2:3.2: Safrai, Shmuel, ed. *The Literature of the Sages.* Vol. 2: *Midrash, Aggada, Midrash Collections, Targum, Prayer.* Assen/Maastricht: Van Gorcum/Philadelphia: Fortress, 1989.

Conzelmann, *Gentiles:* Conzelmann, Hans. *Gentiles—Jews—Christians: Polemics and Apologetics in the Greco-Roman Era.* Philadelphia: Fortress, 1992 [German original: *Heiden—Juden—Christen: Auseinandersetzungen in der Literatur der hellenistisch römischen Zeit.* Tübingen: J. C. B. Mohr, 1981].

Danby: Danby, Herbert. *The Mishnah.* Oxford: Oxford University Press, 1933 [several reprints].

Daniélou, *Theology of Jewish Christianity:* Daniélou, Jean. *The Theology of Jewish Christianity. The Development of Christian Doctrine Before the Council of Nicaea 1.* London: Darton, Longman & Todd, 1964.

Davies/Finkelstein, *Judaism:* Davies, W. D. and Louis Finkelstein, eds. *The Cambridge History of Judaism.* Vol. 2: *The Hellenistic Age.* Cambridge: Cambridge University Press, 1989.

Dix, *Jew and Greek:* Dix, Gregory. *Jew and Greek: A Study in the Primitive Church.* London: A. and C. Black, 1953 [reprint, Dacre Press Westminster, 1967].

Dunn, *Jews and Christians:* Dunn, James D. G., ed. *Jews and Christians: The Parting of the Ways A.D. 70 to 135.* Wissenschaftliche Untersuchungen zum Neuen Testament 66. Tübingen: J. C. B. Mohr, 1992.

Dunn, *Partings:* Dunn, James D. G. *The Partings of the Ways Between Christianity and Judaism and Their Significance for the Character of Christianity.* London: SCM Press/Philadelphia: Trinity Press International, 1991.

Evans, *Jesus and His Contemporaries:* Evans, Craig A. *Jesus and His Contemporaries: Comparative Studies.* Arbeiten zur Geschichte des Antiken Judentums und des Urchristentums 25. Leiden: E. J. Brill, 1995.

Flusser, *Judaism:* Flusser, David. *Judaism and the Origins of Christianity.* Jerusalem: Magnes, 1988.

Frend, *The Early Church:* Frend, William H. C. *The Early Church,* Philadelphia: Fortress, 1982.

Frend, *Martyrdom and Persecution:* Frend, William H. C. *Martyrdom and Persecution in the Early Church: A Study of a Conflict from the Maccabees to Donatus.* Oxford: Basil Blackwell, 1965 [reprint, Grand Rapids, Mich.: Baker, 1981].

Frend, *The Rise of Christianity:* Frend, William H. C. *The Rise of Christianity.* London: Darton, Longman & Todd, 1984 [paperback ed. 1986].

Grabbe, *Judaism:* Grabbe, Lester L. *An Introduction to First Century Judaism: Jewish Religion and History in the Second Temple Period.* Edinburgh: T & T Clark, 1996.

Grant, *Augustus to Constantine:* Grant, Robert M. *Augustus to Constantine: The Rise and Triumph of Christianity in the Roman World.* San Francisco: Harper & Row, 1970 [paperback ed. 1990].

Haase, *Aufstieg:* Haase, Wolfgang, ed. *Aufstieg und Niedergang der Römischen Welt.* Vol. 2: *Principat.* Band 19-27. Berlin/New York: Walter de Gruyter, 1979-1993.

Harnack, *Mission:* Harnack, Adolf von. *Die Mission und Ausbreitung des Christentums in den ersten drei Jahrhunderten.* 2 vols. 4th ed. Leipzig: J. C. Hinrichs'sche Buchhandlung, 1924.

Hengel, *Judaism and Hellenism:* Hengel, Martin. *Judaism and Hellenism: Studies in Their Encounter in Palestine During the Early Hellenistic Period.* 2 vols. [in one vol.] London: SCM Press, 1981 [first English ed. in two vols. 1974].

Hengel, *Kleine Schriften 1-2:* Hengel, Martin. *Judaica et Hellenistica: Kleine Schriften 1; Judaica, Hellenistica et Christiana: Kleine Schriften 2.* Wissenschaftliche Untersuchungen zum Neuen Testament 90; 109. Tübingen: Mohr Siebeck, 1996, 1999.

Horbury, *Jews and Christians:* Horbury, William. *Jews and Christians in Contact and Controversy.* Edinburgh: T & T Clark, 1998.

Jocz, *Jewish People:* Jocz, Jacob. *The Jewish People and Jesus Christ: The Relationship Between Church and Synagogue.* 3rd ed. Grand Rapids, Mich.: Baker, 1979 [first ed. London: SPCK, 1949].

Lieu, *Image:* Lieu, Judith. *Image and Reality: The Jews in the World of the Christians in the Second Century.* Edinburgh: T & T Clark, 1996.

Lieu/North/Rajak, *The Jews:* Lieu, Judith; John North and Tessa Rajak, eds. *The Jews Among Pagans and Christians in the Roman Empire.* London: Routledge, 1992.

Meyers/Strange, *Archaeology:* Meyers, Eric M. and James F. Strange. *Archaeology, the Rabbis, and Early Christianity: The Social and Historical Setting of Palestinian Judaism and Christianity.* Nashville: Abingdon, 1981.

Mimouni, *Judéo-christianisme:* Mimouni, Simon Claude. *Le judéo-christianisme ancien: Essais historiques.* Patrimoines. Paris: Les éditions du Cerf, 1998

Murphy, *Religious World:* Murphy, Frederick J. *The Religious World of Jesus: An Introduction to Second Temple Palestinian Judaism.* Nashville: Abingdon, 1991.

Neusner/Frerichs, *To See:* Neusner, Jacob and Ernest S. Frerichs, eds. *"To See Ourselves as Others See Us": Christians, Jews, "Others" in Late Antiquity.* Chico, Calif.: Scholars Press, 1985.

New Schürer 1-3: Schürer, Emil. *The History of the Jewish People in the Age of Jesus Christ (175 B.C.-A.D. 135).* Revised and edited by G. Vermes, F. Millar and M. Black. 3 vols. Edinburgh: T & T Clark, 1973-1987.

Parkes, *Conflict:* Parkes, James. *The Conflict of the Church and the Synagogue: A Study in the Origins of Antisemitism.* London: Soncino Press, 1934 [reprint, New York: Hermon, 1974].

Rengstorf/Kortzfleisch, *Kirche und Synagoge:* Rengstorf, Karl Heinrich and Siegfried von Kortzfleisch, eds. *Kirche und Synagoge: Handbuch zur Geschichte von Christen und Juden.* Vol. 1. Stuttgart: Ernst Klett Verlag, 1968.

Rokeah, *Conflict:* Rokeah, David. *Jews, Pagans and Christians in Conflict.* Studia Post-Biblica 33. Leiden: E. J. Brill/Jerusalem: Magnes, 1982.

Rowland, *Origins:* Rowland, Christopher. *Christian Origins: An Account of the Setting and Character of the Most Important Messianic Sect of Judaism.* London: SPCK, 1985 [paperback reprint, London, 1933].

Sanders, *Judaism:* Sanders, E. P. *Judaism: Practice and Belief 63 BCE-66 CE.* Rev. ed. London: SCM Press/Philadelphia: Trinity Press International, 1992 [rev. ed. 1994; several reprints].

Sanders, *Self-Definition 1-3:* Sanders, E. P., et al., eds. *Jewish and Christian Self-Definition.* Vol. 1: *The Shaping of Christianity in the Second and Third Centuries.* Philadelphia: Fortress/London: SCM Press, 1980. Sanders, E. P., et al., eds. *Jewish and Christian Self-Definition.* Vol. 2: *Aspects of Judaism in the Greco-Roman Period.* Philadelphia: Fortress/London: SCM Press, 1981. Meyer, Ben F. and E. P. Sanders, eds. *Jewish and Christian Self-Definition.* Vol. 3: *Self-Definition in the Graeco-Roman World.* Philadelphia: Fortress/London: SCM Press, 1982.

Sanders, *Schismatics:* Sanders, Jack T. *Schismatics, Sectarians, Dissidents, Deviants: The First One Hundred Years of Jewish-Christian Relations.* Valley Forge, Penn.: Trinity Press International, 1993.

Sandmel, *Judaism:* Sandmel, Samuel. *Judaism and Christian Beginnings.* New York/Oxford: Oxford University Press, 1978.

Schiffman, *Text to Tradition:* Schiffman, Lawrence H. *From Text to Tradition: A History of Second Temple and Rabbinic Judaism.* Hoboken, N.J.: Ktav, 1991.

Schreckenberg 1: Schreckenberg, Heinz. *Die christlichen Adversus-Judaeos-Texte und ihr literarisches und historisches Umfeld (1.-11.Jh).* Europäische Hochschulschriften, Reihe 23 Theologie, 172. Frankfurt am Main/Bern: Peter Lang, 1982.

Schwartz, *Studies:* Schwartz, Daniel R. *Studies in the Jewish Background of Christianity.* Wissenschaftliche Untersuchungen zum Neuen Testament 60. Tübingen: J. C. B. Mohr (Paul Siebeck), 1992.

Segal, *Rebecca's Children:* Segal, Alan F. *Rebecca's Children: Judaism and Christianity in the Roman World.* Cambridge, Mass./London: Harvard University Press, 1986.

Shanks, *Parallel History:* Shanks, Hershel, ed. *Christianity and Rabbinic Judaism: A Parallel History of Their Origins and Early Development.* Washington D.C.: Biblical Archaeological Society, 1992/

London: SPCK, 1993.

Simon, *Verus Israel:* Simon, Marcel. *Verus Israel: Étude sur les relations entre chrétiens et juifs dans l'Empire Romain (135-425).* Bibliothèque des Écoles francaises d'Athènes et de Rome 166, 1948. Revised and expanded eds. Paris: Éditions E. de Boccard, 1964 and 1983. English trans.: *Verus Israel: A Study of the Relations Between Christians and Jews in the Roman Empire (A.D. 135-425).* 2nd ed. Oxford: Oxford University Press, 1986. I quote the French 1983 edition.

Skarsaune, *Proof from Prophecy:* Skarsaune, Oskar. *The Proof from Prophecy. A Study in Justin Martyr's Proof-Text Tradition: Text-Type, Provenance, Theological Profile.* Supplements to Novum Testamentum 56. Leiden: E. J. Brill, 1987.

Stanton/Stroumsa, *Tolerance and Intolerance:* Stanton, Graham N. and Guy G. Stroumsa, eds. *Tolerance and Intolerance in Early Judaism and Christianity.* Cambridge: Cambridge University Press, 1998.

Strack/Billerbeck 1-4: Strack, Hermann L. and Paul Billerbeck. *Kommentar zum Neuen Testament aus Talmud und Midrasch.* Vols. 1-4. Munich: C. H. Beck'sche Verlagsbuchhandlung, 1924-1928 [several reprints].

Tcherikover, *Hellenistic Civilization:* Tcherikover, Victor. *Hellenistic Civilization and the Jews.* Philadelphia/Jerusalem: The Jewish Publication Society of America, 1961 [paperback reprint, New York: Atheneum, 1977].

van der Horst, *Hellenism:* Horst, P. W. van der. *Hellenism—Judaism—Christianity: Essays on Their Interaction.* Contributions to Biblical Exegesis and Theology 8. Kampen: Kok Pharos, 1994.

Wilken, *Judaism:* Wilken, Robert L. *Judaism and the Early Christian Mind.* New Haven, Conn./London: Yale University Press, 1971.

Wilkinson, *Jerusalem:* Wilkinson, John. *Jerusalem As Jesus Knew It: Archaeology As Evidence.* London: Thames & Hudson, 1978.

Wilson, *Anti-Judaism:* Wilson, Stephen G. *Anti-Judaism in Early Christianity.* Vol. 2: *Separation and Polemic.* Studies in Christianity and Judaism 2. Waterloo, Ont.: Wilfried Laurier University Press, 1986.

Wilson, *Father Abraham:* Wilson, Marvin R. *Our Father Abraham: Jewish Roots of the Christian Faith.* Grand Rapids, Mich.: Eerdmans, 1989.

Wilson, *Strangers:* Wilson, Stephen G. *Related Strangers: Jews and Christians, 70-170 C.E.* Minneapolis: Fortress, 1995.

Winter, *Book of Acts 1-5:* Winter, Bruce W., series ed. *The Book of Acts in Its First Century Setting.* 5 vols. Grand Rapids, Mich.: Eerdmans/Carlisle: Paternoster, 1993-1995. The individual volumes are:

1. Winter, Bruce W. and Andrew D. Clarke, eds. *The Book of Acts in Its Ancient Literary Setting* (1993).
2. Gempf, Conrad H. and David W. J. Gill, eds. *The Book of Acts in Its Graeco-Roman Setting* (1994).
3. Rapske, Brian. *The Book of Acts and Paul in Roman Custody* (1994).
4. Bauckham, Richard, ed. *The Book of Acts in Its Palestinian Setting* (1995).
5. Levinskaya, Irina. *The Book of Acts in Its Diaspora Setting* (1996).

Wright, *The New Testament:* Wright, Nicholas Thomas. *The New Testament and the People of God.* Christian Origins and the Question of God 1. London: SPCK, 1992.

Translations of Sources

Old Testament, Old Testament Apocrypha and New Testament: New Revised Standard Version.

Other translations are quoted as follows:

ANF 1-10: Roberts, Alexander and James Donaldson, eds. *The Ante-Nicene Fathers: Translations of the Writings of the Fathers down to A.D. 325.* Grand Rapids, Mich.: Eerdmans, 1967-1969 [several reprints].

Barrett, *Documents:* Barrett, Charles Kingsley. *The New Testament Background: Selected Documents.*

New York: Harper & Row, 1961.

Charlesworth, *Pseudepigrapha 1-2:* Charlesworth, James H., ed. *The Old Testament Pseudepigrapha.* 2 vols. London: Darton, Longman & Todd, 1983, 1985.

Danby, *Mishnah:* Danby, Herbert. *The Mishnah.* Oxford: Oxford University Press, 1933 [several reprints].

Dix/Chadwick: Dix, Gregory. *The Treatise on the Apostolic Tradition of St. Hippolytus of Rome.* London: SPCK, 1968 [reissued by Henry Chadwick].

Falls: Falls, Thomas B. *Writings of Saint Justin Martyr.* The Fathers of the Church: A New Translation 6. Washington D.C.: Catholic University of America Press, 1948 [reprint, 1965].

Feldman/Reinhold, *Jewish Life:* Feldman, Louis H. and Meyer Reinhold. *Jewish Life and Thought Among Greeks and Romans: Primary Readings.* Edinburgh. T & T Clark/Minneapolis: Augsburg Fortress, 1996.

Frend, *New Eusebius:* Stevenson, J. *A New Eusebius: Documents Illustrating the History of the Church to AD 337.* New edition revised by W. H. C. Frend. London: SPCK, 1987.

Goldin, *Fathers:* Goldin, Judah. *The Fathers According to Rabbi Nathan.* New York: Schocken, 1974.

Hennecke, *Apocrypha 1-2:* Hennecke, E., W. Schneemelcher and R. McL. Wilson. *New Testament Apocrypha.* 2 vols. London: SCM Press, 1973, 1975.

Kirsopp Lake 1-2: Lake, Kirsopp. *The Apostolic Fathers in Two Volumes.* Loeb Classical Library. London: Heinemann/Cambridge, Mass.: Harvard University Press, 1912 [several reprints].

Lawlor/Oulton: Lawlor, Hugh Jackson and John Ernest Leonard Oulton. *Eusebius Bishop of Caesarea: The Ecclesiastical History and the Martyrs of Palestine.* 2 vols. London: SPCK, 1954.

Lewis/Reinhold: Lewis, Naphtali and Meyer Reinhold, eds. *Roman Civilization: Selected Readings.* Vol. 2: *The Empire.* 3rd ed. New York: Columbia University Press, 1990.

Loeb ed.: Colson, F. H., et al. *Philo in Ten Volumes.* Loeb Classical Library 226-35. Cambridge, Mass.: Harvard University Press/London: William Heinemann, 1929-1961 [several reprints].

Lukyn Williams: Lukyn Williams, A. *Justin Martyr: Dialogue with Trypho. Translation, Introduction, and Notes.* London: SPCK, 1930.

NPNF 2nd ser.: Schaff, Philip and Henry Wace, eds. *A Select Library of Nicene and Post-Nicene Fathers.* 2nd ser. Vols. 1-14, Peabody, Mass.: Hendrickson, 1995.

Riessler, *Schrifttum:* Riessler, Paul. *Alt-Jüdisches Schrifttum ausserhalb der Bibel.* Darmstadt: Wissenschaftliche Buchgesellschaft, 1966.

Robinson, *Nag Hammadi Library:* Robinson, James M. *The Nag Hammadi Library in English.* San Francisco: Harper & Row, 1981.

Soncino: Epstein, I., ed. *The Babylonian Talmud.* 35 vols. London: Soncino, 1935-1952. Freedman, H., and Maurice Simon, eds. *Midrash Rabbah.* 10 vols. London: Soncino, 1939 [and reprints].

Stern 1-3: Stern, Menachem. *Greek and Latin Authors on Jews and Judaism.* 3 vols. Jerusalem: The Israel Academy of Sciences and Letters, 1976, 1980, 1984.

Thackeray: Thackeray, H. St. John, et al. *Josephus in Nine Volumes.* Loeb Classical Library 186-94. Cambridge, Mass.: Harvard University Press/London: William Heinemann, 1926.

Whitaker, *Documents:* Whitaker, E. C. *Documents of the Baptismal Liturgy.* London: SPCK, 1970.

PART 1

THE MOTHER SOIL

JUDAISM FROM THE MACCABEES TO THE RABBIS

1

THE CULTURAL DIMENSION

JUDAISM & HELLENISM

*T*his is a book about the history of the early church. So why do we begin our story in 167/166 B.C.? That may seem all too early.

The reason is simple: Modern Christians in general assume that the Judaism that was the mother soil of Jesus, the apostles and the earliest Christian communities was the Judaism Christians know from the Bible. And Protestant Bibles do not include the Old Testament Apocrypha (roughly 200 B.C.-A.D. 1). The common assumption is therefore that the Judaism of, let's say, A.D. 30 was more or less the same as the Judaism of the Mosaic books, the Prophets, the Psalms and the Wisdom books.

This assumption is fundamentally misleading, and many phenomena in the New Testament and the early church are not properly understood unless this assumption is corrected. To put it briefly: Some very important things happened to Judaism and the Jewish people in the period "between the Testaments," and these are essential for understanding the origin of the Jesus movement and the early church. That is why our story begins in the middle of the great historical drama that unfolded in the 160s B.C.

After the Babylonian exile (587-538 B.C.) the Jews in Judea lived under foreign rule for almost four centuries. Persian, Greek and Egyptian rulers generally left the Jews to themselves with regard to their religion. Jewish customs and traditions which centered around the temple and the high priest were respected. Thus the Jews in some

respects enjoyed a limited autonomy, usually with the high priest as the official repre-
sentative of the people. This continued into the first decades after 200 B.C. when the
Syrians were the reigning power in the region. The ruling dynasty in Syria, the
Seleucids, had Greek origins from the time of Alexander the Great. Their capital was
Antioch. From the beginning, they continued the policy of cultural and religious tol-
erance.

Things changed with Antiochus IV Epiphanes, the Syrian king who ruled from
175 B.C.

Introduction: The Maccabean Revolt

We begin with a story. The year is 167 or 166 B.C. and we are in the little village
of Modein, situated on a hill near Lydda (now Lod). There is great turmoil in
the village. One of King Antiochus's officers is carrying a royal decree ordering every inhabitant to offer a sacrifice upon the altar of an idol that has been
erected in the marketplace. The Jews of the village are prepared for this. They
heard what happened in Jerusalem some months ago: an idolatrous altar was
erected on top of the altar in the temple itself, and sacrifices to the heathen
gods were now being offered on it—even pigs! And not only was the God of
Israel blasphemed and his temple profaned, but his people were brutally persecuted. All the scrolls of the law were sought out and burned. Any who were
found in possession of Torah scrolls were killed. Mothers who had their sons
circumcised were also put to death (1 Macc 1:44-64). Thus the inhabitants of
Modein knew what awaited them if they did not obey the royal decree and
offer the required sacrifices. As the author of 1 Maccabees soberly records:
"Many Israelites in Modein went over to the king's officers" (1 Macc 2:15).

In a group by themselves in the marketplace stood the elderly priest Mattathias and his sons, Johanan, Simon, Judas (called Maccabee), Eliezer and
Jonathan, their faces tense with sorrow and anger at what was about to take
place. The tension increased as the king's officers turned their attention
toward Mattathias:

> "You are a leader, honored and great in this town, and supported by sons and
> brothers. Now be the first to come and do what the king commands, as all the
> Gentiles and the people of Judah and those that are left in Jerusalem have done.
> Then you and your sons will be numbered among the Friends of the king, and
> you and your sons will be honoured with silver and gold and many gifts."
>
> But Mattathias answered and said in a loud voice: "Even if all the nations that
> live under the rule of the king obey him, and have chosen to obey his command-
> ments, everyone of them abandoning the religion of their ancestors, I and my

sons and my brothers will continue to live by the covenant of our ancestors. Far be it from us to desert the law and the ordinances. We will not obey the king's words by turning aside from our religion to the right hand or to the left."

When he had finished speaking these words, a Jew came forward in the sight of all to offer a sacrifice on the altar in Modein, according to the king's command. When Mattathias saw it, he burned with zeal and his heart was stirred. He gave vent to righteous anger; he ran and killed him on the altar. At the same time he killed the king's officer who was forcing them to sacrifice, and he tore down the altar. Thus he burned with zeal for the law, just as Phinehas did against Zimri son of Salu.

Then Mattathias cried out in the town with a loud voice, saying: "Let everyone who is zealous for the law and supports the covenant come with me!" Then he and his sons fled to the hills and left all that they had in the town. (1 Macc 2:17-28)

In this way began the Maccabean revolt, a revolt which resulted in the rededication of the temple in 164 B.C. (later celebrated in the festival of Hanukkah), in the establishment of a partially autonomous Judean state recognized by the Syrians, and later in an independent Jewish state which lasted until the Roman conquest in 63 B.C.

What was at stake in this revolt? The answer seems rather obvious: The Maccabean uprising represented Judaism's self-defense against the enforced "Hellenization" carried out by Antiochus. The Maccabean uprising made evident the incompatibility of Judaism and Hellenism. The Maccabean fighters and martyrs should be seen as prominent members in the long chain of Jewish martyrs, who throughout the ages have preferred to give up their lives rather than deny their God and his law. In fact, the martyrs of the Maccabean uprising are probably included in the chain of witnesses to faith in God in Hebrews 11:

Others were tortured, refusing to accept release, in order to obtain a better resurrection.[1] . . . [T]hey went about in skins of sheep and goats, destitute, persecuted, tormented—of whom the world was not worthy. They wandered in deserts and mountains, and in caves and holes in the ground.[2] (Heb 11:35-38)[3]

---

[1]Cf. 2 Macc 6—7: the martyrdom of Eleazar and the seven brothers.
[2]Cf. 1 Macc 2:29-41: pious Jews fleeing to the wilderness and hiding in caves.
[3]On the popularity of the Maccabean martyrs in Christian tradition, cf. Frend, *Martyrdom and Persecution*, pp. 19-22. Cf. also on Heb 11 Pamela Michelle Eisenbaum, *The Jewish Heroes of Christian History: Hebrews 11 in Literary Context*, Society of Biblical Literature Dissertation Series 156 (Atlanta, Ga.: Scholars Press, 1997).

26

Nevertheless, if we look at the background and consequences of the Maccabean revolt, it cannot escape us that the encounter between Judaism and Hellenism was a far more complex phenomenon than suggested above. In a now classic study[4] on the Maccabean uprising, the German Jewish scholar Elias Bickerman made two main points. First, the Jews of Israel were exposed to massive influence from Hellenistic culture long before the attempted "Hellenization" by Antiochus. The violent Hellenization of Jerusalem was instigated not by Antiochus but by influential circles within the political and religious leadership of Jerusalem itself.

> "Let us go and make a covenant with the Gentiles around us, for since we separated from them many disasters have come upon us." This proposal pleased them, and *some of the people eagerly went to the king, who authorized them to observe the ordinances of the Gentiles.* So they built a gymnasium in Jerusalem, according to Gentile custom, and removed the marks of circumcision, and abandoned the holy covenant. They joined with the Gentiles and sold themselves to do evil. (1 Macc 1:11-15, italics added)[5]

Thus, the whole question of "Hellenization" was to a great extent an intra-Jewish conflict, and in the beginning the Maccabees turned their weapons mostly against fellow Jews, not against the representatives of the Seleucid king (1 Macc 2:43-46; 3:5-9).[6]

---

[4]Elias J. Bickerman, *Der Gott der Makkabäer* (Berlin: Schocken, 1937); English ed.: *The God of the Maccabees: Studies on the Meaning and Origin of the Maccabean Revolt,* Studies in Judaism in late Antiquity 32 (Leiden: E. J. Brill, 1979).

[5]Cf. also the more extensive presentation of the Jewish Hellenizers' program in 2 Macc 4:7-16.

[6]Bickerman's interpretation of the events—that King Antiochus was more or less used by rival factions within the Jewish elite at Jerusalem—has not gone uncontested. Victor Tcherikover, *Hellenistic Civilization,* pp. 187-203, has argued that the aim of the Jewish Hellenizing party was only to make Jerusalem a Greek city in a political sense, and that the religious persecution was not instigated by them, but by Antiochus, as a punitive action in response to a pro-Torah Jewish rebellion against the king and his Jewish allies. Martin Hengel in *Judaism and Hellenism,* however, has defended the main lines of Bickerman's theory and brought more nuance to it (1:267-309). Cf. also the instructive review of recent discussion in P. Schäfer, *Geschichte der Juden in der Antike: Die Juden Palästinas von Alexander dem Grossen bis zur arabischen Eroberung* (Neukirchen-Vluyn: Neukirchener Verlag, 1983), pp. 52-62. Cf. also the full treatment of the whole question in J. Goldstein's commentaries on 1 and 2 Maccabees in the Anchor Bible series; and in his essays "The Hasmonean Revolt and the Hasmonean Dynasty," in Davies/Finkelstein, *Judaism,* pp. 292-351; "Jewish Acceptance and Rejection of Hellenism," in Sanders, *Self-Definition* 2:64-87. Further: K. Bringmann, *Hellenistische Reform und Religionsverfolgung in Judäa: Eine Untersuchung zur jüdisch-hellenistischen Geschichte (175-163 v. Chr.)* (Göttingen: Vandenhoeck & Ruprecht, 1983). Probably one should not think of a strict either/or with regard to the initiation of the Hellenizing pro-

Bickerman's second point is that the Maccabean fighters, who eventually established the Hasmonean Kingdom,[7] were themselves deeply influenced by Hellenism. But theirs was a Hellenism of a different sort—a Hellenism adjusted so as not to contradict the fundamental truths of Judaism. At the same time, as the Maccabees secured political freedom for Judea, their religious supporters—the forerunners of the Pharisees—were able to integrate important elements of Hellenistic culture into Judaism in such a way that it was no longer felt as a threat, but as an enrichment. It is this process we are going to study a little later in this chapter.

In this way, the story of the Maccabean uprising against violent Hellenization is seen to represent only one side of the coin, one aspect of the rather complex story of Judaism's encounter with Hellenism. And it is to this more constructive encounter and its effect upon the Judaism of our period that we now turn.

Alexander the Great and the Triumph of Hellenism

In order to understand the issues at stake in the Maccabean revolt, we should do as the author of 1 Maccabees does: place the whole process in a wider framework:

> After Alexander, son of Philip, the Macedonian, who came from the land of Kittim [Macedonia and Greece], had defeated King Darius of the Persians and the Medes [at the battles of Issos, 333 B.C., and Gaugamela, 331 B.C.], he succeeded him as king. (He had previously become king of Greece.) He fought many battles, conquered strongholds, and put to death the kings of the earth. He advanced to the ends of the earth, and plundered many nations. When the earth became quiet before him, he was exalted, and his heart was lifted up. He gathered a very strong army and ruled over countries, nations, and princes, and they became tributary to him. (1 Macc 1:1-4)

When Alexander the Great died in 323 B.C. he had succeeded not only in conquering all the important lands around the eastern half of the Mediterranean, but had also laid the foundation of a cultural revolution that would change the character of the ancient world for centuries to come. Alexander

---

cess; there was likely a measure of mutual understanding and collaboration between the Seleucid king and the Hellenizing circles within Jerusalem right from the beginning. But the king went further in his measures during the persecution period than any Jew could defend.

[7]The first generation of Mattathias's sons is usually referred to as "the Maccabees," while the later dynasty is called "the Hasmoneans," probably after one of their forefathers.

Box 1.1. From Alexander the Great to Herod the Great: Main Events

Greek period:	
332 B.C.	Alexander conquers the Persian Empire, including the land of Israel.
323	Death of Alexander, his empire divided among four generals.
Egyptian (Ptolemaic) period:	
320-198 B.C. Judea ruled by Ptolemies.	
Syrian (Seleucid) period:	
198-143 B.C. Judea ruled by Seleucids.	
175-163	Antiochus IV Epiphanes
From 175	"Hellenization" of Jerusalem, led by the High Priest Jason. Gymnasium built.
167	Temple desecrated (followed by persecution for 3 [or 3.5] years).
166	Mattathias's uprising; Mattathias's son, Judah the Maccabee, leads the revolt.
164	Temple rededicated, 25 Kislev.
160	Major defeat for Maccabees; death of Judah. Seleucids regain control in Judea. Jonathan succeeds his brother Judah.
152	Jonathan occupies Jerusalem and is proclaimed high priest.
Jewish independence:	
143-63 B.C. Judea ruled by Hasmoneans; Galilee colonized.	
143	Death of Jonathan; his brother Simon succeeds him.
142	Simon established as high priest and prince of the people.
134	Death of Simon; his descendants rule as princes and high priests (the Hasmonean Dynasty).
Roman period:	
67 B.C.	Romans defeat the Seleucid Kingdom.
63	The Roman general Pompey conquers Jerusalem.
40-37	Herod made Roman vassal king over Judea and after three years gains control.
27	Theater and amphitheater built in Jerusalem.
20/19	Rebuilding of the temple started.
4	Death of Herod the Great.

himself had envisaged a synthesis between the classical Greek culture and the old cultures of the Orient, and although his empire split apart soon after his death, his visions concerning this cultural synthesis were to a large extent fulfilled. But it should be emphasized that the two elements involved—Greece and the Orient—were not equally balanced. Greek culture was the culture of the conquerors, the rulers, the armies and the new business elite. Greek was the language of government and administration, business and commerce. And Greek literature was taken as the supreme model for all kinds of literary production. In other words, Greek culture was the culture of the new era, and anyone who would belong to the new elite had to adopt it.

The languages and the old cultures of Persia, Syria, Judea and Egypt did not enjoy the same prestige because they were the cultures of peoples who had been conquered, peoples who had not been able to withstand the superior power of Alexander and his successors. It was therefore natural that the representatives of the conquerors should regard these native oriental cultures as inferior. And—as often happens in similar circumstances—this attitude was also adopted by the most socially ambitious elements within the conquered societies. We shall see the relevance of this phenomenon when we turn to the history of the Jews in the last two centuries B.C.

There is, however, another aspect of the picture that somewhat balances the above description. The Greeks may have despised much of the culture of the Orient—the "barbaric" culture—but at the same time they had a great deal of secret admiration for it. Plato told a well-known story in which an Egyptian priest says to the Greek sage Solon, "O Solon, Solon, you Greeks are always children: there is not such a thing as an old Greek. . . . You are young in soul, every one of you. For therein you possess not a single belief that is ancient and derives from old tradition, nor yet one science that is hoary with age."[8] Plato seems to accept this statement, and in fact many Greeks seem to have felt that their culture was inferior to that of the Orient precisely due to its lack of ancient tradition. The Greeks were conscious of having created something new concerning democracy, science, philosophy, the theater and other innovations. They were proud of this, but at the same time felt like newcomers, inferior to those peoples who could boast ancient traditions as the basis of their institutions and cultic rites. A profound respect and admiration of "oriental wisdom" gradually developed among the representatives of Greek culture—not least among the philosophers. To take just one illustrative example, in the second century A.D. one of the leading Platonic philosophers, Numenius, claimed that Plato inherited his most profound teachings from the Semites, and that Plato was, quite simply, a "Moses speaking in Greek."[9]

There were, in fact, two respects in which classical Greek culture was quite incapable of filling the role of the new common culture of the Alexandrian empire:

---

[8]Plato, *Timaeus* 22B (Loeb ed., 9:33).
[9]As Martin Hengel remarks, many of the leading philosophers of the last two centuries B.C. were themselves Semites (Hengel, *Judaism and Hellenism* 1:86-88). One of the founders of the very influential "New Academy" (or, in a more modern term, Middle Platonism), was Antiochus of Ashkelon (ca. 130-68 B.C.). Numenius himself was from Apamea in Syria. Cf. M. J. Edwards, "Atticizing Moses? Numenius, the Fathers and the Jews," *Vigiliae Christianae* 44 (1990): 64-75. In a scholarly tour de force Martin Bernal has argued, quite convincingly, that the ancient writers who claimed Greek culture was in large measure derivative from Semitic and Egyptian cultures were in fact right. See his multivolume work *Black Athena: The Afroasiatic Roots of Classical Civilization* (London: Free Association Books, 1987-1991).

1. The traditional Greek religion could not fill the role of religion for a world empire. Wisely, Alexander and his successors did not try to suppress local deities and their worship. As time went by, this resulted in a large degree of religious syncretism. Oriental religions were Hellenized, but Greek religion was also orientalized.

2. The democratic system of the ancient Greek city-state, the *polis*,[10] could not serve as a working model for the centralized authoritarian government that was required by the new Alexandrian empires, since they were ruling conquered peoples who had no democratic tradition. To maintain their rule, the Ptolemies of Egypt and the Seleucids of Syria established centralized authoritarian governments, which they conducted along traditional Near Eastern lines as "divinely appointed kings."

In two respects, therefore, the Orient had cultural elements to offer that Greek culture could not be without if it was to serve as a common cultural framework for the newly created empires: The Orient had religion, cults, age-old wisdom traditions and the idea of divine kingship.

We can see that a complex process took place in the last three centuries B.C. At the same time as the Orient was Hellenized, Greek culture was to a considerable degree orientalized. It is the resultant mixed and complex culture that we call Hellenism. This became the common cultural heritage of all "civilized" people around the Mediterranean for centuries. This statement holds true even for the land of Israel and the population there—although some unique problems were involved, which created conflicts as well as attempts at compromise and adjustment. Before we return to Jerusalem and the conflict there, we must add a few words on the main strategy followed by the promoters of Hellenistic culture: the founding of Hellenistic cities, the *poleis*.[11]

The Hellenistic City: The *Polis*

One scholar has remarked that Aristotle's famous definition of man as *zoon politikon* should not be translated as "a political being," but "a being living in a *polis*."[12] To the Greek mind, the *polis* was the only framework within which a full human life could be realized. In the Hellenistic period, Greek culture was

---

[10]The Greek *polis* (city) was a state in miniature, and had full independence in conducting its internal affairs. Its residents were divided into two classes: citizens with full rights and foreigners who paid a tax in order to reside in the polis. In time slaves were added to make up a third group.

[11]On the classical Greek polis, see especially H. D. F. Kitto, *The Greeks* (Harmondsworth, U.K.: Penguin, 1951 [several reprints], chap. 5: "The Polis," pp. 64-79.

[12]Kitto, p. 78.

propagated first and foremost by the establishment of new Hellenistic *poleis* in the captured territories. Such cities were either founded in places where no previous city existed—for example Caesarea by the sea in Israel, founded by Herod[13]—or else existing cities were converted into poleis. A polis contained some obligatory institutions: a public town center and marketplace (the square *agora*); a hall for the city council (the *bouleuterion*); baths; temples to the Greek (later Roman) gods; a theater; a gymnasium (a combined higher school and sports training ground); preferably a library and a sports stadium; and if a big city, also a hippodrome.

Of greater importance than the buildings were the activities going on in these institutions. The theater and the gymnasium were, so to speak, mission stations for propagating Hellenistic culture. The same can be said for the entire polis in relationship to its surroundings.

In the Roman period the Hellenistic poleis became interconnected by an excellent network of Roman roads—built so solidly that many of them remain to this day, together with the equally solid aqueducts. The Hellenistic cities and the Roman roads that connected them were the nerve system of the Roman Empire and its spread of Hellenistic culture (see figures 1.1, 1.3 and 1.4). Within this nerve system commerce thrived, armies were transferred and new ideas flowed from city to city. In the cities, a cosmopolitan outlook developed, and what Luke says about the Athenians was no doubt typical of Hellenistic city-dwellers in general: "All the Athenians and the foreigners who lived there spent their time doing nothing but talking about and listening to the latest ideas" (Acts 17:21 NIV). We can think of the typical citizen of a Hellenistic city as an intellectual, with considerable interest in religion and philosophy, who was at the same time profoundly conservative in his political opinions so long as his personal welfare or the prosperity of his city were not involved. If the latter were threatened, he would react violently against any disturbance of the public order—as Paul experienced in Ephesus (Acts 19).

When we speak of Hellenistic civilization, we mainly have in mind this urban culture of the Greek and later Roman empires. It has been estimated that approximately ten percent of the population of these empires lived in Hellenistic cities. These ten percent were the main bearers of Hellenistic culture. The degree to which this culture penetrated into the countryside surrounding the cities no doubt varied from region to region. Language barriers

---

[13]See Kenneth G. Holum and Robert L. Hohlfelder, eds., *King Herod's Dream: Caesarea on the Sea* (New York/London: W. W. Norton, 1988).

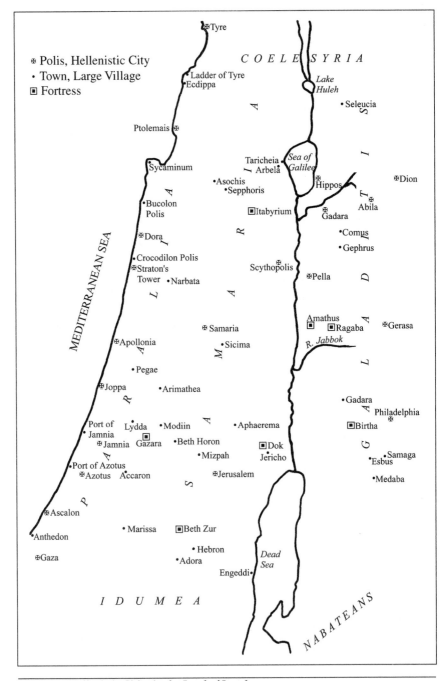

Figure 1.1. Hellenistic Cities in the Land of Israel

may have determined this to a great extent. In Greece and Rome there were no linguistic barriers between the cities and countryside, and the cities had close cultural links to their surroundings. The same may be said of the coastal areas of Asia Minor and even the coastal plains further south: Syria, Israel, Egypt. In other regions, as in the interior of Asia Minor or Syria, in Egypt or the inland of the north coast of Africa, the Hellenistic cities may have been more like islands in a sea of "barbaric" people in the country, who were hardly affected by the culture of the empire.

What was the situation in the land of Israel?

Hellenism in Israel

Let us first notice the great number of Hellenistic cities that were founded or converted in the Ptolemaic and Seleucid periods (marked on figure 1.1, p. 32). They are concentrated along the coastline and in the Transjordan, but also note the large Hellenistic cities in Lower Galilee (Sepphoris and Tiberias), in the Jezreel Valley and in Samaria.[14] Ten of these cities in the Jordan Valley and the Transjordan were later made independent city-states; together they constituted the Decapolis, "the [league of] ten poleis," and the area was named after them (Mk 5:20; Mt 4:25).[15]

This process of Hellenization through Hellenistic cities was carried on, it seems, rather peacefully during the Ptolemaic and Seleucid periods. One region, however, remained unaffected by this process: the central hilly area of Judea, around Jerusalem. Here there were no Hellenistic cities. This was only natural: the only way to Hellenize Judea would have been to convert Jerusalem itself into a Hellenistic city. Jerusalem was the unrivaled capital, the spiritual center and the dominant cultural focus of its region. What happened in Jerusalem would greatly influence life in Judea. Consequently, the Hellenization of Judea depended on the Hellenization of Jerusalem. To this burning problem in the years leading up to the Maccabean revolt the Jews of Jerusalem gave two contradictory answers: support the process of Hellenization or reject it outright.

In order to understand the motives of the extreme "Hellenizers" among

---

[14]Cf. the complete survey of Hellenistic cities in the land of Israel in *New Schürer* 2:85-183. Cf. also the fine essay by M. Avi-Yonah, "Historical Geography of Palestine," in *Compendia 1:1:* 78-116. For a very full discussion of the issue, cf. Aryeh Kasher, *Jews and Hellenistic Cities in Eretz-Israel: Relations of the Jews in Eretz-Israel with the Hellenistic Cities During the Second Temple Period (332 BCE-70 CE),* Texte und Studien zum antiken Judentum 21 (Tübingen: J. C. B. Mohr [Paul Siebeck], 1990).

[15]Cf. esp. Iain Browning, *Jerash and the Decapolis* (London: Chatto & Windus, 1982).

the ruling class in Jerusalem, one must keep in mind what a formidable challenge Hellenistic culture was. It represented, quite simply, "civilization," and Hellenistic rule had brought prosperity and better living conditions to thousands of citizens throughout the known world. To be cut off from this common civilization would be a serious matter indeed: "disaster upon disaster has overtaken us since we segregated ourselves from the Gentiles" (1 Macc 1:11-15, quoted in full above, p. 26). The Hellenizers in Jerusalem wanted to prevent such disaster, but there was one serious obstacle: the Torah. Many commandments in the Torah made closer contact with the Gentiles difficult if not impossible. The naked young men training in the gymnasium were a flagrant contradiction of the Torah commandments prescribing decency; on the other hand circumcision violated all Greek ideals—the Greeks thought it a mutilation of the body.[16] The Sabbath rest and its reasons were unfathomable to the Greeks, and even more so the dietary laws, which to the Greek mind seemed entirely irrational. The Hellenizers thought that in order to become a part of the new world civilization, they would have to accommodate the Torah to the new situation. In plain words, this meant abrogating those parts of the Torah which made the Jews a people apart.[17]

If this Hellenization program had succeeded, Judaism would no doubt have become part and parcel of Hellenistic culture and would gradually have ceased to exist. The Jewish nation would have slowly been assimilated and vanished from world history, as did many of its closest neighbors. The Maccabean fighters were hardly aware of the historical dimensions of their revolt, but in any case their action saved Judaism from extinction at a crucial time. But this is not only due to the repression of the extreme Hellenizers in Jerusalem. Perhaps more important is the constructive way the Maccabees and their religious supporters dealt with the Hellenistic challenge. One should not make the mistake of thinking that the Maccabean period was one of wholesale rejection of Hellenism. For us, who can view the whole period from a

---

[16]Cf. the Greek and Roman sayings on this issue collected in Molly Whittaker, *Jews and Christians: Graeco-Roman Views*, Cambridge Commentaries on Writings of the Jewish and Christian World 200 BC to AD 200, vol. 6 (Cambridge: Cambridge University Press, 1984), pp. 80-85. The words of the Roman author Petronius are rather funny: he quotes a slaveowner who praises one of his slaves for his many talents, yet adds: "He has two blemishes; without these he would be incomparable. He is circumcised and he snores" (*Satyricon* 68.8; Whittaker, 81). Cf. also the survey of pagan attitudes toward circumcision in J. N. Sevenster, *The Roots of Pagan Anti-Semitism in the Ancient World*, Supplements to Novum Testamentum 41 (Leiden: E. J. Brill, 1975), pp. 132-36.

[17]On the Jews being "a people keeping themselves apart," practicing *amixia* (Greek, "not mixing with others"), see the excellent survey in Sevenster, op. cit., pp. 89-144.

bird's-eye perspective, it is easy to see that precisely the period inaugurated by the Maccabean revolt and extending into the first century A.D. was marked by a close encounter between Judaism and Hellenism that profoundly influenced Judaism.

This influence did not, however, destroy Judaism. On the contrary, it introduced a new vitality into the old heritage. Instead of a question of incorporating Judaism into Hellenistic culture on Greek terms, the strategy was now to incorporate elements from Hellenistic culture into Judaism—on the terms of the Torah. This was not a conscious, deliberate strategy; in fact, the Hasmoneans and the religious leaders of their time were hardly aware of the extent they were influenced by Hellenism in their very efforts to defend and express Judaism. Let us look a little closer at two central concepts where we can see this influence at work.

A New Conception of the Torah

In the Hebrew Bible, the Torah is conceived within the framework of salvation history. It is proclaimed at Sinai, at a specific moment in history. And it is given with a specific historic situation in mind: national existence in the promised land. This perspective is eloquently expressed in the speeches of Moses in Deuteronomy. The Bible gives no hint that the Torah existed before it was proclaimed on earth, or that it existed prior to the creation of the world.

Hellenism, however, explained the existence of the world along these lines: the hidden law governing the whole universe is divine reason, *logos*, and the moral task of humanity is to live a life of conformity to this divine reason, which is the law of ethics as well as the law of nature.[18] How did the Jewish sages react to this concept?

They adopted the idea—but applied it to the law of Moses! The Torah is the hidden pattern according to which the world was created, and a life according to the law of nature is therefore a life according to the Torah. The first Jewish writer to apply this idea of pre-existence and cosmic significance to the Torah is the author of Sirach (ca. 190 B.C.). He was helped in this under-

---

[18]This line of thought was especially developed by the Stoic philosophers, cf. the recent study by Maximilian Forschner, *Die stoische Ethik: Über den Zusammenhang von Natur-, Sprach- und Moralphilosophie im altstoischen System* (Darmstadt: Wissenschaftliche Buchgesellschaft, 1995). In the period with which we are concerned, this Stoic concept was synthesized with the Platonic heritage by the so-called Middle Platonists. On this influential synthesis, the modern classic is John M. Dillon, *The Middle Platonists, 80 B.C. to A.D. 220*, rev. ed. (Ithaca, N.Y.: Cornell University Press, 1996 [orig. ed. London, 1977].

standing by the identification of the Torah with *God's preexistent wisdom*, by whom God created the world (Prov 8:22-31). Sirach 24 contains a beautiful hymn in which wisdom praises herself as the preexistent law of creation. The author of Sirach adds, "all this is the covenant of the Most High God, the law that Moses commanded us as an inheritance for the congregations of Jacob" (Sir 24:23).[19]

Later the rabbis elaborated further on this idea by identifying the "beginning" (Hebrew, *reshit*) of Genesis 1:1 with the *reshit* of Proverbs 8:22, which refers to wisdom (= Torah), so that Genesis 1:1 could be read: "By wisdom God created," wisdom being identical to the Torah. A rabbinic midrash on Genesis 1:1 reads:

> As a rule, when a king builds a palace, he does not build it by himself, but calls in an architect, and the architect does not plan the building in his head, but makes use of rolls and tablets. . . . Even so the Holy One, blessed be He, looked in the Torah and created the world. And the Torah declares: "With *Reshit* God created" (Gen. 1:1), and Reshit means none other than Torah, as it is said: "The Lord made me *Reshit* of His way" (Prov. 8:22). (*Gen. Rab.* 1:1)[20]

This is an entirely Jewish concept: The pattern according to which the world was created is the Torah of Moses! At the same time it is entirely Hellenistic. As the Jewish philosopher Maimonides recognized later, this midrash speaks of the Torah in much the same way as Plato spoke about what he called the Ideas, the intellectual pattern behind the material world.[21]

The concept of God's Torah as the preexistent mediator at the creation of the world—the rabbis called it "God's daughter"[22]—is of paramount importance when we come to discuss how the earliest Jewish believers in Jesus conceived of his divinity in relation to that of the Father (see chapter sixteen below).

Though not the only Hellenistic element incorporated into the new con-

---

[19]Cf. the instructive analysis of this important chapter in Eckhard J. Schnabel, *Law and Wisdom from Ben Sira to Paul: A Tradition Historical Enquiry into the Relation of Law, Wisdom, and Ethics*, Wissenschaftliche Untersuchungen zum Neuen Testament, 2. Reihe, 16 (Tübingen: J. C. B. Mohr [Paul Siebeck], 1985); and the critical comments by Boccaccini, "The Problem of Knowledge: Wisdom and Law," in *Middle Judaism: Jewish Thought, 300 B.C.E. to 200 C.E.*, ed. Gabriele Boccaccini (Minneapolis: Fortress, 1991), pp. 81-99.

[20]Soncino translation, p. 1. This midrash was possibly written in the fifth century A.D., but the idea has precedents in the third century and perhaps even earlier (*M Avot* 3:8 and Targums). See further below, chapter sixteen.

[21]Maimonides, *Guide for the Perplexed* 2:6; cf. the valuable comments in Ephraim E. Urbach, *The Sages: Their Concepts and Beliefs*, vol. 1 (Jerusalem: Magnes, 1979 [1st ed. 1975]), p. 199.

[22]*TB Sanhedrin* 101a; *Lev. Rab.* 20; *Num. Rab.* 2 and others. Cf. Strack/Billerbeck 2:355-56.

ception of the Torah, it may be the most important. The following concepts are also significant, especially since many think of them as very typical of rabbinic Judaism.

1. The famous Hillel (a little earlier than Jesus) is credited with seven rules for interpreting biblical texts. David Daube has shown that all of them correspond to Greek methods of exegesis taught in Greek schools of law and rhetoric and applied to codes of law.[23] In the Bible itself, this technical way of interpreting the law does not yet appear.

2. Similarly, the "tradition of the elders," from which the concept of the oral Torah later developed (see chapter five on this subject), has roots in the Greek schools of philosophy. These schools had developed a strong sense of tradition, and it became customary to substantiate the doctrine of the school by citing the chain of famous teachers who had transmitted this doctrine all the way from its authoritative beginning. This way of giving authority to a doctrine was later adopted by the rabbis.[24] A classic text is *M Pirke Avot* 1:1:

> Moses received the Law from Sinai and committed it to Joshua, and Joshua to the elders, and the elders to the prophets, and the prophets to the men of the Great Synagogue.... Simon the Just was of the remnant of the Great Synagogue.... Antigonus of Soko received [the Law] from Simon the Just.... Jose b. Joezer of Zeredah and Jose b. Johanan of Jerusalem received [the Law] from them, [and so on]. (*M Avot* 1:1-4)[25]

The documentation in rabbinic texts, "Rabbi X said in the name of Rabbi Y, who had it as a tradition from Rabbi Z," is a Hellenistic way of substantiating a statement; it is never used in the Bible. Even if we have no certain literary evidence of this way of speaking before the third century A.D., the older concept of the "tradition of the elders" betrays the same Hellenistic model.

3. Another Hellenistic notion resembling the Greek ideal that everyone should study philosophy is the Pharisaic-rabbinic ideal that all Jews should become students of the Torah. Three sayings attributed to the "Great Synagogue" (in the text quoted above) express the prevalent new concept of piety,

---

[23]See David Daube, "Rabbinic Methods of Interpretation and Hellenistic Rhetoric," *Hebrew Union College Annual* 22 (1949): 239-64. In this article Daube very lucidly demonstrates that Hillel's rules—whether or not they actually derive from him—correspond to the way ancient rhetoricians handled codes of law, in order to extract decisions from them in legal conflicts.

[24]Cf. Elias J. Bickerman, "La chaine de la tradition pharisienne," in *Studies in Jewish and Christian History*, vol. 2 (Leiden: E. J. Brill, 1980), pp. 256-79.

[25]Danby, p. 446.

which attains its zenith in the scholar, the student and the scribe: "Raise up many disciples [of the Torah]" (*M Avot* 1:1); "Provide yourself with a teacher and get a fellow disciple" (*M Avot* 1:6); "The more study of the Law, the more life" (Hillel, *M Avot* 2:7).

In these and other ways, Judaism was able to absorb Hellenistic ideas without losing its own identity or compromising its essential principles. These new ideas were used, in the words of *M Avot* 1:1, "to make a fence around the Torah," to glorify it, not to destroy it. It is not the world of Ideas conceived by Plato that is the hidden pattern according to which the world was created—it is the Torah!

Thus, once the exclusiveness of Israel's God and the absolute validity of his Law were recognized, the sages could be quite liberal in applying Greek ideas and concepts to their work with the Torah.

A striking confirmation of this interpretation comes from the Jewish acceptance of Herod the Great's efforts to make Jerusalem a model Hellenistic city, more than 150 years after the failure of the Hellenizers in the Maccabean era. Herod even ventured to Hellenize the exterior of the temple itself—and met with minimal opposition. In the words of Elias Bickerman:

> At the time of Epiphanes, the gymnasium in Jerusalem was enormously dangerous to Judaism. In the time of Philo, the Jews of Alexandria thronged the games without sacrificing any part of Judaism, and the theater, amphitheater, and hippodrome erected in Jerusalem by Herod, were later visited by the Orthodox Jews as well.[26]

The Jerusalem of Jesus was a Hellenistic-Herodian city. To a Greek visitor, the city must have looked familiar: a typical Hellenistic city with regular streets at right angles.[27] The most impressive sight would have been the temple itself, which, except for its enormous size, looked much like other Hellenistic temples. (Herod's temple complex was probably modeled after the "Caesaraeon" erected by Julius Caesar in 48 B.C. in Alexandria.)[28] But if the visitor had been able—which in fact he was not—to visit the interior of the

---

[26]Elias J. Bickerman, *From Ezra to the Last of the Maccabees: Foundations of Post-Biblical Judaism* (New York: Schocken, 1962), p. 181.

[27]Generally on the Hellenistic character of Herod's Jerusalem and the Hellenistic city plan in particular, see John Wilkinson, *Jerusalem as Jesus Knew It: Archaeology as Evidence* (London: Thames & Hudson, 1978) pp. 43-65.

[28]On Herod's expansion of the temple area and its architectonic models, see now Jostein Ådna, *Jerusalemer Tempel und Tempelmarkt im 1. Jahrhundert n. Chr.*, Abhandlungen des Deutschen Palästina-Vereins 25 (Wiesbaden: Harrassowitz Verlag, 1999), pp. 36-71.

sanctuary itself, he would have seen the interior of the old Israelite sanctuary left almost completely intact. This fact may serve as a symbol of the relationship between Judaism and Hellenism in the days of Jesus.[29]

The Concept of Judaism

Before Alexander the Great and his program of "cultural conquest," there hardly existed any "ism" in the old world.[30] People defined themselves and their identities mainly by place of origin and ethnic descent: Greeks were the people inhabiting Greece, the Aegean islands and Asia Minor's western coast; Israelites were the people descending from Jacob's sons and living in parts of the land of Israel and scattered in the Diaspora. Peoples were defined by territory and descent.

After the Babylonian exile and in the Diaspora, the question of *descent* became the crucial one for deciding who did or did not belong to the Jewish nation. We see this principle applied in a paradigmatic way in the famous dissolving of mixed marriages in the time of Ezra: the non-Jewish wives were sent away so as to hinder the "mixing" of "the holy seed" (Ezra 9:2). Either you were born a Jew or you were not, and nothing could change that.

In the wake of Alexander's conquests, a new way of defining identity appeared. People who were not Greeks by descent, began to talk like Greeks, dress like Greeks, live like Greeks, in Greek-style cities. This new way of life was called, in Greek, *hellenismos*—probably the first "ism" on record in history. As a response, Jews began to define themselves in the same way: they had their own way of life, *iudaismos*. This is a term used, probably for the first time, by the author of 2 Maccabees: Judas Maccabee and his brothers "fought bravely for Judaism" (2 Macc 2:21); Judas and his men entered villages "and summoned their kindred and enlisted those who had continued with Judaism" (2 Macc 8:1). "A certain Razis, one of the elders of Jerusalem . . . was accused [before the representative of the Syrian king] of Judaism, and he had most zealously risked body and life for Judaism" (2 Macc 14:38). It is obvious that "Judaism" in these examples does not mean Jewishness in a biological

---

[29]For a fascinating analysis of the long-term encounter and conflict between the Orient and Hellenism, cf. the first chapter in Dix, *Jew and Greek*, "The Conflict of the Syriac and Greek Cultures," pp. 1-18.

[30]For what follows, I am deeply indebted to Daniel R. Schwartz's essay, "Introduction: On the Jewish Background of Christianity," in Schwartz, *Studies*, pp. 1-26. Cf. also Shaye J. D. Cohen, "From *Ethnos* to Ethno-Religion," in *Jewishness*, pp. 109-39.

sense: some born Jews abandoned "Judaism," others fought for it and were faithful. Obviously, the word describes a life according to the Torah; in other words, a certain lifestyle, just like the contrasting concept: "There was such an extreme of *Hellenism* and increase in the adoption of *foreign ways*" by faithless Jews in Jerusalem (2 Macc 4:13).

But just as non-Greeks could become "Hellenists" by turning to and practicing "Hellenism," so too non-Jews could probably become adherents of "Judaism" by adopting the Jewish lifestyle. In fact, we encounter the first known examples of conversion to Judaism in the days of the Hasmoneans. They even forcefully converted non-Jews in order to secure a Jewish population majority in traditional Israelite territory.

In contrast to the episode of the mixed marriages in the days of Ezra, this was a great change in the perception of Jewish identity. Ezra knew no way of making non-Jews Jews; the Hasmoneans did. Ezra did not know the concept of conversion to an "ism"; the Jews of the Hasmonean era did. And if Hellenism had succeeded in becoming a worldwide "ism", why should not Judaism aspire to the same? It takes no great imagination to realize the importance of this new development as a precondition for early Christian self-understanding and mission.

But was not Judaism too bound to a specific culture, and to a language incomprehensible to most non-Jews, for it ever to become a serious competitor of Hellenism?

Greek in Israel

Perhaps the most impressive evidence for the extent to which Judaism and Hellenism were exposed to each other during the crucial centuries around the birth of Christ comes from the study of the languages used in Israel. A Greek visitor would have had no problem being understood in the streets and shops of Jerusalem.

Originally, Greek was a mixture of different local dialects spoken in Greece. After the Alexandrian conquests, Greek became an international language, and the local dialects were worn down and melted into a "common" *(koinē)* Greek used by everyone and understood everywhere. In short, Greek was the English of the ancient Mediterranean world.

Most users of this new *koinē* Greek were not Greek speakers from birth; for them Greek was an acquired language. Judged by classical standards, this new *koinē* Greek seemed inelegant and "barbaric." But it was a rich, nuanced and effective means of communication that was raised to a high literary level by many gifted authors who used it to develop new literary forms in keeping with the spirit of the age.

This is the language employed by several Jewish authors of that time and by the authors of the New Testament. It is the language of the educated elite in all provinces of Alexander's empire, and even became the preferred language of the cultural upper class in Rome itself. Even more remarkable, perhaps, is that Greek gained a certain foothold as a spoken and written language in Israel among the native Jewish population. It did not replace Hebrew or Aramaic, but seems to have been used in addition to these two languages.[31]

Archaeology provides some telling illustrations. Many inscriptions have been found on ossuaries,[32] dating roughly from the 200 years prior to A.D. 135. These inscriptions were intended to be read by family members, and one must presume they were written in the language most familiar to the family. Of a total of 194 known inscriptions, 26 percent are in Hebrew or Aramaic and 64 percent are inscribed in Greek alone. Other Jewish inscriptions have also been found, written in Greek, which were obviously meant to be understood by the majority of literate people. Among the finds in the Cave of Letters in the Judean Desert, which are ascribed to Bar Kokhba and his men, are some letters written in Greek. In the ancient Galilean city of Bet Shearim, many catacombs with burial inscriptions have been found, dating from the first to the sixth century A.D. The oldest catacombs date from the first or second century, and all the inscriptions in them are in Greek. The other catacombs also contain several Greek inscriptions.[33]

It is thus evident that Greek was much in use in Israel during the time that Jesus lived and the early church was established—probably mostly a "pidgin Greek" used in the way and circumstances English is used in Israel today. This should be no surprise to a reader familiar with the New Testament. Two

---

[31]In addition to the works listed in the Suggestions below, one should consult the following: Joseph A. Fitzmyer, "Did Jesus speak Greek?" *Biblical Archaeology Review* 18, no. 5 (1992): 58-63; Pieter W. van der Horst, "Jewish Funerary Inscriptions—Most Are in Greek," ibid., pp. 46-57; G. Mussies, "Greek in Palestine and the Diaspora," in *Compendia* 1:2: 1040-64; Richard A. Horsley, *Archaeology, History and Society in Galilee: The Social Context of Jesus and the Rabbis* (Valley Forge, Penn.: Trinity Press International, 1996), pp. 154-75.

[32]Small coffins for reburial of the bones after the body had completely decayed in the tomb. These were used by Jews in the period ca. 200 B.C.-A.D. 135.

[33]On all of this paragraph, cf. the instructive display of the epigraphic evidence in Meyers/Strange, *Archaeology*, pp. 62-91; but see also the cautions about the Bet Shearim cemetery as not typical for Galilee at large, in Horsley, *Archaeology*, pp. 169-70.

of Jesus' disciples have Greek names—Philip and Andrew—and precisely these two disciples wanted to introduce some "Greeks" (possibly Gentile God-fearers or Greek-speaking proselytes) to Jesus (Jn 12:20-22). The remark made about Philip in this context ("who was from Bethsaida in Galilee"), seems at first sight rather irrelevant, but may indicate that it was well known that Greek was spoken in Bethsaida. The fact that Peter's parents chose to give his brother Andrew a Greek name may indicate that Greek was a familiar language in their family.

If we turn to the rabbinic literature, some of the most famous of the early rabbis are pictured conversing with Roman emperors and other high-ranking Gentiles. However legendary these stories may be, they clearly demonstrate that the rabbinic tradition conceived of these early rabbis as literate men who—when need be—could use the common language of the era without difficulty. It seems that in the first and early second century A.D. the rabbis even favored the use of the Greek translation of the Bible in synagogues, where this would make the Bible better understood.

Active Dissemination of Judaism and Christianity

Why do we emphasize this bi- or trilingual situation among the Jewish population of the land of Israel in this period? Because it has to do with a fundamental characteristic of Judaism in the period of Jesus and the apostles. At this time Judaism was very much on the offensive. The Maccabean era had created new self-confidence among the Jews, and there seems to have been an increasing flow of converts to Judaism, partly as the result of active Jewish mission.[34] Jesus says to the Pharisees, "you cross sea and land to make a single convert" (Mt 23:15), and rabbinic sources confirm this picture of active mission among Gentiles.[35] In the first century A.D.

---

[34]The most ambitious and comprehensive study to push this thesis is Louis H. Feldman, *Jew and Gentile in the Ancient World: Attitudes and Interactions from Alexander to Justinian* (Princeton: Princeton University Press, 1993). On active outreach among Gentiles, cf. also Scot McKnight, *A Light Among the Gentiles: Jewish Missionary Activity in the Second Temple Period* (Minneapolis: Fortress, 1991), and the important comments upon and supplements to this book in Peder Borgen, "Militant and Peaceful Proselytism and Christian Mission," in *Early Christianity*, pp. 45-69.

[35]The classic study is Bernard J. Bamberger, *Proselytism in the Talmudic Period* (Cincinnati, Ohio: Hebrew Union College Press, 1939 [paperback reprint, New York: Ktav, 1968]), esp. pp. 20-24; 275-99. More recently, the active dissemination of Judaism is affirmed persuasively by Feldman, *Jew and Gentile*, 1993; but cf. the cautions in Martin Goodman, *Mission and Conversion: Proselytizing in the Religious History of the Roman Empire* (Oxford: Clarendon, 1994 [paperback ed. Clarendon Paperbacks, 1995]).

many Jews seem to have been convinced that their religion was ultimately to become the religion of all people, and this in a not-too-distant future.[36] Accordingly Judaism had to make itself known in the language of all people: Greek.[37] The earliest Christians shared this conviction, and for them the time of fulfillment had come: "Go therefore and make disciples of all nations" (Mt 28:19). In Jesus, the Messiah, the biblical promises were fulfilled or brought near their fulfillment; now the time had come to gather in "a people for his name" (Acts 15:14) among the Gentiles. Thus, there is nothing un-Jewish about the fact that the New Testament was written in Greek. On the contrary, to write the message of Jesus in Hebrew or Aramaic would have meant to restrict it to a rather narrow audience consisting of native speakers of these languages, which would have been contrary to the spirit of Judaism in this age.

Postscript
In a beautiful passage, Rabbi Leo Baeck has emphasized the "Jewishness" of Paul's reaction to the vision of the risen Christ outside Damascus. In going out to the Gentiles Paul was not un-Jewish; on the contrary, he was true to the deepest Jewish instincts:

> A Greek who had experienced such a vision would have reflected, talked, and mused, or spoken and written about it; he would not have heard the Jewish command: "Go"—"Thou shalt go." The Greek had no God who laid a claim on him and sent him to be his messenger. Only the Jew would be always aware that the revelation entailed the mission, that a prompt readiness to follow the way was the first sign and testimony to the faith. Paul knew now that to him had fallen the apostolate in the name of the Messiah.[38]

---

[36]In Philo this hope seems very clear, cf. *De Vita Mosis* 2.43-44, and the comments in Borgen, "Militant," pp. 56-59. Cf. also Martin Hengel, "Messianische Hoffnung und politischer 'Radikalismus' in der jüdischen Diaspora" in *Apocalypticism in the Ancient Near East and the Hellenistic World,* ed. David Hellholm, 2nd ed. (Tübingen: J. C. B. Mohr [Paul Siebeck], 1989), pp. 655-86.

[37]There has been a lively scholarly debate on the question of whether missionary motives were in part behind the translation of the Bible into Greek by Alexandrian Jews in the third and second centuries B.C. There is hardly any doubt, however, that some non-biblical works within the large body of Jewish Greek literature of the late Second Temple period are rightly called "missionary literature." On this, cf. further below, chapter 3.

[38]Leo Baeck, *Judaism and Christianity* (New York: The Jewish Publication Society of America, 1958), p. 142.

Temple Square

We have emphasized how the Jewish religion, the Jewish way of life, through the encounter with Hellenism redefined itself and became, itself, an "ism": Judaism. The Jewish way of life became an option for non-Jews by birth. The option of conversion to Judaism became a reality. But, unlike Hellenism, Judaism could not sever its links to something that was not an "ism" and never could be. At the heart of Judaism was something local and concrete, not movable: the temple. On the Temple Mount, and there only, was the God of Israel present in a special way. In the temple—and there only—were the sacrifices brought which repaired and restored purity and holiness to Israel whenever these had been lost. It was the pollution of this heart of holiness and purity (the two concepts are mutually inseparable, if not identical) which triggered the Maccabean revolt. The triumph of the revolt was the rededication of the temple. Second Maccabees is a book not about the Maccabees but about the God of Israel defending his temple. The lasting heritage in the Jewish calendar from the Hellenistic period is the festival of Hanukkah, the rededication of the temple—the only Jewish festival in which the temple itself is the *object*, not only the setting, of the festival.

Access to the temple, the sphere of holiness, was only for Jews. That is why adherence to Judaism was something much more serious than adopting Hellenism. You were not qualified to enter the temple simply by adopting a Jewish way of life. You had to be made a Jew formally, you had to become a member of the chosen people, and you had to be cleansed. That is why the ritual of conversion naturally climaxed in the new convert bringing his or her first sacrifice in the temple. In a sense, that was the goal of the whole process. It speaks volumes for what Jewish identity was all about.

This seems like a severe restriction on Judaism's ever becoming a universal "ism", and it was. There is a built-in tension here, with which Judaism had to struggle long and hard, and it goes a long way toward explaining why there arose dissent, disagreements and different schools of thought. At the heart of the disagreements was always the question of purity and holiness. And at the heart of that question was the temple.

Suggestions for Further Reading

An excellent anthology of primary sources in English translation is Feldman/Reinhold, *Jewish Life*. For Gentile views on Jews and Judaism (original texts and translations), see Menachem Stern, *Greek and Latin Authors on Jews and Judaism*, 3 vols. (Jerusalem: The Israel Academy of Sciences and Letters, 1976, 1980, 1984). Cf. also the same author's summary, "The Jews in Greek and Latin Literature," in *Compendia 1:2*: 1101-59. The most important texts among pagan authors on Jews and Christians are gathered in English translation, with short comments, in Molly Whittaker, *Jews and Christians: Graeco-Roman Views*, Cambridge Commentaries on Writings of the Jewish and Christian World 200 BC to AD 200, vol. 6. (Cambridge: Cambridge University Press, 1984).

For a comprehensive survey of the period covered in this chapter, see *New Schürer* 1:125-242. Cf. also Murphy, *Religious World*, pp. 135-62; Schiffman, *Text to Tradition*, pp. 60-119.

There are three classical studies on the encounter between Judaism and Hellenism in the last three centuries B.C.:

1. Elias J. Bickerman, *Der Gott der Makkabäer* (Berlin: Schocken, 1937). This signifi-

cant study of the Maccabean revolt is now available in an English translation: *The God of the Maccabees: Studies on the Meaning and Origin of the Maccabean Revolt*, Studies in Judaism in Late Antiquity 32 (Leiden: E. J. Brill, 1979). Bickerman treated the whole issue once more, and on a broader basis, in his posthumous *The Jews in the Greek Age* (Cambridge, Mass./London: Harvard University Press, 1988). A short and very readable account of his thesis is to be found in Bickerman, *From Ezra to the Last of the Maccabees: Foundations of Post-Biblical Judaism* (New York: Schocken, 1962 [several reprints]), pp. 93-165.

2. Victor Tcherikover, *Hellenistic Civilization and the Jews* (Philadelphia/Jerusalem: The Jewish Publication Society of America, 1961 [paperback reprint, New York: Atheneum, 1977]). Main emphasis on political, cultural, economical and social aspects.

3. Martin Hengel, *Judentum und Hellenismus*, Wissenschaftliche Untersuchungen zum Neuen Testament 10, 2nd ed. (Tübingen: J. C. B. Mohr [Paul Siebeck], 1973). Hengel is placing the theological developments within a framework of political and cultural history. This work is now also available in an English translation: *Judaism and Hellenism: Studies in Their Encounter in Palestine During the Early Hellenistic Period* (London: SCM Press, 1981 [2nd impression in one vol.; reprint, 1991]). This study has since been supplemented by the same author: *Jews, Greeks and Barbarians: Aspects of the Hellenization of Judaism in the Pre-Christian Period* (London: SCM Press, 1980 [German orig., *Juden, Griechen und Barbaren: Aspekte der Hellenisierung des Judentums in vorchristlicher Zeit*, Stuttgarter Bibelstudien 76 (Stuttgart: KBW Verlag, 1976]); and *The 'Hellenization' of Judaea in the First Century After Christ* (London: SCM Press/Philadelphia: Trinity Press, 1989). Cf. also the same author's succinct summary "The Interpenetration of Judaism and Hellenism in the Pre-Maccabean Period," in Davies/Finkelstein, *Judaism*, pp. 167-228.

These major studies, among others, have triggered some more recent large-scale studies of the problem: Jonathan A. Goldstein, *I Maccabees: A New Translation with Introduction and Commentary*, Anchor Bible 41 (New York: Doubleday, 1976); idem, *II Maccabees: A New Translation with Introduction and Commentary*, Anchor Bible 41A (New York: Doubleday, 1983); Louis H. Feldman, *Jew and Gentile in the Ancient World: Attitudes and Interactions from Alexander to Justinian* (Princeton: Princeton University Press, 1993). Emphasizes the vitality and vigor of Judaism faced with the Hellenistic challenges. Cf. also Gabriele Boccaccini, *Middle Judaism: Jewish Thought, 300 B.C.E. to 200 C.E.* (Minneapolis: Fortress, 1991).

For concise archaeological updates on the period, see Andrea M. Berlin, "Between Large Forces: Palestine in the Hellenistic Period," *Biblical Archaeologist* 60 (1997): 2-51; Eric M. Meyers, "The Challenge of Hellenism for Early Judaism and Christianity," *Biblical Archaeologist* 55 (1992): 84-93.

Two classic studies on the diffusion of Greek language and culture in Israel, with main emphasis on rabbinical sources, are Saul Lieberman's *Greek in Jewish Palestine* (New York: Jewish Theological Seminary of America, 1942); and *Hellenism in Jewish Palestine* (New York: Jewish Theological Seminary of America, 1950).

The diffusion and use of Greek in the land of Israel at the transition from B.C. to A.D. are treated in many of the above studies, and specifically in J. N. Sevenster, *Do You Know Greek: How Much Greek Could the First Jewish Christians Have Known?* Supplements to Novum Testamentum 19 (Leiden: E. J. Brill, 1968); Meyers/Strange, *Archaeology*, pp. 62-91; and James Barr, "Hebrew, Aramaic and Greek in the Hellenistic Age," in Davies/Finkelstein, *Judaism*, pp. 79-114.

2

THE POLITICAL
DIMENSION
JEWS & THE
ROMAN EMPIRE

*T*he encounter with the Hellenistic culture of the Hellenistic empires of the
Ptolemies of Egypt and the Seleucids of Syria was of great significance to Judaism.
But perhaps the encounter between Judaism and the political power of Rome was to
become even more fateful. The Romans cared little about Jewish religion as such, and
yet they caused one of the major revolutions in Jewish history: they forced Judaism to
become a religion without a temple. This resulted in one of the deepest transforma-
tions of the whole character of Judaism. In razing the temple in A.D. 70, the Romans
probably only meant to take a wise political precaution. But the religious significance
of this event far outweighed its political effects. It is, however, with the political and
juridical dimensions of the Jewish-Roman relationship that this chapter is concerned.
The religious effects are treated more fully in chapters four and five.

The End of the Hasmonean Dynasty and the Beginning of Roman Rule
Again we begin with a story: In the spring of 63 B.C. three Jewish delegations
appeared before the Roman general Pompey, who had erected his military
headquarters in Damascus. Two of the Jewish groups represented competing
Hasmonean brothers, Hyrcanus and Aristobulus, who were fighting for control of the Hasmonean throne. Each party appealed to the Roman general for

support against the other. The third delegation represented neither of the competing Hasmonean princes, but quite simply "the Jewish people." This third group said that they did

> not desire to be under kingly government [by the Hasmoneans], because the form of the government they received from their fathers was that of subjection to the priests . . . and that these two [Aristobulus and Hyrcanus] . . . sought to change the government of their nation to another form in order to enslave them. (Josephus, *Antiquities* 14.41)[1]

What a sad epilogue to the Hasmonean dynasty. A hundred years after the Maccabean uprising, Jewish leaders appeared before Pompey and appealed to the Roman general to abolish the constitution created by the Hasmonean rulers and their oppressive regime and to restore the ancient priestly theocracy—but now under Roman auspices! How could this be?

It was, in fact, the logical outcome of the process which began only a few years after the outbreak of the Maccabean revolt. The Maccabees could not end their involvement when the Syrian soldiers were ousted from the Holy City. In order to retain their newly gained freedom, the liberators had to become rulers. In 152 B.C., Jonathan, the brother of Judah Maccabee, received the title of high priest from the Syrian rulers, who had kept the power to appoint the high priest. Thus, in their very zeal to protect the Torah and tradition, the Maccabeans did violence to both. They were priests, but not sons of Zadok, and therefore could not claim any hereditary right to the office of high priest (cf. Ezek 40:46; 43:19).

Some pious Jews reacted strongly against this, and a number of them—after some time—even retired to the desert shores of the Dead Sea to build a

---

[1]The Jewish historian Flavius Josephus (ca. A.D. 37-100) belonged to a priestly family and was a commander in Galilee during the first Jewish revolt against Rome (A.D. 66-70). He surrendered to the Romans and later settled in Rome. His works are often somewhat biased towards the Romans, but nevertheless they are the best sources on late Second Temple history. Josephus wrote in Greek. In the 70s he wrote *The War of the Jews*, and in the 90s *My Life* (his autobiography), *Against Apion*, an apology for Judaism, and *Antiquities of the Jews*, a history of the Jewish people from biblical times to his own. For general information on Josephus as a historian, see H. St. J. Thackeray, *Josephus: The Man and the Historian* (New York: Ktav, 1967); Shaye J. D. Cohen, *Josephus in Galilee and Rome: His Vita and Development as a Historian*, Columbia Studies in the Classical Tradition 8 (Leiden: E. J. Brill 1979); Louis H. Feldman, *Josephus and Modern Scholarship (1937-1980)* (Berlin: Walter de Gruyter, 1984); idem, "Flavius Josephus Revisited: The Man, His Writings, and His Significance," in Haase, *Aufstieg* 2 21.2:763-862; Per Bilde, *Flavius Josephus Between Jerusalem and Rome: His Life, His Works and Their Importance*, Journal for the Study of the Pseudepigrapha Supplement Series 2 (Sheffield: Sheffield Academic Press, 1988).

community center at Qumran, vehemently denouncing the "wicked priest" who had persecuted their own leader.[2] The Pharisees, on the other hand, during most of the last 150 years B.C., had varying relations with the Maccabees. Josephus records a break between the Pharisees and Hyrcanus (156-104 B.C.), who was himself originally their disciple (Josephus, *Antiquities* 13.288-98).[3] Pharisaic political influence later reached its peak under the Hasmonean Queen Shlomzion Alexandra in the years 76-67 B.C. (*The Jewish War* 1.110-14).

An increasing tension, however, developed between the pious, learned men of the Torah and the self-conscious Hasmonean princes who would have their say in all sectors of Jewish life. Israel was no longer under foreign rule, but the government prescribed by tradition—a legitimate Davidic king and a legitimate high priest, descending from Zadok—was lacking. In their stead were the Hasmoneans, who were descendants of neither David nor Zadok. And no human effort was likely to provide a better alternative. It must have dawned on many pious Jews that the creation of the true messianic kingdom was in the hands of God, not humans. In the meantime, would it not be better to have no king at all rather than these pseudo-kings? "Later, and in a precisely similar fashion, after the death of Herod, the Jews petitioned that none of the Herodians be named king, but that they be permitted to live without a king, according to the law of their forefathers!"[4]

So, to return to our story above, the Jewish delegation to Pompey very likely thought that the Romans would not interfere with the internal aspects of Jewish life prescribed by the Torah. So why not prefer high-priestly rule under Roman auspices to that of the Hasmoneans?

We have every reason to think that Pompey listened to the delegates from "the Jewish people" with considerable sympathy. He would have greatly appreciated their reverence for the traditions of their fathers. In fact, this was to become a basic element and principle of Roman policy concerning the religions of subjugated peoples: each people should be allowed to follow their ancestral religious traditions and worship the gods of their fathers. The Romans held their own religious traditions in high esteem, and were willing

---

[2]The exact date of this exodus to Qumran is debated among scholars. See further details in chapter six.

[3]Günter Stemberger, *Jewish Contemporaries of Jesus: Pharisees, Sadducees, Essenes* (Minneapolis: Fortress, 1995), pp. 105-10, presents a rather persuasive argument for the view that Josephus mistakenly attached the story of a break with the Pharisees to Hyrcanus, and that it may originally have been told about Alexander Jannaeus (103-76 B.C.).

[4]Elias J. Bickerman, *From Ezra to the Last of the Maccabees* (New York: Schocken, 1962), p. 174.

to respect those of others. Many Jews appreciated this, and when Pompey, in the fall of 63 B.C., advanced to take control of Jerusalem, the city gates were opened to his generals by the Jewish majority in the city. Only a minority voted for resistance. They took control of the Temple Mount, and Pompey had to take this area by force. But once the fierce fighting was over, Pompey was satisfied to merely inspect the temple and its treasures, "yet did Pompey touch nothing of all this, on account of his regard to religion. . . . The next day he gave order to those that had the charge of the temple to cleanse it, and to bring what offerings the law required to God" (Josephus, *Antiquities* 14.72-73).

So it seems that those Jews who favored a Roman take-over were basically right: the Romans respected the ancient Jewish institutions and traditions, and had no intention of interfering in internal Jewish affairs. The following years to a great extent confirmed this. The Romans regarded the Jews as their faithful allies, and the Jews living in Greek cities outside Israel were repeatedly granted special privileges not given to others (Josephus, *Antiquities* 14.185-267). And so it seemed that the Jews had found their ideal government while waiting for full freedom in the kingdom of the Messiah. But this began to change in the days when Herod and his sons became the executors of Roman rule in Israel.

Herod the Great (37-4 B.C.) was not liked by the Jews.[5] As a founder of cities and a master builder, he was one of the greatest Hellenizers in the history of Israel. Even though he was eager to show, when need be, that he respected the Torah and its ordinances, the Pharisees were not duped by his shows. The relationship between him and the Jewish leadership was strained.[6]

Things did not improve when Judea came under direct Roman rule in A.D. 6. It was clear to all that by now the honeymoon between the Jews and Romans was definitely over. The reason involved a conflict between their basic principles and values. Three times, in A.D. 66-70, A.D. 115-117 and A.D.

---

[5]Herod the Great has, understandably, attracted the attention of many scholars. Three comprehensive studies are those of Abraham Schalit, *König Herodes: Der Mann und sein Werk*, Studia Judaica 4 (New York/Berlin: Walter de Gruyter, 1969); Michael Grant, *Herod the Great* (London: Weidenfeld & Nicholson, 1971); Peter Richardson, *Herod: King of the Jews and Friend of the Romans* (Columbia, S.C.: University of South Carolina Press, 1996).
[6]On Pharisaic attitudes toward Herod and his sons, see Gedalyahu Alon, "The Attitude of the Pharisees to Roman Rule and the House of Herod," in Alon, *Studies*, pp. 18-47; esp. pp. 37-42.

Figure 2.1. Roman and Herodian Palestine

132-135, the conflict erupted in outright war,[7] and during the first of these the Jewish people lost their cultic center, the temple in Jerusalem.

What had happened? We shall first take a closer look at the last Jewish revolt (A.D. 132-135). As usual, we begin with a story, this time a Talmudic one.

The Bar Kokhba Revolt

When Rabbi Akiva was taken out for execution, it was the hour for the recital of the Shema, and while they combed his flesh with iron combs, he was accepting upon himself the kingship of heaven (that is, he recited the Shema). His disciples said to him: Our teacher, even to this point? He said to them: All my days I have been troubled by this verse, "with all your soul," which I interpret, "even if he takes your soul." I said: When shall I have the opportunity of fulfilling this? Now that I have the opportunity, shall I not fulfill it? He prolonged the word Èchad [One] until he expired while saying it. (TB Berakhot 61b)

This Talmudic passage recounts another classic story about martyrdom in Jewish tradition. This time the oppressive power was Rome itself, the most impressive political and military power the world had yet seen. The ones torturing Rabbi Akiba were Roman soldiers. But why did they execute the foremost Jewish rabbi of their time? If we had had the opportunity to ask the Roman authorities this question, they would probably have answered in political terms: Rabbi Akiba supported Simon Bar Kosiba, the leader of the second great Jewish rebellion against Rome. He identified him as the "King Messiah" and "The star that comes forth from Jacob" (Num 24:17), thus giving support for his popular name Bar Kokhba, "Son of the Star."[8]

In the years 132-135 Bar Kokhba headed a revolt against Rome that was initially successful, resulting in the establishment of an independent Jewish administration which even struck coins commemorating the liberation of Judea.[9] This, of course, was intolerable to the Romans, and the rebellion was

---

[7]The first and last occurred in the land of Israel, the second in the Diaspora, in Egypt, Cyrenaica (part of present-day Libya) and Cyprus. As I am not going to comment further on the second Jewish rebellion (that of A.D. 115-117 in the Diaspora), I refer the interested reader to the relevant chapter in New Schürer 1, Part One, 21.2, pp. 529-34.

[8]Lam. Rab. 2:2; TJ Taanit 4:7. Cf. Peter Schäfer, "Rabbi Aqiva and Bar Kokhba," in Approaches to Ancient Judaism, ed. William Scott Green, Brown Judaic Studies 9 (Chico, Calif.: Scholars Press, 1980), 2:113-30; and Craig Evans, "Was Simon ben Kosiba Recognized as Messiah," in Evans, Jesus and his Contemporaries, pp. 183-212.

[9]On the Bar Kokhba revolt, cf. the studies listed in the Suggestions below, and in addition, Joseph A. Fitzmyer, "The Bar Kochba Period," in Essays on the Semitic Background of the New Testament, Sources for Biblical Study 3 (London: G. Chapman, 1971), pp. 305-54; Alon, The

brutally crushed. After they killed the last Jewish fighters, the Romans proceeded to take measures that would prevent any future conspiracy or revolt against the empire. Jews were excluded from Jerusalem, and the Holy City was converted into a pagan, Hellenistic city, called *Aelia Capitolina* ("The Capitol-City of the Aelian family"). A shrine to Jupiter was erected on the Temple Mount, and one to Aphrodite on the site held by the Christians to be the place of Calvary and the tomb of Jesus. (The Church of the Holy Sepulchre was built on this site in the fourth century. One of the arches through which Hadrian's temple was entered can still be seen in the "Russian Excavations" inside the Russian convent, to the east of the Holy Sepulchre.) To the south of this temple Hadrian leveled the ground to make room for the Roman forum (now in the Muristan area of the Christian quarter), and he partly changed the pattern of streets to fit this new center in the city. The new main street ran from north to south, passing the facade of the Aphrodite temple and ending at the new forum—along the line of present-day Suk Khan ez Zeit, which runs southwards from the Damascus Gate.[10]

The victory of Hellenism at last seemed complete. Hadrian had succeeded where Antiochus had failed; Jerusalem was now converted to a non-Jewish polis. The sources contain hints that this process had begun prior to Bar Kokhba's uprising, and that it was the main provocation for the revolt.[11]

From this it is evident that for the Jews, the issue at stake was not mainly political. Bar Kokhba and Rabbi Akiba must have felt that Judaism was once again being threatened, just as it was in the days of the Maccabean revolt. For them the uprising had religious motives, and they fought for the God of Israel and his Torah. Akiba's hope for the rebuilding of the temple is reflected in the prayer and benediction he added to the Passover Haggadah:

> Therefore, O Lord our God and the God of our fathers, bring us in peace to the other set feasts and festivals which are coming to meet us, while we rejoice in the building-up of your city and are joyful in your worship; and may we eat

---

Jews 2:570-637; Benjamin Isaac and Aharon Oppenheimer, "The Revolt of Bar Kokhba: Ideology and Modern Scholarship," *Journal of Jewish Studies* 36 (1985): 33-60.
[10]For a recent archaeological assessment of Hadrian's Aelia Capitolina, cf. Hillel Geva, "Searching for Roman Jerusalem," *Biblical Archaeological Review* 23, no. 6 (1997): 34-45, 72-73; Hanan Eshel, "Aelia Capitolina: Jerusalem No More," ibid.: 46-48, 73.
[11]Cf. G. W. Bowersock, "A Roman Perspective on the Bar Kochba War," in *Approaches to Ancient Judaism*, ed. William Scott Green, Brown Judaic Studies 9 (Chico, Calif.: Scholars Press, 1980), 2:131-42. Bowersock argues strongly for the view that Emperor Hadrian had begun to turn Jerusalem into a pagan temple-city before the Jewish revolt broke out, and that this project was among the causes of the revolt.

there of the sacrifices and of the Passover-offerings whose blood has reached with acceptance the wall of your Altar. . . . Blessed are you, O Lord, who has redeemed Israel! (*M Pesahim* 10:6)

The Tension Between Jews and Romans

As noted above, the Romans showed great respect for the religious traditions of conquered peoples. But this tolerance had some very pronounced limitations.[12] For one thing, foreign religions should not contain rites that were offensive to Roman standards of ethics and decency.[13] In this respect there was only one problem with the Jewish religion: the Romans, as Hellenists, strongly disliked circumcision. They considered it a mutilation of the body, contrary to their ideals of physical beauty and proper treatment of the body. Nevertheless, the Romans let their respect for ancestral traditions prevail over their dislike for the rite; besides, the Romans were shrewd realists who must have realized that a ban on circumcision would have been tantamount to a declaration of war on the whole Jewish nation in Israel and abroad. So the Romans grudgingly accepted circumcision, except perhaps in the days immediately prior to and after Bar Kokhba's revolt.

There is evidence to suggest that Emperor Hadrian issued a general ban on circumcision in the early 130s, and that this was one of the provocations that sparked the revolt. From a purely political point of view it was a hopeless decree. The Romans must soon have realized this; it seems that they silently let the ban be forgotten after some decades.

There was, however, another limitation to Roman tolerance that was more fundamental: no foreign religion should refuse to honor the Roman gods. As a rule this created no problems. Most subjects of the Roman Empire were polytheists, who willingly accorded the Roman gods their due honor—and no more. This was all that was required. Among the educated elite, some were philosophical monotheists, some agnostics and some atheists. In any case it did not trouble their conscience to pay homage to the gods—it was mostly a question of social and political expedience.

Not so with the Jews. In the Diaspora, the Gentile neighbors of the Jews had long noticed that the God of Israel was peculiar: he tolerated no other

---

[12]Cf. in general the studies by Juster, Smallwood, and Noetlichs listed in the Suggestions below. For shorter but instructive treatments, cf. W. H. C. Frend, "Rome and First-Century Judaism," in *The Early Church*, pp. 15-23; *New Schürer* 1:243-557; and Alon, "Attitude" (above, n. 6).

[13]A very good survey of Roman policy with regard to "foreign" cults is contained in Frend, *Martyrdom and Persecution*, pp. 104-26.

Box 2.1. Romans and Jews: Some Main Events

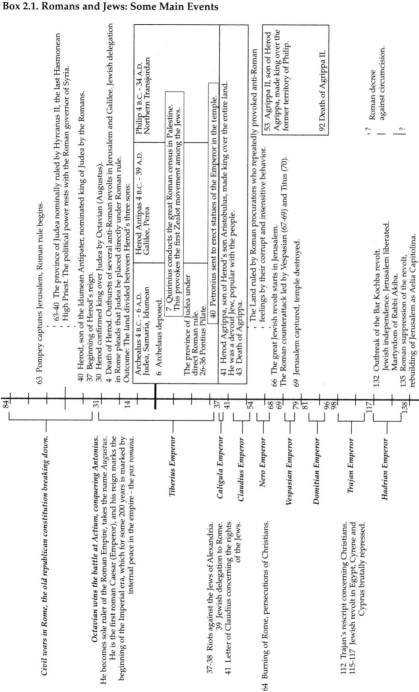

gods. "The Greeks were prepared to accept the God of Israel into their Pantheon, but they were faced with a riddle. The gods of Greece could easily compromise with the God of Israel, but He could not compromise with them. This was hard to understand."[14] Converts to Judaism behaved strangely: they no longer visited the temples of the gods of their fathers and fellow citizens, and avoided dining with their relatives and former friends. It seemed that they despised official religion and avoided close contact with other men, arousing the dislike of their neighbors. The Jews were branded atheists (deniers of the Roman gods) and haters of men. The Roman historian Tacitus was probably speaking for many when he said about the Jews,

> they are extremely loyal toward one another, and always ready to show compassion [towards one another], but toward every other people they feel only hate and enmity. They sit apart at meals and they sleep apart, and although as a race, they are prone to lust, they abstain from intercourse with foreign women; yet among themselves nothing is unlawful. They adopted circumcision to distinguish themselves from other peoples by this difference. Those who are converted to their ways follow the same practice, and the earliest lesson they receive is to despise the gods, to disown their country, and to regard their parents, children, and brothers as of little account. (*Historiae* 5.5.1-2)[15]

Already in pre-Christian times we hear of pogroms against the Jews in

---

[14]Tcherikover, *Hellenistic Civilization*, p. 374.
[15]Quoted according to Stern, *Greek and Latin Authors* 2, no. 281, p. 26. It should be noted that Tacitus also had more positive things to say about the Jews, and that he was by no means among the extreme Jew-haters of antiquity. Cf. esp. David Rokeah, "Tacitus and Ancient Antisemitism," *Revue des études juives* 154 (1995): 281-94. There is a lot of ancient source material on pagan attitudes toward and ideas about the Jewish people, conveniently collected in Stern's three volumes (arranged by author) and in Whittaker's one-volume anthology (arranged according to themes); see the references in the Suggestions in chapter 1. Here it may be pertinent to add some other examples that show part of the tradition to which Tacitus belonged. (1) Diodorus (first century B.C.): "The majority of his [Antiochus Sidetes'] friends advised the king to take the city by storm and wipe out completely the race of the Jews, since they alone of all nations avoided dealings with any other people and looked upon all men as their enemies. . . . [The Jews] had made their hatred of mankind into a tradition, and on this account had introduced utterly outlandish laws: not to break bread with any other race, nor to show them any good will at all. . . . [This was due to Moses] who had ordained for the Jews their misanthropic and lawless customs" (*Bibliotheca Historica* 34-35.1.1-3; Stern no. 63 = 1.183). (2) Apollonius Molon (first century B.C.): "Apollonius reviles us [Jews] in one place as atheists and misanthropes" (Josephus, *Against Apion* 2.145; Stern no. 49 = 1.155). Cf. the following studies: Sevenster (listed above in chapter one, n. 16); David Rokeah, *Jews, Pagans and Christians in Conflict*, Studia Post-Biblica 33 (Leiden: E. J. Brill/Jerusalem: Magnes, 1982), esp. pp. 56-61; John G. Gager, *The Origins of Anti-Semitism: Attitudes Toward Judaism in Pagan and Christian Antiquity* (New York/Oxford: Oxford University Press, 1983), esp. pp. 35-112.

some of the greatest cities of the Roman Empire.

The Romans must have been aware of Jewish objections to worshipping the Roman gods from the very beginning of their alliance with the Jewish people. No homage whatever would be offered to the Roman gods in the temple of Jerusalem. The best the Jews could do was to say prayers and offer sacrifices to the God of Israel for Caesar's well-being. And so they did, from the time of the first emperor, Augustus, and right up to the outbreak of the great revolt in A.D. 66.[16]

Josephus tells a moving story related to this sacrifice. The Emperor Caligula (A.D. 37-41) in a fit of megalomania ordered that statues of himself be erected in all the temples of the empire, Jerusalem included. The Roman general Petronius was sent to Israel with three legions and an order to place the emperor's statue in the temple, and "in the event of the Jews refusing to admit them, his orders were to put the recalcitrants to death and to reduce the whole nation to slavery." In Tiberias, Petronius spent fifty days negotiating with the Jewish leaders and an assembly of the people. He told them that their protests against the images of Caesar were unreasonable, because "all the subject nations . . . had erected in each of their cities statues of Caesar, along with those of their other gods, and that they alone should oppose this practice amounted almost to rebellion, aggravated by insult." But the Jews stubbornly referred to their Law, which did not permit any image at all to be erected in their country, much less in the temple, and said they were ready to suffer for the Law. Petronius then quieted them, and said to them, "Will you then go to war with Caesar?" The Jews replied that they offered sacrifice twice daily for Caesar and the Roman people, but that if he wished to set up these statues, he must first sacrifice the entire Jewish nation. This made such an impression on Petronius that he decided not to carry out Caesar's orders, but rather to try to persuade Caesar to change his mind, and if he should fail in this, "I am ready on behalf of the lives of so many to surrender my own." Josephus concluded his story of this noble Roman officer with great satisfaction: Caesar was indeed enraged and sent a letter threatening Petronius that he would die if he did not immediately carry out the emperor's orders. But this letter was delayed for three months due to a storm, and in the meantime Petronius received another letter—this one informing him of the emperor's

---

[16]For similar practices in earlier times, see Ezra 6:9-10 and 1 Macc 7:33: "After these things Nicanor went up to Mount Zion; and there came some of the priests out of the sanctuary, and some of the elders of the people, to salute him peaceably and show him the whole burnt sacrifice that was being offered for the [Syrian] king [160 B.C.]."

death! (*Jewish War* 2.184-203).

This direct attempt to paganize the temple worship in Jerusalem was not typical of the general Roman attitude. But the Jewish refusal to recognize the gods of Rome continued to irritate and annoy the Romans—to say the least. And the annoyance was mutual.[17]

This incident vividly calls our attention to a new factor that had made itself increasingly evident since the days of Augustus: the worship of the emperor's genius—his personal protecting and sustaining deity.[18] In theory, the Roman emperors did not claim to be gods, and the incense burnt in front of their statues was not meant to be a sacrifice offered to Caesar personally, but only to his genius. This distinction, however, was more easily grasped by the sophisticated Romans than by the citizens of the East, who for centuries had been accustomed to the idea of divine kingship. The Romans were hardly eager to clarify the distinction. To the contrary, this worship of the emperor was of fundamental political significance, as it was tantamount to a declaration of loyalty to Rome. If the orientals held Caesar to be god, so much the better.

To the Jews, the worship offered to Caesar's statues was, of course, completely unacceptable. The Romans were never able to understand the religious motives for this refusal and tended to interpret it in political terms. As Petronius said in the story above, to refuse the emperor's worship "amounted almost to rebellion, aggravated by insult."

The fact that the Jews—however grudgingly—were allowed to not participate in emperor worship can only be explained by the fact that another Roman principle protected the Jews, namely, the Roman respect for ancestral traditions. Besides, the Romans were realists, and they clearly recognized that enforcement of emperor worship among the Jews would have entailed a mass slaughter of terrible proportions. The Romans were not overly sentimental about the value of human life and could be ruthlessly brutal, but their ideals were against unnecessary violence. Petronius again reminds us of the best in Roman morality. So the Jews were left in peace—to some extent. But they were disliked and were considered politically unreliable, especially after the three rebellions. They were treated with suspicion, even though their legal right to remain faithful Jews was recognized. Again a Roman author may speak for many when he said, in the 220s A.D.:

---

[17]We shall return to the Jewish attitude in chapter five (pp. 126-29).
[18]On this, see G. W. Bowersock, "The Imperial Cult: Perceptions and Persistence," Sanders, *Self-Definition* 3:171-82, 238-41.

The Jews have long been in revolt not only against the Romans but against humanity; and a race that has made its own a life apart and irreconcilable, that cannot share with the rest of mankind in the pleasures of the table nor join in their libations or prayers or sacrifices, are separated from ourselves by a greater gulf than divides us from Susa or Bactra or the more distant Indias. What sense then or reason was there in chastising them for revolting from us, whom we had better never annexed? (Philostratus, *Life of Apollonius* 5.35)[19]

There is a revealing sequel to the story related above concerning the Emperor Caligula. On the death of Caligula, Claudius was made emperor (A.D. 41), and the Jews of Alexandria sent emissaries to him—formally to congratulate him on his accession, in fact to win his favor. To the Jews this was especially important because in A.D. 38 there had been an anti-Jewish pogrom in Alexandria, led by the Roman governor, and the former emperor had not taken appropriate action. The reply of the new Emperor Claudius has been preserved. In respect to Roman law the emperor was strictly correct and impartial: both sides had been guilty of riot and were rebuked. The Jews should enjoy the privileges they possessed in the time of Augustus, but no more. After this had been said, the emperor began to betray his own true feelings about the Jews. They should not behave as though they lived in a city separate from their Alexandrian neighbors. They "are not to introduce or invite other Jews who sail down to Alexandria from Syria or Egypt, thus compelling me to conceive the greater suspicion; otherwise, I will by all means take vengeance on them as fomenting a general plague [disorder] in the whole world."[20]

The Legal Position of Jewish and Gentile Believers

The above description of the Roman attitude toward the Jews and their religion contains the clue to understanding the policy followed by the Roman Empire with regard to the believers in Jesus. It is immediately apparent that this policy would be quite different, depending upon whether the believer in Jesus was Jewish or not, at least in the first decades after A.D. 30.

(1) If Jewish, the person remained a Jew in the eyes of the Romans, legally and otherwise, and his or her purely religious convictions were of no concern to them. They would not be involved in internal Jewish disputes and refused to intervene unless social peace and stability were at stake. In other words,

---

[19]Stern no. 403 = 2.342.
[20]The complete text of Claudius's letter is to be found in English translation in Lewis/Reinhold, *Roman Civilization*, pp. 285-88.

Jewish believers in Jesus were basically treated by the Romans on par with other Jews. We see this Roman attitude clearly demonstrated in Acts 18:12-17 (indicated with italics):

> When Gallio was proconsul of Achaia, the Jews made a united attack on Paul and brought him before the tribunal. They said, "This man is persuading people to worship God in ways that are contrary to the law." Just as Paul was about to speak, Gallio said to the Jews, "If it were a matter of crime or serious villainy, I would be justified in accepting the complaint of you Jews; but since *it is a matter of questions about words and names and your own law,* see to it yourselves; I do not wish to be a judge of these matters." And he dismissed them from the tribunal. Then all of them seized Sosthenes, the official of the synagogue, and beat him in front of the tribunal. But Gallio paid no attention to any of these things.

After the crucifixion of Jesus, belief in his messiahship was no longer a political concern for the Romans; if Jews came to believe in Jesus as the Messiah, they nevertheless remained Jews and were entitled to the same protection and privileges as other Jews, including exemption from emperor worship. Throughout Acts, the Romans appear as Paul's protectors, not his persecutors. The Jews who believed in Jesus were not persecuted by the Romans, but—when persecutions occurred, according to Acts—by their fellow Jews.[21]

The situation was different for Gentile converts to Christianity. They could not claim, like the Jews, to be following their ancestral traditions. On the contrary, they broke with the tradition of their fathers in a most provocative way. At baptism, before confessing his faith, the Gentile had to say the following about his past life as a participator in official Greco-Roman religion: "I renounce you, Satan, with all your pomp and splendor." That is, I renounce all my former religious loyalties and obligations, and I now see them as slavery to the devil.[22]

---

[21]After some time, the situation probably became more blurred in practice. When prosecution of people denounced as Christians became the official Roman policy, the status of "Christian" might be more significant to the Roman officials than the status of "Jew" for Jewish Christians. They would probably then regard Jewish believers in Jesus as Jews who had joined an illegal sect. In that case, the Jewish believers would have little protection from their status as Jews. Perhaps we are here touching upon the legal background of John's banishment to Patmos in the days of Domitian (the 90s A.D.).

[22]The first Christian writer to record this renunciation at baptism was Tertullian in the 190s A.D., but very likely it antedated him by several decades. Cf. Tertullian, *On the Crown* 3; *On the Shows* 4 (e.g., in Whitaker, *Documents*, p. 9); and Hans Kirsten, *Die Taufabsage: Eine Untersuchung zu Gestalt und Geschichte der Taufe nach den altkirchlichen Taufliturgien* (Berlin: Evangelische Verlagsanstalt, 1960).

To put it mildly, this was not destined to make the Christians popular with their families and neighbors who remained loyal to the inherited religion of their fathers. If the Jews had been called atheists and haters of men, how much more so the Gentile converts to Christianity! They shared with the Jews the burden of being accused of intolerance, but they did not have the defense the Jews had: they could claim no ancestral or national tradition, for they had no Christian or Jewish forefathers, and they were not a nation. They could be persecuted individually, since there was no question of having to massacre a whole nation. So none of the restraints which prevented the Romans from taking wholesale action against the Jews were at work with regard to the Gentile converts.[23]

In general, the Romans had a strong dislike for any change of religious loyalty. You should respect the Roman gods and worship the gods of your fathers. Period. But this quite simply did not work in the Roman Empire, and the Romans had to take some of the blame themselves. Their excellent administration and communication systems had the effect of breaking down national and linguistic barriers, so people of different religious convictions met and talked with each other and influenced each other. Gods who had been local deities of a tribe or a nation began to travel—they were brought to new cities all along the Mediterranean coast, and ultimately they arrived in Rome. The capital of the empire increasingly became a kind of religious supermarket where you could always hear something new and interesting— as Luke tells about the Athenians (Acts 17:21).[24]

The Romans did not like this,[25] but neither could they stop it. So they established a commission of fifteen men who were to inspect foreign religions and decide which of them should be "recognized" (religio licita). Christianity was never officially allowed by the empire (until it suddenly became the favored religion under Constantine). We have seen the reasons for this. Christianity grew out of Judaism and was, like Judaism, incompatible with emperor worship and respect for the Roman gods. But the Gentile Christians

---

[23]Cf. the excellent treatment of this issue in Frend, *Martyrdom and Persecution.*

[24]One of the best descriptions of migrating religions and the Roman response is found in Arthur Darby Nock, *Conversion: The Old and the New in Religion from Alexander the Great to Augustine of Hippo* (Oxford: Clarendon Press, 1933; paperback reprint London/Oxford/ New York: Oxford University Press 1961/1972), chaps. 3-8.

[25]The Roman historian Tacitus probably spoke for many when he complained that all sorts of foreign cults made their way to Rome, "where all things hideous and shamefull from every part of the world find their centre and become popular" (*Annales* 15.44.3; Barrett, *Documents*, p. 16).

had no excuse which the Romans could understand and accept. How miserable was their legal standing! It has been much disputed among scholars
whether Nero passed a specific law that made Christianity as such illegal. It is
as difficult to prove as to disprove the existence of such a law,[26] but in any
case it would probably have made little difference. The point is not that
Christianity was officially made illegal, but that it was never made legal.

Initially, the Romans took little notice of the Gentile converts, partly
because they were few in number, so few as to escape notice, and partly
because they were regarded as converts to Judaism. But toward the end of the
first century A.D. the Romans must have become increasingly aware that Gentile converts to Christianity did not become Jews and were not recognized as
such by the Jews. In other words, it was the Gentile converts—not the Jewish
believers—who made the Roman authorities aware that Christianity was no
ordinary Jewish sect. But then what was it? It was as hostile to Hellenistic
cults and religions as Judaism ever was. The Christians were not "Greeks,"
but neither were they Jews. Some began to call them "the third race," and
eventually the Christians adopted this designation and applied it to themselves with great pride. They were something new; they belonged to a category unheard of in Hellenistic culture.[27]

The Christians may have been proud of this, but the sentiment of their
contemporaries is summarized bluntly in a phrase quoted by Tertullian: "You
ought not to exist" (*Apology* 4.4). Thus for non-Jews, Christianity was not formally allowed. This meant that Gentile converts to Christianity fell victim to
the changing moods and the personal likes and dislikes of Roman officials,
from the emperor on down. Until the time of Decius (A.D. 250), the Roman
officials were under no obligation to actively investigate Christians. An order
given by Trajan (A.D. 112) expressly said that they were not to be sought out.
Trajan's order came in response to a question from one of his lieutenants,
Pliny the Younger, who had been sent as the emperor's special envoy to the
province of Pontus-Bithynia on the south coast of the Black Sea. The question,

---

[26]The scholarly debate has focused on two passages in Tertullian in which he speaks of an
"institution from Nero" (*institutum neronianum*), *To the Nations* 1.7 and *Apology* 5. Cf. the
discussions in A. N. Sherwin-White, "Early Persecutions and Roman Law Again," *Journal
of Theological Studies*, n.s., 3 (1952): 199-213; J. Zeiller, "Institutum Neronianum," *Revue
d'histoire ecclesiastique* 55 (1955): 393-400; Frend, *Martyrdom and Persecution*, pp. 165-71.
[27]On the Christians as a "third race," see *Preaching of Peter* (ca. A.D. 125), fragm. 2a (in Hennecke, *Apocrypha* 2:100); *Apology* of Aristides, 2; Pseudo-Cyprian *De Pascha Computus* 17.
Cf. esp. Adolf von Harnack, "Die Beurteilung der Christen als drittes Geschlecht seitens
ihrer Gegner," and "Die Botschaft von dem neuen Volk und dem dritten Geschlecht," in
Harnack, *Mission*, pp. 281-89 and 259-67.

as well as the answer, are of considerable interest:

[Pliny:] My Lord: It is my custom to consult you whenever I am in doubt about any matter. Who can better direct my hesitation or instruct my ignorance? I have never been present at trials of Christians. Consequently I do not know the precedents concerning the question of punishment or the nature of the inquisition. I have been in no little doubt whether one should discriminate with regard to age, or whether the young are to be treated no differently from the older; whether renunciation is to be rewarded with indulgence, or if it is of no consequence to have abandoned Christianity if one has once been a Christian; whether the very profession of the name is to be punished, or only the disgraceful practices which go along with the name. So far my procedure when people were charged before me with being Christians has been the following: I have asked the accused if they were Christians. If they said 'Yes' I asked them a second and a third time, warning them of the penalty. If they were stubborn I ordered them to be led off to execution. For I had no doubt that, whatever kind of thing it was that they pleaded guilty to, their very stubbornness and unyielding obstinacy in any case deserved to be punished. There were others afflicted with the same madness whom I decided should be sent to Rome, because they were Roman citizens.[28]

[Emperor Trajan:] My dear Secundus: You have acted absolutely correctly in deciding the cases of those who have been charged before you with being Christians. No general decision can be made by which a standard procedure could be established. They must not be ferreted out. If they are charged and convicted, they must be punished, provided that all who deny that they are Christians and give practical proof of that by invoking our gods, should be pardoned because of this repudiation, no matter what grounds for suspicion may have existed against them in the past. You should pay no attention to anonymous documents which are laid before you. They form a very bad precedent and are quite unworthy of the present age. (Pliny, *Epistles* 10.96, 97; author's translation)

The gist of this correspondence seems pretty clear: The Romans thought

---

[28]In the rest of Pliny's letter, which is too long to be quoted in full here, he goes into some detail as to his interrogation technique and what he found out in his interrogations. Some of this will be quoted later, in chapter nineteen on early Christian worship. Notice the following about his "test" technique in interrogation: "Some [of the denounced persons] denied that they were Christians or had ever been so. When I instructed them to do so, they invoked the gods and did reverence with incense and wine to your image, which I had ordered to be brought for this purpose, and also statues of the gods; they also cursed Christ. *As I am informed that people who are really Christians cannot possibly be made to do any of those things,* I considered that those who did them should be discharged."

that the best one could do with the Christians was to ignore them as much as possible; probably the whole thing would soon die out by itself, whereas too much attention and publicity might have the opposite effect. The number of Christians had increased alarmingly for a while, said Pliny, but with a lenient policy, granting ample opportunity to recant Christian faith, there is good hope: "The temples, which had been almost abandoned, are beginning to have visitors again; and the customary services, neglected for a long time, are beginning to be resumed." So let the whole thing die out through lack of attention.

But once Christians had drawn attention to themselves and were known by the authorities, the normal procedure was to verify the accusations. If the accused persisted in their refusal to sacrifice to Caesar's image, they would usually be executed.

Epilogue

We have seen in this chapter how the Roman policy toward the Jewish people goes a long way in explaining the subsequent Roman policy with regard to the Christians, and why Jewish and Gentile believers in Jesus were treated differently, at least in the early period. Before we continue to look more closely at the religious consequences of the Roman-Jewish encounter, we shall add, in the next chapter, some considerations on what we might call the "Jewish geography" of early Christianity.

Temple Square
In Jerusalem there reigned an invisible king and his visible representative: the high priest. The temple was the palace of the heavenly king. To the Romans, this represented an insoluble dilemma: they knew that if they challenged this center of the Jewish nation, if they tried to occupy it, plain and simple, a mass insurrection and a massacre of the whole people would follow. On the other hand, as long as they did not control this power-base, their control was always incomplete and precarious. The concrete symbol of the Roman attempt to deal with this dilemma was the Roman garrison in the Antonia Fortress overlooking the temple courtyards: control without interference. Whenever the Romans slipped off this tightrope, revolt threatened. When the revolt finally became unavoidable, the rebels took their last stand in the temple. And the Romans had learned their lesson: they razed the temple, eliminating it forever. Only with the temple eliminated was there any prospect of full Roman control.

As in the days of the Hellenistic challenge, this posed a new challenge to Judaism: could it redefine itself once more? We have seen how crucial, how indispensable the temple had been for Jewish identity, for the status of Israel as a holy, a pure people, a people apart. But however this question was answered, however this challenge was met, Judaism would forever bear the mark of the temple, and so would Christianity.

Suggestions for Further Reading

For good treatments of the theme of this chapter, see Murphy, *Religious World*, pp. 247-310; 345-55; Schiffman, *Text to Tradition*, pp. 139-76.

The two classic studies on Rome and the Jews are Jean Juster, *Les Juifs dans l'Empire Romain: Leur condition juridique, économique et sociale*, Vols. 1-2. (Paris: Paul Geuthner, 1914 [reprint, New York: 1966); and Max Radin, *The Jews among the Greeks and Romans* (Philadelphia: Jewish Publication Society of America, 1915).

A selection of more recent studies are: Michael Grant, *The Jews in the Roman World* (London: Weidenfeld & Nicholson, 1973); E. Mary Smallwood, *The Jews Under Roman Rule from Pompey to Diocletian: A Study in Political Relations*, Studies in Judaism in Late Antiquity 22 (Leiden: E. J. Brill, 1976 [reprint with corrections, 1981]); U. Baumann, *Rom und die Juden: Die römisch-jüdische Beziehungen von Pompeius bis zum Tode des Herodes (63 v.Chr.-4 v.Chr.)* (Bern: Peter Lang, 1984); Amnon Linder, *The Jews in Roman Imperial Legislation* (Detroit/Jerusalem: Wayne State University Press, 1987); Karl Leo Noetlichs, *Das Judentum und der römische Staat: Minderheitspolitik im antiken Rom* (Darmstadt: Wissenschaftliche Buchgesellschaft, 1996).

On the Bar Kokhba war: Yigael Yadin, *Bar-Kokhba: The Rediscovery of the Legendary Hero of the Second Jewish Revolt Against Imperial Rome* (London: Weidenfeld & Nicholson, 1971); Peter Schäfer, *Der Bar Kokhba-Aufstand*, Texte und Studien zum Antiken Judentum 1 (Tübingen: J. C. B. Mohr, 1981).

Concerning the legal status of Christians and the Roman persecutions, one should read the excellent chapters on this theme in Frend, *Martyrdom and Persecution*.

3

THE GEOGRAPHICAL
DIMENSION
THE LAND OF ISRAEL
& THE DIASPORA

*I*n the period of early Christianity, Jews were settled in two geographical settings
that were significantly different: the land of Israel and the Diaspora ("the dispersion," meaning all lands outside Israel). This basic "Jewish geography" is crucial to
understanding important aspects of early church history, which we will explore further in chapters nine and ten.

The Diaspora

In order to understand the geography of the Jewish people in the period that
concerns us, we will have to go back to the Babylonian exile (587-538 B.C.).
The first thing to notice is that not all the Jews who had been deported to
Babylon returned to Jerusalem. Some remained in Babylon; they thrived and
multiplied there and were destined to become an influential and even dominant factor in the shaping—centuries later—of rabbinic Judaism. The very
title of the Babylonian Talmud reminds us of this.

To escape the invading Babylonians, some Jews fled to Egypt (Jer 43—44),
perhaps because they had friends and relatives living there already. In any
case, the Egyptian diaspora should be considered at least as old as the Babylonian. Under the friendly rule of the Ptolemies, the Jews in Egypt, and espe-

cially in Alexandria, became a large and influential minority—so large, in fact, that in the first century B.C. they constituted a majority in two of the city's five districts. They were also present as minorities in the other three.[1]

The period of Hellenistic rule proved to be a time in which Jews seized the opportunity to settle in areas previously unknown to them. We do not have sufficient source material to follow this process of emigration in detail, nor is it necessary for our purpose. The result, however, is highly relevant: at the turn of the millennium, Jews were settled in large and small communities from the Persian Gulf in the East and all around the Mediterranean, as far as Spain and possibly Morocco in the West. The words of the Roman historian Strabo, writing at the time of Augustus, are quite to the point: "This people has already made its way to every city, and it is not easy to find any place in the habitable world which has not received this nation and in which it has not made its power felt" (quoted by Josephus, *Antiquities* 14.115).

It should be emphasized that the Jews' gradual settlement of Mesopotamia and the Mediterranean coastlands did not come about as a result of expulsion from the land of Israel. Expulsion was formative for the Babylonian and Egyptian diasporas, but from then on, the spread of Jews throughout the ancient world was mostly a result of their own initiative. The ancient historians were impressed by the rapid growth of these new Jewish communities. It seems as if the vitality of the nation found other ways of expression in the Diaspora than in their native land.[2]

The Land of Israel

During most of the period following the Babylonian exile, the situation in Jerusalem and Judea must have seemed rather discouraging. The Persians allowed the creation of a small Jewish province only surrounding Jerusalem. The rest of the land was inhabited by a mixed population, which Ezra commanded the people of Judah not to recognize as Jews. It was, by the way, in this time that *Jew* (*Judean*)—originally referring to descendants of Judah, and

---

[1] Philo, *In Flacc.* 55. Cf. Tcherikover, *Hellenistic Civilization*, pp. 284-85.

[2] On Jews and Judaism in the Diaspora, cf. the literature listed under this heading in the Suggestions below, and also: Martin Hengel, *Jews, Greeks and Barbarians: Aspects of the Hellenization of Judaism in the Pre-Christian Period* (London: SCM Press, 1980), pp. 83-109; A. T. Kraabel, "The Roman Diaspora: Six Questionable Assumptions," in *Essays in Honour of Yigael Yadin*, ed. Geza Vermes and Jacob Neusner (Totowa, N.J.: Allanheld, Osmun & Co., 1983 [=*The Journal of Jewish Studies* 33 (1982)]), pp. 445-64; John J. Collins, *Seers, Sibyls and Sages in Hellenistic-Roman Judaism*, Supplements to the Journal for the Study of Judaism 54 (Leiden: E. J. Brill, 1997).

later to inhabitants of the southern kingdom—came to include all members of the people of Israel.

The Jewish nation was thus for a long time a mini-nation, only in the Judean hills. It was "a semi-independent province, a kind of enlarged temple estate ruled by a high priest."[3] There were also Jews living outside this mini-nation. By the second century B.C. they were probably the majority in Galilee, but were not part of the Jewish political entity.

The Hasmoneans extended the territory of Judah in all directions. They conquered the Idumeans in the south and forced them to convert to Judaism, and gained dominion over the coastal areas to the west and north of Jerusalem. In the north they gained political dominion over Samaria and Galilee (from 104 B.C.), and even some Transjordan territory. The New Testament also talks about two centers of Jewish population: Judea, including Jerusalem, and Galilee. In between these was Samaria. Ever since the Hasmoneans destroyed the Samaritan temple on Mount Gerizim (128 B.C.) and the city of Shechem, the relationships between Jews and Samaritans was characterized by mutual hostility and distrust (Jn 4:9). When the inhabitants of Galilee went up to Jerusalem for the festivals, they usually avoided the roads which passed through Samaria (but cf. Jn 4:4). Instead, they took the route to the east of the Jordan (Mk 10:1), crossing back over the river near Jericho (Lk 19:1) and from there ascending to Jerusalem (Lk 19:28; Mk 10:32-34). Jesus followed this route on his last journey to Jerusalem.

The Galilee

The Galilee was, agriculturally, the most fertile part of Israel.[4]

> For the land is everywhere so rich in soil and pasturage and produces such variety of trees, that even the most indolent are tempted by these facilities to devote themselves to agriculture. In fact, every inch of the soil has been cultivated by the inhabitants; there is not a parcel of waste land. The towns, too, are thickly distributed, and even the villages, thanks to the fertility of the soil, are all so

---

[3]M. Avi-Yonah, "Historical Geography of Palestine," in *Compendia 1:1*: 78-116; quotation pp. 80-81.

[4]Cf. the paragraph on Galilee in the Suggestions below, and also Eric M. Meyers, "The Cultural Setting of Galilee: The Case of Regionalism and Early Judaism," in Haase, *Aufstieg 2* 19.1:686-702; Meyers/Strange, *Archaeology*, pp. 31-47; Eric M. Meyers, "Galilean Regionalism: A Reappraisal," in *Studies in Judaism and Its Greco-Roman Context*, Approaches to Ancient Judaism, ed. William Scott Green, Brown Judaic Studies 32 (Atlanta, Ga.: Scholars Press, 1985), 5:115-32; Shmuel Safrai, "The Jewish Cultural Nature of Galilee in the First Century," *Immanuel* 24/25 (1990): 147-86.

densely populated that the smallest of them contains above fifteen thousand inhabitants. (Josephus, *Jewish War* 3.3.2 [42-43])[5]

This description brings the Galilee of Jesus' day to life: a fertile, pleasant land, dotted with villages of farmers and craftsmen, with fishing villages on the shores of the Sea of Galilee. Not all of these settlements were Jewish. Although the Hasmoneans had used violent measures against the non-Jewish residents of Galilee during the 104 B.C. colonization, a considerable number of Gentiles remained. The population of Galilee in those days may have reached 150,000,[6] most of whom lived in the region's more than two hundred villages.[7] (Nazareth was a tiny village of less than 500 people; Capernaum had a population of perhaps 1,500.) In the days of Jesus there were two large Hellenistic cities in Galilee: Sepphoris and Tiberias. Sepphoris was the regional capital of Galilee until its destruction in the uprising that followed the death of Herod. His son, Herod Antipas, rebuilt the city and made it a provincial capital in 3 B.C. Up until the days of Trajan (A.D. 117), most of the residents of Sepphoris were Jews. The city was built in the Hellenistic style, and only Jerusalem surpassed it in beauty and size (some 10,000-15,000 residents in the time of Jesus).[8]

---

[5]On Josephus as a "geographer," see Zeev Safrai, "The Description of the Land of Israel in Josephus' Works," in *Josephus, the Bible, and History*, ed. Louis H. Feldman and Gohei Hata (Leiden: E. J. Brill, 1989), pp. 295-324; on his description of Galilee in particular, p. 301. The population numbers given by Josephus are generally considered to be wildly exaggerated, they should sometimes be divided by 10 to arrive at reasonable figures; cf. the remarks on this in Wilkinson, *Jerusalem*, p. 23.

[6]Modern scholarly estimates of the population in villages, towns, and cities in Galilee are widely divergent, and probably not very reliable. Cf. the discussion in Richard A. Horsley, *Galilee: History, Politics, People* (Valley Forge, Penn.: Trinity Press International, 1995), pp. 166-67; 193. I follow his rather conservative estimates, based on an average quota of inhabitants per square hectare in ancient towns (like Pompeii, where it is roughly known).

[7]Josephus, in *Life* 235, says there were 240, and for once he may be quite correct, having some kind of official list (for taxation?) at his disposal.

[8]The recent grand-scale excavations in Sepphoris have resulted in a flood of books and articles. The following is but a narrow selection: Stuart S. Miller, *Studies in the History and Traditions of Sepphoris*, Studies in Judaism in Late Antiquity 37 (Leiden: E. J. Brill, 1984); Eric M. Meyers, Ehud Netzer and Carol L. Meyers, "Sepphoris 'Ornament of All Galilee,'" *Biblical Archaeologist* 49 (1986): 4-19; Eric M. Meyers, Ehud Netzer, and Carol L. Meyers, "Artistry in Stone: The Mosaics of Ancient Sepphoris," *Biblical Archaeologist* 50 (1987): 223-31; Richard A. Batey, *Jesus and the Forgotten City* (Grand Rapids, Mich.: Baker, 1991); Stuart S. Miller, "Sepphoris, the Well Remembered City," *Biblical Archaeologist* 55 (1992): 74-83. There has been considerable debate on how Jewish or pagan Sepphoris was, which has been thought to be significant with regard to the cultural background of Jesus. See recently Mark Chancey and Eric M. Meyers, "How Jewish Was Sepphoris in Jesus' Time?" *Biblical Archaeology Review* 26, no. 4 (2000): 18-33, 61.

Nazareth is only five kilometers from Sepphoris. It is very likely that the young Jesus visited this city and received many impressions about life in a bourgeois metropolis.[9] Craftsmen from Nazareth were probably employed in Herod Antipas's building projects. Perhaps the carpenter Joseph and his son were among them. Jesus' sayings and teachings reveal his familiarity with big city life, and in this he was probably no different from his audience. See, for example, Jesus' words about kings, their rule and life in the royal court in Luke 7:25; 14:31-32; Matthew 18:21-35; 22:1-14; 25:31-46.

One of Jesus' followers was Joanna, the wife of Cuza, the manager of Herod Antipas's household. Joanna was one of the women who traveled with Jesus in Galilee and helped to support him (see Lk 8:1-3; 24:10). Her husband's office makes it highly probable that she and her family were living in Sepphoris.

Sepphoris was the capital of Galilee until approximately A.D. 20, when this honor was transferred to the newly founded city of Tiberias, named for the Emperor Tiberius. Tiberias, under greater Hellenistic influence, soon rivaled Sepphoris in size and significance.[10] In this context see the reference to the Sea of Galilee (or Kinnereth) as the "Sea of Tiberias" in John 6:1 and 21:1. In the second part of the second century A.D., Tiberias became the main rabbinical center in Israel.

On the Jezreel plain and in the Transjordan there were ten more Hellenistic cities, which had been joined together in the "Decapolis league" since the days of Pompey (63 B.C.).[11] Jews living in the Decapolis cities maintained close commercial ties with their brethren in Lower Galilee. Jews living in Galilee were by no means isolated from the Gentile world; it was very close to them. Some of the Galilean villages, including Nazareth, were situated close to a major commercial route, the "Via Maris," connecting Tyre with Sepphoris and ending in Tiberias and Capernaum.[12] Only one part of the Galilee wasn't influenced by

---

[9]On rabbinic responses to the dilemmas of Jewish life in mixed (Hellenistic) cities, cf. Jacob Neusner, "The Experience of the City in Late Antique Judaism," in *Studies in Judaism and Its Greco-Roman Context,* Approaches to Ancient Judaism, ed. William Scott Green, Brown Judaic Studies 32 (Atlanta, Ga.: Scholars Press, 1985), 5:37-52; Peder Borgen, "'Yes,' 'No,' 'How Far?' The Participation of Jews and Christians in Pagan Cults," in *Early Christianity,* pp. 15-43.

[10]Cf. Stuart S. Miller, "Intercity Relations in Roman Palestine: The Case of Sepphoris and Tiberias," *Association of Jewish Studies Review* 12 (1987): 1-24.

[11]Cf. Iain Browning, *Jerash and the Decapolis* (London: Chatto & Windus, 1982).

[12]Cf. Barry J. Beitzel, "The *Via Maris* in Literary and Cartographic Sources," *Biblical Archaeologist* 54 (1991): 64-75. In this article, Beitzel corrects the traditional view that the Via Maris

this exposure: the region called Upper Galilee (see figure 1.1). Here there were no Hellenistic cities, and the region was a hothouse of extreme Jewish nationalism. The Zealots recruited some of their most aggressive leaders and fighters from Upper Galilee. Others came from Gamla, on the Golan Heights, which belonged to the territory of Herod Philip from the year 4 B.C.

It should be added, though, that the above description of Upper Galilee as a hothouse of Jewish zealot nationalism is not entirely uncontested by scholars.[13] It is even more difficult to say something certain and uncontroversial about the religious character of Galilee in general. Were Galilean Jews more or less obedient to the law than the Judeans? And were they less committed to Pharisaical interpretations than their Judean compatriots? Had piety a different character in Galilee? Scholars give widely differing answers to these questions because the available literary evidence is slim and ambiguous, and the archaeological indications from the first-century period extremely scanty. It seems, however, that as the recent "colony" under Judean authority, Galilee was to some extent characterized by its greater distance from the established center of political and religious authority: Jerusalem. It is very likely that "the scribes and Pharisees" represented *Judean* authority and leadership in Galilee, and that their presence there was a kind of continuation of the Hasmonean colonization or conquest policy. (We shall have more to say about this in chapters four and five.)[14]

With regard to our overarching theme—the history of early Christianity—two points should be made concerning Galilee as the region of Jesus' ministry.

1. The first is that although Galilee was in many ways "rural," it was by no means devoid of urban life and culture. It may be anachronistic to think in terms of this dichotomy at all, at least as anything like absolute. Peasants in those days lived in villages and towns, and many of the more urbanized citizens of the big cities like Sepphoris and Tiberias would be landowners. This means that when Paul and other early missionaries took the gospel of Jesus from city to city in the Diaspora at a later date, they did

---

ran along the coastline southward from Tyre (*Via Maris* = "the way along the Sea"). Instead, it went from Capernaum to Tyre: "the way towards the Sea."

[13]Horsley, in his two books on Galilee (see Suggestions), contests the existence of Zealotism as one "movement," and therefore objects to the common theory of Upper Galilee as the mother country of Zealotism.

[14]Sean Freyne's attempt (see references in Suggestions below) to paint a picture of a distinctively Galilean type of Jewish piety has met with criticism by other scholars, see, e.g., Horsley's studies.

not transplant it into a completely different world from that of Jesus and his first disciples. It was different, but it was a difference of degree rather than category.

2. The second point is that the Galilee of Jesus and his disciples was not an isolated Jewish area without Gentiles and contact with Gentiles. The population of Galilee was mixed, as it had always been. It stands to reason that in Galilee the whole question of the relationship between Jews and Gentiles would present itself in other terms than, for example, in Jerusalem. Capernaum, the "headquarters" of Jesus' ministry, was the starting point of the "way towards the Sea," the way to Gentile Tyre. When Jesus said to his disciples, "Do not go among the Gentiles "(Mt 10:5), this was certainly not a self-explanatory or superfluous command: they would have ample opportunity to preach to Gentiles in Galilee itself, and along the main highway to the sea. And when he later supplemented this command by a new one, "[Now] go and make disciples of all nations" (Mt 28:19), it all makes good sense in the Galilean Jewish/Gentile setting.

Jerusalem: The Capital of All Jews
"Jerusalem is my native city, . . . and it is the mother city not only of the land of Judea, but also of many countries" (*Allegorical Interpretation* 281, par.). The man who wrote these words was born, raised and lived his entire life in Alexandria. His name, Philo, was a common Greek name, and he was one of the prominent Greek philosophers of his time. He was a contemporary of Jesus (approximately 20 B.C.-A.D. 50). He lived in the very center of Hellenistic civilization, wrote in perfect Greek, and was able to address the intellectual elite of Alexandria in a way they could understand and appreciate. On the surface, Philo was a successfully assimilated Jew who belonged to the intellectual elite of the Hellenistic world.[15]

And yet, for all his Greek education and background, Philo considered Jerusalem to be his real native town, and he made a pilgrimage to the Holy City at least once during his lifetime. He never forgot—and was never allowed to forget—that he belonged to a threatened minority whose real

---

[15]On Philo, see Peder Borgen, "Philo of Alexandria," in *Compendia* 2:2: 233-82; idem, *Philo of Alexandria: An Exegete for His Time*, Supplements to Novum Testamentum 86 (Leiden/New York/Cologne: E. J. Brill, 1997). Cf. also the older introduction by Samuel Sandmel, *Philo of Alexandria: An Introduction* (New York/Oxford: Oxford University Press, 1979). The great classic on Philo as a philosopher is Harry Austryn Wolfson, *Philo: Foundations of Religious Philosophy in Judaism, Christianity, and Islam*, Vols. 1-2. (Cambridge, Mass.: Harvard University Press, 1947).

homeland was not Egypt. Philo was an observant Jew and wanted to extol the Torah in his writings. In these writings he used the text of the Torah as a point of departure for lofty philosophical ideas, which are inspired by the doctrines of the Stoic and Platonic philosophers of that period. At the risk of his own life he headed a delegation from the persecuted Jewish community of Alexandria to the Roman emperor (A.D. 40-41).

In many ways Philo was representative of the vast majority of Diaspora Jews. Jerusalem was their capital, the center of religious authority and the longed-for goal of pilgrimage. When addressing the emperor on behalf of the Jews of Alexandria, Philo said:

> As for the holy city, I must say what befits me to say. While she, as I have said, is my native city she is also the mother city not of one country Judea but of most of the others in virtue of the colonies [of Jews] sent out at diverse times to the neighbouring lands: Egypt, Phoenicia, the part of Syria called the Hollow and the rest as well and the lands lying far apart, Pamphylia, Cilicia, . . . similarly also into Europe, Thessaly, Boeotia, . . . Corinth and most of the Peloponese. And not only are the mainlands full of Jewish colonies but also the most highly esteemed of the islands: Euboea, Cyprus, and Crete. I say nothing of the countries beyond the Euphrates, for except for a small part they all, Babylon and the other satrapies whose land is highly fertile, have Jewish inhabitants. So that if my own home-city is granted a share of your goodwill, the benefit extends not to one city but to myriads of the others situated in every region of the inhabited world whether in Europe or in Asia or in Libya, whether in the mainlands or on the islands, whether it be seabord or inland. (*Legatio ad Gaium* 281-83)

There was a rather extensive two-way dialogue between the religious authorities in Jerusalem and the Jews of the Diaspora. Envoys were sent out from Jerusalem, carrying letters to the Diaspora communities, instructing them on matters of observance, the ritual calendar and doctrines to be avoided (Acts 9:2; 22:5; 28:21) etc.[16] This continued even after the fall of the temple; many of the leading rabbis of the second century A.D. are pictured in the rabbinic texts as traveling widely among the Jews of the Diaspora. Groups of pilgrims from the Diaspora came to the three great pilgrimage festivals in Jerusalem. They came not only to bring their temple tax and the prescribed sacrifices, but also to hear the famous teachers of the law and to bring

---

[16]On such "encyclical letters," and the Epistle of James being a Christian example of the same genre, see Richard Bauckham, *James*, New Testament Readings (London/New York: Routledge, 1999), pp. 11-28.

back from Jerusalem a renewed zeal for their ancestral faith and its observances.[17]

These close links between Jerusalem and the Diaspora have been rightly
stressed in recent scholarship,[18] partly in opposition to scholars of an earlier
generation who tended to conceive of the Judaism in the land of Israel and
"Hellenistic" (Diaspora) Judaism as two totally separate entities. It may be
worthwhile to add a few words on that topic.

"Palestinian" Judaism and "Hellenistic" Judaism?

The implication of this traditional terminology is that Judaism in the land of
Israel was little affected by Hellenism, so that *Palestinian* almost equals *non-
Hellenistic*.[19] Hellenistic Judaism, on the other hand, is thought to be the religion of Diaspora Jews who spoke Greek and were much more exposed to
Hellenistic influence than the Aramaic/Hebrew-speaking Jews of Israel. The
relevance of this theory to our subject derives from the assumption that "Hellenistic Judaism"—rather than "Palestinian"—was the breeding ground of
Christianity as seen in the New Testament writings and the post-apostolic
period. In chapter one we saw some of the reasons why recent scholarship
has begun to abandon this line of thought.

An increasing amount of evidence shows that Greek was widely used in
the land of Israel throughout the period that interests us. And this Greek
influence went beyond the level of language. We cannot differentiate between
Judaism in Israel and that of the Diaspora by saying that the latter was Hellenistic and the former not.[20] It would also be wrong to say that "Palestinian"

---

[17]Cf. esp. Shmuel Safrai, "The Temple," in *Compendia 1:2:* 865-907.

[18]Cf. Shmuel Safrai, "Relations Between the Diaspora and the Land of Israel," in *Compendia 1:1:* 184-215.

[19]The adjective *Palestinian* is technically an anachronism before the second century A.D.,
when the Romans—most likely Emperor Hadrian after the Bar Kokhba rebellion—officially designated the land of Israel as "Syria Palestina." Before this, the current as well as
the official name of the land of the Jews had been Judea, while Palestine had been the
name of the land of the Philistines (used as such from Herodotus, fifth century B.C.,
onwards.) See on this Louis H. Feldman, "Some Observations on the Name Palestine," in
Studies in Hellenistic Judaism, Arbeiten zur Geschichte des antiken Judentums und des
Urchristentums 30 (Leiden: E. J. Brill, 1996), pp. 553-76. In modern scholarly literature, the
words "Palestine" and "Palestinian" have for a long time been used as geographical terms
for the territory of Judah, Samaria and Galilee. (The name has even been applied to the
land of Canaan in the Israelite and patriarchal period.) In this book the term is generally
avoided, but when reporting on the history of research, it is unavoidable.

[20]The same point is made vigorously in Shaye J. D. Cohen's recent comprehensive history of
Judaism in our period, *Maccabees to Mishnah,* pp. 35-37. He concludes: "This conception of

and "Hellenistic" Judaism were distinct entities, completely separate from each other. Such was not the case. In Israel as well as in the Diaspora we meet great diversity within Judaism.

It should be emphasized that there was no such thing as one distinct "Hellenistic Judaism" shared by all Diaspora Jews. If we were to ask what united the Diaspora Jews and gave them their Jewish identity, the answer would be their loyalty to the basic commandments of the Law and to the temple in Jerusalem. Thus, if we are to use the term "Hellenistic Judaism" at all, we should use it as a comprehensive term referring to Judaism as a whole during the period which concerns us, and not confine it to the Jews of the Diaspora. To put it even more explicitly: their faithfulness to the Torah is what caused the Jews of the Diaspora to reject idolatry and emperor worship, and their faithfulness to Jerusalem and Israel kept alive their feelings of "foreignness" and pushed them to make the pilgrimage to Jerusalem at least once in their life. None of this can be called "Hellenistic."

The Diaspora Jews expressed their theological convictions in a wide range of literary creations, demonstrating a broad theological variety: from the lofty philosophical writings of Philo to the fervently nationalistic lyrics of the *Sibylline Oracles*.[21] Philo and the writers of the *Sibylline Oracles* were all natives of Alexandria, but their writings are more focused on Jerusalem

---

'Hellenism' leads to a redefinition of 'Hellenistic Judaism.' All the Judaisms of the Hellenistic period, of both the diaspora and the land [of Israel], were Hellenized, that is, were integral parts of the culture of the ancient world. Some varieties of Judaism were more Hellenized than others, but none was an island unto itself. It is a mistake to imagine that the land of Palestine preserved a 'pure' form of Judaism and that the diaspora was the home of adulterated or diluted forms of Judaism. The term 'Hellenistic Judaism' makes sense, then, only as a chronological indicator for the period from Alexander the Great to the Maccabees or perhaps to the Roman conquests of the first century B.C.E. As a descriptive term for a certain type of Judaism, however, it is meaningless, because all the Judaisms of the Hellenistic period were 'Hellenistic'" (p. 37).

[21]For comprehensive overviews of the entire body of Jewish Greek literature, see *New Schürer* 3:1-176; and George W. E. Nickelsburg, *Jewish Literature Between the Bible and the Mishnah: A Historical and Literary Introduction* (London: SCM Press, 1981). For the theological ideas, cf. the studies by Barclay, Collins, Gafni, and Van Unnik listed in the Suggestions below, and in addition, John J. Collins, *Seers, Sibyls and Sages in Hellenistic-Roman Judaism*, Supplements to the Journal for the Study of Judaism 54 (Leiden: E. J. Brill, 1997); Peter Dalbert, *Die Theologie der hellenistisch-jüdischen Missionsliteratur unter Ausschluss von Philo und Josephus* (Hamburg: H. Reich, 1954); Jack N. Lightstone, *The Commerce of the Sacred: Mediation of the Divine Among Jews in the Graeco-Roman Diaspora*, Brown Judaic Studies 59 (Chico, Calif.: Scholars Press, 1984); Nikolaus Walter, "Jewish-Greek Literature of the Greek Period," in Davies/Finkelstein, *Judaism*, pp. 385-408.

and the temple than much of the literature of the same period produced in Jerusalem itself.

On the other hand, "Palestinian" Judaism *was* distinguished in some respects from its counterpart in the Diaspora. Conditions of living were markedly different for Jews living in the Land and those outside it. ("The Land" in most cases simply means Jerusalem; we have no certain knowledge of books produced in the land, but outside Jerusalem.) It would be strange if this found no echo in the religious literature of the Land and the Diaspora respectively. There are, indeed, differences, and we shall point out a number of them.

1. Quite naturally, the Jews of the Diaspora were in closer and more frequent contact with the Gentile world than their brethren in Jerusalem. This leads to the fact that the literature of Diaspora Jews is more "evangelistic" than most works produced in Israel. An outstanding example of such evangelistic writings are the *Sibylline Oracles,* apocalyptic writings with origins in Alexandrian Jewry of the Hasmonean period and the decades following the fall of the temple. In these books the Sibylls—legendary Gentile prophetesses—proclaim the central dogmas of Judaism.[22] Gentile readers are asked to leave their paganism and idol worship, and to turn to the one and only God who has made the temple in Jerusalem his dwelling place. A more sophisticated missionary approach is found in the beautiful novel *Joseph and Aseneth* (also from first-century B.C. or A.D. Egypt), which tells the story of how Aseneth, the daughter of an Egyptian priest, was converted to Judaism and married Joseph. Here Aseneth is made the model proselyte, showing the path of truth to other Gentiles.[23]

2. Nowhere in the Diaspora literature do we find examples of those detailed discussions of halakic law which are so characteristic of the rabbinic writings. This alerts us to the fact that Pharisaism and the subsequent devel-

---

[22]On these, see John J. Collins, *The Sibylline Oracles of Egyptian Judaism,* SBL Dissertation Series 13 (Missoula, Mont.: Scholars Press, 1974). English translation in Charlesworth, *Pseudepigrapha* 1:317-472. German translation with extensive introduction and full bibliography on pp. 1071-80: Helmut Merkel, *Die Sibyllinen,* Jüdische Shriften aus hellenistisch-römischer Zeit, 5. 8 (Gütersloh: Gütersloher Verlagshaus, 1998).

[23]English translation in Charlesworth, *Pseudepigrapha* 2:177-247. There are many studies on this somewhat enigmatic work, e.g., Christoph Burchard, *Untersuchungen zu Joseph und Aseneth,* Wissenschaftliche Untersuchungen zum Neuen Testament 8 (Tübingen: J. C. B. Mohr, 1965). A completely new interpretation is attempted by Gideon Bohak, *Joseph and Aseneth and the Jewish Temple in Heliopolis,* SBL Early Judaism and its Literature 10 (Atlanta, Ga.: Scholars Press, 1996). If he is right, the audience of *Joseph and Aseneth* is not Gentiles to be converted, but Jews to be persuaded of the legitimacy of the Jewish temple in Leontopolis, Egypt.

opment of rabbinic halakah were distinctively Palestinian phenomena.[24]

3. As far as we know from the available evidence, there was little fragmentation of Jewry into distinct religious sects in the Diaspora. Josephus's classic enumeration of the four sects of Judaism—Sadducees, Pharisees, Essenes and Zealots—seems to refer only to the land of Israel, and even there participation in the sects was limited to a small minority of the population. As we will see, the Sadducees were concentrated in Israel, mainly in Jerusalem itself. As for the Pharisees, one of their aims was to uphold the standard of purity required of priests. This was difficult enough in the Land; in the Diaspora it would have been quite impractical. Pharisaism as a movement was probably restricted to the land of Israel.[25] In Egypt there were groups similar to the Essenes (Philo calls them Therapeutae), but the type of Essenism found in the Dead Sea Scrolls seems to have been restricted to the Land and somehow connected to the community center in Qumran.

In short, the Jews of the Diaspora seem to have been less prone to form organized factions and parties than their brethren in the Land. They were not primarily Pharisees or Essenes, but quite simply Jews. The supreme focus of authority was not the doctrine of a certain party, but the law and the temple. The law was read and taught in the local synagogue each sabbath, and the situation of the community was such that the focus had to be on the basic and essential. In this way, Judaism in the Diaspora may have been less sectarian and extreme than that of the various parties in Israel, but hardly less pluriform.

4. The last difference may be the most important of all. We have seen that Jerusalem—and the temple service carried out in Jerusalem—was of the utmost importance to many Diaspora Jews. At the same time it was practically out of reach to them, except for the extremely rare occasions when they could make a pilgrimage for some festival, such as the Passover. But this meant that most of the time Diaspora Jews had to practice a temple-less Judaism, without sacrifices, without a Passover lamb, without anything that required an altar and a priest. The very fact that an alternative temple *was*

---

[24]There are rabbinic sayings to the effect that "houses of learning" of the Palestinian type were non-existent in the Diaspora, cf. *TB Eruvin* 21a; and Martin Hengel, *The Pre-Christian Paul* (London: SCM Press/Philadelphia: Trinity Press, 1991), p. 124, n. 184. This does not mean, of course, that Pharisaic/rabbinic *influence* was restricted to the land of Israel (or even Jerusalem). Cf. above on travelling Pharisees and rabbis, and encyclical letters from Jerusalem.
[25]Cf. the magisterial discussion of this issue in Hengel, *Pre-Christian Paul*, pp. 29-34. Paul very likely got his Pharisaic education in Jerusalem, not Tarsus.

established for a period of time in Egypt by exiled Jews demonstrates that this lack of the temple, its sacrifices and its other functions, was not all that easy to compensate for. But the Diaspora Jews really did not have any alternative; they had to develop a way of living as Jews and worshiping their God without access to the temple (which the law said so much about!).

As far as scholars can now tell, one major strategy chosen by Diaspora Jews to cope with this situation was the establishment of the *synagogue* (Greek, "assembly"). From the last couple of centuries B.C. inscriptions turn up that seem to document the erection of special buildings that housed "the assembly," and were called after it: synagogues. In other words, the synagogue, as institution and as building, was an invention of the Diaspora Jews.[26] Only later was the synagogue introduced in the Land, first in Galilee, far away from the temple. In Judea there were for a long time no synagogues; the temple was too close. Only in Jerusalem itself do we find synagogues at the same time as in Galilee, but characteristically they were built by and for *Diaspora* Jews visiting Jerusalem or residing there.

We shall have more to say about the synagogue in later chapters. For the present it is sufficient to state that the synagogue originated as an answer to the needs of Jews who had no access to the temple. It is therefore no wonder that after the destruction of the temple in A.D. 70, the synagogue emerged as the institution that could house a temple-less Judaism. It had done so for some time already; it had tried out some of the necessary strategies for the new situation.

The Geography of Synagogue and Church

The Jews of the Diaspora have been called "the forerunners of Paul." The idea is that the mission of the church was prepared for by the evangelistic efforts of Diaspora Jews.[27] There is much truth in this, although the expression "fore-

---

[26]Cf. esp. J. G. Griffiths, "Egypt and the Rise of the Synagogue," in *Ancient Synagogues: Historical Analysis and Archaeological Discovery*, ed. Dan Urman and Paul V. M. Flesher, Studia Post-Biblica 47, 1 (Leiden/New York/Cologne: E. J. Brill, 1995), 1:3-16; Arye Kasher, "Synagogues as 'Houses of Prayer' and 'Holy Places' in the Jewish Communities of Hellenistic and Roman Egypt," ibid., pp. 205-20; Martin Hengel, "Proseuche und Synagoge, Jüdische Gemeinde, Gotteshaus und Gottesdienst in der Diaspora und in Palästina," in Hengel, *Kleine Schriften* 1:171-95; Levine, *Ancient Synagogue*, pp. 19-41.
[27]Two classic studies along these lines: Frederick Milton Derwacter, *Preparing the Way for Paul: The Proselyte Movement in Later Judaism* (New York: Macmillan, 1930); Ernst Lerle, *Proselytenwerbung und Urchristentum* (Berlin: Evangelische Verlagsanstalt, 1960). Cf. also Rainer Riesner, "A Pre-Christian Jewish Mission?" in Ådna/Kvalbein, *Mission of the Early Church*, pp. 211-50. See also next note.

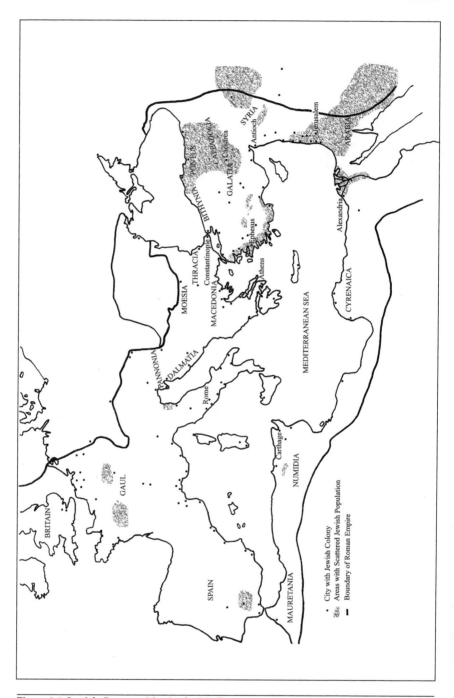

Figure 3.1. Jewish Communities in the Mediterranean Diaspora

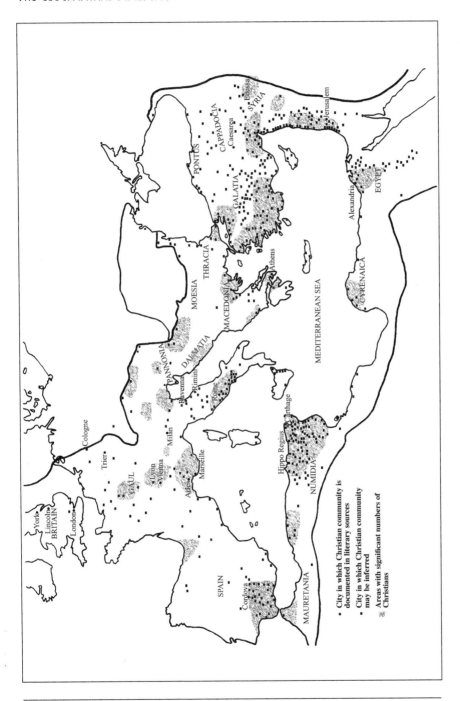

Figure 3.2. Spread of Christianity c. A.D. 300

runners" should not lead us to think that they thought of themselves in this way, or that they ceased to "run" as soon as Paul and the other Christian missionaries came around. What we see in the sources is rather the phenomenon which has been called "missionary competition."[28]

In order better to grasp the reality behind this term, let us visualize a typical Diaspora synagogue, as we meet it, for example, in Acts 13:14-48. It would have had a dual attendance. First, of course, were the loyal and observant Jews, coming each Sabbath to hear the Word of God and to say their prayers. They would have built or equipped the synagogue at their own expense, and were naturally very devoted to it. Their hope was that many outsiders might be attracted to the synagogue and eventually convert to Judaism.

This hope was embodied in the other group attending the synagogue: Gentiles who had become convinced that the God of the Bible was the only true God. They tried to fulfil his ethical precepts; they had a certain familiarity with the Bible; and many of them were contemplating full conversion to Judaism, though few actually took this step. In the New Testament and other ancient sources they are called the "God-fearers." These groups of Gentile God-fearers, attached to almost every Diaspora synagogue, are essential to our understanding of the mission and expansion of the early church.[29] When the gospel message was first addressed to Gentiles, it was addressed primarily to these groups, and among them it found a wide hearing. This would lead us to expect that the geographical spread of Christianity would follow a route populated by Diaspora synagogues. As we know, the Book of Acts testifies that this was true of Paul's missions.

---

[28] On the present hotly debated question of whether the Judaism of this period should be called "missionary" at all, I refer to the literature listed in chapter one's Suggestions and notes 34-36. A recent discussion of "missionary competition," with extensive bibliography, is Reidar Hvalvik, *The Struggle for Scripture and Covenant: The Purpose of the Epistle of Barnabas and Jewish-Christian Competition in the Second Century*, Wissenschaftliche Untersuchungen zum Neuen Testament, 2. Reihe, 82 (Tübingen: J. C. B. Mohr [Paul Siebeck], 1996), pp. 213-322. Cf. also James N. B. Carleton Paget, "Jewish Proselytism at the Time of Christian Origins: Chimera or Reality?" *Journal for the Study of the New Testament* 62 (1996): 65-103.

[29] The literature on the Gentile God-fearers is quite extensive, not least because A. T. Kraabel, in a now famous study, tried to prove they never did exist. Inconveniently for Kraabel, recent finds in Aphrodisias in Asia Minor seem to document their existence beyond reasonable doubt. See A. T. Kraabel, "The Disappearance of the 'God-Fearers,'" *Numen* 28 (1981): 113-26; Thomas M. Finn, "The God-Fearers Reconsidered," *Catholic Biblical Quarterly* 47 (1985): 75-84; Louis H. Feldman, "The Omnipresence of the God-Fearers," *Biblical Archaeological Review* 12, no. 5 (1986): 59-69; idem, "Proselytes and 'Sympathizers' in the Light of the New Inscriptions from Aphrodisias," *Revue des études juives* 148 (1989): 265-305; Irina A. Levinskaya, "The Inscription from Aphrodisias and the Problem of God-Fearers," *Tyndale Bulletin* 41 (1990): 312-18; R. Hvalvik, *Struggle*, pp. 249-67

But let us take a closer look at the maps to see if this correlation might be true in an even wider framework. Figure 3.1 shows all the cities around the Mediterranean and Mesopotamia in which a Jewish colony is known to have existed at the shift from B.C. to A.D., either from literary or archaeological evidence. As you will observe, the Jewish colonies (and synagogues) are not evenly distributed over the area; there are some heavily populated regions, especially in Asia Minor. You will also notice clusters of Jewish settlements around Alexandria and Rome, and a strong Jewish presence in Syria and Greece. Now turn to figure 3.2, which shows the presence of Christian communities ca. A.D. 100-300. One is struck by the almost complete overlap; the two maps exhibit essentially the same pattern. This tells us that Paul's practice was not peculiar to him.

The Christian mission continued for a long time to work primarily among the God-fearing Gentiles surrounding the Diaspora synagogues. Here the gospel of salvation in Jesus the Messiah, without ritual observance of the Law, found its best-prepared audience. From a purely geographical point of view we can assume a close, long-term relationship between Judaism and the early church. In later chapters we will see if this is indeed substantiated by the ancient Christian sources.

Temple Square

Only a small fraction of the total Jewish population lived so near the temple that they could visit it and take part in the temple service on a regular basis. You only had to go as far as Galilee, and visiting the temple became something that required a week or two, and was, for these and other practical reasons, something one did only once or twice a year, or less. For distant Diaspora Jews, pilgrimage to the temple may have been a once-in-a-lifetime experience. This situation calls for two comments, which to a certain extent balance each other:

1. All Jews who did not attend the temple service nevertheless still did attend in that they contributed through the temple tax to cover the expenses of the daily offerings that were brought for all Israel. In this way, all Israel profited from the sacrificial service going on, day in and day out, in the temple. You could be part of it without attending in person. The temple tax meant that also for Jews in the Diaspora the question of Jewish identity was intimately connected with the temple: non-Jews were not allowed to pay it. And speaking of the temple tax, it brought in foreign currency to Jerusalem and therefore necessitated *money-changers* in the temple itself.

2. At the same time, there is no doubt that the Jewish Diaspora had the longest and the most thorough training with regard to living a Jewish life without the temple. When all of Judaism had to redefine itself without a temple after A.D. 70, the Diaspora no doubt had theological resources to offer in the process. In the rabbinic sources, this is to a large extent made invisible, except from one direction: the input from Babylonian sages and immigrants from Babylonia is fully acknowledged.

Suggestions for Further Reading

Introductory readings:

The briefest and most easily read account of the "geographical history" of ancient Judaism and the early church is found in H. G. May, ed., *Oxford Bible Atlas* (London: Oxford University Press, 1962), pp. 76-93. For further study, one should turn to the relevant articles in *Compendia 1:1*, esp. M. Avi-Yonah, "Historical Geography of Palestine," pp. 78-116; M. Stern, "The Jewish Diaspora," pp. 117-83.

General studies of the Jewish Diaspora:

The most comprehensive survey is now probably John M. G. Barclay, *Jews in the Mediterranean Diaspora from Alexander to Trajan (323 BCE-117 CE)* (Edinburgh: T & T Clark, 1996; latest reprint, 1998). This book also includes an excellent review of Diaspora research, pp. 4-9.

For more specialized studies, cf. the following: Victor Tcherikover, *Hellenistic Civilization*, pp. 296-377; John J. Collins, *Between Athens and Jerusalem: Jewish Identity in the Hellenistic Diaspora* (New York: Crossroad, 1983); Aryeh Kasher, *The Jews in Hellenistic and Roman Egypt: The Struggle for Equal Rights* (Tübingen: J. C. B. Mohr [Paul Siebeck], 1985); Paul R. Trebilco, *Jewish Communities in Asia Minor*, Society for New Testament Studies Monograph Series 69 (Cambridge: Cambridge University Press, 1991); Willem Cornelis van Unnik, *Das Selbstverständnis der jüdischen Diaspora in der hellenistisch-römischen Zeit*, ed. P. W. van der Horst, Arbeiten zur Geschichte des Antiken Judentums und des Urchristentums 17 (Leiden/New York/Cologne: E. J. Brill, 1993); J. Mélèze-Modrzejewski, *The Jews of Egypt: From Rameses II to Emperor Hadrian* (Philadelphia: Jewish Publication Society of America, 1995); Douglas R. Edwards, *Religion and Power: Pagans, Jews and Christians in the Greek East* (Oxford: Oxford University Press, 1996); Isaiah M. Gafni, *Land, Center and Diaspora: Jewish Constructs in Late Antiquity*, Journal for the Study of the Pseudepigrapha: Supplement Series 21 (Sheffield: Sheffield Academic Press, 1997). Cf. also the shorter treatments by Harald Hegermann, "The Diaspora in the Hellenistic Age," in Davies/Finkelstein, *Judaism*, pp. 115-66; Schiffman, *Text to Tradition*, pp. 80-97. One should also consult the relevant chapters in *Compendia 1:1*, esp. Shmuel Safrai, "Relations Between the Diaspora and the Land of Israel," pp. 184-215; S. Appelbaum, "The Legal Status of the Jewish Communities in the Diaspora," pp. 420-63; and in *Compendia 1:2*, S. Appelbaum, "The Social and Economic Status of the Jews in the Diaspora," pp. 701-27.

A useful selection of source material in translation, with short introductions, is John R. Bartlett, *Jews in the Hellenistic World: Josephus, Aristeas, The Sibylline Oracles, Eupolemus*, Cambridge Commentaries on Writings of the Jewish and Christian World 200 BC to AD 200, 1, i (Cambridge: Cambridge University Press, 1985); cf. also the primary texts in Feldman/Reinhold, *Jewish Life*, pp. 17-76.

Studies on the region of Galilee:

In recent years, there has been a flood of studies on the cultural and religious character of Galilee, some of which are mentioned here in chronological order: Sean Freyne, *Galilee from Alexander the Great to Hadrian (323 B.C.E. to 135 C.E.): A Study of Second Temple Judaism* (Wilmington: Michael Glazier/Notre Dame: Notre Dame Press, 1980); Meyers/Strange, *Archaeology*, pp. 31-47; Willibald Bösen, *Galiläa als Lebensraum und Wirkungsfeld Jesu: Eine zeitgeschichtliche und theologische Untersuchung* (Freiburg/Basel/Vienna: Herder, 1985); Sean Freyne, *Galilee, Jesus and the Gospels: Literary Approaches and Historical Investigations* (Philadelphia: Fortress, 1988); Lee I. Levine, ed., *The Galilee in Late Antiquity* (New York: Jewish Theological Seminary of America, 1992); Richard A. Horsley, *Galilee: History, Politics, People* (Valley Forge, Penn.: Trinity Press International, 1995); Richard A. Horsley, *Archaeology, History and Society in Galilee: The Social Context of Jesus and the Rabbis* (Valley Forge, Penn.: Trinity Press International, 1996). Horsley's two books challenge many established assumptions about the character and history of Galilee, and scholarship will probably need some time to digest them.

Recent studies of the synagogue and its Diaspora origins:
Dan Urman and Paul V. M. Flesher, eds., *Ancient Synagogues: Historical Analysis and Archaeological Discovery*. vol. 1, Studia Post-Biblica 47, 1 (Leiden/New York/Cologne: E. J. Brill, 1995); Steven Fine, ed., *Jews, Christians, and Polytheists in the Ancient Synagogue: Cultural Interaction During the Greco-Roman Period*, Baltimore Studies in the History of Judaism (London/New York: Routledge, 1999); Lee I. Levine, *The Ancient Synagogue: The First Thousand Years* (New Haven: Yale University Press, 2000). Cf. also A. Th. Kraabel, "The Diaspora Synagogue: Archaeological and Epigraphic Evidence Since Sukenik," in Haase, *Aufstieg* 2 19.1:477-510; S. B. Hoenig, "The Ancient City-Square: The Forerunner of the Synagogue," ibid.: 448-76.

Especially on the relationship between the geography of Judaism and the early church, see James M. Scott, *Paul and the Nations: The Old Testament and Early Jewish Background of Paul's Mission to the Nations with Special Reference to the Destination of Galatians*, Wissenschaftliche Untersuchungen zum Neuen Testament 84 (Tübingen: J. C. B. Mohr [Paul Siebeck], 1995).

4

JERUSALEM
THE CITY OF THE TEMPLE

*W*e said earlier that the deepest impact Roman rule had on Judaism as a religion came almost incidentally, from the Roman perspective: Judaism was deeply transformed through the loss of the temple in A.D. 70. For Second Temple Judaism the temple itself, and the worship going on in the temple, belonged to the very foundation of the religion. Jewish religion centered around the cultic service of the priests and the Levites in the temple. After A.D. 70 Judaism had to be drastically redefined. The earliest believers in Jesus belonged to the Second Temple period, they began their new life as disciples of Jesus when the temple was still standing and in full business. Neither Peter, nor Jacob (or James, Jesus' brother), nor Paul lived long enough to see the temple fall. What was the significance of the temple to the earliest followers of Jesus? And when the temple fell, what did that mean? In hindsight, we observe that two varieties of pre-70 Judaism were able to survive, we should perhaps even say profit from, the fall of the sanctuary: the movement of sages that became the fathers of rabbinic Judaism, and the Jesus movement that became Christianity. In this chapter, we take a closer look at the pre-70 Jerusalem that was their common cradle.

Was Jerusalem Relevant?

There are those who contend that the early church was shaped by events occurring not in Jerusalem or Israel, but in the Hellenistic cities of the eastern empire, Syria, Asia Minor and even in Greece and the city of Rome itself. The argument continues over whether the early Jerusalem community of believers in Jesus soon lost its significance, and whether the New Testament writings reflect the beliefs of Hellenized Christians who had only minimal contact with Jerusalem and the first believers there.

In order to support this theory, the Book of Acts has to be dismissed as a mostly unhistorical record, and this was done by many New Testament scholars in the past. But in recent years the historical credibility of Acts has been re-evaluated, and for good reasons.[1] The centrality of the Jerusalem community and its position as the "mother church" of all Christianity, as reported in Acts, is also substantiated by important evidence in Paul's epistles (to which we will return below).

The Christian church had its decisive beginning in Jerusalem; its first doctrinal decisions were made there; its first organizational patterns were developed there; its basic self-definition was worked out there. Therefore it will be worthwhile to devote some time to describing Jerusalem as it was known to the earliest Christian community.

The Temple and the Pilgrimages

The key to understanding Jerusalem's enormous significance since Old Testament times is the temple. Without the temple, Jerusalem would have been just another provincial city in the Judean hills, lying far from the main commercial routes and geographically isolated. At that time, there were two main roads running from north to south, both far from Jerusalem: one along the coast and one from Damascus southward through the highlands east of the Jordan. In ancient times this latter road was called "the King's Highway." The

---

[1]Cf. C. K. Barrett, *Luke the Historian in Recent Study* (London: Epworth, 1961); Ian Howard Marshall, *Luke: Historian and Theologian*, 2nd ed. (Exeter: Paternoster, 1979); Jacob Jervell, "The Problem of Traditions in Acts," in *Luke and the People of God: A New Look at Luke-Acts* (Minneapolis: Augsburg, 1972), pp. 19-39; Martin Hengel, *Acts and the History of Earliest Christianity* (London: SCM Press, 1979 [Philadelphia: Fortress, 1980]); Colin J. Hemer, *The Book of Acts in the Setting of Hellenistic History*, Wissenschaftliche Untersuchungen zum Neuen Testament 49 (Tübingen: J. C. B. Mohr [Paul Siebeck], 1989); and, most recently, the five-volume series *The Book of Acts in Its First Century Setting*, ed. Bruce W. Winter et al. (Grand Rapids, Mich.: Eerdmans/Carlisle: Paternoster, 1993-1996) For complete listing of the volumes in the series, see the general literature bibliography in the introduction above, p. xix.

main road from east to west ran through the Jezreel plain, far to the north.[2]
Jerusalem's topographical location was backward, being surrounded by mountains on all sides, with only one natural pass to the southeast (along the Kidron). Not a single east-west pass cuts through the mountain ridge upon which Jerusalem is situated. Travelers and merchants from the Transjordan preferred the Jezreel route and did not pass by Jerusalem. Added to this were the facts that the neighborhood of Jerusalem was poor in natural resources and its water supply was always problematic. The only raw material available in large quantities was stone, the Jerusalem stone famous to this day. The only natural resource apart from stone was the olive trees, for which the soil is well suited. The name of the Mount of Olives is a reminder that there was once a thriving olive industry around Jerusalem, but even this was no large-scale export business. In fact, "a proof of how unsuitably placed Jerusalem was for trade is the fact that in the entire course of her history, we find no single trade whose product had ever made her name famous."[3]

In spite of all this, Jerusalem was the unrivaled center not only of Judea, but of the entire Jewish nation, whether in Israel or in the Diaspora. And not only Jews recognized the importance of Jerusalem. Pliny the Elder, a Gentile Roman writer, says that Jerusalem was "by far the most distinguished city not of Judaea only, but of the whole Orient" (*Natural History* 5.14). There is only one explanation for this: the temple and the pilgrimages.[4] "There times a year all the men are to appear before the Sovereign Lord" (Ex 23:17 NIV). This Torah commandment to visit Jerusalem on the three festivals of Pesach (Passover), Shavuot (Festival of Weeks) and Succoth (Festival of Booths), and to bring the prescribed sacrifices to the temple, is the key to understanding life in Jerusalem in the Second Temple period. This commandment did not require that each man make the pilgrimage three times every year. Most Jews could not have fulfilled such a requirement, since making the pilgrimage entailed a great expenditure of time and money, especially for those living in the distant Diaspora. The commandment was taken to belong to the category of "commands which have no limit," that is, commands which encourage that certain actions be done as often as practically possible. For people living

---

[2]For this and the following description of Jerusalem's geographical position, cf. Joachim Jeremias, *Jerusalem in the Time of Jesus* (London: SCM Press, 1969 [many reprints]), pp. 51-54; John Wilkinson, *Jerusalem as Jesus Knew It: Archaeology as Evidence* (London: Thames & Hudson, 1978), pp. 30-43.
[3]Jeremias, *Jerusalem in the Time*, p. 27.
[4]Cf. esp. Shmuel Safrai, "The Temple" (see Suggestions below).

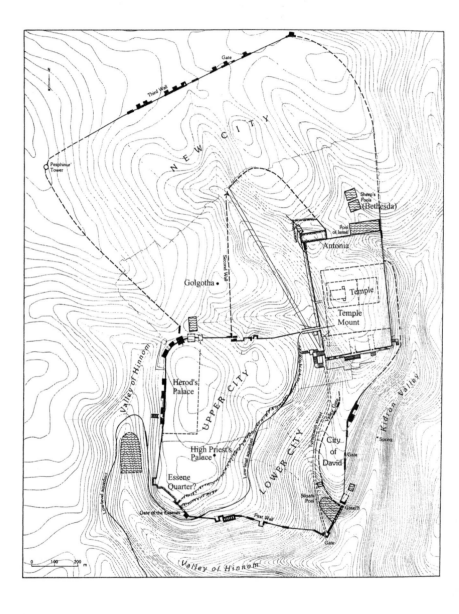

Figure 4.1. Jerusalem

in or near Jerusalem, participation in all the festivals would be possible, but it would be costly for those living in other parts of Israel; the normal practice of observant Jews would be to go once a year—as did the parents of Jesus (Lk 2:41)—or less. Among Diaspora Jews the frequency was no doubt much lower: perhaps only once in a lifetime, depending on religious commitment, traveling distance and personal means.

One—possibly very generous—scholarly estimate of the population inside and outside the land of Israel in the first century numbers the Jewish population in the land at 2.5 million (plus approximately one million non-Jews); and in the dispersion at approximately 5 million Jews.[5] The ratio here is more significant than the absolute figures: the majority of Jews were living outside the land, as they do today. The estimated number of permanent citizens in Jerusalem (within the walls) varies from ca. 50,000 to ca. 100,000. During festivals the population almost doubled, which would mean that approximately 1 percent of the Jewish community outside Jerusalem would attend each festival of pilgrimage. The ancient sources, in one of the few cases in which they give realistic and reliable figures, say that the pilgrims numbered "tens of thousands."

Thus the pilgrimages were at the very foundation of the city's economy and prosperity.

The Temple: The Financial Significance

Let us take a closer look at the pilgrims. What did they bring with them? First and foremost they brought money to spend in Jerusalem. Before they left on their journey, they collected the temple tax from all their kinsmen. Every Jew was obliged to pay this tax, the so-called half-shekel tax (equivalent to two Roman dinars; cf. Mt 17:24-27), once a year. This half-shekel was delivered to the temple treasury in Jerusalem, and it contributed, for example, to the expenses of the offerings made for the whole Israelite community each morning and evening, the "continual burnt offering." The tax more than covered these expenses, resulting in the accumulation of a huge amount of capital in the temple treasury. Pious people often deposited their private funds in this treasury, adding to the capital. The temple thus functioned as a kind of deposit bank, and its treasure chambers were considered the safest place you could keep your fortune.

But the financial significance of the temple was not confined to this. The

---

[5]M. Avi-Yonah, "Historical Geography" (in *Compendia 1:1:* 78-116), pp. 108-10.

pilgrims also brought money to buy the required sacrifices of animals, food and wine. The sacrificial service of the temple generated extensive financial activity in and around the city: the raising of animals and corn products in the countryside; the business of bakers, butchers and wine sellers in the city; and the changing of money that was necessary since the pilgrims could not buy their temple offerings or pay the temple tax in the currency they brought with them from abroad, but only with the stable currency minted in Tyre, also called the "shekel of the Sanctuary" (shekel haqodesh).[6] (The Romans did not grant the Jewish authorities the right to mint their own coins.)

There were also other activities necessary to keep the temple running: some 18,000 priests and Levites had to be supported each year (700 per week), sacred vestments for the priests and the curtains of the temple had to be sewn or repaired, sacred Bible scrolls had to be written, the sacred vessels had to be repaired or replaced by new ones and so on. Thus the temple engaged entire guilds of physicians, scribes, smiths, building maintenance workers, weavers, etc. And of course the daily needs of thousands of pilgrims had to be met—so there were hostels and a huge catering industry. The pilgrims also wanted to bring souvenirs home with them. The ancient sources specifically mention two such mementos: a women's diadem called a "golden city" (ir shel zahav) and intricately engraved signet rings.[7]

The different categories of artisans and entrepreneurs were concentrated in their own streets or markets. Ancient sources mention the clothes market; the poultry market, the wool market, the flour market, the coppersmiths' market, and the weavers', cheesemakers' and bakers' streets, to name a few. The "markets" were mostly vaulted bazaar streets, with small workshops on each side, open towards the street. The houses were mostly small one- or two-story buildings.

In the period from approximately 20 B.C. to A.D. 6, the economic significance of the temple was increased by the enormous and costly reconstruction and enlargement project begun by Herod. When the work began, 10,000 lay workers and 1,000 specially trained priests were employed, and when the work was completed some eighty years later, 18,000 construction workers were suddenly faced with unemployment. The result of their work

---

[6]Cf. Tosefta, Ketubim 13:3 [Zuckermandel ed.] (= 12:6, Neusner trans.); M Bekhorot 8:7. Concerning coins and currencies in the eastern Mediterranean area generally, and in Jerusalem and the temple especially, see New Schürer 2:62-66.
[7]For details and sources to this and the foregoing, see Jeremias, Jerusalem, p. 9; and discussion in E. P. Sanders, Judaism, pp. 77-102.

can still be seen in the lower parts of the walls surrounding the Temple Mount (including the Western Wall).[8]

The Herodian Temple was considered one of the most impressive shrines of the ancient world. Looking at the enormous and perfectly cut stones of its surrounding walls, one can easily understand the outburst of Jesus' disciples: "Look, Teacher! What massive stones! What magnificent buildings!" (Mk 13:1 NIV). The rabbis said, "He who has not seen the Temple of Herod has never in his life seen a beautiful structure" (*TB Bava Batra* 4a).

Having painted the above picture of first-century A.D. Jerusalem, one is struck by the remarkable similarity to the Old City of Jerusalem today. Then as now, Jerusalem was a city living on religious tourism; then as now, the pilgrims probably found the city crowded and noisy, and the local population, only interested in making business out of the holy.

The Temple: The Religious Significance

So far we have seen how the temple and the pilgrimages provided the basis for Jerusalem's significance and prosperity. It is time to enlarge our perspective and look at the significance of the temple as a religious institution. Two concepts must be emphasized. The first is the idea of the temple as God's dwelling on earth. The God of Israel was considered invisibly present in the Holy of Holies, and this gave the whole temple an aura of unparalleled sanctity, and its servants a large measure of authority.

From time immemorial, the priests and the Levites had been the authorized teachers of the law, and even the later rabbis recognized that the Temple Mount had been the supreme seat of authoritative Torah teaching. The authoritative Scripture scrolls, from which other scrolls were copied, were kept in the temple,[9] and the rabbis later told that the highest doctrinal and judicial authority, the Sanhedrin, had gathered there. This remains significant even if the rabbis' concepts about the Sanhedrin should prove to be partly fictional

---

[8]Josephus's description of Herod's rebuilding of the temple is found in *Antiquities* 15.11. On the archaeology of the Herodian Temple Mount, cf. Benjamin Mazar, *The Mountain of the Lord* (Garden City, N.Y.: Doubleday, 1975); idem, "Excavations Near Temple Mount Reveal Splendors of Herodian Jerusalem," *Biblical Archaeological Review* 6, no. 4 (1980): 44-59; idem, "The Temple Mount," *Biblical Archaeology Today: Proceedings of the International Congress on Biblical Archaeology, April 1984* (Jerusalem, 1985): 463-68; K. and L. Ritmeyer, "Reconstructing Herod's Temple Mount in Jerusalem," *Biblical Archaeological Review* 15, no. 6 (1989): 23-42; Meir Ben Dov, *Jerusalem* (see Suggestions below), pp. 38-90; Dan Bahat, "The Western Wall Tunnels," in *Ancient Jerusalem Revealed*, ed. Hillel Geva (Jerusalem: Israel Exploration Society, 1994), pp. 177-90.

[9]On the significance of this for the concept and the history of canon, see chapter fourteen.

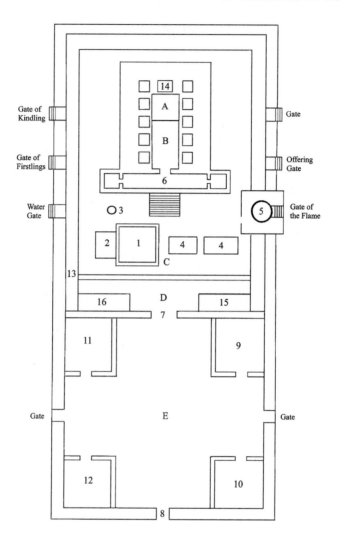

Plan of Herod's Temple

A Holy of Holies
B Sanctuary
C Court of Priests
D Court of Israel
E Court of Women

1 Altar
2 Ramp
3 Laver
4 Slaughter Area
5 Chamber of the Hearth
6 Porch
7 Nicanor Gate
8 Beautiful Gate

9   Chamber of Lepers
10 Chamber of Wood
11 Chamber of Oil
12 Chamber of Nazirites
13 Chamber of Hewn Stone
14 Chambers
15 Chamber of Vestments
16 Chamber of Baked Cakes

Gate of Kindling
Gate of Firstlings
Water Gate

Gate
Offering Gate
Gate of the Flame

Gate
Gate

Figure 4.2. The Temple

(as many scholars now think). Johanan ben Zakkai, the famous rabbi who reestablished rabbinic Judaism after the fall of the temple, used to "sit and teach in the shadow of the sanctuary" (*TB Pesahim* 26a). From the New Testament we know that Jesus taught in the eastern colonnade of the temple forecourts (Jn 10:23), and so did Peter and John (Acts 3:11; 5:12).

The other main concept that explains the religious significance of the temple is that of atonement through the sacrifices brought in the temple. Simon the Just, high priest ca. 200 B.C., said, "On three things does the world stand: on the Torah, on the temple service, and on deeds of loving kindness" (*Avot* 1:2). It is clear that this learned man considered the atoning sacrifices offered in the temple to be indispensable to Israel's relationship with God. When the temple fell in A.D. 70, both rabbinic and Christian sources testify that the most irksome question asked was *How could the people now obtain remission for their sins?*

In the Torah itself, two ideas dominate with regard to the service in the tabernacle: sacrifices and ritual purity. In the Torah there are laws about many different types of sacrifices, not all of them focused on atonement for sin. It seems, however, that in the centuries following the Babylonian exile, atonement for sin became the dominant focus for the entire sacrificial service. Atonement was regarded as the very raison d'être for the temple service, as we observe in a rabbinic story about a friend of Johanan ben Zakkai, Rabbi Joshua. On seeing the temple in ruins shortly after A.D. 70, Rabbi Joshua cried, "Woe unto us! that this, the place where the iniquities of Israel were atoned for, is laid waste!" (*Avot of Rabbi Nathan* 4).

The other important idea associated with the temple was ritual purity.[10] This is a concept difficult to define and difficult for us moderns to understand, but it is a way of making the concept of the holy very concrete, in a sense "physical." In order to enter the sphere where the holy God dwells, one has to be in a state of purity, or else the encounter with God will be destructive. Cultic impurity is treated in very much the same way that we moderns think about infections: impurity is contagious; it infects mainly by touch or through liquids, which means, for example, that the cleansing of vessels becomes very important. Very much like one is "sterilized" before being allowed to enter a strictly disinfected area in a hospital, the Israelite had to be cleansed from impurity before entering the sanctuary, or "the camp," as

---

[10]Here and in what follows I am heavily indebted to Shaye J. D. Cohen's masterful synthesis of recent studies (e.g., Neusner's) in *Maccabees to Mishnah,* chaps. 4 and 5.

sometimes said in the Torah. Sources of infectious impurity were corpses, sexual discharges from men and women, unclean animals, prohibited food, everything connected with idol worship (which implied that Gentiles in general were in a permanent state of impurity, although the relevant sources seem to reveal some uncertainty or disagreement as to the *degree* of this impurity).[11]

The most simple and straightforward understanding of this system of commandments in the Torah would be to think that the priests serving in the temple had to be in a permanent state of purity, whereas the ordinary lay Israelites had to cleanse themselves every time they would enter the sanctuary. This seems to have been the understanding of the majority in the late Second Temple period, probably also of the priests themselves. But was this sufficient, or did the Torah really intend all Israel to permanently constitute "the camp," wherever they lodged? Should laypeople also follow the regulations for priests? This, it seems, was to become the program of the Pharisees. We shall have more to say about that in the next chapter.

Here it is relevant to point out, as Shaye Cohen has done, that all three leading religious "parties" in the late Second Temple period—Sadducees, Pharisees, Essenes—defined themselves in one way or other through their relation to the temple, the temple service and the temple as the area of purity. Their attitudes differed greatly, but the temple was essential to their self-understanding, positively or negatively. That is why the "parties" belonging to the late Second Temple period ceased to exist when the temple disappeared.

We have focused on the significance of the temple for "the locals," those who lived more or less within reach of the temple: the Judeans in general and the Jerusalemites in particular. But let us return to the Diaspora Jews. It seems very reasonable to assume that for them, in their daily dealings with Gentile neighbors, anything like the permanent ritual purity required within "the camp" of Israel was utterly beyond reach. Maybe this was part of their motivation to undertake pilgrimage to Jerusalem and the temple: to experience, for once, the nearness to the holy God himself and the holy purity surrounding him; to bring the atoning sacrifices and be cleansed from sin.

Pilgrims from the land of Israel would normally return home when the festival was over (see Lk 2:43). But pilgrims from the distant Diaspora would

---

[11]See on this Gedalyahu Alon, "The Levitical Uncleanness of Gentiles," in Alon, *Studies*, pp. 146-89; and Sanders, *Judaism*, pp. 72-76.

naturally try to profit as much as possible from their costly and troublesome journey, and we can safely assume that they often prolonged their stay to several weeks, or even several months, to cover more than one festival. Whether they had planned it or not, some pilgrims settled in for a permanent stay, among them some who made the pilgrimage in their old age and settled in Jerusalem in order to die and be buried there. The rabbinic literature mentions synagogues of Jews from Alexandria and Tarsus, and in Acts 6:9 we read about the "synagogue of the Freedmen (as it was called), Cyrenians and Alexandrians, and others of those from Cilicia and Asia." Some remains of a synagogue built for—and possibly by—such pious Jews from the Diaspora were found in 1913, during an excavation led by R. Weill on the Ophel ridge south of the Temple Mount. Weill found a Greek inscription which reads as follows:

> Theodotus the son of Vettenus, priest and archisynagogos, son of the archisynagogos, grandson of the archisynagogos, restored this synagogue for the reading of the Torah and the study of the commandments, and the hostel and the rooms and the [ritual] baths, for needy travellers from foreign lands. The foundations of the synagogue were laid by his fathers and the elders and Simonides.

A synagogue could hardly be restored in Jerusalem after the Bar Kokhba war (A.D. 132-135), which means that the restoration had to take place before A.D. 135, and since the synagogue was founded by his grandfather or even earlier, it certainly must have been in existence in the first century A.D., possibly in the late first century B.C.

Vettenus is a Latin name, and possibly Theodotus's family were Jews who immigrated to Jerusalem from Rome. Some scholars have suggested that they were former slaves who settled in Jerusalem after gaining their freedom. If this is the case, this synagogue may be the "Synagogue of the Freedmen" mentioned in Acts. However, the lack of physical evidence makes this no more than an attractive hypothesis.[12]

This inscription, and the synagogue and people it tells about, opens a window into the piety and the mentality of Diaspora Jews in Jerusalem. The synagogue was built and maintained by a family of Diaspora Jews of priestly descent who immigrated to Jerusalem, and it was built to cater to the needs of pilgrims. And we observe why the pilgrims came: for "the

---

[12]For instructive comments on the Theodotus inscription, see Martin Hengel, *Between Jesus and Paul: Studies in the Earliest History of Christianity* (London: SCM Press, 1983), pp. 17-18; and John J. Rousseau and Rami Arav, eds., *Jesus and His World: An Archaeological and Cultural Dictionary* (Minneapolis: Fortress, 1995), pp. 144-45.

reading of the Torah and the study of the commandments"; and not to forget, to be purified and able to enter the sanctuary (hence "the ritual baths" of the synagogue). Literally built "in the shadow of the Sanctuary," at the foot of the steps to the Huldah gates, this location probably had symbolic significance as well.

Having emphasized the centrality of the temple to all kinds of groups within pre-70 Judaism, it is time to take a closer look at the group of people whose role and significance directly depended upon that of the temple: the priests and the Levites.

The Chief Priests, the Priests and the Levites

First we must emphasize that we are dealing with three distinct groups that can be envisioned as three concentric circles. In the innermost circle we find the high priest, former high priests and other leading functionaries of the temple. Of these, Joachim Jeremias made the following list from rabbinical sources:

☐ The captain *(sagan* or *nagid)* of the temple.[13] He was next in rank to the high priest and could step in to fulfill his duties if necessary.

☐ The director of the weekly division of (ordinary) priests *(rosh ha-mishmar).*

☐ The director of the daily shift *(rosh beit av).*

☐ The seven temple overseers *(ammarkalim).*

☐ The three or more temple treasurers *(gizbarim).*

These are "the chief priests" in plural, a rather narrow group of some fifteen to twenty persons.

The office of high priest was hereditary, and had been so since the days of Zadok, David's priest who anointed Solomon (1 Kings 1:38-40). Whether literally true or not, it was generally believed in the Hellenistic period that the successive high priests had been an unbroken line of Zadok's descendants. Nobody else could legitimately be made high priest. But in the turbulent years of the Hellenistic "reform" in Jerusalem, different branches of the Zadokite clan were utterly neutralized by being labeled as radical "Hellenizers," and the Hasmoneans, who were not Zadokites, grasped the opportunity and had Judah Maccabee's brother Jonathan installed as high priest in 152 B.C. After him, his brother Simon and his descendants served as high priests, and in this capacity they functioned as the supreme leaders of the autonomous Jewish state until the Roman conquest in 63 B.C. Somewhat later, Herod the

[13]Greek *strategos;* cf. Acts 4:1; 5:24, 26.

Great began the practice of installing and deposing high priests as he wanted (Zadokite or not), and this was continued by the Romans after Herod's death and right up to the first Jewish war of A.D. 66-70, which brought the final end of the high priest's office.

We moderns, hearing about this sad line of illegitimate and "politically appointed" high priests, may think that the office was hopelessly compromised and had lost all religious authority and significance during the last hundred years of its functioning. There is no doubt that many pious Jews at that time had great qualms about the state of affairs, but we should probably not conclude that the high priest's office and service were accorded no respect or reverence. After all, he was still the only man to enter the Holy of Holies once a year, there to make atonement for his own sins and for the people's. The significance of the high priest depended more on his office and service than on his personal qualities or lack thereof. We see this in more than one place in the New Testament. The author of John's Gospel was certainly not a fan of the high priest Caiaphas (he had every reason not to be!), but in John 11:49-50 he credits Caiaphas with a true prophecy—not because he was Caiaphas, but because he was high priest that year. The prophetic gift followed the office, not the man. Acts 23:1-5 tells about Paul before the Sanhedrin, speaking some harsh words to Ananias without being aware that he was speaking to the high priest. When informed of the fact, Paul hastily apologized for having insulted "a leader of [God's] people."

Even when the high priest was ever so unworthy as a person and by the way he had been appointed, once installed, he was nevertheless the high priest, and to him the Torah accorded a unique position as mediator between God and his people. Catholics may appreciate this easier than other modern Christians: the Pope is the Pope.

The second circle is the large group of ordinary priests. If the high priest was one and the "high priests" few, the priests were many. Their office was, hereditary, as were the high priest's and the Levites'. One became priest by right of birth, not by "personal call" nor by "ordination." The ordinary priests lived all over the country and only came to officiate in the temple every twenty-fourth week, when the turn of their "division" came (cf. 1 Chron 24:1-19). The number of such priests was considerable. Joachim Jeremias has calculated that 56 priests officiated in the temple each day, with 28 more being necessary on sabbaths. Each priest was on duty for only one day during his division's week, so each of the 24 divisions would number about 300 priests, which makes a grand total of 7,200.[14]

Except for two weeks each year, these priests lived in their towns and villages as ordinary Jews. Their priestly descent and tasks would naturally tend to make them more law-observant than their fellow citizens, and some of them, though possibly not all, were educated men. Here we have to recall that the other main task of a priest—apart from sacrificing in the temple—was to teach and apply the Torah. Some scholars now think that the "scribes" we hear so much about in the New Testament and in other texts from this period were, for the most part, priests. During their long terms "off duty" from the temple, they would make a living by applying their expertise in Torah as local jurists. (We shall have more to say about this in the next chapter.)

In the temple, the priests' primary duty was to receive the sacrifices brought by laypeople: inspect the animals (they should have no blemish), slaughter them, flay them, cut them apart, sprinkle the blood, throw the parts to be burnt up upon the altar, maintain the fire on the altar, clean the area around the altar, etc. Most of this was done outside the sanctuary, in the forecourt of the priests, where the great altar for burnt sacrifices stood. In the main hall of the temple they probably had less to do, but it was there they burnt incense to accompany the daily, fixed prayers.

It is often overlooked that we have an excellent and well informed report on a priest and his service in the New Testament:

> In the days of King Herod [the Great] of Judea, there was a priest named Zechariah, who belonged to the priestly order of Abijah. His wife was a descendant of Aaron, and her name was Elizabeth. Both of them were righteous before God, living blamelessly according to the commandments and regulations of the Lord. . . . Once when he was serving as priest before God and his section was on duty, he was chosen by lot, according to the custom of the priesthood, to enter the sanctuary of the Lord and offer incense. Now at the time of the incense offering, the whole assembly of the people was praying outside. Then there appeared to him an angel of the Lord, standing at the right side of the altar of incense. . . .
>
> Meanwhile, the people were waiting for Zechariah, and wondered at his delay in the sanctuary. When he did come out, he could not speak to them, and they realized that he had seen a vision in the sanctuary. He kept motioning to them and remained unable to speak. When his time [week] of service was ended, he went to his home (Lk 1:5-10, 21-23).

---

[14]The number of Levites was probably comparable to or slightly higher than the number of priests. Josephus gives the total number of priests and Levites as 20,000 (*Against Apion* 2.108), which roughly agrees with Jeremias's calculation, *Jerusalem*, pp. 199-200. Cf., however, the critical remarks on Jeremias's calculation in Sanders, *Judaism*, 78-79.

Temple Square
In this chapter we have been talking about things that were soon to disappear: in A.D. 70 the Jews lost the temple, and with the temple the service of the high priest and the priests and the Levites disappeared, never to be resumed. In A.D. 135 the Jewish people lost Jerusalem itself. And yet, none of these things really disappeared.
  "Jerusalem was not, like Corinth for example, a large city with lots of little temples dotted here and there. It was not so much a city with a temple in it; more like a temple with a small city around it" (Wright, *The New Testament*, p. 225). In this temple, holiness and purity were secured through the atoning sacrifices for all Israel. To all this belong concepts like atonement, purification by blood, sacrificial lambs, a holy people, a sanctified people, a people cleansed from their sins, a purified people, a royal priesthood, a New Jerusalem.
  When reading the New Testament writings, one recognizes everywhere this temple terminology. In the very center of Paul's exposition of justification by faith in Christ (Rom 1—5), we suddenly find ourselves in the midst of the Holy of Holies in the temple, fixing our eyes on the cover of the ark, the *kapporet* upon which the high priest sprinkled the atoning blood on the Day of Atonement: "there is no distinction [between Jew and Gentile], since all have sinned and fall short of the glory of God; they are now justified by his grace as a gift, through the redemption that is in Christ Jesus, *whom God put forward as a sacrifice of atonement* [Hebrew, *kapporet*] *by his blood*, effective through faith" (Rom 3:22-25).

The third circle contains Levites who were the assistants and servants of the priests: they brought the wood for the altar and other accessories into the temple; they maintained order in the temple area (some of them were organized as a local police squad, the "temple guards"); they opened and closed the gates and inspected visitors. They also had liturgical functions: they were the singers of the temple. They rotated their period of service according to an order similar to that of the priests. This means, of course, that the Levites lived scattered around exactly like the priests. In the New Testament we meet at least one Levite: Barnabas, who was to join Paul on his first missionary journey (Acts 13:1-3), was "a Levite from Cyprus" (Acts 4:36).

We have used this much space to describe the temple, the service in the temple and the priesthood doing service there, because all this was still the religious center and heart of the common Jewish religion in the first seventy years of the Christian era. Many handbooks and historical surveys of the Judaism of this period have a lot to say about Pharisees, Sadducees, Essenes, Zealots; and the impression is often created that these were the only people that mattered, religiously, and that discussions about doctrine and law among these groups was all Judaism was about at the time of Jesus and Paul. But this distorts the proportions of the full picture. According to Josephus there were a few Sadducees, some 4,000 Essenes, and well over 6,000 Pharisees, but 20,000 priests and Levites![15] Numbers do not always translate into influence, but in this case Josephus's numbers may be quite significant, the more so as Josephus himself in more than one place ascribes great influence to the priesthood. (He was a priest himself and should know.)

Suggestions for Further Reading

The classical study covering the theme of this chapter is Joachim Jeremias, *Jerusalem in the Time of Jesus: An Investigation into Economic and Social Conditions During the New Testament Period* (London: SCM Press, 1969, and several reprints). This book is very rich in detailed information concerning all aspects of life in Jerusalem. It is also an important sourcebook on the religious parties of the Sadducees and the Pharisees, and should thus be consulted also with regard to the next chapter. It is rather dated, however, in its handling of the rabbinical sources.

A study with more emphasis on the archaeology of Jerusalem is John Wilkinson, *Jerusalem as Jesus Knew It: Archaeology as Evidence* (London: Thames & Hudson, 1978).

The most comprehensive recent treatment of this chapter's theme is Lee I. Levine, ed., *Jerusalem: Its Sanctity and Centrality to Judaism, Christianity, and Islam* (New York: Continuum, 1999). Cf. also Sanders, *Judaism*, pp. 45-189.

The significance of the temple and the pilgrimages is excellently brought out in an article by Shmuel Safrai, "The Temple," in *Compendia 1:2:* 865-907.

On the archaeology of Jerusalem one should also consult: Benjamin Mazar, *The Mountain of the Lord* (Garden City, N.Y.: Doubleday, 1975); Nachman Avigad, *Discovering Jerusalem* (Nashville/Camden/New York: Thomas Nelson, 1983); Meir Ben-Dov, *Jerusalem: Man and Stone: An Archeologist's Personal View of His City* (Tel Aviv: Modan, 1990); Hillel Geva, ed., *Ancient Jerusalem Revealed* (Jerusalem: Israel Exploration Society, 1994).

---

[15]On these figures, and for a discussion of their significance, see E. P. Sanders, *Jesus and Judaism* (London: SCM Press, 1985), pp. 194-98; and the response in N. T. Wright, *The New Testament*, pp. 195-97.

5

HOW MANY "JUDAISMS"?

*J*udaism" used to be an unambiguous concept: Judaism was the religion, or way *of life, of the Jewish people. Throughout the ages it developed and changed, but throughout this development it kept a basic identity and a historic continuity. This was conceived of as organic growth and development, much like a plant grows. In recent years, this picture has been challenged, and for good reasons. For one thing, speaking of the Jewish way of life in the singular is quite misleading, at least for important eras in Jewish history. Secondly, there were dramatic revolutions and upsetting catastrophes in Jewish history, which had a deep impact and sometimes drastic consequences, more like an earthquake. In this chapter we shall look at one example of both: we shall study a period in which Judaism was by no means uniform, and a period in which a major catastrophe took place, a catastrophe that has left indelible marks on Judaism and Jewish history—and also on Christianity.*

Introduction: "Give me Jabne!"

On the eve of the destruction of Jerusalem by the Romans (A.D. 70), the Roman general Vespasian negotiated with the Jewish rebels within the city to bring about their surrender. Rabbi Johanan ben Zakkai, the leading rabbi in the city, urged his compatriots to accept the general's terms, but they refused.

Now, after Rabban Johanan ben Zakkai had spoken to them one day, two and three days, and they still would not listen to him, he sent for his disciples, for Rabbi Eliezer and Rabbi Joshua. "My sons," he said to them, "arise and take me out of here. Make a coffin for me that I might lie in it." Rabbi Eliezer took hold of the head end of it, Rabbi Joshua took hold of the foot; and they began carrying him as the sun set, until they reached the gates of Jerusalem. "Who is this?" the gatekeepers demanded. "It's a dead man," they replied. "Do you not know that a dead man may not be held overnight in Jerusalem?" "If it's a dead man," the gatekeepers said to them, "take him out." So they took him out and continued carrying him until they reached Vespasian. They opened the coffin and Rabban Johanan stood up before him. "Are you Rabban Johanan ben Zakkai?" Vespasian inquired; "tell me, what may I give you?" "I ask nothing of you," Rabban Johanan replied, "save Jabne [English, *Jamnia*], where I might go and teach my disciples and there establish a prayer[house] and perform all the commandments." "Go," Vespasian said to him, "and do as you wish." (*Avot of Rabbi Nathan* 4)[1]

In gratitude towards Vespasian, Johanan prophesied that the general would become Emperor. It took only a couple of days before messengers came saying that the Emperor was dead and Vespasian was his successor.

This famous story has been taken to have great symbolic significance, and indeed it has (regardless of its measure of historical truth). At the same time as Johanan ben Zakkai escaped from the beleaguered city, the priests continued their daily routines in the temple and kept on until they were massacred around the altar doing their duties. They did not escape; they perished, and so did the priesthood and its temple service. The high priest and the Sadducees also disappeared with the temple; they lost everything that gave them power. The Zealots, who had provoked the war with Rome in the first place, prepared a last stand inside the city and were finally massacred almost to the last man. A little earlier—at Qumran by the Dead Sea—the study center of the Essenes was destroyed by the Romans. It devastated them; they never returned or recovered.

Johanan alone, with his disciples, escaped from the disaster unhurt and had a basis upon which to continue with their Jewish way of life. According to rabbinic legend, Johanan emerged as the leader of Judaism after the catastrophe of A.D. 70, and the house of study that he established in Jamnia (Hebrew, *Jabne*), by the coast, became the spiritual lighthouse of a devastated people.

To add to the symbolic significance, we can supplement the story with

---

[1]Goldin, pp. 35-36.

another story about escape from Jerusalem: the escape from Jerusalem to Pella in the Transjordan by the community of the believers in Jesus. According to Eusebius, they had been warned before the outbreak of the war by a prophecy and had heeded the prophecy by fleeing to Pella. Thus, to remain for a while on this level of history charged with symbols: two faith-systems, two ways of life, two "religions," and two only, escaped from the destruction, intact and with a future—rabbinic Judaism and the Christian community.

This way of reading the two stories of escape corresponds to a traditional point of view which for a long time held sway in New Testament scholarship. With one additional assumption we have the traditional theory complete. What we have to assume is that the Judaism of the rabbis after A.D. 70 is the direct and unbroken continuation of the Judaism of the Pharisees before A.D. 70. For a long time this was the established scholarly opinion. What happened to "normative Judaism" around the year 70 was mainly a change of label—"Pharisaic" became "rabbinic"—but in terms of theological content the two were more or less identical. You could think of water running through a channel: for the distance from the Maccabees to A.D. 70 the channel was called "Pharisaic," from A.D. 70 onwards its name changed to "rabbinic," but it was the same water flowing through the same channel.

In Jewish studies this picture resulted in descriptions of "Judaism" in which statements ascribed to Jewish sages within the period of approximately 200 B.C. to A.D. 200 were synthesized into a coherent system.[2] In New Testament studies the result was that when Jesus debated with the Pharisees in the Gospels, he was thought to debate with the representatives of Judaism as a whole. According to this perspective, Jesus himself began the debate between Christianity and Judaism; it was continued by all his followers and disciples. Right from the beginning, Christianity and Judaism were two clearly distinct entities, the one represented by Jesus and his disciples, the other by the Pharisees.

The impact of this way of looking at first-century Jewish and Christian history has been enormous, and is still felt in New Testament scholarship. There is no doubt, however, that a basic "change of paradigm" is taking place. For

---

[2]The classic example is George Foot Moore's *Judaism in the First Centuries of the Christian Era: The Age of The Tannaim* (= vol. 1 of the three-volume work *Judaism in the First Centuries of the Christian Era*) (Cambridge, Mass.: Harvard University Press, 1927-1930, frequently reprinted); a more recent example of this comprehensive approach to "rabbinic" Judaism as one entity is Ephraim E. Urbach's *The Sages: Their Concepts and Beliefs*, 2 vols. (Jerusalem: Magnes, 1975 [and reprints]).

one thing, Jewish scholars have argued with great conviction that Jesus should not be placed *outside* Pharisaism, but within it: when Jesus debates with Pharisees, his own positions can be shown to agree with those of other Pharisaic authorities. In other words, Pharisaism itself was complex; it comprised different opinions; it could comprise those of Jesus. Jesus' debates with Pharisaic opponents is therefore an intra-Pharisaic debate.[3]

Secondly, the simple continuity between Pharisees and post-70 rabbis is being seriously questioned. Few doubt that leading Pharisees were *part* of the reestablished Jewish leadership after 70, and that they contributed to the formation of the Judaism we meet in later rabbinic writings, first and foremost the Mishnah. But more and more scholars have come to realize that the Pharisees were by no means alone in this, that rabbinic leadership after 70 was broader in its composition and partly distanced itself quite emphatically from the Pharisees *as a sect or party*. In rabbinic writings, the pre-70 ancestors of the rabbis are normally not called *perushim* (Hebrew for Pharisees, meaning "sectarians"!), but rather *hakamim*, meaning "sages." Some of those named as sages are also named as Pharisees in Josephus and the New Testament, but not all, and there is no need to identify the pre-70 sages of rabbinic literature—as a group—with the Pharisees of the New Testament and Josephus. It is often overlooked that Johanan ben Zakkai, the recognized father of rabbinic Judaism, in one of his sayings distanced himself from the Sadducees *and* from the Pharisees![4]

As a result of this shift of perspective, one should no longer project the Judaism of the Mishnah and related rabbinic writings into the pre-70 situation and identify it with Pharisaic teaching, the latter being regarded as the normative Judaism of the entire first century. The pre-70 situation must be described on its own terms, and once we turn to the contemporary sources,[5] the picture, in one respect, becomes surprisingly clear.

The common point of reference for all Jews was the temple, and the numerically biggest and probably most widely influential group of religious

---

[3]In recent years, this point of view has been developed by David Flusser in several studies, e.g., *Jesus*, 2nd ed. (Jerusalem: Magnes, 1998). For an overview of Jewish scholarship on Jesus, see Donald A. Hagner, *The Jewish Reclamation of Jesus: An Analysis and Critique of Modern Jewish Study of Jesus* (Grand Rapids, Mich.: Zondervan, 1984).

[4]For this paragraph, see esp. the extensive discussion in John Bowker, *Jesus and the Pharisees* (Cambridge: Cambridge University Press, 1973), pp. 1-38. See also Cohen, *Maccabees to Mishnah*, pp. 226-27; Schiffman, *Text to Tradition*, pp. 177-185.

[5]That is, first-century sources; some New Testament documents and all of Josephus's are *written* after 70, but build on pre-70 personal experiences, traditions and sources.

leaders were the priests. But within the priesthood, especially among its elite, there were factions. And there was at least one non-priestly elite group that competed with the priestly elite: the Pharisees.

When Josephus said that among the Jews there were three philosophical schools—Sadducees, Pharisees and Essenes—he did not mean that all Jews belonged to one of these three "parties." He meant no more than he said: like other cultured peoples, the Jews had their intellectuals (philosophers), and like other philosophers, they belonged to different "schools" of opinion. Josephus was clearly and explicitly speaking about a numerically small elite among the Jewish leadership. And we get the same picture of the Pharisees, scribes and Sadducees in the New Testament. So, what we get in the contemporary first-century sources is a picture of competing religious elites, competing for the position as "teachers of Israel," none of them having anything like a monopoly, none of them being able to define other Jews as being outside of "Judaism" in a way everyone would recognize. It seems clear that Jesus and the early community of his believers fit into this very picture; they take part in this contest from within, not from without. It is meaningless and grossly anachronistic to picture Jesus, Peter or Paul as debating with "Judaism" or its representatives, as if they themselves were outside and represented something else, a non-Jewish position.

I believe, therefore, that one should call this pre-70 situation "Judaism in several varieties," instead of "several Judaisms."[6] However diversified Judaism was, it seems that Jews during the last period of the second temple were no more uncertain about who was a Jew and who was not, than in later periods. Most Jews would think, for example, that the Samaritans were not Jews, in spite of the fact that the Samaritans had the Torah, were circumcised and practiced a Jewish lifestyle. Few, on the other hand, would say the Qumran covenanters were not Jews. The basic criterion may be stated like this: a Jew is one who by descent or conversion belongs to the people who worship the God that (normally) dwells in the temple at Jerusalem. This excludes the Samaritans but includes the Qumranites. It also has the advantage of including the first Jewish believers in Jesus, while at the same time explaining why they gradually came to develop an identity so inwardly independent of the

---

[6]E. P. Sanders, in his *Judaism* and elsewhere, prefers the former approach; whereas Jacob Neusner strongly advocates the abolishment of any talk about "Judaism" in the singular. Cf. his rather temperamental criticism of Sanders in *Judaic Law from Jesus to the Mishnah: A Systematic Reply to Professor E. P. Sanders*, South Florida Studies in the History of Judaism 84 (Atlanta, Ga.: Scholars Press, 1993).

physical temple (even before A.D. 70), that they were, in time, to burst through the definition of Judaism held by most of their compatriots.[7] So, we stick to Judaism in the singular, while recognizing great pluralism, even factionalism, within pre-70 Jewish religion.[8]

This serves as a kind of preface to the following paragraphs, which deal in turn with what we know about the different factions within the religious elite. For some of them, we know surprisingly little, and scholars today claim to know less than scholars did previously.

The Priestly Elite

The most numerous and possibly most influential group among the ordinary people is also the group we know the least about: the some 20,000 ordinary priests and Levites. These are the ones whom the Bible itself clearly mandates to teach and direct the people of Israel according to the law of God; and we must assume they did. These may be the people who are called "scribes" in the New Testament. In any case, it seems unwise to exclude them from this category.[9]

The problem with this group is that we know next to nothing about their teaching or their opinions—for example, with regard to the questions debated between the Pharisees and the Sadducees. It should be emphasized that this large group cannot simply be identified with the Sadducees. Accord-

---

[7]Shaye Cohen in his *Jewishness*, and Richard Bauckham in the article quoted below in this note, both emphasize that the recognition of the Jerusalem temple as the dwelling place of the one true God was a basic criterion of Jewish identity. We see this in the conversation between Jesus and the Samaritan woman in John 4. Against Neusner's way of speaking about several Judaisms, Bauckham also argues the following way: If we define each of the parties within Judaism as "a Judaism," we have no term for the Judaism of the vast majority of Jews who belonged to no party at all. "The mass of the people who did not belong to a party cannot be regarded as another party alongside the others" (Bauckham, "The Parting of the Ways," *Studia Theologica* 47 [1993]: 135-51; quotation p. 137.)
[8]See Shemaryahu Talmon, "The Internal Diversification of Judaism in the Early Second Temple Period," in *Jewish Civilization in the Hellenistic-Roman Period*, ed. S. Talmon, Journal for the Study of the Pseudepigrapha Supplement Series 10 (Sheffield: Sheffield Academic Press, 1991), pp. 16-43; Albert I. Baumgarten, *The Flourishing of Jewish Sects in the Maccabean Era: An Interpretation*, Supplements to the Journal for the Study of Judaism 55 (Leiden: E. J. Brill, 1997).
[9]This identification is argued extensively by Sanders, *Judaism*, pp. 170-89. Others think that "scribes" in the New Testament is only a synonym for Pharisees, see, e.g., Ellis Rivkin, "Scribes, Pharisees, Lawyers, Hypocrites: A Study in Synonymity," *Hebrew Union College Annual* 49 (1978): 135-42. For yet another interpretation, see Daniel R. Schwartz, "'Scribes and Pharisees, Hypocrites': Who are the 'Scribes' in the New Testament?" in Schwartz, *Studies*, pp. 89-101.

ing to Josephus, the Sadducees were a small group *within* the priesthood; possibly also—through family connections—comprising a few members *without*. The Sadducees, according to him, was the priestly aristocracy, a few families of leading priests. And we do not even know if all leading priests belonged to this group. In talking about the large group of ordinary priests and Levites, therefore, we are by no means talking about the Sadducees. In fact, there is substantial evidence in Josephus that some priests were Pharisees.

We should probably not think of the priests as a homogeneous group, having the same opinions everywhere and at all times.[10] It remains a possibility that some leading priestly scribes were among the "sages" who, after A.D. 70, took part in the formation of the body of traditions laid down in the *Mishnah*, and that they may be responsible for the large quantity of material concerning the temple, temple rituals and priestly duties that we find there. One could also suggest the possibility that some of the priests, perhaps the majority, occupied some middle ground between the competing "school" positions of the Pharisees and Sadducees—though here we are merely guessing.

As far as we know, no "ordinary" priest has left us a written document stating his theological convictions. I say "as far as we know," for one should not exclude the possibility that some of the Jewish writings from the intertestamental period (Apocrypha and Pseudepigrapha) are in fact written by priests, priests who were neither Sadducees nor Pharisees nor anything else in particular. The book of Sirach has often been characterized as "proto-sadducaic"; "proto-" because the Sadducees are documented as a separate party only at a later date. But could it be that Sirach is quite simply "priestly"?

Josephus was a priest, but clearly no average priest. Yet Josephus should be able to give us some significant evidence as to what kind of knowledge and theological opinions a priest in his days had, even if Josephus probably knew more than most.

With these tantalizing glimpses into something we would like to know more about, we must be content. It is now time to turn to the "schools" described by Josephus, and we start with the two priestly ones, Sadducees and Essenes.

Priestly Judaism: The Sadducees

Almost everything about the Sadducees is enigmatic, beginning with Jose-

---

[10]Cf. Menachem Stern, "Aspects of Jewish Society: The Priesthood and Other Classes," in *Compendia 1:2:* 561-630.

phus's report on them as a "philosophical school":

> The Sadducees hold that the soul perishes along with the body. They own no observance of any sort apart from the laws; in fact, they reckon it a virtue to dispute with the teachers of the path of wisdom that they pursue. There are but few men to whom this doctrine has been made known, but these are men of the highest standing. They accomplish practically nothing, however. For whenever they assume some office, though they submit unwillingly and perforce, yet submit they do to the formulas of the Pharisees, since otherwise the masses would not tolerate them. (*Antiquities* 18.16-17)

> The Sadducees . . . do away with Fate [divine providence] altogether, and remove God beyond, not merely the commission, but the very sight, of evil. They maintain that man has free choice of good or evil, and that it rests with each man's will whether he follows the one or the other. As for the persistence of the soul after death, penalties in the underworld, and rewards, they will have none of them. . . . Such is what I have to say on the Jewish philosophical schools. (*Jewish War* 2.164-66)

Here Josephus obviously describes the Jewish "schools" according to the conventional patterns in Greek literature of the time. In such descriptions, the school's opinions about divine providence versus free will and about the immortality of the soul were the standard topics. That Josephus singles out these questions and not others may therefore be a courtesy to his readers, and need not imply that these were the crucial questions if the schools were to describe themselves.[11] The Sadducees are clearly portrayed as Epicureans: they hold the same opinions as the Epicurean philosophers. They deny that God interferes in human affairs, and they deny the immortality of the soul. The New Testament gives a description of the Sadducean position that seems less stylized to the Greek pattern: "some Sadducees came to [Jesus], saying there is no resurrection" (Mt 22:23). "The Sadducees say that there is no resurrection, or angels, or spirits; but the Pharisees acknowledge all three" (Acts 23:8).

A tentative interpretation says that the Sadducees did not share the Phari-

---

[11]N. T. Wright interestingly proposes that Josephus has translated something very Jewish (about all the three parties) into something very Greek. The real issue, according to Wright, was how the three schools were thinking about the relationship between human and divine action in history, especially with regard to the liberation and restoration of Israel: Was it God's business alone (roughly the Essenes' position), or was it dependent on man's political prudence alone (roughly the Sadducees' position), or was it a bit of both (roughly the Pharisaic position)? Cf. Wright, *The New Testament*, pp. 200-202.

saic belief in an afterlife through resurrection (Josephus Hellenized this for his Greek readers as a denial of the immortality of the soul). Luke's report in Acts 23:8 about not believing in angels and spirits is not easy to interpret; maybe the Sadducees rejected the flourishing apocalyptic literature of this period with all its angels and visions (cf. Acts 23:9). In any case, the Sadducees were clearly not up to Josephus's own standard of sound theology, which agreed with the Pharisaic on these points, and so he deemed them Epicurean, that is, less than pious.

In one more passage, however, Josephus gives us important information on the Sadducees and their relation to the Pharisees. And in this passage Josephus is not bound by the school presentation pattern:

> For the present I wish merely to explain that the Pharisees had passed on to the people certain regulations handed down by former generations and not recorded in the Laws of Moses, for which reason they are rejected by the Sadducaean group, who hold that only those regulations should be considered valid which were written down [in Scripture], and that those which had been handed down by former generations need not be observed. And concerning these matters the two parties came to have controversies and serious differences, the Sadducees having the confidence of the wealthy alone but no following among the populace, while the Pharisees have the support of the masses. (*Antiquities* 13.297-98)

This passage is of greater importance because of what it says about the Pharisees than what it says about the Sadducees, so we shall return to it below. Here it is sufficient to point out that the Sadducees seems to have rejected the extra-biblical regulations of the Pharisees because the Pharisees *could not and would not found these regulations upon the biblical text.* The Pharisees seem to have admitted that their extra commandments were not in the Bible. When asked why they should nevertheless be observed, they answered by pointing to the authority of their ancestors who made these regulations. That was something the Sadducees refused to accept; they were rather eager to *argue* in such questions (as Josephus said in the first text above), probably requiring a scriptural basis. The same principle could lie behind the Sadducean rejection of belief in the resurrection of the dead and communication of revelation through spirits and angels: they meant this lacked exegetical basis in the Bible. (There is no reliable evidence that the Sadducees rejected the prophetical books of the Old Testament and the rest of the Old Testament writings. Some late church fathers claim this, but may have confused Sadducees with Samaritans.)

The only additional information on the Sadducees of any significance is the Mishnah's reports on discussions between Sadducees and Pharisees concerning details of the law. We will return to these when treating the Essenes; here we quote Schiffman's summary on the matter: "In general, the Sadducees saw the purity laws as referring to the Temple and its priests, and saw no reason for extending them into the daily life of all Israel, a basic pillar of the Pharisaic approach."[12]

In all other respects, we are poorly informed about the Sadducees: their name, their origin, their history and their politics remain shrouded in mystery. The most reasonable explanation of their name is that they supported the Zadokite high priests. As we know already (cf. chapter one), the Zadokite line had been interrupted by the Hasmonean high priests. From this we would expect that the Sadducees/Zadokites would be fierce opponents of the Hasmoneans, but that seems not to have been the case. They seem rather to have cooperated with and even supported the Hasmoneans. Many hypotheses have been put forward to solve this apparent contradiction between name and policy. It is interesting, however, that some new light may be shed on the issue from the history of the other priestly elite: the Essenes. This light does not come from Josephus, but from the most recently edited portion of the Dead Sea Scrolls.

Priestly Judaism: The Community at Qumran and the Essenes

The Community at Qumran

The Dead Sea Scrolls may be divided roughly into three categories: (1) biblical manuscripts, (2) sectarian writings and (3) non- or pre-sectarian writings. The latter category comprises (a) nonbiblical writings used but not produced by the Qumran sect, and (b) nonbiblical writings probably produced by members or predecessors of the sect, but not yet expressing the characteristic points of view that later became typical for the Qumran community. Categories 1 and 2 were published first, and many books on the Qumran sect were based mainly on these texts. Category 3 texts have been published quite recently and have changed the way scholars now perceive the origin, history, character and significance of the sect.[13]

---

[12]Schiffman, *Text to Tradition*, p. 108.
[13]The best comprehensive introduction to the entire Qumran literature, taking the recently published texts into account, is Lawrence H. Schiffman, *Reclaiming the Dead Sea Scrolls: The History of Judaism, the Background of Christianity, the Lost Library of Qumran* (Philadelphia/Jerusalem: The Jewish Publication Society, 1994).

One of the most important of the recently published texts is the so-called *Halakic Letter*, or "Some Deeds of the Law" (*Miqsat Ma'ase ha-Torah* = 4QMMT = 4Q394-399) as the full title runs. In this letter the earliest leaders of the group that fled to Qumran argue with opponents in Jerusalem who apparently belong to the priestly establishment there. The leaders of the Qumran group advocate points of law that agree with opinions ascribed to the Sadducees in later rabbinic literature, while their opponents in Jerusalem advocate opinions later ascribed to the Pharisees. In other words, the Qumran group appears to be "oppositional Sadducees," while the Jerusalem temple establishment appears to conform to Pharisaic positions. We should then combine this with the observation that the Qumran leaders engaged in bitter polemics against a "wicked priest" who persecuted "the teacher of righteousness," one of their own leaders. Scholars almost unanimously conclude that the "wicked priest" must be one of the first Hasmonean high priests, possibly Jonathan (152-143) or maybe Simon (142-134). The easiest way to explain this anti-Hasmonean attitude and the "Sadducaic" position of the Qumranites is to assume that they identified with the deposed Zadokite line of high priests, at least some branch of it, and perhaps had some of the Zadokite descendants in their midst. If so, *these* "Sadducees" exhibit precisely that anti-Hasmonean attitude we missed among the "regular" Sadducees Josephus writes about. But the Qumranites may also help explain why not all of the Zadokite party followed their course: the price they had to pay for their open opposition against the Hasmoneans was high—persecution and exile in the desert. So maybe another branch of the Zadokite opposition chose to remain in Jerusalem, near the center of power, in order to gain influence through cooperation and accommodation rather than open conflict: if you can't beat them, join them. And maybe after some time this strategy brought them such influence that they forgot everything about opposition and instead became masters of the art of compromise and remaining in power—and emerged as Josephus's Sadducees.

In any case it seems very likely that the Qumran community and the Sadducees had some common roots and a tradition of interpreting the law that derived from the same sources. The very priestly character of the Qumran community has long been noticed by scholars. One of the sectarian writings (now commonly called *The Damascus Document*), which somehow made its way to the Cairo Geniza (and from there to the Geniza collection of manuscripts in Cambridge University), was published as early as 1910 by Solomon Schechter. He did not know the provenance of the document, but from the contents he called it a *Zadokite Work*.[14] The latest published texts have indeed proved him right.

But this means that the "pre-sectarian" doctrine of the earliest Qumran documents should be a doctrine not very unlike the Sadducean one at the same early period. The anti-Pharisaic polemic of the *Halakic Letter* also documents the early date of important Pharisaic teachings. In this way the Qumran documents not only throw light on a hitherto little known sect of Judaism. They also illuminate the early history of Sadducees and Pharisees, and allow the Qumran sect itself to appear a lot less marginal and "outside" than it did in the beginning (when only the most sectarian writings were fully edited).

The Qumran community stayed at Qumran from the 140s B.C. until the Roman destruction of the site in A.D. 68, although they probably had to vacate the community center temporarily in the years after 31 B.C., when an earthquake partly destroyed the community buildings and installations. The fault-line in the ground can still be seen. Some one hundred people may have been living in Qumran. The physical isolation of the place in a desert area may have boosted the process of a more and more sectarian self-understanding. Increasingly, the Qumranites understood themselves as the only true Israelites. They were "the sons of light" who, in an apocalyptic end-time battle, were to conquer "the sons of darkness." But throughout the history of the sect, they remained true to their priestly origin (although laypeople soon became the majority). The Qumran community was organized according to the model of the tabernacle community during the forty years in the desert. There was a strictly defined order by rank: first came the priests, then the Levites, then the "many" or the people. They placed a heavy emphasis on ritual immersions and Levitical purity.

The priestly character of the sect also shows up in their attitude toward the Jerusalem temple. Since the days of the "wicked priest," the Essenes regarded the temple as polluted and the sacrifices as invalid. Nevertheless they continued to send votive offerings to the temple, and their rejection of the present temple service was by no means meant as a disparagement of the temple or a declaration that its service was insignificant. To the contrary, they rejected the present polluted service precisely because they valued the temple so much. In fact, they expected to take control of the temple and either cleanse it from

[14]Solomon Schechter, *Fragments of a Zadokite Work,* Documents of Jewish Sectaries 1 (Cambridge: Cambridge University Press, 1910 [reprint, New York: Ktav, 1970]).

pollution or rebuild it in the near future, when the great eschatological war had begun. The spiritual worship and the community meal at Qumran were only temporary substitutes for the temple service, which was to be resumed as soon as possible. In the meantime the Qumran community itself could be called the temple of God: He was present in their midst.

Finally, the messianism of the community had a priestly slant. Like other Jewish groups at the time, the Qumran people awaited *two* messiahs, one anointed priest and one anointed king (cf. Zech 4:11-14 as a biblical foundation for this model). In Qumran the priestly Messiah—presumably the eschatological Zadokite high priest—would rank above the Davidic royal Messiah.[15]

John J. Collins summarizes the role and function of the Davidic Messiah:

> He is the scepter who will smite the nations, slay the wicked with the breath of his lips, and restore the Davidic dynasty. Hence his role in the eschatological war. He is also the Messiah of righteousness, who will usher in an era of peace and justice. He is presumably a human figure, although he is endowed with the Spirit of the Lord. He is expected to restore a dynasty rather than rule forever himself.[16]

The priestly Messiah, on the other hand, is expected to restore the temple worship. It is possible that in speaking of two messiahs, not one, and in extolling the priestly Messiah as a separate figure, different from the royal, the Qumran sect was indirectly criticizing the Hasmonean combination of the two offices.

Such, in rough outline, was the Judaism of the Qumran community. The main point about the Dead Sea Scrolls in our context is that they have opened a completely new window on aspects of Judaism toward the end of the Second Temple period. They have given us firsthand source material from a variety of Judaism we didn't know existed. Or did we?

The Essenes

Two pagan Roman authors, Dio Chrysostom and Pliny, say that a Jewish sect by the Latin name *Esseni*[17] had fled to the shores of the Dead Sea and established itself there; Pliny even located them between Jericho and En Gedi,

---

[15]On the messianism of the scrolls, see esp. John J. Collins, *The Scepter and the Star: The Messiahs of the Dead Sea Scrolls and Other Ancient Literature,* Anchor Bible Reference Library (New York: Doubleday, 1995).

[16]Collins, *Scepter,* p. 67.

[17]Cf. in general *New Schürer* 2:555-97, with extensive bibliography (until 1979) pp. 555-58.

which must mean at Qumran.[18] Philo and Josephus have more information on the same sect, which they identify in Greek as *Essaioi* (Philo and Josephus) or *Essenoi* (Josephus). Josephus and Philo do not mention the settlement at Qumran, but say that the Essenes live scattered around in the whole country. Josephus also speaks about two branches of the sect, one that avoids marriage and one that accepts it (*Jewish War* 2.160-61). He gives a quite detailed description of the Essenes' way of life, which makes it evident that they were very scrupulous about ritual purity and that they dressed in white linen, probably a priestly vestment. Josephus as well as Philo numbered them at over four thousand.

Are these "Essenes" and the Qumran community the same sect? Some scholars answer with a simple *yes;* some with a simple *no.* The majority, however, think we are safer to say that there must be some connection between the Qumran community and the four thousand Essenes, but hardly a complete identity.[19] For one thing, there is the question of numbers and locale. The Qumran community center could probably house some one hundred people, and Josephus and Philo explicitly state that the Essenes lived all over the land of Israel. Josephus said there was no town without them. The better question, therefore, probably asks, what was the relationship between the Qumran community center and the larger Essene movement? Were the people at Qumran a splinter group, an extreme wing? Or was the center at Qumran a kind of spiritual headquarters for the whole movement, the home of its scribal elite and leadership? Perhaps it functioned, at the same time, as a "retreat center" where ordinary Essenes could live for a while to study and practice the purity rules more stringently than possible in their hometowns. While uncertain about the exact answers to these or similar proposals, most scholars agree that there must be some such connection between the Essenes and the Qumran community. There are, in fact, indications in the Scrolls themselves that two different sets of rules were valid: one for people living in Qumran itself, one for sect members living elsewhere, among non-members.

Josephus treats the Essenes within his "three schools" passages, and in what he says about their philosophical ideas, the Pythagoreans seem to be his

---

[18]For a brief and concise discussion of Pliny's and Dio's statements, see *New Schürer* 2:562-63. For more extensive treatment, see Geza Vermes and Martin D. Goodman, *The Essenes According to the Classical Sources,* Oxford Centre Textbooks 1 (Sheffield: JSOT Press, 1989).

[19]The most recent and extensive discussion of Josephus's description compared to the Dead Sea Scrolls is Todd S. Beall, *Josephus' Description of the Essenes Illustrated by the Dead Sea Scrolls,* Society for New Testament Studies Monograph Series 58 (Cambridge: Cambridge University Press, 1988).

model: "The doctrine of the Essenes is wont to leave everything in the hands of God. They regard the soul as immortal and believe that they ought to strive especially to draw near to righteousness. . . . Otherwise they are of the highest character, devoting themselves solely to agricultural labor" (*Antiquities* 18.18-19). Roughly speaking, the Scrolls confirm this somewhat stylized picture of Essene doctrine; the Qumran community did emphasize the sovereign and irresistible will of God more than other varieties of Judaism known to us.

Even before the 1947 discoveries of the Dead Sea Scrolls, scholars had used Josephus's and Philo's material on the Essenes to illuminate certain aspects of Jesus' teaching and that of the early Christian community. The availability of the new and rich material from Qumran led, during the first decades, to considerable enthusiasm and sometimes exaggerated claims about the Scrolls being the real clue to everything about Jesus and the early community. In recent years more sober and balanced assessments have been made, and there is already a large body of literature on Qumran and the New Testament. We shall not pursue this theme here, however, but return to it in chapters six and seven. It is now time to call on stage those teachers of Israel who used to be considered its only teachers: the Pharisees.

Priestly Judaism for Laypeople: The Pharisees
Scholars used to know a lot about the Pharisees, which did not surprise readers of the New Testament because to them the Pharisees seemed very familiar. It therefore comes as somewhat of a surprise that scholars in recent years have come to question much of established "knowledge" about the Pharisees. But if one looks into the matter a little more closely, one can hardly escape the conclusion that the now widespread caution is well founded. One scholar summarized our main problem with regard to the Pharisees thus: "first that there is far too little evidence; and . . . second, that there is far too much."[20]

1. Outside the enormous bulk of rabbinic writings, we have mainly the New Testament and Josephus as roughly contemporary sources for the last period of Pharisaism. These books contain something on the Pharisees, but not as much, and not as clear and unambiguous, as we could wish. This is the problem of too little evidence.

2. The rabbinic writings contain a lot of information, or apparent information, on the early sages and their teaching and rulings, and some of these sages belong to the pre-70 period. It is commonly assumed that these early

---

[20]John Bowker, *Jesus and the Pharisees* (Cambridge: Cambridge University Press, 1973), p. 1.

sages were Pharisees, and also that the body of tradition fostered by the second- and third-century rabbis to a large extent had already been held by the first-century Pharisees. We spoke about this model of continuity above. In addition, the rabbinic writings often refer to people called *perushim*, probably the Hebrew word rendered *Pharisaioi* by Josephus and in the New Testament. Here we are in for a surprise, however, for the *perushim* are often denounced as schismatics or hypocrites by the rabbis, and often seem not to be a specific group at all. In other texts they are obviously the opponents of the Sadducees, and then they resemble the New Testament's and Josephus's Pharisees a lot more. In short, the rabbinic material represents the problem of too much evidence.

In recent years, scholars have tried to tackle these problems one by one, treating Josephus's evidence (and that of the New Testament) on its own terms,[21] and that of the rabbinic sources on their own terms.[22] Only after completing this work may one venture some tentative synthesis into one coherent picture, always keeping in mind the hypothetical nature of some of the conclusions. Leaning heavily on the experts in the field, we make the following attempt along these lines.

According to Josephus, the Pharisees emerge as a distinct group around the middle of the second century B.C. (together with the Sadducees), and he depicts them as scheming politicians who use rather tough methods with their opponents, including murder. After the end of Hasmonean rule, single Pharisees seem to have had some influence on some of Herod's family; then they disappear from the political scene altogether, only to emerge once more during the dramatic year of A.D. 67 when the internal Jewish debate about the great insurrection against Rome reached its peak. Many scholars have had difficulty squaring this picture of the Pharisees as primarily politicians with the pictures in other sources (also in Josephus) that portray them primarily as a theological party concerned with the purity regulations in the Torah.[23] It could be, however, that this contrast between "politics" and "piety" is a modern one that should not be applied to the period we are concerned with here. During both of the two periods in which we meet the Pharisees in a mainly

---

[21]The leading representative of this approach is now Steve Mason, *Josephus on the Pharisees* (see full reference in Suggestions).

[22]The pioneer in this field is Jacob Neusner, *The Rabbinical Traditions about the Pharisees*, 3 vols., and the one-volume selection *The Pharisees* (see Suggestions).

[23]Jacob Neusner observed the two different portraits and tried to understand them as depicting a historic development of the Pharisaic movement: *From Politics to Piety: The Emergence of Pharisaic Judaism*, 2nd ed. (New York: Ktav Publishing House, 1979).

political role, the Jewish people took their political fate into their own hands and established some degree of self-rule. In such circumstances *all* groups wanting to lead and influence the people of Israel had to become politicians— except the ones who quit the political power play altogether and went into exile, as the Qumranites. In the Hasmonean temple-state the question of how to interpret and practice the laws regulating the people's relation to the temple—purity, tithes and so on—would be both religious and political questions at the same time.[24] The Pharisees and the Sadducees disagreed in such matters; the Pharisees advocated some nonbiblical rulings that they did not justify with biblical exegesis, but by appeal to the authority of "the (fore)fathers" who had given these rulings. Josephus and the New Testament writings agree completely on one point: the Pharisees were known to be extremely scrupulous in their observance of these regulations. But in what did this scrupulosity consist?

Here a rabbinic source may help us. *Mishnah Avot* 1:1 as well as many parallel texts state that "the men of the Great Synagogue" said three things: Be deliberate in judgement, raise up many disciples, and make a fence around the law. It is this latter command that concerns us here. Making a fence around the law means giving supplementary rulings that hinder a man or woman from even coming close to breaking a scriptural command. These supplementary rulings have no direct biblical foundation, but are meant to prevent one from getting into a situation in which one might break a biblical command. For example, when Adam heard God say "of the tree of the knowledge . . . you shall not eat" (Gen 2:17) in rendering this command for Eve he "made a fence" by adding "you shall not eat of [it], nor shall you touch it" (Gen 3:3).[25] The attribution of the command to "make a fence" to the rather shadowy "Great Synagogue" may be legend, but there is hardly any doubt that this principle expresses well the idea behind much of the Pharisaic tradition of extrabiblical regulations: they are meant to prevent even the opportunity for breaking scriptural commands.

A considerable bulk of the Pharisaic halakah is concerned with purity regulations (food, drink and vessels) and the laws of tithing. In the Bible most of these laws concern the priests or visitors to the temple: those "within the camp." Most Jews and most priests seem to have taken this quite literally and did not worry much about these regulations in everyday life outside "the

---

[24]Cf. Daniel R. Schwartz, "On Pharisaic Opposition to the Hasmonean Monarchy," in *Studies*, pp. 44-56.
[25]*Avot of Rabbi Nathan* 1; trans. Goldin, *Fathers*, p. 8.

Box 5.1. Pharisaic "Tradition" and Rabbinic "Oral Law"

In *TB Shabbat* 31a there is a story about Hillel the Elder referring to two Torahs, one written and one oral, both originating with Moses at Sinai. This has often been taken as proof that already the early Pharisees knew the concept of an oral Torah transmitted all the way from Sinai to their own time through an unbroken chain of tradents. This idea is later clearly stated in the opening passages of the *Mishnah* tractate *Avot*. It is doubtful, however, that the pre-70 Pharisees knew this idea. It is clearly not known to the New Testament writers in their reports on the Pharisees, and it is unknown to Josephus. What they say about the "tradition" obeyed by the Pharisees seems rather to speak against their knowing an oral law from Sinai: the Pharisees cited "their forefathers" as the originators of and the authorities behind their "tradition," not God or Moses at Sinai. Likewise, the rabbinic writings only very rarely ascribe the concept of oral law to early sages, and the way these early sages treat scribal tradition seems to indicate that they did not accord it the same authority as the written Torah from Sinai. It therefore seems that the concept of oral Torah developed later, possibly to be launched for the first time in the tractate *Avot*, and that it was an alternative attempt to come to terms with the *question of authority*, which had accompanied the Pharisaic extra-biblical tradition from the beginning. The other attempt to bolster the authority of this tradition was to try and give it an exegetical underpinning, to show it could be derived from biblical commands. Possibly these two strategies developed more or less as parallels—in the long run, both were incorporated in the Talmuds.[26]

camp," when not visiting the temple. The Pharisees, however, seem to have applied these regulations in their everyday life, at least within Jerusalem, which they may have defined as being "the camp" spoken of in the Torah.

Jacob Neusner has interpreted this Pharisaic program as aimed at making every Israelite a "priest." They should all live a life not only in accordance with the Torah, but specifically in accordance with the requirements of Levitical purity which the Torah enjoined only on the priests.[27] They sought to realize God's calling for Israel as *Mamlehet Kohanim*, a nation of priests (Ex 19:6). "Their emphasis on the importance of dietary laws and other purity regulations was based on their desire to raise the status of every Jew to equal that of the priests and to consider their table as similar to the table of God in the Jerusalem temple."[28]

In order to help each other achieve this ideal, the Pharisees organized societies, *havurot*, with the main purpose of enabling all members to maintain their purity and share their meals at a completely *kosher* table. It is possible

[26]For bibliography and a very instructive discussion of this issue, see E. P. Sanders, "Did the Pharisees Have Oral Law?" in *Jewish Law from Jesus to the Mishnah: Five Studies* (London: SCM Press/Philadelphia: Trinity Press International, 1990), pp. 97-130.

[27]For discussions of Neusner's thesis, see E. P. Sanders, "Did the Pharisees Eat Ordinary Food in Purity?" in *Jewish Law from Jesus to the Mishnah*, pp. 131-254; Daniel R. Schwartz, "'Kingdom of Priests': A Pharisaic Slogan?" in Schwartz, *Studies*, 57-80.

[28]*New Schürer* 2:388 n. 16.

that the name Pharisee originated with the emergence of this phenomenon. It means "one who separates himself," namely from unclean things and persons, which included the majority of the people. A great deal of Pharisaic halakah is concerned with how members of the *havurot* should deal with those outside so as not to lose their own purity. Those outside, the non-Pharisaic Jews, were called the *am haaretz*, "the people of the land," a rather scornful name in the mouth of a Pharisee.[29]

With this, we have tried to make the scrupulosity of the Pharisees a little more concrete; the nature of the sources hardly allows us to be much more specific.

Like Sadduceeism, Pharisaism was probably a Jerusalem-centered movement. In order to become a Pharisee, Paul went to Jerusalem to study at the feet of Gamaliel. But there are more than one indication in the extant sources that the Pharisees wanted to extend their sphere of influence not only to all the land of Israel but also into the Diaspora, and that therefore some of them traveled. Thus, it is not surprising that we find Pharisees debating with Jesus in the Galilean synagogues (a couple of times they are said to come from Jerusalem, together with "the scribes").

Having previously stressed that all the Jewish groups treated in this chapter held the temple and the temple service at the very center of their concerns, how should we describe the Pharisees in this regard? As we have seen, the Pharisees sought to make every Israelite a priest and every meal a temple meal. Their aim was to extend the sanctity of the temple, not to replace it or make it unnecessary. And yet, once you say that the temple is wherever you are, it is easy to draw the conclusion that the actual temple is insignificant, perhaps even dispensable. The very heart of the temple service was the sacrifices. The prophets of the Bible taught Israel that sacrifices would not suffice if unaccompanied by real heartfelt contrition and a sincere desire to mend one's ways and practice righteousness. One could easily conclude that the sacrifices themselves were nonessential: the change of heart was the real thing.

The sacrifices were expressly commanded by the highest authority, the Torah, and because of this we can expect a certain ambivalence among the Pharisees about them. Because of the Torah the sacrifices were held in high esteem as God's will, but at the same time repentance can be seen as the main

---

[29]Cf. John 7:48-49, in which "the authorities" (the chief priests) and the Pharisees are contrasted to "this crowd, which does not know the law."

factor in atonement. It is interesting to study the approach of Johanan ben Zakkai on this matter. Some sayings of his clearly indicate that he did not regard the cultic rites as necessary or effective in themselves. Thus, he was able to interpret the fall of the temple and the cessation of the sacrifices as God's hint that other means should now replace the temple service.

> Once as Rabban Johanan ben Zakkai was coming forth from Jerusalem, Rabbi Joshua followed after him and beheld the temple in ruins. "Woe unto us!" Rabbi Joshua cried, "that this, the place where the iniquities of Israel were atoned for, is laid waste!" "My son," Rabban Johanan said to him, "be not grieved; we have another atonement as effective as this. And what is it? It is acts of loving-kindness, as it is said, 'For I desire mercy and not sacrifice' [Hos 6:6]. (*Avot of Rabbi Nathan* 4)[30]

Thus the very program of Pharisaism—to make every Israelite a priest and every table a temple meal—had prepared Israel for the post-70 situation. It was perhaps quite unintentional, but we cannot know for sure. There are indications in the rabbinic sources that some rabbis in Jesus' days had forebodings that the temple service would come to an end, and some even prophesied to that effect.[31] The Pharisees were therefore probably not among those who were most concerned about what Jesus had to say about the temple. With or without knowing it, they were themselves preparing the people for the post-70 situation.

Still, the people mourned the loss of the temple deeply. Many of the traditions in the Mishnah are preserved with a view to the eventual rebuilding of the temple. For this rebuilding the rabbis, among them Rabbi Akiba, continued to long and pray, because the temple service was part of the Torah to which they were dedicated.

---

[30]Goldin, *Fathers*, p. 34.
[31]"Our rabbis taught: During the last forty years before the destruction of the Temple the lot ('For the Lord') did not come up in the right hand; nor did the crimson-colored strap become white; nor did the western-most light shine; and the doors of the *Hekal* [sanctuary] would open by themselves, until R. Johanan ben Zakkai rebuked them, saying: *Hekal, Hekal*, why will you be the alarmer yourself? I know about you that you will be destroyed, for Zechariah ben Ido has already prophesied concerning you: Open your doors, O Lebanon, that the fire may devour your cedars" (*TB Yoma* 39b). "R. Zadok observed fasts for forty years in order that Jerusalem might not be destroyed, [and he became so thin that] when he ate anything the food could be seen [as it passed through his throat]. When he wanted to restore himself, they used to bring him a fig, and he used to suck the juice and throw the rest away" (*TB Gittin* 56a).

Judaism Apart from the Temple: The Synagogue

The most concrete expression of this unconscious preparation for the post-70 situation was the establishment of the synagogue.[32] The historical origins of the synagogue are thickly shrouded in uncertainty. The traditional theory is that the first synagogues were established during the Babylonian exile, but there is insufficient evidence to prove this. The earliest archaeological evidence comes from Egypt and suggests that synagogues existed there ca. 250 B.C. From the first century A.D. we have written evidence of their existence in the New Testament, Philo and Josephus. First-century synagogues have been archaeologically documented at Herodium, Masada, Gamla and (one) in Jerusalem. The literary evidence points to several synagogues in Galilee. If we stick to the first-century A.D. picture, the following pattern seems to emerge: the synagogue was by then a well-established institution in the Diaspora, and some Diaspora Jews took this institution with them to Jerusalem when they settled there. Otherwise, there were no ordinary synagogues in Jerusalem or Judea:[33] the temple itself was close and available and made synagogues superfluous. In Galilee the synagogue seems to have become the order of the day in the first century, but was possibly quite young as an institution. We also do not know if there existed special buildings for the synagogue assembly or if the assembly met in the city square or in large private houses. Luke 7:5 indicates that there was a synagogue building in Capernaum at least; possibly it was completely demolished when the big "white" synagogue in Capernaum (the ruins are still standing) was built in the early Byzantine period. There is still a conspicuous lack

---

[32]Selective bibliography: A. Th. Kraabel, "The Diaspora Synagogue: Archaeological and Epigraphic Evidence Since Sukenik," in Haase, *Aufstieg 2* 19.1:477-510; S. B. Hoenig, "The Ancient City-Square: The Forerunner of the Synagogue," ibid.: 448-76; Lee I. Levine, ed., *The Synagogue in Late Antiquity* (Philadelphia: The American Schools of Oriental Research, 1987); Frowald G. Hüttenmeister, "'Synagoge' und 'Proseuche' bei Josephus und in anderen antiken Quellen," in *Begegnungen zwischen Christentum und Judentum in Antike und Mittelalter: Festschrift für Heinz Schreckenberg*, ed. Dietrich-Alex Koch and Hermann Lichtenberger, Schriften des Institutum Judaicum Delitzschianum 1 (Göttingen: Vandenhoeck & Ruprecht, 1993), pp. 163-81; Dan Urman and Paul V. M. Flesher, eds., *Ancient Synagogues: Historical Analysis and Archaeological Discovery*, vol. 1, Studia Post-Biblica 47, 1 (Leiden/New York/Cologne: E. J. Brill, 1995); Steven Fine, ed., *Jews, Christians, and Polytheists in the Ancient Synagogue: Cultural Interaction During the Greco-Roman Period*, Baltimore Studies in the History of Judaism (London/New York: Routledge, 1999); Lee I. Levine, *The Ancient Synagogue: The First Thousand Years* (New Haven: Yale University Press, 2000).
[33]The synagogues at Herodium and Masada are exceptions: they were probably established by Zealots of Galilean origin during the Jewish war of A.D. 66-70.

of hard archaeological data on first-century Galilean synagogue buildings (apart from the extraordinary one in Gamla).

The oldest sources speak of the reading and expounding of the Scriptures—some also of prayer—as the central feature of the synagogue service. It must be stressed that the synagogue was a laymen's institution. Whereas in the temple everything was done by the priests, in the synagogue everything depended on the lay congregation itself. The central part of the service, the reading of the Scriptures, was carried out by the members of the congregation in turn. If a scribe was present, he would be asked to expound the text. But if none were available, everyone was free to speak, and guests would be asked to step forward and greet the congregation with a "word of exhortation" (Acts 13:15). If a priest happened to be there, his status was equal to that of the other members of the congregation. All these features clearly betray the synagogue's Diaspora origins.

Apart from the reading and expounding of the Scriptures, the other main component of the synagogue service was prayer. Here again it was the congregation who prayed, not a priest or someone appointed to this task.[34] Before the time of Jesus, fixed patterns had already developed for both these components of the synagogue service. The Scripture reading consisted of the Torah, read each Sabbath according to a three-year or one-year cycle, and the Prophets, read selectively so as to match the Torah passage.[35] This reading of the Prophets was called the *haftarah* ("ending" or "completion") of the Torah reading. Typical of the availability of sources about the first century, it is the New Testament that gives us the first reliable accounts of the *haftarah* reading in Israel and the Diaspora: Luke 4:17 and Acts 13:15. Some of the main prayers still used in the synagogue service today already existed in the first century A.D.—and some may even be traced back to the last two centuries B.C. This holds true for the principal prayer in each synagogue service, which is often called quite simply the *Teffilah* (the prayer) or the *Amidah* (because it is prayed *standing*), or, more fully, the *Shmoneh Esre* ("the eighteen" [benedic-

---

[34]The custom of having a priest say the Aaronic blessing in the synagogue service probably developed after the fall of the temple, cf. below.

[35]On the reading from the Bible and the cycles of reading in the ancient synagogue, see C. Perrot, "The Reading of the Bible in the Ancient Synagogue," in *Compendia 2:1:* 137-59; Lawrence H. Schiffman, "The Early History of Public Reading of the Torah," in *Jews, Christians, and Polytheists in the Ancient Synagogue: Cultural Interaction During the Greco-Roman Period,* ed. Steven Fine, Baltimore Studies in the History of Judaism (London/New York: Routledge, 1999), pp. 44-56; Lee E. Levine, *The Ancient Synagogue: The First Thousand Years* (New Haven, Conn./London: Yale University Press, 2000), pp. 506-10.

tions]). The individual blessings contained in this prayer are probably older than the compilation of all eighteen benedictions, which apparently took place toward the end of the first century A.D.

In this early phase, the wording of the benedictions seems to have varied, but their main purpose and contents were fixed. In the days of Jesus the wording and sequence of the elements of the synagogue service had attained such stability that we are fully justified in speaking of a synagogal liturgy. The echoes of the synagogal prayers in the Lord's Prayer and other early Christian prayers demonstrate that this liturgy was well known to Jesus and the early disciples. We should not think that the early Christians were antiliturgical in their worship gatherings. It is no accident that in Acts 2:42 Luke does not say that the early community "devoted themselves to the apostles' teaching . . . and *prayer*," but to "*the prayers*," which suggests fixed patterns. All the evidence points to the synagogal liturgy as a source for those prayers. We shall return to this topic in chapters eighteen and nineteen.

The synagogue and its service were from the outset considered supplements, not substitutes, for the temple service. The latter revolved around the sacrifices, while the former revolved around the reading of the Scriptures. Thus, while the synagogue was by no means opposed to the temple, it did not necessarily side with the priesthood. The lay scribes were closer to its heart than the priests. No doubt the Pharisaic scribes were quite influential in the synagogues of the land of Israel during the 100-150 years prior to the fall of the temple, though they never had a complete monopoly.

After the destruction of the temple, the synagogue service became a real substitute for the temple service, but only after important additions had been made. When the Psalms were no longer sung by the Levites in the temple, the synagogue's congregation took up this Levitical task. The blessing of Aaron (the priestly blessing) no longer sounded from the lips of the officiating temple priest; it was solemnly recited in the framework of the synagogue prayers—but still by a priest.

At a somewhat later date, specific prayers were thought to replace the temple sacrifices (according to a rabbinic exegesis of Hosea 14:2: Words of the lips are more valuable than animal sacrifices). It also became customary to recite the biblical and mishnaic passages concerning sacrifices as a substitute for the actual sacrifices. It should be emphasized that none of the sages responsible for these modifications of the synagogal liturgy thought of the synagogue service as a permanent substitute for the temple service. They created prayers for the rebuilding of the temple and the restoration of the sacrifices, and the

synagogue equivalents to the temple service were only meant to be temporary substitutes, until the time of restoration. In theory, this has been the attitude of rabbinic Judaism ever since. But as centuries passed, the whole
temple service became something more and more strange and foreign—until
Maimonides in the twelfth century declared the sacrificial cult to be only a
temporary necessity (there are rabbinic intimations of the idea much earlier).

Nationalistic Judaism: The Zealots

To describe the Zealot movement very briefly, we could say that according to
Josephus it was the nationalistic right wing of the Pharisees. Josephus writes
that the Zealots agreed with the Pharisees in all things, except that "they have
a passion for liberty that is almost unconquerable, since they are convinced
that God alone is their leader and master" (*Antiquities* 18.23).[36]

The Zealot movement was founded, according to Josephus, by Judas of
Gamla and Zadok the Pharisee in response to the census carried out by
Quirinius (cf. Lk 2:2 and Acts 5:37). "They said that the assessment carried
with it a status amounting to downright slavery, no less, and appealed to the
nation to make a bid for independence" (*Antiquities* 18.4). Judas may have
had an ambition to copy the Maccabees, and in one respect he was successful:
many of his descendants became leading Jewish freedom fighters. His sons
Simon and Jacob were engaged in anti-Roman activities and were crucified as
rebels ca. A.D. 47. His descendant Menahem captured Masada at the beginning of the Great War against Rome in A.D. 66 and later was a leader of the
revolt in Jerusalem. Menahem's nephew was Eleazar ben Yair, the famous
leader of those freedom fighters who held out at Masada and finally determined to take their own lives rather than become Roman slaves. There is
therefore some justification for speaking of a whole dynasty of Zealot leaders.
The sources also contain evidence that indicates that at least some of these
leaders made messianic claims for themselves or were regarded as messiahs
by their followers.

Until the outbreak of the large-scale revolt in A.D. 66, these leaders and
their followers mostly used guerilla tactics in their fight against Herodian and
Roman rule, and did not shrink from using political assassination as a
weapon against their enemies. They hid daggers in their clothes and used the
cover of festival crowds to get at their victims—hence their nickname *Sicarii*,

---

[36]Josephus's portrait of the Zealots is analyzed, e.g., in Valentin Nikiprowetzky, "Josephus
and the Revolutionary Parties," in *Josephus, the Bible, and History*, ed. Louis H. Feldman
and Gohei Hata (Leiden: E. J. Brill, 1989), pp. 216-36.

daggermen.[37] It seems that these Sicarii were, during the last years before A.D. 70, distinguished from other Zealot groups.

It seems that there were two things Judas found outrageous about the Roman census under Quirinius. First, counting the people of Israel is prohibited in the Bible, and second, the census was the first step of taxation. The tax had to be paid in heathen coins, bearing a three-dimensional image of Caesar (cf. Mt 22:15-22).

Our sources are inadequate for an extensive description of the development of the Zealot movement starting with Judas and ending in A.D. 70, and many scholars now think that Josephus has exaggerated in portraying the Zealot movement as a continuous movement of a more or less organized nature.

The highly dramatic climax to the activities of the Zealots was the Great War against Rome in A.D. 66-70, which Josephus describes in detail. It is not our purpose here to recount the whole story told by Josephus; but a few relevant points should be noted. The first is that this war did not begin as a revolt by "the Jews" against Rome, but as a Zealot rebellion. There was much Jewish opposition to the revolt. The priestly aristocracy was of course against it, and so were the leading Pharisees. The first phase of the revolt therefore had the character of an internal civil war in Jerusalem, in which the Zealot party gained the upper hand. They crowned their victory by murdering—after treason—the Roman watch force which had taken refuge in the three towers of Herod's Palace in the Upper City (now within the Citadel at the Jaffa Gate).

After this, the war partly changed its character. The priestly aristocracy and the leading men of Jerusalem realized that a massive Roman retaliation could not be avoided, and they joined the rebels and mobilized most of the country. However, when the Roman onslaught came, these leaders and their hastily improvised armies could offer the Roman legions little resistance, and for the duration of the war the leadership and military power

---

[37]It has been suggested that Judas's appellation, Iscariot, means that he belonged to the Sicarii, and that his disapproval of Jesus' non-violence motivated his betrayal. But this is speculation and is linguistically unlikely, since the obvious meaning of Iscariot is *ish Kerioth,* a "man from Kerioth." On the other hand, the second name of Jesus' disciple Simon *the Cananaean* (Hebrew *haKannai*) could indicate that he belonged to the Zealot party, for *kannai* is the Hebrew equivalent of the Greek *zeelotes* (cf. Mk 3:18). But a man being called a zealot, or calling himself a zealot, in the 30s A.D. did not necessarily imply that he belonged to anything like an organized militant group. Paul refers to himself as "a zealot for the traditions of my ancestors" in Gal 1:14, thus demonstrating the rather non-technical meaning of the term in his time (before the Great War against Rome A.D. 66-70, when the term was appropriated by one faction among the freedom fighters).

Temple Square
The temple has been with us throughout this chapter. The different Jewish parties gave different answers to the question of how the purity of the people related to the purity of the temple. Nevertheless, all were thinking within a shared framework: holiness and purity are related to the presence of God according to a system of concentric circles, with the Holy of Holies in the center, then the sanctuary, then the courtyards, then Jerusalem, the Land, the earth. A corresponding system of concentric circles involves human beings: in the center the high priest, the only one to enter the Holy of Holies; around him priests, Levites, Jewish men, Jewish women, Gentiles.

For the Sadducees, that was it; there was nothing more to say, except that Roman occupation did not in any fundamental way interfere with this system.

For the Pharisees, the point was to extend the priestly circle to include themselves as laypersons; to extend the temple realm into their own houses and courtyards. Their intent was not meant to create a replacement, only an extension of the temple. But when the temple in the center disappeared, the temple in their homes did not.

The Qumran community had the biggest problem with the whole system: for them, the very center of holiness was polluted. Accordingly they had to establish a new center elsewhere, and did so at Qumran. Since this was not, to begin with, a sanctified place, the requirements of ritual purity were even harsher at Qumran than anywhere else. Here these requirements had to create a sacred space that did not exist beforehand. But it was all meant to be temporary. For the time being, the Qumran community itself functioned as the temple, but their aim was to recapture the sanctuary in Jerusalem and rededicate it for pure worship.

Josephus's "Fourth Philosophy," more commonly known as the Zealot movement, found Roman presence and Roman control of the Land problematic, and Roman control of the center unacceptable. For them, the king of heaven and the emperor in Rome were rivals when it came to the temple. One had to give way to the other. Gentile-Roman control of the center was itself a pollution.

Samaritanism was not Judaism, for the simple reason that the Samaritans did not recognize the true center.

Finally, we have the lonely figure of John the Baptist (and maybe others like him). We don't know much about him. But apparently he thought that the center of purity and holiness was not the Jerusalem temple, nor any other, nor any specific place at all. For him, the center seems not to have been a place, but something he himself did: his cleansing, sanctifying baptism. The ideal place for his preaching and his baptism of repentance was the desert, not the temple. For John, this raised the question of who constituted the true Israel in a new and radical way.

Approaching Jesus and his followers from this temple background raises many intriguing questions. How did Jesus fit into this picture? Did he?

───

reverted back to the hands of the Zealots.

As the war went on, they all assembled in Jerusalem to protect the temple. They did this with the utmost dedication and courage, while at the same time engaging in brutal acts of revenge amongst themselves and cruel persecution of anyone in the city suspected of sympathizing with Rome.

Thus the Great War began and ended as the war of the Zealots. The Pharisaic opposition should be especially noted. We have already seen that the founder of rabbinic Judaism, Johanan ben Zakkai, slipped silently out of

Jerusalem in the midst of the uprising. His way was not the way of the Zealots. But it was his way that was to provide a future for Judaism.[38]

Suggestions for Further Reading
A useful anthology of older studies is Lee Levine, *Jewish Sects, Parties and Ideologies in the Second Temple Period* (Jerusalem: Hebrew University, 1978).

A comprehensive, balanced and readable account of the traditional picture of Pharisees and Sadducees is contained in *New Schürer* 2:381-414. Cf. also Murphy, *Religious World,* pp. 187-245.

A more recent synthesis, taking account of current developments within Qumran research, is Günter Stemberger, *Jewish Contemporaries of Jesus: Pharisees, Sadducees, Essenes* (Minneapolis: Fortress Press, 1995). Stemberger is highly critical of many established points of view, but may be over-skeptical in some respects. For a more balanced statement of the "new" position, see Grabbe, *Judaism,* pp. 29-50. For E. P. Sander's contribution to the picture of Jewish leadership, see his *Judaism,* pp. 170-89; 315-490.

Martin Hengel and Roland Deines, "E. P. Sanders' 'Common Judaism,' Jesus, and the Pharisees," *The Journal of Theological Studies,* n.s, 46 (1995): 1-70, provide a magisterial evaluation of much recent research on the Pharisees and other leading groups.

On the Pharisees:
A useful anthology of translated source material is John Bowker, *Jesus and the Pharisees* (Cambridge: Cambridge University Press, 1973).

The two classic works on rabbinic theology and practice, assuming a basic continuity within the Pharisaic tradition, are George Foot Moore, *Judaism in the First Centuries of the Christian Era,* 3 vols. (Cambridge: Cambridge University Press, 1927-1930 [reprinted in 2 volumes, Peabody: Hendrickson, 1997]); Ephraim E. Urbach, *The Sages: Their Concepts and Beliefs,* 2 vols. (Jerusalem: Magnes, 1975 [and reprints]). Cf. also Louis Finkelstein, *The Pharisees: The Sociological Background of Their Faith,* 2 vols., 3rd ed. (Philadelphia: Jewish Publication Society of America, 1962). This contains a theory of the social setting of Pharisaism that has been contested by other scholars. For critique of the "old" approach, see e.g., Gerald J. Blidstein, "The Import of Early Rabbinic Writings for an Understanding of Judaism in the Hellenistic-Roman Period," in *Jewish Civilization in the Hellenistic-Roman Period,* ed. Shemaryahu Talmon, Journal for the Study of the Pseudepigrapha: Supplement Series 10 (Sheffield: Sheffield Academic Press, 1991), pp. 64-72; Jacob Neusner, "The Use of the Later Rabbinic Evidence for the Study of First-Century Pharisaism," in *Approaches to Ancient Judaism: Theory and Practice,* ed. William Scott Green, Brown Judaic Studies 1 (Missoula, Mont.: Scholars Press, 1978), pp. 215-28.

---

[38]On Johanan's flight and its significance, cf. Peter Schäfer, "Die Flucht Johanan b. Zakkais aus Jerusalem und die Gründung des 'Lehrhauses' in Jabne," in Haase, *Aufstieg* 2 19.2:43-101.

On the "new" approach in Pharisaic studies:
Jacob Neusner, *The Rabbinic Traditions About the Pharisees Before 70*, 3 vols. (Leiden: E. J. Brill, 1971; reissued as South Florida Studies in the History of Judaism, 202-4 (Atlanta, Ga.: Scholars Press, 1999). An attempt to sift out the historically reliable traditions concerning the Pharisees contained in later rabbinic literature. Cf. also his one-volume summary, *The Pharisees: Rabbinic Perspectives*, Studies in Ancient Judaism 1 (Hoboken, N.J.: 1973); and his historical sketch: *From Politics to Piety: The Emergence of Pharisaic Judaism*, 2nd ed. (New York: Ktav, 1979). Neusner spearheaded the new methodology in Pharisaic studies.

E. P. Sanders, *Jewish Law from Jesus to the Mishnah: Five Studies* (London: SCM Press/ Philadelphia: Trinity Press International, 1990), contains two extensive essays in which he discusses Neusner's theses about the Pharisees: "Did the Pharisees have Oral Law?" (pp. 97-130); and "Did the Pharisees Eat Ordinary Food in Purity?" (pp. 131-254).

Other studies representing the "new" approach, but with different conclusions:
The question of continuity and discontinuity between the Pharisees and later rabbis is instructively dealt with in Alexander Guttmann, *Rabbinic Judaism in the Making* (Detroit: Wayne State University Press, 1970).

Ellis Rivkin, "Defining the Pharisees: The Tannaitic Sources," *Hebrew Union College Annual* 40/41 (1969-1970): 205-49. Idem, *A Hidden Revolution* (Nashville: Abingdon, 1978).

Anthony J. Saldarini, *Pharisees, Scribes, and Sadducees in Palestinian Society* (Wilmington, Del.: Michael Glazier, 1988; Edinburgh: T & T Clark, 1989).

Steve Mason, *Flavius Josephus on the Pharisees: A Composition-Critical Study*, Studia Post-Biblica 39 (Leiden: E. J. Brill, 1991). A landmark in careful reading of Josephus's evidence.

Albert I. Baumgarten, *The Flourishing of Jewish Sects in the Maccabean Era: An Interpretation*, Supplements to the Journal for the Study of Judaism 55 (Leiden: E. J. Brill, 1997). Attempts a cultural-sociological explanation of the phenomenon.

Cf. also Schiffman, *Text to Tradition*, pp. 98-119.

On the history of research:
Roland Deines, *Die Pharisäer: Ihr Verständnis als Spiegel der christlichen und jüdischen Forschung seit Wellhausen und Graetz*, Wissenschaftliche Untersuchungen zum Neuen Testament 101 (Tübingen: Mohr Siebeck, 1997). In its concluding chapter, pp. 534-55, this study makes a significant contribution toward drawing a balanced and updated picture of the Pharisees, at the same time holding on to valid insights in earlier research, which, according to Deines, has been grossly misrepresented by some of the leading representatives of the new paradigm.

On the Sadducees:
The great classic study is J. Le Moyne, *Les Sadducéens* (Paris: J. Gabalda et Cie, 1972). This study may claim to know more about them than we actually do. Cf. Günther Baumbach, "The Sadducees in Josephus," in *Josephus, the Bible, and History*, ed. Louis H. Feldman and Gohei Hata (Leiden: E. J. Brill, 1989), pp. 173-95.

On the synagogue:
Concerning the origin and early history of the synagogue, cf. the titles listed in note 32, page 123 above. On the development of synagogue liturgy, see the recent survey in Raphael Posner, Uri Kaploun and Shalom Cohen, eds., *Jewish Liturgy: Prayer and Synagogue Service Through the Ages* (Jerusalem: Keter, 1975).

The classic monograph on the historical development of the synagogue service is Ismar Elbogen, *Der jüdische Gottesdienst in seiner geschichtlichen Entwicklung* (orig. ed. Leipzig, 1913; 3rd ed. Frankfurt am Main: J. Kauffmann, 1931 [reprint, Hildesheim: Georg Olm, 1967]). English trans.: *Jewish Liturgy: A Comprehensive History*, trans. Raymond P. Scheindlin (Philadelphia: Jewish Publication Society, 1993).

More summarized, but also more readable, is A. Z. Idelsohn, *Jewish Liturgy and Its Development* (New York: Schoken, 1967).

The most recent synthesis of liturgical research and history is Stefan C. Reif, *Judaism and Hebrew Prayer: New Perspectives on Jewish Liturgical History* (Cambridge: Cambridge University Press 1993, paperback ed. 1995).

On Qumran and the Essenes:
For a short introduction, see *New Schürer* 2:550-97, or Geza Vermes, *The Dead Sea Scrolls in English*, 4th ed. (London: Penguin, 1995), pp. 1-64. Another, more complete, one-volume English translation of the scrolls is Florentino García Martínez, *The Dead Sea Scrolls Translated: The Qumran Texts in English* (Leiden/New York/Cologne: E. J. Brill, 1994).

For full-scale and up-to-date treatment, see J. C. VanderKam, *The Dead Sea Scrolls Today* (Grand Rapids, Mich.: Eerdmans, 1994); Lawrence H. Schiffmann, *Reclaiming the Dead Sea Scrolls* (Philadelphia/Jerusalem: The Jewish Publication Society, 1994).

A profiled and provocative study with interesting discussion of the relationship between the Essene movement and John the Baptist, Jesus and the early Christian community, is Hartmut Stegemann, *Die Essener, Qumran, Johannes der Täufer und Jesus*, 4th ed. (Freiburg: Herder, 1994). English trans.: *The Library of Qumran: On the Essenes, Qumran, John the Baptist, and Jesus* (Grand Rapids, Mich.: Eerdmans, 1998). Stegemann also has useful comments on recent sensationalist publishing on Qumran (e.g., Michael Baigent and Richard Leigh, *The Dead Sea Scrolls Deception* [London: Cape, 1991]; Barbara Thiering, *Jesus and the Riddle of the Dead Sea Scrolls: Unlocking the Secrets of His Life Story* [San Francisco: Harper, 1992]; Robert H. Eisenman and Michael Wise, *The Dead Sea Scrolls Uncovered* [Shaftesbury: Element, 1992]).

Full discussion of the unreliable information in these "bestsellers," and reliable up-to-date information is also provided in Otto Betz and Rainer Riesner, *Jesus, Qumran und der Vatikan: Klarstellungen* (Giessen: Brunnen Verlag, 1993). English trans.: *Jesus, Qumran and the Vatican: Clarifications* (London/New York: Crossroad, 1994).

On Qumran and the New Testament:
Krister Stendahl, ed., *The Scrolls and the New Testament* (New York: Harper, 1957; reprint, Westport, Conn.: Greenwood Press, 1975; reprint, New York, 1992); Matthew Black, *The Scrolls and Christian Origins: Studies in the Jewish Background of the New Testament*, Brown Judaic Studies 48 (Chico, Calif.: Scholars Press, 1983 [orig. ed. New York: Charles Scribner's Sons, 1961]); James H. Charlesworth, ed., *John and the Dead Sea Scrolls* (New York: Crossroad, 1990); idem, *Jesus and the Dead Sea Scrolls* (New York: Doubleday, 1992); Jerome Murphy-O'Connor and J. H. Charlesworth, eds., *Paul and the Dead Sea Scrolls* (New York: Crossroad, 1990); Joseph A. Fitzmyer, *The Dead Sea Scrolls and Christian Origins* (Grand Rapids, Mich. and Cambridge, U.K.: Eerdmans, 2000).

On the Zealot movement:
See *New Schürer* 2:598-606. The standard study in large format is Martin Hengel, *Die Zeloten: Untersuchungen zur jüdischen Freiheitsbewegung in der Zeit von Herodes I bis 70 n. Chr.*, Arbeiten zur Geschichte des antiken Judentums und des Urchristentums 1, 2nd ed. (Leiden: E. J. Brill, 1976 [1st ed. 1961]). English trans.: *The Zealots: Investigations into the Jewish Freedom Movement in the Period from Herod I Until 70 A.D.* (Edinburgh: T & T Clark, 1989).

The theory that Jesus had close connections with the Zealots and was, basically, a Zealot himself, is propounded in S. G. F. Brandon, *Jesus and the Zealots: A Study of the Political Factor in Primitive Christianity* (Manchester: Manchester University Press, 1967). This theory has been widely rejected among scholars, we think rightly so. Cf. Martin Hengel, *War Jesus revolutionär?* Calwer Hefte 110 (Stuttgart: Calwer Verlag, 1970). English trans.: *Was Jesus a Revolutionist?* Facet Books, Biblical Series 28 (Philadelphia: Fortress, 1971); idem, *Victory over Violence: Jesus and the Revolutionists* (Philadelphia: Fortress, 1973); Ernst Bammel and Charles F. D. Moule, eds., *Jesus and the Politics of His Day* (Cambridge: Cambridge University Press, 1984).

PART 2

CHRISTIAN BEGINNINGS

FROM JEWISH PARTY TO GENTILE CHURCH

6

JESUS WITHIN JUDAISM

*T*he Yad Vashem museum in Jerusalem displays a picture from wartime Germany. On a fence we read the sign Juden verboten, "Jews no admittance." Inside the fence we see Jesus hanging on the cross: a crucifix on an open-air altar. The terrible irony of the situation is immediately seen by most present-day visitors to the museum, but was probably completely lost on the passers-by in wartime Germany. The idea probably did not occur to them that they were in fact looking at a Jew in a place where Jews were not allowed. They quite simply did not think of Jesus as Jewish; to many pious Christians the idea would have been shocking.

We may like to think that nowadays Christians in general and Bible scholars in particular have repudiated and surrendered this anti-Jewish and unhistorical "un-Jewing" of Jesus. But it gives food for thought to hear a rabbi say, "I have seen pictures and sculptures of Jesus in all kinds of dress and color of skin: as a blond Scandinavian, as a Latin American, as a black African, even as a Chinese. I believe there is only one version of Jesus I have never seen: I have never seen him dressed as a Jew, prayer-shawl, phylacteries and all." When you come to think of it . . .

The purpose of this chapter is not to write a short history of Jesus, nor a history of research on Jesus. Many such exist already,[1] and both subjects require extensive discussion completely beyond the scope of this book. Instead, I will focus on one point: the Jewishness of Jesus. I approach this question through a brief review of some important contributions to Jesus research that are relevant to this issue.

It is customary, especially among scholars who regard German scholarship as being the most significant in this field, to speak of different "quests" for the "historical Jesus." Often you will meet a series of three: "the old quest," "the new quest," and "the third quest."[2] As a convenient way of sorting the material, I use this rubric below, but I will also include more on *Jewish* Jesus research than is usually done in such reviews, partly because it cannot be conveniently subsumed under any of the "quests."

"The Old Quest"

In 1906 Albert Schweitzer took stock of the results of the quest for the historical Jesus so far.[3] Schweitzer demonstrated that modern scholars for the most part had portrayed the supposedly "historical" Jesus in such a way that he resembled themselves. Jesus was made the spokesman of their own favorite religious and philosophical ideas. Schweitzer had no problems in showing that these portraits of Jesus were as unhistorical as the ecclesiastical picture they were meant to supplant. Schweitzer himself launched another and much more unfamiliar Jesus: a Jewish prophet deeply steeped in apocalyptic ideas, whose thinking focused on the imminent catastrophe of the end of the world. In this way Schweitzer's Jesus undoubtedly became more Jewish than he had been in most of the research Schweitzer reviewed.

In German theology two things happened in response: The Jewishness of the "historical" Jesus was partly recognized. On the other hand—and partly because of that—this "historical" Jesus was declared to be of minor relevance to the Christian message. The Gospel *kērygma* (Greek, "message") of the early

---

[1]See the Suggestions below. In the following notes, some of the entries in the Suggestions are referred to by author and short titles only.
[2]See, e.g., Witherington, *Jesus Quest* (esp. pp. 9-13 on terminology); Wright, *Jesus*, pp. 13-124.
[3]Albert Schweitzer, *Von Reimarus zu Wrede: Eine Geschichte der Leben-Jesu-Forschung* (Tübingen: Mohr, 1906; 2nd ed. 1913 under the new title *Geschichte der Leben-Jesu-Forschung;* later several editions, the most recent is a Siebenstern-Taschenbuch in two volumes [77, 78], Munich/Hamburg: dtv, 1966); English trans.: *The Quest of the Historical Jesus: A Critical Study of Its Progress from Reimarus to Wrede* (New York, 1910; several later editions, e.g., A. & C. Black, 1954).

Christian community was not identical with the (Jewish) message of Jesus, but was a (largely non-Jewish) message *about* him, focusing on his death as God's act of salvation.

"The New Quest"

After Rudolf Bultmann and his disciples had launched this program, there was for a long time little interest in historical research concerning Jesus. But then Ernst Käsemann "reopened" the quest for the historical Jesus.[4] Käsemann advocated a simple historical criterion by which it should be possible to discern which of the words attributed to Jesus in the Gospels were actually spoken by him. If a saying of Jesus cannot be explained as expressing contemporary Jewish theology, nor explained as expressing later Christian theology, then there is a good chance that it is authentic. This is often called the "criterion of dissimilarity." Käsemann's idea was that with this criterion one could establish a core that could be regarded as a "critically established minimum of authentic sayings." In practice, this minimum was often identified with the message of the "historical Jesus."[5]

It goes without saying that the historical Jesus reconstructed by this method could not be placed squarely within the Judaism of his own time. The criterion of dissimilarity tended to eliminate the most obviously Jewish sayings of Jesus as non-authentic. The method could hardly result in anything other than a Jesus different from Judaism almost by definition.[6]

Understandably, Jewish scholars interested in Jesus research reacted quite strongly against this methodology. They took it, and not without reason, to be another variety of the old Christian tendency to "de-Judaize" Jesus or deny his Jewishness. Instead, they launched what could be called "the criterion of

---

[4] Ernst Käsemann, "Das Problem des historischen Jesus," *Zeitschrift für Theologie und Kirche* 51 (1954): 125-53; reprinted in *Exegetische Versuche und Besinnung* (Göttingen: Vandenhoeck & Ruprecht, 1967), 1:187-214; English trans.: "The Problem of the Historical Jesus," in *Essays on New Testament Themes*, Studies in Biblical Theology 41 (London: SCM Press, 1964), pp. 15-47.

[5] Since Käsemann's days, there has been an extended discussion of this criterion of dissimilarity, see Meier, *Marginal Jew* 1:171-74; Theissen/Merz, *Historical Jesus*, pp. 115-18; Gerd Theissen and Dagmar Winter, *Die Kriterienfrage in der Jesusforschung: Vom Differenzkriterium zum Plausibilitätskriterium*, Novum Testamentum et Orbis Antiquus 34 (Freiburg, Switzerland: Universitätsverlag/Göttingen: Vandenhoeck & Ruprecht, 1997).

[6] The point is well stated by Theissen/Merz: "*The criterion of difference is dogmatics disguised:* Jesus' uniqueness and originality are posited a priori. This prior assumption leads to a distortion of history: what connects Jesus with Judaism and primitive Christianity is suppressed or underestimated. The criterion of difference thus favours, for example, the rise of an anti-Jewish picture of Jesus" (p. 115; italics added).

continuity": those words of Jesus should be considered authentic which could conceivably be uttered (in Aramaic or Hebrew) by a first-century Jew, whereas sayings that seem not to fit into the religious mindset of such a person or that cannot easily be retroverted into Semitic idiom are suspect.

This is essentially the thesis of David Flusser.[7] But not only Flusser—scholars in general have in great measure come to realize that the criterion of dissimilarity is far too simple in terms of history, and that the basic Jewishness of Jesus should rather be a fundamental premise of all historical research on him.[8] At this point scholars belonging to the "third quest" distance themselves rather emphatically from the representatives of the "new quest."[9]

---

[7]See his chapter 1: "The Sources," in the new edition of *Jesus*, pp. 18-23. Flusser sometimes applies the criterion of continuity with Judaism so rigorously that he may be accused of the opposite kind of dogmatism than the one criticized above. One cannot know in advance that sayings or actions in which Jesus seems to break with contemporary concepts of what a law-obedient Jew could say or do are not authentic, unless one knows in advance, independent of the sources, that Jesus never said or did such things. But this is an unprovable a priori assumption.

[8]For general reviews of recent Jesus research, see the entries listed under this heading in the Suggestions, and also Sanders, *Jesus and Judaism*, pp. 23-58; Charlesworth, *Jesus Within Judaism*, pp. 9-29; Wright, *Jesus and the Victory of God*, pp. 28-124. Especially on the criterion of continuity in recent debate, one should consult the chapters on method in Sanders, *Jesus and Judaism*, pp. 3-22; and Wright, *Jesus and the Victory of God*, pp. 91-98. Both these scholars formulate a nuanced criterion of continuity that was first put forward by the great pioneer of Jewish Jesus research, Joseph Klausner. Sanders puts it as follows: "That reconstruction of Jesus and his message is most credible which fulfil two criteria: it should situate Jesus believably in Judaism and yet explain why the movement initiated by him eventually broke with Judaism" (op. cit., p. 18). It is characteristic of Sanders and Wright that in order to place Jesus within his Jewish setting, they have found it necessary to write separate volumes on Judaism in the time of Jesus: Sanders, *Judaism*; and Wright, *New Testament*.

[9]The most recent representatives of a quest that basically follows Bultmann and Käsemann, stressing the criterion of dissimilarity, are the Jesus Seminar scholars in general and John Dominic Crossan and Burton L. Mack in particular (Crossan, *The Historical Jesus: The Life of a Mediterranean Jewish Peasant* [San Francisco: Harper, 1991]; Burton L. Mack, *The Lost Gospel: The Book of Q and Christian Origins* [San Francisco: Harper, 1993]). These scholars are as unhappy with Jewish religious and political leadership in Jesus' day as they are with Christian leadership after Jesus. They therefore tend to make Jesus their hero by eliminating from him the later typically Christian features, but also by making him rather non-Jewish compared with the Judaism of his times. He is portrayed as not being concerned with the historical destiny of Israel, and as not having an eschatological message. In this, these "new questers" come very close to the old quest so severely criticized by Schweitzer. For two recent, but quite different critiques, see Luke Timothy Johnson, *The Real Jesus: The Misguided Quest for the Historical Jesus and the Truth of the Traditional Gospels* (San Francisco: Harper, 1996); Wright, *Jesus and the Victory of God*, pp. 28-82. Wright says: "Have the New Questers . . . come to terms with the politically problematic analogy between themselves and those German scholars who, in the 1920s and 1930s, reduced almost to nil the specific Jewishness of Jesus and his message?" (p. 79, n. 233).

"The Third Quest": A Jewish Quest

Put very briefly, the third quest has tried to take seriously the challenge put forward, among others, by Jewish scholars: Jesus should be understood within the framework of the Judaism of his time. Jesus was Jewish.[10]

But what does it mean that Jesus was Jewish, that he was inside, not outside Judaism? Here the different pictures of first-century Judaism make a difference. If one thinks of Pharisaic Judaism as a kind of mainstream, normative Judaism, later to emerge as the one and only Judaism, one will also be inclined to include Jesus within this Judaism and make him a Pharisee— although a highly original and somewhat oppositional Pharisee. This approach has been characteristic of much recent Jewish scholarship on Jesus. Flusser, for example, takes most of Jesus' debates with Pharisees to be intra-Pharisaic debates. The position of Jesus in these debates can be shown to square with known Pharisaic positions on the same issues.[11]

In that case, what about Jesus' originality? (The term is not a very happy one, because extremely modern.) For Jewish scholars this has been a very important question. If Jesus was just another rabbi, how do we explain the many controversies that accompanied him? How do we explain the words and acts of his closest disciples after his death? How do we explain the fact that Jesus actually gave rise to something that burst through the limits of Judaism?

Here we shall render the verdict of two prominent Jewish scholars on Jesus' originality. In 1930 Claude Joseph Goldsmith Montefiore published an important study, *Rabbinic Literature and Gospel Teachings*,[12] in which he partly confirmed the view of earlier Jewish scholars that Jesus said nothing that could not be paralleled in rabbinic writings,[13] but also partly corrected it. It is true, Montefiore said, that most of Jesus' sayings, when taken in isolation,

---

[10]In this "school" one might place several scholars; Wright, *Jesus*, lists twenty (p. 84). Among the Jesus books listed in the Suggestions below, nearly all belong to this quest.

[11]With this interpretation, Flusser challenged ingrained presuppositions in most of Christian scholarship. For reasoned and balanced Christian treatments of this issue, see Stephen Westerholm, *Jesus and Scribal Authority*, Coniectanea Biblica, NT Series 10 (Lund: CWK Gleerup, 1978); E. P. Sanders, "The Synoptic Jesus and the Law," in *Jewish Law from Jesus to the Mishnah: Five Studies* (Philadelphia: Trinity Press International, 1990), pp. 1-96.

[12]Claude Joseph Goldsmith Montefiore, *Rabbinic Literature and Gospel Teachings* (London: 1930; reprint, New York: Ktav, 1970). His friend and coworker Israel Abrahams also published two volumes (1917, 1924; full reference in Suggestions) originally intended as rabbinical notes to Montefiore's gospel commentary (in two volumes) from 1909.

[13]Cf. the review of older Jewish scholarship, which claimed that Jesus said nothing new, in Lindeskog, *Die Jesusfrage*, pp. 215-32.

have parallels in the enormous body of the talmuds and the midrashim. But for the totality, the synthesis in Jesus' teaching, no satisfactory parallel can be found elsewhere. There is an intensity, a total involvement of the person, a radical and paradoxical edge to the message that is unique to Jesus. His attitude toward the marginal groups in society is also unique: he treated children, women and sinners differently than did his contemporary colleagues among the Pharisees.

David Flusser thinks along similar lines with regard to Jesus' originality. He puts it very succinctly: "From ancient Jewish writings we could easily construct a whole Gospel without using a single word that originated with Jesus. This could only be done, however, because we do in fact possess the Gospels."[14] In other words, the most original in Jesus is the new whole, the new totality he made out of traditional sayings and thoughts. In the light of this totality, some of his individual sayings also acquire a new radicality or depth that sets him apart.

> Those who listened to Jesus' preaching of love might well have been moved by it. Many in those days thought in a similar way. Nonetheless, in the clear purity of his love they must have detected something very special. Jesus did not accept all that was thought and taught in the Judaism of his time. Although not really a Pharisee himself, he was closest to the Pharisees of the school of Hillel who preached love, and he led the way further to unconditional love—even of one's enemies and of sinners.[15]

Most Christian scholars belonging to the "third quest" would distance themselves from the equation of Pharisaic Judaism with normative pre-70 Judaism and therefore make the question of Jesus' Jewishness a wider one. If one takes as a point of departure the premise that in the pre-70 situation none of the competing religious elites within Judaism could effectively claim a monopoly in terms of defining Judaism, then a wide spectrum of positions and opinions was open to any first-century Jew, without any of these placing him outside Judaism. There were also more role models for a man like Jesus than those of the scribe and the Pharisee, not to speak of the Sadducee and the Qumran Essene. John the Baptist reminds us of the existence of the prophetic role model, and there are, no doubt, several aspects of continuity as well as differences between the Baptist and Jesus.

Geza Vermes has dug out material on the charismatic prophetlike figures

---

[14]Flusser, *Jesus* (1998), p. 90.
[15]Ibid., p. 92.

of rabbinic tradition (esp. Honi the Circle-Drawer and Hanina ben Dosa) and tried to understand "Jesus the Jew" against this background. The result is a Jesus less Pharisaic than Flusser's, but hardly less Jewish.[16]

It may be too early to draw a definitive picture of Jesus' exact position with regard to the then dominating religious elites because the picture of the latter is still very much in a state of flux. He was probably much closer to the Pharisees than to the Qumranites; the priestly character of the Qumran community and its almost obsessive concerns with matters of ritual purity, calendar questions and so on find no echo at all in Jesus' preaching and teaching. Nor was Jesus a Zealot, although some have interpreted a few isolated sayings in a Zealot vein. Most difficult is the task of describing in a precise way his relationship with the Pharisees. With no one else did he discuss more intensely; that in itself may be an indication of closeness: you debate most vehemently with those closest to you. His one and only recorded debate with Sadducees leaves the impression that he did not find them worthy of serious discussion: "you know neither the scriptures nor the power of God" (Mt 22:29). Should Jesus be seen as a representative of neither of the leading schools, but rather as a representative of a distinctively Galilean type of Judaism?[17] But then again, how much do we know for certain about Galilean Judaism?

Jesus and the Hope of Israel

It may reasonably be argued that the questions raised above are too formal to tell us the really important things about Jesus and his relationship with Judaism. The most important question may not be to which "party" or "type" of Judaism Jesus belonged—if to any in particular—but rather what his message and aim were with regard to the national hopes and aspirations of the Jewish people, based, as these hopes were, on the biblical heritage. Two scholars in particular have contributed to this new way of stating the question about Jesus: E. P. Sanders and N. T. Wright. Sanders thinks that what he calls "the restoration of Israel" is the framework within which all of Jesus' words and

---

[16]It should be mentioned that Flusser, in the latest and revised version of his *Jesus*, has emphasized further the non-Pharisaic dimensions of Jesus, and in a very perceptive way enriched the Jewish background with Qumran ideas and aspects of the prophetic-charismatic tradition. For perceptive criticisms of Vermes, see Meier, *Marginal Jew* 2:581-88 ("Jewish Traditions about Honi the Circle-Drawer and Hanina ben Dosa"); and Evans, *Jesus and His Contemporaries*, pp. 215, 227-43 ("Rabbinic Miracle Stories"; with further bibliography).

[17]In Lee, *Galilean Jewishness*, an attempt is made to understand Jesus against the background of Sean Freyne's portrayal of a Galilean variety of Judaism.

actions make the most sense. Characteristically, Sanders begins his treatment of Jesus' message with his action in the temple: if Jesus' main concern is any-

---

Temple Square
Luke begins his story about Jesus in the temple: his relative, the priest Zechariah, received a prophetic announcement about John and Jesus while sacrificing in the temple. Later, when baby Jesus was forty days old, he was presented to the Lord in the temple, and the prophets Simeon and Hanna prophesied about him there, in the sacred place. Twelve-year-old Jesus remained in the temple when his parents left, later to be found by them there because "I must be in my Father's house" (Lk 2:49). During his last week, Jesus returned to the temple, taught there and confronted the temple establishment in a way that caused his death. There is a "yes and no" to the temple that runs through the whole story, and that makes Jesus unique and unlike any of the other parties or figures we have met: unlike the Sadducees, of course, but also unlike the Pharisees, the Qumranites, the nationalists, even unlike John.

The clue to this whole story of Jesus and the temple is hidden in the meaning of his last action in the temple, but should also be indirectly discernible in his Galilean ministry. How did Jesus think about the holiness of God's people? I believe that is the first question to ask. And then, contingent upon that: How did he think about the holiness of the temple?

1. Jesus aligned himself with John in at least two ways: he accepted the baptism of John, and he proclaimed repentance like John. This probably means he thought about purity and holiness very much like John, only perhaps a little more radically. For John, holiness/purity was connected with his own baptism of repentance in the wilderness. For Jesus it seems to have been connected with his own person: with him present, more than the temple was there (Mt 12:6), and more than Jonah, the very prophet of repentance (Mt 12:41). Israel becomes pure by repenting, by entering the kingdom brought near in Jesus, by fulfilling the double commandment of love: repentance towards God, reconciliation with neighbor. Purity is not something acquired by bringing sacrifice in the temple, it is acquired by reconciling oneself with one's neighbor (Mt 5:23-24). Purity springs from within (Mk 7:14-23).

2. Like the prophets of old, Jeremiah in particular (Jer 7; 26), Jesus seems to have thought that Israel misused the sacrifices in the temple by making them a substitute for this inner repentance and purification. In that case, the temple was no longer the source of purity and holiness, quite the contrary. The very symbol of this "substitution" character of the temple service was that the daily sacrifice (the *tamid* sacrifice) and the individual sacrifices were something you bought for money (hence money changers and dove traders in the temple). The action of Jesus in the temple was probably a dramatization, a proclamation in act, of this prophetic criticism.

3. There was a secret in all this that Jesus did not divulge to anyone except his nearest disciples toward the end of his life (Mk 10:45), and most clearly in his last meal with them: he was himself to be the final sacrifice, the sacrifice that (by implication) put an end to all other atoning sacrifices. That would result in a complete redefinition of what—or rather who—the temple would be from now on.

---

where in particular, it should be here, because here he confronts the innermost core of Judaism, its most potent symbol.[18] If Jesus in word and deed proclaimed the destruction of the present temple and the building of a new one,

---

[18]Sanders, *Jesus and Judaism*, pp. 61-76.

this must be seen against the background of what can be learned about the "new temple and restoration [of Israel] in Jewish literature."[19] Furthermore, it was Jesus' confrontation with the institution of the temple, and all it stood for, that caused his death, not his discussions with the Pharisees concerning halakic questions.[20] It was not halakic minutiae, but the restoration of Israel that was Jesus' aim, his mission.

N. T. Wright agrees with Sanders that Jesus' action in the temple during his last week in Jerusalem is crucial for understanding what Jesus wanted to accomplish. But Wright develops another model for describing the "restoration" project he sees as Jesus' aim. According to Wright, the metaphor of the exile of God's people is crucial for understanding how Jesus perceived the plight of his people. God's people are (in part) living in their own land, but in a kind of inner exile. Salvation and redemption are then described in the metaphors of returning home from exile. From this perspective Wright is able to shed fresh light on many well-known passages in the Gospels (his favorite example probably being the parable of the prodigal son, Lk 15:11-32).

I break off here; the purpose of this chapter is not to give anything like a full review of present-day answers to the question of Jesus' Jewishness, but rather to whet the reader's appetite for reading more. Much exciting research is going on in recent Jesus scholarship; the Jewishness of Jesus is now being approached from many interesting angles.

Suggestions for Further Reading
There is an excellent annotated bibliography on recent Jesus research in Charlesworth, *Jesus Within Judaism* (1988), pp. 223-43.

Two recent surveys tell the story of the "new" or "third quest" for the historical Jesus: Ben Witherington III, *The Jesus Quest: The Third Search for The Jew of Nazareth* (Downers Grove, Ill.: InterVarsity Press, 1995); Mark Allan Powell, *Jesus as a Figure in History* (Louisville: Westminster John Knox, 1998), reissued in Great Britain as *The Jesus Debate: Modern Historians Investigate the Life of Christ* (Oxford: Lion, 2000).

Older Jewish research is summarized and evaluated in Gösta Lindeskog, *Die Jesusfrage im neuzeitlichen Judentum: Ein Beitrag zur Geschichte der Leben-Jesu-Forschung* (Uppsala: Almquist & Wiksells, 1938; reprinted with an appendix, Darmstadt: Wissenschaftliche Buchgesellschaft, 1973). For the more recent period, see Donald A. Hagner, *The Jewish Reclamation of Jesus: An Analysis and Critique of the Modern Jewish Study of Jesus* (Grand Rapids, Mich.: Zondervan, 1984).

---

[19]Sanders, op. cit., the title of chapter 2, pp. 77-90.
[20]On this point, Sanders comes close to the position of Flusser.

Studies on Jesus by Jewish scholars:
Israel Abrahams, *Studies in Pharisaism and the Gospels*, 2 vols. (Cambridge: Cambridge University, 1917, 1924; reprint New York: Ktav, 1967); Josef Klausner, *Jesus von Nazareth, seine Zeit, sein Leben und seine Lehre* (Berlin: Jüdischer Verlag, 1930; 2nd ed. Berlin, 1934; 3rd ed. Jerusalem: Jewish Publishing House, 1952); English trans.: *Jesus of Nazareth: His Life, Times and Teaching* (London: George Allen & Unwin/New York: Macmillan, 1925 [reprint, New York: Beacon, 1961; New York: Menorah, 1979]); A. Finkel, *The Pharisees and the Teacher of Nazareth: A Study of Their Background, Their Halachic and Midrashic Teachings, the Similarities and Differences*, Arbeiten zur Geschichte des Spätjudentums und Urchristentums 4 (Leiden: E. J. Brill, 1964); Schalom Ben-Chorin, *Bruder Jesus: Der Nazarener in jüdischer Sicht* (Munich: Paul List Verlag, 1967; paperback ed. Munich: dtv, 1977); David Flusser, *Jesus in Selbstzeugnissen und Bilddokumenten*, Rowohlts Bildmonographien 140 (Hamburg: Rowohlt Verlag, 1968); new and thoroughly revised version: *Jesus*, 2nd ed. (Jerusalem: Magnes, 1998); idem, *Last Days of Jesus in Jerusalem: A Current Study of the Easter Week* (Tel Aviv: Sadan Publishing House, 1980; German trans.: *Die letzten Tage Jesu in Jerusalem: Das Passionsgeschehen aus jüdischer Sicht*, Bericht über neueste Forschungsergebnisse (Stuttgart: Calwer Verlag, 1982); idem, *Die rabbinischen Gleichnisse und der Gleichniserzähler Jesus*, 1. Teil: *Das Wesen der Gleichnisse*, Judaica et Christiana 4 (Bern: Peter Lang, 1981); Pinchas E. Lapide, *Der Rabbi von Nazaret: Wandlungen des jüdischen Jesusbildes* (Trier: Spee-Verlag, 1974); Geza Vermes, *Jesus the Jew: A Historian's Reading of the Gospels* (London: William Collins Sons, 1973; paperback ed. Fontant/Collins, 1976 and reprints); idem, *Jesus and the World of Judaism* (Philadelphia: Fortress, 1983); Gaalyah Cornfeld, *The Historical Jesus: A Scholarly View of the Man and His World* (New York: Macmillan/London: Collier Macmillan, 1982).

Studies on Jesus by Christian scholars:
David Bivin and Roy Blizzard, *Understanding the Difficult Words of Jesus: New Insights from a Hebraic Perspective* (Arcadia, Calif.: Makor Foundation, 1984); Bruce Chilton, *A Galilean Rabbi and His Bible* (Wilmington: Michael Glazier, 1984); E. P. Sanders, *Jesus and Judaism* (London: SCM Press, 1985); idem, *The Historical Figure of Jesus* (London: Penguin, 1995); Gerd Theissen, *Der Schatten des Galiläers: Historische Jesusforschung in erzählender Form* (Munich: Christian Kaiser Verlag, 1986); English trans.: *The Shadow of the Galilean: The Quest of the Historical Jesus in Narrative Form* (London: SCM Press, 1987, and later reprints); Bernard J. Lee, *The Galilean Jewishness of Jesus: Retrieving the Jewish Origins of Christianity*, Studies in Judaism and Christianity: Conversation on the Road Not Taken 1 (New York/Mahwah: Paulist, 1988); James H. Charlesworth, *Jesus Within Judaism: New Light from Exciting Archaeological Discoveries* (New York: Doubleday, 1988/London: SPCK, 1989); Brad H. Young, *Jesus and His Jewish Parables: Rediscovering the Roots of Jesus' Teaching* (New York/Mahwah: Paulist, 1989); John P. Meier, *A Marginal Jew: Rethinking the Historical Jesus*, vol. 1: *The Roots of the Problem*

and the Person; vol. 2: *Mentor, Message, and Miracles;* vol. 3: *Companions and Competitors,* Anchor Bible Reference Library (New York: Doubleday, 1991, 1994, 2001); Craig A. Evans, *Jesus and His Contemporaries: Comparative Studies,* Arbeiten zur Geschichte des antiken Judentums und des Urchristentums 25 (Leiden: E. J. Brill, 1995); N. T. Wright, *Jesus and the Victory of God,* Christian Origins and the Question of God 2 (London: SPCK, 1996).

7

THE EARLY JERUSALEM COMMUNITY OF BELIEVERS IN JESUS

*I*t all began in Jerusalem. That, in any case, is Luke's contention in the first chapters of Acts, and no doubt he was right.[1] The first Christian community was established in Jerusalem, and it stayed there for several years, even though many of its leaders were Galileans and it was in Galilee that Jesus had had the most follow-ers. Jerusalem was the most dangerous place the early community could possibly be, and yet they stayed. This stubborn adherence to Jerusalem sprang from their conception of their divine commission: they could not fail Jerusalem without failing God.

The Importance of Jerusalem to the Early Church
The believers in Jesus were convinced that they had a message that all Israel should hear, a message of the utmost importance and the highest authority. "Therefore let the entire household of Israel know with certainty that God has

---

[1]This, of course, is not uncontested in modern scholarship. Some scholars think that Luke has overemphasized the Jerusalem part of the story, and left out, e.g., the important part Galilee had in the story. The assumption of these scholars is that the early Jesus movement *must have had* a continuation also in Galilee after the death of Jesus in Jerusalem. For sources to this "lost" story one looks to the Gospels on the assumption that sources and traditions

made him both Lord and Messiah, this Jesus whom you crucified" (Acts 2:36). If this message were to have meaning at all, it would have to be proclaimed in Jerusalem, in the center of authority and the focal point of Judaism. For the message was for all Israel, from the priests in the temple and the scribes of the schools to the person in the street and the peasants in the countryside.

Accordingly, we find the apostles preaching and teaching at the very center of authority for all Jews: the Temple Mount itself, the "mountain of the Lord" (Acts 3:11-26; 5:12, 21-26, 42). In this they followed in the footsteps of Jesus, their Messiah, who during his last week in Jerusalem acted as the sovereign master of the temple (Mt 21:1-16).

The rabbis of a later date attached great significance to the words of Isaiah: "The law will go out from Zion, the word of the Lord from Jerusalem" (Is 2:3 NIV). They took it to mean that the authoritative interpretation of the law is the one that issues from the courts on the Temple Mount (where the Sanhedrin had its sessions).[2] The word of the Lord proceeds from Jerusalem to all Israel, at home and abroad; Jerusalem is the seat of authority.

The early believers in Jesus thought in much the same way.[3] Even Paul, who did not recognize any human authority between himself and the risen Christ, showed deep respect for the authority of the early Jerusalem community (see Gal 2:1-10). This can be indirectly seen in his rhetorical question to the Corinthians about a debated issue of Christian "law": "Did the word of God go forth from you?" (1 Cor 14:36, author's translation). Paul is obviously alluding to Isaiah 2:3, and the correct answer to his question would be that God's word goes forth from Jerusalem, and so does the word of Christ.[4]

---

used by the authors of the canonical Gospels derive from early communities of believers in Galilee. By doing a kind of literary archaeology on the Gospels one digs out older layers of the texts, and behold, the lost story comes to light. The main problem with this approach, in my opinion, is the extremely hypothetical nature of each and every step in this type of research. The leading exponent today of this approach is probably John Dominic Crossan, *The Birth of Christianity: Discovering What Happened in the Years Immediately After the Execution of Jesus* (Edinburgh: T & T Clark, 1999). For an important critique of one of the basic assumptions of this approach, viz., that the Gospels express the theology and concerns of specific local communities, see Richard Bauckham, ed., *the Gospels for All Christians: Rethinking The Gospel Audiences* (Edinburgh: T & T Clark, 1998).

[2]Cf. *M Sanhedrin* 11:2. When a matter cannot be decided by any other court, it is to be taken "to the Great Court that was in the Chamber of Hewn Stone *[Gazit], whence the Torah goes forth to all Israel* [Isa 2:3]" (Danby, *Mishnah*, p. 399, italics added).

[3]See Richard Bauckham, "James and the Jerusalem Church" (in Winter, *Book of Acts* 4:415-80), especially the part entitled "Jerusalem at the Centre," pp. 417-27; and Martin Hengel, "The Geography of Palestine in Acts" (ibid., 4:27-78), pp. 35-37.

[4]See the comments on this in Birger Gerhardsson, *Memory and Manuscript: Oral Tradition and*

The significance of Isaiah 2:3 shines through in Jesus' command to the disciples as reported in Luke 24:47: repentance and forgiveness of sins should be preached in his name to all nations, *beginning in Jerusalem* (cf. Paul in Rom 15:19: "*From Jerusalem* all the way around to Illyricum I have fully proclaimed the gospel of Christ"). Perhaps even more pronounced is the commission given in Acts 1:8: "You shall be my witnesses in Jerusalem, and in all Judea and Samaria, and to the ends of the earth."

The disciples therefore had no choice: they had to address all Israel with their message and they had to do it from Jerusalem, the seat of authority for all Jews. They had to begin their teaching and preaching in the temple itself. But the content of their message was such that it made the temple superfluous. Did they fully realize that?

Conflict in the Temple: Sympathy from the People
It was not an easy path. The temple authorities were not inclined to allow Galilean fishermen, who believed in the resurrection of their Messiah, to teach and preach on the very Temple Mount. According to Acts, the first two clashes between the disciples and the authorities occurred precisely because the disciples had been teaching in the temple. "While Peter and John were speaking to the people, the priests, the captain of the temple, and the Sadducees came to them, much annoyed because they were teaching the people and proclaiming that in Jesus there is the resurrection of the dead" (Acts 4:1-2, cf. Acts 5:17, where the high priest and the Sadducees take action against the apostles).

We get the impression that the opposition came from the Sadducean chief priests, who denied the resurrection of the dead (Mt 22:23-33; Acts 23:6-9). They were especially offended by the fact that the apostles carried their message of the resurrection of Jesus right into the temple, which the Sadducees regarded as their domain (Acts 4:1-2). The offensive and daring strategy implemented by the disciples had its price, but it also bore great fruit: "So those who welcomed his message were baptized, and that day about three thousand persons were added. . . . And day by day the Lord

---

Written Transmission in Rabbinic Judaism and Early Christianity, Acta Seminarii Neotestamentici Upsaliensis 22 (Lund: C. W. K. Gleerup/Copenhagen: Munksgaard, 1964), pp. 275-76. He aptly quotes a rabbinic parallel to Paul's rhetorical question, implying the same reference to Is 2:3. Rabbi Nathan upbraids Rabbi Hananiah of Nehar-Paqod because he had made decisions which no local rabbi had authority to make. Nathan's retort was, "Does the Torah proceed from Babel, and the word of God from Nehar-Paqod?" (*TJ Nedarim* 6:13; *TJ Sanhedrin* 1:3; cf. more parallels in Strack/Billerbeck 3:469).

added to their number those who were being saved" (Acts 2:41, 47). "Many of those who heard the word believed; and they numbered about five thousand" (Acts 4:4). "More than ever believers were added to the Lord, great numbers of both men and women. . . . A great number of people would also gather from the towns around Jerusalem" (Acts 5:14, 16). "The word of God continued to spread; the number of the disciples increased greatly in Jerusalem, and a great many of the priests became obedient to the faith" (Acts 6:7).

Some scholars claim that Luke is exaggerating, and that the message of the apostles found little hearing in Jerusalem. But if we assume, as is commonly done, that the normal population of Jerusalem was at that time around 100,000, and that it almost doubled during festivals, 5,000 believers is not an unrealistic number. There is no reason to doubt Luke's statement that the message of the apostles found a considerable hearing among the Jews of Jerusalem—both residents and pilgrims present in the city during the festivals.[5]

One additional feature in Luke's portrait of the circumstances of the early community deserves notice: the populace of Jerusalem—apart from the priestly aristocracy—is portrayed as being favorably disposed toward the new group (Acts 2:47). Beyond that, "the people" of Jerusalem protected the disciples against persecution by the authorities (Acts 4:21; 5:26). This is hardly Luke's fiction. In fact, interesting evidence in Josephus confirms that as late as the 90s, Jesus and his brother James had excellent reputations among nonbelievers such as Josephus. We shall return later to his words about James. See the text box below for a brief discussion of Josephus's words about Jesus (*Antiquities* 18.63-64).

Reading through this text, one can hardly disagree with the Jewish scholar P. Winter's conclusion regarding Josephus's attitude to Jesus:

> he was not on the whole unsympathetic towards Jesus. . . . Josephus viewed the execution of Jesus as a "dreadful event." . . . He referred to Jesus as a wise man. And this indicates that Jews belonging to the circle to which Josephus belonged—a Pharisaic group, no doubt—had not at that time (ca. 93 AD) given Jesus a bad name as a heretic, or denounced him as a rebel.[6]

---

[5]Cf. especially Wolfgang Reinhardt, "The Population Size of Jerusalem and the Numerical Growth of the Jerusalem Church," in Winter, *Book of Acts*, 4:237-65.
[6]*New Schürer* 1:440-41.

Box 7.1. Josephus on Jesus

Josephus's one and only passage on Jesus has almost certainly been tampered with by Christian scribes who were not fully satisfied with what Josephus had to say. Most of these editorial additions are easy to recognize, and if we remove them we are left with a text that should be pretty close to what Josephus actually wrote.[7] Such a reconstruction can now be substantiated by an Arabic version of this passage found by the Israeli scholar Shlomo Pines.[8] Here we have arranged the Greek and Arabic versions of Josephus's text side by side. In the Greek version we have put brackets around those portions thought to have been added or changed by Christian scribes. It is hard to imagine that the Arabic text was written by a Christian, and it therefore seems likely to be close to Josephus's original (pay special attention to the italicized words).

Greek	**Arabic**
At this time there appeared Jesus, a wise man [if indeed one might call him a man].	At this time there was a wise man who was called Jesus.
For he was a doer of startling deeds, a teacher of people who receive the truth with pleasure.	And his conduct was good, and he was known to be virtuous [variant reading: his learning was outstanding].
And he gained a following both among many Jews and among many of Greek origin. [He was the Messiah.]	And many people from among the Jews and other nations became his disciples.
And when Pilate, because of an accusation made by the leading men among us, condemned him to the cross, those who had loved him previously did not cease to do so.	Pilate condemned him to be crucified and to die. And those who had become his disciples did not abandon his discipleship.
[For he appeared to them on the third day, living again, just as the divine prophets had spoken of these and countless other wondrous things about him.]	*They reported* that he had appeared to them three days after his crucifixion and that he was alive; accordingly, *he was held* to be the Messiah concerning whom the Prophets have recounted wonders.
And up until this very day the tribe of Christians, named after him, has not died out.	And the people of the Christians so-called after him, has to this day not disappeared.

---

[7] The bibliography on this is extensive. One of the most recent extensive discussions of the issue is probably also one of the best, and contains extensive bibliography: John P. Meier, *A Marginal Jew: Rethinking the Historical Jesus*, vol. 1: *The Roots of the Problem and the Person*, The Anchor Bible Reference Library (New York: Doubleday, 1991), pp. 59-69.

[8] S. Pines, *An Arabic Version of Testimonium Flavianum and Its Implications* (Jerusalem: The Israel Academy, 1971).

Thus there is every reason to believe Luke's report of the mostly peaceful relationship between the early community and their Jerusalem neighbors.

This does not mean that there was no tension at all, but that it was kept on a level below conflict. Within a few years, however, this would change. A single man, Stephen, seems to have provoked the latent opposition to the believing community. In doing so, he became the first Christian martyr.

Increased Conflict: The "Hellenists"

At first, the story about the "Hellenist" Stephen and his martyrdom seems straightforward and simple (Acts 6—7). On further reflection, however, the story raises many intricate historical questions, and Acts 6 becomes one of the most enigmatic and controversial passages in the New Testament.[9]

Here we first encounter two groups within the Jerusalem community, the "Hellenists" and the "Hebrews." These terms probably refer to the Greek-speaking and Aramaic- or Hebrew-speaking parts of the community. Luke says that the conflict between the two groups concerned administrative matters. He does not say that theological disagreements were involved. It is common among modern scholars, however, to assume that such was the case. This is based on an inference from Acts 8:1, where Luke says that immediately following the martyrdom of Stephen a great persecution broke out "against the church in Jerusalem, and all except the apostles were scattered throughout the countryside of Judea and Samaria." The argument goes like this: since the apostles, the leaders of the Aramaic-speaking part of the church, were not affected by the persecution, this must mean that the Aramaic-speaking group as a whole was not affected, for it would have been inconsistent to leave only the leaders in peace. In other words, the implication of Acts 8:1 must be that only the Hellenists were persecuted, and this—so the argument continues—was because they had a theology more offensive to normative Judaism. As a rule, this theological difference is seen as related to the temple: while the "Hebrews" recognized the temple and the temple worship—and even participated in it (Acts 3:1)—the "Hellenists," led by Stephen, rejected the temple and, conse-

---

[9]Cf. the very extensive bibliography in Jervell, *Die Apostelgeschichte*, pp. 214-15. In addition, Daniel R. Schwartz, "Residents and Exiles, Jerusalemites and Judaeans (Acts 7:4; 2:5, 14): On Stephen, Pentecost and the Structure of Acts," in Schwartz, *Studies*, pp. 117-27; Craig C. Hill, *Hellenists and Hebrews: Reappraising Division Within the Earliest Church* (Minneapolis: Fortress, 1992); Oskar Skarsaune, "Were the Hellenists 'Liberals'?" *Mishkan* 24, no. 1 (1996): 27-35.

quently, the portions of the Torah relating to the sacrifices. Hence the accusation against Stephen: "This man never stops saying things against this holy place and the law; for we have heard him say that this Jesus of Nazareth will destroy this place and will change the customs that Moses handed on to us" (Acts 6:13-14).[10]

Further confirmation of this theory is found in Stephen's speech (Acts 7), in which verses 47-50 are taken to imply rejection of the temple and its service. It is further argued that the "Hellenists" were more liberal and universalistic in their outlook than the "Hebrews," and that they accordingly became the bearers of the gospel to the Gentiles. See for example the first attempts to share the gospel in Acts 8:26-40; 11:19-21.

This is, no doubt, an attractive and rather convincing theory at first glance. But on closer inspection it turns out that each step in the argument is extremely weak and open to objection. First, Luke says expressly in Acts 8:1 that the whole Jerusalem church was persecuted and that they were scattered due to this persecution. True, he says that the apostles alone stayed in Jerusalem, but he does not say that they were not persecuted.[11] According to Luke, it was the apostles' duty to stay in Jerusalem, for their work there was not yet completed. Accordingly, none of the apostles really leave Jerusalem until Peter does so in Acts 12:17. When, before that, we meet Peter in Lydda or Jaffa or Caesarea (Acts 9:32—10:48) he is only staying for a short visit, and he always returns to Jerusalem (Acts 11:2). In conclusion: what Luke portrays in Acts 8:1 is a general persecution of the whole community, with the apostles nevertheless stubbornly refusing to leave Jerusalem.

Secondly, Luke does not indicate that the persecution was triggered by Stephen saying something new that no one among the "Hebrews" had said before. What Stephen said concerning the temple had been said by Jesus himself, and we have no certain evidence that any group in the early community would disagree with his theology on this point. What was new about Stephen was not the message he proclaimed, but the audience he proclaimed it to. "Then some of those who belonged to the synagogue of the Freedmen (as it was called), Cyrenians, Alexandrians, and others of those from Cilicia and Asia, stood up and argued with Stephen" (Acts 6:9). Here we see *Diaspora*

---

[10]This theory about the Stephen episode was first launched by the Tübingen scholar Ferdinand Chr. Baur in 1845. For an extensive review of its history to the present, see Hill, *Hellenists and Hebrews*, pp. 5-17.

[11]For this point, see Bauckham, "James," pp. 428-29.

Jews who had settled in Jerusalem.[12] In Acts 9:29 we meet the same group of people—this time called "Hellenists" (i.e., Greek-speakers)—who opposed Paul as vehemently as they had opposed Stephen. And in Acts 21:27-31 it is these same Diaspora Jews who try to kill Paul (cf. also Acts 23:12-15). Again the accusation is the same as the one leveled against Stephen: "This is the man who is teaching everyone everywhere against our people, our law, and this place [the temple]; more than that, he has actually brought Greeks into the temple and has defiled this holy place" (Acts 21:28). To conclude: Stephen was not persecuted because he introduced a new theology, but because he encountered a new group of adversaries—the resident Diaspora Jews in Jerusalem, the "Hellenists."

The violent reaction of precisely this group should not surprise us. The very fact that they had taken the trouble to leave their native countries and settle in Jerusalem proves that they were not average Jews.[13] They were zealous Jews, and their main reason for settling in Jerusalem was probably to be close to the temple; they wanted to participate in the temple worship and to sacrifice. Being Diaspora Jews, they would not automatically belong to one of the three parties within Judaism in Israel—the Sadducees, Pharisees or Essenes—but would quite simply be "Torah Jews," zealous for the Torah and the temple. This very zeal had brought them to Jerusalem in the first place.

It was when the Greek-speakers within the Jerusalem community came into contact with this group that open conflict and persecution broke out. Thus it would seem that the reason for the persecution of the Jerusalem church, following the execution of Stephen, was not new theological tendencies within the Jerusalem community, but contact with a new group of Jerusalem residents, the "Hellenists."[14]

Let us try to piece together the evidence reviewed so far. We are faced with two rounds of persecution. The first affected the apostles who were preaching and teaching on the Temple Mount. This primarily offended the Sadducees, partly because the apostles proclaimed the resurrection, and partly because

---

[12]Concerning the early synagogues in Jerusalem being synagogues precisely for Diaspora Jews, see above chapter 3, and cf. the discussion of Acts 6:9 in Rainer Riesner, "Synagogues in Jerusalem" (in Winter, *Book of Acts* 4:179-211), pp. 204-6.

[13]I cannot avoid thinking that present day English-speaking Brooklyn Jews, settling in Jerusalem's ultra-orthodox quarters, are a close modern parallel to the "Hellenists" of Jerusalem in the pre-70 city.

[14]I should warn the reader that the interpretation advocated here is definitely a minority position. The great majority of scholars still think the Baur interpretation, or some modified version of it, is the best.

they did it within the temple, the domain of the Sadducean priests. The Pharisee Gamaliel defended the apostles' freedom to preach. The second round of persecution affected the whole Jerusalem church, and was instigated by resident Diaspora Jews zealous for the temple and the law. They were offended by Stephen, who repeated the sayings of Jesus about the temple (compare Jn 2:19; Mk 13:2).

Jesus' declaration that the temple would be destroyed and raised by him in three days appears in all the Gospels, and was no doubt a tradition shared by all the believers in Jerusalem at that time. True, most of the references to Jesus' words come from false witnesses and mockers (see Mt 26:61; 27:40; Mk 14:58; 15:29), but John 2:19 seems to indicate that their falsehood consisted in distorting the intention of Jesus rather than his actual words. It seems that these sayings about the temple upset the priests and the zealous Diaspora Jews, but there is no direct evidence that the Pharisees were particularly troubled by them.[15]

The First Believers' View of the Temple

Let us glance at the catastrophe of the year 70. The destruction of the temple was a devastating blow to Judaism, except for two groups: the Pharisees and the Christians. Or let me put it a little more cautiously: there were at least some Pharisees, and probably many believers in Jesus, who were mentally prepared to cope with the new situation without too many problems. Jerusalem and the temple were important to both groups, but the temple was not an essential, irreplaceable institution. It is of considerable symbolic significance that representatives of both groups left Jerusalem during the years of the great Jewish revolt. Johanan ben Zakkai left the turmoil of Jerusalem to build Judaism anew at Jamnia with his fellow scholars. All or some of the Jewish believers' community made a (temporary?) wartime refuge in Pella east of the Jordan.[16]

---

[15]Cf. the very extensive discussion in Craig A. Evans, "Predictions of the Destruction of the Herodian Temple in the Pseudepigrapha, Qumran Scrolls, and Related Texts," *Journal for the Study of the Pseudepigrapha* 10 (1992): 89-147; and Evans, *Jesus and His Contemporaries*, pp. 367-80. Evans here assembles a large number of Jewish texts containing prophecies of doom and destruction of the temple, including Pharisaic/rabbinic ones.

[16]The historicity of the flight to Pella has been hotly debated, cf. Marcel Simon, "La Migration à Pella: Légende ou Réalité?" *Recherches de science religieuse* 60 (1972), 40-52 (reprinted in *Le Christianisme antique et son contexte religieux: Scripta Varia*, vol. 2, Wissenschaftliche Untersuchungen zum Neuen Testament 23 (Tübingen: J. C. B. Mohr, 1981), pp. 477-94; B. E. Gray, "The Movements of the Jerusalem Church During the First Jewish War," *Journal*

An interesting document which seems to have some connection with the Pella community has been preserved. It is part of the so-called Pseudo-Clementine *Recognitions*, and is preserved more or less as one continuous block in book 1:27-71 (it is sometimes called "The Ascents of James (II)," and appears to have been written about A.D. 150).[17] This text contains some interesting similarities to Acts. Its beginning and end are missing, which is unfortunate, especially since the fragment ends just as Paul is about to meet the Lord on the road to Damascus. Apparently the writer disagreed with Paul and his mission, but had much praise for Jesus' brother James. The author draws a picture of salvation history beginning with Abraham and ending with the Jerusalem community under the leadership of James. He is friendly toward mission among the Gentiles, but is himself mainly concerned with Israel.

The author is a pious, law-obedient Jew, who accepts circumcision and the eternal validity of the Torah, except for one element in it: that portion which is concerned with sacrifices. These, he writes, were only a temporary accommodation made necessary by the bad habit of offering sacrifices which the Israelites had acquired in Egypt.[18] Thus Moses began correcting the problem, "leaving the other half to be corrected by another, and at a future time; by him, namely, concerning whom he said himself, 'A prophet shall the Lord God raise unto you' (Deut 18:15, 18)" (*Recognitions* 1.36).[19] Moses made a par-

---

of *Ecclesiastical History* 24 (1973): 1-7; Gerd Luedemann, "The Successors of Pre-70 Jerusalem Christianity: A Critical Evaluation of the Pella-Tradition," in Sanders, *Self-Definition* 1:161-73; Ray A. Pritz, "On Brandon's Rejection of the Pella Tradition," *Immanuel* 13 (1981): 39-43; C. Koester, "The Origin and Significance of the Flight to Pella Tradition," *Catholic Biblical Quarterly* 51 (1989): 90-106; Jerome Murphy-O'Connor, "The Cenacle: Topographical Setting for Acts 2:44-45" (in Winter, *Book of Acts* 4:303-21), pp. 316-17, with reference to recent literature. Eusebius is apparently contradictory. He seems to imply that the whole community settled permanently in Pella, while at the same time he says that there was a church of Jewish believers in Jerusalem between the two wars (i.e., between A.D. 70 and 132).

[17]The fundamental study of the Pseudo-Clementine *Recognitions* 1:27-71 is Strecker, *Judenchristentum*, pp. 221-54. Cf. also Schoeps, *Theologie und Geschichte*, pp. 384-417; J. L. Martyn, "Clementine Recognitions 1,33-71, Jewish Christianity, and the Fourth Gospel," in *God's Christ and His People: Studies in Honour of Nils Alstrup Dahl*, ed. J. Jervell and W. A. Meeks (Oslo: Scandinavian University Press, 1977), pp. 265-95; Robert E. Van Voorst, *The Ascents of James: History and Theology of a Jewish-Christian Community*, SBL Dissertation Series 112 (Atlanta, Ga.: Scholars Press, 1989); F. Stanley Jones, *An Ancient Jewish-Christian Source on the History of Christianity: Pseudo-Clementine Recognitions 1.27-71*, Text and Translations Christian Apocrypha Series (Atlanta, Ga.: Scholars Press, 1995).

[18]There is rabbinic evidence that makes it almost certain that this theory is of Jewish origin, cf. *Lev. Rab.* 22:8 (in a midrash attributed to R. Levi, ca. A.D. 300). Cf. the discussion of this in Skarsaune, *Proof from Prophecy*, pp. 297-98, 316-19.

[19]Quoted here according to the translation of the Pseudo-Clementines in *ANF* 8:87.

tial correction by abolishing sacrifices to idols; Jesus abolished sacrifices altogether. The writer here has Jesus' own sacrifice in mind. The atoning death of Christ is applied to the believer in baptism, and therefore the author states that baptism takes the place of sacrifices: "Lest they might suppose that at the cessation of sacrifice, there was no remission of sins for them, he instituted baptism by water amongst them, in which they might be absolved from all their sins on the invocation of his name" (*Recognitions* 1.39).[20] The devastation of Jerusalem, says the author, was a direct result of the sinful continuance of temple sacrifices after the appearance of Jesus.

There is evidence in Justin Martyr that suggests that the view of the sacrifices held by the author of *Recognitions* 1.27-71 is actually much older than the document itself.[21] Therefore we may assume that this Judeo-Christian document from the second century does not differ radically in its view of the temple from that of the pre-70 Jerusalem community.

We have already seen that from the very beginning the apostles valued the temple as the place from which the authoritative word of God was to go forth to all Israel and to the nations, according to Isaiah's prophecy (Is 2:3). We further heard of the earliest community that they were in the temple "day by day" (Acts 2:46). But what did they do there? First we should note that with one exception, we never read that they brought sacrifices. (The exception is Paul, who in Acts 21:23-26 brings sacrifices for himself and four others in fulfillment of a Nazirite vow. Romans 3:25 shows that Paul could have attached no atoning quality to these sacrifices, which in any case were probably not conceived of as having such a quality.)[22]

What we do read is that they went up to the temple to teach and pray (Acts 3:1). We have already seen the significance of their teaching in the temple. Their praying there should probably be seen in the light of Jesus' words when he "cleansed" the temple: "It is written, 'My house shall be called a house of prayer'; but you are making it a den of robbers" (Mt 21:13). It seems as if the early believers purposefully ignored the sacrificial cult going on in the temple. To put it a little more pointedly, they treated the temple as if it were the supreme synagogue. In the synagogue you teach

---

[20]Ibid., p. 88.
[21]Cf. the discussion in Skarsaune, *The Proof from Prophecy*, pp. 316-20.
[22]The sacrifices to be brought at the end of the Nazirite period are described in Num 6:13-20, and although one of the many sacrifices to be brought is described, technically, as a "sin-offering" (it may also—perhaps better—be rendered "impurity-offering"), there is hardly any doubt that the whole complex of sacrifices should be seen essentially as votive sacrifices, which belonged to the thanksgiving category, cf. esp. Lev 7:11-18.

and pray, but you do not sacrifice.[23]

While the cessation of the atoning sacrifices posed a problem for the rabbis after A.D. 70, there is no trace in early Christian literature that this situation was ever considered a problem. On the contrary, in *Recognitions* 1.33-71 it is rather the *continuation* of the sacrifices between A.D. 30 and 70 which is seen as a grave sin.

The concept of the temple as a house of prayer rather than a place for propitiatory sacrifices is beautifully brought out in an old account of the martyrdom of James, the brother of Jesus, ca. A.D. 62. This fascinating account has been preserved thanks to the author Hegesippus[24]—himself possibly a Jewish believer—who wrote it down during the latter half of the second century, and thanks to Eusebius, who quoted the story in his *Ecclesiastical History*.

> James became leader of the Jerusalem assembly. From his mother's womb he had been consecrated a Nazirite.[25] He alone was permitted to enter the sanctuary, and there "was found on his knees asking forgiveness on behalf of the people, so that his knees became hard like a camel's. . . . On account of his exceeding great justice,

---

[23]Cf. Martin Hengel, with reference to the tradition about James quoted below: "Precisely because the Temple no longer served as a place of sacrifice and atonement, but had become 'a house of prayer,' . . . the tradition could develop that James went alone to the Temple and there 'constantly went down on his knees to pray to God and ask him for forgiveness for his people.' He, James, the brother of Jesus, as earthly intercessor for disobedient Israel, corresponded to Jesus the Son of Man as the heavenly intercessor at the right hand of God. By contrast, the Temple cult itself had lost its atoning effect" (Hengel, *The Atonement: The Origins of the Doctrine in the New Testament* [London: SCM Press, 1981], p. 57). Jostein Ådna in his treatment of this issue makes the interesting proposal that for the early Jerusalem community a kind of "reversal" took place: the *atoning sacrifice* of Jesus was commemorated in the eucharistic celebration in their homes, which thereby functioned as "temples," whereas the temple became a non-sacrificial "house of prayer." Cf. Jostein Ådna, *Jesu Kritik am Tempel: Eine Untersuchung zum Verlauf und Sinn der sogenannten Tempelreinigung Jesu, Markus 11,15-17 und Parallelen* (Tübinge/Stavanger: Dissertation, 1993), pp. 554-59. To all of this, and to my own statements above, I add the following caution: It may, in reality, have taken some time before the full implications of a sacrificial interpretation of the death of Jesus were drawn, especially with regard to the temple service. On the psychological level, things may change more slowly than on the conceptual.

[24]He also, very likely, embellished it a great deal. Richard Bauckham has shown how the basic story, which Hegesippus used, can in part be reconstructed with the help of one of the Nag Hammadi texts, which also seems to build on the same story. See Bauckham, "For What Offence Was James Put to Death?" in *James the Just and Christian Origins*, ed. Bruce Chilton and Craig A. Evans (Leiden: Brill, 1999), pp. 201-6 (article, pp. 199-232).

[25]Or rather, maybe, a Rechabite. What is said about the restrictions James took on himself agrees in part with those of the Rechabites (Jer 35:6-11). There were probably no Rechabites any longer at the time of James, and Hegesippus or his source may just have drawn a rather free portrait of James as a great ascetic.

he was called 'The Just,' and 'Oblias,' which is in Greek 'bulwark of the people,' and 'Justice,' as the prophets show concerning him."[26] James was held in such high regard that many believed because of his testimony, and the Jewish leaders had to appear before James and entreat him that on the coming Passover he should "restrain the people; for it is gone astray in regard to Jesus, as if he were the Messiah. We beseech you to persuade all who come for the Day of the Passover concerning Jesus; for in you do we all put our trust. For we bear you witness, as do all the people, that you are just, and that you do not respect persons." They requested that James should stand on the pinnacle of the Temple so as to be heard by all. Standing there, James is asked, "'Who is the gate of Jesus?'[27] And he replied with a loud voice, 'Why do you ask me concerning the Son of Man, since He is sitting in heaven at the right hand of the Mighty Power, and shall come on the clouds of heaven?' And when many were fully persuaded and gave glory at the testimony of James, and said, 'Hosanna to the Son of David,'" the Jewish leaders regretted having given James this opportunity to witness. They threw him down from the pinnacle, and afterwards began stoning him, for he was not killed by the fall. While being stoned, he prayed, "Forgive them, for they know not what they do." Finally he was killed by a fuller's club (*Ecclesiastical History* 2.23.2-18).[28]

There are many interesting features in this story,[29] especially when we compare it to the following account given by Josephus. After having described the corrupt behavior of the high priest Ananus (son of the Annas mentioned in the Gospels), Josephus goes on to say:

---

[26]I think Richard Bauckham has shown quite convincingly that all three names for James are derived from specific prophetic texts: "The Just One" recalls Is 3:10 (LXX), "Let us do away with The Just One, for he is inconvenient to us." "Oblias" is certainly a distortion of a Hebrew name, probably *Gevul-am*, "protecting wall of the people," based on Is 54:12: "I will make . . . your wall (*gevul*) of precious stones." "Righteousness" might then be taken from Is 54:14: "In righteousness you shall be established." Bauckham argues that the two latter names should be understood against the background of the early community being envisaged as the new temple, and different leaders being called after different parts of the building: "rock [of foundation]" (Peter), "pillars," "wall," etc. See Bauckham, "For What Offence," pp. 206-9.

[27]This question is rather peculiar, because it is obvious that the right answer is "Jesus." Bauckham suggests that the original question was formed on the basis of Ps 118:20: "This is the gate of the LORD," assuming that the temple imagery is still being employed: Who is "the gate of the Lord" leading into the new temple? Answer: Jesus. One could also consider the possibility that there is a Hebrew substratum here: Who is *the gate of salvation?* (Hebrew, gate of *Yeshuah*).

[28]Lawlor/Oulton 1:59-60, paraphrased in part.

[29]Bauckham, in the analysis mentioned above, argues strongly that it is, to a large extent, based on Ps 118, which is conceived as being spoken by James. Metaphorical expressions in the psalm are taken literally in the story. For other comments, see Bernheim, *James, Brother of Jesus*, pp. 246-58.

Ananus, therefore, being of this [corrupt] character, and supposing that he had a favorable opportunity on account of the fact that Festus [the new Roman procurator] was still on the way, called together the Sanhedrin, and brought before them the brother of Jesus, the so-called Christ, James by name, together with some others, and *accused them of violating the law,* and condemned them to be stoned. (*Antiquities* 20.200, italics added)

This accusation of breaking the law, coming from the high priest, gives the impression that the issue is some offence or disregard for the temple worship. The case seems strikingly similar to the charges against Stephen and Paul. Josephus is certainly right in judging the high priest and his fellows responsible for James's death. Josephus then writes that those of the people who were most eager to keep the law (meaning the Pharisees) complained to King Agrippa and the new Roman procurator Albinus about what Ananus had done, leading to his deposal (cf. the story of the Pharisee Gamaliel I in Acts 5:33-40).

If we try to pull together this direct and indirect evidence, we get a picture in agreement with the letter of James, whether it was directly or indirectly written by him: The faction led by James—presumably the whole Aramaic-speaking portion of the early community[30]—seems to have completely ignored the sacrificial cult of the temple. This created tension between them and the Sadducees, and later with the Diaspora Jews who were zealous for the temple. The early Jerusalem community seems to have regarded the temple as the supreme synagogue, the ultimate place for teaching and praying. The remission of sins was no longer obtained by the sacrifices offered there, but by the supreme sacrifice of Christ. In 1 Corinthians 15:3-7, Paul passes on a tradition probably derived from the earliest Jerusalem community, in which the sacrificial death of Christ is already spoken of in unambiguous terms.

What About the Torah?
In light of this, how should we characterize the attitude of the earliest community toward the Torah as a whole? It seems we should emphasize the concept of Jesus being the fulfiller of all aspects of the Torah (Mt 5:17-18). His ethical teaching summed up the central ethical teachings of the Torah, stressing the priority of the commandments to love God and your neighbor, which

---

[30]Concerning the question of how and when James succeeded the Twelve as main leader of the Jerusalem community, see Bauckham, "James and the Jerusalem Church" (in Winter, *Book of Acts* 4:415-80), pp. 427-50.

are actually found in the Torah. The teaching of Jesus was thus both old and new regarding the Torah, but there was a significant shift of authority: for the earliest believers, the ultimate authority was Jesus. When he interpreted the Torah, he did so as if he was the authority speaking through it (Mt 5:21-48; cf. chapter sixteen below).

In the same way, the Torah sacrifices were no longer the means of salvation because the sacrifice of Christ had fulfilled the sacrifices prescribed in the Torah. The death of Jesus inaugurated the age of the new covenant that will "not be like the covenant that I made with their ancestors . . . to bring them out of the land of Egypt" (Jer 31:32; see vv. 31-34; see also Jesus' words in Lk 22:20). Living in the times of the Messiah, the earliest believers reacted in a consistently Jewish way by no longer holding the Torah to be the ultimate authority. There are ancient rabbinic sayings that indicate that in the messianic age there will be changes in the Torah,[31] with some commandments being abrogated. Although these sayings are largely suppressed in later rabbinic tradition, they show that the attitude of the early community was hardly un-Jewish in the context of pre-70 Israel. Their entire attitude was determined by their conviction that they were living in the days of the Messiah.

Having said all this, we must add that the early Jewish believers saw no reason *not* to observe the Torah. On the contrary, believing in Jesus did not deprive them of their Jewish identity, neither in their own eyes nor in the eyes of other Jews, as the stories about James clearly demonstrate. Living in the time of fulfillment, why should they not fulfill the Torah in their own lives? (They probably had no consciousness of breaking the Torah by not bringing the prescribed sacrifices to atone for sin or impurity, because they meant to be in a state of sanctity and purity prior to all such sacrifices, because of their participation in the cleansing and atoning death of Jesus. The remedies prescribed in the Torah, rather than being bad, were simply superfluous.) Accordingly, we read that many of the first believers were even "zealous for the Law" (Acts 21:20). A direct divine revelation was necessary to make Peter transgress the Torah concerning unclean food (Acts 10). The Pharisaic halakic tradition was given considerable respect (Mt 23:2-3), but was not considered an absolute authority, and was increasingly disregarded after A.D. 70 (the Gospels of Matthew and Luke are important sources for this). Instead, a

---

[31]See W. D. Davies, *Torah in the Messianic Age and/or the Age to Come*, JBL Monograph Series 7 (Philadelphia: Society of Biblical Literature, 1952), pp. 50-94; Jacob Jervell, "Die offenbarte und die verborgene Tora: Zur Vorstellung über die neue Tora im Rabbinismus," *Studia Theologica* 25 (1971): 90-108.

halakic tradition specific to the believers' community developed, still unmistakably Jewish, but not rabbinic. In this way, by no means did they discard their Jewish identity, and we can understand their general reputation as pious, law-obedient Jews.

But this still leaves two unanswered questions: What about Torah-obedience as a means of salvation, and what about the Gentiles who became believers in Jesus? What was required of them with regard to Torah-observance and inclusion in the Jewish people through conversion? These are the central questions of the next chapter.

Temple Square
This chapter has looked largely at the early community's relation to the temple. Here we shall focus on another aspect: the early community regarded *itself* as the true, eschatological temple. Scattered references to this idea in several New Testament writings fit together if one presupposes that the early community regarded itself this way. (1) According to Matthew, Jesus said he would *build* his *ekklēsia*, "assembly, church," on Peter as the rock, the foundation (Mt 16:18). Together with the verb *build*, the saying about the "gates of Hades" not prevailing against the *ekklēsia* is probably an indication that the *ekklēsia* is not only envisaged as a house, but precisely as the temple (temples have gates). See also Matthew 12:3-8. (2) According to Paul in Galatians 2:9, James and Peter ("Cephas") and John were regarded as "pillars" of the Jerusalem community (it is not said if they alone or also others were so regarded), again a metaphor presupposing the overarching temple metaphor. Notice Revelation 3:12: "If you conquer, I will make you a pillar in the temple of my God." (3) In Eusebius's *Ecclesiastical History*, Hegesippus (mid second century A.D.) reports that James, the Lord's brother, was called "Oblias," which is probably a distortion of Hebrew *gebul-am*, "[protecting] wall of the people," referring to Isaiah 54:11-12, in which Jerusalem or the temple (the two often coalesce) is said to have stones, foundation, pinnacles, gates and a [protecting] wall.

In a temple there are priests; who are the priests of this new temple? The early evidence is silent about this, but if we go by the later evidence of 1 Peter, the priests of the new temple are not any particular group, but *the whole new people as such*. They are "a chosen race, a royal priesthood, a holy nation, God's own people" (1 Pet 2:9); they are also, at the same time, "built into a spiritual house [temple]," of which they are the "holy priesthood, to offer spiritual sacrifices acceptable to God" (1 Pet 2:5). This temple is built upon Jesus as the foundation, the stone laid in Zion, "a cornerstone chosen and precious" (1 Pet 2:6; cf. Is 28:16).

This corresponds to a striking fact about the early ministries of leadership in the Christian community: since the whole people is priestly, all leadership ministries are called by entirely non-priestly, non-cultic terms: "elder" (Greek, *presbyteros*; English, presbyter), "overseer" (Greek, *episkopos*; English, bishop), "assistant" (Greek, *diakonos*; English, deacon). The new people of God are not *in* a temple, attending a service led by priests, they *are* the temple and they *are* its priests, themselves conducting the service.

Suggestions for Further Reading
The main source for the theme treated in this chapter is, of course, Acts 1—12.

A scholarly yet eminently readable account of the earliest years of the Christian community is contained in F. F. Bruce, *New Testament History* (New York: Anchor, 1972), pp. 205-33. Bruce is closer to the traditional theory about the "Hellenists" than is the present author.

The same is true of Martin Hengel, who has two excellent studies: *Between Jesus and Paul: Studies in the Earliest History of Christianity* (London: SCM Press, 1983), and *Acts and the History of Earliest Christianity* (London: SCM Press, 1979/Philadelphia: Fortress, 1980).

For the "Jewishness" of Luke's own perspective, one should study carefully the fascinating book by Jacob Jervell, *Luke and the People of God: A New Look at Luke-Acts* (Minneapolis: Augsburg, 1972); and now also the same author's commentary on Acts: *Die Apostelgeschichte,* Kritisch-exegetischer Kommentar über das Neue Testament 3 [17. Aufl.] (Göttingen: Vandenhoeck & Ruprecht, 1998). Cf. also the fascinating perspectives in Dix, *Jew and Greek,* pp. 29-60.

For the history of the Jerusalem community until the Great War A.D. 66-70, see esp. Richard Bauckham, "James and the Jerusalem Church," in *The Book of Acts in Its Palestinian Setting,* vol. 4 of *The Book of Acts in Its First Century Setting* (Carlisle: Paternoster/ Grand Rapids, Mich.: Eerdmans, 1995), pp. 415-80.

On the Jewish Christianity of sources in the Pseudo-Clementines, see Hans Joachim Schoeps, *Theologie und Geschichte des Judenchristentums* (Tübingen: J. C. B. Mohr, 1949); Georg Strecker, *Das Judenchristentum in den Pseudoklementinen,* Texte und Untersuchungen 70 (Berlin: Akademieverlag, 1958; 2nd ed., 1981).

An important study of the attitude of Jesus and the early community vis-à-vis the temple and the temple service is Jostein Ådna, *Jesu Stellung zum Tempel,* Wissenschaftliche Untersuchungen zum Neuen Testament, 2. Reihe, 119 (Tübingen: Mohr Siebeck, 2000).

James, the brother of Jesus, has attracted a lot of interest recently. See, e.g., W. Pratscher, *Der Herrenbruder Jakobus und die Jakobustradition,* Forschungen zur Religion und Literatur des Alten und Neuen Testaments 139 (Göttingen: Vandenhoeck & Ruprecht, 1987); Pierre-Antoine Bernheim, *James, Brother of Jesus* (London: SCM Press, 1997); J. Painter, *Just James: The Brother of Jesus in History and Tradition* (Columbia: University of South Carolina Press, 1997); Bruce Chilton and Craig A. Evans, eds., *James the Just and Christian Origins* (Leiden: E. J. Brill, 1999).

8

THE MISSION TO THE GENTILES & THE QUESTION OF THE TORAH

*D*uring *his early ministry, Jesus' goal was to go to the "lost sheep of the house of Israel" (Mt 15:24), not to the Gentiles, and he gave his disciples the same commission (Mt 10:5-6). But on several occasions Gentiles came to Jesus, and in one case he testified that "in no one in Israel have I found such faith" (Mt 8:10). These episodes hint that one day there would be no limitations on the spreading of the good news, and after his resurrection Jesus explicitly told his disciples to go and make disciples of all nations (Mt 28:19-20; Lk 24:45-47; Acts 1:8).*

Problems?

We have no evidence whatsoever of any opposition within the early community to the inclusion of Gentiles in the new people of the Messiah. The Old Testament was unambiguous on this point: the Messiah was to be "a light unto the Gentiles" (Is 42:6-7; 49:6; cf. Lk 2:32), who were to join themselves to the people of God (Is 2:2-4; etc.). While there was hardly any disagreement among the early believers about this, some rather important questions were still left unanswered.

The Old Testament prophecies could easily be interpreted to mean that salvation in the Messiah was first to be preached to Israel, so that all Israel, or at least most of Israel, would have a share in it. The resultant glory for Israel would be so great that the Gentiles would be attracted, and hardly need any exhortation to come and share in Israel's salvation (Is 2:3).

Those who thought this way would not be opposed in principle to mission among the Gentiles, but would say that as long as Israel had not recognized Jesus as its Messiah, the time for missions among the Gentiles had not yet come. The best evidence that such thinking existed is Romans 11. Here Paul takes issue with this concept and turns it upside down: God's plan now is not to wait for the salvation of Israel, but to first preach the gospel to the Gentiles—and then, through this, for Israel to be saved.[1]

But an even more urgent problem faced them. What about the Gentiles who joined the people of God? Should they be accepted in the usual Jewish way, that is, by circumcision and obedience to the Torah? Christians living over 1900 years later have become so used to the practical outcome of this debate that we can hardly understand how difficult the question was. We tend to forget, for example, that Jesus said nothing about it, at least not directly. This silence of Jesus, perhaps more than anything else, explains why the leaders of the Jerusalem church had to wait—and did wait—for direct divine intervention before deciding this issue.

The intervention came in the moving episode of Peter and Cornelius in Acts 10. (Read the whole chapter and the sequel in Acts 11:1-18.) This, says Luke, silenced the circumcision party (Acts 11:2, the "circumcised believers" critical of Peter), and made them "praise God, saying, 'Then God has given even to the Gentiles the repentance that leads to life'" (Acts 11:18).

Only after this divine intervention favoring the inclusion of non-circumcised Gentiles does Luke feel free to recount that some of the Jewish believers who were scattered abroad, during the persecution after Stephen's death, began to preach to Gentiles:

> Now those who had been scattered by the persecution in connection with Stephen travelled as far as Phoenicia, Cyprus and Antioch, telling the message only to Jews. Some of them, however, men from Cyprus and Cyrene, went to Antioch and *began to speak to Greeks also*, telling them the good news about the Lord Jesus. (Acts 11:19-20 NIV, italics added)

This interesting passage yields no support for the theory that attributes the

---

[1]For this interpretation of Romans 11, see Nils Alstrup Dahl, "Promise and Fulfillment" and "The Future of Israel" in *Studies in Paul: Theology for the Early Christian Mission* (Minneapolis: Augsburg, 1977), pp. 121-36 and 137-58.

mission to the Gentiles to the "universalistic" outlook of the "Hellenistic" party of the Jerusalem community. As we recall from the last chapter, the Baur theory says that the ones persecuted and fleeing from Jerusalem were the Hellenists, and they began the mission among the Gentiles, due to their more open attitude. But this text says that the ones scattered preached to Jews only, in keeping with the prevalent notion in Jerusalem. It was only after a while that some of them began preaching to Gentiles as well. And this may have had a very simple explanation: Preaching in the synagogue(s) of Antioch, they could hardly, in the long run, avoid this, because at the synagogue they certainly had a mixed audience: Jews, proselytes and God-fearing Gentiles.[2]

The mission to the Gentiles was not bound up with the Jerusalem Hellenists as a group, but with the Antioch community, born of the first community in Jerusalem. It was in the framework of this community that some of the newcomers from Jerusalem, Jews from Cyprus and Cyrene, began to address their preaching specifically to (God-fearing) Gentiles.

In the beginning, this seems not to have created trouble back in Jerusalem. It should not, if everyone in Jerusalem was happy with the conclusion reached over the Cornelius affair. Nevertheless, the Jerusalem community sent Barnabas as their special envoy to inspect and guide matters in Antioch (Acts 11:22-26), and according to Luke, he was overjoyed to see the Gentile believers. He went to fetch Paul, and together they acted as the liaisons between Jerusalem and Antioch (Acts 11:25-30; 12:25). This rather harmonious situation was not to last, however.

The Role of Paul and the Apostolic Council

Some scholars speak of Paul as the second, or sometimes even the only, founder of Christianity.[3]

They imply that Paul represents a Christianity totally different from that of the early community in Jerusalem. Paul is said to be a product of Hellenistic Judaism and Hellenistic Christianity, having minimal contact with the Aramaic-speaking community in Jerusalem and disregarding its theology and authority.[4]

---

[2]Josephus says about Antioch: "The Jews made proselytes of a great many of the Greeks all the time" (*Jewish War* 7.3.3 [45]), which also would indicate a broad fringe of God-fearing Gentiles around the synagogue.
[3]For this paragraph, see the fascinating analysis in Dix, *Jew and Greek*, pp. 35-51.
[4]A recent statement of this view is Hyam Maccoby, *The Mythmaker: Paul and the Invention of*

Acts provides no evidence to substantiate this theory.[5] Paul is brought to Antioch by a member of the Jerusalem church, and he acts under the authority of Jerusalem in his teaching ministry (Acts 11:22-26). The pupil of Gamaliel the Elder was no peripheral figure to Judean Jews, whether believers or not. Paul's own letters substantiate the evidence in Acts. In Galatians 2:2 Paul makes it abundantly clear that he considered it essential to be recognized by the Jerusalem church, and this recognition was in fact accorded him (Gal 2:3-10). During his first visit to Jerusalem, Paul stayed with Peter for fifteen days (Gal 1:18) and visited James as well. As C. H. Dodd once remarked, we can be sure that during those fifteen days Paul and Peter had more important things to discuss than the weather![6] The traditions he received from the Jerusalem community were fundamental for Paul (1 Cor 11:23-26; 15:3-7).[7]

Second, it should be stressed that Paul was neither the initiator nor the sole undertaker of a mission among the Gentiles. When Paul came to Antioch, the mission among the Gentiles was in full swing, and it was begun by converted Diaspora Jews from the Jerusalem community (Acts 11:19-26). At this early stage, it seems to have caused no major problems in Jerusalem, as we have just seen.

This, however, was to change within a few years. Apparently a group in the Jerusalem community could not accept the admission of Gentiles without circumcision and ritual observance of the Torah. Paul calls them "false brethren" in Galatians 2:4-5, and in Galatians 2:12 it is the same group that Paul calls "certain men from James." This must mean that they claimed the authority of James for their own views. The evidence in Acts as well as in Galatians 2 shows that they were hardly justified in this appeal to James, but they were influential enough to win Peter over to their side while he was visiting Antioch (Gal 2:11-14; read the whole passage). Peter now refused to dine with non-kosher Gentiles, apparently forgetting the insight gained in the Cornelius episode in Acts 10 (cf. Gal 2:12). With Peter courting the "circumcision party," a summit meeting in Jerusalem now became necessary to settle this internal conflict.

Christianity (London: Weidenfeld & Nicholson, 1986); and idem, *Paul and Hellenism* (London: SCM Press, 1991).

[5]In the following interpretation of Acts, I owe much to the studies of Jacob Jervell listed in the Suggestions to chapter 7, although he would probably not subscribe to everything I say.

[6]C. H. Dodd, *The Apostolic Preaching and Its Development: Three Lectures*, new ed. (London: Hodder & Stoughton, 1963), p. 16.

[7]See Birger Gerhardsson, *Memory and Manuscript: Oral Tradition and Written Transmission in Rabbinic Judaism and Early Christianity*, Acta Seminarii Neotestamentici Upsaliensis 22 (Lund: C. W. K. Gleerup/Copenhagen: E. Munksgaard, 1964), pp. 274ff.

Box 8.1. Synchronizing Galatians 2 and the Acts Account

The synchronization of Galatians 2 and Acts 10-15 is notoriously difficult, and there are several options.
1. The most common is to synchronize Gal 2:1-10 with Acts 15:1-31. The two accounts do match on several points, but there are also problems with harmonizing them, and many conclude that if Paul is correct in Gal 2 about the outcome of the "council," Luke's report on the "apostolic decree" in Acts 15 must be displaced: Paul seems unaware of any such decree when writing Gal 2.[8] Or was he consciously ignoring it?[9]
2. This has led some scholars to propose another solution:[10]
  • Paul's first visit to Jerusalem: Gal 1:18 = Acts 9:26-30.
  • Paul's second visit to Jerusalem: Gal 2:1-10 = Acts 11:30; 12:25.
  • The conflict at Antioch: Gal 2:11-14 = Acts 15:1-3.
  • The writing of Galatians (= *before* the council of Acts 15).
  • Paul's third visit to Jerusalem (the apostolic council): Acts 15:2-29.
As with all other attempts to synchronize Paul's report in Galatians with Acts, there are difficulties with this solution, too.
In the account of the present chapter, I have taken as a premise that the "answer" provided by the apostolic decree in Acts 15 admirably fits the "question" posed by the episode related by Paul in Gal 2:11-14. I leave undecided whether this should be explained by (a) Gal 2:11-14 being a flash-back, recounting an episode *preceding* Gal 2:1-10;[11] or (b) Luke having telescoped into one meeting in Acts 15 decisions really taken at two meetings, the second after the writing of Galatians.[12]

---

[8]Many scholars realize that the decree from the Jerusalem council looks very much like the solution to the Antiochene conflict reported by Paul in Gal 2:11-14, and that therefore the decree should have been agreed upon after and not before the clash between Peter and Paul in Antioch. But if so, it must have been agreed upon later than the Jerusalem Council, which Paul places before his conflict with Peter (Gal 2:1-10). This would also explain Paul's ignorance in Galatians with regard to the decree. See for this interpretation, Taylor, *Paul, Antioch and Jerusalem,* pp. 140-42. One may, however, interpret the chronological sequence in Gal 2 differently; see below and note 11.
[9]This is assumed by Jervell, *Apostelgeschichte,* pp. 406-7.
[10]Cf. Richard Bauckham, "Barnabas in Galatians," *Journal for the Study of the New Testament* 2 (1970): 61-70; F. F. Bruce, *The Epistle to the Galatians: A Commentary on the Greek Text,* The New International Greek Testament Commentary (Exeter: Paternoster/Grand Rapids, Mich.: Eerdmans, 1982), pp. 105-128.
[11]This is argued by Gerd Lüdemann, *Paul Apostle to the Gentiles: Studies in Chronology* (London: SCM Press, 1984), pp. 75-77.
[12]It may alert the reader to the complexity of the problem if I mention here two recent proposals for different solutions to the puzzle. Marcus Bockmuehl has argued that the area mentioned in the covering letter of the apostolic decree, "Antioch, Syria, Cilicia" (Acts 15:23), was in fact reckoned as, theologically, belonging to the land of Israel. Accordingly, the commandments concerning "resident aliens" in Lev 17—18 could be applied to Gentiles in these areas, but not beyond. That would explain why Paul in Gal 2 says nothing about the decree: it was not relevant for the areas in which Paul conducted his mission ("Antioch and James the Just," in *James the Just and Christian Origins,* ed. Bruce Chilton and Craig A. Evans, Supplements to Novum Testamentum 98 [Leiden: Brill, 1999], pp. 155-98).

We read about the so-called apostolic council in Acts 15. Peter seems to have taken to heart the lesson taught him by Paul at Antioch (Acts 15:7-11, cf. Gal 2:14). Even more importantly, James sides with Peter, Paul and Barnabas against the "circumcision party" (Acts 15:13-21). Gentiles need not be circumcised or subjected to the ritual observances of the Torah. On one point only are the Gentile believers told to make a concession to their Jewish brethren: they should not eat meat sacrificed to idols, or meat from strangled animals, that is, meat with blood in it (Acts 15:20, 29; 21:25). In the Torah the stranger living among Israelites, the "resident alien," was told to observe these commandments: "If anyone of the house of Israel or of the aliens that reside among them eats any blood, I will set my face against that person who eats blood" (Lev 17:10; cf. further Lev 18:26; 20:2).[13]

In the light of this, the meaning of the "apostolic decree" becomes clear: the Gentiles need not become circumcised Jews in order to be fully accepted into the people of God, but they are requested to keep those commandments of the Torah which are obligatory for Gentiles living among Jews.[14] Among these commands, special emphasis is laid on those related to table fellowship—in other words, the decree is specifically aimed at the unity of mixed congregations. The Jewish believers are asked to recognize their uncircumcised brethren as belonging fully to the new people of the Messiah, while the Gentiles are asked to respect the sensitivities of their Jewish brethren and not to violate the Torah commandments valid for Gentiles living among Israelites.

With this the Jerusalem leaders took a decisive stand against the "circumcision party." Paul and the Antioch community could go on with their mission among the Gentiles, knowing that Jerusalem would support them as it had done previously. (Paul seems to have widened the intention of the decree con-

Peder Borgen, on the other hand, argues that the essence of the decision reached at the Jerusalem summit was twofold: (1) Gentile believers were not to be circumcised; (2) they were to be admonished to keep the other requirements that were usually enjoined on converts (to quit pagan sins and habits); the exact wording of the latter was left open, which explains why the so-called decree exists in many variants. Luke, in Acts 15 and 21, quotes the version known to him; Paul presupposes another wording, and can therefore write what he writes in Gal 2 without contradicting or being ignorant of the agreements of the Jerusalem meeting. ("Catalogues of Vices, the Apostolic Decree, and the Jerusalem Meeting," in Borgen, Early Christianity, pp. 233-52.)

[13]Cf. the rabbinic material collected in Strack/Billerbeck 2:721-22. On the interpretation of James's speech, see Jostein Ådna, "James' Position at the Summit Meeting of the Apostles and the Elders in Jerusalem (Acts 15)," in Ådna/Kvalbein, Mission of the Early Church, pp. 125-61.

[14]For this interpretation of the apostolic decree, see esp. Jervell, Luke and the People of God, pp. 143-46.

cerning table fellowship and formulated a general principle of Christian brotherly love: respect the sensitivities of your Christian brother in all matters related to the ritual aspects of food [1 Cor 10:25-33; Rom 14:13-23].)[15]

The Mission to the God-Fearing Gentiles

On reading Galatians 1:16; 2:7-9, one may get the impression that Paul in his mission went exclusively to Gentiles. But Romans and Acts clearly prove that such was not the case. On the contrary, throughout his mission Paul acted on the principle that the Gospel was "to the Jew first and also to the Greek" (Rom 1:16). In every city, Paul first went to the synagogue to preach and debate (Acts 9:20-22; 13:5, 14-52; 14:1-43; 16:13; 17:1-5, 10, 17; 18:4).[16] And more often than not, some, even many, of the Jews attending the synagogues became believers (see Acts 13:43; the Jews and converts mentioned here are probably not included among the Jews mentioned in v. 45; see also Acts 14:1; 17:4, 11-12; 18:4, 8; 19:9. Only some were "stubborn and disbelieved" [Acts 28:24]).

The normal result of Paul's preaching was a split among the Jews: some believed, some not. The sometimes violent measures taken by the latter are proof that they considered Paul a real threat to their community. It was only after this split had been established that Paul turned to address the Gentiles (Acts 13:46-49; 18:6; 28:28). It is important to grasp the exact meaning of this "turning to the Gentiles." It seems to mean that Paul left the synagogue and ceased to address the synagogue community as such. But it does not mean that he was no longer willing to proclaim the gospel to the Jews. Acts 19:8-10 shows he still did preach to Jews, and it is very likely that Jews are included in Acts 18:11 and 28:30.

Next, it is important to notice what kind of Gentiles Paul was addressing. Acts is very clear on this point: they were not just any Gentiles, but "God-fearers," that is, Gentiles who believed in the God of Israel, lived according to the moral precepts of the Torah and visited the synagogue.[17] Very often they are mentioned as being present in the synagogue while Paul was still primarily

---

[15]This seems to me a more natural interpretation of these passages than Jervell's assertion that in these texts Paul flatly contradicted or ignored the decree, *Apostelgeschichte*, p. 406.

[16]Some scholars find difficulties with this because the Paul of the letters seems to understand his mission as being to the Gentiles exclusively. But this may be a simplistic reading of the letters. It is obvious from Romans 9—11 that the mission to Israel was not something Paul had put behind himself once and for all, and the type of Gentiles that made up the communities Paul founded clearly speak in favor of the picture in Acts (see below).

[17]Cf. the bibliography on the God-fearers listed in the Suggestions and notes 28-29 in chapter three above. A special Acts-related study of the Diaspora synagogues and their God-fearers is Levinskaya, *Book of Acts in Its First Century Setting*, vol. 5, *The Book of Acts in Its Diaspora Setting*, pp. 51-126.

addressing the Jewish community. In Acts 13:16 Paul even makes special mention of this group in his opening address in the synagogue of Antioch in Pisidia: "You Israelites, and others who fear God, listen." The same double address appears again in Acts 13:26. It is this group of God-fearing Gentiles that is mentioned in 13:48 as having gladly received the gospel. In several instances, many God-fearing Gentiles are part of the synagogue audience and come to believe before Paul leaves their congregation (Acts 14:1; 17:4, 12; 18:4). "Turning to the Gentiles" does not therefore indicate a radical change in missionary procedure. It does not mean that Paul began to address an entirely new audience. It only means that, from now on, he focused on the God-fearers and established himself somewhere else than in the synagogue for the rest of his stay in that city.

The story in Acts 18:5-11 carries a great deal of symbolic significance: having been rejected in the synagogue of Corinth, Paul "went to the house of a man named Titius Justus, a worshipper of God; his house was next door to the synagogue" (Acts 18:7). Luke adds that Paul stayed there for one and a half years.

It is a remarkable fact that almost all Gentile converts whose names are given in Acts belong to this category of God-fearing Gentiles. Cornelius was "a devout man who . . . prayed constantly to God" (Acts 10:2). He even observed the Jewish hours of prayer (Acts 10:3, 30). The proconsul Sergius Paulus kept company with a Jewish prophet and was eager to hear the word of God (Acts 13:6-12). Lydia was "a worshipper of God" (Acts 16:14). We have already met Titius Justus (Acts 18:7).

Only twice in the whole of Acts does Paul address Gentiles who do not belong to the God-fearers. The first time is in Acts 14:8-18, where Paul is forced to address the Gentile crowd to prevent them from sacrificing to Barnabas and himself, and the whole of his speech is concerned with preventing this. He does not proclaim the gospel to this crowd of "raw" Gentiles! The second time is in Athens (Acts 17:16-34). Here Paul seems to have widened his outreach to include philosophically educated Greeks, many of whom were no doubt theoretical monotheists who would agree with Paul's polemic against temples and idols in Acts 17:22-31. But once again we see that the speech on the Areopagus was not given on Paul's initiative: "they took him and brought him to the Areopagus and asked him, 'May we know what this new teaching is that you are presenting?'" (Acts 17:19).[18]

---

[18]On Paul's Areopagus speech, see Bertil Gärtner, *The Areopagus Speech and Natural Revelation*, Acta Seminarii Neotestamentici Upsaliensis 21 (Uppsala: 1955); Karl Olav Sandnes, "Paul and Socrates: The Aim of Paul's Areopagus Speech," *Journal for the Study of the New Testament* 50 (1993): 13-26. We will return to the theme in chapter twelve.

Thus we find that the two apparent exceptions to the rule stated above substantiate rather than contradict it. What does this mean? It means that viewed from the outside, from the standpoint of the Roman authorities or the average person on the street, Paul's mission to the Gentiles was still an essentially Jewish affair, affecting mainly the Jewish community. The Gentile God-fearers among whom Paul found such a receptive hearing for his message were probably regarded as half-Jews by their Gentile neighbors, and their new faith in a Jewish Messiah would hardly be noticed were it not for the fact that some of them began to witness in a new way. In any case, this mission among the God-fearers would still be regarded as a mainly intra-Jewish affair. That is why we so seldom hear of persecutions initiated by Gentiles in Acts. In the only two cases in which Paul is attacked by Gentiles, he is treated as a Jew, and in both cases the reason is that they felt that their income from pagan businesses was threatened (Acts 16:16-23; 19:23-41). In the last instance, it is interesting to note that the Gentile rage against Paul seems to make no distinction between Jesus-believers and other Jews; they directed their campaign against Jewish preaching in general (cf. vv. 33-34). In all other instances, the persecution was instigated by Jews who were jealous of Paul's success among the God-fearers (see Acts 13:50-51; 14:2-6, 19; 17:5-9, 13; 18:12-17).

What about the keeping of the commandments by Jewish believers? The final accusation made against Paul by those in the Jerusalem community who were still skeptical of him does not even mention his mission to the Gentiles. His accusers are concerned with what he has been teaching *Jews* throughout the Diaspora. James tells Paul:

> You see, brother, how many thousands of believers there are among the Jews, and they are all zealous for the law. They have been told about you that you teach all the Jews living among the Gentiles to forsake Moses, and that you tell them not to circumcise their children or observe the customs. (Acts 21:20-21)

According to Acts, these are false accusations. Paul taught no such thing. There is no evidence in Paul's letters to indicate that Luke portrays Paul as being more Jewish than he really was. The author of Romans 9:4-5 and 11:1-6, to mention just two relevant passages, could not possibly have told believing Jews to stop being Jews (see also 1 Cor 7:18 and 9:20).

What Paul had to say against observance of the law concerns Gentile believers, but is based on assumptions that are true for Jewish believers as well. Here his opposition was consistent and vehement, for the only good reason to impose circumcision and the law on Gentiles would be that salvation came from the law, and in that case "Christ died for nothing" (Gal 2:21). In his insistent emphasis that the source of salvation is Christ's death and resurrection—and not the law—Paul was in basic agreement with the leaders of the Jerusalem community.

But—like the Jerusalem community—Paul recognized the law as a national prerogative of Israel. It is highly significant that in his final defense before the Jewish leaders in Rome, Paul emphasized that he had never spoken or acted "against our people or the customs of our ancestors," that is, the halakah (Acts 28:17). This connection between Jewish nationality and law observance is highly significant (cf. above on the position of the Jerusalem community).

What, then, can we learn from the book of Acts about Paul's mission? We meet a very Jewish Paul, who conducted his mission almost entirely within the bounds of the synagogue and the circle of God-fearing Gentiles attached to it. This was fundamental to Paul's understanding of himself as a missionary. Romans 11:13-14 clearly shows the historical accuracy of the picture of Paul in Acts: in his mission to the Gentiles, Paul never went far from the synagogue.

The fact that occasionally people outside the circle of Gentile God-fearers were attracted and came to faith does not, of course, contradict the above picture of Paul's missionary strategy (there is evidence of this in Acts 19:17-20). In his letters Paul sometimes addresses the Gentile believers as if they had been full-fledged Gentiles (Eph 2:1-3; 4:17-24; but this is one of his last letters, when the gospel had already been preached by many others). In his letters to the Corinthians, it is evident that some of the believers were from a Gentile background.

Furthermore, another feature of Paul's letters clearly substantiates Luke's evidence. In his main letters—those to Galatia, Corinth and Rome—Paul clearly presupposes that his readers are not only familiar with the Old Testament, but also with the rabbinic methods of arguing a point from a given text. Considering the short interval between the establishment of the congregations and Paul's writing to them, this cannot be explained by Paul's own teaching or that of other teachers. In later days, when the influx of real Gentiles became greater, Paul's letters were considered "hard to understand" (2 Pet 3:16). No wonder! Paul wrote to converted Jews and God-fearers, and they were equipped to understand him.

Before we leave the evidence in Acts, it remains to say a few words on the situation of the converted Gentile God-fearers and their Jewish brethren. One can easily suggest a simple reason for Paul's success among the God-fearers. They were attracted to Judaism and would gladly become members of the people of God, but two obstacles held them back: circumcision (which for adults was a painful and dangerous operation) and the cumbersome ritual observances concerning food, etc. It would seem that Paul offered all of the rewards with none of the cost: as Christians they received full citizenship in Israel (Eph 2:11-22) without circumcision or ritual observance.

In other words, was Paul's success due to ulterior motives among the God-fearers? Were they simply opportunists choosing the easier way? That may have been a real danger in Paul's mission, and part of the reason that so many of his congregations caused him so much worry and trouble. But one should not forget the other side of the coin. As we saw in chapter three, the legal position of Gentile converts to Christianity was utterly precarious, once the Romans and the populace took notice of them. The convert to Judaism joined a *religio licita* and had the protection of the imperial decrees. The Gentile converts to Christianity were in a legal no man's land and became the victims of arbitrary persecution.

In the middle of the second century the Gentile convert Justin—who was later to prove his faith with martyrdom—implicitly answers an accusation of opportunism:

> If we endure all that men and evil demons work out for us to bear, so that even in the extremity of pains too great to tell, and death and punishments, we pray that even they who ordered us such sufferings may obtain mercy, . . . how should we not also, Trypho, be able to keep those (lesser) things that hurt us not at all, namely circumcision of the flesh and Sabbaths and the festivals? (*Dialogue with Trypho* 18.3)

In their willingness to accept persecution and martyrdom, the Gentile converts were equal to their Jewish brethren, and much more exposed. They would not have had this readiness for martyrdom had not the gospel gripped their hearts and determined their lives.

The Reaction of the Roman Authorities

We have emphasized repeatedly that in general the Roman populace and authorities took little notice of the Gentile mission in the first century. There were some exceptions to this rule, however, in cities in which the community was of some size and significance. Such was the case in Antioch. Here the populace seems to have noticed that converts to Christianity did not become ordinary Jews—and they were always speaking of their founder as *Christos,* "the anointed one." So the Antiochenes put the somewhat derogatory label *Christianoi,* "the Christ-sect," on these Gentile converts.

It was several years later that the Gentile believers began to apply this designation to themselves; the Jewish believers never adopted it, nor were they called Christians by their adversaries among the Jews. In Acts 24:5 Paul is called "a ringleader of the sect of the Nazarenes." Notice, by the way, that Paul is depicted here as a leader of the Jewish believers! "Nazarenes" later became a common designation of Jewish believers, but to that we shall return in a later chapter.

Another city in which the Christians soon made themselves noticed by the populace was Rome itself. To begin with, however, the controversy over the new faith was seen as an entirely intra-Jewish affair. The Roman historian Suetonius writes about an action taken by the Emperor Claudius in A.D. 49: "He expelled the Jews from Rome, on account of the riots in which they were constantly indulging, at the instigation of Chrestus." It is commonly supposed that Suetonius is a little misinformed, and that the real reasons for the unrest among the Jews were intense discussions, and perhaps internal persecutions, over the question of Christus, the Messiah (this expulsion of the Jews from Rome is probably alluded to in Acts 18:2).[19]

But in A.D. 64 the populace of Rome and the Emperor Nero seem to have been better informed. The Christians were probably still considered a Jewish sect, but not an ordinary one. The Roman historian Tacitus tells how Nero tried to dispel suspicions of his being the cause of Rome's fire by blaming "the Christians." Tacitus's report eloquently brings out how detested and dangerous the label "Christian" was:

> To get rid of the report [of arson], Nero fastened the guilt and inflicted the most exquisite tortures on a class hated for their abominations, called Christians by the populace. Christus from whom the name had its origin, suffered the extreme penalty during the reign of Tiberius at the hands of one of our procurators, Pontius Pilate, and a most mischievous superstition thus checked for the moment, again broke out not only in Judaea, the first source of the evil, but even in Rome, where all things hideous and shameful from every part of the world find their center and become popular. Accordingly, an arrest was first made of all who

[19]See Helga Botermann, *Das Judenedikt des Kaisers Claudius: Römischer Staat und Christiani im 1. Jahrhundert,* Hermes, Einzelschriften 71 (Stuttgart: Steiner Verlag, 1996).

Temple Square
Many times the prophets said that in the end time the (Gentile) peoples will take part in the temple service. The "wall of separation" (Eph 2:15), the fence around the inner sanctuary in the Jerusalem temple, beyond which Gentiles were not allowed to enter, signified by its very existence that this was not the end-time temple, the final temple.

In other words, in the end time the Gentiles would become holy and pure and fully qualified to enter within the most sacred part of the sanctuary. One might think, on the basis of first-century A.D. Judaism, that this would come about by all the Gentiles becoming Jews through the ritual of conversion. But the early believers, and James among them, found otherwise. They found that the prophets, when speaking about the Gentiles and their participation in end-time salvation, were speaking about them *as (still) Gentiles*. They would and should not become Jews. And that meant they were not supposed to observe the Torah given to Israel by God. They were pure and holy without the Torah, without "works of the law." God would be "cleansing their hearts by faith" (Peter in Acts 15:9). As Gentiles, they were the equal of Jews by birth as priests of the new temple.

In a way, this thoroughly relativized Jewish identity. In another way, it did not. Through the apostolic decree Gentile believers were put under the purity regulations for resident aliens as contained in the Torah of Holiness in Lev 17–18. By entering the new temple through cleansing in water (baptism), by abstaining from meat sacrificed to idols in pagan temples, and by abstaining from "whatever has been strangled and from blood" (Acts 15:20), the Gentile believers were reminded that they now belonged to a community that was in origin a temple community. (The problem with consumption of animal blood was of course that God had reserved this blood to be the very means of atonement in the temple worship [Lev 17:10-11].)

---

pleaded guilty; then, upon their information, an immense multitude was convicted, not so much of the crime of firing the city, as of hatred against mankind. Mockery of every sort was added to their deaths. Covered with the skins of beasts, they were torn by dogs and perished, or were nailed to crosses, or were doomed to the flames and burnt, to serve as a nightly illumination when daylight had expired. Nero offered his gardens for the spectacle, and was exhibiting a show in the circus, while he mingled with the people in the dress of a charioteer or stood aloft in a car. Hence, even for criminals who deserve extreme punishment, there arose a feeling of compassion; for it was not, as it seemed, for the public good, but to glut one man's cruelty, that they were being destroyed. (Tacitus *Annals* 15.44)[20]

In this horrible story, the charge leveled against the Christians stands out: they were found to be "haters of mankind"—the classic anti-Jewish accusation. Yet the Christians obviously did not have the protection of belonging to a *religio licita*. They were not recognized as ordinary Jews.

It must be emphasized, however, that this Neronian persecution in Rome—terrible as it was—represented the exception rather than the rule con-

---

[20]Barrett, *Documents*, pp. 15-16.

cerning official Roman policy in the first century A.D. For the most part, Christians lived unnoticed by the authorities, and the isolated occurrences of persecution were caused by neighbors who took offense at their faith and reported them to the authorities.

With this we conclude our survey of the mission to the Gentiles prior to A.D. 70. It was seen by outsiders as a primarily intra-Jewish affair, which affected mainly the synagogue and those Gentiles affiliated with it.

Suggestions for Further Reading

Most of the entries listed in chapter seven are relevant for this chapter also. In addition, note the following (in chronological order):

Johannes Munck, *Paul and the Salvation of Mankind* (London: SCM Press, 1977).

Martin Hengel, *Between Jesus and Paul: Studies in the Earliest History of Christianity* (London: SCM Press, 1983).

Jacob Jervell, *The Unknown Paul: Essays on Luke-Acts and Early Christian History* (Minneapolis: Fortress, 1984).

Nicholas Taylor, *Paul, Antioch and Jerusalem: A Study in Relationships and Authority in Earliest Christianity,* Journal for the Study of the New Testament: Supplement Series 66 (Sheffield: Sheffield Academic Press, 1992).

Rainer Riesner, *Die Frühzeit des Apostels Paulus: Studien zur Chronologie, Missionsstrategie und Theologie,* Wissenschaftliche Untersuchungen zum Neuen Testament 71 (Tübingen: J. C. B. Mohr [Paul Siebeck], 1994). English trans.: *Paul's Early Period: Chronology, Mission Strategy, Theology* (Grand Rapids, Mich./Cambridge, U.K.: Eerdmans, 1998).

Jerome Murphy-O'Connor, *Paul: A Critical Life* (Oxford: Clarendon, 1996).

Martin Hengel and Anna Maria Schwemer, *Paul Between Damascus and Antioch: The Unknown Years* (London: SCM Press, 1997).

9

THE LAND OF ISRAEL
THE CHURCH OF
JEWISH BELIEVERS

*S*cholars have had great problems in agreeing on a definition of "Judeo-Chris-
*tians" or "Jewish Christians," and most present-day Jewish believers reject any name
for themselves which contains the word "Christian" at all. For them, "Christian"
means "Gentile" and "un-Jewish," so they prefer to call themselves "Messianic
Jews" or something similar. To call first- or second-century Jews who believed in
Jesus "Messianic Jews" would be grossly anachronistic, however. But we do need a
short term to refer to them, and since "Jewish believers [in Jesus]" is more or less
neutral, we use it here. It refers in this book to Jews (by birth or conversion) who came
to believe in Jesus as the Messiah of Israel.*

Internal Diversity
In the first few centuries A.D. the practice and doctrine of the Jewish believers,
like that of their Gentile brethren, varied widely. We must remember that this
term refers to a complex and multi-hued phenomenon. Jewish believers seem
to have had many degrees of keeping or not keeping a clear Jewish identity
by observing the commonly practiced halakah.[1] (This itself was by no means

---

[1]For literature discussing the different types of Judeo-Christianity, see the following:

uniform in all places or throughout our period.)

While keeping this in mind, we nevertheless still suggest that it would be fruitful to consider the early Jewish believers as falling into two main groups, based on which circumstances they lived under. For Jewish believers living in the land of Israel or the greater province of Roman Syria who spoke Aramaic (some perhaps Hebrew) as their first and everyday language, the practical possibility of keeping a Jewish identity and practicing a Jewish way of life would be good indeed. And when these Jewish believers formed local communities, quite small perhaps, they would probably tend to be almost exclusively made up of Jewish believers. Gentile Christian members would probably be rare, if only because of language. In these communities it is easy to imagine their Jewish observance as something communal, practiced by the community as such. The Jewish festivals would be a case in point.

In the Diaspora, on the other hand, one easily imagines a different scenario. Here we have mixed communities right from the beginning (based on the mixed synagogue attendance). Soon, or right from the start, the Jewish believers were the minority in such communities; after a while, a tiny minority. Under these circumstances, Jewish observance could hardly be a communal affair, it had to be individual, unless the few Jewish believers segregated themselves and formed their own group. (We have little if any evidence to determine whether this happened.) But if individual, Jewish observance was also difficult, and one may easily imagine a wide variety of individual solutions to the many dilemmas. For example, when and how to celebrate Passover? The apostolic council in Acts 15 and the decisions reached there prove

---

Johannes Munck, "Jewish Christianity in Post-Apostolic Times," *New Testament Studies* 6 (1959/1960): 103-16; Gilles Quispel, "The Discussion of Judaic Christianity," *Vigiliae Christianae* 22 (1968): 81-93; Robert Alan Kraft, "In Search of 'Jewish Christianity' and its 'Theology'. Problems of Definition and Methodology," *Recherches de science religieuse* 60 (1972): 81-92; A. F. J. Klijn, "The Study of Jewish Christianity," *New Testament Studies* 20 (1974): 419-31; Robert Murray, "Defining Judaeo-Christianity," *Heythrop Journal* 15 (1974): 303-10; Marcel Simon, "Réflexions sur le Judéo-Christianisme," in *Christianity, Judaism and other Greco-Roman Cults: Festschrift Morton Smith*, vol. 2 (Leiden: E. J. Brill, 1975), pp. 53-76; reprinted in idem, *Le Christianisme antique et son contexte religieux: Scripta Varia*, Wissenschaftliche Untersuchungen zum Neuen Testament 23 (Tübingen: J. C. B. Mohr, 1981), 2:598-621; Bruce J. Malina, "Jewish Christianity or Christian Judaism: Toward an Hypothetical Definition," *Journal for the Study of Judaism* 7 (1976): 46-57; S. K. Riegel, "Jewish Christianity: Definitions and Terminology," *New Testament Studies* 24 (1978): 410-15; Raymond E. Brown, "Not Jewish Christianity and Gentile Christianity but Types of Jewish/Gentile Christianity," *Catholic Biblical Quarterly* 45 (1983): 74-79; James F. Strange, "Diversity in Early Palestinian Christianity," *Anglican Theological Review* 65 (1983): 14-24; Joan E. Taylor, "The Phenomenon of Early Jewish-Christianity: Reality or Scholarly Invention?" *Vigiliae Christianae* 44 (1990): 313-34.

that Jewish-Gentile coexistence was not necessarily easy, and it required concessions and adaptation from both sides.

I would suggest that this distinction between two types of Jewish Christian life—one communal in the land of Israel and the Semitic-speaking Jewish colonies in Syria; one individual in the rest of the Diaspora—is fruitful when it comes to tracing the history and influence of the early Jewish believers.

As the years passed, the Jewish believers of the Diaspora became a smaller and smaller minority in the rapidly growing church, and it probably became harder for them to keep their Jewish identity. Some managed to do so against the odds, and as we will see in the next chapter they would leave a lasting mark on the church as a whole. These Jews, who were members of largely Gentile communities, were for the most part forgotten or ignored by church historians.

On the other hand, most of the churches in Israel/Syria remained completely Jewish (especially those where Aramaic or Hebrew was spoken), a fact that influenced the continued observance of Jewish customs. These traditions and ceremonies—circumcision or a kosher meal, for example—were community events, a virtual impossibility in mixed congregations. Evidence from the fourth and fifth centuries suggests that this was still the situation in the land of Israel and its environs.[2] There were Jewish Christian communities, not just individual Jewish believers scattered among the general population. This chapter will focus on these Jewish Christian communities in Israel.

The Sources

Our source material concerning the Jewish believers is not as rich and explicit as we could have wished. We know that they wrote books; but unfortunately only sparse fragments of them have been preserved, mostly in the works of Epiphanius of Salamis and Jerome.[3]

It may be, however, that some of the earliest Christian writings known as the Apostolic Fathers[4] were written by Jewish believers.[5] If so, they were defi-

---

[2]See, first and foremost, Ray A. Pritz, *Nazarene Jewish Christianity: From the End of the New Testament Period Until Its Disappearance in the Fourth Century*, Studia post-biblica 37 (Leiden: E. J. Brill/Jerusalem: Magnes, 1988).

[3]See Pritz, 1988.

[4]The Apostolic Fathers were defined as a group of writings only in 1672 by the editor J. B. Cotelier. He thought they were all the work of personal disciples of the apostles. Today this group is defined more loosely as the first generation of Christian writers after the New Testament period, who did not write in the format of pseudo-apostolic gospels, acts or apocalypses (the latter group is usually classified among the New Testament Apocrypha, which is also a very loosely defined group). See the separate text box on the Apostolic Fathers at the end of chapter 10.

[5]The strongest candidates are *1 Clement*, the *Didache* and *The Shepherd of Hermas*. None of

Box 9.1. The Ambiguity of Archaeological Evidence: The Sign of the Cross

On several "ossuaries" (some found in the grounds of Dominus Flevit on the Mount of Olives, others in Talpiot and other locations) one discerns crosses.[6] (An ossuary is a small stone coffin or box for reburial of bones. They were used by Jews in the period ca. 400 B.C.-A.D. 135.) Are these crosses Christian symbols? The Franciscan fathers think yes. The well-known archaeologist Jack Finegan supports this position with the following argument:[7] the early Christian cross symbol is rooted in the Hebrew tav (+) symbolism. He demonstrates that the + (cross) mark is used in the margin of some Qumran scrolls to indicate passages about the Messiah or the messianic age. He points to the fact that although the + was a Jewish symbol, it was never previously used as a burial symbol in the Jewish tradition. Thus he supports the Franciscan view that the ossuary crosses are messianic symbols of Jewish Christian origin.

Others argue that the letter tav could be a Jewish symbol, recalling Ezekiel 9:3-11.

Still others are not convinced that the crosses are symbols at all. They may be "artisan signs intended to indicate matching places, between lid and receptacle, and conveying the simple meaning 'this is the spot.'"[8] Others, again, take these "crosses" as examples of the rosettes that occur on almost all Jewish ossuaries.[9]

Thus, until archaeologists develop greater certainty about assigning archaeological remains to Jewish believers rather than Jews in general, we have to view archaeological evidence of this kind with caution.

nitely living in mixed congregations and made no point of stressing their Jewish identity. That may be part of the reason it is so hard to know with certainty whether or not they were Jewish believers. The same holds true for a few other Christian writings from the pre-Constantinian period that scholars suspect may be written by Jewish believers.

The writings of the (Gentile) church fathers make some references to Jewish believers and, in some cases, extensive reports on their beliefs and practices. The richest source material stems from the period after the second and third centuries. Nevertheless, even from the second and third centuries we can get valuable glimpses that reveal much if we learn to read them properly.[10]

There is a considerable amount of literary evidence on Jewish believers in Jewish sources, especially the rabbinic literature. This evidence is of course

---

these, however, though rich in Jewish tradition, can be proved conclusively to have been written by Jewish believers.
[6]See the most recent survey and discussion in Sanders, *Schismatics*, pp. 30-37.
[7]See his highly interesting chapter on the history of the cross mark in Jack Finegan, *The Archaeology of the New Testament: The Life of Jesus and the Beginning of the Early Church* (Princeton: Princeton University Press, 1969), pp. 220-60.
[8]Meyers/Strange, *Archaeology*, p. 104.
[9]For this interpretation, see esp. Sanders, *Schismatics*, pp. 30-37.
[10]Cf. the excellent review in Pritz, *Nazarene Jewish Christianity*, pp. 19-28.

polemic in character, but that does not detract from its value and interest. It is often difficult, however, to know for sure whether the heretics described in the rabbinic texts were Jewish believers, Gentile Christians or other deviants.

Finally, there is the forthcoming archaeological evidence. This source, however, is the most difficult to interpret, and for obvious reasons. For each text, each inscription, each pictorial symbol claimed to be derived from Jewish believers, the following two questions must always be asked—and often left unanswered: could it be Jewish rather than Jewish Christian? Conversely, could it be simply Christian and not specifically Jewish Christian?[11] A third alternative is that signs supposed to be symbols are really not symbols at all.

Jewish Believers in the Land of Israel (I): The Archaeology of Holy Places
Jerusalem: The Holy Sepulchre
When Hadrian converted Jerusalem into Aelia Capitolina in the latter half of the 130s, he laid out a Roman forum in what is now the Muristan Quarter of the Old City. In the days of Jesus this area was just outside the city walls; in fact it was situated in the corner between the walls called the first and second by Josephus. In Old Testament times the area had been a quarry; in its center a piece of rock of poorer quality had been left intact, like a hill in the middle of the quarry. In the walls of the quarry there were rock-cut tombs, some of which were in use at the time of Jesus. The quarry itself was by then overgrown with grass and plants, and may have looked like a garden. The place was very near a gate in the corner between the first and second wall, the so-called Gennath gate (possibly found by N. Avigad during recent excavations in the Jewish Quarter). Very soon after Jesus' death, in A.D. 44, King Agrippa I began building a new city wall (the so-called third), which enclosed this garden, the hill and the tombs within the city. Then Hadrian placed his forum here, as mentioned above. He covered over the entire area with an enormous fill of earth and sand, and at the north end of his forum, on top of the hill, he raised an even higher platform as the base for a Roman temple dedicated to Jupiter.

All of this is considered uncontestable historical fact, proved by archaeological and literary evidence. It is also uncontestable fact that Constantine in the late 320s gave orders that Hadrian's temple was to be torn down and the platform fill removed. When this was done, the hill and the tomb(s) re-emerged into daylight, and were believed to be the tomb of Jesus and the rock of Calvary. Over

---

[11]The otherwise stimulating books by the Franciscan fathers Bagatti, Testa and Mancini are not always sufficiently critical in their handling of these two questions.

these remains Constantine's architects erected two churches, the remains of which are in the present Church of the Holy Sepulchre in the Old City.

Now, were the Christians of Constantine's time correct in their identification of the hill and the tomb? That is the crucial question regarding the authenticity of the places within the present Church of the Holy Sepulchre. There seem to be two possibilities: (1) Constantine's architects simply wanted to demolish the pagan shrine of Hadrian, and had to remove its platform to make a more solid foundation for a church planned to go there. They and everybody else were surprised to find a hill and a tomb beneath Hadrian's temple, and concluded, without any foundation in older local traditions, that this must be Calvary and Jesus' tomb. In this case, they were not necessarily wrong, but would be right only by chance. We cannot know they were right. However, this scenario has one weak point: Why should they plan to build a large church in this place? Was it only to replace a pagan temple with something both bigger and Christian? In any case, why go to all the trouble of removing Hadrian's temple platform all the way down to bedrock—and over a more extensive area than needed even for the planned church (the so-called Martyrion)?

These questions make me opt for the other possibility: (2) Christians in Jerusalem already knew that Calvary and Jesus' tomb had been buried under Hadrian's shrine. That was why Constantine's architects launched their excavation project in the first place. They knew what they were digging for. There are several indications that local Christians knew the location of Calvary and the tomb at this place, and some of this evidence may point to Jewish believers. First, in Constantine's day, as in ours, the place is in the middle of the city, in clear contradiction to the New Testament record that Christ was crucified and buried outside the city. But this speaks in favor of the location's authenticity: if anyone at a later time freely should invent the place of Jesus' death, he would choose a place outside the city of his own time, that is, outside Agrippa's third wall and outside Hadrian's Aelia. In the 150s or 160s A.D. Melito of Sardis visited the Holy Land. Afterwards he wrote in his Paschal homily that Christ was crucified "in the middle" of Jerusalem. It contradicts the New Testament, but it agrees perfectly with the location of Hadrian's temple within Aelia Capitolina! Most likely, local Christians had pointed out precisely this place to Melito.[12]

---

[12]Joan Taylor's argument that Melito's words ("in the middle of the *plateia*") would rather indicate a place in the middle of Hadrian's forum, south of the present Holy Sepulchre,

But who were these Christians? Possibly they were Gentile, because in A.D. 135 Hadrian had expelled all Jews from Jerusalem (there is no evidence to suggest he made an exception for Jews believing in Jesus). On the other hand, Hadrian's decree may have been effectively enforced only for a short period; soon Jews would have silently filtered back into Jerusalem. Here we find an interesting piece of evidence in Origen's commentary on Matthew 27:33: "Concerning the place of the skull, it came to me that Hebrews hand down [the tradition that] the body of Adam has been buried there; in order that 'as in Adam all die' both Adam would be raised and 'in Christ all will be made alive' [1 Cor 15:22]."

In Jewish tradition the tomb of Adam was placed under the rock upon which the second temple was built. The tradition recorded by Origen should therefore be seen as a Jewish "temple" tradition transferred to Golgotha, which is now seen as the new temple rock. This tradition is attributed to "Hebrews" [=Jews] by Origen; they could hardly be other than Jewish believers.[13]

It is therefore probable that local Christians in Jerusalem knew the place of Jesus' death and burial prior to Hadrian's erecting the Aelia with its temples, and that there were Jewish believers among those Christians—certainly prior to A.D. 135, but possibly also afterwards. After Golgotha and the tomb came to be included within the city walls, as early as A.D. 41, we simply have to assume the local Jewish Christian community continued to keep the memory of the authentic place.[14]

Jerusalem: A Community Center on Mount Zion?
Present-day visitors to the so-called Mount Zion in Jerusalem are shown a two-story building, whose present form dates from the late crusade period, as the gothic pillars and arches show. On the ground floor tourists are shown "the tomb of David" in the northeastern corner; the upper floor is the "coenaculum," the "room of the [last] supper." The lower parts of the southern, eastern and northern walls of the building are made of massive Herodian

---

seems to me very weak, because it presses the text beyond any reasonable preciseness for a poetic preacher (Taylor, *Christians and Holy Places*, pp. 117-20).

[13]Again, Taylor's criticism of this line of reasoning seems to me unconvincing and partly artificial; (Taylor, *Christians and Holy Places*, pp. 124-27).

[14]For a recent and detailed argument concerning the possible authenticity of the location of the Holy Sepulchre, see Martin Biddle, *The Tomb of Christ* (Phoenix Mill, Stroud, Gloucestershire: Sutton Publishing, 1999), esp. pp. 53-65. The argument in John J. Rousseau and Rami Arav (*Jesus and His World: An Archaeological and Cultural Dictionary* [Minneapolis: Fortress, 1995], pp. 112-18) that the tomb in the Holy Sepulchre is too close to the temple to be authentic, seems strangely unaware of the Second Temple period tomb in the Syrian Orthodox chapel in the Holy Sepulchre.

stones in secondary use. Some unknown builders re-used these stones when building the structure sometime during the Roman or Byzantine periods. The crusaders found this building in ruins, but chose to use some of the ruined walls in their own building.

But what was the building found in ruins by the crusaders? According to the Jewish archaeologist Pinkerfeld it was in fact a Jewish synagogue built before the Byzantine period (= a pre-Constantinian building), since the original floor was lying 10 cm beneath an early Byzantine mosaic floor. It was a synagogue because a large niche in the north wall was oriented northwards—roughly toward the Temple Mount—and not eastwards, as it would have been in a church.[15] B. Bagatti accepted the latter argument and agreed it was a synagogue, not a church. He argued, however, that some of the graffiti found on fragments of plaster from the walls proved that the synagogue was Jewish Christian rather than simply Jewish.[16] The graffiti are not extensive and not easy to interpret; but Bargil Pixner has bolstered Bagatti's conclusion with a new argument: the niche in the north wall is in fact not oriented toward the Temple Mount, nor exactly north, but exactly toward the Holy Sepulchre. What better proof that this synagogue was not Jewish, but Jewish Christian! Pixner assumes that this building was erected soon after A.D. 70 when the early community of Jewish believers returned from Pella, and that this community was able to hang on to their small synagogue-church throughout the entire period until Byzantine times, when they were at last swallowed up by the Gentile church, and their synagogue building made an appendix to a great Byzantine church. Pixner further assumes that the Jewish Christian synagogue-church was erected in about A.D. 72 on the very spot of the upper room in which Jesus celebrated his last Passover meal (the first Holy Supper) with his disciples, and in which the apostles were assembled on the Day of Pentecost. This would then also be the first place of worship for the early community in Jerusalem.[17]

---

[15]J. Pinkerfeld, "David's Tomb: Notes on the History of the Building, Preliminary Report," *Bulletin of the Louis M. Rabinowitz Fund for the Exploration of Ancient Synagogues* 3 (1960) [Jerusalem]: 41-43; J. W. Hirschberg, "The Remains of an Ancient Synagogue on Mount Sion," in *Jerusalem Revealed: Archaeology in the Holy City 1968-1974*, ed. Yigael Yadin (Jerusalem: Israel Exploration Society, 1975), pp. 116-17.

[16]See his statement of the argument in Bagatti, *The Church from the Circumcision: History and Archaeology of the Judaeo-Christians*, Studium Biblicum Franciscanum, Collectio Minor 2 (Jerusalem: Franciscan Printing Press, 1971, reprint, 1984), pp. 118-22.

[17]Pixner has stated his theory a number of times: Bargil Pixner, "Church of the Apostles Found on Mt. Zion?" *Biblical Archaeological Review* 16, no. 3 (1990): 16-35, 60; "Church of the Apostles on Mt. Zion," *Mishkan* 13, no. 2 (1990): 27-42; "Die apostolische Synagoge auf dem Zion," in *Wege des Messias und Stätten der Urkirche: Jesus und das Judenchristentum im Licht neuer archäologischer Erkenntnisse* (Giessen/Basel: Brunnen Verlag, 1991), pp. 287-326.

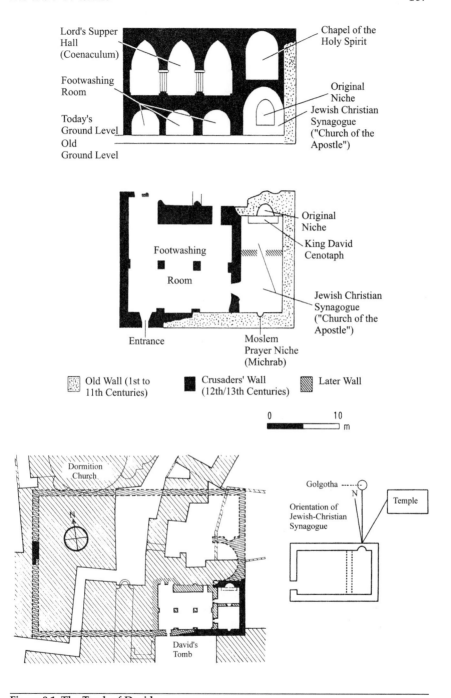

Figure 9.1. The Tomb of David

Pixner has combined and supported this theory with another.[18] He thinks that a gate found in the first wall on the west side of the Mount Zion hill is the "gate of the Essenes" mentioned by Josephus, and that therefore the "Essene quarter" in Jerusalem should be located inside this gate. The ritual baths found in this area provide additional evidence. They are very similar to those at Qumran. This means the Essene quarter and the Jewish believers' community center were very close neighbors on Mount Zion. This could explain Jesus' command to his disciples when he asked them to find a place for his Passover meal: follow a man carrying a pitcher of water. Why a man, when this was typical women's work? Because the man came from the Essene quarter, where Essenes lived like monks, without women, since sexual unions were not allowed in the city of the temple. This means that Jesus celebrated his last meal in the house of an Essene host, and Pixner finds additional evidence for this in the fact that, according to the Gospel of John, Jesus celebrated the Passover *before* the ordinary Jewish Passover night. That was because he followed the Essene calendar, by which Passover eve fell on Tuesday night.

This impressive chain of evidence has influenced many local guides and quite a few scholars to accept Pixner's theory, and to speak of Mount Zion as the quarter of the earliest Christian community and the "Tomb of David" building as the oldest Christian (Jewish Christian, that is) place of worship.[19] On closer inspection, however, each link in Pixner's argument is open to objection.

The existence of an Essene quarter inside the so-called Essene Gate is not a proven fact.[20] One cannot safely conclude such a quarter from simply the name of the gate, for gates were often named after what they led *out* to, not *in* to (as later, for example, the Damascus and Jaffa gates). It could be that Jeru-

───────────────────────────

[18]Cf. "Das Essenerquarter in Jerusalem und dessen Einfluss auf die Urkirche," *Das Heilige Land* 113 (1981): 3-14; "An Essene Quarter on Mount Zion?" in *Studia Hierosolymitana*, vol. 1: *Studi archeologici in onore di P. Bellarmino Bagatti*, Studium Biblicum Franciscanum, Collectio Maior 22 (Jerusalem: Franciscan Printing Press, 1976), pp. 245-85; "Das Essener-Quartier in Jerusalem" and "Essener-Viertel und Urgemeinde," in Pixner, *Wege des Messias,* pp. 180-207, 327-24; "Archäologische Beobachtungen zum Jerusalemer Essener-Viertel und zur Urgemeinde," in *Christen und Christliches in Qumran?* ed. Bernhard Mayer, Eichstätter Studien N. F. 32 (Regensburg: Verlag Friedrich Pustet, 1992), pp. 89-113.
[19]Cf., for example, Rainer Riesner, "Essener und Urkirche in Jerusalem," in Mayer, *Christen und Christliches in Qumran?* pp. 139-57.
[20]See esp. Benedikt Schwank, "Gab es zur Zeit der öffentlichen Tätigkeit Jesu Qumran-Essener in Jerusalem?" in Mayer, *Christen und Christliches in Qumran?* pp. 115-30; Taylor, *Christians and Holy Places,* pp. 207-20.

salemites left through this gate to go down the Hinnom and Kidron valleys to Qumran. The ritual baths with one or more dividing ledges on the steps are not found only on Mount Zion and in Qumran, but also in other rich neighborhoods in Jerusalem and elsewhere. The common denominator for all the baths seems to be *priestly* rather than Essene. And this relates to a weightier argument against Mount Zion as a good place for the Essenes: if anything is evident from recent archaeology, it is that the entire western hill, all the way from the southeastern corner of the Temple Mount and up to the crest of Mount Zion, was the quarter of the wealthy priestly aristocracy of Jerusalem.[21] Would the Essenes choose to live in the neighborhood of their deadly enemies?

The archaeology of the supposed "synagogue" is also problematic. The old wall on the southern side extends way beyond the natural limit on the building's western side, and there is no trace of a western wall at all, nor a trace of the necessary corners, if ever they existed. The niche in the northern wall is placed strangely out of center, and seems too big to serve as a place for Torah scrolls.[22] The walls are also too massive to be the walls of a building as small as the supposed synagogue. This and more has led several scholars to suppose that the Roman/Byzantine remains in the present building must have been part of something quite big, namely, a Byzantine basilica. From literary evidence we know that one was in fact built on Mount Zion, and it is depicted on the Madaba Map.[23] This basilica *may* have been built on a spot pointed out by old local tradition as the place of the first community, but it may also have

---

[21]Cf. esp. Magen Broshi, "Excavations in the House of Caiaphas, Mount Zion," in *Jerusalem Revealed*, ed. Yigael Yadin (Jerusalem: The Israel Exploration Society, 1975), pp. 57-60; Nahman Avigad, *Discovering Jerusalem* (Nashville: Thomas Nelson), pp. 64-204.

[22]The period envisaged by Pixner—the early 70s A.D.—may also be too early for a fixed niche for the Torah ark. It seems rather that the Torah was kept in movable arks even at a time later than this, before they were replaced by fixed installations inside the synagogue buildings. See Eric M. Meyers, "The Torah Shrine in the Ancient Synagogue: Another Look at the Evidence," in *Jews, Christians, and Polytheists in the Ancient Synagogue*, ed. Steven Fine (London/New York: Routledge, 1999); pp. 201-23; Lee I. Levine, *The Ancient Synagogue* (New Haven/London: Yale University Press, 2000), pp. 328-31.

[23]For the theory that the Tomb of David building represents the ruined southeastern corner of the Byzantine Hagia Sion, see Wilkinson, *Jerusalem*, pp. 169-70; Jerome Murphy-O'Connor, *The Holy Land: An Oxford Archaeological Guide from Earliest Times to 1700*, 4th ed. (Oxford: Oxford University Press, 1998), p. 106; and Taylor, *Christians and Holy Places*, pp. 215-19. The main objection to taking the old walls as belonging to a Byzantine building is the original floor beneath the Byzantine one. But as Taylor rightly says, two floors on top of each other are not unusual in Byzantine buildings and churches—both of them being Byzantine. Another possibility is that an earlier building was more or less razed, and the Byzantine Hagia Sion erected on top of it (so Murphy-O'Connor).

been attached to the church secondarily.[24] Jerome Murphy-O'Connor has recently made a good case for the view that literary evidence may prove the existence of a Christian community center in this area prior to the Byzantine buildings.[25] The Pilgrim of Bordeaux (A.D. 333) and Epiphanius (A.D. 394) both speak of a synagogue remaining on Mount Zion until Byzantine times, the only one remaining of an original seven. It may be the same building Epiphanius refers to as "a little church of God," and it may well be that this was in fact the assembly house of the Christian community of Jerusalem in pre-Byzantine times. If so, the place was very difficult to reach in the period of Aelia Capitolina (135-325) because the tenth Roman Legion was stationed between the residential areas north in the city and the southern part of Mount Zion. This would indicate that the Christians had strong reasons to hold on to this location of their place of assembly. Epiphanius gives the following reason: the "little church of God" was on the place "where the disciples went to the upper room on their return from the Mount of Olives after the Ascension of the Redeemer [Acts 1:13]."[26] It speaks for the authenticity of this tradition that Epiphanius does not mention any very glorious event as the reason for the location, such as the Last Supper or the Day of Pentecost, but quite simply that this was the place of assembly for the primitive community, and continued to be so until Byzantine times. Epiphanius was born in the land of Israel in 315 in present-day Bet Guvrin; he had certainly visited Jerusalem several times and should have been well informed.

This leaves us with the possibility that there was a small house of assembly on Mount Zion on the grounds of the present-day Tomb of David/Coenaculum building, and that this house was either destroyed when the first Byzantine church was built on the spot (before 348, when Cyril of Jerusalem refers to it), or perhaps incorporated into the Byzantine Church. Only further archaeological investigations can shed more light on this issue.

It speaks for the authenticity of Epiphanius's rather modest report on the "small church" being the assembly place of the first community that the place was identified as the scene of the Pentecost event only after the building of

---

[24]The latter is the argument of Taylor, op. cit., pp. 218-19.
[25]See his interesting article "The Cenacle: Topographical Setting for Acts 2:44-45," in *The Book of Acts in Its Palestinian Setting*, ed. Richard Bauckham (*The Book of Acts in Its First Century Setting*, vol. 4 [Grand Rapids, Mich.: Eerdmans/Carlisle: Paternoster, 1995]), pp. 303-21. Murphy-O'Connor also accepts Pinkerfeld's conclusion that the original floor of the present Tomb of David building is pre-Byzantine, probably from the second century.
[26]Epiphanius, *De mensuris et ponderibus* 14; quoted here according to Murphy-O'Connor, "Cenacle," p. 307.

the first Byzantine basilica, and further identified with the location of the Last Supper only in the fifth century.[27]

If this location is authentic, it allows us to see the early community assembling in a rich man's or woman's spacious villa on Mount Zion. The whole question of a continuous presence of Jewish believers in Jerusalem through the two wars and after will be treated below.

Capernaum: The House of Peter?

If you visit Capernaum, you will be shown "the House of Peter." The justification for this rather immodest claim runs as follows: excavators have found three building phases on this spot. The latest is an octagonal church built sometime during the latter half of the fifth century. In the center of this church there was a large room that seems to have originally belonged to a private house built during the first century B.C. During the fourth century this room was expanded and turned into a church. As such it was seen and described by Egeria on her visit in the 380s.

Obviously the builders of the church considered this room a holy place. They were probably not the first to do so, because the room seems to have been previously redecorated and equipped with more solid floors than usual in private homes in this poor area of the city.[28] Common sense arguments (which house in Capernaum would most likely be chosen by the first Christians of that city as their house of worship?) point to the possibility that this room was the house mentioned in Mark 1:29-34 and 2:1-12 (see also the reference in Mt 9:1 to Capernaum as Jesus' "own town"). So perhaps this is the house used by the earliest Christian community of Capernaum as their place of meeting? No doubt this community was mainly Jewish. In the rabbinic writings we read of *minim* living in Capernaum, and when *minim* refers to Christians, as it probably does in this case, it most often refers to Jewish believers.

Nazareth

Another glimpse of a community of Jewish believers may be provided by the

---

[27]Cf. Murphy-O'Connor, "Cenacle," p. 318.

[28]For archaeological details, see Meyers/Strange, *Archaeology*, pp. 59-60, 114-16, 128-30; Sanders, *Schismatics*, pp. 37-39, 70-74; cf. also the critique of the Franciscan interpretations of the archaeological evidence in Joan E. Taylor, "Capernaum and its 'Jewish-Christians': A Re-examination of the Franciscan Excavations," in *Bulletin of the Anglo-Israel Archaeological Society* 9 (1989-1990): 7-28; idem, *Christians and Holy Places*, pp. 268-94.

archaeological finds beneath the Churches of the Annunciation and of St. Joseph in Nazareth. Among the most interesting finds are some caves in the bedrock beneath the churches. The Franciscan archaeologists take graffiti on the repeatedly plastered walls to indicate that these caves had been the object of Christian pilgrimages from the third century. They also claim to have found, in the nave of the Church of the Annunciation, the remains of a synagogue which was later rebuilt as a church. Christian graffiti were found on the walls of the synagogue, which may indicate that it belonged to a Jewish Christian community. Another possible interpretation is that the synagogue was Jewish, but that Christian visitors were allowed to enter it, or that the graffiti are all Byzantine.[29] It must be said, therefore, that the archaeological evidence for a pre-Constantinian Jewish believers' community in Nazareth is quite ambiguous, and it seems wise to confess ignorance with the present state of affairs.[30]

Jewish Believers in the Land of Israel (II): Literary Evidence
The Relatives of Jesus
The possibility of a Jewish Christian community in Nazareth brings us to the New Testament traditions about the believing relatives of Jesus.[31] Apart from the New Testament evidence—which is richer than often assumed—we have in Eusebius fragments of two writers, both of them possibly Jewish believers themselves, who report on Jesus' relatives: Hegesippus and Julius Africanus. Eusebius himself also adds some material without indicating his sources.

1. We have already quoted Hegesippus's account of the martyrdom of James, the brother of Jesus. In addition, he tells a most moving story concerning some relatives of Jesus arrested by Domitian. The emperor seems to have conducted a hunt for descendants of David among the Jews, presumably

---

[29]On the archaeological evidence, see Meyers/Strange, *Archaeology*, pp. 130-37; and Sanders, *Schismatics*, pp. 74-78.
[30]See, e.g., the criticism of the Franciscans by Taylor, *Christians and Holy Places*, pp. 221-67. She presents a good argument for the view that the basins identified as Judeo-Christian *mikvehs* by Bagatti were in reality collecting basins for wine: the whole area beneath the Church of the Annunciation and the Church of St. Joseph seems to have been filled with installations for wine and olive processing. I have not deemed it necessary to include in this brief discussion of Judeo-Christian archaeology the complex issue of the interpretation of "symbols" in graffiti and stone structures. Emanuele Testa has developed an interpretation of such "symbols" as well as inscriptions, and takes a lot of such material to derive from Judeo-Christians. He also maps a specific Judeo-Christian theology on this basis. His whole construction, however, is extremely speculative, and can sometimes be shown to depend on simple misreading of the evidence.
[31]The book with which to start on this theme is now Richard Bauckham, *Jude and the Relatives of Jesus in the Early Church* (Edinburgh: T & T Clark, 1990).

because he saw them as politically dangerous, as they might produce messianic candidates. Two grandsons of Jesus' brother Jude were arrested. They said that they were just ordinary peasants, and they showed their hard, callused hands as proof that they spoke the truth.

> And when they were asked concerning Christ and His Kingdom, of what sort it was and where and when it was to appear, they answered that it was not a temporal nor an earthly kingdom, but a heavenly and angelic one, which would appear at the end of the world, when he should come in glory to judge the living and the dead, and to give unto everyone according to his works. (*Ecclesiastical History* 3.20.4)

Upon this answer, they were released as innocent, and afterward "they ruled the churches, inasmuch as they were both martyrs and of the Lord's family; and, when peace was established, remained alive until Trajan" (*Ecclesiastical History* 3.20.6).

2. Apart from this, we also meet Jesus' relatives as church leaders and travelling missionaries in some other scraps of information in Hegesippus and others. Paul speaks in 1 Corinthians 9:5 about the rights of a traveling apostle, rights that were used by "the other apostles and the brothers of the Lord and Cephas." Some 170-80 years later Julius Africanus said that Herod, being a non-Jew, had all Jewish family records burned so that no one should have an advantage on him, yet

> a few careful people had private records of their own, . . . priding themselves on preserving the memory of their noble birth. Of such were the persons mentioned above, called *Desposyni* [Relatives of the Lord] from their connexion with the Saviour's family. Coming from the Jewish villages of Nazareth and Cochaba, they travelled over the rest of the land, explaining the aforesaid genealogy, as far as they could trace it, and from the Book of the Days [= Chronicles]. (*Ecclesiastical History* 1.1.14)[32]

Africanus's concern in context is to explain the differences between the genealogies of Jesus in Matthew and Luke; this explains why he makes it sound as if the main contents of the preaching of the relatives of Jesus was their genealogy. The tradition on which he depends, however, could contain correct historical information: in proclaiming Jesus as the Messiah, his relatives emphasized his (and their) Davidic descent. That this was an important element in the earliest version of the Christian message is witnessed to by

---

[32]Lawlor/Oulton 1:21. In commenting on this passage, I am leaning heavily on the fascinating treatment in Bauckham, *Relatives of Jesus*, pp. 61-69.

Paul in Romans 1:3-4, where he quotes an old Jewish-Christian kerygmatic formula.[33]

These wandering missionaries of our Lord's family are said to have preached in the land of Israel and lived in the villages of Nazareth and Cochaba. The latter is very likely modern Kaukab, sixteen kilometers north of Nazareth. It is interesting that Jesus' relatives lived in two villages having "messianic" names: Nazareth = "little *nezer*" (Is 11:1); Cochaba = "the star" (Num 24:17: a star shall rise from Jacob). Bargil Pixner speculates that Jesus' ancestors, when they immigrated to Galilee sometime during the first century B.C., may have given their villages these names because of a strong consciousness of belonging to the messianic/Davidic line. However that may be (perhaps the other way round: they settled in these villages because of the messianic names the villages already had), it is hard to believe that Jesus' larger family was located in these two villages entirely by accident.

3. If we return to Jerusalem, after this glimpse from Galilee, Hegesippus and Eusebius both have interesting information on the leadership of the Jerusalem community after the death of James, Jesus' brother. Obviously James had risen to be the effective leader of the Jerusalem community at the time of his death by martyrdom in A.D. 62, probably because the Twelve were either dead or often away on missionary journeys. Who should replace the Lord's brother as head and leader of the Jerusalem community?

> After the martyrdom of James . . . it is recorded that those apostles and disciples of the Lord who were still surviving met together from all quarters and, together with our Lord's relatives after the flesh (for the more part of them were still alive), took counsel, all in common, as to whom they should judge worthy to be the successor of James; and, what is more, that they all with one consent approved Symeon the son of Clopas, of whom also the book of the Gospels makes mention [Jn 19:25], as worthy of the throne of the community in that place. He was a cousin—at any rate so it is said—of the Saviour; for indeed Hegesippus relates that Clopas was Joseph's brother. (*Ecclesiastical History* 3.11)[34]

According to Hegesippus, Symeon proved himself worthy of the trust shown him: he is portrayed as a true *zaddiq*, reaching the maximum age allowed for humans (Gen 6:3), 120 years, and at that age he was martyred while still in his full powers:

---

[33]Bauckham, *Relatives*, chap. 7, makes an interesting case for the view that the genealogy in Luke actually derives from this preaching activity of Jesus' relatives, pp. 315-73.
[34]Lawlor/Oulton 1:78.

It has been handed down that [in the persecution under Trajan] Symeon, the son of Clopas, who, as we showed, was appointed second bishop of the church at Jerusalem, ended his life by martyrdom. . . . "Certain [Jewish Christian heretics] accused Simon the son of Clopas of being of the house of David and a Christian; and so he was martyred at the age of a hundred and twenty years, when Trajan was Caesar and Atticus consularis" [= quote from Hegesippus]. . . . When he had been tortured in various ways and for very many days for being a Christian, and had filled the judge himself and his attendants with the greatest amazement, he was at last awarded an end similar to that which the Lord suffered. (*Ecclesiastical History* 3.32.1-3)[35]

The context in which Hegesippus has placed these scraps of evidence on the life and death of Symeon is interesting also in our context: he considers Symeon a pillar of orthodoxy. It was only after his death that heretics dared to come out into the open. While in Hegesippus this picture of orthodoxy/heresy is stereotypical, nevertheless it is interesting to notice that in the second half of the second century the Jewish Christian leadership of the Jerusalem community was considered, and probably was well-known as, orthodox by second-century standards. This may be idealizing history, but it could hardly have been claimed by anyone if it were a well-known fact that the Jerusalem leadership had been, for example, Ebionitic (see further below).

Eusebius's List of Jewish Christian "Bishops"

As to the bishops of Jerusalem, however, I have quite failed to find their dates preserved in writing (for indeed it is recorded that they were exceedingly short-lived); but this much I have learnt from writings: that up to the siege of the Jews under Hadrian [end of Bar Kokhba war, 135] there had been fifteen bishops in succession, all of whom, it is said, were of Hebrew origin, but received the knowledge of Christ with a sincere heart, insomuch that the persons capable of judging such matters approved them as worthy of the ministry of a bishop; for [it is said] that their whole church at that time consisted of believing Hebrews, who continued from the days of the apostles right down to that siege in which the Jews, having again revolted from the Romans, were conquered after severe fighting. It will be right, then, since the bishops of the circumcision came to an end at that time, to give here a list of them from the first.

The first, therefore, was James, the Lord's brother, as he was called; after him the second, Symeon; the third, Justus;

---

[35]Lawlor/Oulton 1:92-93.

Zacchaeus, the fourth;
the fifth, Tobias;
the sixth, Benjamin;
John, the seventh;
the eighth, Matthias;
the ninth, Philip;
the tenth, Seneca;
the eleventh, Justus;
Levi, the twelfth;
Ephres, the thirteenth;
the fourteenth, Joseph;
last of all, the fifteenth, Judas.

Such is the number of the bishops in the city of Jerusalem, from the apostles to the time of which we are now speaking. All of whom were of the circumcision. (*Ecclesiastical History* 4.5.1-4)[36]

There is obviously something wrong with this list: from the death of James (A.D. 62) until A.D. 135 (73 years) there is not room for fifteen leaders in succession; all the more so since we are told that Symeon alone reigned into the time of Hadrian; his martyrdom may have occurred sometime ca. A.D. 100-110. This leaves the remaining thirteen "bishops" with something like two years each, and explains Eusebius's bewilderment that no dates were given in his source for the list, and his conclusion that the Jewish bishops must have been exceedingly short-lived! There are other sources, however, which supplement Eusebius and may give us the clue he lacked. Some of the last twelve names on his list occur in an apocryphal *Letter of James to Quadratus*, in which these names are said to be the names of the elders who assisted James in leading the church. This could mean that only the first three on Eusebius's list succeeded each other as "bishops," while the last twelve were members of a presbyter-circle formed on the pattern of the twelve apostles. In that case Symeon could have reigned some forty years as leader, and after him Justus some thirty years.[37]

Again, the available evidence gives us only a tantalizing glimpse of a chapter of early church history that we should have liked to know a lot more about. But one very relevant conclusion is inevitable in the light of what we

---

[36]Lawlor/Oulton 1:106-7. On this list, cf. Bauckham, *Relatives*, pp. 70-79; Y. Lederman, "Les évêques juifs de Jérusalem," *Revue biblique* 104 (1997): 211-22.
[37]I have here followed Bauckham, *Relatives*, see him for details, additional evidence, and supportive argument, pp. 70-79.

have seen here: it has often been claimed that the Jewish community's flight to Pella before or during the Jewish-Roman war in A.D. 66-70 served to estrange the Jewish believers from their fellow Jews because they were seen as national traitors. There is no evidence to support this view, and the presence of a Jewish church in Jerusalem after the war speaks strongly against it. The Jewish believers were not the only ones to leave Jerusalem during the war (and we do not know that they *all* left). Afterwards they seem to have come back in strength. There is much indirect evidence which suggests that the years A.D. 70-135 were the classic period of Jewish Christianity, in which it continued to influence Gentile Christianity deeply, while at the same time presenting a challenge to Judaism that the rabbis had to take seriously.

The Rabbis and the Minim

The rabbinic evidence seems to indicate that the Jewish believers in Israel continued their dialogue with the rabbis, sometimes in a friendly atmosphere, though this may not have been the general rule.[38] We have evidence that the rabbis took the challenge from the Jewish believers seriously, and that they responded to it. The first thing they did was to introduce the so-called *Birkat Haminim*, the twelfth benediction, within the prayer of the synagogue service. In the Babylonian Talmud the following question is asked:

> Why is the prayer called the "Eighteen" benedictions when it is actually made up of nineteen benedictions? R. Levi said: the benediction relating to the *minim* was subsequently instituted at Yavne [Jamnia]. . . . Our Rabbis have taught: Simeon the cotton-dealer arranged the eighteen benedictions in order in the presence of Rabban Gamaliel at Yavne [Jamnia]. Rabban Gamaliel asked the sages: Is there anyone who knows how to word the benediction relating to the *minim*? Samuel the small stood up and worded it. . . . Rab Judah has said in the name of Rab: If a reader made a mistake in any of the other benedictions, they do not

[38]Extensive bibliography in Mimouni, *Judéo-christianisme*, pp. 177-78, n. 2. The most important studies include: Adolph Büchler, "The Minim of Sepphoris and Tiberias in the Second and Third Centuries," in *Studies in Jewish History* (London/Oxford: Oxford University Press, 1956), pp. 245-74; S. T. Lachs, "Rabbi Abbahu and the Minim," *Jewish Quarterly Review* 60 (1970): 197-212; Stuart S. Miller, "The *Minim* of Sepphoris Reconsidered," *Harvard Theological Review* 86 (1993): 377-402; Burton L. Visotzky, "Prolegomenon to the Study of Jewish-Christianities in Rabbinic Literature," in *Fathers of the World: Essays in Rabbinic and Patristic Literatures*, Wissenschaftliche Untersuchungen zum Neuen Testament 80 (Tübingen: J. C. B. Mohr [Paul Siebeck], 1995), pp. 129-49; Martin Goodman, "The Function of Minim in Early Rabbinic Judaism," in *Geschichte—Tradition—Reflexion: Festschrift für Martin Hengel zum 70. Geburtstag*, vol. 1: *Judentum*, ed. H. Cancik et al. (Tübingen: J. C. B. Mohr [Paul Siebeck], 1996), pp. 501-10; Simon Claude Mimouni, "La question des 'minim,'" in *Judéo-christianisme*, pp. 177-85.

remove him, but if in the benediction of the *minim,* he is removed, because we suspect him of being a *min. (TB Berakhot* 28b-29a)

This probably happened sometime between A.D. 70 and 100. No doubt the Jewish believers are included among the *minim* (separatists, heretics).[39] At a somewhat later date, it seems the meaning of *minim* became more vague, and to keep the sting against the Jewish believers they were singled out for special mention:

> For the renegades (*meshumadim*) let there be no hope, and may the arrogant kingdom [Rome?] soon be rooted out in our days, and the Nazarenes (*ha Notzrim*) and the *minim* perish as in a moment and be blotted out from the book of life and with the righteous may they not be inscribed. Blessed art Thou, O Lord, who humblest the arrogant. (From an ancient version of the *Amidah.*)[40]

The Talmud specifically states that all present in the synagogue should say this without signs of hesitation or stumbling. In other words, this benediction was meant to be a test passage that would expose any Jewish believers present in the synagogue.

This usage calls for the following inferences: (1) At this time the Jewish believers were still in the habit of visiting the synagogue. (2) They were so numerous and influential that the rabbis had to take them seriously. We should also note the introductory statements in the Talmudic passage that connect *Birkat Haminim* with God's glory and oneness—both important themes in the believers' dispute with the rabbis, who saw this benediction as a vertebra, a vital part of the body, in the test of orthodox belief.

This view of *Birkat Haminim,* its introduction and purpose, is supported by the fact that Justin (ca. A.D. 160) and later Epiphanius and Jerome (fourth century) state that the Nazarenes/Christians are cursed three times a day in the synagogue.[41]

---

[39]Some scholars speculate that *minim* could be a derogatory perversion of *maaminim:* the (Jewish) *believers* (in Jesus). See Jozc, *Jewish People,* p. 177, with references to older scholarship. The literature on the *Birkat-Ha-Minim* is even more extensive than that on *minim* in general (cf. previous note). For an extensive list, see Mimouni, *Judéo-christianisme,* pp. 168-69 n. 2. Here also is a good review of older and newer scholarship, pp. 168-88. See also the summary of the status of the question in Pieter W. van der Horst, "The Birkat Ha-minim in Recent Research," in idem, *Hellenism,* pp. 99-111.

[40]First published from a Cairo Geniza fragment by Solomon Schechter, "Genizah Specimens," *Jewish Quarterly Review* 10 (1898): 657 (article, pp. 654-59). Cf. most recently the discussion of the textual variants of this prayer in Mimouni, pp. 169-77.

[41]Cf. William Horbury, "Early Christians on Synagogue Prayer and Imprecation," in Stanton/Stroumsa, *Tolerance and Intolerance,* pp. 296-317.

The *Birkat Haminim* is not the only evidence of Jewish believers' presence and numbers. Some other changes in the synagogal liturgy regarded as stemming from the same time may have been prompted by the presence of Jewish believers in the synagogues. Of special relevance is the omission of the Decalogue from the synagogal liturgy, "because of the cavelling of the heretics, for they might say: 'These only were given to Moses on Sinai'" (*TB Berakhot* 12a). Apparently, so as not to play into the hands of the Jewish believers, among others—who claimed that the Decalogue was the original law and the remaining commandments were added as secondary amplification after the golden calf incident—the rabbis excised the Decalogue altogether. We have already seen evidence that proves some Jewish believers took this position regarding the Decalogue (see chapter seven on the Jewish Christian tradition in *Recognitions* 1.27-71, p. 157).[42]

A few references to Jewish Christian *minim* in rabbinic literature may refer to the period we are now studying. The most well known is a story concerning a certain Jacob of Kfar Sekaniah, ca. A.D. 100-120.[43] It goes like this: Rabbi Eliezer (ca. 135) is arrested on suspicion of heresy. Asked by Rabbi Akiba if he could possibly have listened to *minut* with pleasure at some time, he suddenly remembered: "By heaven you have reminded me! Once I was walking up the main street of Sepphoris when there came towards me a man named Jacob of Kfar Sekaniah who told me something in the name of the So-and-So [namely Jesus] which pleased me" (*Midrash Qohelet Rabbah* 1 8:3).[44] According to the midrash, the tradition which Jacob handed on in the name of Jesus was concerned with a halakic question: what is to be done with money earned by a harlot when it is given as an offering to the temple? Rabbi Eliezer had no good answer, but was pleased

---

[42]A Judeo-Christian influence of quite a different kind on the synagogue was postulated in 1984 by the orthodox Jewish scholar Yehuda Liebes (original Hebrew article, "Matzmiah qeren Jeshuah" in *Jerusalem Studies in Hebrew Thought* 3 [1984]: 313-48; English summary: Yehudah Liebes, "'Who Makes the Horn of Jesus to Flourish,'" *Immanuel* 21 [1987]: 55-67). He claimed that the final wording of the fifteenth benediction in the *Amidah*, *Tsemach David*, was phrased by Jewish Christians in the latter part of the first century. His main arguments were the parallels between this benediction and Luke 1:68-79 (esp. vv. 68-69), and the fact that in the expression *qeren X* ("horn of X") one would expect the X to be a person rather than an abstract noun. Other scholars find it hard to believe that nascent rabbinic Judaism would allow such influence on the very liturgy by Jewish believers in Jesus.
[43]Many have commented on this story, see now Richard Bauckham, *Jude and the Relatives of Jesus in the Early Church* (Edinburgh, T & T Clark, 1990), pp. 117-21.
[44]The story occurs in several other rabbinic texts, see synopses in Travers Herford, *Christianity in Talmud and Midrash*, pp. 137-40; and Bauckham, *Jude and the Relatives of Jesus in the Early Church* (Edinburgh, T & T Clark, 1990), pp. 106-9.

with the solution Jacob gave in the name of Jesus: "From the filth it came and on the filth it should be expended . . . let it be spent on privies for the public." It is rather remarkable that a leading rabbi like Eliezer was on speaking terms with a Jewish believer like Jacob. Later, Eliezer was excommunicated by the Sanhedrin at Jamnia. "It is therefore possible that behind his confession to have taken pleasure in a certain exposition coming from a heretical source is more than would appear on the surface."[45]

Once Rabbi Eleazar ben Dama had been bitten by a serpent, and Jacob of Kfar Sama (or Sekaniah)[46] came to heal him. But his uncle Rabbi Ishmael would not allow it because Jacob was a *min*, and before ben Dama had finished his argument to the contrary he died (*Midrash Qohelet Rabbah* 1 8:3; TB *Avodah Zara* 27b). It is obvious that Jacob was endowed with the gift of healing, and that it was disputed among the rabbis whether Jews were allowed to take advantage of that gift or not.

It is interesting to note the rabbinic evidence that suggests that some of the leading rabbis were not unaffected by Jewish Christian teaching, as in the story of Rabbi Eliezer above. The most baffling example is the case of Rabbi Elisha ben Abuyah, who is said to have hidden books of *minim* in his clothes, and whose orthodoxy was so questionable that in later tradition he was called Aher, "The Stranger." According to one Talmudic passage, he asked the question whether there could be "two powers [divinities] in heaven"; and this seems from early times to have been an expression referring to Christian belief in the divinity of Jesus.[47] Maybe Elisha took strong interest in the Gospels.[48]

These scattered glimpses do not amount to very much, but at least they show that Jewish believers in Jesus were known to the rabbis and that they were influential enough to be taken seriously by them. Perhaps these stories

---

[45]Jocz, *Jewish People*, p. 181. Cf. also the interesting comments on this passage in Richard Bauckham, op. cit., pp. 106-16; and Daniel Boyarin, "Martyrdom and the Making of Christianity and Judaism," *Journal of Early Christian Studies* 6 (winter 1998): 578-91 (article pp. 577-628). Bauckham argues that this Jacob of Sikhnin could possibly be the grandson of Jude, the brother of Jesus.

[46]He is often taken to be the same as the Jacob of our previous story, but see the argument to the contrary in Bauckham, op. cit., pp. 116-21.

[47]The most extensive discussion of this famous passage, TB *Hagigah 15A*, is in Alan F. Segal, *Two Powers in Heaven: Early Rabbinic Reports About Christianity and Gnosticism*, Studies in Judaism in Late Antiquity 25 (Leiden: E. J. Brill, 1977), pp. 60-67.

[48]It is to be noted that most scholars interpret the traditions about Elisha ben Abuyah as indicating that he fell into a form of Gnosticism. See in particular Gedaliahu G. Stroumsa, "Aher: A Gnostic," in *The Rediscovery of Gnosticism*, ed. Bentley Layton, Studies in the History of Religions 41 (Leiden: E. J. Brill, 1981), 2:808-18.

could also be taken to indicate that the rabbis were worried about grass-roots socializing between Jewish believers and other Jews.[49]

Bar Kokhba and the Jewish Believers

Our final scrap of evidence comes from the turbulent years of the Bar Kokhba revolt. Apparently the Jewish believers did not support the revolt, mainly, perhaps, because they would not do anything to support the messianic claims of Bar Kokhba. The most reliable information on the fate of Jewish believers during the revolt is the following: "In the Jewish war recently Bar Kokhba, the leader of the revolt of the Jews, ordered Christians only to be subjected to terrible punishments, unless they would deny Jesus the Christ and blaspheme him" (Justin, *First Apology* 31.6; remember that Justin was a native of Samaria in the time of the revolt).

In the so-called *Apocalypse of Peter* (possibly a Jewish Christian[50] writing from Israel or Egypt ca. A.D. 150), the following words are attributed to Jesus, explaining the meaning of his parable about the fig tree (Lk 13:6-9):

> Have you not grasped that the fig tree is the house of Israel? Verily, I say to you, when its boughs have sprouted at the end, then shall deceiving Christs come [Mk 13:22], and awaken hope [with the words]: "I am the Christ [Mt 24:5], who am (now) come into the world." And when they shall see the wickedness of their deeds (even of the fake Christs), they shall turn away after them and deny him to whom our fathers gave praise, the first Christ whom they crucified and thereby sinned exceedingly. But this deceiver is not the Christ. And when they reject him, he will kill with the sword and there shall be many many martyrs. Then shall the boughs of the fig tree, i.e. the house of Israel, sprout, and there shall be many martyrs by his hands: they shall be killed and become martyrs. (Ethiopic text, chap. 2)[51]

This text, written a few years after the revolt, is an obvious reference to Bar Kokhba's persecution of the Jewish believers.

The recently found Bar Kokhba letters confirm that Bar Kokhba dealt ruth-

---

[49]This is how I would interpret the evidence that Boyarin takes to mean there were no practical differences between Jews and Christians in the period of the composition of these stories. See his article referred to in note 45.

[50]Richard Bauckham has argued that the author of this early Christian writing was a Jewish believer; see his articles "The *Apocalypse of Peter*: A Jewish Christian Apocalypse from the Time of Bar Kokhba," *Apocrypha* 5 (1994): 7-111; "Jews and Jewish Christians in the Land of Israel at the Time of the Bar Kochba War, with Special Reference to the *Apocalypse of Peter*," in Stanton/Stroumsa, *Tolerance and Intolerance*, pp. 228-38.

[51]Hennecke, *Apocrypha* 2:669.

lessly with fellow Jews who opposed him or disobeyed his orders, support-
ing the credibility of the Christian evidence quoted above. For Jewish
believers the Bar Kokhba revolt must have been a challenge; it seemed that a
messiah had come who accomplished what Jesus had not: freeing the land
and the people from Roman oppression. What would the Jewish believers say
in response to this? Perhaps we have a trace of their response in an expanded
quotation of Numbers 24:17 (Bar Kokhba's slogan) in Justin Martyr (*First
Apology* 32:12):

1. A star shall rise out of Jacob [Num 24:17]
2. and a flower will come forth from the root of Jesse [Is 11:1]
3. and upon his arm will the nations hope [Is 51:5].

When Jewish believers wanted to point out the falsehood of Bar Kokhba's
messianic claims while the revolt was still successful, they would argue that
he was not of Davidic origin (cf. line 2 in the quote), and that he did not fulfill
the universalist task assigned to the Messiah by the prophecies (line 3 in the
quote).

After the revolt had failed, the rabbis also came to the conclusion that Bar
Kokhba had been a false messiah and they distorted his name to Bar Koziba,
"Son of the Lie." But the Jewish believers' lack of participation in the revolt
and their resultant persecution by Bar Kokhba seem to have had lasting
results: the rift between Jewish believers and their fellow Jews widened.

Another fact was also of considerable consequence: after the revolt had
been crushed by the Roman legions, Emperor Hadrian issued a decree that
made it illegal for all circumcised persons to live in Jerusalem or even to come
within sight of the city. Along with their Jewish brethren, the Jewish believers
were also affected by this decree. It meant the cessation of the community of
Jewish believers in Jerusalem, at least for some years. They lost their spiritual
headquarters, so to speak. The most influential and oldest community of Jewish believers was dissolved. In their stead, Gentile Christians invaded Jerusalem and established a purely non-Jewish community there.

The Nazarenes

Despite the considerable symbolic significance of the event just mentioned,
it should not mislead us to think that Jewish Christianity completely disappeared. In the middle of the second century, some twenty-five years
after the Bar Kokhba revolt, Justin knew of Jewish believers who had two
characteristics: (1) They believed in Jesus as the Messiah and Son of God,
and (2) they continued to observe the law of Moses without requiring that

their Gentile brethren do the same.[52]

In the third and fourth centuries there is still solid evidence for the existence of such Jewish believers. In the fourth century they are called "the Nazarenes," and from Jerome and Epiphanius we get the following information: they are few, mainly to be found in the region of Israel and Syria. They recognize Jesus as the Son of God, they accept the virgin birth, they recognize the apostleship of Paul and the Gentile mission, and they have a gospel in Hebrew. These two church fathers—who were zealous hunters of all heresies—found nothing wrong with the doctrines of the Nazarenes. But they took offense at another aspect of this Jewish Christian group: they continued to keep the law, that is, circumcision and the Sabbath. By this time there was no longer any willingness in the Gentile church to accept such Christians; the spirit of brotherly recognition, as seen in Justin, was gone.

After the fourth century the Nazarenes—very likely direct descendants of some from the early Jerusalem community who fled to Pella in A.D. 70—disappeared from the record of history.[53]

We have deliberately put great emphasis on the existence of this "orthodox" Jewish Christian church. In the writings of the church fathers we find a bewildering variety of Jewish Christian sects, all of them heretical. This creates the misleading impression that all Jewish believers were sectarians and heretics. We know next to nothing about the relative numerical strength of these sects compared with the "orthodox" Jewish believers, but the nature of the sources accounts for the fact that the heretics get much more attention than the orthodox. This should not mislead us to conclude that the heretical groups were the majority.

There is one such group, however, that deserves special mention: the Ebionites.

The Ebionites

The ancient sources indicate that the Ebionites were a splinter group derived

---

[52]On this group of Jewish believers, see first and foremost the study by Pritz listed in the Suggestions below, but then also the collection of texts in A. F. J. Klijn and G. J. Reinink, *Patristic Evidence for Jewish-Christian Sects,* Supplements to Novum Testamentum 36 (Leiden: E. J. Brill, 1973), pp. 154-229, and their analysis of the testimonies on Nazarenes, pp. 44-52; see also Wolfram Kinzig, "'Non-Separation': Closeness and Co-Operation Between Jews and Christians in the Fourth Century," *Vigiliae Christianae* 45 (1991): 27-53; Martinus C. de Boer, "The Nazoreans: Living at the Boundary of Judaism and Christianity," in Stanton/Stroumsa, *Tolerance and Intolerance,* pp. 239-62.
[53]For an extensive discussion of the sources, see Pritz, *Nazarene Jewish Christianity,* pp. 71-82.

from the Nazarenes. It is not certain that this is correct. The first to mention them by name is Irenaeus in the 180s A.D. The characteristic feature that distinguished the Ebionites from the Nazarenes was their doctrine about Christ. They rejected the ideas of divine pre-existence and virgin birth, and they claimed that Jesus won the right to be elected as the Messiah by his extremely faithful observance of the law. They further regarded the baptism of Jesus as his messianic anointing. Justin, writing about A.D. 160, knew of such people and may have been referring to this group when he spoke of Jewish believers who require that Gentile believers be circumcised and keep the law. Other evidence indicates that the Ebionites rejected Paul—a natural consequence of their position concerning the Torah.

The problem with the Ebionites, as far as the historian is concerned, is the very confused state of the ancient sources. This has to do with the strange fact that another heretical group, the gnostics,[54] took great interest in the doctrines of the Ebionites and adopted them to a considerable extent. In other respects the Ebionites and the gnostics differed widely, but the church fathers seem to have had difficulty distinguishing between genuine Ebionite doctrine and later gnostic modifications. The result is a rather blurred and confused picture of the Ebionites.

To add to this confusion, there actually seem to have existed groups of Jewish believers who incorporated gnostic elements in their teaching. Such a group may stand behind the curious piece of literature called the Pseudo-Clementine writings. In their preserved form they derive from the fourth century A.D., but several scholars have presented a strong case for the theory that they build on older sources; the main one perhaps dates from the middle of the third century, and an even older one from the middle of the second century. Hans Joachim Schoeps[55] considered the Pseudo-Clementines as a whole a main source for early Ebionite Christianity, which he took to represent the authentic theology of the early Jerusalem community. It seems that Schoeps was wrong in this respect: the theology of the early Aramaic- (or Hebrew-)

[54]Gnosticism was a religious movement with different branches. It flourished in the Hellenistic world of the second and third centuries A.D., drawing inspiration from oriental religions and mystical cults, from the Old Testament and from Jewish and Christian traditions. The gnostics viewed the creation and the body as something negative, from which the soul (the divine spark that remains in human beings) should seek to be redeemed and unified with its divine origin, this by means of the gnostic cult and the sect's esoteric tradition. Gnostic sects close to Christianity denied Jesus' being a man of flesh and blood who suffered bodily and was resurrected. See more on Gnosticism in chapter twelve.
[55]Hans Joachim Schoeps, *Theologie und Geschichte des Judenchristentums* (Tübingen: J. C. B. Mohr, 1949).

Temple Square
The evidence in Origen that some he calls "Hebrews" transferred motifs from the Temple Mount to the cliff of Golgotha is intriguing indeed. It would seem to indicate that Jewish believers—possibly before Hadrian's paganization of Jerusalem in general and the area of Golgotha in particular—regarded the cliff of Golgotha as the functional equivalent or substitute for the Temple Mount. Why? The best explanation I can think of is the belief that the death of Jesus on the cross was the functional equivalent of the atoning sacrifices brought in the temple, and at the same time the ultimate sacrifice that substituted, and thereby made the others superfluous. The temple mount had now moved to Golgotha.
In the eastern wall surrounding the Temple Mount, a little south of the Lions, or Stephen's, Gate, we find the so-called Golden Gate, now blocked. It was not always blocked: that gate led into a gate building on the inside of the wall. The present building may date from the Ummayad period (late seventh century A.D.), but was probably preceded by a Byzantine structure. The striking thing about the whole gate structure is its axis. When elongated westward, it literally bypasses the temple (north of it), but directly hits the cliff of Golgotha. Is this sheer accident? Or is the orientation of this gate a remnant from pre-Muslim times, when Christians built a first version of this structure and made it a gate to the new temple mount?[56] If so, it would be a telling symbol for an early piece of Jewish Christian theology.

speaking community of Jerusalem was carried on in a more representative way by the Nazarenes than by the Ebionites.

With this, our rapid sketch of the different groups of Jewish believers comes to an end. The source material is tantalizingly fragmented, and there are many unanswered questions. But some main conclusions can be considered beyond doubt:

1. In Israel, and later also in Syria, congregations of Jewish believers remained until at least the fourth century. Their doctrine did not differ significantly from that of the dominant Gentile Christian church: they recognized the divine status of Jesus and his birth by the virgin, as well as the Gentile mission and the apostleship of Paul. In the second century Justin recognized them as brothers in the faith, and in the fourth century Jerome and Epiphanius found nothing wrong with their doctrine.

2. The Jewish believers continued to observe circumcision, the sabbath and

---

[56]I do not want to be dogmatic about this, because the axis also skirts the "Dome of the Spirits" north of the Dome of the Rock on the temple platform. If that was the original orientation, the axis alignment with Golgotha in the Holy Sepulchre would indeed be accidental. But a look at any good map reveals what an unlikely coincidence that is. So, if accidental, maybe also providential? The larger, ascending part of present day Via Dolorosa follows the same axis, only some meters to the north. Inside the Convent of the Small Sisters of Jesus (sixth station) you can see part of a much older street, some meters to the south of the present one: perhaps at some time the (Byzantine?) street leading from the Golden Gate to Golgotha? I am speculating, of course. And the first gate on the spot could be Hadrianic, oriented toward his Aphrodite temple.

other parts of the law. They had a gospel in Hebrew, probably a version of Matthew. They seem to have been engaged in an intense and at times amiable dialogue with the rabbinic teachers.

3. It is these Jewish believers with their belief in the divine sonship of Jesus whom we encounter in some of the polemics against *minim* in the rabbinic writings.

4. A splinter group that possibly broke away from these orthodox Jewish believers is the Ebionites. They regarded Jesus as a mere man, elected to be the Messiah. They rejected Paul and probably required that Gentiles be circumcised before they were admitted into the church.

5. At a later stage, some Jewish Christian groups were influenced by gnostic doctrines, and thus we get the varied picture of several Jewish Christian sects depicted by the church fathers.

Suggestions for Further Reading

A classic treatise on the evidence and the history of Jewish believers in antiquity is contained in Jocz, *Jewish People,* chap. 5. The most recent comprehensive survey is Mimouni, *Judéo-christianisme.*

The archaeological evidence as interpreted by the Franciscan Fathers is presented most fully in Bellarmino Bagatti, *The Church from the Circumcision: History and Archaeology of the Judaeo-Christians,* Studium Biblicum Franciscanum, Collectio Minor 2 (Jerusalem: Franciscan Printing Press, 1971 [reprint, 1984]). For a shorter, more sober, very instructive review of their work, one should consult Meyers/Strange, *Archaeology.* The major critic of the Franciscan archaeologists is Joan E. Taylor, *Christians and the Holy Places: The Myth of Jewish-Christian Origins* (Oxford: Clarendon, 1993).

On the rabbinic evidence, one should consult the very extensive collection of texts in Robert Travers Herford, *Christianity in Talmud and Midrash* (London: Williams & Norgate, 1903; reprint, Ktav: New York, 1975). Herford's comments on the texts are not always sufficiently critical. See now Burton L. Visotzky, "Prolegomenon to the Study of Jewish-Christianities in Rabbinic Literature," in *Fathers of the World: Essays in Rabbinic and Patristic Literatures,* Wissenschaftliche Untersuchungen zum Neuen Testament 80 (Tübingen: J. C. B. Mohr [Paul Siebeck], 1995), pp. 129-49.

The evidence in the church fathers concerning the different sects of (heretical) Jewish believers is most conveniently offered and analyzed in A. F. J. Klijn and G. J. Reinink, *Patristic Evidence for Jewish-Christian Sects,* Supplements to Novum Testamentum 36 (Leiden: E. J. Brill, 1973).

A special study devoted to the Nazarenes, evaluating the evidence of the church fathers as well as the rabbinic writings, is Ray A. Pritz, *The Jewish Christian Sect of the Nazarenes* (Jerusalem: Magnes, 1988).

On the Jewish Christianity of sources in the Pseudo-Clementines, see Hans Joachim

Schoeps, *Theologie und Geschichte des Judenchristentums* (Tübingen: J. C. B. Mohr, 1949); Georg Strecker, *Das Judenchristentum in den Pseudoklementinen*, Texte und Untersuchungen 70 (Berlin: Akademieverlag, 1958 [2nd ed. 1981]).

A fascinating study of Jewish terminology, imagery and thought patterns in early Christian theology is Daniélou, *The Theology of Jewish Christianity*, The Development of Christian Doctrine Before the Council of Nicaea 1 (London: Darton, Longman & Todd, 1964).

10

THE DIASPORA
THE CHURCH OF JEWS
& GENTILES

*W*e have stressed repeatedly in the foregoing chapters that the mission of the early church throughout the Jewish Diaspora would, by its very nature, result in mixed congregations composed of Jews and Gentiles. It is this Diaspora church of the late first and early second century A.D. that we are going to study a little closer in this chapter. The sources we have for telling its story are more or less disconnected documents and fragments, scattered pieces of evidence that are far too few to allow any big and coherent jigsaw puzzle to be put together. We have no "Luke the historian" for this period. What Eusebius has to offer is not a connected narrative, but rather some more fragments of documents otherwise lost. Eusebius's Ecclesiastical History *is as much an anthology of sources as it is a history. For the period that now concerns us, though, some documents that have been preserved independently of Eusebius can teach us the most about how things developed within the church: the so-called Apostolic Fathers.*

The Apostolic Fathers

If we limit ourselves to the period after A.D. 70 and prior to A.D. 150, not much source material is available, which makes the few documents and fragments we do have all the more valuable. One feature is quite striking in most of these writings: they are very "internal." They address church problems within the church. Whereas the New Testament writings, which precede them, and the works of the Apologists, which follow them, are more missionary and outward oriented, these documents are "in house" to an almost surprising degree. Or maybe not so surprising: we see in these documents a young movement in the process of defining itself. The outer limits are more or less clear, sometimes less clear, but within these limits there is still much fluidity and uncertainty as to what constitutes the new Christian identity.

The writings we are talking about are traditionally called the Apostolic Fathers. They shed some interesting light on the Diaspora church in the period ca. A.D. 70-150, and we will now examine their evidence more closely.

1 Clement

First Clement (commonly dated to A.D. 96) is probably the earliest Christian document apart from the New Testament writings.[1] The anonymous author, according to reliable tradition, was named Clement, a presbyter of the Roman community. His letter has several striking features. First, the author is unusually familiar with the entire Old Testament. He is able to quote verses appropriate to everything he is saying, often from rather out-of-the-way places in the Old Testament. In other words, he has the entire Old Testament at his fingertips.

Secondly, the author regards the pious men of the Old Testament as his own ancestors and the history of the Christian community as a direct continuation of Israel's history. Throughout the letter the author demonstrates great familiarity with Jewish ways of thinking and expressions, and when he concludes his letter with a great prayer (1 Clement 59.3—61.3), the language and phrases of his prayer display striking parallels to Jewish prayers from antiquity.[2]

---

[1]On 1 Clement, see L. W. Barnard, "The Early Roman Church, Judaism, and Jewish-Christianity," Anglican Theological Review 49 (1967): 371-84; Donald A. Hagner, The Use of the Old and New Testaments in Clement of Rome, Novum Testamentum Supplements 34 (Leiden: E. J. Brill, 1973); Otto Knoch, "Im Namen des Petrus und Paulus: Der Brief des Clemens Romanus und die Eigenart des römischen Christentums," in Haase, Aufstieg 2 27.1:3-54; Horacio E. Lona, Der erste Clemensbrief, Kommentar zu den Apostolischen Vätern 2 (Göttingen: Vandenhoeck & Ruprecht, 1998).

[2]This was pointed out already by A. Z. Idelsohn, Jewish Liturgy and Its Development (New York: Schocken, 1967 [orig. ed. Cincinnati: Holt, Rinehart and Winston, 1932]), pp. 301-4. Sanders, Schismatics, pp. 219-20, is so impressed with the Jewish character of 1 Clement that he thinks the author was himself a Jewish believer.

Box 10.1. The Apostolic Fathers

1 Clement (ca. A.D. 96): A letter from the Roman community to the community in Corinth, where a "coup" by younger leaders has ousted the older leaders. The community of Rome protests against this. Main theme: end strife, restore harmony.

Didache, The Teaching of the Twelve Apostles (ca. A.D. 100): Catechism and regulations for baptism, prayer, fasting, Eucharist, charismata, church leadership, Sunday worship.

The Letters of Ignatius (ca. A.D. 110): Five letters to communities in Asia Minor, one to the community in Rome, one to bishop Polycarp of Smyrna, all of them written during Ignatius's journey (in captivity) towards martyrdom in Rome. Themes: warnings against quasi-Jewish practices and docetic Christology, admonitions to gather around the bishop.

Barnabas (ca. A.D. 130): Letter of advice concerning the relationship between Judaism and Christianity, Christian faith and the law. The last chapters contain a Jewish/Christian ethical catechism based on the same source as the one in *Didache*.

2 Clement (first half of second century): A written sermon, exhortations to keep baptismal grace intact in a life without sin. Polemics against Gnostic denial of the resurrection of the flesh.

Hermas, *The Shepherd* (ca. A.D. 140-45): A book of exhortation in the form of visions and parables, proclaims one more chance of repentance before the return of the Lord.

Letter of Polycarp (ca. A.D. 115-130): Possibly two letters combined. Admonitions to Christian life, recommendation of the Ignatian letters.

Martyrdom of Polycarp (possibly a first version of it was written shortly after the event in ca. A.D. 156, later expanded and revised): Tells the story of Polycarp's arrest, trial and martyrdom; contains important material on early Christian prayer, especially the eucharistic prayer.

Letter to Diognetos (ca. A.D. 170 ?): A small Christian apology, possibly addressed to Emperor Marcus Aurelius's teacher of philosophy, Diognetos.

There is no doubt that *1 Clement* is a Christian document: the letter's salutation greets the addressees as "those who are called and sanctified by the will of God through our Lord Jesus Christ"; Peter and Paul are mentioned as model witnesses and martyrs (*1 Clement* 5.4-7); there are scattered references to "Christ" throughout the letter; one passage in chapter 36 displays a high Christology (inspired by Hebrews). But if we removed these features from the text we would hardly destroy its main structure, and we would have a text that is rather characteristic of Diaspora Judaism, in style as well as content.[3] If the author was not a Jewish believer, but a Gentile, his background was certainly among the God-fearers of some Roman synagogue.

So what does he think about the Jews; how does he define his Christian identity vis-à-vis Israel? In a strange way, he more or less avoids the whole issue by simply taking for granted that the Christian church is now the people of God, the continuation of the biblical Israel. There is no anti-Jewish polemic in

---

[3]See, for this, Lona's commentary, pp. 58-65.

1 Clement, no aggressive self-definition vis-à-vis the Jews. In explaining this, one would probably be wise to remember the statement above about these writings being mainly "in-house" Christian writings. *First Clement* perhaps provides the clearest example of this internal tendency. The author was concerned with an intra-Christian conflict in Corinth and found no reason to expand on outer-limit problems for the Christian community. Otto Knoch, in his study of *1 Clement*'s attitude to Israel and Judaism, interprets the silence of the letter as indirect proof of a friendly, positive, even grateful attitude toward biblical Israel as well as the contemporary synagogues in Rome.[4] This should probably not be ruled out, but may also be an overinterpretation of Clement's silence. We are on the safe side if we say that there is a remarkably strong positive identification with biblical Israel and the Scriptures of Israel (Old Testament) in this writing, and an accidental or conscious ignoring of any identity problems vis-à-vis the Jews of this strikingly Jewish church.[5]

Didache

The Jewish background of the fascinating document called *The Teaching (Didache) of the Lord to the Gentiles Through the Twelve Apostles* is quite conspicuous.[6] The first part of the writing (chaps. 1-6) is made up of a so-called proselyte catechism, which recurs in a basically identical form in the *Epistle of Barnabas*, chapters 18-20, and in a Latin document called *Doctrine of the Apostles*. In the *Didache* version of this catechism, some words of Jesus are interpolated (they are absent from the two other versions). If we remove these insertions (*Didache* 1.3-5), we are left with an entirely Jewish

---

[4]Otto Knoch, "Die Stellung der apostolischen Väter zu Israel und zum Judentum: Eine Übersicht," in *Begegnung mit dem Wort: Festschrift für H. Zimmermann*, ed. J. Zmijewski and E. Nellessen, Bonner biblische Beiträge 53 (Bonn: Anton Hain, 1980), pp. 348-50 (article pp. 347-78).

[5]For more points of view on Jewish/Christian relations in *1 Clement*, see James C. Walters, "Romans, Jews, and Christians: The Impact of the Romans on Jewish/Christian Relations in First-Century Rome," in *Judaism and Christianity in First-Century Rome*, ed. Karl P. Donfried and Peter Richardson (Grand Rapids, Mich./Cambridge, U.K.: Eerdmans, 1998), pp. 175-95, esp. pp. 190-95; William L. Lane, "Social Perspectives on Roman Christianity During the Formative Years from Nero to Nerva: Romans, Hebrews, *1 Clement*," ibid., pp. 196-244, esp. pp. 224-44.

[6]On *Didache*, the richest material on Jewish background is collected in Jean-Paul Audet, *La Didaché: Instructions des apôtres*, Études bibliques (Paris: J. Gabalda, 1958). Cf. also the older work of C. Taylor, *The Teaching of the Twelve Apostles with Illustrations from the Talmud* (Cambridge/London, 1886). A recent full-scale commentary is Kurt Niederwimmer, *Die Didache*, Kommentar zu den Apostolischen Vätern 1 (Göttingen: Vandenhoeck & Ruprecht, 1989). In addition, see Wilson, *Strangers*, pp. 224-27; Mimouni, *Judéo-christianisme*, pp. 193-201.

document, a kind of ethical instruction for would-be converts[7]—or perhaps for Gentile God-fearers. This is clearly indicated in chapter 6, which is more than strange in a Christian text, but which makes excellent sense if addressed to God-fearers by Jews: "If you can bear the whole yoke of the Lord, you will be perfect, but if you cannot, do what you can. And concerning food, bear as much as you can [of the dietary laws], but keep strictly from that which is offered to idols, for it is the worship of dead gods."

Moreover, chapters 7-15, which contain a short church order with prescriptions for baptism, prayer, fasting and eucharistic celebration,[8] have a Jewish foundation that is easy to recognize. We shall treat all this in some detail later, in chapters seventeen through nineteen. Here it is sufficient to point out that being so close to Jewish tradition and Jewish practices, the author of *Didache* obviously has felt a need to emphasize some boundary markers, so as not to be identified with the local Jews.

> Let not your fasts be with the hypocrites, for they fast on Mondays and Thursdays, but do you fast on Wednesdays and Fridays. And do not pray as the hypocrites, but as the Lord commanded in his Gospel, pray thus: "Our Father . . . [in a Matthean version]." Pray thus three times a day (*Didache* 8.1-3).[9]

There can hardly be any doubt that this urge to act differently than the Jews (the "hypocrites") is necessitated precisely by otherwise great similarity.

It is commonly assumed that *Didache* dates from ca. A.D. 100 (some think it is earlier), and that it comes from the church of Syria. Matthew seems to be a main influence behind this writing, or maybe *Didache* and Matthew are so close in time that they rather come from a shared background. It is striking that *Didache* can in many ways be seen as a natural "sequel" to Matthew: in *Didache* we meet the Apostolic *teaching* to the Gentiles, the teaching Jesus commissioned his disciples to deliver according to Matthew 28:20. Compared with *1 Clement* in Rome, the Syrian community speaking to us in the *Didache* is as Jewish (perhaps more) as the one in Rome, but the relationship to the Jews is more conscious and more polemical.

---

[7]A lot has been written on this source, see as an excellent introduction Willy Rordorf, "Un chapître d'éthique judéo-chrétienne: Les Deux Voies," in idem, *Liturgie*, pp. 155-74; and also Niederwimmer, *Didache*, pp. 48-64 (with extensive bibliography).
[8]Some scholars think the sequence of ethical instruction (chaps. 1-6), baptism (7), fasting and prayer (8), and Eucharist (9-10) is not accidental, but mirrors the different stages in Christian initiation. See quite recently J. A. Draper, "Ritual Process and Ritual Symbol in *Didache* 7-10," *Vigiliae Christianae* 54 (2000): 121-58.
[9]Kirsopp Lake 1:321.

The deep familiarity with Jewish traditions we have met in *1 Clement*, as well as the *Didache*, is hardly conceivable unless we imagine Jewish believers as the theological tutors of the authors and/or communities behind these documents.

Ignatius

The third of the earliest Apostolic Fathers, Ignatius, is the most enigmatic of them all.[10] He was bishop of Antioch in Syria, was arrested and sent to Rome, and en route visited some Christian communities in the province of Asia and spoke with envoys of others. His seven letters, written during his journey to martyrdom in Rome, ca. A.D. 110, are linguistically peculiar, theologically original, and their interpretation is highly controversial among scholars. The special relevance of Ignatius in our context is due to the fact that if *1 Clement* and the *Didache* seem very Jewish, Ignatius does not.

In Ignatius, the Jewish context of Christianity seems much more remote than in any Christian writing before him (or immediately after him, as we shall see). In part, this may be due to the character of his letters. On his journey through Asia Minor, Ignatius was shocked to see that a specific heresy was threatening to gain a foothold in the congregations, and his letters are entirely devoted to warnings against this heresy. Their range of interest and topics is therefore rather limited. But the heresy envisaged throws interesting light on Gentile Christianity in Asia Minor in the early second century, and Ignatius's reply may tell us something of Gentile Christianity in Antioch, where he was bishop:

> Be not led astray by strange doctrines or by old fables which are profitless. For if we are living until now according to Judaism, we confess that we have not received grace. For the divine prophets lived according to Jesus Christ. Therefore they were also persecuted, being inspired by his grace, to convince the disobedient that there is one God, who manifested himself through Jesus Christ his son, who is his Word. (*To the Magnesians* 8.12)[11]

> It is monstrous to talk of Jesus Christ and to practice Judaism. For Christianity did not base its faith on Judaism, but Judaism on Christianity, and every tongue

---

[10]On Ignatius and the Jews, see Charles Kingsley Barrett, "Jews and Judaizers in the Epistles of Ignatius," in *Essays on John* (London: SPCK, 1982), pp. 133-58; Lloyd Gaston, "Judaism of the Uncircumcised in Ignatius and Related Writers," in Wilson, *Anti-Judaism*, pp. 33-44; Lieu, *Image*, pp. 23-56; Graham N. Stanton, "Other Early Christian Writings: 'Didache,' Ignatius, 'Barnabas,' Justin Martyr," in Barclay/Sweet, *Early Christian Thought*, pp. 174-90, esp. pp. 176-81.

[11]Kirsopp Lake 1:205.

believing on God was brought together in it. (*To the Magnesians* 10:3)[12]

And the prophets also do we love, because they also have announced the Gospel, and are hoping in him and waiting for him, by faith in whom they also obtain salvation, being united with Christ Jesus, for they are worthy of love and saints worthy of admiration, approved by Jesus Christ, and numbered together in the Gospel of the common hope. But if anyone interpret Judaism to you do not listen to him; for it is better to hear Christianity from the circumcised than Judaism from the uncircumcised. (*To the Philadelphians* 5.2—6.1)[13]

I heard some men saying, "if I find it not in the ancient [Scriptures, the Old Testament], I do not believe in the Gospel." And when I said to them that it [the Gospel] is in the charters [the Old Testament], they answered me, "that is exactly the question." But to me the charters are Jesus Christ, the inviolable charter [Scripture] is his cross and death and resurrection, and the faith which is through him. (*To the Philadelphians* 8.2)[14]

He [Christ] is the door of the Father, through which enter Abraham and Isaac and Jacob and the Prophets and the Apostles and the Church. All these things are joined in the unity of God. But the Gospel has somewhat of pre-eminence, the coming of the Saviour, our Lord Jesus Christ, his passion, and the resurrection. For the beloved prophets had a message pointing to him, but the Gospel is the perfection of incorruption. (*To the Philadelphians* 9.1-2)[15]

He [Christ] is in truth of the family of David according to the flesh, God's Son by the will and power of God, truly born of a Virgin, baptised by John that "all righteousness might be fulfilled [Mt 3:15] by him," truly nailed to a tree in the flesh for our sakes under Pontius Pilate and Herod the Tetrarch (and of its fruit are we from his divinely blessed Passion) that "he might set up an ensign" [Is 5:26] for all ages through his Resurrection, for his saints and believers, whether among Jews, or among the heathen, in one body of his Church. For he suffered all these things for us that we might attain salvation, and he truly suffered even as he also truly raised himself, not as some unbelievers say, that his Passion was merely in semblance—but it is they who are merely in semblance. . . . For I know and believe that he was in the flesh even after the Resurrection; . . . He ate and drank with them as a being of flesh, although he was united in spirit to the Father. (*To the Smyrnaeans* 1.1—3.3)[16]

There are some who ignorantly deny him, but rather were denied by him, being

[12]Ibid., p. 207.
[13]Ibid., pp. 243-45.
[14]Ibid., p. 247.
[15]Ibid., p. 249.
[16]Ibid., pp. 253, 55.

advocates of death rather of the truth. These are they whom neither the prophecies nor the law of Moses persuaded, nor the Gospel even until now.... [They] blaspheme my Lord, and do not confess that he was clothed in flesh? (*To the Smyrnaeans* 5.1-2)[17]

It is right to refrain from such men and not even to speak about them in private or in public, but to give heed to the Prophets and especially to the Gospel, in which the Passion has been revealed to us and the Resurrection has been accomplished. (*To the Smyrnaeans* 7.2)[18]

Reading through these texts, we first notice that for Ignatius the church is composed of Jewish and Gentile believers, and he considers the possibility of "hearing Christianity from the circumcised." No wonder—the community of Antioch had from its very beginning been a mixed one, and although the Jewish believers were probably a minority in Ignatius's day, he no doubt knew some Jewish believers whom he recognized as fully orthodox brethren.

Second, we find that the heretics are not Jews, but uncircumcised Gentiles who propagate something Ignatius calls "Judaism." This probably means that they observe a rather arbitrary selection of Old Testament commands. *To the Magnesians* 9.1 seems to imply that they observed the sabbath. They accord great authority to the Old Testament, placing it decidedly above the Gospels. These Gentile believers may correspond to the type of believers who at a later period were called "Judaizers."

Scholars dispute whether this group is identical with the next group of heretics: those who deny the physical reality of the incarnation. These heretics said that the flesh of Christ was not real flesh; it only seemed like flesh, and Christ did not really suffer.

If these two types of heresy were represented by the same group of people,[19] the combination of ideas may seem strange to the modern reader. But we have ample evidence from the second century that it really existed, namely among the people we usually call Gnostics. We shall have more to say about the Gnostics in chapter twelve. Here it is sufficient to mention that among the Gnostics we often find what may be called a romantic fascination with Judaism—or perhaps with the Old Testament. Many of the Gnostics seem to have been full-fledged Gentiles with little contact with real-life Judaism. But they were fasci-

---

[17]Ibid., p. 257.
[18]Ibid., pp. 259, 61.
[19]This was the thesis of Einar Molland, "The Heretics Combatted by Ignatius of Antioch," *Journal of Ecclesiastical History* 5 (1954): 1-6.

nated by the Old Testament and read and interpreted it eagerly, although, as we shall see, they were utter strangers to its doctrine and spirit.

Ignatius had no patience with this pseudo-Judaism. It was much better to hear sound Christian doctrine from believers who are real, circumcised Jews! For Ignatius, the Old Testament is a book about Christ, its central message is the death and the resurrection of Christ. The prophets were disciples of Christ; Ignatius speaks of Abraham, Isaac and the others as fellow Christians.

One gets the impression that Ignatius's relationship to the Old Testament was mainly a literary one. For him, the Old Testament was a book, not a living past which, through traditions and observances, determined his own life and thinking. It is this, more than anything else, that betrays the Gentile Christian. The position of Ignatius may perhaps best be characterized as New Testament orthodoxy. It was the apostolic writings that made him value the Old Testament and love the prophets. The authority of the Old Testament is undisputed, but it is derived from the authority of the gospel.

This was probably one of the most characteristic differences between Jewish believers and believers coming from an entirely Gentile background. It was not a question of doctrinal differences but rather a difference of mentality. For both groups the Old Testament was an authoritative book, and the church of the Gentiles was later to defend the Old Testament bravely and at considerable cost against attacks from within the church and without. But to them the Old Testament was and remained a book, describing a history that was past and finished. To the Jewish believers, it was so much more. Through innumerable cords of tradition, festivals, daily practices, religious concepts, etc., the Jewish believers were bound up with the Old Testament; it was part of their lives.

What we observe in Ignatius may perhaps best be described as a loss of Jewish context. The constant reference to the Old Testament in the authoritative apostolic preaching nevertheless saved him from neglecting or ignoring the Old Testament. And the fact that he had to oppose heretics who denied the physical reality of the incarnation seems to have had a very healthy effect on his own theology. He vigorously opposed any Hellenistic degradation of the body and stressed the concrete, physical reality of all elements in the creed: Jesus was truly of the family of David, he truly suffered, etc. This emphasis makes him come out with statements that were shockingly crude to Greek ears, such as "the suffering of my God" (*To the Romans* 6.3).

Barnabas

Before we leave the apostolic fathers, we shall comment briefly on the strange writing that is called *The Epistle of Barnabas* in the ancient manuscripts.[20] This is actually an anonymous document, as the author nowhere names himself. The letter was probably written around A.D. 130-132; the place of origin is not known (though often believed to be Alexandria).

Chapters 1-17 are devoted to the question of how Christians should understand the Old Testament, especially the ritual commandments. Briefly summarized, the author's point of view is this: The ritual commandments are all valid for Christians, but they were never meant to be taken literally. They all have spiritual significance, but the Israelites were misled by an evil angel to take them literally, and consequently Moses withdrew the covenant. This same covenant is now offered anew in Christ, and Christians are the ones who understand the true meaning of the Old Testament law, while the Jews continue in their tragic misunderstanding. The Christians, not the Jews, are the people of God; in fact, the Jews never were the people of God. The author strongly objects to those fellow-Christians who speak of the covenant as common to Jews and Christians.

How should we evaluate this? One way to react to *Barnabas* is to say that it is an extreme example of Gentile Christian arrogance. Our task, however, is to try to understand even those phenomena that we do not like. How should we understand a document like *Barnabas*? Let us first notice that the author takes the Old Testament to be identical with the Scriptures; all his scriptural quotations—more than seventy together—are taken from the Old Testament. To him the Old Testament law is eternally valid. More than that, in his paraphrases of Old Testament texts, the author sometimes includes details from rabbinic tales as if they were part of the biblical text itself. This has made

---

[20]See the studies listed in the Suggestions below, as well as the following articles: A. Marmorstein, "L'Épitre de Barnabé et la polémique juive," *Revue des etudes juives* 60 (1910): 213-20; Leslie W. Barnard, "The Epistle of Barnabas and the Dead Sea Scrolls," *Scottish Journal of Theology* 13 (1960): 45-59; idem, "The 'Epistle of Barnabas' and Its Contemporary Setting," in Haase, *Aufstieg* 2 27.1:159-207; S. Lowy, "The Confutation of Judaism in the Epistle of Barnabas," *Journal of Jewish Studies* 11 (1960): 1-33; Karen K. Chandler, "The Rite of the Red Heifer in the Epistle of Barnabas and Mishnah Parah," in *Approaches to Ancient Judaism*, vol. 5: *Studies in Judaism and Its Greco-Roman Context*, ed. William Scott Green, Brown Judaic Studies 32 (Atlanta, Ga.: Scholars Press, 1985), pp. 99-114; Martin B. Shukster and Peter Richardson, "Temple and *Bet Ha-midrash* in the Epistle of Barnabas," in Wilson, *Anti-Judaism*, pp. 17-31; Wilson, *Strangers*, pp. 127-42; William Horbury, "Jewish-Christian Relations in Barnabas and Justin Martyr," in Dunn, *Jews and Christians*, pp. 315-45; Graham N. Stanton, "Other Early Christian Writings: 'Didache,' Ignatius, 'Barnabas,' Justin Martyr," in Barclay/Sweet, *Early Christian Thought*, pp. 174-90, esp. pp. 181-84.

some scholars wonder whether the author might not be a Jewish believer after all.[21] This is hardly the case, because at times his renderings of rabbinic lore are marred by grave misunderstanding.

An illustrative example of this use occurs in his treatment of Leviticus 16. In the following table Barnabas's additions to the biblical text are quoted, together with the relevant portion of the Mishnah.[22]

Barnabas 7	*Mishnah* parallel
Let them eat of the goat which is offered . . . for all their sins . . . and let all the priests alone eat the entrails unwashed with vinegar. . . .	If The Day of Atonement was a Friday, the he-goat . . . was consumed at evening. The Babylonian [priests] used to eat it raw since they were not squeamish. (*Menahot* 11:7)
Take two goats, goodly *and alike,* and offer them. . . .	The two he-goats . . . should *be alike in appearance,* in size, and in value. (*Yoma* 6:1)
And do ye all spit on it, and goad it,	The Babylonians . . . used to pull its hair. (*Yoma* 6:4)
and bind the scarlet wool about its head, and so let it be cast into the desert.	He bound a thread of crimson wool on the head of the goat and he turned it towards the way by which it was to be sent out. (*Yoma* 4:2)
He who takes the goat into the wilderness drives it forth,	They delivered it to him that should lead it away (*Yoma* 6:3).
and takes away the wool, and puts it upon a shrub which is called Rachel.	He divided the thread of crimson wool and tied it to the rock and the other half between its horns, and he pushed it down into the ravine from behind. (*Yoma* 6:6)

---

[21]Mimouni, *Judéo-christianisme,* pp. 231-55, thinks he is.
[22]For further comment on this passage, see Prigent, *Les Testimonia,* pp. 99-110; Prostmeier, *Barnabasbrief,* pp. 284-316.

The interesting feature here is Barnabas's saying that the man who led the goat into the wilderness bound the scarlet wool "on a shrub which is called *Rachel*" (or, in other manuscripts, *Rache* or *Rachil*). This does not agree with the *Mishnah*, which instead mentions a rock. The text of the *Mishnah* is logical: where there is a ravine (into which the goat was pushed to be killed in a merciful way), there would also be a rock; but the shrub of which Barnabas speaks must have been quite rare, for it cannot be found in any other texts from antiquity. So there is quite likely something wrong with Barnabas's version. The solution to the puzzle is probably quite simple: there is in Greek a very rare word for rock or cliff, namely *rachis*. Barnabas, having no first-hand knowledge of rabbinic lore, but taking his information from a Greek source, misread this word and took it to be the name of some shrub with which he happened to be familiar.

This and some other indications strongly suggest that Barnabas's knowledge of rabbinic haggadah was not first-hand, but transmitted to him via written sources which he used while writing his own letter. A closer study of his many Old Testament quotations suggests that the same is true for great parts of the Old Testament. Only rarely does Barnabas quote directly from the Greek version of the Bible; most often his quotations are copied from earlier Christian writings.

In other words, this author is not entirely at home in the Old Testament— the very book that is his highest authority! He is heavily dependent on one or more Christian precursors who were thoroughly familiar with the Bible and with rabbinic haggadah. Once we observe this, it is easy to make the additional observation that the Christian sources which furnished Barnabas with most of his Old Testament quotations and all of his rabbinic lore were not nearly so anti-Jewish as he himself was. Maybe these sources were written by Jewish believers, a possibility that makes *Barnabas* an even more fascinating document.[23]

Two concluding remarks on *Barnabas*: (1) It is often assumed that the author of *Barnabas* did not have any close real-life contact with Jews and Judaism, and that his anti-Jewish polemic is merely a literary exercise, bent on strengthening insecure Christians in their own identity. But Reidar Hval-

---

[23]In Skarsaune, *Proof from Prophecy,* it is argued that Justin Martyr, some 20-30 years after *Barnabas,* had access to some of the same source material as the author of *Barnabas* used, and that this accounts for the similarities between the two authors, rather than Justin having used *Barnabas* directly. The best analysis of sources in *Barnabas* is, in my opinion, that of Prigent (see Suggestions below).

vik has recently argued,[24] to my mind quite convincingly, that conversion to Judaism was a very real option for some of those whom Barnabas is addressing in his letter, and that this explains some of the urgency in the letter's anti-Jewish stance. This would correspond to a situation in which the lines of demarcation between Jews and Christians are not that clear-cut; the author wants to make them so.

(2) It is often assumed that the question of whether non-Jewish believers should observe the Torah or not was a problem only to the very first generation of Gentile believers, who began reading the Greek Bible without having received much instruction on how to understand what they read. After some time, the Pauline solution to this problem was universally accepted. But this was clearly not the case; Barnabas in the early 130s seems completely unaware of Paul's theology. The author of *Barnabas* was (probably) a Gentile facing the Old Testament law, and learning that it was eternally valid, while at the same time facing the fact of not observing it in his own life, nor in that of his community. Being convinced of the permanent validity of the law, he had only two options: either he must become a full-fledged Jew, observing the law on all points, or he must thoroughly spiritualize all ritual aspects of the law.

He chose the latter, but the very vehemence with which he rejects the Jews' literal observance of the law may be an indication that this possibility had not been very far from him, and that the question continued to trouble him. So the *Epistle of Barnabas* shows us a Gentile Christianity not yet quite sure of itself, searching for simple answers to complex questions. Behind the arrogant facade of *Barnabas* there may very well be hidden a troubled heart.

It remains to be added that *Barnabas's* solution was not adopted by the Gentile church at large—fortunately so, one might add. The position of *Barnabas* remained an isolated one, and when Gentile Christian theology came to greater maturity later in the century, it was the New Testament orthodoxy of Ignatius that was carried on. It also seems that Gentile theologians in increasing measure were able to profit from the theological heritage of their Jewish brethren in the faith, to which we will return later.

Concluding Remarks: The Jewish Believers as the Theological Teachers of Gentile Christianity

In this chapter we have reviewed some of the writings deriving from the early church of the Diaspora, and we have found confirmation of the hypoth-

---

[24]In his study listed in the Suggestions below.

esis with which we started: These documents are best understood against the background of mixed communities, in which a minority of Jewish believers acted as the teachers and theological experts for the greater Gentile majority. Despairingly little evidence has survived which could help us draw a detailed picture of the numeric strength of the Jewish believers, their relationship to the increasing number of Gentile converts, and their relationship with the synagogue.

Concerning their theological convictions and their development of Christian doctrine, the direct evidence is almost nil. But the indirect evidence is considerable. We have seen that some of the Apostolic Fathers may contain a great deal of Jewish Christian material, as in 1 *Clement*, the *Didache* and even *Barnabas*. In his fascinating study *The Theology of Jewish Christianity*, Jean Daniélou has tried to create a synthesis of what he considers to be Jewish Christian tradition in the Apostolic Fathers and other Christian writings from the second century. It is a book immensely rich in material, with brilliant detailed analysis of concepts and ideas of Jewish origin in early Christian literature.[25]

But most scholars would like to add that the last step taken by Daniélou—namely synthesizing this material and presenting it as *the* theology of Jewish Christianity—is unwarranted. The fact that an idea or concept can be seen to be of Jewish origin does not automatically imply that it belongs to "Jewish theology" as distinct from "Gentile theology"—especially if "Jewish origin" refers to material from the Old Testament or other Jewish writings held in high esteem by most Christians, for instance, apocalyptic writings such as 1 *Enoch.*

A more appropriate title for Daniélou's book would probably have been "Jewish Forms of Thought in Early Christian Theology." This criticism does not, of course, in any way reduce the value of Daniélou's work. What he has shown, and shown convincingly and brilliantly, is the extent to which the whole of early Christian theology was Jewish in its concepts and modes of expression. This is especially true in those cases in which theology takes the form of exposition of the Scriptures.

There can be no doubt that the biblical scholars of the early church were almost without exception Jewish believers or God-fearers with a good "Jewish" education—people who from their childhood had known the sacred

---

[25]On Daniélou's book, listed in the Suggestions below, see also my review in *Mishkan* 13 (1990): 54-57.

Temple Square
In all the writings reviewed in this chapter, and also in *The Shepherd of Hermas*, we meet repeatedly the concept of the Christian community as the spiritual temple. (*Barnabas* also seems to show negative concern about Hadrian's beginning to build a Jupiter temple on the "old" Temple Mount [*Barnabas* 16.3-4, cf. Hvalvik, pp. 18-23]). This is all in line with New Testament teaching. At the same time we see something new coming up. In *1 Clement* a parallel is drawn between Israel of old and the present church: at that time the people of God was a well-structured hierarchy of high priest, priests, Levites and laymen; and in the same way it should be now. The ministers of the church—overseers/presbyters and deacons—are not directly identified with the old priests and Levites; they are instead compared to them. But the identification is not far away. We see intimations of it also in the *Didache*. And it was to be completed within some hundred years: in Hippolytus (ca. A.D. 210) the bishop has become the new high priest. There is a corresponding loss of the priestly character of the laypeople. We observe the first phases of a development that would end in the Christian community being an assembly of non-priestly laypeople gathering *in* a temple—the church building—and being serviced by the new temple personnel, the Christian priests and Levites: the bishops, presbyters and deacons. And most important of all, the celebration of the Eucharist was increasingly interpreted as an actualization of the sacrificial act of Jesus, and the Christian ministers were accordingly seen as priests bringing God a propitiatory sacrifice (see more on this in chapter twenty). In a sense the cultic temple service of the Old Testament was back, with a physical sanctuary, priests, sacrifice and all. It is thought-provoking that this happened in Christianity, but not in rabbinic Judaism. The latter has done, and apparently done well, without sacrifices and temple to the present day.

Scriptures and had learned the appropriate methods of interpretation in the synagogue. This they liberally passed on to the church at large, so that much of their exegetical work with the Old Testament later turned up in typically Gentile Christian writings.

Let me emphasize that as far as the evidence goes, there is no reason to suspect great doctrinal differences between Jewish believers and other Christians in this period. Jewish believers were the leading theologians of the church, and the Gentiles had mostly learned their theology from Jewish tutors, either by reading their writings (Ignatius reading the New Testament) or by copying their Old Testament expositions (Barnabas). At this time, Jewish believers in mixed communities were not a separate sect apart from the "Great Church," they were quite simply the kernel of the "Great Church." It was they who helped the church define what orthodoxy was. We shall see the significance of this in chapter twelve.

Suggestions for Further Reading
Perhaps the best general survey of the period between the two Jewish wars, A.D. 70-135, is to be found in Frend, *The Rise of Christianity*, pp. 119-60 (= chapter 4, "The Christian Synagogue 70-135").

An excellent review of the Apostolic Fathers with special emphasis on their Jewish heritage, is Jean Daniélou, *The Theology of Jewish Christianity, The Development of Christian Doctrine Before the Council of Nicaea* 1 (London: Darton, Longman & Todd, 1964), pp. 28-54. Apart from this, the whole book is relevant to the theme of this chapter.

See also Leslie W. Barnard, *Studies in the Apostolic Fathers and their Background* (Oxford: Blackwell 1966); Leonhard Goppelt, *Christentum und Judentum im ersten und zweiten Jahrhundert: Ein Aufriss der Urgeschichte der Kirche,* Beiträge zur Förderung Christlicher Theologie, 2. Reihe, 55 (Gütersloh: Bertelsmann, 1954); Otto Knoch, "Die Stellung der apostolischen Väter zu Israel und zum Judentum. Eine Übersicht," in *Begegnung mit dem Wort: Festschrift für H. Zimmermann,* ed. J. Zmijewski and E. Nellessen, Bonner biblische Beiträge 53 (Bonn, 1980), pp. 347-78; J. Klevinghaus, *Die theologische Stellung der Apostolischen Väter zur alttestamentlichen Offenbarung,* Beiträge zur Förderung Christlicher Theologie 44, 1 (Gütersloh: Bertelsmann, 1948); Graham N. Stanton, "Aspects of Early Christian-Jewish Polemic and Apologetic," *New Testament Studies* 31 (1985): 377-92.

On Barnabas, see Pierre Prigent, *Les Testimonia dans le Christianisme Primitif: L'Épître de Barnabé I-XVI et ses sources,* Études bibliques (Paris: J. Gabalda, 1961); James Carleton Paget, *The Epistle of Barnabas: Outlook and Background,* Wissenschaftliche Untersuchungen zum Neuen Testament, 2. Reihe, 64 (Tübingen: J. C. B. Mohr [Paul Siebeck], 1994); Reidar Hvalvik, *The Struggle for Scripture and Covenant: The Purpose of the Epistle of Barnabas and Jewish-Christian Competition in the Second Century,* Wissenschaftliche Untersuchungen zum Neuen Testament, 2. Reihe, 82 (Tübingen: J. C. B. Mohr [Paul Siebeck], 1996); Ferdinand R. Prostmeier, *Der Barnabasbrief,* Kommentar zu den Apostolischen Vätern 8 (Göttingen: Vandenhoeck & Ruprecht, 1999).

11

ENCOUNTER WITH PAGANISM—&THE JEWISH HERITAGE

*T*he picture of Christian mission that we get from Acts is a mission whose pri-
mary target groups were the Jewish members and Gentile visitors of the Diaspora
synagogues. This picture would probably still be valid in the first decades of the sec-
ond century A.D. But increasingly, Christian outreach would take the Christian mes-
sage outside these groups, that is, outside the circle of Jewish and Gentile
monotheists. It would be presented to pagan Gentiles also. This made the church face
new challenges. Or rather, it made the young church face old challenges in a new way
and on a more massive scale than before.

What did this do to the church? Did it serve to alienate the church from its Jewish
roots, or did it rather force the church to an appreciation of the work of Jewish apolo-
gists, who had faced this challenge for a long time already?

It is in the work of the so-called Apologists of the second century that we find the
answer to this question.

Introduction
It is a remarkable fact that almost none of the missionary preaching that has
come down to us from the early period (before A.D. 135) has much polemic
against idol worship. In the New Testament we find such polemic in two

unusual circumstances, which we have discussed already, Acts 14:15-17; 17:22-31 (cf. chapter eight). Aside from this there is a warning not to participate in sacrificial meals at the pagan temples in 1 Corinthians 10:19-21, and there is a hint of polemic against idol worship in 1 Thessalonians 1:9. That is all there is of direct polemic against paganism in the New Testament. (Romans 1:19-32 is not concerned with paganism as a reality in which the readers of the letter are ensnared, but is a theological statement about the sinfulness of idol worship.)

The Christian mission of the New Testament period operated within Jewish spiritual territory, inside which Judaism had already fought and won the decisive battles against paganism. In the New Testament we hear only distant echoes of that battle: paganism is, for the most part, a distant phenomenon, present all the time in the communities' surroundings, but not much of a threat or challenge because the Christians had for the most part done away with idolatry even before becoming Christians.

The same is very much true about the Apostolic Fathers of the first half of the second century. Here we find even less direct polemic against paganism. For the authors and readers of these writings, paganism is more or less a past reality, or perhaps better, a conquered reality. The real threat comes from elsewhere: from various distortions of biblical doctrine (cf. chapter twelve), from factions and false ambitions among the Christians themselves.

But once we have passed, say, A.D. 130, all this changes dramatically. Suddenly we meet a group of authors known as the Apologists (See box 11.2, p. 231). Here the polemic against paganism is the main concern, the very purpose for which these documents were written. What had happened? Why this change?

Let us return to the picture of "spiritual territory." So far, the Christian mission operated within the spiritual territory of the synagogue. In other words, the Christian missionaries mainly addressed themselves to Jews and Gentile God-fearers who were biblical monotheists. The missionaries operated in a nonpagan, monotheistic territory already cleared by the synagogue. During the second century this changed. The outreach of the church extended beyond the spiritual territory of the synagogue. "Raw" Gentiles, pagan Gentiles, became interested in the church. This meant that the church could no longer rely on preparatory antipagan work done by the synagogue. The church had to fight that battle itself.[1] For this reason we have entitled this

---

[1]For general overviews of the history of the church and its mission during the first part of the second century A.D., see Frend, *Rise of Christianity,* pp. 126-92; Grant, *Augustus to Constantine,* pp. 77-120.

Box 11.1. Jewish Apologetics and Missionary Literature

Wisdom of Solomon (written ca. 150-100 B.C., probably in Alexandria): This contains a classic Jewish refutation of idol worship.

The Letter of Aristeas (last century B.C.): Tells the story of the translation of the Septuagint, "The Seventy" (LXX), the Torah rendered in Greek by seventy Jewish elders, having come from Jerusalem to Egypt. The *Letter* is at the same time a commendatory document for the Torah and the excellence of the Mosaic legislation.

Joseph and Aseneth (last century B.C. or first century A.D.): A love-story about the wife of Joseph, the daughter of an Egyptian priest. She plays the role of the model proselyte, a figure with which proselytes—especially women—could identify.

Philo of Alexandria, *Against Flaccus* and *Embassy to Gaius* (shortly after the event, A.D. 40): Here Philo tells of persecution in Alexandria and his subsequent journey to Rome as a leader of a Jewish delegation that appealed to the emperor. In a wider sense, all of Philo's books may be said to be apologetic and missionary on behalf of Judaism.

The Sibylline Oracles, especially Books 3 (written in Egypt ca. 100 B.C.) and 4 (possibly written in the land of Israel, end of first century A.D.): These are the supreme examples of a special genre of missionary literature in which figures of authority within Greek-Roman culture are made the spokespersons of Judaism. The Sibyls were originally pagan prophetesses of antiquity, whose oracles were regarded as divine revelations by many, including some prominent politicians. Other examples of Jewish authors using pagan authorities as pseudonyms include Pseudo-Orpheus, Pseudo-Hekataios (a famous historian), Pseudo-Hystaspes, etc.

Josephus, *Against Apion* (written shortly after A.D. 100): A skilled defense of Judaism against attacks. Gives valuable insight into early anti-Semitism. In a wider sense, Josephus's great historical work *Jewish Antiquities* may also be called apologetic.

period "encounter with paganism."

What weapons should the church use? By what arguments should idolaters be convinced to quit idol worship and embrace faith in the one God of the Bible? The rather obvious answer is that the Christian Apologists had to learn from their Jewish precursors, for the Jews had been engaged in this battle for some time.

We do not possess more than scraps and fragments of the rich Jewish literature concerned with refuting paganism and inviting Gentiles to join the elect people. But the preserved writings (or fragments of writings) are sufficient to give us a rich and nuanced picture of how Jews had addressed their Gentile neighbors during the period ca. 200 B.C.-A.D. 100 (See box 11.1, above).[2] They are also sufficient to indicate the quite massive take-over of Jewish apologetics and missionary preaching by the

---

[2]See the sources and literature listed in the Suggestions below, and in addition cf. the following: A. Causse, "La propagande juive et l'hellénisme," *Revue d'histoire et de philosophie religieuses* 3 (1923): 397-414; Robert McLachlan Wilson, "Jewish Literary Propaganda," in *Paganisme, Judaisme, Christianisme: Mélanges offerts à Marcel Simon*, ed. A. Benoit et al. (Paris: E. de Boccard, 1978), pp. 61-71.

early Christian Apologists.[3]

One may state this situation in a way that sounds paradoxical: precisely when the church extended its outreach into "raw" Gentile territory, the Jewish heritage became more indispensable than ever.

Conversion in Judaism and Christianity

Let us review some revealing illustrations of this thesis. When a Gentile converted to Judaism, one thing was obligatory: a complete break with all forms of pagan religion and worship. Pagan religion was regarded as slavery to God's adversary or evil demons, and you had to renounce all that when you turned to the God of Israel. This is beautifully expressed in the prayer of repentance put in the mouth of Aseneth, the future wife of Joseph, in the fascinating missionary novel called *Joseph and Aseneth*.[4] Aseneth is portrayed as a model proselyte. She was the daughter of an Egyptian priest and had her chamber full of Egyptian idols. When turning from her ancestral religion, she says the following:

> I have committed lawlessness and irreverence. . . . My mouth is defiled from the sacrifices of the idols and from the tables of the gods of the Egyptians. I have sinned, Lord, before you I have sinned much in ignorance, and have worshipped dead and dumb idols. . . . With you I take refuge, Lord. . . . For behold, the wild old lion persecutes me, because he is the father of the gods of the Egyptians, and his children are the gods of the idol maniacs. And I have come to hate them . . . and have thrown all of them from me and destroyed them. (*Joseph and Aseneth* 12:5-9)[5]

Most of the first Gentile converts to Christianity, the God-fearers, had this break with paganism behind them when they became Christians. In the second century this changed. An increasing number of converts came directly from paganism. They went, so to speak, directly from the "table of the demons" (1 Cor 10:21) to the table of the Lord. This posed a challenge to the growing church. It had to see to it that the required break with paganism really took place.[6] Accordingly, two rituals developed which were used prior

---

[3]Studies that emphasize this takeover include Erwin R. Goodenough, *The Theology of Justin Martyr: An Investigation into the Conceptions of Early Christian Literature and Its Hellenistic and Judaistic Influences* (Jena: Frommann, 1923 [reprint, Amsterdam: Philo, 1968]); Robert M. Grant, *Greek Apologists of the Second Century* (Philadelphia: Westminster Press, 1988), pp. 9-18.

[4]For references to recent studies of this novel, see chap. three, note 23, p. 77.

[5]Charlesworth, *Pseudepigrapha* 2:220-21.

[6]In an emphatic way Thomas M. Finn brings out the drama involved in the conversion of

to the administration of baptism.

The first was the repeated exorcism of baptismal candidates. Shortly after A.D. 200, Hippolytus of Rome wrote down the exorcism formula used in his church: "He (the bishop) shall exorcise every evil spirit to flee away from them and never return to them henceforward" (*Apostolic Tradition* 20.8).[7] Hippolytus does not seem to imply that all candidates are possessed by demons. Rather, the exorcisms are thought to have a diagnostic function: any demon will have to betray itself and yield when faced with the commandment to leave the person in Jesus' name. But the pre-baptismal exorcism was also open to another, more spiritual interpretation, in which all human servitude to Satan and his host was seen as "possession": "Before we believed in God the habitation of our heart was corrupt and weak, like a temple really built with hands, because it was full of idolatry, and was the house of demons through doing things which were contrary to God" (*Barnabas* 16:7).

The second measure was to introduce the renunciation into the baptismal liturgy. Before confessing their faith and going down into the baptismal font, the candidates had to affirm the following formula (or a very similar one): "I renounce you, Satan, and all service of you and all your works."[8] This meant that the baptismal candidates implicitly declared that all religious practice they had hitherto been engaged in was *servitio Satanae*, slavery under Satan. And they explicitly renounced all of this; very much like the literary figure of Jewish proselyte Aseneth.

We do not know at what time the pre-baptismal exorcisms and the formal renunciation of Satan were introduced into the baptismal liturgy. In the New

---

stark pagans: "Catechesis was only half the battle, and 'battle' is the correct word: The purpose of the catechumenate was literally to 'reform' the candidate. . . . Thus, as the catechumens' convictions changed from old values to new, their conduct had also to change from old ways to new. This formative task was assigned to exorcism, because the obstacle to conversion was a literally terrifying field of forces—physical, psychological, and spiritual—which the catechists identified with graphic specificity: the gods, their cultic processions, the races, the theater, the gladiatorical extravaganzas, every conceivable vice. . . . The unseen enemy, however, was Satan and his legions—the real obstacle to conversion. . . . As a result, catechesis was linked to exorcism. For the Holy Spirit to enter, . . . the evil spirit had to be driven out. Thus, exorcist was counterpart of catechist" (Thomas M. Finn, *Early Christian Baptism and the Catechumenate: West and East Syria*, Message of the Fathers of the Church 5 [Collegeville, Minn.: Liturgical Press, 1992], pp. 5-6).
[7] Dix/Chadwick, p. 32.
[8] This formula is taken from Hippolytus, *Apostolic Tradition* 21.9 (Dix, p. 34), but is attested earlier in Tertullian. Cf. collection of texts in E. C. Whitaker, *Documents of the Baptismal Liturgy*, 2nd ed. (London: SPCK, 1970), pp. 7-10.

Testament we find no trace of either element, so a reasonable guess is that they were added during the beginning of the second century.[9]

A very vivid picture of the pagan world into which the church penetrated during the second century is provided in Hippolytus's prescriptions for how different categories of pagans should be received when they asked for baptismal instruction:

> If a man be a pander who supports harlots either let him desist or let him be rejected. If a man be a sculptor or a painter, he shall be taught not to make idols. If he will not desist, let him be rejected. . . . A charioteer likewise or one who takes part in the games or who goes to the games, either let him desist or let him be rejected. A man who is a gladiator or a trainer of gladiators or a huntsman or one concerned with wild-beast shows or a public official who is concerned with gladiatorial shows, either let him desist or let him be rejected. (*Apostolic Tradition* 16.10-24)[10]

It is quite obvious from these requirements for candidates for baptism that the church is no longer in the world of the God-fearers. It has been plunged into the world of paganism and must take the required measures to ensure that new converts do not bring their paganism with them into the church.

In the world of antiquity, the Jews and the Christians were the only ones who required this absolute break with all other religious allegiances,[11] and the Christian rituals of conversion must have made the church look very Jewish to the average pagan. In fact, it may easily be observed that the development of Jewish proselyte baptism during the first two centuries A.D. continued to influence Christian baptismal rites long after the New Testament period (see more on this in chapter eighteen below).

The Apologists

We should keep this new setting clearly in mind when we approach the Christian Apologists of the second century. Some of their writings are so exclusively devoted to attacking pagan idolatry and defending biblical monotheism and ethics—for example, *Apology* by Aristides and *To Autoclytus* by Theophilus—that specific Christian elements such as the name of Jesus or

---

[9]Cf. Hans Kirsten, *Die Taufabsage: Eine Untersuchung zu Gestalt und Geschichte der Taufe nach den altkirchlichen Taufliturgien* (Berlin: Evangelische Verlagsanstalt, 1960).
[10]Dix, pp. 25-28.
[11]The best study to bring this out very clearly is still Alfred Darby Nock, *Conversion: The Old and the New in Religion from Alexander the Great to Augustine of Hippo* (Oxford: Oxford University Press, 1961 [or reprints]).

Box 11.2. The Apologists

The Preaching of Peter (ca. A.D. 125): Fragments preserved in Clement of Alexandria. Missionary preaching defending the Gospel against Jews and Greeks.

The Apology of Quadratus (ca. A.D. 125): Delivered to Emperor Hadrian; one little fragment preserved in Eusebius. Some of those healed or raised from the dead by Christ still alive in the [early] days of Quadratus.

Aristides, *Apology* (ca. A.D. 140): Similar to *The Preaching of Peter,* heavy emphasis on the rationality of monotheism and the irrationality of idolatry.

Justin Martyr, Two *Apologies* (ca. A.D. 150-160): Greek philosophy (Socrates) said to be an ally of Christians. Truth of Christianity proved from the Old Testament prophets, who foretold the Messiah.

Tatian, *Oration to the Greeks* (A.D. 165-70): Tatian was Justin's pupil, and made full use of his master's philosophical arguments against paganism. The truth is to be found in the Prophets.

Melito of Sardis, *Apology* (ca. A.D. 172): The church and the empire should make peace with each other, to the profit of both. (Only fragments preserved, in Eusebius's *Ecclesiastical History*).

Athenagoras, *Supplication for the Christians* (ca. A.D. 177): A very scholarly and philosophical defense of Christianity.

Theophilus of Antioch, *To Autolycus* (ca. A.D. 180): Represents a massive takeover of Jewish apologetics.

Tertullian, *Apology* (A.D. 197): The classic defense of Christianity and the first major presentation of Christianity in Latin.

Clement of Alexandria, *Exhortation to the Greeks* (slightly before A.D. 200): The most learned defense of Christianity written until then.

---

the title Christ (which would distinguish them from corresponding Jewish writings) are only hinted at. Christ is only spoken of in connection with the doctrine of creation, that is, as the Wisdom or Word of God, which acted as a mediator when the world was created.

It is this new setting and emphasis that make the Apologists seem so unfamiliar and so different from the New Testament writers. In reality, they think in very Jewish ways and carry on important Jewish concerns vis-à-vis paganism. Let us make a detailed case study to give some substance and color to the above generalizations.

We will use Justin Martyr as our example and start with a passage that on the surface sounds rather Hellenistic and unbiblical. After having stated that the gods of the Gentiles are really demons (derived from the illegal cohabitations mentioned in Gen 6:1-4), Justin goes on to say:

Taken captive by fear and not understanding that these were evil demons, men called them gods and gave each of them the name which each of the demons had chosen for himself. When Socrates tried by true reason and with due inquiry to make these things clear and to draw men away from the demons, they, working through men who delighted in wickedness, managed to have him

put to death as godless and impious, saying that he was bringing in new divini-
ties. And now they do the same kind of thing to us. For these errors were not
only condemned among the Greeks by Logos, through Socrates, but among the
barbarians, by Logos himself, who took on the form of a man and was called
Jesus Christ. (*First Apology* 5.3-4)[12]

This passage deserves careful reading. On the surface, Justin is stating that
Socrates in some sense was a Christian and that Greek philosophy, represented by Socrates, is some kind of revelation outside Scripture. Some modern theologians have thought they discerned here a doctrine about the
"hidden Christ in non-Christian religions."[13] But that is not what Justin has in
mind. One might say the contrary: hidden behind the non-Christian religions
of the Roman Empire Justin does not detect Christ, but evil demons. What
Justin is saying is that we Christians are not the first to undertake this criticism of pagan religions—unmasking the gods as evil demons. Socrates let
himself be guided by Logos, reason, which Christ, the true Reason, as a mediator of God's creation, has placed in every human being. Human rational
thought should be sufficient to unmask idol worship as nonsense and
depravity, and Socrates is a witness against the rest of humanity that they
have no rational excuse for their paganism.[14]

This is not very far from Paul, who in Romans 1:19-21 said that God's
greatness as a creator should be sufficiently evident in nature to deter people
from idol worship, "so they are without excuse" (see also Acts 17:24-28).

But this makes Justin's portrait of Greek philosophy all the more interesting. Let us compare a few rabbinic passages. "Whoever acknowledges idolatry disavows the whole Torah, and whoever disavows idolatry acknowledges the whole Torah" (*Sifre Deut.* 28). "Idolatry is so heinous that he who

---

[12]E. R. Hardy in C. C. Richardson, ed., *The Library of Christian Classics*, vol. 1: *Early Christian Fathers* (London: SCM Press, 1953), pp. 244-45.

[13]For this interpretation, see George Khodr, "Christianity in a Pluralist World: The Economy of the Holy Spirit," *The Ecumenical Review* 23 (1971): 118-28; republished in *Living Faiths and the Ecumenical Movement*, ed. Stanley J. Samartha (Geneva: WCC, 1971), pp. 131-42.

[14]For this interpretation of Justin, see Ernst Benz, "Christus und Sokrates in der alten Kirche (Ein Beitrag zum altkirchlichen Verständnis des Märtyrers und des Martyriums)," *Zeitschrift für die neutestamentliche Wissenschaft* 43 (1950/1951): 195-224; David F. Wright, "Christian Faith in the Greek World: Justin Martyr's Testimony," *Evangelical Quarterly* 54 (1982): 77-87; Arthur J. Droge, "Justin Martyr and the Restoration of Philosophy," *Church History* 56 (1987): 303-19; Graham Keith, "Justin Martyr and Religious Exclusivism," *Tyndale Bulletin* 43 (1992): 57-80; Oskar Skarsaune, "Judaism and Hellenism in Justin Martyr, Elucidated from His Portrait of Socrates," in *Geschichte—Tradition—Reflexion: Festschrift für Martin Hengel zum 70. Geburtstag*, Band 3: *Frühes Christentum*, ed. H. Cancik et al. (Tübingen: J. C. B. Mohr [Paul Siebeck], 1996), pp. 585-611.

rejects it is as though he admits the whole Torah" (*TB Qiddushin* 40a). "For anyone who repudiates idolatry is called 'a Jew'" (*TB Megillah* 13a). The meaning of these sayings is not that circumcision and the rest of the commandments can be dispensed with if you want to become a Jew. The meaning is rather that anyone who makes the remarkable feat of breaking with the idolatry of family and surroundings—as Abraham did, according to the rabbis—is an "honorary Jew." Such a person is behaving like a Jew on the essential point.

According to the rabbis, Abraham originally shared the idolatrous practices of his father. But he abandoned the idols, was persecuted and was even thrown into a fiery furnace, like the three men of Daniel 3 (Hananiah, Azariah and Mishael) who also rejected idolatry.[15] Now let us return to a passage in Justin:

> Those who lived in accordance with Logos (that is, rejected idolatry) are "Christians," even though they were called atheists, such as, among the Greeks, Socrates and Heraclitus and others like them; among the barbarians, Abraham, Ananiah, Azariah and Mishael." (*First Apology* 46.3)

The parallel to the rabbinic idea is perfect: just as Gentiles who rejected idolatry could be regarded as "Jews" by the rabbis, so Greek philosophers who rejected pagan religion were regarded as "Christians" by Justin.

This corresponds to a further parallel: just as the Gentile who rejects idolatry is said by the rabbis to acknowledge the whole Torah, so Justin portrays Christ as fulfilling the essential function of the Torah when he turns people from idol worship to the God of Abraham:

> As an eternal and final Law was Christ given to us. . . . By the name of Him who was crucified, Jesus Christ, men part from idols and all other iniquity, and draw near to God, and make confession of Him, and worship, enduring unto death . . . (and from this) all can understand that He is the new Law. (*Dialogue with Trypho* 11.2-4)[16]

Justin here conceives of the work of Christ in typical Torah terms: Christ fulfills the essential function of the Torah, which is to destroy paganism and lead people to recognition of the one true God. And so, when Justin met with a true philosopher, a true lover of wisdom like Socrates, he was willing to rec-

---

[15]The earliest versions of this legend occur in *Jubilees* 11:14—12:21 (second century B.C.) and Pseudo-Philo, *Biblical Antiquities* 6.1-18 (first century A.D.), later it is often repeated in rabbinic midrashim. See Louis Ginzberg, *The Legends of the Jews* (Philadelphia: The Jewish Publication Society of America, 1937), 1:189-217, for a full review of all the different traditions.

[16]Williams, p. 23.

ognize in him the working of God's Wisdom, which is Christ. The rabbis shared this approach to Gentile philosophy: "Our Rabbis taught, 'On seeing the sages of Israel one should say, "Blessed be He who has given a portion of His wisdom to them that fear Him." On seeing the sages of the idolaters, one should say, "Blessed be He who has given of His wisdom to his creatures"'" (*TB Berakhot* 58a). So, on closer inspection, Justin's teaching on Christ as the universal Logos, active in the Greek philosophers, turns out to be strikingly Jewish, and part of his vehement rejection of all pagan religion.

Basically the same picture emerges if we turn to Clement of Alexandria, usually regarded as the most significant Hellenizer among the theologians who are of interest here. His apologetic and missionary work *Exhortation to the Greeks* (*Protreptikos pros hellenas*) harshly critiques the Greek and Roman gods and traditional religion (chaps. 2-4). Then the philosophers are taken to task (chaps. 5-6). Most of the philosophers are not much better than the idolaters, for they exalt the four elements or "the first principles" as if they were gods, and pay them divine tribute. Some of the philosophers, however, have rejected this, and have thereby seen glimpses of the truth. Foremost among these is Plato (chap. 6). What Clement especially values in Plato is his recognition that God is incomprehensible. God cannot be identified with anything in the created world. He is one and he is good. Just as Moses by means of the Law turned Israel from idolatry to the true God, so the philosophers, through glimpses and fragments of the truth, have unmasked and destroyed idolatry and prepared the Greeks for their encounter with the true God. But only the incarnated Logos leads us all the way to God.

Now all this may seem to take us into an atmosphere of advanced, well-educated Christians who were able to speak the jargon of the sophisticated intellectual elite of the Roman cities. It would be entirely misleading, however, to suppose that this intellectual fight for biblical monotheism was confined to the literary salons. Every Christian had to stand up and take the consequences of the baptismal renunciation: "I renounce you, Satan."

The rejection of paganism was an everyday reality with everyday consequences that could be heavy. Sometimes it meant martyrdom; Justin Martyr reminds us that the Apologists would have written on more harmless themes if they were only seeking intellectual exercise. Most early Christian writers knew that they might have to answer with their lives for what they wrote, because their writing made them publicly known. Equally exposed, of course, were the renowned leaders of the Christian community, the bishops. Not a few martyrs of this period were bishops, such as Polycarp or other leading figures of the church.

Even the average rank-and-file Christians always ran the risk of being exposed to their neighbors' hatred because they rejected their neighbors' religion. Then it was not so much a question of making a convincing intellectual defense, but of simple personal integrity and perseverance. Or, as the martyrs themselves would have put it, it was a question of faithfulness to the Lord who had redeemed them.

When the Roman official enticed the aged Polycarp: "Swear and I set you free: Curse Christ," Polycarp answered, "Eighty and six years have I served Him, and He did me no wrong. How can I blaspheme my King, that saved me?" (Martyrdom of Polycarp 9.3).

We come closest, perhaps, to the average Christian in a moving document preserved by Eusebius (Ecclesiastical History 5.1-4). It is a letter from the communities of Vienne and Lyons in southern France, addressed to their sister congregations in Asia Minor. The year is A.D. 177, and the letter was written while the cruel persecution of about forty-eight members was still fresh in the bereaved communities' minds.

The Martyrs of Lyons

Exactly what caused the riot against the Christians is not known; one gets the impression that it was the outlet for a general hatred that had been building up over time. It began with a social excommunication of the Christians. They were banned from the baths and the marketplaces and eventually from all public places. Shortly afterward, when the Roman governor was absent from the city, the mob took the law into their own hands and started a regular pogrom against the Christians.

They were insulted, beaten and stoned. At the intervention of the authorities, they were jailed. Some of the wealthier Christians had slaves in their household. These were arrested and tortured in order to produce evidence that the Christians had secretly committed incest and cannibalism. Some yielded to the torture and "testified" as they were told.

After this, the rage of the populace knew no bounds. The authorities also tortured the Christians themselves in order to produce evidence for criminal actions. They were given inhuman treatment in prison, and not a few of them perished, among them Photinus, the bishop of Lyons. Most of the prisoners withstood the torture, including one Sanctus, who "would not [even] state . . . his own name, or the people or city whence he came, or whether he were bond or free. But to every question he replied in Latin: 'I am a Christian,' . . .

and no other word did the heathen hear from his lips" (*Ecclesiastical History* 5.1.20).[17]

For most of the prisoners the heaviest part of their torture was still ahead: they were condemned to serve as public entertainment in the wild-beast show at the amphitheater of Lyons. Two by two they were led into the arena, tortured, and then thrown to the beasts. With special love and compassion the narrative expands on the martyrdom of Blandina, a young female slave whom no one thought could survive long, because her body was weak.

> When we were all afraid, and her mistress according to the flesh (who was herself a combatant among the martyrs) was in a state of agony, lest the weakness of her [Blandina's] body should render her unable even to make a bold confession, Blandina was filled with such power that those who by turns kept torturing her in every way from dawn till evening were worn out and exhausted, and themselves confessed defeat. . . . They marvelled that breath still remained in a body all mangled and covered with gaping wounds. . . . But the blessed woman, like a noble champion, in confession regained her youth; and for her, to say "I am a Christian, and with us no evil finds a place" was refreshment and rest and insensibility to her lot. (*Ecclesiastical History* 5.1.18-9)[18]

This torture Blandina endured while still in prison. At last her turn came to be exposed in the theater. She was

> suspended on a stake, . . . exposed as food to wild beasts which were let loose against her. Even to look on her, as she hung cross-wise in earnest prayer, wrought great eagerness in those [other martyrs] who were contending, for in their conflict they beheld with their outward eyes in the form of their sister Him who was crucified for them. . . . And as none of the wild beasts at that time touched her, she was taken down from the stake and cast again into prison . . . that she might conquer in still further contests, and so both render irrevocable the sentence passed on the crooked serpent, and encourage the brethren—she the small, the weak, the despised, who had put on Christ the great and invincible Champion, and who in many rounds vanquished the adversary and through conflict was crowned with the crown of incorruptibility. (*Ecclesiastical History* 5.1.41-42)[19]

So Blandina had to go into the arena a second time. She became, in fact, the last to give up her life for Christ. On the last day of the shows she was again brought into the arena, this time together with the fifteen-year-old boy Ponti-

---

[17]Lawlor/Oulton 1:142.
[18]Ibid.
[19]Ibid., p. 145.

cus. Again they were exposed to all imaginable kinds of torture, but to the amazement of the watching crowd, Blandina even had the strength to encourage Ponticus, so that he passed away without denying his faith.

> But the blessed Blandina last of all, having, like a highborn mother, exhorted her children and sent them forth victorious to the King, travelled herself along the same path of conflicts as they did, and hastened to them, rejoicing and exulting at her departure, like one bidden to a marriage supper, rather than cast to the wild beast. And after the scourging, after the wild beasts, after the frying-pan, she was at last thrown into a basket and presented to a bull. For a time the animal tossed her, but she had now lost all perception of what happened, thanks to the hope she cherished, her grasp of the objects of her faith, and her intercourse with Christ. Then she too was sacrificed, and even the heathen themselves acknowledged that never in their experience had a woman endured so many and terrible sufferings. (*Ecclesiastical History* 5.1.53-56)[20]

Not even then was the populace satisfied. After the deaths of the martyrs, their bodies were left unburied to be devoured by dogs, and finally the remains were burned, and the ashes thrown into the river Rhone, "that not a fragment of them might be left on earth" (*Ecclesiastical History* 5.1.62).

It is a fascinating and terrible story the survivors had to tell, fascinating for the light it throws both on the Christian community and on its surroundings. Let us first take a look at the attitude of the populace. One gets the impression that at the bottom of their hate and rage there lies fear. "The intense fury of the people and their fear that somehow or other the Christians might triumph over their gods, stands out on every page of the . . . story."[21] This is most clearly seen in the treatment of the martyrs' dead bodies. Their persecutors no doubt feared that the martyrs' death in the arena might not be the last act of the drama, and that their hope of resurrection might come true. The thoughts of the persecuters are expressed thus in the narrative: they burned the bodies of the martyrs

> "in order," as they themselves said, "that they may not even have the hope of a resurrection, in faith of which they introduce into our midst a certain strange and new religion, and despise dread torments, and are ready to go to their death, and that with joy. Now let us see if they will rise again, and if their god can help them, and deliver them out of our hands." (*Ecclesiastical History* 5.1.63)[22]

---

[20]Ibid., p. 146.
[21]Frend, *Martyrdom and Persecution*, p. 9.
[22]Lawlor/Oulton 1:147.

238 — IN THE SHADOW OF THE TEMPLE

Whether or not these pagans felt quite at ease and were fully reassured that their own gods had been vindicated, we do not know. What we do know is that some were left wondering. The narrative says that some Gentiles asked, "Where is their God, and of what profit is their religion to them, which they preferred even to their lives?" (*Ecclesiastical History* 5.1.60). To some, this wondering at what the martyrs found so immensely valuable in Christianity might have been the first step toward closer investigation, knowledge and eventually conversion.[23] A few years later Tertullian was to put it tersely and eloquently: "The blood of the Christians is a seed" (*Apology* 50).

Of even greater interest in our study is the attitude of the community that produced these martyrs and wrote the account of their martyrdom. Some striking features in the description of the martyrs require an explanation. The martyrs are regularly called fighters, combatants, athletes; they are engaged in a contest; and enduring unto death they conquer and win this contest. Rather peculiar language is used about Blandina: She is likened to "a high-born mother," and the other martyrs are her "children," whom she has "sent before her, victorious to the King."

Nothing of this is strange, however, to one who is familiar with the story of the Maccabean martyrs in Second and Fourth Maccabees. In 2 Maccabees 7 we read the story about the mother and her seven sons who were martyred by Antiochus Epiphanes. An expanded version appears in 4 Maccabees 8—17. Here the mother and her sons are described as fighters in exactly the same way as in the Christian account of the Lyons martyrs. The account of the mother's martyrdom obviously provides the literary model for the account of Blandina. This means that the author of the narrative was quite familiar with the Jewish martyr tradition contained in the Maccabean books, and that he presupposed the same familiarity in his readers. Obviously, the Lyons community regarded the Maccabean martyrs as their spiritual forebears and as inspiring examples to be followed when need be.[24]

---

[23]A well-known example is the story Justin Martyr tells about himself in his *Second Apology*, chap. 12.

[24]In this analysis, I have followed Frend, *Martyrdom and Persecution*, rather closely. The thesis put forward in Glen W. Bowersock, *Martyrdom and Rome*, The Wiles Lectures (Cambridge: Cambridge University Press, 1995)—that the concept of martyrdom in early Christian texts is a purely Christian invention in a Roman context and that the passages in 2 Maccabees that seem to anticipate it are later redactional modifications—does not seem convincing. Daniel Boyarin ("Martyrdom and the Making of Christianity and Judaism," *Journal of Early Christian Studies* 6 [1998], pp. 577-627) argues that both authors are wrong because rather than thinking of Judaism and Christianity as two separate entities, the one influenc-

Was this contact with the proud Jewish martyr tradition only a literary affair? Or did the Lyons community have direct contact with real-life Judaism in their own town? There is an interesting hint in the narrative itself. Under torture, a girl named Biblias in a sudden burst of indignation said, "How can those eat children, who are forbidden to eat the blood even of brute beasts?" This clearly indicates that the community of Lyons still observed the apostolic decree of Acts 15 concerning kosher meat.[25] As Frend aptly remarks, "the question arises, where did the Christians get their meat from? The only possible answer is, from a kosher market established for the Jews, and this in turn indicates fairly close personal relations between the Jews and Christians in the city. At Lyons . . . the Jews are not mentioned among the church's enemies."[26]

The Christians in Lyons are thus an excellent test-case for the thesis stated in this chapter. Directly confronted with paganism, the Jewishness of the Christian faith becomes pronounced and palpable. In the account of the martyrs of Lyons, the Maccabean martyr tradition comes dramatically back to life.

And there is more. There is evidence that Jews on their part were impressed by the testimony given for Israel's God by Gentile Christian martyrs. Almost unwillingly, Trypho the Jew admits to Justin that Christian readiness for martyrdom impresses him: when you are willing to endure martyrdom, he says, how come you do not bother to keep the ritual commandments of the law, which are easier? (*Dialogue with Trypho* 19.1). At a later time, during the Diocletian persecution, the Jews of Lydda were amazed to watch the Gentile Christian martyrs from Egypt who had been sent to their city to be tortured there. They heard the Roman officer call these Egyptian Gentiles by Hebrew names: Elijah, Isaiah, Jeremiah, Daniel. And true to their names, they rejected idol worship and stood firm in their confession of the God of Israel:

> The Jews . . . stood around, seeing and hearing, while the Egyptians renounced the gods of their own fathers and confessed the God who was also the God of the Jews, and witnessed for him whom the Jews had many times renounced. . . . And at the men and at their names, at their words and at their actions, the Jews

---

ing the other, one should think of them as overlapping to such an extent that they rather share one common history. I have problems buying this thesis wholesale, but cf. below.
[25]Meat from animals slaughtered in such a way that no blood was left in the meat. Jews were not allowed to eat blood.
[26]Frend, *Martyrdom and Persecution*, p. 18.

were greatly amazed. (Eusebius, *Palestinian Martyrs* 8.1)[27]

Daniel Boyarin feels convinced that it must be such Gentile Christians the rabbis had in mind when they spoke about righteous Gentiles who because of their faithfulness to monotheism would certainly inherit the world to come. He quotes Saul Liebermann:

> What did the Rabbis think of the Gentile who did not avail himself of the [offered] exemption and did suffer martyrdom for His Name? All pious Gentiles were promised their share in the future life, those of them who suffered for their good deeds were especially singled out, and there can be no doubt that the pious Gentiles who suffered martyrdom for their refusal to offer sacrifices to idols were deemed deserving of one of the noblest ranks in the future world.[28]

I should probably like to qualify this somewhat by saying that there seems to be no reason to exclude Christian martyrs for monotheism from such rabbinic statements, but maybe the rabbis also had other Gentiles in mind—why not Socrates, for example?[29]

In conclusion, we have no unambiguous evidence that many of the Vienne and Lyons Christians were Jewish; very likely the great majority were Gentile, maybe all of them. Their strikingly "Jewish" behavior in the face of aggressive paganism is all the more striking, and so is the approach toward paganism by the early church in general. Justin defined the task of philosophy as turning Gentiles from pagan idols to the true God (of Israel). If anything, that is a remarkably "Jewish" definition of philosophy! And in defining Christianity as a "philosophy," in this sense of the word, he is certainly not "Hellenizing" Christianity away from its Jewish roots.

Suggestions for Further Reading
Sources:

The Apologists are most conveniently available in English translations in Alexander Roberts and James Donaldson, eds., *The Ante-Nicene Fathers*, vols. 1-3 (Grand Rapids, Mich.: Eerdmans, 1970; several reprints). For a separate, annotated, translation of Justin, see Leslie William Barnard, *Justin Martyr: The First and Second Apologies*, Ancient Christian Writers 56 (New York: Paulist, 1997).

---

[27]Eusebius's tract on the Palestinian martyrs is an appendix to his *Ecclesiastical History.* Quoted hereafter Lawlor/Oulton 1:365.
[28]Boyarin, "Martyrdom," p. 626; the quote from Liebermann is from Saul Liebermann, "The Martyrs of Caesarea," *Annuaire de l'institut de philologie et d'histoire orientales et slaves* 7 (1939-1944): 411.
[29]Cf. above, pp. 232-33.

Temple Square

Temples, bringing of sacrifice, temple meals—all this was the order of the day in the everyday world of early Christians. When they were arrested and accused of being Christians, it was a temple function that was used as the acid test of who were really Christians and who not. Pliny wrote:

> When I instructed them [people accused of being Christians] to do so, they invoked the gods and did reverence with incense and wine to your image, which I had ordered to be brought for this purpose, and also statues of the gods; they also cursed Christ. *As I am informed that people who are really Christians cannot possibly be made to do any of those things,* I considered that those who did them should be discharged. (*Epistles* 10.96, italics added)

For Jews, belonging to a recognized religion (*religio licita*), it was easier to explain their rejection of the official Roman and the local cult of the cities: they had their own temple and their own cult in Jerusalem, and sacrifices were daily brought in the Jerusalem temple on behalf of the emperor and the empire. The Maccabean martyrs had been martyrs for a God dwelling in a concrete, visible temple. After 70, the temple was no more, but the Romans knew they had destroyed it themselves. They could not blame the Jews for not having a temple. But they could not understand why Christians, who had no such ancient loyalty to a visible temple anywhere, should be so adamant in refusing to have anything to do with any other temple or worship. There is in early Christianity an almost obsessive concern with the pollution, the uncleanness, the unholiness that goes with all kinds of idol worship or pagan temples. This is difficult to explain from merely theoretical convictions concerning idol worship. It has all the marks of a living temple community, deeply imbued with the feeling of holiness surrounding the only true temple, and the impurity and unholiness emanating from all other temples. Their own temple was invisible; their loyalty to it, and to its Lord, was for all to see.

Jewish apologetics and missionary literature are available in German translation in the one-volume classic, Paul Riessler, *Alt-Jüdisches Schrifttum ausserhalb der Bibel* (Heidelberg: Kerle, 1927; reprint, Darmstadt: Wissenschaftliche Buchgesellschaft, 1966). For English translations, one should turn to Charlesworth, *Pseudepigrapha 2.*

Studies:

On the second-century Christian Apologists in general, the best introduction is Robert M. Grant, *Greek Apologists of the Second Century* (Philadelphia: Westminster Press, 1988); cf. also the same author's *Gods and the One God: Christian Theology in the Graeco-Roman World* (London: SPCK, 1986).

On Justin in particular, see Leslie W. Barnard, *Justin Martyr: His Life and Thought* (Cambridge: Cambridge University Press, 1967); and Eric F. Osborn, *Justin Martyr,* Beiträge zur historischen Theologie 47 (Tübingen: J. C. B. Mohr, 1973). The Jewishness of Justin's theology is analyzed in Erwin R. Goodenough, *The Theology of Justin Martyr: An Investigation into the Conceptions of Early Christian Literature and Its Hellenistic and Judaistic Influences* (Jena: Frommann, 1923 [reprint, Amsterdam: Philo, 1968]). On Justin and Greek philosophy, see Niels Hyldahl, *Philosophie und Christentum: Eine Interpretation der Einleitung zum Dialog Justins,* Acta Theologica Danica 9 (Copenhagen: Munksgaard, 1966); Robert Joly, *Christianisme et philosophie: Etudes sur Justin et les Apologistes grecs du deuxième siècle,* Université Libre de Bruxelles, Faculté de Philosophie et Lettres 52 (Brussels: Editions de l'Université de Bruxelles, 1973); also O. Skarsaune, "The Conversion of Justin Martyr," *Studia Theologica* 30 (1976): 53-73; idem, "Judaism and Hellenism in Justin Martyr, Elucidated from His Portrait of Socrates," in *Geschichte—Tradition—Reflexion: Festschrift für Martin Hengel zum 70. Geburtstag,* Band 3: *Frühes Christentum,* ed. H. Cancik et al. (Tübingen: J. C. B. Mohr [Paul Siebeck], 1996), pp. 585-611; Arthur J. Droge, "Justin Martyr and the Restoration of Philosophy," *Church History* 56 (1987): 303-19.

On Jewish apologetic and missionary literature, some older studies are still valuable: Moritz Friedländer, *Geschichte der jüdischen Apologetik als Vorgeschichte des Christentums* (Zürich, Amsterdam: Philo, 1973); Paul Krüger, *Philo und Josephus als Apologeten des Judentums* (Leipzig: Verlag der Dürr'schen Buchhandlung, 1906); Peter Dalbert, *Die Theologie der hellenistisch-jüdischen Missionsliteratur unter Ausschluss von Philo und Josephus* (Hamburg: H. Reich, 1954). Among the newer studies, the best general surveys are John J. Collins, *Between Athens and Jerusalem: Jewish Identity in the Hellenistic Diaspora* (New York: Crossroad, 1983); and John M. G. Barclay, *Jews in the Mediterranean Diaspora from Alexander to Trajan (323 BCE-117 CE)* (Edinburgh: T & T Clark, 1996), pp. 125-228, 336-80, 445-52 (excellent overview and rich in bibliographical information). Cf. also the following: John J. Collins, *The Sibylline Oracles of Egyptian Judaism,* SBL Dissertation Series 13 (Missoula, Mont.: Scholars Press, 1974); Louis H. Feldman, *Jew and Gentile in the Ancient World: Attitudes and Interactions from Alexander to Justinian,* Princeton N.J.: Princeton University Press, 1993), pp. 305-22;

A major study on apologetics and martyrdom in the early church, stressing the "Jewishness" of early Christianity in general, is Frend, *Martyrdom and Persecution.* The first chapter in this extensive study is especially recommended as an excellent commentary on the story of the martyrs of Lyons.

A counterpoint to Frend is Glen W. Bowersock, *Martyrdom and Rome,* The Wiles Lectures (Cambridge: Cambridge University Press, 1995). A highly original alternative to both of these is Daniel Boyarin, *Dying for God: Martyrdom and the Making of Christianity and Judaism,* Figurae—Reading Medieval Culture (Stanford, Calif.: Stanford University Press, 1999).

12

ORTHODOXY & HERESY
THE CHALLENGE FROM
GNOSTICISM & MARCION

*D*ifficult as the encounter with Roman authority and power was for the early church, rather than threatening the church's process of defining itself, that encounter actually helped the process. The Romans had to know exactly who were Christians when put to trial, and so did the Christians themselves. This was not the case with the phenomenon we are to study in this chapter. Quite early in their history, the communities of believers had to cope with the fact that some within their own ranks promoted views that seemed to differ from received tradition, and there were other communities with similar doctrines who claimed to represent true Christianity. On this front, the challenge of self-definition was more difficult.

It is argued in this chapter that this challenge, too, forced the church back to its Jewish identity. This time the object of strife was the Old Testament and the God of creation.

The Basic Definition of Heresy

I made it clear to you that those who are Christians in name, but in reality are godless and impious heretics, teach in all respects what is blasphemous and godless and foolish. . . . If you yourselves have ever met with some so-called Christians, who . . . dare to blaspheme the God of Abraham, and the God of Isaac, and the God of Jacob, and who say too that there is no resurrection of the dead, but that their souls ascend to heaven at the very moment of their death—do not suppose that they are Christians. . . . But I, and all other entirely orthodox Christians, know that there will be a resurrection of the flesh, and also a thousand years in a Jerusalem built up and adorned and enlarged, as the prophets Ezekiel and Isaiah, and all the rest, acknowledge. (Justin Martyr, *Dialogue with Trypho* 80.3-5)[1]

[The heretics] all had one law, that they should not employ the Torah and the Prophets, and that they should blaspheme God Almighty, and should not believe in the resurrection. (Syrian *Didascalia Apostolorum* 23 [vi.10])[2]

About one hundred years separate the above passages: Justin Martyr wrote ca. A.D. 160; the Syrian church order *Didascalia Apostolorum* was written in the middle of the third century. And yet they say exactly the same point; they give the same definition of heresy, and this definition is entirely Jewish. Compare the following Mishnah passage: "These are they that have no share in the world to come: he that says that there is no resurrection of the dead prescribed in the Law, and he that says the Law is not from Heaven, and an Epicurean [a blasphemer and immoral person]." (*Sanhedrin* 10:1)[3]

It is fairly evident from the first two passages that for the early Christians the distinction between orthodoxy and heresy amounted to something very simple and basic: Do you confess faith in the God of the Old Testament as the one and only God, creator of heaven and earth, or do you not? The more specific point mentioned in the texts above—the resurrection from the dead—is only a concretization of that basic criterion. Those who denied the resurrection of the body were the same who denied that creation was good and that God was creator of heaven and earth.[4]

To modern Christians this may seem an all too simple criterion—we can hardly think of someone today wishing to be regarded as a Christian and at the same time denying the first article of the creed: "I believe in God, the Father Almighty, creator of heaven and earth." Did such people really exist in the days of the early church?

---

[1]This and the following quotations from Justin's *Dialogue* are rendered according to Lukyn Williams (this quote pp. 169-70).
[2]R. Hugh Connolly, *Didascalia Apostolorum: The Syriac Version Translated and Accompanied by the Verona Latin Fragments* (Oxford: Clarendon, 1929; reprint, 1969), p. 202.
[3]Danby, *Mishnah*, p. 397.
[4]In this and the following paragraphs I am following an idea developed by Adelbert Davids, "Irrtum und Häresie, 1 Clem.—Ignatius von Antiochien—Justinus," *Kairos*, n.s., 15 (1973): 165-87. In my own article, "Heresy and the Pastoral Epistles," *Themelios* 20 (1994): 9-14, I tried to take Davids's concept a little further. Cf. also George W. MacRae, "Why the Church Rejected Gnosticism," in Sanders, *Self-Definition* 1:126-33.

Justin speaks about men who "pretend to be Christians and confess the crucified Jesus as their Lord and Christ," and yet "blaspheme the Creator of the universe . . . and the God of Abraham and Isaac and Jacob" (*Dialogue with Trypho* 35.2.5). And in other church fathers we meet with more detailed information concerning the doctrine of the heretics.[5] According to these sources, the answer to the above question is, no doubt, *yes!*

Not only did people who combined faith in Christ with rejection of the God of the Old Testament exist—these people were a major threat to the church, because they found considerable hearing among members of the church. But the reports of the church fathers are strongly polemical. Could it be that they distorted and caricatured the opinions of their opponents?

Happily, we are now in a position to compare the reports of the ecclesiastical writers with documents stemming directly from their opponents. In 1945, a sensational find was made by an Egyptian peasant at Nag Hammadi (not very far from Luxor). He found a sealed jar containing twelve ancient books. Through various and complicated routes and circumstances, reminiscent of the fate of the Dead Sea Scrolls, these twelve books eventually all found their way to the Coptic museum of Cairo, where they are kept today. The entire collection is called The Nag Hammadi Library, and is available in an English translation.[6]

The significance of this "Library" is that it provides us with numerous texts (52 tractates in all) written by the opponents of the church fathers. These opponents are usually called Gnostics by modern scholars, from the Greek word *gnosis*, meaning knowledge.[7] In the Nag Hammadi texts we hear them speak for themselves. What they have to say substantiates the reports of the church fathers as basically correct;[8] but the Nag Hammadi

---

[5]First and foremost in Irenaeus's major work *Against Heresies,* ca. A.D. 185, Books 1 and 2.

[6]James M. Robinson, ed., *The Nag Hammadi Library* (New York: Harper & Row, 1981 [paperback]; and later editions [orig. ed. Leiden: E. J. Brill, 1977]).

[7]There were in antiquity some persons or groups who either called themselves Gnostics, or were so-called by others, but only some of these would be called Gnostics in the modern scholarly meaning. On the other hand, most ancient Gnostics—according to the modern definition—were not called by that name in their own time. The abstract *Gnosticism* is altogether a modern term. Cf. Morton Smith, "The History of the Term *Gnostikos,*" in *The Rediscovery of Gnosticism,* vol. 2: *Sethian Gnosticism,* ed. Bentley Layton, Studies in the History of Religions 41 (Leiden: E. J. Brill, 1981), pp. 796-807.

[8]It should be added that the church fathers sometimes quoted large fragments of Gnostic writings, sometimes even whole works, so it is not true to say that before the Nag Hammadi discovery there were no original Gnostic works around. The first volume of a major source anthology on Gnosticism is based, to a large extent, on such material: Werner Foerster, *Gnosis: A Selection of Gnostic Texts,* 2 vols. (Oxford: Clarendon, 1972, 1974; orig. German ed. *Die Gnosis* [Zürich 1969, 1971]).

texts supplement and enrich our picture of Gnostic teaching.

The Fundamentals of Gnostic Doctrine

It may be worthwhile to dwell a little on the teaching of the Gnostics, partly because it is by no means an outdated phenomenon of only historical interest. This will become evident once we try to summarize what Gnosticism was all about.[9]

There are several Gnostic "systems," with a great deal of variety in details, but one can nevertheless discern a basic pattern that is common to most or all Gnostic texts: There exists a highest God, who within himself comprises several divine powers. The Gnostics called these powers *aeons*, and there were different systems of arranging the aeons. For some reason one of the aeons fell out of the divine sphere (often called "the fullness" [Greek, *pleroma*]) and sank downwards. This aeon, confused and in despair, created the material world, which is evil because material. On this point all Gnostics were consequent dualists: matter is opposed to spirit as evil to good. The fallen aeon somehow mingled with the created matter, so that fragments of the divine substance were imprisoned in material bodies. These divine fragments are the souls of men. But the human souls no longer know of their heavenly, divine origin. They have forgotten it; they live in estrangement from their true nature. And in this estrangement they are lost; they perish unless they are reminded of who they really are. This knowledge of who we really are is the gnosis that Gnosticism is all about. Once the soul has regained this knowledge of its own true nature, it is ready for a return to the divine sphere when death has set it free from the prison of the body. During this ascent to God, the soul has to pass hostile planetary powers watching the gates of heaven. In some Gnostic systems, part of the saving gnosis was to know the passwords which would open the gates and render the hostile forces powerless.

In this way salvation was conceived of as an ongoing process in which all the fallen divine substance was gradually reabsorbed into the Godhead from which it had originally fallen. When the process is finished, the whole material universe will vanish as a bad dream.

---

[9]In recent years there has been a strong tendency among scholars not to treat Gnosticism as one homogeneous movement or -ism, but rather to treat different types of Gnostics separately. This is no doubt a sound method. Nevertheless, few scholars would deny that there is in most, if not all, of the different Gnostic systems a common pattern or scheme which is easily recognized. For a comprehensive and authoritative introduction, see Kurt Rudolph, *Gnosis: The Nature and History of Gnosticism* (San Francisco: Harper & Row/Edinburgh: T & T Clark, 1983).

Box 12.1. The Gnostics: Teachers and Documents (selective)

Simon the Magician (Acts 8:9-24): According to the church fathers, he was the founder of Gnostic heresy. It is difficult to assess the truth of this; we know next to nothing about Simon's teaching.

Basilides (ca. A.D. 120-140): A teacher in Egypt. He taught that the human body is material and lies outside the divine plan of salvation; it is of no religious consequence to let the body have its share of carnal pleasures. Salvation comes through gnosis, revealed by Christ. He was not crucified; Simon of Cyrene was crucified in his stead.

Valentinus (ca. A.D. 135-160): The founder of that branch of Gnosticism that became the most influential among church members in the West. An Alexandrian by birth, he mainly propagated his doctrines in Rome. His system is classically Gnostic and is known through the reports of the church fathers and through one of the writings found in Nag Hammadi, the so-called *Gospel of Truth*, probably written by Valentinus or one belonging to his circle. Valentinus's system may be summarized like this: From the highest deity, the *pleroma*, "fullness," there issue aeons in pairs. Their ultimate offspring, the son of one of the lowest aeons, Sophia, "Wisdom," is the Demiurge, the creator-God of the Old Testament. Redemption is effected by the aeon Christ who united himself to the man Jesus at Jesus' baptism. Christ brings humans gnosis, but only the "pneumatics" (i.e., the Valentinians) are able to receive it. Salvation consists in entering the pleroma as pure spirit.

Ptolemy and Heracleon (ca. A.D. 150-160): Two of Valentinus's disciples. Ptolemy is known through his *Letter to Flora* in which he discusses how Gnostics should understand the Mosaic legislation. Heracleon wrote the first known commentary on the Gospel of John. It has survived through extracts in Origen's commentary on John.

Bardesanes (ca. A.D. 180-220): The main representative of Syrian Gnosticism. A great missionary and hymnwriter, he became very influential in Syriac-speaking Christianity. The apocryphal *Acts of Thomas* may derive from him or his school.

The Nag Hammadi Documents (ca. A.D. 150-400): A collection of diverse Gnostic documents, some of them heavily influenced by Jewish or Christian ideas, others without any discernible contacts with biblical doctrine. Among the most well-known of the 52 documents in this collection are

> *The Gospel of Thomas* (ca. A.D. 150-170?)—generally Gnostic
> *The Gospel of Truth* (ca. A.D. 160-170?)—Valentinian
> *The Treatise on Resurrection* (= *Letter to Rheginus*) (ca. A.D. 170-200)—Valentinian
> *The Apocryphon of John* (ca. A.D. 170-200)—another classic formulation of the Gnostic system
> *The Gospel of Philip* (ca. A.D. 250-300)—Valentinian

Gnosticism and Christianity

Several Gnostic systems were related to the Old Testament on one point and to Christianity on another.[10]

1. Many Gnostics took great interest in the first three chapters of the

---

[10]There are a great many studies of this relationship; only a few are mentioned in the Suggestions below. Cf. also the very careful study by Robert McLachlan Wilson, *Gnosis and the New Testament* (Oxford: Blackwell, 1968).

Bible.[11] They accepted the biblical account of the creation of the world, but totally re-interpreted the significance of it. For them, the creation of the world was a disaster or a big misunderstanding, and the God of the Old Testament was an inferior deity, incompetent, ignorant or even wicked. He was by no means identical with the real, the highest Divine Reality. Regarding the account of the Fall in Genesis 3, the Gnostics tended to reverse the roles: For them the serpent was the hero, teaching humans how to gain knowledge and how to befoul the stupid creator-god. (There were even some Gnostics called Ophites, serpent-worshipers.) For none of the Gnostics was Genesis 3 the story of the Fall, for the Fall had taken place already, before creation. Genesis 3 was rather the first step in the process of salvation.

2. The other point of contact was with Christianity. It should be evident from the above that Gnosticism could easily find a place for Christ in its concept of salvation: Christ could be conceived of as a bringer of knowledge, sent down to humans from the divine realm to remind them of their divine, heavenly origin. Christ was thus not a messenger from the creator-god of the Old Testament, but from the unknown Divine Reality. The Gnostics therefore conceived of Christ as a teacher, a revealer.

This last point is typically expressed in a gospel produced by Gnostics during the second century, the so-called *Gospel of Thomas* found among the Nag Hammadi texts.[12] It has only sayings of Jesus, often twisted so as to express Gnostic theology. It contains no miracle stories and no passion narrative, and the sayings of Jesus have no narrative framework. Jesus transmits isolated sayings, he does not place himself in any role within or relationship to Israel's history.[13]

Let us just look at one saying in this gospel to get an impression of how well-known sayings of Jesus were twisted so as to express Gnostic thought.

---

[11]Some also were interested in the biblical story beyond that. On Gnostic interpretation of the Old Testament, see, Birger A. Pearson, "Use, Authority and Exegesis of Mikra in Gnostic Literature," in *Compendia 2:1:* 635-52.

[12]When this complete Coptic text of *Thomas* was found, it turned out that some scattered fragments of an unknown Greek Gospel, which had been known for a long time, seem to represent an earlier Greek version of the *Gospel of Thomas*. These fragments also indicate that the translation of *Thomas* from Greek to Coptic was no literal translation, but rather a rephrasing and rearrangement of the Greek text.

[13]There is a vast literature on *The Gospel of Thomas*, partly because an American school of thought believes that this Gospel contains some sayings of Jesus that are preserved here in a more original form than in any of the New Testament Gospels. As a representative of this school, see Stevan L. Davies, *The Gospel of Thomas and Christian Wisdom* (New York: Seabury, 1983); for a very pertinent critique, see John P. Meier, *A Marginal Jew: Rethinking the Historical Jesus*, vol. 1: *The Roots of the Problem and the Person*, Anchor Bible Reference Library (New York: Doubleday, 1991), pp. 124-39.

The following saying should be compared with Luke 17:20-21:

Jesus said, "If those who lead you say to you, 'See, the kingdom is in the sky,' then the birds of the sky will precede you. If they say to you, 'It is in the sea,' then the fish will precede you. Rather, the kingdom is inside of you, and it is outside of you. When you come to know, yourselves, then you will become known, and you will realize that it is you who are the sons of the living father. But if you will not know yourselves, you dwell in poverty and it is you who are that poverty." (*Gospel of Thomas* 3)[14]

For the Gnostic, salvation is to know oneself, that is, know one's true nature and heavenly origin. Salvation is not to become a son or daughter of God; salvation is to realize, to know, that we *are* children of the Father.

Christ as bringer of this knowledge could thus easily find a place in the Gnostic system. But he was not indispensable. There are Gnostic texts in which Christ plays no role at all—the heavenly knowledge is transmitted through visions or dreams or other messengers. This fact brings before us the very complex and much disputed question of the origins of Gnosticism.

The Origins of Gnosticism

The church fathers regarded Gnosticism as a Christian heresy; the Gnostics were Christian apostates; the true gospel had been there first, then came Gnostic perversion. Some modern scholars still hold this view,[15] while others think that Gnostic systems existed prior to and independent of Christianity. Some scholars, notably in Germany, have even argued that Gnosticism has deeply influenced the New Testament writings, starting with Paul.

We have no opportunity here to enter into an extensive discussion of these complex problems.[16] The following points should be made, however.

1. There is no literary evidence for the existence of Gnostic systems in the first century A.D. Some of the Gnostic texts stem from the second century, most of them from the third and fourth centuries. This corresponds to the fact that in the church fathers we do not come across polemics against full-fledged Gnosticism before the latter half of the second century, but then suddenly it becomes outspoken, vehement and extensive. What we find in earlier sources are casual polemics against certain tendencies which were later

---

[14]Robinson, *Nag Hammadi Library*, p. 118.
[15]Most notably Simone Pétrement, *A Separate God: The Christian Origins of Gnosticism* (San Francisco: Harper Collins, 1990; London: Darton, Longman & Todd, 1991).
[16]For extensive reports on and discussion of this thesis, see the works by Yamauchi and Colpe listed under Suggestions for further reading.

to become fully developed in the Gnostic systems of the second century. To be a little more precise, before the second century there is no trace of the typically Gnostic identification of the God of the Old Testament as a stupid or wicked creator-god. But there are traces of a general contempt for the created world. In early first-century gnosis, it seems as if the God of the Old Testament is still identified with the highest God, the Father. But he is not directly responsible for the creation of the material universe. This world is made by one or more angels, lower than God himself (as in Irenaeus's report on Simonian gnosis, *Against Heresies* 1.23.2). This may be one example of how first-century tendencies developed and were radicalized into full-fledged Gnosticism in the second century.[17]

2. Everywhere in Gnostic literature where we meet a Savior descending to earth to teach the saving knowledge, Christian influence seems to be at work. In definitely non-Christian Gnosticism this redeemer figure is lacking. It is therefore an error to take New Testament Christology to be dependent on a "gnostic Redeemer myth"; it is rather the other way around.

3. Concerning the much-debated question of the origins of Gnosticism, we should distinguish two questions: (a) What is the origin of the different concepts and motifs that have been integrated into the Gnostic system? (b) What is the origin of the basic Gnostic conception of the material universe as inherently bad, and of the creator-god as evil?

In recent scholarship there has been a marked tendency to derive Gnosticism from Jewish roots. And there are no doubt many ideas and concepts of Jewish origin in the Gnostic systems.[18] But obviously one is then asking the first of the above questions, not the second. For example, in several Gnostic systems the aeon that falls away from God and is responsible for the creation of the world is called Wisdom (*Sophia*). This is no doubt an echo of the Jewish concept that God's Wisdom was active when God created the world (cf. above, chapter one, and below, chapter sixteen). But it is precisely this creating activity of Wisdom which makes her the villain of the Gnostic system. And this basic negative attitude towards everything connected with the creation of the world is certainly not of Jewish origin.

---

[17]I have argued this point in my article "Heresy and the Pastoral Epistles," *Themelios* 20 (1994): 9-14. Cf. also the very interesting study by Nils A. Dahl, "The Arrogant Archon and the Lewd Sophia: Jewish Traditions in Gnostic Revolt," in Layton, *Rediscovery of Gnosticism* 2:689-712.

[18]See Birger A. Pearson, "Jewish Elements in Gnosticism and the Development of Gnostic Self-Definition," in Sanders, *Self-Definition* 1:151-60.

Some scholars have suggested that this entirely negative evaluation of the created world may ultimately derive from Indian religion, and there are some striking parallels between Gnostic and Hindu, even Buddhist, ways of thinking. But we lack solid evidence which would make this more than an attractive hypothesis.

What is more solidly documented is the fact that a fundamentally negative attitude towards this world was widespread in certain circles of Roman society in antiquity.[19] There were many reasons for this, some cultural and some political. On the cultural and religious level one notices the very widespread belief in astrology. People believed that they were ruled irresistibly by astral powers or by Fate, and once you conceived of these powers as hostile, you would groan and long for liberation. On the political level, most people must have felt that, confronted with the empire, they were totally insignificant. What a relief to hear that you were immensely significant, the bearer of a divine spark in your soul, and that this knowledge would liberate you from the hostile powers ruling this world!

Gnostic Elitism

There is a striking feature about Gnosticism that confirms that much of its attraction had to do with making people feel significant.[20] The Gnostics did not present their message as something that everybody should and could hear and grasp. On the contrary, they addressed themselves to the few, to an exclusive circle of initiates who, through their participation in this superior knowledge, belonged to the elect part of humanity. Those Gnostics who regarded themselves as Christians did not regard themselves as ordinary Christians. By their share in the secret knowledge of spiritual things they were highly elevated above average Christians, with their all-too-materialistic ways of thinking.

Take the concept of the resurrection. To the Gnostics the usual Christian concept of the resurrection of the body was hopelessly naive and materialistic. The whole point was to be freed from the bodily prison—what a tragic anticlimax to be clothed once again with a material body in the hereafter! Of course you should conceive of the resurrection in much more spiritual

---

[19]The classic statement of this point of view is Hans Jonas, *Gnosis und Spätantiker Geist*, vol. 1, Forschung zur Religion und Literatur des Alten und Neuen Testaments 51 (Göttingen: Vandenhoeck & Ruprecht, 1934). Cf. also the same author's English book on Gnosticism: *The Gnostic Religion: The Message of the Alien God and the Beginnings of Christianity* (Boston: Beacon, 1958; new ed. London: Routledge, 1992).
[20]Cf. Jacques E. Menard, "Normative Self-Definition in Gnosticism," in Sanders, *Self-Definition* 1:134-50.

terms; it concerned your soul, not your body.[21]

Similarly, the usual Christian conception of the incarnation was all too crude for the Gnostics. If the whole point of Christ's mission was to free humans from the material universe, he could himself be no part of it by carrying a real body. So Christ had no real, physical body, he only appeared (Greek, *dokein*) to have one. The Gnostics had a docetic Christology, and we have already seen Ignatius fight valiantly against it.

The following excerpt from the Gnostic *Acts of John* conveys an impression of how the Gnostics themselves liked to conceive of Christ's apparent body:

> Sometimes when I (John) meant to touch him I encountered a material, solid body; but at other times again when I felt him, his substance was immaterial and incorporeal, and as if it did not exist at all.... And I often wished, as I walked with him, to see his footprint in the earth whether it appeared—for I saw him raising himself from the earth—and I never saw it. (*Acts of John* 93)[22]

This makes one understand why Ignatius always inserted "truly" in his creed (cf. above p. 215).

Such was the Gnostic position. It must have had much to recommend it to Hellenistic minds. And there was one added attraction: Gnosticism was tolerant. For most Gnostics, burning incense before Caesar's image or fulfilling other socially necessary religious obligations was no problem. It was in any case a merely outward rite, it did not affect one's soul.

There are some Gnostic texts ridiculing ordinary Christians because of their zeal for martyrdom.[23] In the Nag Hammadi tractate *The Testimony of Truth* we read the following:

> The foolish—thinking in their heart that if they confess, "We are Christians," in word only but not with power, while giving themselves over to ignorance, to a human death, not knowing where they are going nor who Christ is, thinking that they will live, when they are (really) in error—hasten towards the principalities and the authorities (NHL IX,3 31.22—32.5).[24]

Not all Gnostics were as hostile to martyrdom as this, but Irenaeus is

---

[21]This is the basic tenet also in a Gnostic treatise which is otherwise closer to "orthodox" teaching than most Gnostic texts: "The Treatise on the Resurrection," cf. Malcolm M. Peel, *The Epistle to Rheginos: A Valentinian Letter on the Resurrection* (London: SCM Press/Philadelphia: Fortress, 1969).

[22]Hennecke, *Apocrypha* 2:227.

[23]On the theme of martyrdom in orthodoxy versus Gnosticism, there is an excellent discussion in Elaine H. Pagels, *The Gnostic Gospels* (New York: Vintage Books [Random House], 1981), pp. 84-122.

[24]Robinson, *Nag Hammadi Library*, p. 407.

hardly guilty of great exaggeration when he writes about the Gnostics he knew: "They have reached such a pitch of audacity that they even pour contempt upon the martyrs, and vituperate those who are killed on account of confessing the Lord" (*Against Heresies* 3.18.5). "During the whole time since Christ appeared on earth, only one or two of them have occasionally along with our martyrs borne the reproach of the Name . . . and been led forth to death" (*Against Heresies* 4.33.9).[25]

The Nag Hammadi texts confirm also the implicit polemic of Ignatius: Those who denied the reality of Jesus' body and the reality of his suffering also denied the value of Christian martyrdom. They found it unnecessary and meaningless.

It is interesting to speculate which social groups in Roman society were especially prone to lend an ear to the Gnostic message. Here, however, it is sufficient to emphasize that Gnosticism was never meant to be, and probably never became, a mass movement. It was exclusive in character, and may primarily have appealed to a certain kind of intelligentsia in the Roman cities. It was probably not because Gnosticism found wide hearing among the rank and file Christians that it was taken so seriously by the church. It was rather because it threatened to invade the intelligentsia of the church. That was serious enough. The church was in no position to easily give away competent preachers, teachers and leaders to the Gnostics—the church needed them badly herself.

Due to their elite character, their exclusivism, the Gnostics never established a church of any duration (with the significant exception of Manichaeism from the third century onward). The typical Gnostic community was a group of persons adhering to a charismatic teacher, rapidly dissolving with the disappearance of the leader. There were many teachers and many systems, and a considerable amount of rivalry between the various groups. This emphatic exclusivism led to a never-ending process of creating new systems and groups. Irenaeus remarks ironically on this: Among the Gnostics, everybody had the ambition of being a teacher of others and establishing his own group (*Against Heresies* 3.2.2).

So there was never established a Gnostic church in the second century. There was, however, one man who succeeded in establishing a church which lasted more than a few decades, and which became a real competitor for the established church. His name was Marcion.

---

[25]*ANF* 1:447, 528.

Marcion

According to the ancient sources, Marcion[26] was the son of the Christian bishop of Sinope, a city on the coast of the Black Sea. He was a wealthy man and a gifted man, in other words, a man of great value to the early church. Nevertheless he was excommunicated from his native church, and when on his way to Rome he met the aged bishop Polycarp in Asia Minor, Polycarp de-nounced him as "the first-born of Satan."

Arriving in Rome shortly before A.D. 140, Marcion was able to win the favor of the Roman community, something that may have been related to the fact that he donated 50,000 silver *denarii* to this community. But as it turned out, the integrity of the Roman congregation was not for sale, and Marcion got his money back when he was excommunicated in A.D. 144. After that, he founded his own church, which was to last for some centuries, although it never had much appeal to the masses. Nevertheless it represented a challenge so serious that the church father Tertullian devoted years of writing and rewriting to produce five monumental books refuting Marcion several years after the heretic's death.

What was Marcion's heresy? The church fathers generally grouped him together with the Gnostics. Modern scholars have questioned whether this is appropriate. There are some peculiar features in Marcion that set him off from the Gnostics. He has none of their predilection with fanciful mythological exegesis of the Bible, and he takes no interest in their elaborate systems of aeons and their mythological account of the world's origin.

But in other respects he shares the basic Gnostic convictions. The God of the Old Testament is not the Father of Jesus Christ, but an inferior deity who was ignorant and vengeful, foreign to the principle of unlimited love taught by Jesus. The miserable world we live in is the product of this inferior deity. It was this creator who devised the degrading method of sexual reproduction; and the mere thought of how a child is born was enough to fill Marcion with nausea. Accordingly, Marcion rejected marriage and required that his followers should live single so as not to help the creator god of the Old Testament to keep the miserable show going on. In this he was in agreement with most of the Gnostics, though some Gnostics turned the argument the other way and said that since this mortal body will perish in any case, it does not hurt the divine spark within you if you let the body have the sensual (that is, gastronomical and sexual) pleasures it longs for.

---

[26]On Marcion, see the studies listed in the Suggestions below.

Because Marcion rejected any spiritualization of the Old Testament, he agreed with the Jews that the Messiah predicted in the Old Testament had not yet come. The Messiah of the Old Testament, according to Marcion, was a cruel warrior whose aim was Jewish nationalism. Jesus had been totally different. His Father was not the God of the Old Testament, but the Highest God who had been unknown before Jesus came and revealed him. This God, the real Father, was merciful towards sinners: his forgiving love knew no limits.[27]

But did not Jesus himself recognize the God of the Old Testament as his Father and quote Old Testament passages as authoritative words of God? And didn't the apostles do the same? Marcion was aware of the problem and had a ready solution which seems to be his personal invention: The Gospels and the apostolic epistles did not faithfully reproduce the message of Jesus, because the apostles misunderstood Jesus. They were so determined by their Jewish background that they were unable to grasp the radical newness of Jesus and his message, with the sad consequence that they re-Judaized Jesus. Marcion thus became the first Bible critic in the early church. His heroes were Jesus and Paul; Paul was the only one who really understood Jesus. But even Paul's letters had been interpolated by Judaizing scribes, and it was only after he had excised these Jewish interpolations that Marcion was able to recognize ten letters as genuine (he did not recognize, or possibly did not know, the letters to Timothy and Titus). Among the Gospels Marcion thought Luke had preserved the teachings of Jesus in the purest form, though here also there were several interpolations he removed.

Marcion thus came out with a critically (we moderns would say quite uncritically) reconstructed New Testament, which became the sole Holy Scriptures for the Marcionite church. Modern scholars have assumed that Marcion thereby provoked the established church to define its collection of holy apostolic writings (to be placed beside the Old Testament). In other words, Marcion was the indirect cause of what we usually call the canonization of the New Testament within the church.[28] This is a suggestion to be kept

---

[27]Adolf von Harnack, who wrote the classic study on Marcion (see Suggestions), was so impressed by the "evangelical" elements in Marcion's thought that he pronounced him the only real follower of Paul in second-century Christianity and a pioneer ahead of his time with regard to rejecting the non-evangelical nature of the Old Testament.

[28]The foremost exponent of this thesis is Hans von Campenhausen, *The Formation of the Christian Bible* (Philadelphia: Fortress, 1972). For a summary and some discussion of it, see Lee M. McDonald, *The Formation of the Christian Biblical Canon*, 2nd ed. (Peabody, Mass.: Hendrickson, 1995), pp. 154-69.

in mind when we return to a fuller treatment of the issue in chapter fourteen.

In his treatment of the Old and New Testaments, Marcion differed markedly from the Gnostics. They tended to accept the New Testament writings as they were, only supplementing them with supposed oral traditions deriving from Jesus via traditional channels other than the New Testament writings. They also did not reject the entire Old Testament the way Marcion did, but rather tended to distinguish between more or less valuable parts of the Old Testament. They may be said to be the first Bible critics of the Old Testament.[29]

Conclusion: Heresy and Orthodoxy

With this sketch of the basic doctrinal positions of the Gnostics and of Marcion we should be better equipped to grasp the significance of the concept of heresy in the second century. Heresy was a concept applied to anyone who claimed to be a Christian but denied the basic dogmas of the Old Testament, first and foremost by defaming creation and blaspheming the Creator, denying that the God of the Old Testament is the Father of Jesus Christ. This is the essence, the basic definition of heresy in our time period. Whether this denial of creation and the Creator betrayed itself in docetic Christology, ascetic denial of marriage, denial of the bodily resurrection, or in other things, was of less importance. The early Christian writers all had a sure instinct which made them react intensely against all symptoms of denial of the first article of their creed: I believe in the God *who created heaven and earth.*

The following observation confirms this analysis of the meaning of heresy: Neither Jews nor Jewish Christians were called heretics by the earliest Christian writers. The Jews not believing in Jesus were called disbelievers and other, worse names, but they were never called heretics—they did not deny belief in the Creator. Those Jewish believers who denied the divine pre-existence of Christ and regarded him as a mere man, elected to become the Messiah, were not called heretics. This does not mean that their Christology was regarded as acceptable. It only means that they did not exhibit the distinctive mark of heresy: rejection of belief in the Creator.[30]

What we have found in this chapter amounts to something like a guiding principle that helped the young Gentile Christian church of the second century to navigate its doctrinal course. This guiding principle was a basic

---

[29]See especially *Ptolemy's Letter to Flora* (quoted in Epiphanius's *Panarion* 33.3-7), English translation (selective) in Frend, *New Eusebius*, pp. 85-89.
[30]This is seen particularly clearly in Justin's *Dialogue with Trypho,* chaps. 48-49. Cf. also above, chapter nine on the Ebionites.

dogma of Old Testament revelation: belief in the Creator of heaven and earth; belief that creation is good, that the human body is God's work, that marriage is a blessed institution, that the gifts of creation are to be received with thanksgiving. In the Syrian *Didascalia Apostolorum* (ca. 250) there is a charming creed which beautifully summarizes the criteria of orthodoxy:

> We have established . . . that you
> worship God Almighty
> and Jesus Christ
> and the Holy Spirit;
> that you employ the Holy Scriptures
> and believe in the resurrection of the dead,
> and that you make use of all his creatures with thanksgiving;
> and that men should marry. (*Didascalia Apostolorum* 24 [vi.12]).[31]

Temple Square

There is a massive *materiality* to the temple cult in the Bible. The holiness of the sanctuary, its sacred objects, the Ark, is in a sense *dinglich*, "thing-ish," to an extent that often embarrasses readers of later, supposedly more "spiritual" times. In the temple the people of God bring their Lord the firstfruits of his own creation—grain, wine, oil, cattle—and much of the purpose of the temple cult is to bring concrete blessing on concrete physical life: fecundity on the fields, among cattle, among people. Gerhard von Rad speaks about a penetrating *Immanenzwille*, "will towards becoming immanent," in the God of the temple. It is certainly not by accident that God's indwelling of the temple/tabernacle became the most powerful metaphor of the incarnation in John's Prologue: the Word became flesh and *tabernacled* among us (Jn 1:14). And it is hardly by accident that the scene of life eternal is depicted in the last two chapters of Revelation as a new Jerusalem coming down to earth and having the dimensions of a cosmic *Holy of Holies:* a great cube, "fifteen hundred miles, its length and width and height are equal" (Rev 21:16).

There is a massive materiality in all of this that is never lost, not in the first, and not in the last book of the New Testament. But no wonder it caused great offence to Gnostic and other spiritualists, who could only think of God and matter, the divine and the material, as opposites. This dualism is foreign to the God of the temple service; it is foreign to earliest Christianity; but it invaded central segments of Christianity at a later period.

In the words of a modern scholar not very sympathetic toward second-century orthodoxy, "orthodox tradition implicitly affirms bodily experience as the central fact of human life. What one does physically—one eats and drinks, engages in sexual life or avoids it, saves one's life or gives it up—are all vital elements in one's religious development."[32] In this, the orthodox church had no quarrel with the Jews.

---

[31]Connolly, p. 204.
[32]Pagels, *Gnostic Gospels*, p. 101.

Suggestions for Further Reading

The Nag Hammadi texts are now available in English translation in the one-volume collection: James M. Robinson, ed., *The Nag Hammadi Library* (New York: Harper & Row, 1981 [orig. ed. Leiden: E. J. Brill, 1977]). The other preserved documents of Christian Gnosticism are collected in Hennecke, *Apocrypha 1-2;* Werner Foerster, *Gnosis: A Selection of Gnostic Texts,* 2 vols. (Oxford: Clarendon, 1972, 1974); Bentley Layton, *The Gnostic Scriptures* (Garden City, N.Y.: Doubleday, 1987).

Good surveys of Gnosticism:

Hans Jonas, *The Gnostic Religion: The Message of the Alien God and the Beginnings of Christianity* (Boston: Beacon, 1958; new ed. London: Routledge, 1992); Kurt Rudolph, *Gnosis: The Nature and History of Gnosticism* (San Francisco: Harper, 1987); Alastair H. B. Logan, "Gnosticism," in *The Early Christian World,* ed. Philip F. Esler (London and New York: Routledge, 2000), 2:907-28 (with updated bibliography). Cf. also the critical study of Michael Allen Williams, *Rethinking "Gnosticism": An Argument for Dismantling a Dubious Category* (Princeton: Princeton University Press, 1996).

Instructive studies on Gnosticism and its relationship to early Christianity:

Carsten Colpe, *Die religionsgeschichtliche Schule: Darstellung und Kritik ihres Bildes vom gnostischen Erlösermythus,* Forschungen zur Religion und Literatur des Alten und Neuen Testaments, N. F., 60 (Göttingen: Vandenhoeck & Ruprecht, 1961); Robert M. Grant, *Gnosticism and Early Christianity,* 2nd ed. (New York: Harper & Row, 1966); Edwin M. Yamauchi, *Pre-Christian Gnosticism: A Survey of the Proposed Evidences* (London: Tyndale , 1973). Cf. also the somewhat controversial book by Elaine H. Pagels, *The Gnostic Gospels* (New York: Random House, 1979; paperback ed. New York: Vintage Books [Random House], 1981).

The two classic studies of Marcion:

A. von Harnack, *Marcion: Das Evangelium vom fremden Gott,* 2nd ed. (Leipzig: J. C. Hinrichs Verlag, 1924; reprint, Darmstadt: Wissenschaftliche Buchgesellschaft, 1985). This book contains all the source material in original texts.

E. C. Blackman, *Marcion and His Influence* (London: SPCK, 1948).

Cf. also J. Knox, *Marcion and the New Testament* (Chicago: University of Chicago Press, 1942; reprint, New York 1980); R. Joseph Hoffmann, *Marcion: On the Restitution of Christianity. An Essay on the Development of Radical Paulinist Theology in the Second Century* (Chico, Calif.: Scholars Press, 1984); Ulrich Schmid, *Marcion und sein Apostolos,* Arbeiten zur neutestamentlichen Textforschung 25 (Berlin/New York: Walter de Gruyter, 1995).

13

ELDER & YOUNGER
BROTHERS
THE SECOND-CENTURY
DEBATE WITH JUDAISM

*I*n previous chapters we have seen repeatedly that the young Gentile Christian church increasingly depended on its Jewish heritage when it gradually came to include a growing number of Gentiles with no prior contact with Judaism. The demarcation line between Christianity and paganism, and between right and wrong Christianity, had to be drawn firmly, and on these demarcation lines Christians had to emphasize those points that they shared with the Jews: biblical monotheism, biblical ethics, rejection of idolatry.

But how was the situation on the other demarcation line—between the church and Judaism? We would, perhaps, expect that precisely the common front against paganism and the deniers of Old Testament religion would tend to bring Christians and Jews close together. In a certain sense that was no doubt the case, Christianity had begun as a movement within the Jewish community, and it continued to operate within a mainly Jewish framework for several decades into the second century. In more than one sense the church was next door to the synagogue (cf. Acts 18:7).

But this closeness did not necessarily mean friendship. You often have the most violent and passionate quarrels with those who are closest to you—precisely because they are close. The logic of this is not difficult to grasp: you tend to regard the error that comes closest to the truth as the most dangerous one.

Introduction: The Bitterness of Family Strife

In many ways Jews and Christians were close; so close that it became necessary for both parties to draw a clear-cut line of demarcation between themselves and the other party, and to emphasize that Judaism was not Christianity and vice versa.[1] In their outreach, Jews and Christians addressed much the same audience, and the potential converts had to be told in very plain terms that they should become Christians and not Jews, or vice versa.[2]

We have seen already (chapter nine) how the rabbis took precautions that should have hindered Jewish believers from participating in the synagogue service. Scholars have often claimed that the rabbis were only concerned with *Jewish* believers in Jesus; in other words, *Gentile* Christians were of no concern to the rabbis. This is not what the sources suggest, however. Some early Christian texts expressly say that the Jews took an active part in the prosecution of Gentile Christians, the classic example being the *Martyrdom of Polycarp*. Is there a historical setting in which these sources make sense?

Such a setting would be precisely the phenomenon of "missionary competition": Jews and Christians reaching out for the same converts. If the Jews saw Christian missionaries snapping their potential converts away from them, they would naturally resent them deeply even if they were Gentiles, and the Jews would do anything legally in their power to stop the Gentile missionaries. The bitterness of the Christians when the Jews were helpful in handing them over to the authorities is as understandable as the bitterness of the Jews when the church "stole" their sympathizers and potential proselytes. Thus, whenever a conflict with the Roman authorities was involved, the feelings between Jews and Christians tended to become poisoned. A

---

[1] In much recent research, the concept of "self-definition" has therefore been the focus of interest, cf. especially the three volumes edited by E. P. Sanders et al., *Self-Definition 1-3*. In a recent article and book, Daniel Boyarin has argued that the very necessity of making such self-demarcations, on both the Jewish and Christian sides, indirectly shows that on a grassroots level the Jews and the Christians were indistinguishable; the attempt to draw demarcations is a project of the leaders alone. I believe Boyarin has overstated the case, but he has certainly contributed some stimulating input on this question. Cf. Boyarin, "Martyrdom and the Making of Christianity and Judaism," *Journal of Early Christian Studies* 6 (1998), pp. 577-627; idem, *Dying for God: Martyrdom and the Making of Christianity and Judaism*, Figurae—Reading Medieval Culture (Stanford, Calif.: Stanford University Press, 1999).

[2] On the phenomenon of missionary competition, and on the question whether Jews conducted anything like mission in the modern sense, see discussion and literature in chapters one and three above (esp. pp. 42-43 notes 34-36, and p. 80 note 28). See also the very thorough discussion by Martin Hengel and Anna Maria Schwemer, "The Problem of the 'Sympathisers' and Jewish Propaganda," in *Paul Between Damascus and Antioch: The Unknown Years* (London: SCM Press, 1997), pp. 61-76.

modern reader cannot but be sad when he or she discerns in the Christian writers of the second century the unconcealed satisfaction they took in the crushing of the second Jewish revolt A.D. 135. Not a word of compassion or comfort is found in any Christian writer. What lay behind such anti-Jewish feelings among the Gentile Christians?[3]

From Jewish Self-Criticism to Anti-Jewish Slogans

Let us go back a little in time. When Stephen came to the end of his speech before the Jewish council in Jerusalem, he finished with the following words:

> You stiff-necked people, uncircumcised in heart and ears, you are forever opposing the Holy Spirit, just as your ancestors used to do. Which of the prophets did your ancestors not persecute? They killed those who foretold the coming of the Righteous One, and now you have become his betrayers and murderers. You are the ones that received the law as ordained by angels, and yet you have not kept it. (Acts 7:51-53)

What was Stephen doing here? Was he borrowing from Gentile anti-Jewish propaganda? Not at all. He was acting out the role of a prophetic preacher of penitence to Israel, and almost all he said was borrowed from sermons or prayers of penitence in the Old Testament. Compare the following: "But they [the desert generation] and our ancestors . . . stiffened their necks and did not obey your commandments. . . . They were disobedient and rebelled against you and cast your law behind their backs and killed your prophets, . . . and they committed great blasphemies" (Neh 9:16, 26; read the whole of 9:6-37).

---

[3]Most of the studies on Jewish/Christian relations listed in the Suggestions below are immediately relevant to this theme. In addition, note the following: F. Blanchetière, "Aux sources de l'antijudaïsme chrétien," *Revue d'histoire et de philosophie religieuses* 53 (1973): 353-98; idem, *Aux sources de l'anti-judaïsme chrétien: IIe-IIIe siècles* (Jerusalem: n.p., 1995); Peter Richardson, ed., *Anti-Judaism in Early Christianity,* vol. 1: *Paul and the Gospels,* Studies in Christianity and Judaism 2 (Waterloo, Ont.: Wilfrid Laurier University Press, 1986); Herbert Frohnhofen, ed., *Christlicher Antijudaismus und jüdischer Antipaganismus* (Hamburg: Steinmann and Steinmann, 1990); G. I. Langmuir, "The Faith of Christians and Hostility to Jews," in *Christianity and Judaism,* ed. Diana Wood, Studies in Church History 29 (Oxford: Oxford University Press, 1992), pp. 77-92; Lee Martin McDonald, "Anti-Judaism in the Early Church Fathers," in *Anti-Semitism and Early Christianity: Issues of Polemic and Faith,* ed. Craig A. Evans and Donald A. Hagner (Minneapolis: Fortress, 1993), pp. 215-52; Miriam S. Taylor, *Anti-Judaism and Early Christian Identity: A Critique of the Consensus,* Studia Post-Biblica 46 (Leiden: E. J. Brill, 1994); Guy G. Stroumsa, "From Anti-Judaism to Antisemitism in Early Christianity?" in *Contra Iudaeos: Ancient and Medieval Polemics Between Christians and Jews,* ed. Ora Limor and Guy G. Stroumsa, Texts and Studies in Medieval and Early Modern Judaism 10 (Tübingen: J. C. B. Mohr [Paul Siebeck], 1996), pp. 1-26; Stanton/Stroumsa, *Tolerance and Intolerance.*

"All the house of Israel is uncircumcised in heart" (Jer 9:26). "The godless say, 'Let us bind the Righteous One, for he is inconvenient to us'" (Is 3:10 LXX).

These texts pose no question of anti-Semitism; one might say on the contrary: in these and similar texts Israel exposes herself to heart-searching self-criticism under God's judgement, and this ability to exert self-criticism is her real strength.[4]

When the early Jewish believers addressed their non-believing Jewish brethren with the harshest words of the Old Testament prophets, they did so as inheritors of this Old Testament tradition of Jewish self-criticism. We should read Stephen's speech in this light. It is not only a defense against accusations; it is a prophetic call to repentance. Stephen's words can only be uttered in their true spirit by one who is able to say with Paul "I have great sorrow and unceasing anguish in my heart. For I could wish that I myself were accursed and cut off from Christ for the sake of my own people, my kindred according to the flesh" (Rom 9:2-3).

All this changed radically when this way of preaching penitence to Israel passed into the hands of Gentile Christians without this deep sense of solidarity with Israel. In their hands, these harsh Old Testament words to Israel became a weapon to discredit the Jewish people as disbelieving by nature, while the Gentile Christians exalted themselves as more willing to believe and obey God. We see this clearly in Justin Martyr:

> If you [Jews] will confess the truth, you yourselves cannot deny that we [Gentiles] are more faithful than you in relation to God. For we, having been called of God by means of the mystery of the cross, which is so despised and full of shame; and (suffering) punishments even unto death for our confession and obedience and piety, . . . we, I say, endure all things lest we should deny Christ even in word. But you were redeemed from Egypt with a high arm and a visitation of great glory [there follows an extensive enumeration of all the wonders

---

[4]In a groundbreaking study, Odil Hannes Steck demonstrated that there is in the Old Testament and in intertestamental Jewish literature a certain pattern of preaching repentance, which Steck deems to be of Deuteronomistic origin, and which he calls the Sin-Exile-Return pattern. In most of the cases where this pattern is used, Israel's sin is seen in their rejection of God's Word or Law, climaxing in their killing the messengers, the prophets. See Steck, *Israel und das gewaltsame Geschick der Propheten: Untersuchungen zur Überlieferung des deuteronomistischen Geschichtsbildes im Alten Testament, Spätjudentum und Urchristentum,* Wissenschaftliche Monographien zum Alten und Neuen Testament 23 (Neukirchen-Vluyn: Neukirchener Verlag des Erziehungsvereins, 1967). Steck also follows this pattern into the New Testament. In Skarsaune, *The Proof from Prophecy,* an attempt is made to pursue the use of this pattern, and its transformation into anti-Jewish slogans, in the early Patristic period, pp. 278-80, 288-95.

worked by God for the benefit of Israel during the desert wandering]. In spite of all this you made a calf, and eagerly committed fornication with the daughters of the aliens, and committed idolatry, and did so again afterwards when the land had been entrusted to you with such great power. . . . You are convicted by the prophets, even after Moses' warnings, of having gone so far as to sacrifice your own children to demons, and of having, in addition to all this, dared so much against Christ, and still do dare. (*Dialogue with Trypho* 131.2—133.1)[5]

As can be seen from this excerpt, Justin has full biblical support for everything he says about the Jewish nation. And yet the distance from the Old Testament and from Stephen's speech is enormous. For in Justin the enumeration of Israel's sins is no longer meant to be a call to repentance and return to God. In Justin it has become something quite different: Justin takes the biblical record of Israel's sins to mean that the Jews have a natural inclination toward disbelief and sin, while on the other hand the Gentiles have a natural inclination toward belief and obedience. The ruthless Jewish self-criticism contained in several passages in the Old Testament—unparalleled in the ancient world and one of the finest fruits of mosaic and prophetic teaching—is misused by Justin as if it were some kind of ethnological description of the peculiarities of the Jewish people.

Corresponding to this, he seems to mean that the faith of the Gentiles is their own merit, and that this makes them worthy to receive salvation, since it betrays their natural inclination toward faith. In short, Justin has fallen prey to precisely that danger against which Paul warns in Romans 11:17-18: "If some of the branches [of the olive tree that is Israel] were broken off, and you, a wild olive shoot, were grafted in their place to share the rich root of the olive tree, *do not boast over the branches.*" It is this boasting we observe very clearly in Justin, and, sad to say, he was quite representative of the Gentile Christian church from the second century onward.[6]

There is a particular point on which this general process of turning Jewish self-criticism into anti-Jewish slogans can be instructively observed. In the Old Testament scheme of penitence preaching, the emphasis is on Israel's sin and guilt. This corresponds to the fact that when the earliest Christians con-

[5]Lukyn Williams, pp. 270-74.
[6]On Justin's anti-Judaic attitude, see further Ben Zion Bokser, "Justin Martyr and the Jews," *Jewish Quarterly Review,* n.s., 64 (1973/1974): 97-122, 204-11; Harold Remus, "Justin Martyr's Argument with Judaism," in *Anti-Judaism in Early Christianity,* vol. 2: *Separation and Polemic,* ed. Stephen G. Wilson (Waterloo, Ont.: Wilfrid Laurier University Press, 1986), pp. 59-80; Stephen G. Wilson, *Strangers,* pp. 258-84; Judith M. Lieu, "Justin Martyr's *Dialogue with Trypho,*" in Lieu, *Image,* pp. 103-53.

Box 13.1. Polemic Against the Jews: Main Documents

The Letter of Barnabas (ca. A.D. 130): A treatise on how Christians should understand the Mosaic legislation. The author claims that the Old Testament precepts were never meant to be taken literally, but that the Jewish people did so because they were misled by an evil angel. As a punishment, God's covenant was withdrawn and is now offered anew in Christ. The suffering of Christ and the substitution of the "old" people with the "new" (= the Christians) is foretold in the Old Testament.

The Controversy between Jason and Papiscus (ca. A.D. 140?): Written by Aristo of Pella and only known through a few fragments in later church fathers. Jason, a Jewish believer, and Papiscus, an Alexandrian Jew, debate the question whether Jesus is the Messiah promised in the Old Testament. The discussion ends with Papiscus coming to faith in Jesus. It is commonly assumed that this dialogue was used as a source for similar dialogues written later (as late as the fifth and sixth centuries).

The Dialogue with Trypho (ca. A.D. 160): Written by Justin Martyr, probably in Rome. The book presents itself as a report on an actual debate between Justin and Trypho taking place shortly after the Bar Kokhba revolt, and probably taking place in Ephesus. Justin was born in Neapolis (now Nablus) in Samaria as the son of a Roman colonist (officer?). He had considerable knowledge of Judaism and Jewish arguments against Christianity, but no first-hand knowledge of Hebrew. The three main questions debated in the *Dialogue* are (1) the eternal or temporal validity of the ceremonial precepts in the Law; (2) the messiahship of Jesus; and (3) the claim that Christians have now replaced the Jews as the people of God. It is possible, but not provable, that Justin used Aristo's *Controversy* as one of his sources.

Against the Jews (shortly before A.D. 200): Written in Latin by Tertullian of Carthage. It is not directly addressed to Jews, but rather to Christians contemplating conversion to Judaism. It claims to be based, however, on an actual debate between a Jew and a Christian. Tertullian depends on, among others, Justin's *Dialogue with Trypho*, but enriches the dossier of arguments by some very learned arguments not used by Justin.

---

fronted their Jewish brethren with the serious sin of rejecting Jesus and bringing him to the cross, the only relevant guilt to talk about was the guilt of those Jerusalem Jews whom they were addressing. But when this preaching passed into the hands of Gentile Christians, it easily changed character. It was (mis)taken to mean that the Jewish nation as such was in a special way guilty of the Lord's death, while Pilate and the other Gentiles were guiltless. The peak of this development was reached already in Melito of Sardis (ca. A.D. 175). Here the Gentile Christian church hurled against the Jewish people the words "You murdered God," which were to resound for centuries to come.[7] We are here facing the specifically Christian element in European anti-Semitism.

---

[7]On Melito and his anti-Jewish charges, see Eric Werner, "Melito of Sardis: The First Poet of Deicide," *Hebrew Union College Annual* 37 (1966): 191-210; K. W. Noakes, "Melito of Sardis and the Jews," *Studia Patristica* 13 (Berlin: Akademie-Verlag, 1975), pp. 244-49; Stephen G. Wilson, "Passover, Easter and Anti-Judaism: Melito of Sardis and Others," in Neusner/Frerichs, *To See* pp. 337-55; idem, "Melito and Israel," in Wilson, *Anti-Judaism*, pp. 81-102; Lieu, *Image*, pp. 199-240.

The Assertiveness of the Younger Brother

What lies behind this vehement Gentile Christian self-assertion vis-à-vis the Jews? There are certainly many dimensions to the causes for this phenomenon: theological, social, political. In many respects, the Gentile Christians were the underdogs with regard to the Jews: they were not a recognized religion; they were culturally less at home in the biblical heritage than their Jewish neighbors. When they proclaimed to Gentiles that Jesus was the Messiah, fulfilling the Old Testament promises, it was always an effective counterargument to say, "Then why did his own people reject him? They should know their own Scriptures better than you!"

The more one considers these different reasons for anti-Jewish attitudes among early Christians, the more one feels that there was probably a strong psychological dimension to all this. It seems plausible to say that part of what we are facing is the inferiority complex of the younger—the much younger—brother. Let us try to visualize the situation in which the young Gentile Christian church found itself vis-à-vis Judaism.

First, there was the very palpable fact that while Judaism was a *religio licita,* a recognized religion, Christianity was not. The political and social security of the Jews was vulnerable and fragile, but their rights were nevertheless stated clearly in imperial decrees. In certain circles of the Roman intelligentsia, Jews were recognized and respected.[8] The Jew had a defined position in society and enjoyed a certain amount of security.

The Gentile Christians had no such security—not as Christians. If they were betrayed to the authorities and did not give up their confession, execution was the most likely outcome. Many Christians must have envied the Jews their greater security and their recognized position. At the same time we observe that many Christians compensated for this by taking pride in their inferior position. Justin Martyr is again an eloquent witness to this: You Jews fail the noble martyr tradition of the Old Testament, but we Christians carry it on!

Second, the Jew had the religious and cultural security of hundreds of years of unbroken tradition. The Christians were newcomers with no prehistory, and they were painfully aware of it. The rabbis handed on a tradition of scriptural exegesis which could claim the authority of generations of excellent teachers, reaching all the way back to Moses on Mount Sinai. They had

---

[8]See John M. G. Barclay, *Jews in the Mediterranean Diaspora from Alexander to Trajan (323 BCE-117 CE)* (Edinburgh: T & T Clark, 1996), pp. 292-98.

perfect command of the entire Old Testament, and they could argue their point from minute details in the original Hebrew text. And there was a basic consistency in their approach to the Bible: they not only recognized the Torah as divine, they also observed it.

The Gentile Christians were at an obvious disadvantage on all points. In many respects their interpretation of the Bible was startlingly new. They found meanings in biblical verses that no one had found there before. And they could quote no recognized tradition or authority to support them. Worst of all, they had no direct access to the original text, and their knowledge of the Old Testament was often limited to selected passages and proof texts.[9]

To a neutral outside observer it must have seemed rather preposterous when such people nevertheless dared to challenge the authority of the learned rabbis. In this battle, the Christians were by all objective standards the underdogs. One should keep this in mind when one reads the many harsh and derogatory remarks about the rabbis and rabbinic theology and exegesis in the Christian writers of the second century. Many of the church fathers betray an awareness that the rabbis far excelled them in biblical scholarship; and in later centuries Origin and Jerome were to seek Jewish instructors in order to read the Old Testament in the original text and to understand it better.[10] In the eyes of the Christians, Judaism was not only the elder brother, Judaism was also the mightier and the more learned brother—which no doubt corresponded to the objective facts.

The only thing the Christians had to set against this scholarly superiority was their basic conviction that the rabbis had nevertheless failed to recognize the Messiah when he came, and that therefore their scholarship was combined with a fundamental blindness with regard to the meaning of the Scriptures. What a man like Justin Martyr has to set against rabbinic scholarship is not superior scholarship, but something Justin calls "the grace to understand": "I am about to relate passages of Scripture to you, though I am not

---

[9]See on this Oskar Skarsaune, "From Books to Testimonies: Remarks on the Transmission of the Old Testament in the Early Church," in *The New Testament and Christian-Jewish Dialogue: Studies in Honor of David Flusser*, ed. Malcolm Lowe [*Immanuel* no. 24/25] (Jerusalem: Ecumenical Theological Research Fraternity, 1990), pp. 207-19; and idem, "The Development of Scriptural Interpretation in the Second and Third Centuries," in *Hebrew Bible/Old Testament: The History of Its Interpretation*, ed. Magne Sæbø (Göttingen: Vandenhoeck & Ruprecht, 1996), 1:373-442.

[10]The standard treatment of Origen's relationship to Judaism and his many references to information obtained from a "Hebrew tutor" is Nicholas R. M. de Lange, *Origen and the Jews* (Cambridge: Cambridge University Press, 1976).

anxious to present a merely artistic arrangement of arguments. For I have no ability to do this, but this grace alone was given me of God, that I might understand His Scriptures" (*Dialogue with Trypho* 58.1).[11]

Justin was convinced that his way of expounding the Old Testament had been handed over to the church by the apostles, and that the apostles had learned it from the risen Christ, when "he opened their minds to understand the scriptures" (Lk 24:45).[12] Thus, while Justin himself was convinced that his exegesis derived from the highest authority, he was not able to appeal to an authority that would be recognized by his Jewish opponents nor by neutral on-lookers. That he should try to tear down the authority of the rabbis as much as possible, is in this perspective understandable, but not sympathetic.

In another field one also has the feeling of encountering the effects of a Gentile Christian inferiority complex. Paul had written to those of Gentile origin within the church: "you are no longer strangers and aliens, but you are citizens with the saints and also members of the household of God" (Eph 2:19). For the first Gentile converts it must have been an overwhelming experience to feel that in Christ they had become full members of the people of God, without the least stain or blemish attaching to them because of their Gentile background. To begin with, they were a minority, and they no doubt recognized that the people of God was something that existed prior to them, something they were taken into. They were "fellow citizens," but by no means the only citizens of the new kingdom.

In the second century one observes a marked change. The Christians of Gentile origin by now far outnumbered those of Jewish origin. Gradually, this fact came to influence the concept of the church. In Justin Martyr, the church is an essentially non-Jewish entity. It is made up of believing Gentiles, and over against this church of the Gentiles Justin places the Jewish nation as essentially non-believing. The border between believers and non-believers tends to coincide with the border between Gentiles and Jews. True, Justin knows of Jewish believers. But whereas in Paul the Gentiles are added to the true Israel of Jewish believers to share in their inheritance, in Justin it is the other way round: the few Jewish believers are added to the church of the Gentiles to share in their inheritance.

This shift of perspective had far-reaching consequences. While in Paul the

---

[11]Lukyn Williams, p. 119.
[12]Cf. also *Dialogue with Trypho* 78.10; 92.1; 100.2; 119.1; and comment in Skarsaune, *Proof from Prophecy*, pp. 11-13.

Gentiles share in the promises given to true Israel, in Justin the promises are transferred from the Jewish people to the church of the Gentiles. This church replaces the Jewish people. It takes over the inheritance of Israel while at the same time disinheriting the Jews. One might express this development by using Paul's image from Romans 11. In Paul, God has cut off some of the branches of Israel's old olive tree, and in their place he has grafted some wild branches—the Gentiles. In Justin, God has cut down Israel's olive tree, and in its place he has planted an entirely new tree—the church of the Gentiles. Onto this tree he has grafted a few branches from the old tree—those branches are the believing Jews.[13]

Once Christians began to think this way, they would naturally pose the question of election as an either/or alternative: Either the Jewish people or the (Gentile) church is the inheritor of the Old Testament heritage. No one in antiquity fostered the idea of God having two peoples; it had to be the church or the Jews. In this way, Christians of the second century were never able to assert their election in Christ without at the same time lashing out against the Jews.

One fact seems to emerge clearly from the above analysis: the numerical reduction of the Judeo-Christian element within the church was part of the reason why the church of the second century came to think of itself as essentially Gentile, a non-Jewish entity set over against the Jewish people as such.

This means, on the other hand, that by their very existence the Judeo-Christians were a moderating factor in this process of "gentilization" in the self-understanding of the church.[14] The Judeo-Christians had become a

---

[13]Since I have taken Justin to task here for radicalizing a Pauline model, one could ask if Justin's perspective is not in fact anticipated in other New Testament texts, e.g., in Matthew. Matthew 8:11-12 would be a case in point: Gentiles joining the patriarchs in the kingdom, while the "heirs of the kingdom" are thrown out. This is not the place for an extensive argument on the issue, I would like only to submit the following: there is no doubt in Matthew that *some* in Israel are expected to miss the kingdom because of their unbelief, and that many Gentiles are to *join* the kingdom. But this may still be basically compatible with Paul's perspective in Rom 11, and it is possible to make a good case for the view that Matthew has combined the commission to evangelize the nations (Mt 28:16-20) with an implicit motif of the restoration of Israel. See Peter Stuhlmacher, "Matt 28:16-20 and the Course of Mission in the Apostolic and Postapostolic Age," in Ådna/Kvalbein, *Mission of the Early Church,* pp. 17-44; Hans Kvalbein, "Has Matthew Abandoned the Jews?" ibid., pp. 45-62; Oskar Skarsaune, "The Mission to the Jews—A Closed Chapter? Some Patristic Reflections Concerning 'The Great Commission,'" ibid., pp. 69-83.

[14]See especially Jacob Jervell, "The Mighty Minority," in *The Unknown Paul: Essays on Luke-Acts and Early Christian History* (Minneapolis: Augsburg, 1984), 26-51.

minority within the church not because they had become so few, but because the Christians of Gentile origin had become so many. The influence and significance of the Judeo-Christians are still easily recognized in many of the writers of the second century: Justin Martyr, Theophilus of Antioch, Irenaeus. And very likely we should credit these Judeo-Christians with the fact that despite all bitterness and bad feelings a real dialogue with Judaism was carried on in the second century, as in Justin's *Dialogue with Trypho*. A modern reader may not be very satisfied with the tenor and tendency of much that Justin has to say—we have taken him to task for some of it above—but nevertheless it is a real dialogue in the sense that the objections put forward by Trypho are the real Jewish objections, and some of Justin's answers betray deep theological insight and make much sense. It may thus be of some relevance to make a very brief summary of this dialogue.

Justin's *Dialogue with Trypho*

Justin begins with his *Dialogue with Trypho*[15] a most emphatic denial of any ideas resembling those of Marcion:

> "There will never be any other God, Trypho, and there never was from all eternity," so said I to him, "save He who made and established this universe. Nor do we consider that we have one God, and you another, but Him only who brought

---

[15]The literature on this very interesting document is extensive; studies with a focus on the Jewish/Christian debate on the interpretation of Scripture in the *Dialogue* include Moritz Friedländer, "Justins Dialog mit dem Juden Tryphon," in *Patristische und talmudische Studien* (Vienna: Alfred Hölder, 1878; reprint, Westmead: Gregg International Publishers, 1972); pp. 80-137; Leslie W. Barnard, "The Old Testament and Judaism in the Writings of Justin Martyr," *Vetus Testamentum* 14 (1964): 395-406; Willis A. Shotwell, *The Biblical Exegesis of Justin Martyr* (London: SPCK, 1965); David E. Aune, "Justin Martyr's Use of the Old Testament," *Bulletin of the Evangelical Theological Society* 9 (1966): 179-97; A. J. B. Higgins, "Jewish Messianic Belief in Justin Martyr's *Dialogue with Trypho*," *Novum Testamentum* 9 (1967): 298-305; Ben Zion Bokser, "Justin Martyr and the Jews," *Jewish Quarterly Review*, n.s., 64 (1973/1974): 97-122, 204-11; Theodore Stylianopoulos, *Justin Martyr and the Mosaic Law*, SBL Dissertations Series 20 (Missoula, Mont.: Scholars Press, 1975); Demetrius C. Trakatellis, *The Pre-Existence of Christ in the Writings of Justin Martyr*, Harvard Dissertations in Religion 6 (Missoula, Mont.: Scholars Press, 1976); Frederic Manns, "L'exégèse de Justin dans le Dialogue avec Tryphon: Témoin de l'exégèse juive ancienne," in *Essais sur le Judéo-Christianisme*, Studii Biblici Fransiscani Analecta 12 (Jerusalem: Franciscan Printing Press, 1977); Skarsaune, *The Proof from Prophecy* (1987); Robert S. MacLennan, *Early Christian Texts on Jews and Judaism*, Brown Judaic Studies 194 (Atlanta, Ga.: Scholars Press, 1990); pp. 49-88 (with full bibliography on Jewish/Christian relations in the second century, pp. 162-98); William Horbury, "Jewish-Christian Relations in Barnabas and Justin Martyr," in Dunn, *Jews and Christians*, pp. 315-45; M. Hirschman, "Polemic Literary Units in the Classical Midrashim and Justin Martyr's *Dialogue with Trypho*," *Jewish Quarterly Review* 83 (1992-1993): 369-84.

your fathers out of the land of Egypt by a mighty hand and a stretched out arm, nor have we set our hopes on any other (for there is none), but only on Him on whom you also have set yours, the God of Abraham, Isaac and Jacob." (*Dialogue with Trypho* 11.1)[16]

But then, says Trypho, how is it that you Christians, who claim to worship the God of the Bible, do not observe his law? Justin answers by claiming that a distinction must be made with regard to the law. (1) Some commandments are ethical and agree with the law God had written in every human heart. This law is eternal and is observed by Christians. (2) But there is a second element in the law, ritual commandments which were given to the Jews only, to discipline them after the episode of the golden calf. These are not universal, and they are not necessary any longer after Christ has come and made all who believe in him truly pious and law-obedient.

To bolster his claim that with the coming of Christ the ceremonial part of the law should be abolished, Justin quoted, among others, Isaiah 51:4 and Jeremiah 31:31. Isaiah 51:4 reads: "Listen to me, my people, and give heed to me, my nation; *for Torah will go forth from me.*" This verse does not explicitly speak about changes in the Torah, but some of the rabbis took this to be implied, since it speaks of the giving of Torah at a time when the Torah of Moses was already given long ago. Accordingly we read in the *Midrash Rabbah* on Leviticus: "Rabbi Abin Bar Kahana said: The Holy one, blessed be he, said: 'A new law shall go forth from me' [Is 51:4], that is, *a renewal* of the Law" (*Lev. Rab.* 13:3).[17]

Apparently, there were some rabbis who made a distinction within the law between commandments for which rational reasons could be given, and commandments for which no such reasons could be found. The context of the above midrash passage is concerned to prove that in the world to come some of the unexplained commandments are to be abolished. There are other rabbinic texts that speak of the law becoming in some sense "new" in the messianic age, although sayings with this tendency seem to have been suppressed in later rabbinic tradition—possibly because Christians exploited this concept.[18] In any case it is obvious that Justin, in quoting Isaiah 51:4 as scriptural support for the idea of an abolishment of parts of the law, is in close contact

---

[16]Lukyn Williams, p. 22.
[17]H. Freedman and M. Simon, eds., *Midrash Rabbah: Leviticus* (London: Soncino, 1939), p. 167, quote modified.
[18]See Jacob Jervell, "Die offenbarte und die verborgene Tora: Zur Vorstellung über die neue Tora im Rabbinismus," *Studia Theologica* 25 (1971): 90-108; and Skarsaune, *Proof from Prophecy*, pp. 357-59 (with references to further literature).

with rabbinic discussions about the law. This familiarity with Jewish exegesis may well have been transmitted to him by Judeo-Christian sources.

It is thus evident that for Justin his attitude toward the law is intimately bound up with his conviction that he is living in the messianic age, in other words, his conviction that Jesus is the Messiah. And this is the second main theme of the dialogue.[19] Trypho raises the following objection: The prophecies of the Bible depict "one who is great and glorious, and takes over the everlasting kingdom. . . . But this your so-called Christ is without honour and glory, so that He has even fallen into the uttermost curse that is in the Law of God [Deut 21:23], for He was crucified" (*Dialogue with Trypho* 32.1).[20]

The point of Trypho's objection is this: what he misses in Jesus' messiahship is any sign that the messianic age came with him. Nothing has changed in the world. The peoples have not beaten their swords into plowshares and their spears into pruning hooks; the nations still lift up swords against each other, and they still learn war (cf. Is 2:4). In Jewish eschatology, the words of Isaiah 2:2-5 describe the essence of the messianic age. The pointing out that it did not come with Jesus may be called the timeless Jewish objection against his messiahship.

In order to better understand Justin's answer, it may be useful to compare it with the answer traditionally given in much modern teaching and preaching. This traditional answer says the Jews misunderstood the messianic prophecies by taking them in an outward, much too literal sense; but peace brought by the Messiah is not outward, political peace; it is peace of the heart, peace with God. Messianic liberation does not mean political or social liberation, but liberation from sin and guilt. And Jesus brought all this and more. The Jews did not recognize him because their expectation was wrong.

It is interesting to notice that Justin says nothing of the sort. He does *not* say that the messianic expectation of the Jews is false, crude, unspiritual, etc. He does not say that the Jews are wrong in their ideas of the messianic age. What he does say is something else. You have not observed, he says, that in the Old Testament the career of the Messiah has two phases, two stages. The Messiah is to come two times. In his first coming he will be dishonored and despised, he will suffer and die, thereby conquering the devil, atoning for our sins, and rising victoriously from the dead, thereby putting all evil spirits to shame. In his second coming he will come triumphantly, establishing in power and glory the messianic kingdom. Then all those things will be present

---

[19]We will return to parts of his proof for the messiahship of Jesus in chapter fifteen.
[20]Lukyn Williams, p. 62.

which Trypho misses in the first coming of Jesus. Then all messianic prophecies of the Old Testament will be fully realized.[21]

In order to prove that the Messiah has already come once, Justin makes
much out of *Genesis 49:10:* Since the kingdom has now failed from Judah, the
Messiah must have come. (This was to become a classic Christian argument
in debates with Jews for centuries to come.) Other important proof texts are
Numbers 24:17 (the star from Jacob); Isaiah 11:1 (the shoot from Jesse); *Psalm
72:17, Zechariah 6:12* (the dayspring); Isaiah 7:14 (the birth of the Messiah); *Isaiah 9:5a* (the hidden growth of the Messiah); Isaiah 11:2-3 (the messianic
anointing with the Spirit); Psalm 22; Isaiah 53 (the passion and death of the
Messiah); *Psalm 24:7-8* (the ascension of the Messiah); Psalm 110:1 (the
enthronement of the Messiah); Daniel 7:13 (the return of the Messiah); Zechariah 12:10-12 (the recognition of the Messiah by the Jews at his second coming). In this list, there are some important "new" texts (italicized above)
compared with the proof texts quoted most often in the New Testament. It is
interesting to notice that they correspond closely to the most often quoted
messianic proof texts of the Talmuds.[22] This probably means that Justin is
using a proof text tradition developed among Jewish Christians engaged in
intense dialogue with their nonbelieving kinsmen.[23]

In addition to this proof that Jesus is the Messiah promised in the Bible,
Justin wields an extensive scriptural argument concerning the divine nature
of the Messiah. On this topic, Trypho says the following:

> To my mind . . . they who say He [Jesus] has been a man (only), and has been
> anointed and made Messiah by election, speak with greater acumen than you
> and yours who say what you now affirm [namely that the Messiah pre-exists
> and is divine]. For all of us Jews expect that the Messiah will be a man of human
> origin [Greek, *anthropos ex anthropōn*], and that Elijah will come and anoint Him.
> But if this man [Jesus] seems to be the Messiah, one must certainly acknowledge
> that He is man of merely human origin. (*Dialogue with Trypho* 49.1)[24]

The main thrust of Justin's answer is to prove that the Old Testament

---

[21]In order to see the present-day relevance of this line of argument, cf. the interesting article
by Rabbi Chaim Pearl, "Some Thoughts on Jewish-Christian Dialogue," in *Israel and
Yeshua: Festschrift Celebrating the Tenth Anniversary of Caspari Center for Biblical and Jewish
Studies*, ed. Torleif Elgvin (Jerusalem: Caspari Center, 1993), pp. 85-90; esp. pp. 87-88.
[22]Cf. the list with references in Skarsaune, *Proof from Prophecy*, pp. 261-62.
[23]See also Oskar Skarsaune, "Schriftbeweis und christologisches Kerygma in der ältesten kirchli-
chen Schriftauslegung," in *Schrift und Auslegung*, ed. Heinrich Kraft, Veröffentlichungen der
Luther-Akademie e.V. Ratzeburg 10 (Erlangen: Martin-Luther-Verlag, 1987), pp. 45-54.
[24]Lukyn Williams, p. 97.

knows another "God" and "Lord" besides God the Father. Genesis 1:26; 19:24; Exodus 3:1-6; Psalm 110:1; and Psalm 45:7 are among the main proof texts. We have every reason to believe that this kind of argument was developed among Judeo-Christians with a knowledge of Hebrew. Let us compare a passage in Justin with a passage in the Babylonian Talmud.

> [Justin: the "Lord" conversing with Abraham in Gen 18:22-23 is not God the Father, nor an angel.] "He is 'Lord,' receiving from the Lord who is in heaven, namely the Maker of the universe, the duty of bringing those punishments on Sodom and Gomorrah which the word enumerates, saying thus: 'The Lord rained on Sodom and Gomorrah brimstone and fire from the Lord out of heaven' [Gen 19:24]. (*Dialogue with Trypho* 56.23)[25]

The argument is that: in this verse there are two "Lords": one on earth conversing with Abraham and bringing the brimstone and fire down on Sodom and Gomorrah; and one in heaven. Compare this with the following Talmudic passage:

> A *Min* [heretic] once said to R. Ishmael b. Jose [ca. A.D. 180]: It is written "Then the Lord caused to rain upon Sodom and Gomorrah brimstone and fire from the Lord," [Gen 19:24] but "from him" should have been written! A certain fuller said, Leave him to me, I will answer him. It is written, "And Lamech said to his wives, Ada and Zillah, Hear my voice, ye wives of Lamech"; but he should have said, "my wives." But such is the Scriptural idiom—so here too, it is the Scriptural idiom. —Whence do you know that? asked he [R. Ishmael]. I heard it in a public discourse of R. Meir, [he answered]. (*TB Sanhedrin* 38b)[26]

Rabbi Meir was Justin's contemporary, which means that Justin's argument was already known to the rabbis of the land of Israel at that time. Certainly they had not read it in Justin; they knew it from those who had been Justin's teachers, the Judeo-Christians of Israel or the nearby regions. In the context of the Talmudic passage several other arguments of the *minim* for the existence of a second God are mentioned. Most of these arguments presume a knowledge of the Hebrew text; in other words, here we observe Jewish Christians engaged in exegetical argument with the rabbis.

This brief review of Justin's *Dialogue with Trypho* does not in any way exhaust the richness of the arguments and scriptural passages used to prove his point. Scripture is quoted so extensively that later generations of Christian apologists and polemicists against Judaism had little to add; Justin's main

---

[25]Ibid., p. 117.
[26]Soncino translation, *Sanhedrin*, p. 246.

Temple Square

In days to come the mountain of the LORD's house shall be established as the highest of the mountains, and shall be raised above the hills; all the nations shall stream to it. Many peoples shall come and say, "Come, let us go up to the mountain of the Lord, to the house of the God of Jacob; that he may teach us his ways and that we may walk in his paths." (Is 2:2-3)

Early Christian believers shared the conviction—across ethnic and theological differences—that this prophetic vision was now being realized. A man like Justin was even convinced it would be realized in a quite concrete way. He spiritualizes nothing when he says: "Come with me all who fear God, who wish to see the good things of Jerusalem. Come, let us go in the light of the Lord, for he has set his people free, even the House of Jacob. Come, all ye nations, let us be gathered together at Jerusalem" (*Dialogue with Trypho* 24.3). The very proof of how concretely he envisages this, is, at the same time, the sad backside of his glorious vision: the Hadrianic decree expelling all Jews from Jerusalem is seen by Justin as the negative preparation for this conquest of the city by the believers from the Gentiles. The nations do not come to Jerusalem to join the elect Israel of God there, but to oust and replace them. God's house was to become a house of prayer for all the Gentiles—only.

---

proof texts recur in all later disputations, right up to our own times.

The first to excerpt extensively from Justin's work was Tertullian, at the end of the second century. His *Adversus Judaeos (Against the Jews)* is no longer a real dialogue, but a monologue aimed at fellow Christians who felt attracted towards Judaism and may have been on the verge of conversion.[27]

Two main observations emerge from the evidence surveyed in this chapter. (1) We have seen behind the text of Justin's *Dialogue* Jewish Christians engaged in an intense dialogue with rabbinic Judaism, eager to convince their Jewish kinsmen that Jesus is the divine Messiah, God's Son. (2) We have seen among the Gentile Christians an increasing tendency to define the church as essentially non-Jewish, an entity set over against the Jewish people. This means that in claiming the Old Testament heritage for the church, they felt the necessity of denying it to the Jews.

Suggestions for Further Reading

Justin Martyr's *Dialogue with Trypho* is most conveniently accessible in an English translation in *ANF* 1:194-270. A fully annotated translation is A. Lukyn Williams, *Justin Martyr: The Dialogue with Trypho: Translation, Introduction, and Notes* (London: SPCK, 1930). Selected parts are translated in R. P. C. Hanson, *Selections from Justin Martyr's Dialogue with Trypho, a Jew,* World Christian Books 49 (London: Lutterworth, 1963). For a complete American translation of all Justin's works (and the spurious as well), see

---

[27]The best commentary on this neglected but important work of Tertullian is Hermann Tränkle, *Q. S. F. Tertulliani Adversus Iudaeos, mit Einleitung und kritischem Kommentar* (Wiesbaden: Franz Steiner Verlag, 1964).

Thomas B. Falls, *Writings of Saint Justin Martyr,* The Fathers of the Church: A New Translation 6 (Washington: The Catholic University of America Press, 1948 [and later reprints]).

In recent years, a vast literature has been produced on the relationship between Jews and Christians in antiquity. The pioneer and classic is James Parkes, *The Conflict of the Church and the Synagogue: A Study in the Origins of Antisemitism* (New York and London: Soncino, 1934 [reprint, New York, 1969]). The more recent standard work is Marcel Simon, *Verus Israel: Étude sur les relations entre chrétiens et juifs dans l'Empire Romain (135-425),* Bibliothèque des Écoles francaises d'Athènes et de Rome 166 (Paris, 1948). Revised and expanded eds. Paris: Éditions E. de Boccard, 1964 and 1983). English trans.: *Verus Israel: A Study of the Relations Between Christians and Jews in the Roman Empire (AD 135-425),* 2nd ed. (Oxford: Oxford University Press, 1986).

Some newer studies:
    (Those listed in the general bibliography at the end of the Introduction are only mentioned here by short title and year of publication.) Amos B. Hulen, "The 'Dialogues with the Jews' as Sources for the Early Jewish Argument Against Christianity," *Journal of Biblical Literature* 51 (1932): 58-70; Sandmel, *Judaism* 1978; Rokeah, *Conflict* (1982); John G. Gager, *The Origins of Anti-Semitism: Attitudes Toward Judaism in Pagan and Christian Antiquity* (New York and Oxford: Oxford University Press, 1985), esp. part 3, pp. 113-91; Segal, *Rebecca's Children* (1986), chaps. 6 and 7; Stephen G. Wilson, ed., *Anti-Judaism in Early Christianity,* vol. 2: *Separation and Polemic* (Waterloo, Ont.: Wilfrid Laurier University Press, 1986); Flusser, *Judaism* (1988); Robert S. MacLennan, *Early Christian Texts on Jews and Judaism,* Brown Judaic Studies 194 (Atlanta, Ga.: Scholars Press, 1990); Dunn, *Partings* (1991); Dunn, *Jews and Christians* (1992); Conzelmann, *Gentiles* (1992); Schwartz, *Studies* (1992); Craig A. Evans and Donald A. Hagner, eds., *Anti-Semitism and Early Christianity: Issues of Polemic and Faith* (Minneapolis: Fortress, 1993); Sanders, *Schismatics* (1993); Wilson, *Strangers* (1995); Lieu, *Image* (1996); John Barclay and John Sweet, eds., *Early Christian Thought in Its Jewish Context* (Cambridge: Cambridge University Press, 1996); Ora Limor and Guy G. Stroumsa, eds., *Contra Iudaeos: Ancient and Medieval Polemics Between Christians and Jews,* Texts and Studies in Medieval and Early Modern Judaism 10 (Tübingen: J. C. B. Mohr [Paul Siebeck], 1996); Horbury, *Jews and Christians* (1998); Karl P. Donfried and Peter Richardson, eds., *Judaism and Christianity in First-Century Rome* (Grand Rapids, Mich./Cambridge, U.K.: Eerdmans, 1998); Graham N. Stanton and Guy G. Stroumsa, eds., *Tolerance and Intolerance in Early Judaism and Christianity* (Cambridge: Cambridge University Press, 1998); Guy G. Stroumsa, *Barbarian Philosophy: The Religious Revolution of Early Christianity,* Wissenschaftliche Untersuchungen zum Neuen Testament 112 (Tübingen: Mohr Siebeck, 1999).

General works on early Jewish and early Christian interpretations of the Bible:
    R. Loewe, "The Jewish Midrashim and Patristic and Scholastic Exegesis of the Bible,"

in *Studia Patristica,* ed. Kurt Aland and F. L. Cross, Texte und Untersuchungen 63 (Berlin: Akademie-Verlag, 1957), 1:492-514; Jakob J. Petuchowski, "Halakah in the Church Fathers," in *Essays in Honor of Solomon B. Freehof,* ed. W. Jacob et al. (Pittsburgh: Rodef Shalom Congregation, 1964), pp. 257-74; Roger le Déaut, "La tradition juive ancienne et l'exégèse chrétienne primitive," *Revue d'histoire et de philosophie religieuses* 51 (1971): 31-50; Kurt Hruby, "Exégèse rabbinique et exégèse patristique," *Recherches de science religieuse* 47 (1973) 341-72; Judith R. Baskin, "Rabbinic-Patristic Exegetical Contacts in Late Antiquity: A Bibliographical Reappraisal," in *Approaches to Ancient Judaism,* vol. 5: *Studies in Judaism and Its Greco-Roman Context,* ed. William Scott Green, Brown Judaic Studies 32 (Atlanta, Ga.: Scholars Press, 1985), pp. 53-80 (with very full bibliography on pp. 75-80); William Horbury, "Old Testament Interpretation in the Writings of the Church Fathers," in *Compendia 2:1:* 727-87; Martin Hengel and Hermut Löhr, eds., *Schriftauslegung im antiken Judentum und im Urchristentum,* Wissenschaftliche Untersuchungen zum Neuen Testament 73 (Tübingen: J. C. B. Mohr [Paul Siebeck], 1994); Burton L. Visotzky, "Jots and Tittles: On Scriptural Interpretation in Rabbinic and Patristic Literatures," in *Fathers of the World: Essays in Rabbinic and Patristic Literatures,* Wissenschaftliche Untersuchungen zum Neuen Testament 80 (Tübingen: J. C. B. Mohr [Paul Siebeck], 1995), pp. 28-40; Günter Stemberger, "Exegetical Contacts between Christians and Jews in the Roman Empire," in *Hebrew Bible/Old Testament: The History of Its Interpretation,* ed. Magne Saebø (Göttingen: Vandenhoeck & Ruprecht, 1996), 1:569-86.

PART 3

THE PERSISTENCE
OF THE JEWISH HERITAGE

*FAITH & ORDER
IN THE EARLY CHURCH*

14

WHICH BOOKS BELONG IN THE BIBLE?
THE QUESTION OF CANON

*F*or us moderns, the Bible is something very concrete and definite: a book between two covers. In antiquity, the question of which books belonged to the Bible was
not that simple, because "the Bible"—Greek, ta biblia, "the [sacred] books"—was
not one, but several books. From the beginning, these existed only as scrolls, and one
scroll could contain only one of the larger biblical books, such as Genesis or Isaiah.
This means that the Bible existed concretely only as a collection of scrolls, in no particular order, or abstractly as a list of the biblical books. And lists always have to have
a certain order.

The early church very soon adopted a new book format for its sacred books: the
codex, the equivalent and precursor of the modern book. This allowed the church to
produce codices containing the whole Bible in one volume. Such codices are preserved
from the fourth century onwards. Before that, it is likely that the New Testament
books were published together in codex format quite early, some scholars think early
in the second century. It seems the church was also a pioneer in using the codex format for the Old Testament books, possibly from the same time as this format was used
for individual New Testament books or the whole New Testament.[1]

---

[1]On these two paragraphs see, e.g., Peter Katz, "The Early Christian's Use of Codices Instead

We shall have to keep these facts in mind when we speak of "the Bible" and "the canon" in the following pages. We are not, from the beginning, speaking of different books being collected between two covers in one book, but of something more abstract: a group of books being accorded an authority that set them apart from other books.

What Is "Scripture"?

For the first believers in Jesus, the word *Scripture* had the same meaning as for all other Jews; it meant the books of the Hebrew Bible,[2] what Christians later came to call the Old Testament.[3] In Justin's *Dialogue with Trypho*, this is still the case. Trypho speaks of Scripture, and Justin speaks of Scripture, and they mean exactly the same: the books of the Hebrew Bible. Justin never uses the introductory formula "as it is said in Scripture" (or equivalents) when he quotes from the New Testament writings. His pupil Tatian (ca. A.D. 170-175) is the first, to our knowledge, to quote a New Testament writing as Scripture.[4] But he only does so once.[5] We have to turn to Athenagoras (ca. 180) and his contemporary, Theophilus of Antioch, to find Christian authors who use the same formulas of quotation when they quote the New Testament as when they quote the Old Testament. For them, Scripture is composed of the Hebrew Bible *plus* the apostolic writings.

This would seem to imply that the only real question of canon in the early church was over the New Testament books. How and why were these books recognized as being on the same level of authority as the Old Testament, and

---

of Rolls," *The Journal of Theological Studies* 46 (1945): 63-65; C. H. Roberts and T. C. Skeat, *The Birth of the Codex* (London: Oxford University Press, 1983 [reprint, 1985]).

[2]Here and in the following I use "Hebrew Bible" as the name of the collection of books that came to be the Jewish Bible, and also corresponds to the Protestant Old Testament. It is called the *Hebrew* Bible to distinguish it from the somewhat larger collection of books contained in most manuscripts of the Greek Bible, the so-called Septuagint. In Jewish parlance, the Hebrew Bible is often called *Tanak*, short for *Torah, Neviim* and *Ketuvim* (The Law, The Prophets and The Writings), the three parts of the canon in traditional Jewish Bibles.

[3]The first author to use the term is Melito of Sardis around A.D. 175, in a fragment preserved in Eusebius's *Ecclesiastical History* 4.26.13-14: "I got precise information about the books of the Old Covenant [Greek, *ta tēs palaias diathēkēs biblia*], of which I now send you a list." In Clement of Alexandria, a decade or two later, the term is already traditional.

[4]In *2 Clement* 2:4 and *Barnabas* 4:14 isolated sayings of Jesus are quoted as "Scripture." It is probable that these quotations are meant to be quotes from Jesus rather than from the Gospels as writings. In Polycarp, *Letter to the Philippians* 12:1, Eph 4:26 is quoted as "holy Scriptures" (plural!). It is possible that Polycarp mistook the whole of Eph 4:26 to be a Psalms quotation (therefore the plural), whereas only the first part really is: Ps 4:5. Cf. in general von Campenhausen, *Entstehung*, pp. 143-44.

[5]*Oration to the Greeks* 13.1. The quotation formula is not very specific, however: "as it is said" [Greek, *to eiremenon*].

which books should belong in the New Testament?

It is evident, however, that the early church also had a problem with the Old Testament canon. Since the days of the Reformation, this problem has been clearly visible in the difference between the Catholic (and Orthodox) Old Testament and the Protestant Old Testament. The Protestant Old Testament comprises exactly the same books as the Hebrew Bible, whereas the Catholic Old Testament has some more books, which Protestants call the Apocrypha. And both Bibles—the Catholic and the Protestant—can claim early church authority!

The Catholic Bible is an indication that the Old Testament of the early church was larger than the Hebrew Bible. How do we explain that? There is also one more difference between the Christian Old Testament (whether Catholic or Protestant) and the Jewish Bible: the order of books is not the same. All Bibles begin with the five books of Moses, and most of them continue with the historical books from Joshua through 2 Kings. But from there on it varies. The Jewish Bible continues with the longer prophetical books: Isaiah, Jeremiah, Ezekiel, and the collection called The Twelve (the Minor Prophets). These are taken together with the historical books Joshua through 2 Kings and called the Prophets. The third part of the Jewish canon, the Writings (Hebrew, *Ketuvim*) is a rather peculiar collection of books, comprising three poetical books (Psalms, Lamentations, Song of Solomon); three wisdom books (Proverbs, Job, Ecclesiastes); six "historical" books (Ruth, Esther, Ezra, Nehemiah, 1-2 Chronicles); and one prophetic book (Daniel). The internal order among these books is also rather peculiar, apart from the fact that it varies slightly even in the medieval manuscripts.[6]

If we compare this with the Christian Old Testaments from antiquity— either lists of books or the order of the Old Testament codices—we see a marked difference (apart from the difference that the Christian Bibles vary much more among themselves than do the Jewish). The rather artificial distinction between the Prophets and the Writings in the Jewish Bible is usually not observed in the Christian Bibles, and a general tendency is to move the prophetical books towards the end. In other words, while the Jewish Bible

---

[6]The established order is Psalms, Proverbs, Job, Song of Songs, Ruth, Lamentations, Ecclesiastes, Esther, Daniel, Ezra, Nehemiah, 1-2 Chronicles. Perhaps the guiding principle behind this is to group the books into two categories: first the Davidic and Solomonic books from Israel's golden days (Psalms through Ruth); then different books from the days of the Babylonian exile and its aftermath (Lamentations through 2 Chronicles).

Box 14.1. The Old Testament Apocrypha

Tobit (early second century B.C.): An edifying short story about the rewards of true piety. Originally written in Hebrew or Aramaic; fragments of both versions found at Qumran.

Judith (second century B.C.): A legendary short story of how the Jewess Judith saved her people during a siege. Originally written in Hebrew; only the Greek version extant.

Wisdom (of Solomon) (composed late second or early first century B.C.): Written in Alexandria, originally in Greek. Not short proverbs as in Proverbs, but rather a connected treatise on how God through salvation history leads and saves those who trust in him and his wisdom.

Sirach (Hebrew original composed ca. 190 B.C.; translated by Jesus son of Sirach's grandson into Greek ca. 132 B.C.): Fragments of the Hebrew found in Qumran, on Masada and in the Cairo Geniza. A wisdom book in the style of Proverbs, but with longer and partly more argumentative units. Salvation history seen from the perspective of Wisdom. Presented as a study guide to the threefold biblical canon. Among the Apocrypha, Sirach was the one book that remained popular and was widely read among Jews for a very long time, right through the Middle Ages.

Baruch (composed around A.D. 1): A "prophetic" book in the style of the Old Testament prophetical books, but deeply influenced by the Wisdom tradition. Attributed to Jeremiah's scribe and secretary Baruch.

The Letter of Jeremiah (composed before 100 B.C.): Hebrew fragments found at Qumran. A polemical homily against idolatry.

1 Maccabees (composed in Hebrew ca. 100 B.C.): Only the Greek version is extant. Tells the story of the dramatic events of 175-134 B.C., in the style of Kings and Chronicles.

2 Maccabees (first century B.C.): A summary of Jason of Cyrene's five books on the Maccabean uprising and its prehistory, roughly covering the period 180-161 B.C. Written in Greek, in the style of the Greek historians.

Prayer of Manasseh (ca. 100 B.C.): Prayer of penitence, cf. 2 Chronicles 33:18-19.

ends with the historical Ezra-Nehemiah-Chronicles group, the Christian Bibles tend to end with the three or four major (longer) prophetical books, the twelve minor (shorter) prophetical books or Daniel. The Christian Old Testament ends on a prophetical note; the Jewish Bible does not.

The Old Testament Canon in Judaism and the Early Church

Some decades ago, most scholars agreed to a simple and elegant explanation of the difference between the Jewish Bible and the Christian Old Testament (= Jewish Bible + Apocrypha). The explanation was sought in Alexandrian Judaism and the Greek translation of the Bible, the so-called Septuagint ("[The translation of] the Seventy," based on the old legend of how this translation was made).[7] Scholars assumed that the Jews in Alexandria regarded the

---

[7]The two oldest versions of the legend occur in the so-called *Letter of Aristeas* and in Philo, *On the Life of Moses* 2.25-44. Josephus tells the story mainly according to Aristeas (*Antiquities* 12.12-118). Later many of the church fathers took it over from one or more of these Jewish sources.

Apocrypha as part of their Bible, and since the early church took over the Greek Old Testament as the Bible of the church, the larger canon of Alexandria also came to be the canon of the church.[8]

An alternative version of this "Alexandrian" hypothesis runs as follows: The Jews in Alexandria did not have a larger, but a more *restricted* canon. They regarded only the Torah as Scripture in the strict sense. But this also meant that they were more liberal with regard to all other writings and made no fundamental distinction between the books belonging to the categories of the Prophets, the Writings and the Apocrypha. For the early church, some of the latter books were the most important, and so the Christian Old Testament became very inclusive, making no distinction between Prophets, Writings and Apocrypha.[9]

There are two problems with either version of this Alexandrian hypothesis.[10] (1) There is no evidence whatsoever that the Jews of Alexandria had a canon that differed from that of Jews elsewhere, say, in the land of Israel. On the contrary, Alexandrian Jewish writers like Philo seem to presuppose the normal Jewish canon of Torah, Neviim and Ketuvim. (2) The hypothesis presupposes that the early church, universally and unanimously, regarded the Apocrypha as part of its Old Testament. That—as we shall see shortly—was not the case. In fact, when the church fathers on occasion produced lists of their Old Testament canon, they regularly mentioned the books of the Jewish Bible, but did not include the Apocrypha. At the same time, these same writers on occasion quoted the Apocrypha as Scripture. This clearly points to the conclusion that there was a certain ambiguity or inconsistency in the early church regarding the canon of the Old Testament.

But this phenomenon gives no indication that we should look to Alexandria in particular for an explanation. Alexandrian church fathers reproduced the standard Jewish Bible in their lists of Old Testament books, not the supposed "Alexandrian Bible."[11]

---

[8]The fascinating story of how this theory came to be formulated in the late eighteenth century is told in Albert C. Sundberg, *The Old Testament of the Early Church*, Harvard Theological Studies 20 (Cambridge, Mass.: Harvard University Press/London: Oxford University Press, 1964). Cf. also J. Shaper, "The Rabbinic Canon and the Old Testament of the Early Church: A Social-Historical View," in *Canonization and Decanonization: Papers Presented to the International Conference of the Leiden Institute for the Study of Religions (LISOR), held at Leiden 9-10 January 1997*, ed. A. van der Kooij and K. van der Toorn, Studies in the History of Religions 82 (Leiden: E. J. Brill, 1998), pp. 93-106; esp. 93-95.

[9]As a representative statement of this theory, see Aage Bentzen, *Introduction to the Old Testament*, 6th ed. (Copenhagen: G. E. C. Gad, 1961), 1:35-41.

[10]The standard refutation of the Alexandrian hypothesis is Sundberg's book.

[11]Sundberg's critique of this hypothesis was in part anticipated in Peter Katz, "The Old Test-

In recent years, scholars have for the most part abandoned the Alexandrian hypothesis and launched an alternative explanation, this time in terms of chronology, not geography. The idea is that during the first century A.D. the group of Writings within the Jewish canon was still open; it was not clearly defined. The early church took over an open-ended canon and was free to define a more extensive collection of Writings (including some or all of the Apocrypha). Rabbinical Judaism made up its mind about the Writings at the so-called Synod of Jamnia around A.D. 90-100 and settled for a more restricted number of Writings (excluding the Apocrypha). The church did not feel it had to follow this rabbinical decision and kept the older, more inclusive canon.

This hypothesis is vulnerable to the second objection against the Alexandrian hypothesis, referred to above. One cannot state without qualifications that the Old Testament canon of the early church included the Apocrypha. If the supposed definition of the Writings by the rabbis in Jamnia was a novelty, why should the church have paid any attention to it, and why should early and late church fathers have obeyed it each time they produced lists of their canon?

But the most serious objection against this hypothesis concerns the very idea of a "synod" in Jamnia making decisions about the extent of the Writings. This idea is a modern scholarly construct, with less than a flimsy basis in the sources.[12] It is built on *one* Mishnaic text, *Yadayim* 3:5, which we shall take a closer look at now.

All the Holy Scriptures render the hands unclean.[13] Rabbi Judah [ca. A.D. 150]

---

ament Canon in Palestine and Alexandria," *Zeitschrift für die neutestamentiche Wissenschaft* 47 (1956): 191-217.

[12]For criticism of the theory of a "synod" at Jamnia, cf. W. M. Christie, "The Jamnia Period in Jewish History," *The Journal of Theological Studies* 26 (1925): 347-64; Jack P. Lewis, "What Do We Mean by Jabneh?" *Journal of Bible and Religion* 32 (1964): 125-32; Peter Schäfer, "Die sogenannte Synode von Jabne," *Judaica* 31 (1975): 54-64, 116-24; R. C. Newman, "The Council of Jamnia and the Old Testament Canon," *The Westminster Theological Journal* 38, no. 3 (1976): 319-49; Leiman, *Canonization*, pp. 120-24; G. Stemberger, "Die sogenannte Synode von Jabne und das frühe Christentum," *Kairos* 19 (1977): 14-21; Beckwith, *The Old Testament*, pp. 276-77.

[13]"Making the hands unclean" is thus a mark of canonical status; the exact background of this principle is not known. Some scholars suspect that the explanation given in *TB Shabbat* 14a is secondary, but Sid Leiman thinks it is to the point: the priests and other scholars used to keep the biblical books in the same place as the priestly dough-offering, thus exposing the books to danger (from mice and other animals attracted to the dough). In order to enforce separation of scrolls and food, it was decided that the books made their hands unclean (they could not eat and handle the scrolls at the same time). See Leiman, *Canonization*, pp. 115-20.

says: The Song of Songs renders the hands unclean, but about Ecclesiastes there is dissension. Rabbi Jose [ca. A.D. 150] says: Ecclesiastes does not render the hands unclean, and about the Song of Songs there is dissension. Rabbi Simeon [ca. A.D. 150] says: Ecclesiastes is one of the things about which the School of Shammai adopted a more lenient, and the School of Hillel the more stringent ruling. Rabbi Simeon ben Azzai [ca. A.D. 110] said: I have heard a tradition from the seventy-two elders on the day [ca. A.D. 90-100] when they made Rabbi Eleazar ben Azariah head of the college (of Sages), that the Song of Songs and Ecclesiastes both render the hands unclean. Rabbi Akiba [died A.D. 135] said: God forbid!—no man in Israel ever disputed about the Song of Songs (that he should say) that it does not render the hands unclean, for all ages are not worth the day on which the Song of Songs was given to Israel; for all the Writings are holy, but the Song of Songs is the Holy of Holies. And if anything was in dispute the dispute was about Ecclesiastes alone. Rabbi Johanan ben Joshua, the son of Rabbi Akiba's father-in-law, said: According to the words of Ben Azzai so did they dispute and so did they decide.[14]

The only thing that is clear from this text is that there was an ongoing debate about two of the "fringe" books among the Writings *(Ketuvim)* right into the middle of the second century (and there is additional rabbinic evidence that debates over single books, even including the Prophets, continued beyond that period). One episode in these debates was the vote of the seventy-two elders who gathered to make Rabbi Eleazar ben Azariah head of the college of sages. This was not anything like a council of bishops, making binding decisions for all the people. But it seems that a form of Christian ecclesiastical institution is somehow read back into the rabbinic text by many (Christian) scholars.

Exactly *what* the discussion about Song of Songs and Ecclesiastes—and later some other books—was all about is a question we shall postpone for the present.

Delimiting the Hebrew Canon
We shall consider some evidence that points to the conclusion that the whole Hebrew biblical canon was a clearly defined—and closed—unit *prior* to the supposed "synod."[15]

---

[14]Danby, *Mishnah*, p. 781.
[15]For the following, see Martin Hengel, "'Schriftauslegung' und 'Schriftwerdung' in der Zeit des Zweiten Tempels," in *Schriftauslegung im antiken Judentum und im Urchristentum*, ed. Martin Hengel and Hermut Löhr, Wissenschaftliche Untersuchungen zum Neuen Testament 73 (Tübingen: J. C. B. Mohr [Paul Siebeck], 1994), pp. 1-71.

First and foremost there is the evidence of Josephus.[16] Around A.D. 95 Josephus wrote the following about the Jews and their holy books:

We have given practical proof of our reverence for our own Scriptures. For, although such long ages have now passed, no one has ventured either to add, or to remove, or to alter a syllable; and it is an instinct with every Jew, from the day of his birth, to regard them as the decrees of God, to abide by them, and, if need be, cheerfully to die for them. Time and again before now the sight has been witnessed of prisoners enduring tortures and death in every form in the theatres, rather than utter a single word against the laws and the allied documents. What Greek would endure as much for the same cause? Even to save the entire collection of his nation's writings from destruction he would not face the smallest personal injury. (*Against Apion* 1.42-44)[17]

It is very clear in this passage that Josephus is proud of belonging to a people who possess a collection of books that are regarded as unique, compared with all other books. This, in itself, is sufficient to indicate that for Josephus this collection was clearly defined; that is, that he was in no doubt as to which books belonged to it. And he has explicit statements about this in the same passage:

With us it is not open to everybody to write the [historical] records [of our people]. . . . There is no discrepancy in what is written, . . . on the contrary, the prophets alone had this privilege [of writing], obtaining their knowledge of the most remote and ancient history through the inspiration which they owed to God, and committing to writing a clear account of the events of their own time just as they occurred. It follows . . . that we do not possess myriads of inconsistent books, conflicting with each other. Our books, *those which are justly accredited, are but twenty-two*, and contain the record of all time. Of these, five are the books of Moses, comprising the laws and the traditional history from the birth of man down to the death of the lawgiver. . . . From the death of Moses until Artaxerxes

---

[16]For the following treatment of Josephus on canon, see esp. Sid Z. Leiman, "Josephus and the Canon of the Bible," in *Josephus, the Bible, and History*, ed. Louis H. Feldman and Gohei Hata (Leiden: E. J. Brill, 1989), pp. 50-58 (with references to earlier literature); Steve Mason (with Robert A. Kraft), "Josephus on Canon and Scriptures," in *Hebrew Bible/Old Testament: The History of Its Interpretation*, ed. Magne Saebø, vol. 1: *From the Beginnings to the Middle Ages (Until 1300)*, part 1: *Antiquity* (Göttingen: Vandenhoeck & Ruprecht, 1996), pp. 217-35; A. van der Kooij, "The Canonization of Ancient Books Kept in the Temple of Jerusalem," in Kooij and Toorn, *Canonization*, pp. 17-40, esp. pp. 19-23.

[17]Josephus is here and elsewhere quoted according to Thackeray's Loeb edition. This quote: pp. 179-81.

[18]Josephus probably reckoned Lamentations as one book with Jeremiah, and Ruth as one book with Judges. That gives the following list of "historical" books written by prophets:

... the prophets subsequent to Moses wrote the history of the events of their own times in thirteen books.[18] The remaining four books[19] contain hymns to God and precepts for the conduct of human life. (*Against Apion* 1.37-41, italics added)[20]

From Josephus, then, we may conclude that his biblical canon comprised exactly the same books as we now reckon to the Hebrew Bible. The important thing to notice here is that Josephus—at exactly the same time as the "decision" at Jamnia was supposedly made—speaks about the whole canon as being held in a category by itself by all Jews, and that it has been so for a long time. Josephus was writing this in Rome—far away from Jamnia—and he wrote as if the question of canon (including the Writings) had long been settled in Judaism. But he also testifies to the variability of the *order* of books. His division between prophetical and "remaining books" does not correspond to the later division between the Prophets and Writings in Jewish Bibles.[21]

Josephus's evidence provides a good argument for the view that the number of canonical books was settled quite some time before he wrote. There is corroborative evidence prior to Josephus: (1) the attitude of the Qumran people and (2) the attitude of Sirach's Greek translator.

1. The canon in Qumran. Shemaryahu Talmon has argued convincingly that the Qumran sect believed that a new period of "holy history" and of contemporary revelation had been opened in their own time. They themselves felt they had authority to produce new writings more or less of a "biblical" nature.[22] So we would not expect the Qumran people to pay very much atten-

---

(1) Joshua, (2) Judges/Ruth, (3) 1-2 Samuel, (4) 1-2 Kings, (5) 1-2 Chronicles, (6) Ezra/Nehemiah, (7) Esther, (8) Job, (9) Isaiah, (10) Jeremiah, (11) Ezekiel, (12) The Twelve Prophets, (13) Daniel. Josephus seems to have arranged the canonical books according to a simple "historical" principle: in what he took to be their chronological sequence. Notice that this part of his canon ends with the prophetical books and Daniel.
[19]Psalms, Proverbs, Ecclesiastes, Song of Songs.
[20]Thackeray, p. 179.
[21]The earliest literary evidence for the traditional internal arrangement of the Writings and the Prophets, which is found in what we might call the "rabbinic Bible," is *TB Bava Batra* 14b. Cf. the discussion of this passage in Beckwith, *The Old Testament*, pp. 122-30. A. van der Kooij, in the article listed in note 16, argues that Josephus's order of thirteen prophetical books and only four "remaining Scriptures," was not created by him, but was traditional. He thinks it is the same, or roughly the same, order as can be discerned in the Prologue to Sirach (cf. below), in 4QMMT (the so-called *Halakic Letter* from ca. 150 B.C.), in 2 Macc 2:13-14, and also in Luke 24:44.
[22]Talmon has stated this in several articles, see e.g., "Between the Bible and the Mishnah," in his *The World of Qumran From Within: Collected Studies* (Jerusalem: Magnes/Leiden: Brill, 1989), pp. 11-52; "The Community of the Renewed Covenant: Between Judaism and Christianity," in *The Community of the Renewed Covenant: The Notre Dame Symposium on the Dead Sea Scrolls*, ed. Eugene Ulrich and James Vanderkam, Christianity and Judaism in Antiq-

tion to, or to respect, a "closed" canon of the Bible, even if it existed in their time. It is all the more striking that they *do* in fact seem to presuppose the ordinary canon.[23] The fact that the Qumran people seem to regard the writings enumerated by Josephus as being in a category by themselves gives a very clear indication of the strength of the tradition of doing so already established. Otherwise these people would have little or no reason to so regard these writings.

2. The evidence of Sirach.

> Many great teachings have been given to us through the Law and the Prophets and the others [or other books] that followed them, and for these we should praise Israel for instruction and wisdom. Now, those who read the Scriptures must not only themselves understand them, but must also as lovers of learning be able through the spoken and written word to help the outsiders. So my grandfather Jesus, who had devoted himself especially to the reading of the Law and the Prophets and the other books of our ancestors, and had acquired considerable proficiency in them, was himself led to write something pertaining to instruction and wisdom, so that by becoming familiar also with his book those who love learning might make even greater progress in living according to the law. (Sirach, Prologue)

This quote is from the preface to Sirach's book, written in Greek around 132 B.C. by the translator of the Hebrew original. He shows much of the same reverence vis-à-vis a unique collection of books as does Josephus, although not as explicit as he. He even indicates the three groups of books this collec-

---

uity Series 10 (Notre Dame, Ind.: University of Notre Dame Press, 1994), pp. 3-24. The primary example of a "biblical" type of book produced by the sect itself would be the *Temple Scroll*. On the question whether this book was conceived as a candidate for the canon, see J. L. Lust, "Quotation Formulae and Canon in Qumran," in *Canonization and Decanonization: Papers Presented to the International Conference of the Leiden Institute for the Study of Religions (LISOR), Held at Leiden 9-10 January 1997*, ed. A. van der Kooij and K. van der Toorn, Studies in the History of Religions 82 (Leiden: E. J. Brill, 1998), pp. 67-77; esp. pp. 72-75.

[23] For substantiation of this somewhat controversial statement, see G. W. Anderson, "Canonical and Non-Canonical," in *The Cambridge History of the Bible*, vol. 1: *From the Beginnings to Jerome*, ed. P. R. Ackroyd and C. F. Evans (Cambridge: Cambridge University Press, 1970), pp. 113-59, esp. pp. 149-55; Lawrence Schiffmann, *Reclaiming the Dead Sea Scrolls* (Philadelphia/Jerusalem: The Jewish Publication Society, 1994), pp. 161-80; and J. L. Lust's article, referred to in the preceding note (with extensive recent bibliography). These and other scholars emphasize that introductory formulas like "as it is written" or "as it is said" are used only with reference to the 22 (24) books of the later biblical canon, and to none else. This speaks for a recognition in practice that these books have unique authority also in Qumran. The same seems to be indicated directly in a passage in the so-called *Halakic Letter* (4QMMT), which speaks of "the Book of Moses and the Books of the Prophets and [the writings of] David" (cf. Lk 24:44; and comment in van der Kooij's article, pp. 26-27).

tion comprises: the Law, the Prophets and the (other) Writings.[24] These books, more than any others, should be studied. The Hebrew work of his grandfather, which he now translates into Greek, is itself not a book of the same order as the sacred books, but is a result of study of the Scriptures and aims at obedience to the Law. The book of his grandfather is thus not meant to replace or supplement the ancient Scriptures, but to encourage study of them and obedience toward them. The author obviously did not pretend to write as an inspired prophet, but as a student of the prophetic writings. Jesus, Sirach's grandson, does not say explicitly that the collection of holy books was "closed" in his time, but that seems a reasonable inference from the general tenor of what he says.

In general, the New Testament seems to confirm that by the first century A.D. the Old Testament canon was for all practical purposes an established reality. All the canonical books are quoted or alluded to as Scripture, except Esther.[25] Only one non-canonical book is verbally quoted—and once only, and not explicitly as Scripture (*1 Enoch* 1:9 in Jude 14-15).[26]

Before we return to the rabbinical debates about certain books, let us pose the question, what was the basic criterion for regarding a book as canonical? It is once more Josephus who provides us with the most direct evidence: "From Artaxerxes to our own time the complete history has been written, but has not been deemed worthy of equal credit with the earlier records, *because of the failure of the exact succession of the prophets*" (*Against Apion* 1.41, italics added).[27]

In this passage, we find a very clearly expressed idea: the idea of the "canonical epoch" or the "period of revelation." The distinctive mark of this

---

[24]A. van der Kooij, "Canonization," argues that Sirach's Prologue presupposes more or less exactly the same order of prophetical and other books as Josephus. One could add to this that the very fact that several authors seem to use "Law and Prophets" as partly equivalent to "Law, Prophets and Psalms/David's Books/Other Books," is a strong indication that the four Davidic/Solomonic Wisdom and Poetical Books were regarded as some kind of supplement to or extension of the Prophets' Books, thus forming practically one group with them. David as well as Solomon were regarded as Spirit-inspired, therefore prophetical authors.

[25]Interestingly, this corresponds to practice in Qumran. Esther was known there, but was not quoted with the quotation formulae reserved for holy books: "as it is said," "as it is written"; and is not represented among the manuscript fragments of biblical books (all the others are). See Shemaryahu Talmon, "Was the Book of Esther Known at Qumran?" *Dead Sea Discoveries* 2 (1995): 249-67.

[26]On this quotation and the canon-historical debates around it, see Richard Bauckham, *Jude and the Relatives of Jesus in the Early Church* (Edinburgh: T & T Clark, 1990), pp. 137-41.

[27]Thackeray, p. 179.

epoch was the presence of the prophetical Spirit in Israel. Before and after this period the prophetical Spirit was not present in the same way as during that epoch.[28]

This idea of a holy epoch in which revelation took place is not found only in Josephus. It is implied in several texts concerned with the question of revelation and canon and collecting the sacred books. In most cases, the period is thought to last from Moses to Ezra or from Moses to Nehemiah.[29]

The conviction that the prophetical epoch had ended seemed to be, so to speak, the other side of the consciousness that the biblical books had an authority higher than other books. They stemmed from the period of prophetic revelation: the Torah, written down by Moses; the Prophets written down by prophets and their disciples. Torah and Prophets—Mosaic content and prophetical inspiration—also provide a criterion for the remaining writings that were to end up as the Writings. Even they were believed to come from this epoch and from inspired authors (both David and Solomon were regarded as inspired, and therefore prophetical, authors), and were found to agree with and support the Torah and the Prophets: David's and others' Psalms; the three books of Solomon. The book of Job was thought to have been written by Moses; Ruth was regarded as an appendix to Judges; Lamentations as an appendix to Jeremiah; and Daniel as a prophetic book from the exile period. Ezra, Nehemiah and Chronicles formed the appropriate end of the story of the canonical period. Even Esther told a story from the canonical period. Of all these books, only three would seem to cause some problem with regard to their content: Ecclesiastes, because it seemed to teach hedonism; Song of Songs, if taken literally (God and his commandments are not mentioned); and Esther, because God is not mentioned and the book introduces a festival not prescribed in the Torah.

Let us turn back to the rabbinical debates on canon. If we observed correctly that the basic canonical criteria are origin in the canonical epoch and agreement with the Torah/Prophets, then we would expect some "fringe" books about which there could be disagreement. Did they match the canonical criteria fully? This would not be a debate on the canon as such; rather, the

---

[28]On this theme, see esp. Odil Hannes Steck, *Der Abschluss der Prophetie im Alten Testament: Ein Versuch zur Frage der Vorgeschichte des Kanons*, Biblisch-Theologische Studien 17 (Neukirchen-Vluyn: Neukirchener Verlag, 1991); and Rebecca Gray, "Josephus and the Belief That Prophecy Had Ceased," in *Prophetic Figures in Late Second Temple Jewish Palestine: The Evidence from Josephus* (New York/Oxford: Oxford University Press, 1993), pp. 7-34.
[29]See evidence for this in Sirach 49:13; 2 Maccabees 2:13-14; 4 *Ezra* 14:18-47; *TB Bava Batra* 14b-15a.

canon as such is already a reality at the time this debate about the fringe books begins.

And this is exactly what we find in the sources. The debate concerns the three problematic books of Ecclesiastes, Song of Songs and Esther. They are fringe books in the sense that they were, in the end, retained within the canon. Not a single debate, however, is on record concerning any book outside the final biblical canon. Accordingly, the recorded rabbinical debates are not debates on the closing of the Writings group, but debates on fringe books within the established canon.

The Old Testament Apocrypha

What we have seen so far leaves us with the problem of the Apocrypha within the Christian Old Testament as an unresolved question. The following remarks and observations are not an established scholarly theory. I only submit them for careful consideration.[30]

We begin with an author living considerably later than the period which concerns us in this book, but his remarks are too instructive to be bypassed. It is Augustine, who frequently discusses questions of canon in his famous work *The City of God*.

> Solomon also is found to have prophesied [about Christ] in his books, of which three are received as of canonical authority: Proverbs, Ecclesiastes, and Song of Songs. But it has been *customary* [in the church] to ascribe to Solomon two others also, of which one is called Book of Wisdom, the other Ecclesiasticus [= Sirach], on account of some resemblance of style, but *the more learned* have no doubt that they are not his; yet of old the Church, especially the Western, received them into authority. (*The City of God* 17.20, italics added)[31]

This passage is a clear indication of a fact we can observe from many other sources also: in the church there were two Old Testament canons in actual use. When the learned bishops and theologians of the church—from the second to the fourth centuries—felt a need to produce lists of the Old Testament canon, they almost invariably reproduced a list of the books in the Jewish Bible, and of these books only. We find such lists in Melito (Asia Minor, ca. A.D. 175); Origen (Alexandria, ca. A.D. 230-40); Athanasius (Alexandria, 349); and others. When criteria are mentioned, the Christian authors show that

---

[30]Cf. E. Earle Ellis, "The Old Testament Canon in the Early Church," in *Compendia* 2:1: 653-90; Martin Hengel, "Die Septuaginta als von den Christen beanspruchte Schriftensammlung bei Justin und den Vätern vor Origenes," in Dunn, *Jews and Christians*, pp. 39-84.

[31]*NPNF* 2:357, quote modified.

they think very much along the lines of Josephus (whom some of them no doubt had read): Only the books of the Hebrew Bible stem from the period in Israel's history in which the Spirit of prophecy inspired the authors; the other books (the Apocrypha) were written after that period, and therefore should not be reckoned as canonical.

But the other thing that comes through very clearly in Augustine's statement is that many Christians—the rank and file majority of "the church"— were less critical and from old days had accepted these books. This had to do with the fact that the majority of the Apocrypha claimed to be written by authors belonging to the canonical epoch. This was the case, for example, with the book called Wisdom of Solomon, which claimed to be written by Solomon. If this claim was believed at face value, the book should be considered canonical according to the Jewish and Christian canon criterion.

In another passage in *The City of God* (15.24.4) Augustine complains that there are some believers who are overly uncritical: they are willing to believe anything; they therefore also accept the alleged books of Enoch, Noah and others as genuine. But all wise men reject the alleged authorship of these books as utterly incredible; they are simply not genuine. Augustine seems all the time to imply that if they actually were written by Enoch, Noah, etc., he too would consider them canonical.

We can observe here how the Jewish and Christian canon principle— authorship in the canonical period of inspiration—would naturally lead to a discussion about which books claiming to stem from this period actually did so; in other words, a discussion about genuineness. And here it seems that the rank and file laypeople on the one hand, and the learned theologians on the other, to a certain extent parted company: "The church" accepted more books (some or all of the Apocrypha), while "the learned" stuck to the Jewish canon.

When the learned Jerome in the years around A.D. 400 was commissioned to make a complete and new Latin translation of the Bible, he only wanted to translate and include in his Bible the books of the Hebrew Bible. But pressure from less learned clergy, and even bishops, not to speak of emotional pleas from lay Bible readers who loved some of the Apocrypha, induced him to a practical compromise: He translated the Apocrypha, too, but put them apart from the canonical books proper, and explained his reason for doing so in prefaces to the apocryphal books.[32] (In this he became Luther's mentor at the

---

[32]On Jerome as a critic of canon, see John N. D. Kelly, *Jerome: His Life, Writings, and Controversies* (London: Duckworth, 1975), pp. 159-67, 263-72.

time of new Bible editions during the Reformation; Luther did exactly like Jerome and repeated his principles in his own preface to the Apocrypha.)

This, I think, goes a long way toward explaining why and how we meet two effective Old Testament canons in the early church, one "folkish" including the Apocrypha, one "learned" excluding them.

Let us finally return to the other difference between the Jewish (Talmudic) Bible and the Christian Old Testament: the order of books within the Prophets and the Writings. Simply put, the Christian order of books is much closer to the order attested by Josephus and, implicitly, by older witnesses such as Sirach's Prologue, compared with the later Talmudic order. When the whole of Scripture is shortly characterized as "The Law and The Prophets," the whole canon is understood as a prophetic collection, and it is only natural to let it conclude on a prophetical note, for example, with Nahum (the last of the twelve Minor Prophets) or Daniel. This may not be a Christian creation, but rather a takeover from ordinary Jewish practice prior to the later rabbinic rearrangement into Prophets and Writings.[33]

The New Testament as Canon

It was emphasized above that the early church from the beginning only called the Hebrew Bible *Scripture*, not the apostolic writings.[34] This does not mean, however, that the teaching of Jesus, the stories about him, and the teaching and preaching of the apostles were regarded as of less authority. On the contrary, the relative grading of authority is well expressed in Hebrews 1:1: "Long ago God spoke to our ancestors in many and in various ways by the prophets, but in these last days he has spoken to us by a Son, whom he appointed heir of all things." The two ultimate authorities are Scripture (the prophets) and the Son (speaking himself or through his apostles). Jesus himself had authorized his apostles as speaking for him: "whoever listens to you, listens to me" (Lk 10:16). This corresponds to the very structure of the New Testament: Jesus speaking in the four Gospels (and in another way in Revelation), his apostles speaking for him in Acts and the Epistles.

This new authority beside the "old" Scripture did not at once take over all

---

[33]For the whole of this treatment of the Old Testament canon, I gratefully recognize my debt to input from my colleague Terje Stordalen (Norwegian School of Theology, Oslo). See his "Law or Prophecy? On the Order of the Canonical Books" in *Tidsskrift for Teologi og Kirke* 72 (2001), pp. 131-50.

[34]See the literature listed under this heading in the Suggestions below, and also von Campenhausen, *Formation*, chaps. 4-7; McDonald, *Formation*, chaps. 6-9 (= pp. 137-249).

the roles and functions of Scripture. But very soon the Gospels took on one of Scripture's main functions: They were read during the weekly worship of the community, alongside Scripture. The earliest direct evidence of this is a famous report in Justin, ca. A.D. 150:

> On the day called Sunday, all who live in cities or in the country gather together to one place, and the memoirs of the apostles [Justin's usual name for the Gospels] or also the writings of the prophets are read, so long as time permits; then, when the reader has ceased, the president makes a speech and instructs and exhorts us to the imitation of these good things. (*First Apology* 67.3-4)[35]

Probably this reading of the Gospels ("the memoirs of the apostles") during worship—on a par with the biblical writings—was the most important reason why, after a while, the New Testament writings also were quoted as Scripture. But which writings belonged to this new part of Scripture? What was the canon criterion or criteria?

Delimiting the New Testament Canon

In order to approach this problem, we have to ask the question of who—apart from Scripture—were the absolute authorities for early believers? The entire New Testament leaves us in no doubt: the Lord and his apostles. "Whoever listens to you listens to me, whoever rejects you rejects me, and whoever rejects me rejects the one who sent me" (Lk 10:16).

In the beginning, believers had direct access to these authorities; they could literally listen to them. After Jesus' death and resurrection, his words and actions were told in an authoritative way by those whom he had chosen to this ministry: first and foremost the Twelve, but then also a wider circle around them: "those who from the beginning were eyewitnesses and servants of the word" (Lk 1:2). As long as there was abundant access to this direct oral transmission of Jesus' words and deeds, there was probably little need to fix everything in writing. But when the first generation of disciples—and especially the Twelve—grew old, and a second generation, the disciples of the disciples, were to carry the tradition on, there arose a need to put down in writing the authentic tradition from the Lord. One of these second-generation disciples, Luke, says that "many have undertaken to set down an orderly account of the events that have been fulfilled among us, just as they were handed on to us by those who from the beginning were eyewitnesses" (Lk 1:1-2).[36]

---

[35]*ANF* 1:186.
[36]On the whole of this paragraph, see Nils A. Dahl, "Anamnesis: Memory and Commemora-

As time went by, this became the simple criterion of establishing which gospel writings should be regarded authentic and therefore authoritative: those written by apostles (Matthew, John) or personal followers of apostles (Mark, Luke). Modern scholars may think that all four Gospels belong to the last category (Matthew being produced within "the school of Matthew" rather than by the apostle himself, and John coming from "the Johannine circle"), but even so, the fact remains undisputed even in the most critically-minded scholarly circles: the four Gospels in the New Testament are the only such writings produced in the first century A.D. and deriving from the first-through-second generations of disciples. When scholars nowadays try to reconstruct "the Jesus of history," the canonical Gospels are still their main and superior sources. That in itself is a tribute to the sound historical sense displayed by the early church in delimiting the New Testament canon.[37]

The fixing in writing of oral tradition did not mean that the latter immediately died out. In the first half of the second-century Bishop Papias of Hierapolis—himself an important source of information on the written Gospels of Mark and Matthew—had the following to say about how he exploited all reliable sources of information about the Lord:

> I will not hesitate also to set down for your benefit, along with the interpretations, all that ever I carefully learnt and carefully recalled from the elders, guaranteeing its truth. For I did not take delight, as most men do, in those who have much to say, but in those who teach what is true; not in those who recall foreign commandments, but in those who recall the commandments given by the Lord to faith, and reaching us from the truth itself. And if anyone chanced to come who had actually been a follower of the elders, I would enquire as to the discourses of the elders, what Andrew or what Peter said, or what Philip, or what Thomas or James, or what John or Matthew or any other of the Lord's disciples; and the things which Ariston and John the elder, disciples of the Lord say. For I supposed that things out of books did not profit me so much as the utterances of a voice which lives and abides [cf. 1 Pet 1:23]. (Eusebius, *Ecclesiastical History* 3.39.3-4)

---

tion in Early Christianity," in *Jesus in the Memory of the Early Church* (Minneapolis: Augsburg, 1976), pp. 11-29; and Birger Gerhardsson, *The Gospel Tradition*, Coniectanea biblica, New Testament Series 15 (Lund: Glerup, 1986).

[37]There are, of course, some scholars who would elevate the apocryphal *Gospel of Thomas* to a prominent place among the earliest sources, but I think they are mistaken. See especially the very careful discussion of this whole issue in John P. Meier, *A Marginal Jew: Rethinking the Historical Jesus*, vol. 1: *The Roots of the Problem and the Person*, The Anchor Bible Reference Library (New York: Doubleday, 1991), pp. 112-66.

Papias almost sounds like a second-century rabbi when he sets the value of oral transmission so high.[38] At the same time it seems evident from other glimpses of his work preserved by Eusebius that he based his expositions primarily on canonical Mark and Matthew, and added tradition from other sources mainly to substantiate his interpretations of the Lord's words. It is also evident that his concept of reliable tradition was based on a sound historical principle: there should be as direct access as possible to the first generation, as few as possible intermediaries.

The importance of having apostolic gospel tradition documented in writing no doubt increased in the second century, when the gnostics claimed to have access to alternative channels of oral tradition, and when several written documents claiming apostolic authorship emerged. With regard to the latter, the church was faced with the simple question of genuineness: Were these "gospels" in fact written by Peter or Philip or Thomas—in the first century— or were they pseudonymous fabrications of the second century? If genuine, they would have to be reckoned as authoritative.[39]

Eusebius, in the fourth century, gives us the most insight into the reasoning behind the church's stand on the issue of fake apostolic writings. He mentions the following arguments: (1) If a writing has been unknown in most of the local churches and only recently has become known in some or just a few places, it is certainly a fake. This holds true, even if the contents are quite orthodox. (2) If a writing contains teaching at variance with the teaching of the well-established, genuine apostolic writings, it is certainly a fake.[40] In addition to this, learned theologians such as Origen or Bishop Dionysius of Alexandria could argue about authorship from rather advanced studies of stylistic peculiarities: Origen concluding that Hebrews was not penned by Paul (the style too polished),[41] and Dionysius concluding that John's Gospel and Revelation could not be written by the same author (the styles too different).[42]

[38]Cf. in particular Birger Gerhardsson, *Tradition and Transmission in Early Christianity*, Coniectanea neotestamentica 20 (Lund: Gleerup, 1964).
[39]Cf. Armin Daniel Baum, "Literarische Echtheit als Kanonkriterium in der alten Kirche," *Zeitschrift für die neutestamentliche Wissenschaft* 88 (1997): 97-110.
[40]See Eusebius, *Ecclesiastical History*, 3.3.1-2 (Lawlor/Oulton, p. 65); 3.25.1-7 (Lawlor/Oulton, pp. 86-87). In his way of thinking, Eusebius is very much in line with his great model Origen, cf. his quotations from Origen in 6.25.3-14 (Lawlor/Oulton, pp. 197-99). We later see Augustine reason along the same lines, *On Christian Teaching* 2.8.12 (*NPNF* 2:538).
[41]See the quotation from Origen in Eusebius's *Ecclesiastical History* 6.25.11-12 (Lawlor/Oulton, p. 198).
[42]*Ecclesiastical History* 7.25 (Lawlor/Oulton, pp. 236-40).

It should be evident that the rather arrogant assumption prevalent in much modern scholarship—namely, that ecclesiastical authorities in the second and third centuries, when the New Testament canon was shaped, were extremely naive and credulous—is quite simply mistaken.[43] Their judgement seems to have been on the whole sound and critical, and when they were in doubt, they said so.

The main books of the New Testament canon are enumerated as such already by Irenaeus, and the discussions which continued right into the fourth century were concerned with a few fringe books—very similar to the rabbinic debates over fringe books in the Hebrew canon. The result of the formation process of the New Testament canon is that we do have in the New Testament a unique collection of first-century Christian documents (possibly one book belonging to the very early second: 2 Peter), and outside the New Testament only one or two documents of comparable age (but definitely third generation documents: *Didache* and *1 Clement*).

In conclusion, the basic principle behind the New Testament canon is as clear and self-evident as that behind the Old Testament: the normativity of the documents is defined by author and period of authorship, which makes the debate about the extent of the canon basically a debate about "genuine" or "fake" attributions. This also means that this debate is probably never closed once and for all; at different periods of later church history it may surface again, as it certainly did during the reformation period, when Luther felt free to resume the early church's argument concerning James, Hebrews and Revelation.

---

[43]It is often assumed in present scholarship that all people in antiquity were extremely naive in questions of authorship and literary forgery, and, more specifically, that our moral condemnation of pseudonymity (one author borrowing a more famous author's name for his own product) was utterly foreign to them. Nothing could be further from the truth. See the very illuminating chapter "Literary Criticism in Early Christian Times," in Robert M. Grant, *Heresy and Criticism: The Search for Authenticity in Early Christian Literature* (Louisville, Ky.: Westminster/John Knox, 1993), pp. 15-32. He documents here that philologians as well as rhetoricians were well aware of the problem of forgeries and false attributions, and that they (1) developed quite sophisticated techniques to expose false attributions (basically the same as in modern scholarship: differences of style, anachronisms, contradictions within a text), and (2) condemned forgeries severely. Tertullian has a very interesting note which proves that Christians were by no means an exception to this rule. When a presbyter in Asia Minor was exposed as the author of the *Acts of Paul and Thecla*— in itself a theologically absolutely unobjectionable piece of hagiography—he was deposed from his position as presbyter! (Tertullian, *On Baptism*, chap. 17; *ANF* 3:677).

Temple Square

Josephus and other ancient sources frequently mention a specific aspect of the canonical books: they were sacred scrolls *kept in the temple*. Many scholars now think that this idea was no fiction, but did correspond to historical fact.[44] In rabbinic Judaism after A.D. 70 and the loss of the temple (and its collection of sacred books), the rabbis were able to continue the propagation of these sacred books, and these only, as the ancient norm and authority. However, this knowledge was lost among the rank and file Gentile Christians, and there was no "central authority" within the church comparable to that of the rabbis. Learned theologians might have known which books had this authorization from the temple collection, but they were in the minority and were not heeded in the Christian communities the way the rabbis were among their own.

Suggestions for Further Reading

An extensive and helpfully annotated bibliography (through 1997), very instructive, is J. A. M. Snoek, "Canonization and Decanonization: An Annotated Bibliography," in *Canonization and Decanonization: Papers presented to the International Conference of the Leiden Institute for the Study of Religions (LISOR), Held at Leiden 9-10 January 1997*, ed. A. van der Kooij and K. van der Toorn, Studies in the History of Religions 82 (Leiden: E. J. Brill, 1998), pp. 435-506.

On the Hebrew Bible/Old Testament canon:

The most recent full-scale treatments of the pre-Christian formation of the Jewish Bible canon are Philip R. Davies, *Scribes and Schools: The Canonization of the Hebrew Scriptures*, Library of Ancient Israel (Louisville, Ky.: Westminster John Knox, 1998); Stephen B. Chapman, *The Law and the Prophets: A Study in Old Testament Canon Formation*, Forschungen zum Alten Testament 27 (Tübingen: Mohr Siebeck, 2000). Cf. also Sid Z. Leiman, *The Canonization of Hebrew Scripture: The Talmudic and Midrashic Evidence*, Transactions of the Connecticut Academy of Arts and Sciences 47 (Hamden: Archon, 1976); idem, "Inspiration and Canonicity: Reflections on the Formation of the Biblical Canon," in Sanders, *Self-Definition* 2:56-63; Odil Hannes Steck, *Der Abschluss der Prophetie im Alten Testament: Ein Versuch zur Frage der Vorgeschichte des Kanons*, Biblisch-Theologische Studien 17 (Neukirchen-Vluyn: Neukirchener Verlag, 1991).

On the Old Testament canon of the early church:

A classic study anticipating the theory of "folkish" and "learned" canon expounded in this chapter is Bruce Foss Westcott, *The Bible in the Church: A Popular Account of the Collection and Reception of the Holy Scriptures in the Christian Churches*, 3rd ed. (London/Cambridge: Macmillan, 1870).

The following two modern studies should be regarded as standard: Albert C. Sund-

---

[44]See, e.g., van der Kooij, op. cit.; Beckwith, *The Old Testament*, pp. 80-86.

berg, *The Old Testament of the Early Church,* Harvard Theological Studies 20 (Cambridge, Mass.: Harvard University Press/London: Oxford University Press, 1964); Roger Beckwith, *The Old Testament Canon of the New Testament Church and Its Background in Early Judaism* (Grand Rapids, Mich.: Eerdmans, 1985). Cf. also J.-D. Kaestli and Otto Wermelinger, eds., *Le Canon de L'Ancien Testament: Sa formation et son histoire,* Le monde de la Bible (Geneva: Labor et Fides, 1984).

On the New Testament canon:

Harry Y. Gamble, *The New Testament Canon: Its Making and Meaning,* Guides to Biblical Studies (Philadelphia: Fortress, 1985); Bruce M. Metzger, *The Canon of the New Testament: Its Origin, Development, and Significance* (Oxford: Oxford University Press, 1987 [paperback ed. 1997]); David Trobisch, *Die Endredaktion des Neuen Testaments: Eine Untersuchung zur Entstehung des christlichen Bibel,* Novum Testamentum et Orbis Antiquus 31 (Freiburg: Universitätsverlag Freiburg Schweiz/Göttingen: Vandenhoeck & Ruprecht, 1996).

Comprehensive studies of the Christian two-testament canon:

Hans Freiherr von Campenhausen, *Die Entstehung der christlichen Bibel,* Beiträge zur historischen Theologie 39 (Tübingen: J. C. B. Mohr [Paul Siebeck], 1968). English trans.: *The Formation of the Christian Bible* (Philadelphia: Fortress, 1972); Frederick Fyvie Bruce, *The Canon of Scripture* (Downers Grove, Ill.: InterVarsity Press, 1988); Lee M. McDonald, *The Formation of the Christian Biblical Canon,* 2nd expanded ed. (Peabody, Mass.: Hendrickson, 1995); John Barton, *Holy Writings, Sacred Text: The Canon in Early Christianity* (Louisville: Westminster John Knox, 1997); the same book published in London, 1997, under the title *The Spirit and the Letter: Studies in the Biblical Canon.*

15

CHRISTOLOGY IN THE MAKING (1)
THE MESSIAH

*I*n this chapter we shall try to understand how and why the confession that Jesus is Messiah was formulated by the early community, how it developed and how it was defended against different forms of objections and denials. We shall concentrate on the formulation of messianology vis-à-vis Jewish objections. There is a remarkable consistency in the Jewish objections against Jesus being the Messiah, from ancient times to ours.

Jesus: The Messiah?
As early as the 130s A.D., the Jew Trypho—according to Justin Martyr—formulated his opposition to Jesus' being the Messiah this way:

> Sir, these and suchlike passages of Scripture [Dan 7:9-28 et al.] compel us to await one who is great and glorious, and *takes over the everlasting kingdom* from the Ancient of days as Son of man. But this your so-called Messiah is without honour and glory, so that He has even fallen into the uttermost curse that is in the Law of God, for he was crucified. (*Dialogue with Trypho* 32.1, italics added)[1]

In short, Jesus is not the Messiah because he failed to bring the messianic kingdom.

---

[1]Lukyn Williams, p. 62.

A modern formulation of the same objection occurs in a book by David Berger and Michael Wyschogrod, *Jews and "Jewish Christianity."*[2] It comes in the form of a story: A rabbi once overheard a conversation between a Christian missionary and some pious but uneducated Jews. The Jews said they trusted the opinion of the old rabbinic authorities concerning the question of the Messiah; therefore they would not believe in the messiahship of Jesus.

> "In that case," asked the Christian, "how can you explain the fact that Rabbi Akiva initially thought that Bar Kokhba was the Messiah?" The Jews were taken aback and could find no answer. The rabbi, who had been listening quietly, turned to the Christian and asked, "How do you know that Bar Kokhba wasn't the Messiah?" "That's obvious," he replied; "Bar Kokhba was killed without bringing the redemption."[3]

With this story the authors want to demonstrate a simple but basic point: when it comes to Messiah-candidates other than Jesus, Christians reason along exactly the same lines as all Jews have done at all times. The basic Jewish criterion for evaluating a candidate for Messiah is this: Does he bring about the messianic age? Or, as Berger and Wyschogrod state it:

> The only way to define "the Messiah" is as the king who will rule during what we call the Messianic age. The central criterion for evaluating a Messiah must therefore be a single question: Has the Messianic age come? It is only in terms of this question that "the Messiah" means anything. What, then, does the Bible say about the Messianic age? Here is a brief description by a famous Christian scholar: "The recovery of independence and power, an era of peace and prosperity, of fidelity to God and his law, of justice and fair-dealing and brotherly love among men, and of personal rectitude and piety" (G. F. Moore, *Judaism*, II, p. 324). If we think about this sentence just for a moment in the light of the history of the last two thousand years, we will begin to see what enormous obstacles must be overcome if we are to believe in the messianic mission of Jesus. If Jesus was the Messiah, why have suffering and evil continued and even increased in the many centuries since his death?[4]

This modern Jewish objection to Jesus being the Messiah is in substance the same as the one we quoted from Trypho (ca. A.D. 130) above and could be quoted from innumerable Jewish polemicists in ancient, medieval and modern times.

---

[2]New York: Ktav, 1978.
[3]Berger and Wyschogrod, p. 20.
[4]Ibid., p. 19.

It is the contention of this chapter that early belief in Jesus as the Messiah was formulated in constant dialogue and debate with this Jewish objection—right from the beginning. It will also be argued that the common Jewish picture of early Christian messianism—that it solves the problem of the non-appearance of the messianic age by "spiritualizing" this concept[5]—is not correct during the first centuries A.D. Christians did *not* say that something was wrong when the Jews expected an outward peace, independence and justice, to be inaugurated by the Messiah's coming. On the contrary, Christians agreed that the Bible was speaking about a messianic kingdom that could be seen, felt, experienced. But in that case, how and why did they claim that Jesus actually brought the kingdom?

Very likely this question was the one that already troubled John the Baptist: If Jesus was the Messiah, how is it that the messianic kingdom seems not to have arrived?

> When John heard in prison what the Messiah was doing, he sent word by his disciples and said to him, "Are you the one who is to come, or are we to wait for another?" Jesus answered them, "Go and tell John what you hear and see: the blind receive their sight, the lame walk, the lepers are cleansed, the deaf hear, the dead are raised, and the poor have good news brought to them. And blessed is anyone who takes no offence at me. (Mt 11:2-6)

Notice that Jesus directs the attention of John's disciples to something they can see and hear, that is, something manifest and observable, not to something "spiritual" and invisible. It is, in fact, a fascinating experience to read through the Gospels from the perspective of the Jewish objection: Where are the signs of the kingdom to be seen? Such a reading seems to prove beyond doubt that the Gospel writers, as well as Jesus himself, constantly addressed an audience for whom this question was vital.

In general, the New Testament answer to this Jewish objection is surprisingly nuanced. This, no doubt, has partly to do with the fact that Jewish expectations about the Messiah were nuanced and to a certain extent divergent at the time of Jesus.

In fact, we have many indications in the extant sources that more than one

---

[5]As an example, Berger and Wyschogrod may be quoted once again: Early Christians shifted the function of the Messiah "from a visible level, where it could be tested, to an invisible one, where it could not. The Messiah's goal, at least the first time around, was not the redemption of Israel (which had clearly not taken place) but the atonement for original sin, which was seen as a sort of inner redemption. . . . At least no one could *see* that it hadn't happened" (p. 21).

"model" of the messiah was alive in Jewish expectations.[6] Different kinds of messiahs were envisaged. In Qumran, for example, they awaited a messiah of Israel and a messiah of Aaron (that is, a royal and a priestly). This corresponds roughly to the messianology of the so-called *Testaments of the Twelve Patriarchs*, in which we hear about two anointed ones, one of Judah and one of Levi. In both cases, the Old Testament offices of king and priest are clearly in the background.[7]

In the rabbinic sources we find another model of two messiahs, probably based on Genesis 49 (Blessing of Jacob) and Deuteronomy 33 (Song of Moses), in which both Judah and Joseph are called the leader of their brethren. Corresponding to the double kingdom in the time after Solomon, this recurs in the rabbinic texts as the two messiahs of David and Ephraim: the first one victorious, the other dying in battle. It is difficult to ascertain whether this concept was already well known in New Testament times or developed later—for example, during the second century A.D. as an aftermath of the Bar Kokhba incident.[8]

What about Jesus with regard to this rather complex picture? According to his descent, Jesus could only be Messiah of David, not of Ephraim and

---

[6]The most recent and quite extensive study of this theme is John J. Collins, *The Scepter and the Star: The Messiahs of the Dead Sea Scrolls and Other Ancient Literature*, The Anchor Bible Reference Library (New York: Doubleday, 1995). Cf. also Shemaryahu Talmon, "Types of Messianic Expectation at the Turn of the Era," in *King, Cult and Calendar in Ancient Israel: Collected Studies* (Jerusalem: Magnes/Leiden: E. J. Brill, 1986), pp. 202-24; idem, "The Concept of *Mashîah* and Messianism in Early Judaism," in *The Messiah: Developments in Earliest Judaism and Christianity*, ed. James H. Charlesworth (Minneapolis: Fortress, 1992); pp. 79-115; Jacob Neusner, William Scott Green and Ernest S. Frerichs, eds., *Judaisms and Their Messiahs at the Turn of the Christian Era* (Cambridge: Cambridge University Press, 1987); P. D. Hanson, "Messiahs and Messianic Figures in Proto-Apocalypticism," in Charlesworth, *The Messiah*, pp. 67-78.

[7]In addition to the studies listed in the preceding note, one may consult the shorter studies of J. Liver, "The Doctrine of the Two Messiahs in Sectarian Literature in the Time of the Second Commonwealth," *Harvard Theological Review* 52 (1959): 149-85; Louis Schiffman, "Messianic Figures and Ideas in the Qumran Scrolls," in Charlesworth, *Messiah*, pp. 116-29; Craig A. Evans, *Jesus and His Contemporaries: Comparative Studies*, Arbeiten zur Geschichte des antiken Judentums und des Urchristentums 25 (Leiden: E. J. Brill, 1995), pp. 83-154 (extensive bibliography on the two messiahs theme, pp. 84-86).

[8]On the enigmatic Messiah of Ephraim, the following studies may be called classics: Joseph Klausner, *The Messianic Idea in Israel: From Its Beginning to the Completion of the Mishnah* (London: Allen & Unwin, 1956); pp. 483-501; S. Hurwitz, *Die Gestalt des sterbenden Messias: Religionspsychologische Aspekte der jüdischen Apokalyptik*, Studien aus dem C. G. Jung-Institut 8 (Zürich/Stuttgart: Rascher Verlag 1958); J. Heinemann, "The Messiah of Ephraim and the Premature Exodus of the Tribe of Ephraim," *Harvard Theological Review* 68 (1975): 1-15. See discussion in Skarsaune, *The Proof from Prophecy*, pp. 217, 395-96.

not of Levi. (If he was to be considered a priestly messiah after all, it had to be according to the model of another non-Levitic priest: Melchizedek. Psalm 110:3 provides the biblical basis for this, and Hebrews spells it out in full.) Accordingly, should we look at the Jewish concept of a Davidic messiah in order to draw a picture of what messiah meant as applied to Jesus?

Very likely we should. But we should also keep in mind that our Jewish sources are either pre-New Testament or post-New Testament, and we should not neglect the New Testament itself as an important source on Jewish messianology. All the relevant sources taken together seem clearly to indicate that even if we limit our quest to the Messiah of David, there is still reason to speak of a great *diversity* among the pictures drawn of this figure. This will become evident when we look a little closer at the New Testament picture of Jesus as the Messiah.

The Messianic Task

In many Old Testament texts the focus is on the Messiah's *works* rather than on his person or his being. The Messiah completes his messianic task by setting the people of God free, liberating them from their enemies. The other titles of the Messiah—especially Son of God—also seem to have primary reference to his work rather than to the essence of his being. In short, they are functional rather than ontological. This remains so in some well-known New Testament texts too. And this fact raises the interesting question: According to the New Testament writers, *when* does Jesus begin his messianic work, strictly speaking?[9] Three basic answers seem to be given.

1. Jesus will begin his messianic work at his return, his second coming.

Repent therefore, and turn to God so that your sins may be wiped out, so that

---

[9]In New Testament scholarship there has been a widespread reluctance to make the Messiah a primary category for interpreting Jesus' significance. This is partly because many scholars doubt that Jesus himself understood his own task in terms of the traditional Messiah. Some are quite convinced he did not. In that case, all one can do with the messiah concept is to explain how it came to be applied to Jesus after all, so to speak in spite of everything. But this does not provide any basis for making the messiah concept central for understanding Jesus' significance. The present writer does not share this view, but this is not the place for the quite extensive argument necessary to establish an alternative point of view. For a refreshingly novel attempt to understand Jesus as placing himself squarely within contemporary concepts of the Messiah and his task, see Craig A. Evans, *Jesus and His Contemporaries: Comparative Studies,* Arbeiten zur Geschichte des antiken Judentums und des Urchristentums 25 (Leiden: E. J. Brill, 1995), pp. 83-211, 437-56.

times of refreshing may come from the presence of the Lord, and that he may send the Messiah appointed for you, that is, Jesus, who must remain in heaven until the time of universal restoration that God announced long ago through his holy prophets. (Acts 3:19-21)

In this remarkable text, Jesus is, so to speak, stored in heaven until the time of his messianic coming, the second coming. Then the prophecies will come true. Likewise, other sayings about the second coming view the return of Christ as the coming of the kingdom in fullness.

This line of thought is continued in the writings of the church fathers.[10] Justin Martyr's response to the objection of Trypho, quoted above, runs like this: It is true that Scripture proclaims a victorious Messiah who puts an end to all injustice and makes peace on earth, a Messiah coming with great power and glory—and Jesus will fulfil all this at his second coming. But it is also true that Scripture proclaims a first coming of the Messiah in which he is lowly and meek, dying for the sins of all (e.g., Is 53).[11]

Tertullian takes the idea of two messianic comings a step further: The Jews only paid attention to the second messianic advent, because it was more clearly put forward in the prophecies and was perceived as more worthy of the Messiah. They ignored the first advent proclaimed by the prophets, "because of the greater obscurity of the prophecies [concerning this advent], and because it was to be so unworthy [of the Messiah]" (*Against Marcion* 3.7.8).

Time and again the church fathers quote Zechariah 12:10 as a biblical proof text indicating *both* of the two advents: "When they look on the one whom they have pierced." He was pierced in his first, lowly coming, but at his second coming they will look at him with great astonishment.

One can summarize this line of thought by saying that in a certain sense the first coming of Jesus was not in the strict sense messianic. If the task of the Messiah is defined only from those prophecies that speak of the restoration of outward peace and justice, it is the second, not the first coming of Jesus that is messianic.

This, however, is not the only line of thought in the New Testament and

---

[10]For this and the following, see Oskar Skarsaune, "Altkirchliche Christologie—jüdisch/unjüdisch?" *Evangelische Theologie* 59 (1999): 267-85, esp. pp. 268-81.
[11]E.g., *Dialogue with Trypho* 32; 34.2; 49; 52; 110.2; etc. See the discussion of this "two comings" theme in Skarsaune, *The Proof from Prophecy*, pp. 285-87. It also occurs in the Jewish Christian source employed in the Pseudo-Clementine *Recognitions* 1.27-71, and is probably of Jewish Christian origin.

the early church. We shall look a little more closely at two others.

2. Jesus began his messianic work at his resurrection and ascension to God's right hand.

> This Jesus God raised up, and of that all of us are witnesses. Being therefore exalted at the right hand of God, and having received from the Father the promise of the Holy Spirit, he has poured out this that you both see and hear. For David did not ascend into the heavens, but himself says, "The Lord said to my Lord, 'Sit at my right hand, until I make your enemies your footstool.'" Therefore let the entire house of Israel know with certainty that God has made him both Lord and Messiah, this Jesus whom you crucified. (Acts 2:32-36)

It seems clear that in this case it is as the exalted one that Jesus may fully be called the Messiah.

The same idea (indicated with italics) is very likely contained in a formula we find in Romans 1:3-4, which is probably quoted, not created, by Paul (author's translation):

> God's Son,
> who was descended from David according to the flesh
> and was *installed as Son of God*[12] with power according to the Spirit of holiness *by the resurrection from the dead,*
> Jesus Christ our Lord.

In this text "God's Son" is not an ontological description of Jesus' status, but a functional messianic title: he entered his messianic office by being raised and exalted from the dead. According to this line of thought, Jesus executes his messianic task as enthroned at God's right hand through and after his resurrection. Jesus is Messiah as the risen and exalted one.[13]

---

[12]Most Bible translations, beginning from the King James Version, feel embarrassed by the Greek text at this point, because it seems to speak of Jesus being somehow *made* God's Son by the resurrection. They therefore water this down: KJV: "declared to be the Son of God with power"; NEB: "declared Son of God by a mighty act"; RSV: "designated Son of God in power"; NRSV: "declared to be Son of God with power"; TEV: "he was shown with great power to be the Son of God"; NIV: "declared with power to be the Son of God," alternative in footnote: "was appointed to be the Son of God with power." The only translation I have come across that renders the Greek text in a straightforward way is the Catholic NAB: "was made Son of God in power." The word *made* here (Greek, *horizein*) has the same meaning as in "he was made bishop": appointed and installed in office.

[13]There is extensive literature on this theme. See e.g., Jean Daniélou, "La session à la droite du Père," in *Études d'exégèse judéo-chrétienne (Les Testimonia)*, Théologie historique 5 (Paris: Beauchesne, 1966), pp. 42-49; David M. Hay, *Glory at the Right Hand: Psalm 110 in Early*

This line of thought is also continued in the church fathers. The signs of the messianic age are really present here and now, according to Justin, because the Messiah Jesus is now reigning. Having quoted the classic biblical prophecy of the messianic age, Isaiah 2:1-5 (= Micah 4:1-4), Justin continues:

> Gentlemen, I am aware that your teachers admit that this whole passage refers to the Messiah; I also know that they affirm that the Messiah has not yet come, *. . . as if not a word of the prophecy had yet been fulfilled.* What brainless beings! For they have missed the point of all the cited passages, namely, that two advents of Christ have been proclaimed: the first, in which He is shown to be subject of suffering and the crucifixion, without glory or honor; and the second, in which He will come from the heavens in glory. . . . For we Christians who have gained a knowledge of the true worship of God from the Law and from the word which went forth from Jerusalem by way of the Apostles of Jesus, have run for protection to the God of Jacob and the God of Israel. *And we who delighted in war, in the slaughter of one another, and in every other kind of iniquity have in every part of the world converted our weapons of war into implements of peace—our swords into ploughshares, our spears into farmer's tools.* (Dialogue with Trypho 110.1-3)[14]

If Justin were asked to pinpoint the most manifest sign of the present reign and power of the Messiah, he would no doubt point to the defeat of demons, a spectacular phenomenon made manifest in exorcisms through Jesus' name. In the *Dialogue*, chapter 83, he discusses the interpretation of Psalm 110, which he says the Jewish teachers referred to Hezekiah.

> "He shall send forth the sceptre of power upon Jerusalem, and He shall rule in the midst of Thy enemies . . ." [Ps 110:2]. Now, who will not concede that Hezekiah was not a priest forever according to the order of Melchisedek? And who is not aware that he was not the redeemer of Jerusalem? And who does not know that he did not send the sceptre of power upon Jerusalem, and did not rule in the midst of his enemies? . . . But, although our Jesus has not yet returned in glory, He has sent forth into Jerusalem the sceptre of power, namely, the call to repentance to all the nations over which the demons used to rule, as David testifies: "The gods of the Gentiles are demons" [Ps 96:5 LXX]. And the power of

Christianity, SBL Monographs Series 18 (Nashville/New York: Abingdon, 1973); W. R. G. Loader, "Christ at the Right Hand—Ps. CX in the New Testament," *New Testament Studies* 24 (1978): 199-217; M. Gourgues, *A la droite de Dieu: Resurrection de Jesus et actualisation du Psaume 110:1 dans le Nouveaux Testament,* Études Bibliques (Paris: J. Gabalda, 1978); Martin Hengel, "'Sit at My Right Hand!'" in *Studies in Early Christology* (Edinburgh: T & T Clark, 1995), pp. 119-225.
[14]Falls, pp. 317-18, italics added.

His word compelled many to abandon the demons whom they used to obey, and through Him to believe in Almighty God, because the gods of the Gentiles are demons. (*Dialogue with Trypho* 83.2-5)[15]

Justin returns to this theme again and again:

> Some of you dare to explain the following words, "Lift up your gates, O ye princes, and be ye lifted up, O eternal gates, that the King of Glory may enter," [Ps 24:7] as if they referred to Hezekiah, while others of you apply them to Solomon. On the contrary, we can prove that they were spoken neither of the one nor of the other, nor of any of your kings, but only of our Messiah, who appeared (first) without beauty or honor—as Isaias, David, and all the Scriptures testify—who is lord of hosts by the will of the Father who bestowed that honor upon him; who arose again from the dead and ascended into Heaven—as is stated in the Psalm and other Scriptural passages which also declared Him to be Lord of hosts. *You can easily see the truth of this, if you will but open your eyes and look at the things that are happening around you:* Every demon is vanquished and subdued when exorcised in the name of this true Son of God. (*Dialogue with Trypho* 85.1-2)[16]

According to this line of thought, Jesus executes his messianic task, "making his enemies his footstool," during his reign at God's right hand from his first to his second coming, as the risen, exalted and enthroned one. But there is also a third line of thought.

3. Jesus began his messianic work when he was baptized by John.
In his *Dialogue*, Justin attributes to Trypho the conviction—allegedly shared by all Jews—that the Messiah is to be anointed by Elijah (*Dialogue with Trypho* 49.1). Justin himself held the opinion that this actually happened at the baptism of Jesus by John: John acted in the role of Elijah, endowed with the spirit of Elijah; Jesus was anointed by the Spirit (*Dialogue with Trypho* 87—88).[17] But Justin is more than a little reticent in developing this idea, because he fears a possible implication: that Jesus was *made* Son of God by the proclamation of

---

[15]Falls, pp. 280-81.
[16]Ibid., pp. 282-83, italics added.
[17]On this, see Daniel Alain Bertrand, *Le baptême de Jesus: Histoire de l'exégèse aux deux premiers siècles,* Beiträge zur Geschichte der biblischen Exegese 14 (Tübingen: J. C. B. Mohr [Paul Siebeck], 1973); Skarsaune, *Proof from Prophecy,* pp. 196-99, 391-93; Peter Pilhofer, "Wer salbt den Messias? Zum Streit um die Christologie im ersten Jahrhundert des jüdisch-christlichen Dialogs," in *Begegnungen zwischen Christentum und Judentum in Antike und Mittelalter: Festschrift für Heinz Schreckenberg,* ed. Dietrich-Alex Koch and Hermann Lichtenberger, Schriften des Institutum Judaicum Delitzschianum 1 (Göttingen: Vandenhoeck & Ruprecht, 1993), pp. 335-45.

the heavenly voice and the anointing descent of the Spirit. The same reticence is beginning to show forth already in the Gospel narratives about Jesus being baptized by John. If you understand "Son of God" more in an ontological sense (as Justin does, for example), Jesus cannot be made or appointed something he is already, and indeed has been from eternity. If, however, you understand "Son of God" in a more functional, messianic sense, there is no great problem in saying that Jesus was anointed—that is, designated, consecrated—for his messianic task when he was baptized by John. And that probably is the meaning of the story in its oldest versions.[18]

When the baptism of Jesus by John is understood as the inauguration of the messianic task of Jesus, the task of the Messiah includes his suffering and death. Indeed, one may even say that in more than one text it is precisely the suffering messiah that is the main focus within this line of thought.

It is extremely difficult to ascertain whether—and if so, to what extent and in which circles—the idea of suffering messiah was known in Judaism at the time of Jesus. As is well known, standard Jewish exegesis of Isaiah 53 applied—or came to apply—this text to the people of Israel collectively, not to the Messiah. On the other hand the Targums apply the passage to the Messiah, although at the same time removing the suffering from him. Some medieval and even modern Jewish interpretations read Isaiah 53 as a prophecy of a messiah suffering vicariously for his people. Is this a recalling of a very ancient reading, which was suppressed in Judaism after the text was applied to Jesus?[19]

In any case, what seems clear beyond doubt from the Gospels is that those closest to Jesus, his own disciples, were *not* familiar with the sufferings of the Messiah. When Jesus warned them that he had to suffer and die,

---

[18]I find my compatriot Ragnar Leivestad's interpretation of Jesus' baptism very fascinating. Leivestad thinks that Jesus understood himself to be designated as the Messiah at his baptism, and therefore that he understood his own actions and preaching afterwards as those of the designated but not yet reigning Messiah. See Leivestad, *Jesus in His Own Perspective: An Examination of His Sayings, Actions, and Eschatological Titles* (Minneapolis: Augsburg, 1987).

[19]This has been claimed by Joachim Jeremias in Walter Zimmerli and Joachim Jeremias, *The Servant of God,* Studies in Biblical Theology 20 (London: SCM Press, 1957). Cf. the criticism of this thesis in Oscar Cullmann, *The Christology of the New Testament* (London: SCM Press, 1963); pp. 52-60. Cf. now the extensive and careful reevaluation of the material in Martin Hengel, "Zur Wirkungsgeschichte von Jes 53 in vorchristlicher Zeit," in Hengel, *Kleine Schriften* 2:72-114. The whole volume in which this article was first published, is relevant to our theme: Bernd Janowski and Peter Stuhlmacher, eds., *Der leidende Gottesknecht: Jesaja 53 und seine Wirkungsgeschichte,* Forschungen zum Alten Testament 14 (Tübingen: J. C. B. Mohr [Paul Siebeck], 1996).

they protested or did not understand.

It is also clear beyond reasonable doubt that early Christian interpretation of Scripture—in which hints at the suffering and death of the Messiah was found in many more texts than Isaiah 53—was the most original and innovative contribution of the early community in the field of exegesis.[20] According to Luke, it was Jesus himself, after his resurrection, who taught his disciples this new approach to the biblical testimony of the Messiah:

> "Oh, how foolish you are, and how slow of heart to believe all that the prophets have declared! Was it not necessary that the Messiah should suffer these things and then enter into his glory?" Then beginning with Moses and all the prophets, he interpreted to them the things about himself in all the scriptures.

> Then he opened their minds to understand the scriptures, and he said to them, "Thus it is written that the Messiah is to suffer and to rise from the dead on the third day, and that repentance and forgiveness of sins is to be proclaimed in his name to all nations, beginning from Jerusalem." (Lk 24:25-27, 45-48)

In this teaching of Jesus after his resurrection, when he "opened the scriptures" (Lk 24:32) and expounded the biblical message about the Messiah, the question of the messianic kingdom or the messianic age was certainly not forgotten. Luke makes that plain when he repeats his report on Jesus' teaching in Acts: "Appearing to them over the course of forty days and speaking about the kingdom of God" (Acts 1:3). "When they had come together, they asked him, 'Lord, is this the time when you will restore the kingdom to Israel?'" (Acts 1:6).

It is plain from this, however, that the kingdom is envisaged as still future and that the Messiah's passage through suffering and death is regarded as in some way a necessary preparation for the establishment of the kingdom. And it is probably along these lines that the Gospel authors want us to conceive of Jesus' work prior to his suffering also: He is announcing and preparing the kingdom, bringing it near in signs, healings and effective preaching. But this is only the first stage of a total messianic task that comprises several stages.

To this total task Jesus was baptized by John, and there is no doubt that Jesus' baptism was understood, at the earliest stage, as a messianic *anointing*. In Scripture, anointing and the Spirit of God are closely related concepts, as in Isaiah 61:1: "The Spirit of the Lord GOD is upon me, because the

---

[20]The splendid little study of Charles Harold Dodd is still to be recommended as the classic on this theme: *According to the Scriptures: The Sub-Structure of New Testament Theology* (London: James Nisbet & Co., 1952; reissued as Fontana Paperback 1965).

LORD has anointed me; he has sent me to bring good news to the oppressed."

The baptism conferred by John therefore provides the answer to the question: If Jesus was the anointed one, the Messiah, when and how was he anointed? It also follows biblical precedents that the king is anointed by a prophet: Samuel anointed Saul (1 Sam 10:1); Samuel anointed David (1 Sam 16:13); a prophet anointed Jehu (2 Kings 9:1-13); and so on.[21]

If, in conclusion, we apply these three answers to the question, *when* did Jesus begin his function as the Messiah? we can observe that they are not mutually exclusive or contradictory. Taken together, they say something like this: There is no simple answer to the question of when Jesus established the messianic kingdom simply because the establishment of the kingdom is not something that happens in an instant, but is a drama with several acts. Jesus could even compare it to a slow, almost hidden process, like leaven doing its work in a lump of dough (Mt 13:33). He could also point out that everything big—as the kingdom was surely expected to be—must begin as something very small, like a mustard seed (Mt 13:31-32). But neither Jesus nor his early followers thought that his kingdom was without any visible manifestation, or that nothing had happened and nothing changed in the world as a consequence of Jesus' being anointed as Messiah and beginning his messianic task through its different stages. "Go and tell John what you hear and see" (Mt 11:4). "You can easily see the truth of this, if you will but open your eyes and look at the things that are happening around you" (Justin, *Dialogue with Trypho* 85.1).

Confessing Belief in the Messiah: The Apostolic Creed

Belief and confession are two words that belong intimately together in the New Testament. In your heart you believe; with your mouth you confess what you believe. Paul makes the classic statement in Romans 10:9-11:

> If you confess with your mouth, "Jesus is Lord,"
> and believe in your heart that God raised him from the dead,
> you will be saved.
> For it is with your heart that you believe and are justified,
> and it is with your mouth that you confess and are saved. (NIV)

The gospel message about Jesus the Messiah asks for the assent of the per-

---

[21]On this theme, see now Craig A. Evans, "From Anointed Prophet to Anointed King: Probing Aspects of Jesus' Self-Understanding," in Evans, *Jesus and His Contemporaries*, pp. 437-56.

son addressed; this assent is made verbal in confessing with one's mouth the belief of one's heart. This may sound very "theological," but it all becomes very concrete when a person asks for admission to the people of the Messiah through baptism. Then it is necessary to ask the candidate the question, do you (really) believe . . . ? And the candidate has to affirm that belief.

Believe exactly *what?* At the moment of baptism, it is necessary to know exactly *how* the question of faith should be formulated: What should be included as the absolutely necessary summary of faith, and what can be left out?

Very early, it seems, the so-called baptismal questions acquired a more or less fixed format.[22] In the beginning we find it may be one single question, as we can reconstruct from Acts 8:37 (according to some manuscripts, but not the earliest):

Ethiopian eunuch: "May I be baptized?"
Philip: "Do you believe with all your heart in Jesus?"
Eunuch: "I believe that Jesus the Messiah is the Son of God."

Very soon, however, Matthew 28:19 was understood as an instruction by Jesus of how to formulate the baptismal questions. Accordingly, the questions and answers ran like this:

Q. Do you believe in God the Father?
A. I do.
Q. Do you believe in Jesus the Messiah, his Son?
A. I do.
Q. Do you believe in the Holy Spirit?
A. I do.

We find traces of these baptismal questions in Justin and Irenaeus, but also indications that the first and especially the second question were expanded a little. That was probably done to make sure that the candidate had a sound faith and was not, for example, a gnostic or a Marcionite in disguise. In the second question, it was relevant to add something that ensured that the baptismal candidate genuinely believed in the reality of Jesus' suffering and death on the cross. From Justin we may reconstruct the following second question: "Do you believe in Jesus the Messiah, God's Son, *who was crucified*

---

[22]For this and the following, cf. J. N. D. Kelly, *Early Christian Creeds*, 3rd ed. (London: Longman, 1972), pp. 40-49; and, more recently and in greatest detail, Wolfram Kinzig; Christoph Markschies and Markus Vinzent, *Tauffragen und Bekenntnis*, Arbeiten zur Kirchengeschichte 74 (Berlin/New York: Walter de Gruyter, 1999).

under Pontius Pilate?" (*First Apology* 61.13).

In Tertullian, this connection between Matthew 28:19 and the baptismal questions of faith is made explicit, as also the continued expansion of the questions:

> When we are going to enter the water [of baptism]—but also a little before, in the presence of the congregation, and under the hand of the president—we solemnly confess that we renounce the devil, and his pomp, and his angels. Hereupon we are thrice immersed, *making a somewhat fuller pledge than the Lord has appointed in the Gospel* [= Mt 28:19]. (*The Crown* 3)[23]

The "somewhat fuller pledge" no doubt refers to more extensive questions than the simple ones deducible from Matthew 28:19. Tertullian's text is also interesting in showing us exactly *how* baptism was conferred in his day (the 190s A.D.): On answering "yes, I believe" to each of the baptismal questions, the candidate was immediately immersed into the baptismal basin (or into a river), altogether immersed three times.

The development we have traced thus far reached its climax in the prescriptions for baptism by the Roman presbyter Hippolytus,[24] ca. A.D. 220:

> When the presbyter takes hold of each one of those who are to be baptised, let him bid him renounce, saying:
>
> *I renounce you, Satan, and all your service and all your works.*
>
> And when he has said this let him anoint him with the oil of exorcism saying:
>
> *Let all evil spirits depart far from you.*
>
> Then after these things let him give him over to the presbyter who stands at the water [to baptise]; and let them stand naked in the water. And let a deacon likewise go down into the water. And when he [who is to be baptised] goes down to the water, let him who baptises lay his hand on him saying thus:
>
> *Do you believe in God the Father Almighty?*
>
> And he who is being baptised shall say:
>
> *I believe.*
>
> Let him immediately baptise him once, having his hand laid upon his head. And after this let him say:
>
> *Do you believe in the Messiah Jesus, the Son of God,*

---

[23]*ANF* 3:94, quote modified.

[24]Almost everything about *The Apostolic Tradition* and its attribution is being discussed in present scholarship. The document has not been preserved as such, but is a modern reconstruction based on several later Church Orders. The attribution of the reconstructed document to Hippolytus is also contested, as well as the authenticity of the baptismal questions in the original document. I am not in a position to form any independent opinion on these questions, and have chosen to follow conventional wisdom, as found in Kelly's book (see note 22). In the study of Kinzig et al., all the new questions are raised and fully discussed.

Who was born of the Holy Spirit and the Virgin Mary,
Who was crucified in the days of Pontius Pilate,
and died,
and rose the third day living from the dead
and ascended into the heavens
and sat down at the right hand of the Father,
and will come to judge the living and the dead?

And when he says: *I believe,* let him baptise him the second time. And again let him say:

Do you believe in the Holy Spirit in the Holy Church,
and the resurrection of the flesh?

And he who is being baptised shall say: *I believe.* And so let him baptise him the third time. (Hippolytus, *The Apostolic Tradition* 21.9-18)[25]

It is clear that if we took these three questions and turned them into positive statements beginning with "I believe," we would have a text very similar to the well-known Apostle's Creed. In fact, it seems that in the community of Rome during the third century this change actually took place, and that a declaratory creed of this type was recited by the baptism candidates prior to their baptism. This creed is therefore called "The Old Roman Creed," and it is the mother of all later creeds in Latin, among them the so-called "Apostolic," which got its present form sometime during the fifth century and replaced other local versions in the West during the reign of Charlemagne (eighth-ninth centuries).[26]

There is a loose end, however, in this story about how the creed developed, and it is time to tie it up. We have repeatedly translated the Greek *(ho) Christos* and Latin *Christus* as "the Messiah," and one may ask if that is justified. To many Greek-speaking Christians the title "anointed" (Greek *Christos*) soon lost its meaning as a title and became only a second name of Jesus, so that "Jesus Christ" was only a double name, and the meaning "the anointed one," or "Messiah," was lost.

There is, however, undeniable evidence that Christians who were themselves Jews or retained contact with Jews were always aware of the meaning, semantically as well as ideologically, of the title *Christos*. In Justin's *Dialogue with Trypho* it is not only Trypho who uses *Christos*—often with the definite article—in the sense of "the Messiah," but also Justin himself. Two characteristics of the use of *Christos* always indicate that the word may still be used as a title:

---

[25]Gregory Dix, *The Treatise on the Apostolic Tradition of St. Hippolytus of Rome,* 2nd ed. by Henry Chadwick (London: SPCK, 1968), pp. 34-37, quote modified.
[26]The standard monograph on the origin and history of the Old Roman and Apostolic Creed is Kelly's book, chapters 1-5 and 12-13.

(1) If it is prefixed, that is, comes before the name Jesus (and especially if it has the article), the chances are good that *Christos* is a title. In Hippolytus's second question and in the Old Roman Creed *Christos* is prefixed to the name Jesus, whereas in almost all later versions of the creed it comes after the name Jesus. (2) More importantly, the summary of the career of Jesus contained in the second article of this creed is of a peculiar type. We can easily observe the same type in similar summaries from the first and second centuries:

> What I received I passed on to you at the first: that
> Christ died for our sins
> > *according to the Scriptures,*
> that he was buried,
> that he was raised on the third day
> > *according to the Scriptures,*
> and that he appeared. (1 Cor 15:3-5)[27]

> We, *unrolling the books of the prophets* which we possess, who name Jesus Christ, partly in parables, partly in enigmas, partly expressly and in so many words, find [predicted in them]
> > *His coming*
> > *and death,*
> > *and cross,*
> > *and all the rest . . .*
> > *and his resurrection*
> > *and assumption to heaven. . . .*
> We have believed in God in consequence of *what is written* [in the Scriptures] respecting Him [Jesus the Messiah]. . . . For we know that God enjoined these things, *and we say nothing apart from the Scriptures.* (*Preaching of Peter,* ca. A.D. 125)[28]

> *In the books of the prophets* we found Jesus our Messiah foretold as
> > *coming,*
> > *born of a virgin,*
> > *reaching manhood, and healing every disease . . .*
> > *and being hated, and unrecognized, and crucified,*
> > *and dying,*
> > *and rising again, and ascending into heaven, being called and [really] being the*

---

[27]NIV with alternative footnote reading in v. 3.
[28]This writing was apparently an early second-century imitation of the canonical book of Acts, probably focusing more on missionary speeches by Peter. It has not been preserved in its entirety, but some fragments, among them the one given here, are contained in quotations from the book in Clement of Alexandria. Translation, *ANF* 2:510, italic added.

Son of God. . . .
All this was prophesied before he appeared. (Justin, *First Apology* 31.7-8; ca. A.D. 150)[29]

The Church . . . has received from the apostles and their disciples this faith:
(1) [She believes] in one God, the Father Almighty, Maker of heaven and earth and the sea and all things that are in them;
2) and in one Christ Jesus, the Son of God, who became incarnate for our salvation;
(3) and in the Holy Spirit,
who proclaimed through the prophets the dispensations [of God] and the [two] comings [of the Messiah]:
the birth from a virgin,
the passion,
and the resurrection from the dead,
and the ascension into heaven . . .
and his future coming from heaven in the glory of the Father . . .
to raise up anew all flesh . . .
and execute just judgement. (Irenaeus, *Against Heresies* 1.10.1; ca. A.D. 190)[30]

The common feature of these summaries leaps to the eye: In his historical career, *Jesus fulfilled the messianic prophecies.* He *began* to fulfill them—if such an expression is allowed—at the point when he entered history and was born of Mary. Therefore the virgin birth from Mary is always the starting point in summaries like this. There is no mention of the Son of God existing with God before he became human, or even being with God before the creation of the world and from eternity. In this type of summary the focus is not on the nature, the essence of the Messiah's person, but on the messianic *task*, which was predicted in the prophets and fulfilled by Jesus from the moment he entered history. In other words, to link back to the beginning of this chapter, the emphasis in this type of summary—and therefore in the Old Roman Creed, second article—is on the Messiah's work, his function, rather than on the nature of his person as such. The second article of the baptismal confession of the Western (Latin) church is thus a strikingly "Jewish" confession of a Messiah with markedly "Jewish" characteristics.[31]

---

[29]*ANF* 1:173.
[30]*ANF* 1:330.
[31]This is not to say that the Roman community, or Roman theologians, in the middle of the hird century were unfamiliar, with the "high" Christology of a divine and preexistent Son of God. This high Christology is easily documented in Roman authors right from the beginning of the second century. It is all the more striking that the Roman community should choose to stick to this "Jewish" or "low" Christology in its baptismal confession.

Suggestions for Further Reading

On Jewish messianism:

Joseph Klausner, *The Messianic Idea in Israel: From Its Beginning to the Completion of the Mishnah* (London: Allen & Unwin, 1956).

Jacob Neusner, *Messiah in Context: Israel's History and Destiny in Formative Judaism* (Philadelphia: Fortress, 1984).

Jacob Neusner; William Scott Green and Ernest S. Frerichs, eds., *Judaisms and Their Messiahs at the Turn of the Christian Era* (Cambridge: Cambridge University Press, 1987).

John J. Collins, *The Scepter and the Star: The Messiahs of the Dead Sea Scrolls and Other Ancient Literature,* The Anchor Bible Reference Library (New York: Doubleday, 1995).

Jewish and Christian messianism:

James H. Charlesworth, ed., *The Messiah: Developments in Earliest Judaism and Christianity* (Minneapolis: Fortress, 1992).

Ithamar Gruenwald et al., eds., *Messiah and Christos: Studies in the Jewish Origins of Christianity Presented to David Flusser on the Occasion of His Seventy-Fifth Birthday,* Texte und Studien zum antiken Judentum 32 (Tübingen: J. C. B. Mohr [Paul Siebeck], 1992).

William Horbury, *Jewish Messianism and the Cult of Christ* (London: SCM Press, 1998).

On New Testament Christology:

There is a wealth of studies. The following should be regarded as central:

Oscar Cullmann, *The Christology of the New Testament* (London: SCM Press, 1963).

Nils Alstrup Dahl, *Jesus the Christ: The Historical Origins of Christological Doctrine* (Minneapolis: Fortress, 1991).

Martin Hengel, *Studies in Early Christology* (Edinburgh: T & T Clark, 1995); see esp. the essay "Jesus, the Messiah of Israel," pp. 1-72.

On the formation of Christology as messianology in the early church:

Surprisingly little has been written on this topic. See the following:

Aloys Grillmeyer, *Christ in Christian Tradition,* vol. 1: *From the Apostolic Age to Chalcedon (AD 451),* 2nd ed. (London and Oxford: Mowbrays, 1975), pp. 3-76.

Oskar Skarsaune, *Incarnation: Myth or Fact?* Concordia Scholarship Today (St. Louis: Concordia, 1991).

On the formation of the Apostolic Creed:

John Norman Davidson Kelly, *Early Christian Creeds,* 3rd ed. (London: Longman, 1972 [or later eds.]); chapters 1-5 and 12-13.

Cf. also the shorter, more popular account contained in Frances M. Young, *The Making of the Creeds* (London: SCM Press, 1991).

16

CHRISTOLOGY IN THE MAKING (II)
THE INCARNATE WORD

*A*round the middle of the third century, the Roman community fixed the word-ing of their creed, in which they confessed their belief in a remarkably "Jewish" Mes-siah Jesus. Some 70-80 years later, in Nicaea A.D. 325, the Eastern church also agreed on a common formula of faith, later to be revised and somewhat expanded at Constan-tinople A.D. 381. It is commonly known as The Nicene Creed (for full text see p. 336). During the fourth and the following centuries this creed became the universal creed of Christendom. One could say that this creed, more than anything else, defines Christian belief. If it is true that this creed severed Christianity from the very roots of Jewish monotheism, it becomes more significant in our history than perhaps anything else.

Eastern and Western Christology

Many scholars may agree that the messianology we surveyed in chapter fif-teen has a basically Jewish character. But can we claim the same for the Christology of the most famous of the creeds from the early church: the Nicene?

The creed now recited in churches all around the world as the Nicene Creed is really a later modification of the original creed of the council of

Nicaea (A.D. 325). The original runs like this:

We believe in one God, the Father Almighty,
Maker of things visible and invisible.
And in one Lord Jesus Christ, the Son of God,
begotten from the Father, onlybegotten,
  that is, from the substance of the Father,
God from God,
light from light,
    true God from true God,
    begotten, not made,
    of one substance with the Father,
through whom [the Son] all things came into being,
things in heaven and things on earth,
Who—because of us men and because of our salvation—
came down and became incarnate,
becoming man,
suffered,
and rose again on the third day,
ascended to the heavens,
will come to judge the living and the dead.
And in the Holy Spirit.[1]

Before we comment further on this creed, it may briefly be pointed out that there is good evidence[2] for the view that the creed was made in the following way: The "drafting committee" took as textual basis a typical *eastern* baptismal creed—possibly the one of Jerusalem—and inserted into it only the four lines that are italicized in the quotation above. These lines are the only controversial statements in the creed; apart from them there is nothing special about it. But even without these lines, we easily observe that this creed is very different indeed from the Old Roman we studied in the previ-

---

[1] J. N. D. Kelly, *Early Christian Creeds*, pp. 215-16, italics added. In the creed as formulated at Nicaea, there was also appended the following clause (cf. Gal 1:8-9): "But as for those who say, There was when He was not, and before being born He was not, and that He came into existence out of nothing, or who assert that the Son of God is of a different being or substance, or is subject to alteration and change—these the Catholic and Apostolic Church condemns" (Kelly, p. 216).

[2] The two main sources for the creed-making of the 250 bishops gathered at Nicaea are both eyewitness reports: Eusebius of Caesarea (the author of the famous *Ecclesiastical History*), writing home to his congregation immediately upon conclusion of the council; and Athanasius, writing a book *On the Decrees of the Nicene Council* some 25 years afterward. Both are to be found in English translations in *NPNF* 2nd Ser. 4:74-76 and 150-72.

ous chapter.[3] We can display the differences in a synopsis:

Second Article, Nicaea	Second Article, Old Roman
And in one Lord Jesus Christ,	And in Messiah Jesus,
the Son of God,	God's only Son,
begotten from the Father,	our Lord
onlybegotten,	
God from God,	
light from light,	
through whom [the Son]	
all things came into being, things	
in heaven and things on earth,	
Who—because of us men and	Who was born of the
because of our salvation—	Holy Spirit
came down and became incarnate,	and the Virgin Mary,
becoming man,	
suffered,	was crucified under
	Pontius Pilate,
	was buried
and rose again	arose from the dead
on the third day,	on the third day
ascended to the heavens,	ascended into heaven
	and sits at the
	Father's right hand
	from whence
will come to judge	He will come to judge
the living and the dead.	the living and the dead.

Some differences in format and style leap to the eye: The longest passage in the eastern creed concerns the being of the Son with God before the world was created; then there is a weighty statement that he *participated in creating the world.* The Old Roman creed includes nothing that corresponds to this. The statements about the Son's human birth are also different: the Old Roman states, in a simple, narrative fashion, that he was born of the Holy Spirit and Mary—basically the same way of telling the story as we have in Matthew and Luke. The eastern creed expresses the same fact much more "theologically," roughly the same way as in John: the Son became flesh, was

---

[3]For analyses of the origin and meaning of the creed from Nicaea, cf. Kelly, *Early Christian Creeds,* chaps. 7 and 8; Oskar Skarsaune, "A Neglected Detail in the Creed of Nicaea (325)," *Vigiliae Christianae* 41 (1987): 34-54; Richard P. C. Hanson, *The Search for the Christian Doctrine of God: The Arian Controversy 318-381* (Edinburgh: T&T Clark, 1988), chap. 6 (= pp. 152-78).

incarnate,[4] became man. Up to this point, the eastern creed has been much more extensive than the western (Roman), but now the picture changes. In the eastern creed the entire life story of Jesus, including his suffering, crucifixion, death and burial, is condensed into the one word "suffered." Notice also that in the eastern creed the session at God's right hand—which we interpreted as the statement about the exalted Jesus' *messianic reign*—is left out.

To conclude, while the Old Roman creed portrays Jesus as the Messiah doing the task predicted by the prophets; the eastern creed portrays him as a divine being becoming incarnate, as the mediator of creation who himself became man, suffered for his own creatures, and was then exalted. While the Roman creed is oriented "horizontally" along the time axis—prophetic promises, fulfillment—the eastern creed is oriented "vertically": the one who was with God and created the world with him "came down," suffered, rose again, shall finally descend once more as the final judge. The "movement" in this creed is "vertical" the whole time.

Eastern Christology: Hellenistic?

Jewish scholars in antiquity, the Middle Ages and modern times have almost unanimously claimed that the idea that Jesus is the incarnate Word of God is un-Jewish, a product of Christianity's transplantation from a Jewish milieu to a Gentile-Hellenistic milieu.[5] Liberal Christian scholars in modern times have said much the same thing, as for example, the great historian of dogma, Adolf von Harnack. His saying has become famous: "The Christological dogma . . . is a product of the spirit of Hellenism on the soil of the Gospel."[6]

Now, as Harnack was well aware, there is no way of holding the eastern creed to be basically Greek and un-Jewish, while at the same time holding John the Evangelist, or for that matter Paul, to be un-Greek and Jewish in their Christology. Therefore, according to many critical scholars, the process of "Hellenizing" Christianity must have begun very early, underway already in Paul, and seems to have reached a first climax in John 1:1-18 (the so-called Johannine Prologue).

In our time, the Jewish writer Pinchas Lapide has tried to understand this

---

[4]In Latin, the Son's coming "in the flesh" is *in carne,* from which derives *incarnatus* and, in English, "incarnation."
[5]A brief review of some selected examples is in Skarsaune, *Incarnation,* pp. 13-15.
[6]Adolf von Harnack, *Lehrbuch der Dogmengeschichte,* vol. 1, 5th ed. (Tübingen: J. C. B. Mohr, 1931), p. 20: "Das Dogma ist in seiner Conception und in seiner Ausbau ein Werk des griechischen Geistes auf dem Boden des Evangeliums." After Harnack, almost every scholar writing on the subject of early church dogma in general, and Christology in particular, has had to take issue with this thesis.

"Hellenization" in Christology as a conscious cultural adaptation. He says about Paul:

> He brought the message of the Jewish Messiah to the pagan world with a commitment of complete faith. . . . He was successful in being a Greek for the Greeks and a Jew for the Jews. He possessed courage to display religious imagination. He knew that he would be rejected if he came either to Corinth or Rome and preached about an anointed Jewish Messiah who was David's son. They would not understand what he was talking about. But for Greek and Roman ears, he would fare extremely well talking about an incarnate Son of God and a Logos, a divine Word who had descended in order to redeem the world. On the other hand, this made no sense to Galilean fishermen and shepherds. That was why Paul appeared in Jerusalem as a devout, faithful Jew proclaiming a Jewish Messiah, while for Greeks he spoke of a Saviour who was the Son of God.[7]

So this is the challenge we face in this chapter: Are Harnack, Lapide and a score of other experts correct in their evaluation of eastern Christology as utterly Hellenistic and un-Jewish?

Let us begin with an observation on the typical Hellenistic reaction to the dogma of the incarnate Son of God. Lapide would have us believe that this was something Gentile Hellenists would really appreciate, something they craved for, something they would embrace enthusiastically. But we have several authentic reports on the Gentile Hellenistic reaction, and it does not correspond to this picture at all. The available evidence shows, on the contrary, that most Hellenists reacted with disgust and contempt at the very idea of a divine incarnation, and with charges of blasphemy when they heard that the incarnate Son of God had suffered the uttermost shame of crucifixion. We will let one Gentile author speak for all. He is Celsus, a Platonist philosopher writing a polemical book against Christianity ca. A.D. 175.

> God is good and beautiful and happy, and exists in the most beautiful state. If then he comes down to men, he must undergo change, a change from good to bad, from beautiful to shameful, from happiness to misfortune, and from what is best to what is most wicked. Who would choose a change like this? It is the nature only of a mortal being to undergo change and remolding, whereas it is the nature of an immortal being to remain the same without alteration. Accordingly, God could not be capable of undergoing this change. . . . Either God does change, as the Christians say, into a mortal body; and it has already been said

---

[7]The quotation is from a published transcript of an interview on Norwegian television April 24, 1977. (Contained in Pinchas Lapide, *Jøder og kristne: Bidrag til en dialog* [Oslo: Dreyers Forlag, 1978], pp. 94-95, my translation.)

that this is an impossibility. Or he does not change, but makes those who see him think that he does so, and leads them astray, and tells lies. . . . Dear Jews and Christians, no God or child of God has either come down or would want to come down (from heaven)![8]

Tertullian once made a point of this difficulty, the offensiveness of the fact of the incarnation. It is as if he were striving to express the basic intuition that the offensiveness of the christological dogma is precisely what makes it ring true. Nobody would have dreamt of inventing anything so offensive! Besides, Tertullian reminds us, Paul has warned us that in the gospel we meet the foolishness of God. But, he says to Marcion, if you eliminate the birth and the suffering of the divine Son from the gospel, there is no foolishness left.

> Which is more unworthy of God, which is more likely to raise a blush of shame, that God should be borne, or that he should die? That he should bear the flesh, or the cross? be circumcised, or be crucified, be cradled or be coffined, be laid in a manger, or in a tomb?

> The Son of God was crucified. I am not ashamed of it, because it seems shameful. And the Son of God dies, it is by all means to be believed, because it is absurd. And He was buried, and rose again; the fact is certain, precisely because it is impossible. (*De carne Christi* 5.1, 4)[9]

Thus, according to Tertullian, the very offensiveness of the christological confession carries the conviction of its truth. This is not something we have made up.[10]

So Celsus and Tertullian have made us aware of the true response to the concept of incarnation in the Hellenistic world. And that means that the Christian doctrine of the incarnation can hardly be the product of a milieu— the Hellenistic—that regarded this doctrine as a philosophical and theologi-

---

[8]Celsus's book is preserved almost in its entirety through quotations in Origen's refutation of it, *Contra Celsum*; the best English translation is Henry Chadwick's *Origen: Contra Celsum. Translated with an Introduction and Notes* (Cambridge: Cambridge University Press, 1965). The quotation is from *Contra Celsum* 4.14; 4.18; 5.2; Chadwick, pp. 192-93, 195, 264.

[9]*ANF* 3:525, quote modified.

[10]In modern times C. S. Lewis has eloquently made the same point: "[The story of the incarnation] is not transparent to the reason: we could not have invented it ourselves. It has not the suspicious *a priori* lucidity of Pantheism or of Newtonian physics. It has the seemingly arbitrary and idiosyncratic character which modern science is slowly teaching us to put up with in this wilful universe. . . . If any message from the core of reality ever were to reach us, we should expect to find in it just that unexpectedness, that wilful, dramatic anfractuosity which we find in the Christian faith. It has the master touch—the rough, male taste of reality, not made by us, or, indeed, for us, but hitting us in the face" (*The Problem of Pain* [London: Collins, Fontana Books, 1957], p. 13).

cal monstrosity. Nor can it be the brilliant idea of someone trying to speak the way Hellenists liked.

Now if we could ask the church fathers themselves what they thought was the background of the Christology of the eastern creed, they would no doubt have answered, this creed is biblical through and through, not only in substance, but also in wording. And by "biblical" they would have meant that every word and clause in the creed can be substantiated from the Old Testament, not only the New. Their Old Testament sometimes included the so-called Apocrypha, and did so in this case (cf. chapter fourteen above). But there is no question of the Jewishness of the Apocrypha; they belong to mainstream Judaism of the two last centuries B.C.

Gradually, modern scholars have come to realize that the church fathers were quite simply right in this claim for the biblical foundation of their Christology. The Christology of the eastern creeds is certainly other than the messianic confession of the Roman Creed, but that does not automatically imply that it is less rooted in Jewish tradition. Let us try to trace these roots.

Wisdom Incarnate

We begin by simply giving an overview of the New Testament passages that are most similar to the first part of the christological statement of the Nicene Creed.

> For us there is one God, the Father, from whom are all things and for whom we exist, and one Lord, Jesus Christ *through whom are* all things and through whom we exist. (1 Cor 8:6)

> He is the image of the invisible God, the first-born prior to all creation; for *by him all things were created,* in heaven and on earth, . . . *all things were created through him* and for him. He is before all things, and *in him all things hold together.* (Col 1:15-17, author's translation)

> But in these last days he has spoken to us by a Son [or the Son], whom he appointed heir of all things, *through whom he also created the worlds.* He is the reflection of God's glory and the exact imprint of God's very being, *and he sustains all things by his powerful word.* (Heb 1:2-3)

> The words of the Amen, the faithful and true witness, *the origin of God's creation.* (Rev 3:14)

> In the beginning was the Word (Greek, *logos*), and the Word was with God, and the Word was God. He was with God in the beginning. *Through him all things were made, without him nothing was made that has been made. In him was life.* (Jn 1:1-4 NIV)

This list calls for several comments. The first is that the Johannine prologue is by no means an isolated and singular text in the New Testament as far as Christology is concerned. John has Paul and the author of Hebrews to support him in what he says of the Word in John 1. And maybe we should add two more supporters, if Revelation was written by another John than the Evangelist, and if Paul is quoting a pre-Pauline hymn in Colossians 1:15-20 (as many scholars think).

Second, it is easy to see what is common to all these passages about the preexistent[11] Son of God: the common feature is the saying that he assisted God at the creation of the world; that God created *through him* or *by him*. Let us call this the idea of *mediatorship in creation*. The Son or the Word is God's *mediator* in creating the world.

This idea helps us to pose the right question when we ask for the Jewish roots of this Christology. Scholars have often searched in general for ideas of pre-existence in Judaism and found many and diverse answers as to what could qualify as the background of Christology. But if we ask more precisely which thing or person—which X—is playing an important role in Judaism in sayings like "God created the world through X," then the answer is obvious and easy to find in the extant sources. In Jewish writings of the Second Temple period there is one such X and one only: the Wisdom of God.

Here is a sample of such sayings:

> The Lord *by wisdom* founded the earth. (Prov 3:19)
>
> [Wisdom speaking:] When God assigned to the sea its limit, . . . when he marked out the foundations of the earth, *then I was beside him, like a master worker.* (Prov 8:29-30)
>
> She [wisdom] is an initiate in the knowledge of God, and *an associate in his works.* (Wisdom of Solomon 8:4)
>
> *By your wisdom* you have formed humankind. (Wisdom of Solomon 9:2)

It may seem surprising at first that God's wisdom, which is not a person, should be such an important model for God's Son, who certainly is a person. But here we should notice two things: (1) This background makes it easier to understand that in the Johannine prologue the Son is also identified with something that is seemingly not a person: the Word. It is interesting to notice that in Wisdom of Solomon God's wisdom is also

---

[11]In scholarly literature, the terms *preexistence* and *preexistent* are used to designate the existence of the Word or the Son of God *before* (Latin, pre-) his incarnation.

identified with God's word (*Logos*). (2) In several texts in the Old Testament and the Apocrypha God's Wisdom is in fact described—or behaves— as if it were a person. Scholars have for a long time wrestled with the problem of how to explain this phenomenon properly. Some think it should be described as nothing more than a poetic personification of an aspect of God, while others think that this does not do full justice to the texts that identify God's Wisdom with something that is to a certain extent exterior to God. Foremost among these identifications is the one which identifies God's Wisdom with the Torah (on this more in a moment). Some scholars have therefore come to the conclusion that Wisdom in these texts is an aspect of God which has at the same time a kind of quasi-personal existence outside him, and they call this a hypostatization[12] of one of God's attributes.

Before we go on exploring this idea further, let us see to what extent this Wisdom concept may clarify the terminology used in the christological texts representing this Wisdom Christology.

1. In Hebrews the Son of God is said to be a radiance (Greek, *apaugasma*) of God's glory and an imprint/image (Greek, *charaktēr*) of his being. This is a free quotation, actually, of Wisdom of Solomon 7:26, which says of Wisdom: "She is a radiance *(apaugasma)* of the eternal Light, an undistorted mirror of God's energy and an image *(eikōn)* of God's goodness."

2. In Colossians 1:15 the Son is said to be, like Wisdom, the image *(eikōn)* of the invisible God, and then "the first-born *(prōtotokos)* prior to all things created." In Proverbs 8:22, in the Hebrew version, Wisdom says: "He begat me as the first *(qanani reshit)*," and further: "Before he made the earth and the deep places, before water came forth from the sources . . . he begat me" (Prov 8:22-25).

3. The most striking parallel is yet to be mentioned. It comes in a Wisdom text not yet quoted, namely, the self-praise of Wisdom in Sirach 24. This text also has the idea of Wisdom being present with God when he created the world—but then an important idea is added: Wisdom began to seek a place *to dwell on earth* ("become incarnate," we could perhaps say), but found none, until "the Creator of all things . . . chose the place for my tent *(ten skēnēn mou).*

---

[12]The Greek word *hypostasis* is taken from Christian terminology, in which it became the word to describe the three persons of the Trinity. It is interesting to notice that when scholars tried to find an appropriate term for the unique position of Wisdom—being an aspect of the one God and at the same time somehow external to him—they had to turn to trinitarian terminology!

He said, *pitch your tent*[13] *(kataskēnōson)* in Jacob, and in Israel receive your inheritance. . . . In the holy tent I ministered before him, and so I was established in Zion" (Sirach 24:8-10). As is well known, this is exactly the same terminology that is applied to the Word's incarnation in John 1:14, which literally says, "The Word became flesh and *pitched his tent (eskēnōsen)* among us." The Sirach background makes clear why the metaphor of tent is used in John 1:14; the glory and name of God dwelling in the tabernacle/temple explains the tent imagery. This also makes it easier to understand why seeing the glory plays such a great role in the Johannine Prologue: the glory and the cloud of glory were intimately associated with the holy tent and its successor, the temple.

Taken together, this leads us to the following conclusion: The Christology of the New Testament passages we have surveyed is a Jewish "Wisdom Christology" (1 Cor 8:6; Col 1:15-20; Heb 1:2-3; Rev 3:14; Jn 1:1-18). Jesus not only possessed wisdom, was not only a wise man, he was himself God's Wisdom in person, he was Wisdom incarnate, the Word made flesh.

Once we have seen the Wisdom background of these passages, we can recognize it in other important christological passages as well; first and foremost in Philippians 2:6-11, where we have the same vertical movement as in the eastern creed.

This is a Christology other than the messianic, but no less Jewish, and not necessarily later in time. We shall return to this last question shortly.

In Sirach 24, Wisdom is identified with another important object in God's plan of creation: the law of Moses, the Torah. "All this is the book of the covenant of the Most High God, the law that Moses commanded us as an inheritance for the congregations of Jacob" (Sirach 24:23). This identification of Torah and Wisdom became stock in trade with the rabbis, and is universal in rabbinic literature.[14]

In the rabbinic writings we find an interesting midrashic reading in which the two sayings about creation in Genesis 1:1 and Proverbs 8:22 are combined and referred to the Torah. In Proverbs 8:22-31 the rabbis read that Wisdom

---

[13]NRSV: "make your dwelling." I have chosen the more literal translation in order to make my point more clearly.

[14]See the material gathered in Strack/Billerbeck 2:353-57.

was begotten "as the beginning" (NRSV footnote) *before* the rest of creation; this made them read Genesis 1:1 in the following manner: "By (means of) 'Beginning' (= Wisdom), God created the heavens and the earth." In the Targums (Jerushalmi and Neofiti) we find this exegesis in an interesting double translation of *bereshit: "mileqadim bekhokmah bara elohim":* "In the beginning, by Wisdom, God created." And in *Midrash Rabbah* on Genesis 1:1 we find the further identification of Wisdom and Torah spelled out in a magnificent story of creation:

> The Torah declares: "I was the working tool of the Holy One, blessed be He" [cf. Prov 8:29: "I was with him as a master worker" (Hebrew, *amon*)]. In human practice, when a mortal king builds a palace, he builds it not with his own skill but with the skill of an architect. The architect moreover does not build it out of his head, but employs plans and diagrams to know how to arrange the chambers and the wicket doors. Thus God consulted the Torah and created the world, while the Torah declares, "By 'The Beginning' God created" [Gen 1:1], "The Beginning" referring to the Torah, as in the verse, "The Lord made me *The Beginning* of His way" [Prov 8:22].

In the *Midrash Rabbah* this specific midrash is anonymous, and could be too late to be of interest to us. Basically the same midrash is preserved in Philo,[15] however, and Rabbi Akiba seems to hint at it when he says: "Beloved are Israel, for to them was given the precious instrument; still greater was the love, in that it was made known to them that to them was given the precious instrument by which the world was created" (*M Avot* 3:14).[16]

The position accorded to the Wisdom/Torah in such texts as these prompted the rabbis to call the Torah "God's daughter" (*TB Sanhedrin* 101a; *Lev. Rab.* 20:10 etc.).[17]

The fact that mainstream Judaism came to identify God's Wisdom, his assistant at the creation of the world, with the Torah, while believers in Jesus

---

[15]*De opificio mundi (On the Making of the World),* 17-20.
[16]Very likely, the instrumental reading of *bereshit,* equating *reshit* with Wisdom/Torah, was already known to the author of Revelation, because when he calls Jesus "the *archē,* 'beginning,' of God's creation" (Rev 3:14) he may allude to Gen 1:1 Greek: "By *archē* God created."
[17]Both Wisdom and Torah are female words in Hebrew; Wisdom is female in Greek too. This may be sufficient reason why the term *Wisdom* never caught on among believers in Jesus as the term for the preexistent Son of God, although it was extensively used as a christological title in the church fathers. But when the Jewish texts already contained the masculine *Logos* as an equivalent to Wisdom, it is no wonder that believers in Jesus preferred this word—the more so, since God's Logos evoked not only the idea of God's creative plan, as Wisdom did, but also his creative word of Gen 1:3-31 and Ps 33:6.

identified it with Jesus the incarnate Word/Wisdom, explains why Jesus came to play much the same functional role in Christian belief as the Torah does in Jewish.

But has this identification of Jesus and the Wisdom of God any foundation in the words and deeds of Jesus himself—or is it a later projection of speculative ideas?

Jesus and Wisdom/Torah

Let us begin by reading a modern rabbi's characterization of Jesus' teaching in the Gospels. The following is a quote from the Swedish Rabbi Marcus Ehrenpreis:

> A difference [between Jesus and the Jewish rabbis] appears immediately that from the very beginning constituted an unbridgeable wall of separation between Jesus and the Pharisees. Jesus spoke in his own name. Judaism, on the other hand, knew only one *I*, the divine *Anochi* [Hebrew for "I"] who gave us the eternal commandments at Sinai. No other superhuman I has existed in Judaism other than God's. Jesus' sermons begin, "I say to you." The prophets of Israel introduced their preaching, "Thus says the Lord." Here is a difference that goes to the inner core of religion. . . . Jesus' voice had an alien sound that Jewish ears had never heard before. For Judaism, only the revealed teaching of God was important, not the teacher's personal I. Moses and the prophets were human beings encumbered with shortcomings. Hillel and his successors sat on the seat of Moses. Every leading scholar is a link in an unbroken chain of tradition that stretched from Moses to our own time. Jesus seemingly breaks this chain and begins a new one. A man arose in Israel who cried, "I say to you." This was the new and strange element that arose between Jesus and the Pharisees.[18]

It seems that Ehrenpreis is right in this: Jesus spoke in a manner that placed him above the highest category allowed for humans in Judaism, that of the prophet, to say nothing of that of the rabbi. The rabbi may say, "I have received as a tradition from Rabbi A who heard it from Rabbi B," thus authenticating his halakic ruling by the authority of tradition, ultimately deriving its authority from the oral Torah from Moses. The prophet speaks more directly from God, "Thus says the Lord: I . . ." But the prophet also is only a representative of God. He speaks in God's name, not in his own. He wants to restore or strengthen the people's relationship with God, not their relationship with the

───

[18]Marcus Ehrenpreis, *Talmud, Fariseism, Urkristendom* (Stockholm: Hugo Gebers Förlag, 1933), pp. 108-10, my translation.

prophet. His own person is not important. He does not have God's word in himself, it "comes to him"; sometimes he has to wait for it.

Jesus, obviously, never authenticated his teaching the way the rabbis did. He never said "I have received as a tradition." "He taught them as one having authority, and not as the scribes" (Mk 1:22). Nor did he speak like a prophet. He never made himself a representative of God by using the prophetic messenger formula.

He spoke God's word, he said God's Law, *in his own name*. "You have heard that it was said [by God] to those of ancient times [at Sinai], . . . but *I* say to you" (Mt 5:21-22, 27, 31, 33, 38, etc.). For Jewish ears, this must have been shocking. They must have asked, "who are you, to set your own authority above that of the Law?" And this was not the only way Jesus entered God's domain, according to the Gospels. He forgave sins. The reaction of the audience was spontaneous: "It is blasphemy! Who can forgive sins but God alone?" (Mk 2:7). The prophets could ask people to turn to God, to come to God for help and rest. Jesus said, "Come to me, all you that are weary and are carrying heavy burdens, and I will give you rest" (Mt 11:28). The rabbis could speak of taking upon oneself the yoke of the Torah or the yoke of the kingdom; Jesus said, "Take my yoke upon you, and learn from me" (Mt 11:29).[19] The rabbis could say that if two or three men sat together, having the words of Torah among them, the *shekhina* (God's own presence) would dwell on them (*M Avot* 3:2). Jesus said, "Where two or three are gathered in my name, I am there among them" (Mt 18:20). The rabbis could speak about being persecuted for God's sake, or for his Name's sake, or for the Torah's sake; Jesus spoke about being persecuted and even loosing one's life for *his* sake. In the Old Testament, God is the only one to master the forces of nature with his word alone. He threatens the stormy waters, for example (Ps 104:7; cf. Ps 29:3; 77:16). When the disciples saw Jesus threaten the storm on the lake of Galilee, they were terrified with awe: "Who then is this, that even the wind and the sea obey him?" (Mk 4:41). Some charismatic teachers had the gift of doing miracles and healing people—before, during and after the time of Jesus—like Honi the Circle-Drawer or Hanina ben Dosa.[20] But they did so by

---

[19]For a rabbinic parallel, see *Avot* 3:5: "He that takes upon himself the yoke of the Law, from him shall be taken away the yoke of the [oppressing foreign] kingdom and the yoke of worldly care; but he that throws off the yoke of the Law, upon him shall be laid the yoke of the kingdom and the yoke of worldly care" (Danby, p. 450).

[20]On Honi, cf. the study by William Scott Green, "Palestinian Holy Men: Charismatic Leadership and Rabbinic Tradition," Haase, *Aufstieg* 2 19.2:619-47.

their effective prayers; they were great intercessors for other people. Jesus did not heal or perform other miracles by invoking God's power—he had the power in himself and healed by a simple command.[21] Likewise in his exorcisms. Other exorcists tried to frighten the spirit by invoking some divine power other than themselves or by appealing to great charismatics of the past, like Solomon, who was reputed to have produced very effective spells against demons.[22] Jesus made them depart with his own word of power, it was *him* they feared.

And this is only a narrow selection of many similar features in the works and words of Jesus.[23] No wonder that people marveled at him. And if we look to the Old Testament for role models of this characteristic of Jesus' behavior— this *I* beside God, speaking and acting as if this *I* were God's own—we find only one: God's Wisdom (cf. esp. Prov 1:20-33; 3:13-26; 8:32-36; 9:4-6).[24]

---

[21]In his fascinating study *Jesus the Jew: A Historian's Reading of the Gospels* (London: William Collins Sons, 1973; paperback ed. Fontana/Collins, 1976 and later), Geza Vermes has tried to understand Jesus as another charismatic prophet like Hanina and Honi. The analogy is interesting, but breaks down on the decisive point, as we have argued above. For critical evaluation of Vermes's charismatic-prophet Christology, see now John P. Meier, *A Marginal Jew: Rethinking the Historical Jesus*, vol. 2: *Mentor, Message, and Miracle*, The Anchor Bible Reference Library (New York: Doubleday, 1994), pp. 581-88 ("Jewish Traditions About Honi the Circle-Drawer and Hanina ben Dosa"); and Craig A. Evans, *Jesus and His Contemporaries*, pp. 215, 227-43 ("Rabbinic Miracle Stories," with further bibliography).

[22]See, for example, the famous story of the Jewish exorcist Eleazar in Josephus, *Antiquities* 8.45-49 (Loeb ed. 5:594-97); and cf. the rich material on Solomon as the chief exorcist in Louis Ginzberg, *The Legends of the Jews* 4:149-54; 6:291-93. Cf. also D. C. Duling, "Solomon, Exorcism, and the Son of David," *Harvard Theological Review* 68 (1975): 235-52. On the relationship between Eleazar's kind of exorcistic activity and that of Jesus, see Evans, *Jesus and His Contemporaries*, pp. 236-38; and Meier, *Marginal Jew* 2:593.

[23]An important study by my teacher in the New Testament, Sverre Aalen, has, regrettably, only been published in Norwegian: "Jesu kristologiske selvbevissthet: Et utkast til 'jahvistisk kristologi,'" *Tidsskrift for Teologi og Kirke* 40 (1969): 1-18; reprinted in idem, *Guds Sønn og Guds Rike: Nytestamentlige studier* (Oslo: Universitetsforlaget, 1973), pp. 271-88. I am much indebted to him for the ideas set forth above.

[24]Here also Sverre Aalen made an important contribution: "Visdomsforestillingen og Jesu kristologiske selvbevissthet," *Svensk Exegetisk Årsbok* 37/38 (1972/1973): 35-48; reprinted in *Guds Sønn og Guds Rike*, pp. 313-24. There are also several more recent studies: Hartmut Gese, "Die Weisheit, der Menschensohn und die Ursprünge der Christologie als konsequente Entfaltung der biblischen Theologie," *Svensk Exegetisk Årsbok* 44 (1979): 77-114, esp. pp. 97-102; Max Küchler, *Frühjüdische Weisheitstraditionen: Zum Fortgang weisheitlichen Denkens im Bereich des frühjüdischen Jahweglaubens*, Orbis biblicus et orientalis 26 (Freiburg, Switzerland: Universitätsverlag, 1979), pp. 572-97; Oskar Skarsaune, *Incarnation: Myth or Fact?* (St. Louis: Concordia, 1991), 33-43; Ben Witherington III, *Jesus the Sage: The Pilgrimage of Wisdom* (Minneapolis: Fortress, 1994), pp. 147-208; M. Hengel, "Jesus as Messianic Teacher of Wisdom and the Beginnings of Christology," in *Studies in Early Christology* (Edinburgh: T & T Clark 1995), pp. 73-117.

It is therefore not sufficient to say that Jesus was a supremely wise man. He is not a *spokesman* for Wisdom. He *is* Wisdom in person. He is Torah in person. That is why he, in his own name, with his own *I*, can deepen, radicalize, even correct the Torah; not by abrogating it, not by doing it away, but by making it complete.[25]

It goes without saying that a Christology like this could only arise in a Jewish setting among disciples steeped in the Old Testament and Jewish categories of thought.

The Father and the Son

When a man makes something, that something is not of the same nature as its maker precisely because it is made. An artist can make a perfect statue of himself, a copy of himself in every detail. But it is not of the same nature as the artist; it is not of the same living stuff as the artist, does not share his kind of life. On the other hand, when the artist begets a son, the son may not be his exact copy, but he is definitely of the same nature, the same stuff as his father. He shares his kind of life. He is "from his father's being," "of the same essence" as his father.

The very simple point of Nicene Christology is that the last, not the first, analogy is the correct one when it comes to finding the right way to express the relationship between the Father and the Son. We are made by God, therefore different from him in nature, not sharing his kind of life. But the Son is begotten by God, therefore of the same nature, sharing God's kind of divine life.

If we take a new look at the creed of Nicaea, we observe that the inserted clauses stress only this point. Apart from the inserted clauses, the creed is a simple paraphrase of biblical sayings about Jesus as Wisdom. When it says, for example, that the preexistent Logos is "light from light," this is a short expression for what is said in Wisdom 7:26 (and repeated in Heb 1:3): Wisdom is "a radiance of the eternal Light." And when the Nicene Creed says that the Son is born from the Father "before the ages," that is an encapsulated version of Proverbs 8:22-31 (e.g., "from the primeval times before the earth's existence," Prov 8:23, author's translation).

The church fathers, from the very beginning, found in the Wisdom texts (Old Testament, Apocrypha and New Testament) several metaphors to

---

[25]On Jesus' being a wise man and at the same time more than a wise man, Wisdom in person, see esp. Ben Witherington III, *Jesus the Sage*.

describe the relationship between God and his Wisdom, which they then applied in Christology. The Father is to the Wisdom/Son as the root is to the tree (Prov 3:18; Sirach 24:12-17); as the light is to its radiance (Wisdom 7:26) or a variant of this metaphor, as the sun is to its ray (Sirach 24:32); and as the source is to the river (Baruch 3:12, God as the fountain of Wisdom; Sirach 24:25-31, Wisdom as an overflowing river of paradise).

Tertullian uses all these metaphors to describe the relationship between the Father and the Son,[26] and once says that "the Paraclete (Holy Spirit) teaches" these metaphors,[27] no doubt a reference to the Wisdom metaphors in Scripture.

In these metaphors, the church fathers recognized the same basic unity of nature as in the birth metaphor: God and his Wisdom, the Father and the Son, were "of the same stuff," as the water is the same in the fountain and the river, etc. To explain the metaphors with a concept, Tertullian used the word *substance:* the same substance is in the fountain and in the river, and so it is with the Father and the Son: "There is no division of substance, but merely an extension, as when a light is kindled from a light. . . . [Thus Christ is] Spirit of Spirit, and God of God" (*Apology* 21.12-13).[28]

Thus, the concept of substance and the Wisdom metaphors explain each other mutually. When Tertullian wants to elucidate the meaning of the metaphors, he uses the concept of substance; when he wants to make clear the meaning of the concept, he uses the metaphors. We see the same in the Greek fathers, except they had no exact equivalent to Latin *substantia,* so they normally used the concept of "being" (Greek, *ousia*) instead.

What happened before the council of Nicaea was that a presbyter in Alexandria, Arius, totally rejected every notion of a common nature of the Father and the Son. The Son was made, and therefore of a different nature. He was a creature, although in a category by himself, because Arius, too, believed that the rest of creation had been created through the Son. But he firmly rejected any notion that the Son's being was an extension of the Father's. He therefore also rejected all the Wisdom metaphors traditionally used in pre-Nicene Christology, as in the following letter to Bishop Alexander of Alexandria (ca. A.D. 320):

---

[26]Esp. in *Against Praxeas,* chaps. 5-8, his most extensive treatment of Wisdom Christology (in *ANF* 3:597-27; esp. 600-603).

[27]Ibid. 8:5: "For God sent forth the Word, as the Paraclete also declares, just as the root puts forth the tree, and the fountain the river, and the sun the ray" (*ANF* 3:603).

[28]This is my own translation, as the *ANF* 3 translation of the *Apology* is clearly based on a precritical text. Cf. *ANF* 3:34.

[The Son is] a perfect creature of God, . . . an offspring, . . . but not as Valentinus said, that the offspring of the Father was an emanation;[29] nor as Mani taught that the offspring was a part of the Father, consubstantial [*homoousios*], . . . nor as Hieracas (said:) of one torch from another, or as a lamp divided into two.[30]

Adolf von Harnack, himself by no means an admirer of orthodoxy, said the following about Arius's doctrine:

Arianism is a new teaching in the Church. . . . It is not new only because it contended so sharply and publicly that the Logos was created, . . . but it is new because it explicitly denies every substantive connection between the Logos and the Father. The old images which were nearly as old in the Church as the Logos doctrine itself, the spring and the brook, the sun and the light, the original picture and its reflection, are here cast away. But that signifies nothing less than that the Christian doctrine of the Logos and God's Son is discarded. All that remains, are the old names.[31]

In light of this, the meaning of the inserted clauses in the creed of Nicaea becomes plain. They are not intended to introduce a new, revolutionary interpretation of the old eastern creed; on the contrary, they are intended as safeguards around the old meaning of the creed.

Certainly the Fathers at Nicaea did not "Hellenize" Christology by this creed. We have seen already how offensive the very idea of the real God becoming incarnate, and even suffering, was in the Hellenistic setting. In Nicaea the church confessed that the Son, of one being with the Father, had indeed suffered. And there was no way of softening this by explaining that the divine nature in the Son was of a less divine or semi-divine character. In Christ, God suffered. That was as offensive to Hellenists as to anybody, but the fathers at Nicaea understood this to be the doctrine of Scripture.

In a televised interview Pinchas Lapide said the following: "I used to think that becoming incarnate was impossible to God. But recently I have come to the conclusion that it is un-Jewish to say that this is something the God of the

---

[29]Tertullian, *Against Praxeas* 5-8., had used precisely this term to describe the relationship between the Father and the Son: just as the river is an emanation from the spring, so the Son from the Father. Tertullian was aware that the gnostics (Valentinus) had used this term, but was confident it was nevertheless useful to express orthodox doctrine. Arius, of course, is out to discredit the word by attaching it to a well-known heretic.

[30]This metaphor, making the "light from light" concrete, was in fact one of the favorite metaphors of the pre-Nicene fathers, beginning with Justin. Arius's letter is found in English translation in *New Eusebius*, no. 284, p. 326.

[31]*Lehrbuch der Dogmengeschichte*, vol. 2, 5th ed. (Tübingen: J. C. B. Mohr, 1931), p. 221, my translation.

Bible cannot do, that he cannot come that close. I have had second thoughts about the incarnation."[32]

Box 16.1. The Nicene Creed (381)

After the council in Nicaea had agreed in 325 on the creed quoted on page 320, the debate on the christological issue was carried on with undiminished intensity for more than fifty years; the emperors favoring the Arian position most of the time. There was also a debate on the divinity of the Spirit. In 381 a council gathered in Constantinople. It reaffirmed the position of the Nicene council, and adopted a creed very similar to the one from 325 in the first and second articles. In the third article some new precisions were made concerning the nature of the Spirit. The Nicene precisions in the second article, and the new precisions in the third, are italicized in the following quote. Apart from these, the creed from 381, which later became known as the Nicene Creed (scholars call it the Niceno-Constantinopolitan Creed), contains only traditional phrases, some of which are borrowed from the Old Roman Creed (in bold face).

We believe in one God, the Father, almighty,
     maker of heaven and earth, of all things visible and invisible;
And in one Lord Jesus Christ,
     the onlybegotten Son of God,
     begotten from the Father before all ages,
     light from light,
     true God from *true* God,
       begotten, not made,
       of one substance with the Father,
     through Whom all things came into existence,
     Who because of us men and because of our salvation
     came down from heaven,
     and was incarnate **from the Holy Spirit and the Virgin Mary**
     and became man,
     and **was crucified** for us **under Pontius Pilate,**
     and suffered **and was buried,**
     and rose again on the third day according to the Scriptures
     and ascended to heaven,
     and **sits at the right hand of the Father,**
     and will come again with glory to judge living and dead,
     of Whose kingdom there will be no end;
And in the Holy Spirit,
     the Lord and life-giver,
     Who proceeds from the Father,
     Who with the Father and the Son is together worshipped and together glorified,
     Who spoke through the prophets;
in one **holy Catholic** and apostolic **Church.**
We confess one baptism to **the remission of sins;**
we look forward to the **resurrection** of the dead
and the life in the world to come.
Amen.

---

[32]Norwegian television, April 1978. There seems to be no taped copy of this interview preserved by Norwegian Broadcasting, but Lapide's words made such an impression upon me that they stuck in my mind.

Temple Square

"The Word became flesh and tabernacled among us" (Jn 1:14, author's translation). In the Wisdom poem of Sirach 24, Wisdom becomes incarnate as the Torah given at Sinai—and at the very center of that Torah is the sacrificial service of the tabernacle (temple). That is probably the meaning when Wisdom is said to make priestly service in the holy tent on Zion (Sirach 24:10). If Jesus was Wisdom incarnate, this could make us understand that he not only *taught* the way of life, but that he also had to be the true high priest, bringing the final sacrifice, doing the final priestly service in "the holy tent." At the very center of the Mosaic Torah are atoning sacrifices. Jesus, the Torah in person, atoned with his own blood. We see this in the Holy of Holies imagery in Romans 3:25. Hebrews also links the Wisdom Christology of chapter 1 to the theme of Jesus as the high priest in chapters 5-11.

Suggestions for Further Reading

Generally on high Christology in the New Testament and its Jewish background, see the masterly survey of a very large body of material in Martin Hengel, *Der Sohn Gottes: Die Entstehung der Christologie und die jüdisch-hellenistische Religionsgeschichte*, 2nd ed. (Tübingen: J. C. B. Mohr [Paul Siebeck], 1977); English trans.: *The Son of God: The Origin of Christology and the History of Jewish-Hellenistic Religion* (Philadelphia: Fortress Press/ London: SCM Press, 1976). See now also the important study of William Horbury, *Jewish Messianism and the Cult of Christ* (London: SCM Press, 1998).

Two studies focusing on the relationship between monotheism and high Christology, but approaching it from very different angles: Larry W. Hurtado, *One God, One Lord: Early Christian Devotion and Ancient Jewish Monotheism* (Philadelphia: Fortress, 1988). Hurtado's approach is through very high mediator figures in early Jewish thought. Richard Bauckham, *God Crucified: Monotheism and Christology in the New Testament*, Didsbury Lectures 1996 (Carlisle: Paternoster, 1998), thinks that the clue to high Christology is not mediating figures, but the startling fact that early Christians, from the earliest times and in all strata of New Testament literature, included Jesus in God's divine identity. A truly fascinating study. Cf. also Oskar Skarsaune, "Is Christianity Monotheistic? Patristic Perspectives on a Jewish/Christian Debate," in *Studia Patristica*, vol. 29: *Historica, Theologica et Philosophica, Critica et Philologica*, ed. Elizabeth A. Livingstone (Leuven: A. Peeters, 1997), pp. 340-63.

On the wisdom-of-God concept in the Bible and in early Judaism:

Helmer Ringgren, *Word and Wisdom: Studies in the Hypostatization of Divine Qualities and Functions in the Ancient Near East* (Lund: H. Ohlssons, 1947).

Burton L. Mack, *Logos und Sophia: Untersuchungen zur Weisheitstheologie im hellenistischen Judentum*, Studien zur Umwelt des Neuen Testaments 10 (Göttingen: Vandenhoeck & Ruprecht, 1973).

Max Küchler, *Frühjüdische Weisheitstraditionen: Zum Fortgang weishtlichen Denkens im Bereich des frühjüdischen Jahweglaubens*, Orbis biblicus et orientalis 26 (Freiburg, Switzerland: Universitätsverlag, 1979).

On Wisdom Christology in the New Testament:

James D. G. Dunn, *Christology in the Making: A New Testament Inquiry into the Origins of the Doctrine of the Incarnation* (Philadelphia: Westminster Press, 1980), pp. 163-250.

Gottfried Schimanowski, *Weisheit und Messias: Die jüdischen Voraussetzungen der urchristlichen Präexistenzchristologie,* Wissenschaftliche Untersuchungen zum Neuen Testament, 2. Reihe, 17 (Tübingen: J. C. B. Mohr [Paul Siebeck], 1985).

Ben Witherington III, *Jesus the Sage: The Pilgrimage of Wisdom* (Minneapolis: Fortress/Edinburgh: T & T Clark, 1994).

Martin Hengel, "Jesus as Messianic Teacher of Wisdom and the Beginnings of Christology," in *Studies in Early Christology* (Edinburgh: T & T Clark, 1995), pp. 73-117.

On high Christology before and at Nicaea:

A comprehensive study covering the period from the New Testament to Nicene Christology is Oskar Skarsaune, *Incarnation: Myth or Fact?* Concordia Scholarship Today (St. Louis: Concordia, 1991).

John Norman Davidson Kelly, *Early Christian Doctrines,* 4th ed. (London: Adam & Charles Black, 1968 [or later editions]), chaps. 6 and 9.

T. E. Pollard, *Johannine Christology and the Early Church* (Cambridge: Cambridge University Press, 1970).

Aloys Grillmeier, *Christ in Christian Tradition,* vol. 1: *From the Apostolic Age to Chalcedon (451),* 2nd ed. (London and Oxford: Mowbrays, 1975), pp. 85-273.

Rowan Williams, *Arius: Heresy and Tradition* (London: Darton, Longman & Todd, 1987).

Richard P. C. Hanson, *The Search for the Christian Doctrine of God: The Arian Controversy 318-381* (Edinburgh: T & T Clark, 1988).

17

THE CREATIVE SPIRIT

*T*he second century A.D. is the period in which the organization of the church gained stability and structure. At the end of this century we find the communities in most places well organized with one bishop at the head, under him a group of presbyters, and third in rank the deacons, who were the assistants of the bishop. In the New Testament writings only faint beginnings of this hierarchy is to be found, if at all. On the other hand, we find prophets in the New Testament communities, and charismatics like evangelists and teachers, and those with gifts of healing. At the end of the second century have they completely disappeared and been replaced by institutionalized offices only? This is commonly assumed by many. But let us look at it a little more closely.

From Spirit to Organization?
To the first believers, the presence of the Holy Spirit in their midst was an overwhelming experience which is reflected on almost every page of the New Testament. The Spirit was the great gift and blessing that God had promised that he would pour out on "all flesh" at the end of days. And now these "last times" had come.

Comparing this first-century charismatic enthusiasm with second- and third-century emphasis on ecclesiastical structures and organization, many scholars have come to the conclusion that the spiritual fervor of the first generations soon cooled down and was replaced by other concerns. The French scholar Alfred Loisy (1857-1940) put it proverbially: Jesus proclaimed the kingdom of God—instead came the church!

With regard to the Spirit, this would mean that instead of spontaneous charismatic gifts there developed organized ministries; instead of spontaneous participation of the whole congregation during worship, there developed a fixed liturgy monopolized by the professional clergy; and the expectation and practice of signs and miracles vanished.

It would be futile to argue that this picture corresponds to nothing in the sources. But I would like to argue that it is greatly exaggerated, and that the historical realities present us with a much more nuanced picture.

If we turn to the sources from the second- and third-century church, we meet believers who, at every step in their coming to faith and in their lives as Christians, experienced the Spirit as the mover and the life-giving force. When Justin sought to convince Trypho the Jew that after all the messianic age *had* been inaugurated with the coming of Jesus, he pointed first and foremost to the now manifest presence of the Spirit. Before Jesus came, certain gifts of the Spirit were granted to prophets and kings in Israel:

> Solomon had the spirit of wisdom, Daniel that of understanding and counsel, Moses of might and piety, Elijah of fear [of the Lord], and Isaiah of knowledge; and others also in the same way either had one each, or alternately one power and then another, as had Jeremiah, and the Twelve, and David, and in fact all the other prophets. (*Dialogue with Trypho* 87.4)[1]

In Jesus, the Spirit dwelt in the fullness of all his gifts, and through Jesus the Spirit is now granted in his fullness—not to chosen individuals as in former times, but to the new people of God:

> When [these gifts of the Spirit] had taken their rest in Christ, they should again, as was prophesied, be given by the grace of the power of that Spirit to them that believe on Him. . . . It is said therefore, "He ascended on high; He led captivity captive; He gave gifts to the sons of men [Ps 68:18 as quoted in Eph 4:8]. And again it is said in another prophecy: And it shall be after these things that I will pour out my Spirit upon all flesh, and upon my maid-servants, and they shall prophesy [Joel 2:28]. (*Dialogue with Trypho* 87.5-6)[2]

---

[1]Lukyn Williams, p. 186.
[2]Ibid. When Justin speaks of the gifts of the Spirit granted to the Messiah for distribution to believers, he has Is 11:2-3 in mind, which in Jewish tradition was the basis of the concept of the "sevenfold" Spirit granted to the Messiah; cf. also for this concept Rev 3:1; and the fine

As manifest proof of the Spirit's presence, Justin triumphantly states:

> Every day some are becoming disciples unto the name of God's Messiah, and are leaving the way of error. They also receive gifts. . . . For one receives the spirit of understanding, another of counsel, another of might, another of healing, another of foreknowledge, another of teaching, another of the fear of God. (*Dialogue with Trypho* 39.2)[3]

In the following presentation of the teaching about the Spirit in the early church, we shall try to make clear the biblical foundation as well as the experiential aspect of the doctrine.

The Spirit Who Creates

We have seen already that the Son is a mediator of creation, according to the New Testament and unanimous church doctrine. But the Spirit also is a mediator at creation! In several writers of the second century we encounter the idea of a double mediatorship in creation. A classical formulation occurs in Irenaeus:

> There is declared one God, the Father, uncreated, invisible, maker of all things. . . . And God is rational (*logikos*), and therefore produced creatures by *His Logos;* and God is spiritual, and so fashioned everything *by His Spirit,* as the prophet also says: *"By the word* of the Lord the heavens were established, and all their power *by His Spirit* [Ps 33:6]. Hence, since the Logos "establishes," that is, works bodily and consolidates being, while the Spirit disposes and shapes the various "powers," so the Logos is fitly and properly called the Son, but the Spirit (is called) the Wisdom of God (*Proof of the Apostolic Preaching* 5).[4]

Since Irenaeus here (as in *Against Heresies* 3.24.2 and 4.20.2-4) operates with a double mediatorship, he is at pains to distinguish between the roles of the Son and the Spirit: the Son produces the substance of creation, the Spirit forms and adorns.

The scriptural basis for this is twofold. (1) On the one hand, Judaism had developed—as we have seen already—a Wisdom reading of Genesis 1:1: *reshit/archē,* "beginning," was identified with God's eternal Wisdom, *by which* (instrumental *beh/en*) God created. In the New Testament and some of the earliest fathers, as we have seen, this concept was interpreted christologically:

---

study of C. Oeyen, "Die Lehre der göttlichen Kräfte bei Justin," *Studia Patristica* vol. 11, Texte und Untersuchungen 108 (Berlin: Akademie-Verlag, 1972), pp. 215-21.
[3]Lukyn Williams, p. 77, translation modified.
[4]Joseph P. Smith, *St. Irenaeus: Proof of the Apostolic Preaching,* Ancient Christian Writers 16 (Westminster, Md.: Newman/London: Longmans, Green & Co., 1952), p. 50, italics added.

God's Wisdom, by which he created, is his Son, the Logos.[5] Soon, however, this christological reading of Genesis 1:1 seems to have been felt so self-explanatory and obvious to Christians that they no longer had to rely on the christological reading of Genesis 1:1 to justify it. Accordingly, Genesis 1:1 could be given a new reference—this time to the Spirit. This resulted—in good targumic-midrashic fashion—in a double translation of the *bereshit* of Genesis 1:1. We encounter it for the first time—and very clearly—in the apologist Theophilus of Antioch (ca. A.D. 180): "God made everything through Logos and Wisdom, for 'by his Logos the heavens were made firm and by His Spirit all their power' [Ps 33:6]. His Wisdom is most powerful: 'God by Wisdom founded the earth' [Prov 3:19-20]" (*To Autolycus* 1.7).[6]

Here the Logos and Wisdom are put side by side as mediators of creation. An identification of Wisdom with the Spirit is clearly implied, and this is explicitly brought out in Irenaeus, who develops this line of thought, as quoted already. We also observe how Psalm 33:6 and Proverbs 3:19 are brought in to support the implicit Wisdom reading of *reshit* in Genesis 1:1.

There was, however, another scriptural basis that was more explicit and closer to the experience of believers because it concerned specifically (2) the creation of human beings. In Genesis 1:2 the Spirit is said to move or hover over "the face of the deep" (KJV)—the fathers would have added, teeming with creative, formative, life-giving power.[7] This becomes manifest at a crucial moment: the creation of the first human (Gen 2:7). Here the breathing of God easily suggested the mediatorship of the Spirit "joining and uniting the Spirit of God the Father with what God had fashioned, so that man became according to the image and likeness of God" (Irenaeus, *Proof of the Apostolic Preaching* 97).[8]

Irenaeus could also recognize the Logos and the Wisdom/Spirit of God in God's two hands doing the creating:

"And God formed man, taking clay from the earth, and breathed into his face the breath of life" [Gen 2:7]. It was not angels, therefore, who made us, nor who

---

[5] For example, Jn 1:1-3; Col 1:15-20; Heb 1:2-3; Rev 3:14; Justin, *Dialogue with Trypho* 61; Athenagoras (ca. A.D. 175), *Plea for the Christians* 24:2, etc. See chapter sixteen above.
[6] Robert M. Grant, *Theophilus of Antioch: Ad Autolycum*, Oxford Early Christian Texts (Oxford: Clarendon, 1970), p. 11.
[7] There is evidence to suggest that this idea was also widespread in early Jewish reading of Gen 1:2, but that the idea of the Spirit's mediatorship in creation (Judith 16:14; Syriac Baruch 21:4; 23:5) was later suppressed and removed from the interpretation of this verse, possibly due to concerns about heretical reading of the text in this vein. See Martin Hengel, "Jesus as Messianic Teacher of Wisdom and the Beginnings of Christology," in *Studies in Early Christology* (Edinburgh: T & T Clark, 1995), pp. 73-117, esp. p. 95.
[8] Smith, p. 108.

formed us. . . . For God did not stand in need of these . . . as if He did not possess His own hands. For with Him were always present the Word and Wisdom, the Son and the Spirit, by Whom and in Whom, freely and spontaneously, He made all things, to Whom also He speaks, saying "Let us make man after Our image and likeness." (*Against Heresies* 4.20.1)[9]

In Jewish literature we find the idea that God, in the "Let *us*" of Genesis 1:26, was addressing his Wisdom.[10] In the earliest Christian documents this is turned into a christological reading: the Father addressed the Son (*Barnabas* 5.5; 6.12; Justin, *Dialogue with Trypho* 62.1-3). But in Theophilus we observe the same reduplication here as in Genesis 1:1: "God is found saying 'Let us make. . .' as if He needed assistance; but He said 'Let us make' to none other than His own Logos and His own Wisdom" (*To Autolycus* 2.18). Thus, from being a dialogue between God and his Wisdom in Jewish writings, Genesis 1:26 is first read as a dialogue between the Father and the Son, then as a trialogue between the Father, the Son and the Spirit.

The Spirit is therefore seen as a mediator in creation generally and in the creation of humankind especially. Why did the fathers stress the latter idea? Because they had a vivid perception of the Spirit as mediator not only in humanity's first creation but in a person's re-creation in the rebirth of baptism.

Barnabas 6.12 implicitly refers Genesis 1:26 to the new creation of persons that takes place through conversion and baptism. Christ is the new Adam (*Barnabas* 6.9 refers to Gen 2.7), and in baptism the believers are made new people (*Barnabas* 6.11-14). *Barnabas* 11.11 beautifully expresses the regenerating power of the Spirit in baptism in the following saying: "We go down into the water full of sins and foulness, and we come up bearing the fruit of fear in our hearts, and having hope on Jesus in the Spirit."[11]

Therefore, when the early believers taught that the Spirit was a mediator in creation, they immediately associated that with the creative act of God through Christ and the Spirit that they themselves had experienced in conversion and baptism. This association comes out in vivid imagery in Tertullian's booklet on baptism: Spirit and water belonged together already in Genesis 1:2, as they still do in baptism.

---

[9] *ANF* 1:487.
[10] E.g., *Slavonic Enoch* 11.30; and Jewish substratum in *Apostolic Constitutions and Canons* 8.12.16. The same idea is probably presupposed in Wisdom of Solomon 9:1-2. Cf. on this issue Jacob Jervell, *Imago Dei: Gen 1,26f im Spätjudentum, in der Gnosis und in den paulinischen Briefen*, Forschungen zur Religion und Literatur des Alten und Neuen Testaments 76 (Göttingen: Vandenhoeck & Ruprecht, 1960), pp. 46-50.
[11] Kirsopp Lake, p. 383.

"The Spirit of the Lord was hovering over the waters." The first thing, o man, which you have to venerate, is the age of the waters in that their substance is ancient; the second, their dignity, in that they were the seat of the Divine Spirit, more pleasing to Him, no doubt, than all other then existing elements. . . . Water alone—always a perfect, gladsome, simple material substance, pure in itself—supplied a worthy vehicle to God. . . . Water was the first to produce that which had life [Gen 1:20-21], that it might be no wonder if in baptism waters know how to give life. For was not the work of fashioning man himself [Gen 2:7] also achieved with the aid of waters [Gen 2:6]? Suitable material is found in the earth, yet not apt for the purpose unless it be moist and juicy. (*On Baptism* 3)[12]

But the water in itself does not have this capacity of giving life; only water over which the Spirit hovers as in the beginning:

All waters, therefore, in virtue of the pristine privilege of their origin, do, after invocation of God, attain the sacramental power of sanctification; for the Spirit immediately supervenes from the heavens, and rests over the waters, sanctifying from Himself; and being thus sanctified, they imbibe at the same time the power of sanctifying. (*On Baptism* 4)[13]

The first life on earth originated in the waters: the fish. We Christians are likewise born in the water, we are "small fishes," *pisciculi,* says Tertullian (*On Baptism* 1).

But there was yet another aspect of the Spirit's work of re-creating which was called to mind when the early Christians thought about his mediatorship in creation. Genesis 2:7 suggested another biblical text, namely, Ezekiel 37:1-14, especially verses 5-6, 9 and 14: "I will put my [S]pirit within you, and you shall live." In the early church, Ezekiel 37 was taken as a testimony on the resurrection of the dead at the end of days.[14] A passage in Irenaeus (*Against Heresies* 5.15.1) is especially instructive. He quotes Isaiah 26:19; 64:13 and Ezekiel 37:1-14 to the effect that "He who at the beginning created man [Gen 2:7], did promise him a second birth after his dissolution into earth."[15] In both the first and the last creation, the Spirit is the life-giving power; in the Septuagint of Ezekiel 37:5 he has *pneuma zoes,* "spirit of life."

---

[12]*ANF* 3:670.
[13]Ibid., p. 671
[14]See *1 Clement* 50.4; Justin, *First Apology* 52.5-6; Irenaeus, *Against Heresies* 5.15.1; Tertullian, *On the Resurrection* 29-32. Cf. Jean Daniélou, "Les ossements desséchés (Éz., 37,1-14)," in *Études d'exégèse judéo-chrétienne (Les Testimonia),* Theologie Historique 5 (Paris: Beauchesne, 1966), pp. 111-21.
[15]*ANF* 1:542.

Spirit, Eucharist and Ministry

The concept of the Spirit as re-creating and life-giving was not restricted to conversion/baptism and resurrection of the flesh. The idea and the reality were equally influential in early Christian thinking about the Eucharist. When the eucharistic prayer was said, the Holy Spirit descended upon the bread and wine, making them "the medicine of immortality, the antidote that we should not die, but live for ever in Jesus Christ" (Ignatius, *Ephesians* 20.2).[16]

In the eucharistic prayer of Hippolytus (ca. A.D. 220), the minister says:

> We pray You that You will send Your Holy Spirit upon the oblation of Your holy Church and that You will grant to all Your saints who partake to be united to You so that they may be filled with the Holy Spirit for the confirmation of their faith in truth. (*Apostolic Tradition* 4.12)[17]

To say the eucharistic prayer is regarded in the *Didache* as a charismatic function. The charismatic prophets should "make Eucharist as they will" (*Didache* 10.7). But in order to secure a permanently available charismatic to preside at the Eucharist—when there was no spontaneous one around—every congregation should consecrate some persons for this task, laying hands on them (*Didache* 15.1). Probably the *Didache* here foreshadows the charismatic concept of ordination which in Hippolytus is stated in so many words: The laying on of hands, accompanied of prayers, confers the charismatic gifts necessary to function as an "overseer" (Greek, *episkopos,* hence modern "bishop"), an "elder" (Greek *presbyteros,* hence modern "priest") or a "servant" (Greek *diakonos,* hence modern "deacon").[18] Therefore Hippolytus can state that a believer who is in jail for refusing to deny Christ when prosecuted—a so-called confessor—may be appointed a deacon or a presbyter *without* ordination, because the charismatic endowment is already made manifest by confessing Christ in the face of death (*Apostolic Tradition* 10.1). Nor is it necessary to ordain someone who has a gift of healing, for the gift is manifest in any case (*Apostolic Tradition* 15).

---

[16]Kirsopp Lake, p. 195.

[17]Dix/Chadwick, p. 9, translation modified. This element in the eucharistic prayer is traditionally called the *epiclesis,* Greek for "the-calling-upon [the Holy Spirit]." On this element in Hippolytus, see Bernhard Botte, "L'éoiclèse de l'anaphore d'Hippolyte," *Recherches de théologie ancienne et médiéval* 14 (1947): 241-51; and Enrico Mazza, *The Origins of the Eucharistic Prayer* (Collegeville, Minn.: Liturgical Press, 1885), pp. 169-74.

[18]Prayer for the ordination of a bishop: *Apostolic Tradition* 3.1-6 (Dix/Chadwick, pp. 4-6); a presbyter: 8:2-5 (Dix/Chadwick, pp. 13-14); a deacon: 9:10-12 (Dix/Chadwick, pp. 17-18).

This charismatic understanding of the ministries of the ordained clergy therefore corresponds to the dominant role accorded to the Spirit in the Eucharist as well as in baptism. Without the Spirit, baptism and Eucharist would be empty rites, conferring nothing on those partaking. Where there is no Spirit, there cannot be any real sacraments. This was a commonly shared conviction in the early church, and it created problems when one had to deal with sacraments administered by those who were deemed to be without the Spirit themselves.

The Spirit lives in the believers' hearts and in the congregation as in a temple. But where these temples have been polluted by deadly sins or heresy, the Spirit will depart and no longer be operative. This conviction was most pointedly expressed by the Carthaginian bishop Cyprian in the third century. He was willing to draw all the logical conclusions of this idea: Sacraments administered by people outside the true body of Christ were nonentities. Those who had been baptized by heretics or schismatics had to be baptized once more if they repented and joined the true church. Their former baptism was no baptism at all. Those who do not themselves have the Holy Spirit cannot impart him to others.[19]

While sharing Cyprian's premises, not everyone drew the same conclusions. In Rome they felt constrained by the biblical precedent not to repeat baptism as a rite. But they agreed that a baptism conferred by heretics or other people without the Spirit was of no effect. Accordingly, when a person, having been baptized by heretics, repented and sought admittance to the true church, the baptism would be made effective or complete by conferring the Spirit by laying on of hands.[20]

The typical early church concept of the church is thus the charismatic community, the temple in which the Spirit dwells, the body which the Spirit makes come alive. We may sum up this concept in a well-known passage by Irenaeus:

> This gift of God has been entrusted to the Church, as breath was to the first created man, for this purpose, that all members receiving it may come alive. And the means of communion with Christ has been distributed throughout it, that is, the Holy Spirit, the pledge of incorruption, the means of confirming our faith, and the ladder of ascent to God. "For in the Church," it is said, "God has set

---

[19]It was particularly in his letters nos. 70-75 (*ANF* 5:375-97 [here = nos. 69-74]), on the baptism of heretics, that Cyprian developed this theme.
[20]The most crucial documents from this debate between Carthage and Rome are given as nos. 212-17 in *New Eusebius*, pp. 237-43.

apostles, prophets, teachers" [Eph 4:11], and all the other means through which the Spirit works; of which all those are not partakers who do not join themselves to the Church, but cheat themselves of life through their perverse opinions and infamous behavior. *For where the Church is, there is the Spirit of God; and where the Spirit of God is, there is the Church and every kind of grace.* . . . Those, therefore, who do not partake of Him, are neither nourished into life from the mother's breasts, nor do they enjoy that most clear fountain which issues from the body of Christ; but they dig for themselves broken cisterns . . . fleeing from the faith of the Church lest they be convicted; and rejecting the Spirit, that they may not be instructed. (*Against Heresies* 3.24.1)[21]

Charismatic Gifts

What did the early church teach and experience with regard to the gifts of the Spirit, the *charismata*?

The first thing to notice is that many different spiritual gifts continued to be practiced in the church—in varying degrees, no doubt—throughout the entire period with which we are concerned. We have quoted already Justin's enumeration of the charismatic gifts (*Dialogue with Trypho* 39.2; 87.4.; cf. above p. 341). Irenaeus, in *Against Heresies* 2.31-32, contrasts the magical and immoral practices of the gnostics with the exercise of the true charismata in the church.

Those who are in truth His disciples, receiving grace from Him, do in His name perform miracles, so as to promote the welfare of other men, according to the gift which each one has received from Him. For some do certainly and truly drive out devils, so that those who have thus been cleansed from evil spirits both believe [in Christ], and join themselves to the Church. Others have foreknowledge of things to come: they see visions, and utter prophecies. Others still, heal the sick by laying their hands upon them, and they are made whole. Yea, moreover, as I have said, the dead even have been raised up, and remained among us for many years. And what shall I more say? It is not possible to name the number of the gifts which the Church throughout the whole world has received from God, in the name of Jesus Christ. (*Against Heresies* 2.32.4)[22]

Two charismatic gifts especially remained a focus of interest in the early church: the gift of exorcism and the gift of prophecy. In Hermas (140s A.D., Rome) we see how the exercise of prophecy in the midst of the congregation was still a matter-of-course experience in the Roman community in the mid-

---

[21]*ANF* 1:458, italics added.
[22]*ANF* 1:409.

dle of the second century (cf. *Mandate* 11).[23]

Shortly after Hermas wrote his book, a great "charismatic awakening" broke out in Phrygia, Asia Minor, lead by a certain Montanus and two female prophets, Prisca and Maximilla. They prophesied in ecstasy, and in their ecstasy fully identified themselves with one of the persons in the Trinity (i.e., they apparently did not introduce their messages with the messenger formula, "thus says the Lord"). The movement spread rapidly; in North Africa Tertullian became an adherent towards the end of his life.[24]

Many manuals on early church history state without discussion that the Montanist awakening scared the established church sufficiently to make the church anticharismatic and especially afraid of the gift of prophecy. This may, however, be a projection into that period of modern experiences, because this description of the church's reaction is not borne out by the sources, most of which are gathered in Eusebius's *Ecclesiastical History*. On reading Eusebius's report on—and excerpts from—the controversy (*Ecclesiastical History* 5.16-19),[25] one is rather struck by the quite "charismatic" character of many of the ecclesiastical *critics* of the movement. One does not find any criticism directed against the gift of prophecy as such. Many of the anti-Montanists were quite familiar with this gift and mentioned well-known prophets in their own community. One of the critics even used *against* the Montanists the argument that among them no new prophets had arisen after the first one passed away— whereas Paul said that the gift of prophecy should be a lasting ministry in the church, which in fact it was in the non-Montanist church. "But they cannot produce anyone, though it is [now] the fourteenth year or so since the death of Maximilla" (*Ecclesiastical History* 5.17.4).[26]

In addition, another critic, Miltiades, held against the Montanists the fact that their prophets spoke in a state of ecstasy, which a true prophet does not. Another offence was the enormous self-consciousness of the Montanist prophets: they identified their own persons with one of the persons in the

---

[23]Cf. the specialized study on this chapter by J. Reiling, *Hermas and Christian Prophecy: A Study of the Eleventh Mandate*, Supplements to Novum Testamentum 37 (Leiden: E. J. Brill, 1973).

[24]There has been a lot of renewed interest in the Montanist movement in recent scholarship. The following studies are recommended: Christine Trevett, *Montanism: Gender, Authority and the New Prophecy* (New York: Cambridge University Press, 1996); William Tabbernee, *Montanist Inscriptions and Testimonia: Epigraphic Sources Illustrating the History of Montanism*, Patristic Monographs Series, North American Patristic Society 16 (Macon, Ga.: Mercer University Press, 1997).

[25]Lawlor/Oulton 1:158-65.

[26]Lawlor/Oulton 1:162.

Trinity while delivering their messages, and they seemed to have implied that the distinction between true and false Christians coincided with the distinction between those who accepted and those who rejected the Montanist prophecy. Here the non-Montanist church in Asia Minor understood this to mean recognizing a spirit other than the Lord's.

But maybe the Montanist intermezzo in the long run had a negative effect on the practice of the prophetic gift within the church. Some may have felt that the Montanists had incriminated it and to some extent monopolized it. In any case it seems as if it dwindled and was nearly extinguished as a communal gift in the first half of the third century, if the silence of our sources does not deceive us.[27]

Certainly no similar statement can be made about the gift of exorcism—a gift which the early church was convinced was given to every Christian. It is easy to list innumerable instances of continued use and appreciation of this gift, from Justin Martyr to Augustine and later fathers.[28] Why was this gift accorded such a prominent position?

The answer seems to be because in Christian exorcism a direct and victorious confrontation with the gods of the Gentiles was believed to take place. Prophecy, healing, glossolalia etc.—all these gifts had parallels in pagan religion. Pagans could argue that Jesus was just another miracle-working divine person or a magician, and that Christians in their miracle-working were no better than other magicians. In exorcism, however, a direct *confrontation* took place between Jesus and his supposedly divine competitors.

> Let a person be brought before your tribunals, who is plainly under demoniacal possession. The wicked spirit, bidden to speak by a follower of Christ, will . . . make the truthful confession that he is a demon, as elsewhere he has falsely asserted that he is a god. . . . What [can be] clearer than a work like that? What more trustworthy than such a proof? The simplicity of truth is thus set forth, . . . no ground remains for the least suspicion. Do you say that it is done by magic or some trick of that sort? You will not say anything of the sort, if you have been allowed the use of your ears and eyes. For what argument can you bring against a thing that is exhibited to the eye in its naked reality? If, on the one hand, they [the spirits in the possessed] are really gods, why do they pretend to be demons? Is it from fear of us? In that case your divinity is put in subjection to Christians. . . . If,

---

[27]The standard monograph on prophecy in the early church is David E. Aune, *Prophecy in Early Christianity and the Ancient Mediterranean World* (Grand Rapids, Mich.: Eerdmans, 1983).

[28]E.g., Justin, *Dialogue with Trypho* 30.3; 76.6; 85.1-3; Celsus, *True Doctrine* [in Origen, *Contra Celsum* 1.6]; Tertullian, *Apology* 23-27; Origen, *Contra Celsum* 7.4; Athanasius, *On the Incarnation of the Word* 48-50.; *Life of Anthony,* passim; Augustine, *The City of God* 22.

on the other hand, they are demons or angels, why ... do they presume to set themselves forth as acting the part of gods? (Tertullian, *Apology* 23.4-9)[29]

When confronted with a Christian who commands them in the name of Christ, the demons (the pagan gods) are forced not only to speak the truth about themselves, but also the truth about who Christ is and where he is now positioned: that he is God's Son, reigning at the right hand of the Father. When the church was engaged in direct confrontation with paganism, exorcism amounted to a practical proof of Christ's superiority over all the gods of the pagans. "It has not been an unusual thing ... for those testimonies of your 'deities' [in exorcism] to convert men to Christianity; for in giving full belief to them, we are led to believe in Christ" (Tertullian, *Apology* 23.18).[30]

In the early church, demon possession was regarded a Gentile phenomenon associated with the practice of idolatry, that is, demon worship. As we have seen already in chapter eleven, before a candidate for baptism was baptized, several exorcisms were pronounced over him or her in order to secure the person's freedom from any demonic possession (Hippolytus, *Apostolic Tradition* 19.3.8). This was preparatory for the new indwelling of God's Spirit, imparted in baptism itself:

> Before we believed in God the habitation of our heart was corrupt and weak, like a temple really built with hands, because it was full of idolatry, and was the house of demons through doing things which were contrary to God.... When we received the remission of sins, and put our hope on the Name, we became new, being created again from the beginning; wherefore God truly dwells in us, in the habitation which we are. How? His word of faith, the calling of His promise, the wisdom of the ordinances, the commands of the teaching, Himself prophesying in us, Himself dwelling in us.... This is a spiritual temple being built for the Lord. (*Barnabas* 16.7-10)[31]

This beautiful passage in many ways sums up the doctrine of the work of the Spirit: he creates; he gives life; he dwells in believers; he makes them obey the commandments (new life with respect to ethics); he makes them prophesy (provides charismatic gifts).

In conclusion it should be pointed out how the work of the Spirit is portrayed as strikingly parallel to the work of Christ. If the Christology of the early church is biblical and Jewish in its character, so is its pneumatology.

---

[29]*ANF* 3:37-38.
[30]*ANF* 3:38.
[31]Kirsopp Lake 1:399.

Temple Square

In rabbinic theology, there was a widespread notion that the Spirit of God had dwelt in the first temple, but had been lost in the second, only to be restored in the temple of the end time. This notion probably reflects older ideas.[32] It means that there would be a strong eschatological dimension to the early Christian community's self-understanding as the Spirit-filled new temple: they were the true end-time temple. According to the rabbis, the Spirit indwelling the temple was prophetic in nature, It enabled the high priest to prophesy. *Barnabas* 16.6-10 says:

> It is written, "And it shall come to pass when the [last] week is ended that a temple of God shall be built. . . ." God truly dwells in us, in the habitation which we are. How? His word of faith, the calling of His promise, the wisdom of the ordinances, the commands of the teaching, *Himself prophesying in us,* Himself dwelling in us. . . . This is a spiritual temple being built for the Lord. (Italics added. Cf. also the quotation of other parts of *Barnabas* 16 immediately above)

Suggestions for Further Reading

There is, to my knowledge, no modern full-scale monograph on the pneumatology of the early church—in itself a thought-provoking fact. Cf., however, H. B. Swete, *The Holy Spirit in the Ancient Church* (London: Macmillan, 1912).

Stanley M. Burgess, *The Spirit and the Church: Antiquity* (Peabody, Mass.: Hendrickson, 1984); 3rd printing, 1997 under the title *The Holy Spirit: Ancient Christian Traditions*.

John N. D. Kelly, *Early Christian Creeds,* 3rd ed. (London: Longman, 1972 [or later editions]), chap. 5, pp. 4-5.

Geoffrey W. H. Lampe, *The Seal of the Spirit: A Study in the Doctrine of Baptism and Confirmation in the New Testament and the Fathers* (London/New York: Longmans, Green, 1951; 2nd ed. London: SPCK, 1967) (on the Spirit and baptism).

Hans von Campenhausen, *Ecclesiastical Authority and Spiritual Power* (London: Black, 1969; reprint, Peabody, Mass.: Hendrickson, 1997).

David E. Aune, *Prophecy in Early Christianity and the Ancient Mediterranean World* (Grand Rapids, Mich.: Eerdmans, 1983).

---

[32]Cf. Peter Schäfer, *Die Vorstellung vom Heiligen Geist in der rabbinischen Literatur,* Studien zum Alten und Neuen Testament 28 (Munich: Kösel-Verlag, 1972)

18

CONVERSION, BAPTISM & NEW LIFE

*B*efore *Jews could enter the temple, they had to immerse themselves in "living water," so as to become ritually clean. Pharisaic Judaism extended this practice to situations in which visits to the temple were not possible because the temple was far away or because the temple was no more. In the repeated immersions that are still practiced by pious Jews, Judaism carries with it another heritage from the temple and the temple period. And so does Christianity, but with a difference. The difference has very much to do with John the Baptist (or, the Immerser, as some scholars prefer to say presently). John separated his immersion completely from the temple and, it seems, made it a once-only rite of repentance. It probably also took on, by the very nature of its purpose, an element of initiation. One of those who were baptized by John was Jesus. Christians later came to consider this event as having instituted Christian baptism. The difference between the baptisms of John and Jesus was that baptism in the name of Jesus imparted the Spirit. So, baptism and the Spirit belong closely together in the early Christian consciousness. The development of baptism as a rite, as well as of the theological ideas connected with it, is well worth studying.*

Conversion and Baptism in the Early Community:
The Double Background

Conversion can mean two things. For a member of the people of God, conversion means (1) *repentance:* confession of sins, prayer for forgiveness, resolve to mend one's life. John the Baptist addressed Israel with a message of repentance, and for reasons not entirely clear to us, he accompanied this message with the offer to *baptize* those who repented. The baptism of John was a "baptism of repentance for the remission of sins" (Mk 1:4 KJV and parallels); it was intended for Jews, not for Gentiles, and the purpose of ordinary immersions according to the Torah—ritual cleansing of the body—seems not to have played a major role in John's baptism. It also seems to have been a one-time ceremony; it was not repeated, as were the ordinary immersions for uncleanness.[1]

The New Testament leaves no doubt that the baptism of John was in many respects an important precursor of Christian baptism, not least because Jesus himself was baptized by John. Like John's baptism, Christian baptism was from the beginning offered to Jews and did not imply the idea of converting from paganism to Judaism. But this, of course, is the other meaning of *conversion.*

For a Gentile, conversion means to seek admittance into the people of God, it means (2) a change of religion, peoplehood and lifestyle. Judaism had a baptism to offer in this context, too. Modern scholars often call it "proselyte baptism." Since it is probably less known than John's—at least to some readers of this book—it may be wise to present it here briefly.[2] It is the second

---

[1]Several ambitious attempts at reconstructing the theology of John's baptism and the meaning of his ministry have been made, e.g., Heinrich Kraft, *Die Entstehung des Christentums* (Darmstadt: Wissenschaftliche Buchgesellschaft, 1981), pp. 1-43 (further literature listed p. 43); Hartmut Stegemann, *Die Essener, Qumran, Johannes der Täufer und Jesus: Ein Sachbuch* (Freiburg/Basel/Vienna: Herder, 1993), pp. 292-313; Robert L. Webb, *John the Baptizer and Prophet: A Socio-Historical Study,* Journal for the Study of the New Testament: Supplement Series 62 (Sheffield: Sheffield Academic Press, 1991); John P. Meier, *Marginal Jew* 2:19-99 (with extensive bibliography on pp. 63-64).

[2]Select bibliography: still fundamental are two older studies, Wilhelm Brandt, *Die jüdischen Baptismen, oder Das religiöse Waschen und Baden im Judentum mit Einschluss des Judenchristentums,* Beihefte zur Zeitschrift für die alttestamentliche Wissenshaft 18 (Giessen: Töpelmann, 1910); and Strack/Billerbeck 1:102-12. Cf. also Bernard J. Bamberger, *Proselytism in the Talmudic Period* (Cincinnati, Ohio: Hebrew Union College Press, 1939; 2nd ed. New York: Ktav, 1968), pp. 38-52; H. H. Rowley, "Jewish Proselyte Baptism and the Baptism of John," *Hebrew Union College Annual* 17 (1940): pp. 313-34; T. M. Taylor, "The Beginnings of Jewish Proselyte Baptism," *New Testament Studies* 2 (1955/1956): 193-98; Shaye J. D. Cohen, "The Rabbinic Conversion Ceremony," *Journal of Jewish Studies* 41 (1990): 177-203; S. Legasse, *Naissance du baptême,* Lectio Divina 153 (Paris: Editions du Cerf, 1993); pp. 93-101.

background to Christian baptism, after John's.[3]

A pagan, according to the rabbis, was unclean because of his contact with idols. Idols conferred the same uncleanness as corpses, because they were regarded as "dead," or as flux or leprosy.[4] In addition, the Gentiles themselves were regarded as "dead" because of their idolatry—hence the rabbinic saying, "He who separates himself from the uncircumcision is like him who separates himself from the grave" (*M Pesahim* 8:8).[5]

When, therefore, Gentiles converted to Judaism, they had to be washed in ritual immersion to become clean. This first ritual immersion was given increased significance, it seems, during the first or early second century A.D. For women proselytes, the first immersion was the formal mark of their entry into Judaism; through this immersion, they became Jews—and at this period female converts to Judaism were in the majority over male. But even for male proselytes this baptism became an important conversion rite, competing with circumcision in importance.[6] A third element in the conversion rite clearly speaks for a pre-70 A.D. origin of the entire ritual: the convert was to bring his or her first sacrifice. After 70 and the destruction of the temple, the rabbis had to think of substitutes for this rite or dispense with

---

[3]There has been much debate on when proselyte baptism became part of the conversion ritual. Many scholars think the silence of *Joseph and Aseneth*, Philo, Josephus, and the New Testament is sufficient proof that proselyte baptism was not practiced in the first century A.D., and therefore belongs to the second century A.D. It is possible to argue, however, that the question is wrongly put. It is very likely that the first ritual immersion the proselyte underwent was given some special significance from an early date, without necessarily being regarded as an integrated rite within the conversion ritual. The "introduction" of proselyte baptism would in that case mean no more than that the first immersion of the proselyte was being formalized and included in the conversion ritual, and given an increased significance. This could very well have happened gradually, and seems to have been completed during the middle of the second century A.D., at the latest.

[4]The best treatment of this theme is Gedalyahu Alon, "The Levitical Uncleanness of Gentiles," in Alon, *Studies*, pp. 146-89. Alon here refutes the influential theory of Adolph Büchler, who maintained that the theory of Gentile uncleanness was a later construction of the second century A.D. (Büchler, "The Levitical Impurity of the Gentile in Palestine Before the Year 70," *Jewish Quarterly Review*, n.s., 17 [1926/1927]: 1-81).

[5]Cf. the very illuminating comments on this passage in David Daube, *The New Testament and Rabbinic Judaism* (London: School of Oriental and African Studies, The University of London, 1956 [Peabody: Hendrickson, reprint without date], pp. 109-10).

[6]The rabbinic evidence is conveniently displayed in Strack/Billerbeck 1:102-12. The Rabbis Eliezer ben Hyrkan (ca. C.E. 90) and Jehoshua ben Chananja disagreed concerning the question whether circumcision or immersion made a man a Jew. This was probably not a debate on whether either rite was dispensable, but rather concerning the question: *At which point* in the total conversion ceremonies did the transition from Gentile to Jew take place? Cf. esp. Bamberger, *Proselytism*, pp. 45-52.; and also Alon, *Studies*, pp. 172-79.

it.[7] In the rites of Christian baptism, we shall see several parallels between these and the Jewish rituals of conversion.

In the Bible we often read of strangers (Hebrew, *gerim*) joining the Jewish people; therefore *gerim* became the standard term for converts among the rabbis. In Greek a new term was coined, deriving from a verbal root meaning "come near": the *prosēlytos* is "the one who has come near" to the God of Israel.

What was the status, legally and religiously, of a new convert, a proselyte? The basic principle was simple as well as radical: at his conversion the proselyte began a completely new life as a Jew; he was "like a new-born child."[8] His entire Gentile past was annulled, which meant two things: (1) his sins were wiped out, together with his past;[9] and (2) his former family relations were annulled, from now on he had no father or mother, and only such offspring and family as he made after his conversion. So complete was this break with the past that in theory a proselyte could marry any of his or her former relatives.[10] Accordingly, the rabbis had to make special rulings to regulate this.[11]

The rabbis were under the obligation to find Torah support for their ideas and their practice concerning proselytes. They found this according to a simple principle: what happens to the proselyte is the same as what happened to the Israelites when they were rescued out from Egypt or when they entered

---

[7]Cf. Bamberger, pp. 44-45. The sacrifice was thought of as analogous to the covenant sacrifice brought by the Israelites at Sinai (Ex 24:6-8). It was therefore essential that the proselyte should be sprinkled with the blood from the sacrifice, as was Israel at Sinai.

[8]*TB Yevamot* 48b; 98a. Cf. the rabbinic material presented in Joachim Jeremias, *Die Kindertaufe in den ersten vier Jahrhunderten* (Göttingen: Vandenhoeck & Ruprecht, 1958), pp. 39-43.

[9]Cf. *TJ Bikkurim* 3:3, "God forgives the proselyte all his sins [at the moment of his conversion]."

[10]The remark of David Daube is worth quoting: "It is obvious that the notion of a new birth was taken seriously; more seriously (a strange thought) than it seems to be taken by modern Christianity" (*New Testament and Rabbinic Judaism*, p. 113).

[11]Cf. Joachim Jeremias, *Jerusalem in the Time of Jesus* (London: SCM Press, 1969 [or later]), pp. 323-25. The rabbinic material is conveniently gathered in Strack/Billerbeck 3:353-58. Interestingly, the incident of incest condemned by Paul in 1 Cor 5:1 could probably be defended according to the rabbinic principles if the convert was cohabiting with his widowed stepmother. The rabbis, however, tried to restrict such liasons by the principle that one should not offend Gentiles by being more permissive than they themselves were; cf. Paul's remark in 1 Cor 5:1: "that is not found even among pagans." See the instructive comments in Daube, *The New Testament and Rabbinic Judaism*, pp. 112-13. Shaye Cohen, "The Rabbinic Conversion Ceremony," in *The Beginnings of Jewishness: Boundaries, Varieties, Uncertainties* (Berkeley: University of California Press, 1999), pp. 198-238, finds that the conversion ritual itself, as described in *TB Yevamot* 47a/b, is almost completely devoid of such ideas. That may be so, but this text is concerned with regulating ritual, not interpreting it.

the covenant at Sinai. The Israelites were cleansed from their Egyptian defilement by going through the waters (cf. Paul in 1 Cor 10:1-2); or they took a bath when they were asked to make themselves clean before entering the covenant at Mount Sinai.[12]

In this way the description of what happens to the proselyte at his or her conversion is the same as the description of what happened to the Israelites in the exodus and at Sinai: it is a transition from death to life, from darkness to light, from bondage to freedom. The proselyte takes upon himself "the yoke of the kingdom" or "the yoke of the Torah"; he becomes a member of the "kingdom of priests" established at Sinai. The proselyte, in other words, could make his own the well-known saying in the Passover Haggadah:

> He has brought us forth
> from slavery to freedom,
> from sorrow to joy,
> from mourning to holyday
> from darkness to great light,
> and from bondage to redemption.[13]

All of this will prove to be relevant background material when we now turn to look at conversion and baptism among the first Christian believers.

Jewish and Christian Baptism

Christian baptism shared with John's the character of not being concerned with the ritual cleanness of the body, but with repentance and remission of sins: Acts 2:38; 22:16; 1 Peter 3:21 and so on. At the same time, Christian baptism was more than John's: it conferred the Spirit, which John's did not (Mk 1:8 and par.; Acts 19:1-7).

But as the church gradually won more Gentile believers than Jewish, the pattern of Jewish proselyte baptism seems to have exerted more influence on

---

[12]Ex 19:10: since the people were asked to wash their clothes, the rabbis concluded that they also washed themselves, since the latter would be included (as a duty) in the former (concluding from the less to the more obvious, the so-called light and heavy principle, in Hebrew *qal wahomer*). The same could be concluded from the fact that they were (later) sprinkled with blood from their sacrifice (Ex 24:8), "and we have a tradition that there must be no sprinkling without ritual ablution" (*TB Yevamot* 46b).

[13]*The Haggadah: A New Edition* (London: Soncino, 1959), p. 37. The Passover Haggadah contains many sayings describing the whole people of Israel as proselytes undergoing the proselyte experience. For example, "In the beginning, our Fathers were worshippers of strange gods: but now the All-Present has *brought us near* [Hebrew, *qervanu*, the same verbal root as in Greek proselyte] to His service" (p. 18, italics added).

the Christian rite, especially in matters of ritual.[14] That is hardly surprising; we have called attention already to the phenomenon of "missionary competition" between Judaism and the church. They were addressing much the same audience, God-fearing Gentiles, and it is not surprising that the rituals of conversion/initiation should show points of contact, even similarity. The baptism of John increasingly became something belonging to the past; proselyte baptism persisted all the time as a competitor to the baptism of the church.

This parallelism between conversion to Judaism and conversion to Christianity can be seen in terminology, rituals and ideas. We shall begin this survey by commenting briefly on one early Christian name for baptism; a name that otherwise could be taken to derive from the influence of the Hellenistic mystery religions.

In *First Apology* 61.12, Justin tells his readers that "this washing is called illumination." If we turn to Jewish texts in Greek, written in the centuries before and after A.D. 1 and describing Gentiles converting to Judaism, the metaphor of light and enlightenment is central. And the meaning of this is plain: enlightenment comes through the Torah, which is the great light. Pagan life is a life in great darkness; the "illumined ones" seems to have been a stock Jewish name for proselytes.[15] In fact, Justin himself indicates this in his *Dialogue with Trypho.* He quotes Isaiah 49:6 (the Servant of the Lord is the "light for the Gentiles," NIV) and Isaiah 42:6-7 (the same expression), and then comments that these prophecies do not speak of proselytes enlightened by "your Law," but by Christ. To this, one of Trypho's companions responds, "Why shouldn't the prophet mean the Law and those who are enlightened by it?

---

[14]It also stands to reason that Jewish conversion rites became more influential as they themselves became more clearly defined and gained significance among Jews. It is therefore likely that Jewish proselyte baptism exerted a greater influence on Christian ritual in the second century A.D. than in the first.

[15]Cf. the following samples of Greek Jewish texts: "We must rejoice with the proselytes, as if, though blind at first they had recovered their sight and had come from the deepest darkness to behold the most radiant light" (Philo, *On the Virtues* 179). Joseph praying for his future wife Aseneth, the daughter of an Egyptian priest, to make her a proselyte: "O Lord God . . . you who make all alive, who calls from darkness to light and from error to truth, and from death to life" (*Joseph and Aseneth* 8:10). Aseneth's own prayer: "Blessed be the Lord God, who has sent you [the archangel Michael] to deliver me from darkness and lead me to light" (*Joseph and Aseneth* 15:13). The patriarch Levi to his sons: "If you fall back to darkness by your ungodliness—what shall the Gentiles do, who walk in blindness? You will bring a curse on your people, to which the light of the Law was given, to enlighten every man. You will put this light aside, teaching commandments contrary to God's" (*Testament of Levi* 14:4, MS alpha). Cf. further *Testament of Gad* 5:7; *Testament of Levi* 18:9; and in rabbinic literature *Deut. Rab.* 7:3 (the Torah a "light to the world"); *Ex. Rab.* 36:3; *TB Bava Batra* 3b/4a.

These are, of course, the proselytes [to Judaism]" (*Dialogue with Trypho* 122.4).[16]

> No, I replied, . . . for if the Law had the power to enlighten the Gentiles and all those who possess it, what need would there be for a new covenant? But, since God foretold that He would send a new covenant . . . we should not apply the above-quoted passage to the Old Law and its proselytes, but to Christ and His proselytes, that is, us Gentiles whom he has enlightened. (*Dialogue with Trypho* 122.5)[17]

What we see here is a fight over the right to use an established law-related Jewish term for proselytes ("the illuminated ones") as a name for Christians. But not only is the terminology concerning conversion/baptism much the same in Judaism and early Christianity, the rituals also bore striking parallels.

Jewish and Christian Rituals of Conversion

We shall collect examples from three important sources—the *Didache* (ca. A.D. 100?, Syria), Justin Martyr (A.D. 150-160, Rome); and Hippolytus, *Apostolic Tradition* (ca. A.D. 210-220, Rome)—and compare them with Jewish evidence, rabbinic and Greek. Before going into some detail; we make the following overall comparison:[18]

Christian baptism	Jewish proselyte baptism
The candidates are asked about their motives for conversion (*Apostolic Tradition* 16.2).	The candidates are asked about their motives for conversion (*TB Yevamot* 47a).
The candidates must have witnesses who can guarantee their sincerity (*Apostolic Tradition* 16.2).	[Two or three witnesses required at baptism (*TB Yevamot* 46b)].
Pre-baptismal instruction in ethical catechism (*Didache* 1—5; Justin, *First Apology* 61; *Apostolic Tradition* 16—17).	Instruction in some of the heavier and some of the lighter commandments (*TB Yevamot* 47a).

---

[16]My translation.
[17]Falls, p. 337, translation modified.
[18]In the following table, I somewhat anachronistically combine elements from different periods and settings, especially in the Jewish column to the right. There is no reason why the Christian baptism ritual should not combine different elements in Jewish conversion procedure, belonging to different settings. E.g., immersion is not attested in *Joseph and Aseneth*, renouncing idols is not attested in *Yevamot*.

Christian baptism	Jewish proselyte baptism
Immediately before baptism: Exorcisms, prayer and fasting (*Didache* 7; *First Apology* 61; *Apostolic Tradition* 20.3-10).	Proselyte Aseneth praying and fasting (*Joseph and Aseneth* 10—13).
Candidate renouncing the Devil = rejection of idol worship (*Apostolic Tradition* 21.9).	Aseneth renouncing the Devil and idols (*Joseph and Aseneth* 10:8-13; 12:9-12).
Baptism preferably in "living [running] water," but also in a basin (*Didache* 7).	Baptism in "flowing water" (*Sibylline Oracles* 4:162-70), or in a *mikveh*.
Water to touch every part of the body, women should loosen their hair and take off all jewelry, nobody bring an alien object with them (*Apostolic Tradition* 21.5).	Water to touch every part of the body, women should untie their hair and nobody let an object come between the water and their body (*TB Bava Qamma* 82a/b).
After baptism: participation in first eucharist, bringing bread/wine as first offering (*First Apology* 65; *Apostolic Tradition* 20.10; 23.1).	After baptism: participation in first Passover meal; bringing of sacrifice (*M Pesahim* 8:8; *Keritot* 2:1).

This list could easily be prolonged, but it is sufficient to substantiate the impression voiced by two scholars who have studied the early Christian rituals in depth: "The one who studies Proselyte baptism closely, is surprised to see how many points of contact there are with early Christian baptism."[19] "Hippolytus's whole initiation rite is derived from the initiation of *Jewish* proselytes. His baptismal rite is derived directly from the baptismal rite for Jewish proselytes."[20] We shall now study some details more closely.

Pre-Baptismal Instruction
Didache 7.1 says, "Baptise, having first rehearsed all these things." "These things" refer to the catechism in *Didache* 1—6. This early Christian baptismal catechism is a very interesting document. One thing may be considered

---

[19]Joachim Jeremias, *Die Kindertaufe*, p. 34.
[20]Gregory Dix in the Introduction to Dix/Chadwick, p. xl.

beyond dispute: it is based on a Jewish catechism addressed to Gentiles; scholars therefore often refer to it as a "Jewish proselyte catechism."[21] That may be somewhat misleading, however. The original group of addressees becomes quite conspicuous in *Didache* 6.2-3: "If you can bear the whole yoke of the Lord, you will be perfect, but if you cannot, do what you can. And concerning food, bear what you can, but keep strictly from that which is offered to idols, for it is the worship of dead gods."[22] This is the only passage in the whole catechism concerned with ritual commandments; the rest is ethical. The most natural setting for an exhortation like this is to think of it as addressed to the God-fearing Gentiles who assembled in the synagogues of the Diaspora; *not* undergoing full conversion to Judaism, and therefore not obliged to obey all the ritual commandments of the Torah.[23]

So, very likely *Didache* chapters 1-6 were based on a Jewish catechism for Gentile God-fearers. The same document also seems to have been used by the author of the *Epistle of Barnabas* (ca. A.D. 130), chapters 18-21.

The format of this catechism is the simple scheme of "two ways": "There are two ways, one of life and one of death, and there is a great difference between the two ways. The way of life is this" (*Didache* 1.1-2). "The way of death is this" (*Didache* 5.1). Scholars have always recognized this pattern as typically Jewish,[24] even before the evidence now available in the Dead Sea Scrolls.[25] The teaching of the way of life is introduced by this significant summary:

First, you shall love the God who made you,
secondly, your neighbor as yourself;
whatever you wouldn't like to happen to yourself,
don't do it to another. (*Didache* 1.2, author's translation)

Two characteristics separate this summary from corresponding summaries by Jesus in the Gospels and unite it with Jewish parallels: (1) The "golden rule" is given in a negative, not positive, version; and (2) the golden rule is presented as an explanation of what it means to love your neighbor as yourself (Lev

---

[21]See Kurt Niederwimmer, *Die Didache*, Kommentar zu den Apostolischen Vätern 1 (Göttingen: Vandenhoeck & Ruprecht, 1989), pp. 48-64 (with full bibliography). English trans.: *The Didache: A Commentary*, ed. Harold W. Attridge (Minneapolis: Fortress, 1998).
[22]Kirsopp Lake 1:319.
[23]One is here reminded of the title of the *Didache*, which could contain the original title of the original Jewish document underlying chaps. 1-6 (with the words in parenthesis added by the Christian author): "The Lord's Teaching *to the Gentiles* (by the Twelve Apostles)."
[24]E.g., Adolf von Harnack, *Die Apostellehre und die jüdischen beiden Wege*, 2nd ed. (Leipzig: J. C. Hinrichs'sche Buchhandlung, 1896).
[25]See especially 1QS III, 20—IV, 14.

19:18). According to the rabbinic sources, Hillel the elder used the negative golden rule as a summary of the whole Torah precisely when addressing a prospective proselyte: "Whatever is hateful to you, do it not unto your fellow. This is the essence of the Torah, the rest being just its corollary; now go and study that!" (*TB Shabbat* 31a). That this principle is really a free quotation of "love your neighbor as yourself," is made plain in *Targum Jonathan*. Here Leviticus 19:18 is rendered: "Love your fellow man: what you dislike, do not unto him."[26]

In the exposition that follows this summary in the *Didache*, different commandments concerning the love of one's neighbor are combined; one may say that the author made a selection of commandments easy and difficult (beginning with some difficult sayings of Jesus about loving your enemy).

We now turn to an interesting rabbinic parallel to this catechism.[27] In *TB Yevamot* 47b we read that the candidate for conversion was (1) first to be asked for his reasons. If acceptable, (2) he was "given instruction in some of the minor and some of the major commandments." (3) Then he was given specific instructions concerning the sin of neglecting the commandments about "gleanings [Lev 19:9; 23:22], the forgotten sheaf [Deut 24:19], the corner [Lev 19:9; 23:22], and the poor man's tithe." Why precisely these commandments? A little earlier in tractate *Yevamot*, these same commandments were enumerated as such that were given for the profit of the (poor) proselyte, and consequently could attract proselytes for the wrong reasons: "they might be attracted by the gleanings, the forgotten sheaf, the corner and the poor man's tithe" (*Yevamot* 47a). Now, in the pre-baptismal instruction, the proselyte is reminded that as a full-fledged Israelite he is first and foremost obliged to do to others what he might crave for himself. In other words, the teaching about gleanings, etc. was probably to be seen as a concretization of Leviticus 19:18, "love your neighbor as yourself."[28]

In what follows, the catechism of the rabbis emphasized the grave consequences of becoming a full convert to Judaism: before, one would not be punished for eating forbidden fat or profaning the sabbath, but once the

---

[26]The same rendering of "as yourself" also in Lev 19:34. Cf. on this whole issue David Flusser, "A New Sensitivity in Judaism and the Christian Message," in Flusser, *Judaism*, pp. 469-89; esp. 478-79.

[27]In the following, I am using an extremely interesting study by David Daube, "A Baptismal Catechism," in Daube, *The New Testament and Rabbinic Judaism*, pp. 106-40.

[28]We know from other rabbinic sources that the rabbis of the first centuries A.D. were reluctant to quote only summaries of the Torah, such as the Ten Words or the Two Great Commandments, because they feared that by so doing they might support the opinion of the heretics, who only regarded such ethical commandments as valid, and all the others (ritual) as abrogated.

candidate has become a Jew, there is a death penalty for both violations. Finally, the candidate is given notice of the reward granted for the fulfilment of the commandments.

The parallel with *Didache* 1—6 is of course not perfect; it shouldn't be, because the talmudic instructions concern full converts to Judaism, while *Didache* 1—6 was probably based on a catechism for God-fearers only, who would not commit themselves to all the ritual commandments. But this basic difference granted, the remaining similarities in pre-baptismal instructions for Jews and Christians are significant. We move now to a variety of other similarities.

Fasting, Prayer and Exorcism

The most striking parallels to these three components of Christian preparation for baptism are to be found in Greek Jewish literature of a missionary nature, such as the third and fourth books of the *Sibylline Oracles* and the charming and somewhat mystical novel *Joseph and Aseneth* (probably first century B.C.).

Due to contact with idols, the convert from paganism was unclean as well as suspect of being possessed by an unclean spirit. The fasting and prayers were therefore mainly understood as "spiritual cleansing" (for the exorcistic effect of fasting and prayer, cf. Mt 17:21; Mk 9:29) and as expressions of repentance (this is especially emphatic in *Joseph and Aseneth*). The exorcisms were a kind of negative preparation for receiving the Holy Spirit in baptism. The temple of the body must be clean and ready to receive the Spirit; no foreign spirit may occupy it. *Barnabas* 16.7-10 says:

> Before we came to belief in God the habitation of our heart was corrupt and weak, like a temple really built with hands, because it was full of idolatry, and was the house of demons through doing things which were contrary to God. . . . But when we received the remission of sins, and put our hope on the Name, we became new, being created again from the beginning; wherefore God truly dwells in us, in the habitation which we are. . . . This is the spiritual temple being built for the Lord.[29]

Renouncing the Devil, Confessing Faith

Again it is *Joseph and Aseneth* which provides the closest parallels, and they are striking indeed. Tertullian and Hippolytus give us the wording of the

---

[29]Kirsopp Lake 1:399.

Christian renunciation formula:[30]

> We affirm that we renounce the devil and his pomp and his angels. (Tertullian, *The Crown* 3)

> We bear public testimony that we have renounced the devil, his retinue, and his works. (Tertullian, *The Shows* 4)

> I renounce you, Satan, and all your service and all your works. (Hippolytus, *Apostolic Tradition* 21.9)

Compare to this the following excerpts from Aseneth's prayer of penitence:

> I have come to hate their gods, and have destroyed them.

> Behold, the wild old lion persecutes me, because he is the father of the gods of the Egyptians, and his children are the gods of the idol maniacs. And I have come to hate them, because they are the lion's children, and have thrown all of them from me and destroyed them.

> Behold now, all the gods whom I once used to worship in ignorance: I have now recognized that they were dumb and dead idols, and I have caused them to be trampled underfoot by men. (*Joseph and Aseneth* 11:4; 12:9; 13:11)[31]

The meaning in both cases is quite clear: to renounce the devil is the same as to promise to take part no more in pagan worship.

Immediately upon the renunciation followed confession of faith in the Father, the Son and the Holy Spirit, in compliance with Jesus' command in Matthew 28:19. We have studied this part of the ritual in chapter fifteen. The parallels in *Joseph and Aseneth* are again quite close:

> Lord God of the ages, who created all things and gave life to them, who gave breath of life to Your whole creation. . . . You, Lord, spoke and they were brought to life, because Your word, Lord, is life for all Your creatures. With You I take refuge.

> With You I take refuge, Lord, . . . for just as a little child who is afraid flees to his father, and the father, stretching out his hands, snatches him off the ground . . . likewise You too, Lord, stretch out Your hands upon me as a child-loving father, and snatch me off the earth. (*Joseph and Aseneth* 12:1-3, 8)[32]

---

[30]The material is conveniently displayed in E. C. Whitaker, *Documents of the Baptismal Liturgy* (London: SPCK, 1970), pp. 5-10. The following translations of texts from Tertullian and Hippolytus are taken from this source.
[31]Charlesworth, *Pseudepigrapha* 2:218, 221, 223.
[32]Ibid., pp. 220-21.

The "Living Water" of Baptism

The rabbis used to distinguish between the cleansing power of different types of water according to two criteria:[33] "living" water ranked above "drawn" water,[34] and cold above hot. According to these criteria, six grades were established (enumerated in *Mishnah, Mikwaot* 1:1-8, from the lowest to the highest):

1. the water in ponds, cisterns, etc., containing less than forty seahs of undrawn water
2. the water of a rain-pond before the rain-stream has stopped
3. standing water in a pool of forty seahs or more
4. the water of a well, even if it has to be enriched with drawn water to reach forty seahs
5. smitten waters when running ["smitten": meaning salty or from a hot spring]
6. running water directly from a natural source

Category 6 was the real "heavy duty" cleansing water; it was required for the cleansing for flux (Lev 15:13: "He must immerse himself in living water," [author's translation]), for leprosy (Lev 14:5: cleansing by "living water"), and for the production of the cleansing water with ashes of the red heifer (Num 19:17). For ordinary immersion of men and women, water down to category 3 was acceptable; the same held true for proselyte baptisms.

In *Didache* 7 we find the following prescriptions concerning the water of baptism:

Baptise in the Name of the Father and of the Son and of the Holy Spirit
(a) in "living" water,
(b) but if you have no "living" water, baptise in other water,
    (1) and if you cannot in cold,
    (2) then in warm.
(c) But if you have neither, pour water three times on the head in the Name of the Father, Son and Holy Spirit.[35]

As is plain to see, the prescriptions about different kinds of immersion water are very close to the ruling of the *Mishnah*, at least in the evaluating principles applied. From the outside, no big difference would be observed

---

[33]See on this the very instructive excursus in Strack/Billerbeck 1:102-13, esp. pp. 108-9.
[34]This is often rendered as "running" water (for "living" water) and "stationary" (for "drawn"). But the real definition of "living water" is not that it is running, i.e., moving, but that it flows or has flown from a natural source of water, and has come from this source through an unbroken stream (as, e.g., a river or brook, a channel or pipes). "Drawn" water is water cut off from natural sources, as water in a bucket or rainwater in a pond when the rain has ceased.
[35]Kirsopp Lake 1:319/321, letters and numbers added.

between Jewish and Christian immersion of converts. If the community to which the *Didache* is addressed had no suitable river in the neighborhood and decided to build a baptismal pool, they would very likely build it according to the same standards as the Jewish ritual baths.

One also notices that one of the closest analogies to Gentile defilement, that of corpses, required sprinkling with the purifying water (Num 19:13-20). This could be the background for the emergency alternative of baptism by effusion in the *Didache*.

"Going Down, Coming Up"

In his analysis of Jewish proselyte baptism, David Daube called attention to the frequent use of the term "come up" (Hebrew, *'ala*) in connection with baptism. "When he has immersed and come up *[tabhal we'ala]* he is like an Israelite in all respects" (*TB Yevamot* 47b). Daube comments:

> The "coming up" was the decisive moment because of its symbolic meaning. . . .
> It is, for example, conceivable that among the reasons why the Baptist chose to
> baptize in the Jordan was that he saw in the "coming up" a new entry into the
> Promised Land. . . . Moreover, *'ala* figures prominently in the scene where
> Joshua [and the priests and the whole people] cross the Jordan dry-shod [Josh
> 4:14—5:18]. . . . As for Hillel's interpretation of proselyte baptism as a passage
> from death to life—*'ala* may denote "to rise from the grave." In fact, the "coming
> up" is expressly noticed in the narrative of Jesus' baptism as told by Matthew
> and Mark; conclusive evidence—if any still were needed—that Christian baptism originated in Jewish proselyte baptism.[36]

Having reconstructed the original idea attached to proselyte baptism— namely, the Gentile's belonging to the realm of the dead, and coming up alive from the waters of baptism, like a new-born child, like a newly created being—Daube compares this idea with some New Testament passages. But in early Christian writings after the New Testament, to which Daube does not refer, the parallels are even closer. Let us again look at a passage in *Barnabas*: "We go down into the water full of sins and foulness, and we come up, bearing the fruit of fear [of the Lord] in our hearts, and having hope on Jesus in the Spirit" (*Barnabas* 11.11).[37] Barnabas is here apparently using a quite conventional scheme of speaking about baptism and its significance: we "go down" in such-and-such a state; we "come up" in such and such a state.

---

[36]Daube, *New Testament*, pp. 111-12.
[37]Kirsopp Lake 1:383.

Compare the following saying of Hermas (Rome, ca. A.D. 140):

> Before a man bears the Name of the Son of God, he is dead. But when he receives the seal he puts away mortality and receives life. The seal, then, is the water [of baptism]: They go down into the water dead, and come up alive. (Shepherd of Hermas, *Similitude* 9.16.3-4)[38]

The rabbis could say that bringing a Gentile to conversion is like creating that person; that is, a new human being, a Jew, has come into existence (*Genesis Rabbah* 39). In *Barnabas*, Genesis 1:26 is referred to what happens in baptism: a new human being is created in the image of God (*Barnabas* 6.11-12). In several eastern baptismal liturgies, the "going down" and the "coming up" is interpreted as a going down to Sheol and a rising up from there to new life. This idea is probably already expressed in *Barnabas* 11.4, and certainly in the vision of Hermas in *Similitude* 9, in which "the stones" (believers) are brought into the "tower" of the church by being dragged through the water surrounding the tower. This water is the realm of Sheol; the patriarchs were waiting at the bottom of the water to be raised by baptism.[39] The stones laying around the tower (people now alive) have to pass through the water to be born again.[40]

Since we have emphasized the close parallels between Christian and Jewish ideas on baptism as a passage through (or rising from) Sheol and a birth to new life, it should be mentioned that there is one aspect of Christian baptismal theology which from the very beginning is uniquely Christian: that is the idea—most fully developed by Paul in Romans 6:1-11—that the baptized, through the baptismal experience, *is united with Christ:* dies with him, is buried with him, rises with him. But it is all the more striking that this uniquely Christian understanding is expressed most clearly by Paul at this early stage. In contrast, in Justin and the other writers of the second century, this idea is partly lost sight of, while Christian baptismal understanding is largely assimilating contemporary Jewish ideas.

---

[38]Kirsopp Lake 2:263.

[39]The whole concept of the descent into the waters of baptism being a descent to Sheol—and a subsequent raising to new life—has been extensively analyzed by Per Lundberg, *La typologie baptismale dans l'ancienne église,* Acta seminarii neotestamentici upsaliensis (Leipzig/Uppsala: Alfred Lorentz, 1942). His analysis is accepted by Daniélou, *Theology of Jewish Christianity,* pp. 233-48.

[40]Thus, when David Daube says (quotation in note 10 above) that "it is obvious that the notion of a new birth was taken . . . more seriously [by ancient Judaism] than it seems to be taken by modern Christianity," this statement is certainly not true about early Christianity!

Undressing and Dressing Anew

It was characteristic of Jewish immersions in general, therefore also of proselyte baptism, that no foreign object should intervene between the body and the water; therefore baptisms required complete nudity.[41] This means, of course, that prior to baptism there was a complete undressing, and after it a new clothing. It seems that very early this was accorded symbolic significance; Paul speaks repeatedly of undressing, "putting off" the old, sinful self and "putting on" Christ (Rom 13:12-14; Eph 4:24-25). "All of you who were baptized into Christ have clothed yourselves with Christ" (Gal 3:27 NIV).

We have solid evidence in the fourth century for the practice of reclothing the candidates after baptism, not with their own clothes, but with white garments. The symbolic significance of this is obvious and needs no explanation.[42] But it is difficult to know how old this rite of the white baptismal garment is. Jean Daniélou postulates that it may be of Judeo-Christian origin, and therefore integral to the baptismal rite from the beginning.[43] But his evidence is circumstantial and hardly conclusive. The silence about this in Hippolytus's otherwise very complete description should make one cautious about sweeping generalizations.

Post-Baptismal Anointing

In all bathing in antiquity, the use of oil or chrism played the same role as soap and lotions today. It is therefore hardly necessary to ask when and how anointing became part of the baptismal rite; one should rather ask when the anointing was given a ritual significance, a theological interpretation. This is difficult to answer, but the following passage in Justin *may* indicate that post-baptismal anointing was interpreted as part of the baptismal ritual already in his days: "The mystery of the lamb which God ordered you to sacrifice at the Passover was truly a type of Christ, with whose blood the believers . . . *anoint* their homes, that is, themselves" (*Dialogue with Trypho* 40.1).[44] This might also facilitate Justin's concept of all believers as anointed priests (*Dialogue with*

---

[41]Cf. p. 360 above.

[42]Cf. the material gathered in Daniélou, *The Bible and the Liturgy*, pp. 49-53.

[43]*Theology of Jewish Christianity*, pp. 326-29. Daniélou, points to the white garments worn by initiates of the Essene community according to Josephus, *Jewish War* 2.8.7 [137], the white robes associated with the festival of Tabernacles (mainly New Testament evidence, esp. in the heavenly scenes in Rev 4:4; 6:11; 19:14), and the white robes mentioned in a tabernacles setting in Hermas, *Similitude* 8.2.1-4.

[44]Falls, p. 208, italics added.

Trypho 116-17). Tertullian is more explicit:

> After that we come up from the washing and are anointed with the blessed unction, following that ancient practice by which, ever since Aaron was anointed by Moses, there was a custom of anointing them for priesthood with oil out of a horn. That is why [the high priest] is called an anointed [a "christ"], from *chrism* which [is Greek for] anointing: and from this also our Lord obtained his title, though it had become a spiritual anointing, in that he was anointed with the Spirit by God the Father. (*On Baptism* 7)[45]

In Hippolytus the post-baptismal anointing by the bishop—and *only* by the bishop—had definitely developed into a separate rite with its peculiar significance. Exactly *which* significance is difficult to ascertain, due to the uncertainty concerning which reading of Hippolytus's text at this point should be considered original. There is a long and a short version:

Long	**Short**

The Bishop shall lay his hand upon them invoking and saying:
"O Lord God, who did count these worthy of deserving the

forgiveness of sins by the laver of regeneration, make them worthy to be filled with Thy Holy Spirit and send upon them Your grace,	*forgiveness of sins by the laver of regeneration through the Holy Spirit, send upon them Your grace,*

that they may serve You according to Your will; to You be the glory, to the Father and to the Son with the Holy Spirit in the Holy Church, both now and ever and without end. Amen." After this, pouring the consecrated oil and laying his hand on his head, he shall say: "I anoint you with holy oil in God the Father Almighty and Christ Jesus and the Holy Spirit." And sealing him on the forehead, he shall give him the kiss [of peace] and say: "The Lord be with you." And he who has been sealed shall say: "And with your spirit." And so he shall do to each one. (*Apostolic Tradition* 22.1)[46]

According to the long text, the anointing on the forehead by the bishop confers the Holy Spirit. This corresponds to the opinion of Tertullian, some fifteen to twenty years earlier, except that Tertullian focuses on the bishop's laying on of hands, rather than the anointing: "Next [after the anointing] follows the imposition of the hand in benediction, inviting and welcoming the

---

[45]Whitaker, *Documents*, p. 8.
[46]Translation of the long version according to Dix/Chadwick, *Apostolic Tradition*, p. 38. The short version is my own translation and emphasis.

Holy Spirit" (*On Baptism* 8).[47] This interpretation of the anointing/laying on of hands after baptism became standard in the Western church, and when this rite, for practical reasons, was postponed some years in the case of children, it developed into the separate sacrament of *(con)firmation:* the anointing by the bishop conferred a new *strengthening* (Latin, *firmatio*) by the Spirit.

But this agreement of the long text in Hippolytus with later ecclesiastical practice makes it suspect as an adaptation to the opinions of a later time, whereas the short text is not subject to any such suspicion. Moreover, the short text is difficult to explain as an accidental shortening of the long text. This is so because the short text is an almost literal allusion to Titus 3:5: "the washing of rebirth and renewal by the Holy Spirit."[48]

According to the short text, then, the Holy Spirit was conferred in the baptismal immersion itself, which agrees with the view of *Barnabas* quoted above. This leaves the post-baptismal anointing uninterpreted in Hippolytus's text, but it would be no unlikely assumption that the interpretation hinted at in Justin, and made manifest in Tertullian—*priestly* anointing—is the right one in Hippolytus, too.

The new element in Hippolytus's description of the anointing is that the bishop—presumably with his finger in the oil on the candidate's oiled forehead—"seals" the baptized ("sealing him on the forehead"). All later evidence indicates that this means that the bishop signed him with the sign of the cross.[49] Now, the letter *tav* in old Hebrew script was a simple cross, and this reminds us of Ezekiel 9:4: "Go throughout the city, Jerusalem, and put a mark [tav] on the foreheads of those who grieve and lament" (NIV). We do not have evidence that allows us to conclude with any certainty that signing with the cross/tav on the forehead was an old baptismal rite, deriving from Judeo-Christians familiar with the original meaning of Ezekiel 9:4. But the following notice in Origen (A.D. 230s) is of considerable interest. When a Jewish believer in Jesus was asked about the meaning of Ezekiel 9:4, the man gave the following answer:

---

[47]Whitaker, p. 8.

[48]The short reading in Hippolytus is preserved in Latin only: *per lavacrum regenerationis sp[irit]u[s] s[an]c[t]i.* The old Latin of Tit 3:5 is: *per lavacrum regenerationis et renovationis Spiritus sancti.* Bernard Botte, in his comment on the issue, claims that this correspondence with Tit 3:5 was created by sheer "accident graphique"—in my view highly unlikely. Bernard Botte, *Hippolyte de Rome: La Tradition Apostolique,* Sources Chrétiennes 11bis. (Paris: Du Cerf, 1968), p. 89. Cf. the extensive discussion in G. W. H. Lampe, *The Seal of the Spirit* (London: SPCK, 1967), pp. 139-45.

[49]Cf. Daniélou, *Bible and the Liturgy,* pp. 54-69.

The old way of writing the Taw was in the form of the cross, so here [Ezek 9:4] we have a prophecy of the sign that later was to be signed on the foreheads of Christians; and also of what believers now do, when they sign themselves whenever they begin a work, and especially before prayers and the holy readings.[50]

The Baptismal Eucharist

Most early descriptions of Christian baptism emphasized that from the baptismal waters the candidate was immediately introduced to the community of the "brethren" and shared with them his or her first Eucharist. Two features of this "baptismal Eucharist" deserve mention in this context. (1) The first is the idea that bringing bread and wine forward to the altar—to be used in the Eucharist—was considered *an offering*, a sacrifice. (We shall have more to say on the concept of the Eucharist as sacrifice in chapter nineteen). As we remember, bringing a sacrifice was the third and last element of the three requirements for converts to Judaism. (2) At the baptismal Eucharist, and in this one only, the baptized was given milk and honey in addition to bread and wine. This liturgical practice is mentioned by Hippolytus (*Apostolic Tradition* 23.2) and is probably presupposed already by *Barnabas* (ca. A.D. 130): Milk and honey, the nourishment of the land promised to the fathers, he says, is the food of *new-born babies*; we enter the promised land as new-born, being created anew [in baptism] (*Barnabas* 6.8-19).[51]

When we consider the Eucharist as a remodeled Passover meal, we have the interesting sequence of baptism followed by the baptized person's first Passover meal. Could this be relevant to the question of Jewish background? To this subject we now turn.

The Season for Baptism

When one reads in Hippolytus the very extensive instruction program and the many ceremonies to be conducted on and by the baptismal candidates, it

---

[50]Origen, *Selecta in Ezechielem* 9. Cf. on this whole issue Hugo Rahner, "Das mystische Tau," in *Symbole der Kirche: Die Ekklesiologie der Väter* (Salzburg: Otto Müller Verlag, 1964), pp. 406-31; and the shorter but instructive comments in Daniélou, *Theology of Jewish Christianity*, pp. 154-56.

[51]The classic study of this midrash-like passage in *Barnabas* is Nils A. Dahl, "La terre où coulent le lait et le miel selon Barnabé 6,8-19," *Aux sources de la tradition chrétienne: Mélanges offerts à M. Maurice Goguel*, Bibliothèque théologique (Neuchâtel: Delachaux & Niestlé, 1950), pp. 62-70. Cf. also Leslie W. Barnard, "A Note on Barnabas 6,8-17," in *Studia Patristica* 4.2, Texte und Untersuchungen 79 (Berlin: Akademie-Verlag, 1961), pp. 263-67.

seems obvious that this was not repeated for individual candidates each week, but that we should rather think of a large baptismal "class" being gathered, then baptized together at a fixed point in time. This is directly confirmed by Tertullian, who has the following to say:

> The Passover provides the day of most solemnity for baptism, for then was accomplished our Lord's passion, and into it we are baptized. . . . After that, Pentecost is a most auspicious period for arranging baptisms, for during it our Lord's resurrection was several times made known among the disciples, and the grace of the Holy Spirit first given.[52] . . . For all that, every day is a Lord's day: any hour, any season, is suitable for baptism. If there is a difference in solemnity, it makes no difference to the grace. (*On Baptism* 19)[53]

No rabbinic text is explicitly concerned with the season preferred for proselyte baptism; but it is nevertheless interesting to notice the following: in the period when sacrifice had to be offered by the proselyte (i.e., before A.D. 70), conversion and baptism had to be combined with pilgrimage to the temple in Jerusalem. And it may be more than a coincidence that the rabbinic discussions in the Mishnah, concerning when and how a proselyte should be considered fit for full participation in worship, concern only his first participation in the Passover meal. It is not at all unlikely that pilgrimage for Passover was the prime occasion for the conversion ceremonies in Jerusalem.[54] As we have seen, the proselyte was thought to make the same experience in his or her conversion as the Israelites did during the exodus.

But one could also say that the proselyte during conversion was placed at Sinai, receiving the Torah; which means that Shavuot could also be a natural season for conversion. But there is no direct evidence to substantiate this assumption.

---

[52]It is obvious that by "Pentecost" Tertullian here means the whole fifty-day period between Passover and Shavuot. Cf. further comments on this text in chapter nineteen.
[53]Whitaker, p. 9.
[54]Cf. the argument to this effect in Daube, p. 122. David Flusser states without any reservations: "It is an unknown fact that the custom of baptism of neophytes at the night of Easter is the sequel of the Jewish custom of baptism of proselytes in the evening of Passover. . . . This custom is well attested in Jewish sources, and it is clear why the proselytes liked to be baptized at the evening of Passover, having been circumcised some days before: they were permitted to eat the Passover lamb, which is, according to the Law of Moses, forbidden to the uncircumcised. Thus, this Jewish custom passed to Christianity; those who became Christians were baptized at the night of Easter and were admitted to the Eucharist, a symbol of Christ—the Paschal lamb" ("Some Notes on Easter and the Passover Haggadah," *Immanuel* 6 [1976]: 52-60; quotation p. 60).

Baptism, Spirit and New Life

Having reviewed the many parallels between Jewish and Christian baptismal rites, it may be time to emphasize an aspect of Christian baptism which is markedly new, at least with regard to the emphasis it has in the early sources: Christian baptism *confers the Spirit* and the effective power at work in baptism is the Spirit. We have displayed some of the material on this already in chapter seventeen.

Here it should be added that there is clearly an *ethical* side to the theme of baptism and the Spirit. The Holy Spirit simply cannot coexist with sin. That is why Hippolytus has his long list of occupations that are incompatible with admission to the catechumenate (cf. above, p. 230). That is why many of the earliest fathers say that *after* baptism one is not supposed to continue in sin.

The meaning of this is clearly not to teach a doctrine of general sinlessness among believers. It should rather be understood in the context of conversion from paganism: a Christian cannot continue to live as a pagan. The typical sins of paganism were three, according to the rabbis, and these three cardinal sins were mentioned as those a Jew should under no circumstances commit, even under threat of death: idolatry, murder, fornication.[55]

One can easily observe in many early Christian enumerations of sins that a Christian should put behind at conversion, that they are organized according to these three cardinal sins. Many sins are quite simply variants—perhaps sophisticated variants—of the three basic ones; for example, greed for money being a variant of idol worship.

At baptism the Spirit is conferred; the Spirit cannot coexist with sin. We can see how this motif is often used in early Christian exhortations to lead a new life. Here one example must suffice. The Roman writer Hermas (140s) seems not to have been a very high-cultured man, but possibly a representative of the lower strata of the Christian community at Rome. He had, however, a profound perception of the ethical dimension of the Spirit's presence in the life of believers.

> Guard this flesh of yours pure and undefiled, that the Spirit which dwells in it may bear it witness, and your flesh may be justified. See to it, lest the idea enter your heart that this flesh of yours is mortal, and you abuse it in some defilement. For if you defile your flesh you defile also the Holy Spirit, and if you defile the flesh you shall not live. (Shepherd of Hermas, *Similitude* 5.7.1-2)[56]

---

[55]Cf. the rabbinic material gathered in Strack/Billerbeck 1:255.
[56]Kirsopp Lake 2:169.

Be . . . long-suffering and prudent and you shall have power over all evil deeds and shalt do all righteousness. For if you are courageous the Holy Spirit which dwells in you will be pure, not obscured by another evil spirit, but will dwell at large and rejoice and be glad with the body in which it dwells, and will serve God in great cheerfulness, having well-being in itself. But if any ill temper enter, at once the Holy Spirit, which is delicate, is oppressed, finding the place impure, and seeks to depart out of the place, for it is choked by the evil spirit, having no room to serve the Lord as it will, but is contaminated by the bitterness. (Shepherd of Hermas, *Mandate* 5.1.1-3)[57]

In this charmingly simple and perhaps naive way, Hermas gives expression to the profound insight that the Spirit and sin are opposites, just as the Spirit and death are irreconcilable. In his own way, Hermas is repeating the warning of Paul: "Do not grieve the Holy Spirit of God, with which you were marked with a seal for the day of redemption. Put away from you all bitterness" (Eph 4:30).

In conclusion, it has become clear through the foregoing presentation that a strong consciousness of living in the realm and time of the Spirit permeates every aspect of early Christian faith and practice, not just baptism. According to the New Testament texts, the gift of the Spirit was the new element in Christian baptism, the new element that distinguished it from John's. Turning from sin and idolatry, turning to fellowship with the true God and his renewed people, being included in the new Spirit-filled temple, the Christian community—all of this was experienced pneumatology. (Since this whole chapter has brought out the temple dimension of the theme, it has been a sufficient "Temple Square" for this chapter.)

Suggestions for Further Reading

A useful collection of source texts in translation is André Benoît and Charles Munier, eds., *Die Taufe in der Alten Kirche (1.-3. Jahrhundert)*, Traditio Christiana 9 (Bern: Peter Lang, 1994). Cf. also Whitaker, *Documents.*

Important studies:

Bernard J. Bamberger, *Proselytism in the Talmudic Period* (Cincinnati, Ohio: Hebrew Union College, 1939; 2nd ed. New York: Ktav, 1968), esp. pp. 38-52; Per Lundberg, *La typologie baptismale dans l'ancienne église*, Acta seminarii neotestamentici upsaliensis 10 (Leipzig/Uppsala: Alfred Lorentz, 1942); G. W. H. Lampe, *The Seal of the Spirit: A Study in the Doctrine of Baptism and Confirmation in the New Testament and the Fathers* (London/

---

[57]Ibid., pp. 87, 89, translation modified.

New York: Longmans, Green, 1951; 2nd ed. London: SPCK, 1967); André Benoît, *Le Baptême chrétien au second siècle: La théologie des Pères,* Études d'histoire et de philosophies religieuses de l'Université de Strasbourg 43 (Paris: Presses Universitaires de France, 1953); David Daube, "A Baptismal Catechism," in *The New Testament and Rabbinic Judaism* (London: School of Oriental and African Studies, The University of London, 1956 [Peabody, Mass.: Hendrickson, reprint without date]), pp. 106-40; Joachim Jeremias, *Die Kindertaufe in den ersten vier Jahrhunderten* (Göttingen: Vandenhoeck & Ruprecht, 1958); Jean Daniélou, *The Bible and the Liturgy* (Notre Dame, Ind.: Notre Dame University Press, 1966), chaps. 2-7; Gedalyahu Alon, "The Levitical Uncleanness of Gentiles," in Alon, *Studies,* pp. 146-89; Simon Légasse, *Naissance du baptême,* Lectio Divina 153 (Paris: Éditions du Cerf, 1993); Lars Hartmann, *'Into the Name of the Lord Jesus': Baptism in the Early Church* (Edinburgh: T & T Clark, 1997); Thomas M. Finn, *From Death to Rebirth: Ritual and Conversion in Antiquity* (New York: Paulist, 1997); Shaye J. D. Cohen, "Crossing the Boundary and Becoming a Jew," and "The Rabbinic Conversion Ceremony," in *The Beginnings of Jewishness: Boundaries, Varieties, Uncertainties* (Berkeley: University of California Press, 1999), pp. 140-74 and 198-238.

19

WORSHIP &
CALENDAR
THE CHRISTIAN
WEEK AND YEAR

*O*nly rarely do people put down in writing what they do on a regular basis, day in, day out, week by week, year by year. That is why our sources on early Christian worship are indeed meager and mainly consist of scattered, often accidental references to practices that were so self-explanatory to the author and audience that no one saw the necessity of expanding on the issue. The most explicit evidence for the early period occurs in texts written for or by outsiders.

Claiming that Christian worship and order of worship (liturgy) sprang from Jewish roots is today a commonplace in scholarly work. Opinions vary, however, as to how soon and how radically Christian worship broke out of the Jewish mold. In this chapter we will mainly review the pre-Constantinian evidence.

Freedom and Order

Many modern readers, reading 1 Corinthians 12 and 14, think of the worship life of the early Christians as rather unstructured, informal, very spontaneous, very charismatic—much like a modern pentecostal prayer and witness meeting. One should not forget, however, that many of the first believers—also in the Diaspora—came from a background with a very structured form of worship and prayer: that of the ancient synagogue. Before A.D. 70 believers in Jerusalem also regularly attended the times of prayer in the temple (Acts 2:46; 3:1; 5:12).

A comparison of Jewish and Christian patterns of worship and prayer during the first century A.D. seems to show a basic similarity: in both camps there was a combination of freedom in wording and stability in themes and patterns. (It does not even take one generation, by the way, before the same phenomenon characterizes even the most charismatically "free" Christian groups; they are much more stereotyped in their prayer formulations and their order of procedure than they themselves realize.)

It is the stability in themes and patterns that is most easily documented by the written sources, of course, but even the freedom and variation in wording is sometimes mentioned or presupposed. After presenting some model prayers for use at Holy Communion—which we here call by its early name, *Eucharist*—the *Didache* (ca. A.D. 100) says, "But allow the prophets to say the eucharistic prayer the way they like" (*Didache* 10.7). Some hundred or more years later, the Roman presbyter Hippolytus, having produced a complete handbook of liturgic rituals, says the following as an epilogue to his model prayers: Let the bishop pray according to these models, and let no one hinder him or judge him if he simply does so. But if he deviates, "no one shall prevent him. Only let his prayer be thanksgiving to God, but let each one pray according to his ability. If indeed he is able to pray suitably with a grand and elevated prayer, this is a good thing. But if . . . he should pray and recite a prayer according to a fixed form, no one shall prevent him" (*Apostolic Tradition* 10.3-5).[1]

Our sources in the New Testament and the earliest Christian writings after the New Testament are neither sufficient nor explicit enough to allow us to reconstruct in detail how the first believers modified and re-structured their Jewish ways of worship. Some rough outlines, however, and a few scraps of detailed information can be discerned. We shall try to put some of it together in the following exposition—but must warn the reader that this is a very complex subject, and the experts who master the Jewish as well as the early Christian material perfectly are few indeed. What we offer here is no complete survey, but rather an attempt to draw some main contours.

The Big Novelty of Christian Worship: The First Day

When studying the links between Jewish and Christian worship, we have to

---

[1]Dix/Chadwick, p. 19.

distinguish (1) the daily prayer; (2) the weekly worship; and (3) the annual festivals. In first-century Judaism, prayer—privately and in the temple—was daily; Scripture reading weekly (each Sabbath in the synagogue); and the Passover meal once a year. In second-century Christianity all three elements—prayer (communal), Scripture reading (with exposition = sermon) and the eucharistic meal—were combined in the *weekly* assembly each Sunday morning. This shows how important *the first day*[2] was to the early Christians, and that the cycle of the *week* became the most important one. Otherwise it is difficult to explain that the Christian version of the Passover meal, the Eucharist, was celebrated weekly, on Sunday, rather than annually.

This central position accorded to Sunday, especially Sunday morning, is no doubt something distinctly new in Christian worship, compared with Jewish. This in itself is sufficient to indicate—from a purely historical point of view—that Sunday owes its central position to a startlingly important event associated with that day. According to the New Testament, there is no doubt as to what that event was: the resurrection of Jesus from the dead and the encounters of the disciples with the risen one (these seem mostly to have happened during the first day of the week; cf. Jn 20:1-9; 20:19; and 20:26).[3]

If we use our imaginations and try to feel ourselves into the experience of the first believers when they came together only a few weeks or a few months after the resurrection of their Lord, it is not difficult to understand that they wanted to celebrate the renewed fellowship with him and among themselves frequently—indeed, if possible, continuously. (Conversely, only once a year: an impossible idea!) This makes Luke's brief notice in Acts 2:46 ring true: in the beginning they met daily.[4] But as time went on, it was the weekly meeting on Sunday that attracted to itself most attention and most elements of Christian worship. Some scholars believe that the meal which believers shared during their weekly assembly may originally have been meant to celebrate the renewed table-fellowship with Jesus, the risen one, as a resumption of the

[2]In the New Testament, "the first day of the week" is most often called by this Jewish name (Greek, *hē mia [hēmera] tōn sabbatōn*) (Lk 24:1; Acts 20:7; Jn 20:1,19; 1 Cor 16:2, etc.); once "the day of the Lord" (Rev 1:10). Justin, writing for a Gentile audience, is the first to use the Roman-pagan name of the day: "the day of the Sun[god]."
[3]On early Christian Sunday celebration, see Willy Rordorf, *Sunday*, and Richard Bauckham, "The Lord's Day," in *From Sabbath to Lord's Day: A Biblical, Historical, and Theological Investigation*, ed. D. A. Carson (Grand Rapids, Mich.: Academie Books, Zondervan, 1982), pp. 221-50.
[4]Their meeting place, the temple, was also a place for daily worship, unlike the synagogue, which in the first century A.D. was only used for regular communal worship on the sabbath.

table fellowship they had with him before the last Passover. It was not celebrated as a memory of Jesus' death and his last Passover meal. This latter
idea was Paul's invention; he was the first who understood the story of Jesus'
last meal as instituting a new, permanent liturgical celebration in the church.
According to this theory, Paul's version of the Lord's meal was to become the
dominant view, gradually superseding or being combined with the first.[5]
This theory would no doubt help to explain the strange phenomenon of a
weekly Passover meal, but we are on very feeble grounds here and should
not dress hypotheses, however brilliant, as facts.[6]

What can hardly be doubted, though, is that the Christian custom of making the weekly Sunday service the very center of all worship life cannot be
understood except as something that originated during that early period—
weeks and months of enthusiasm; a feeling of living in a definitely new age;
the days of the resurrection![7]

There is and was, however, a relevant parallel in Judaism to this custom of
celebrating an event weekly, an event which is also celebrated annually: each
Sabbath is in some measure a small *Sederabend*, a Passover night in miniature,
in which the exodus is remembered. In the same way each Sunday is an Easter Sunday; the same event is celebrated annually as well as weekly. Maybe
this parallel helped the first believers to establish their double pattern of celebrating the resurrection: each week, as well as once a year.

So much by way of introduction to the Christian week. The same principle
may be observed at work behind the Christian year. What happened to Jesus
was what shaped the Christian week; what happened to Jesus (and his community of believers) also shaped the Christian year. Of the main Jewish
annual festivals—Passover, Shavuot (Pentecost), Tabernacles, New Year's
Day, Yom Kippur, Hanukkah—only Passover and Shavuot were taken over

---

[5]This is—very simplified—the ingenious theory put forward in Hans Lietzmann's groundbreaking study *Mass and Lord's Supper* (for full reference, see Suggestions to chapter twenty).
[6]In Lietzmann's study, the meal prayers and liturgy of *Didache* 9—10 belong to the non-
Pauline, non-Passover type of meal fellowship with the risen Lord. In the next chapter (on
the Eucharist) I am going to argue that the eucharistic prayers of the *Didache* are best understood precisely from a Passover meal background.
[7]In the study of Samuele Bacchiocchi, *From Sabbath to Sunday: A Historical Investigation of the
Rise of Sunday Observance in Early Christianity* (Rome: Pontifical Gregorian University, 1977,
and several later editions), the author does his best to downplay any significance of the first
day of the week prior to the middle of the second century A.D., when, according to him, the
community of Rome was able to impose on the rest of the church Sunday worship, which
was invented in Rome. For cogent criticism of Bacchiocchi, see Richard Bauckham, "Sabbath and Sunday in the Post-Apostolic Church," in Carson, *Sabbath to Lord's Day*, pp. 251-
98, esp. pp. 270-73; and otherwise in other articles in that volume.

and reinterpreted among Christians. Very likely Jewish believers continued to take part in the ordinary celebration of all the Jewish festivals, but they do not seem to have changed them or wanted them observed by Gentile believers—except, that is, Passover and Pentecost. At these festivals, and these only, something new and fundamental happened to Jesus: he died and rose from the dead, ascended to heaven and fulfilled his promise of giving the Spirit.

On the other hand, the significance of the fact that these events *did* coincide with major Jewish festivals should not be underestimated. Sunday was the only new festal day the early believers instituted. It would not have been strange had they also celebrated the birth of Jesus or, for example, his baptism by John. But in the New Testament records, these events are not dated to any existing Jewish festival. Accordingly, it was only after some three hundred years that the Gentile church began celebrating these events, and then they were fixed according to the Roman calendar, not the Jewish.

Having stated this concerning the newness as well as the continuity of the Christian week and year, compared with the Jewish background, let us look a little more closely into the development of the order of worship.

Sunday Worship

In the New Testament we find only short notices about regular Sunday worship (e.g., Acts 20:7; 1 Cor 16:2; Rev 1:10), but scholars have tried to piece together the few scraps of information contained in these passages and others. In Acts 20:7 there is a meal and a sermon on Sunday evening; the meal could be the Eucharist described by Paul in 1 Corinthians 10:14-17; 11:17-34.[8] In Revelation, many scholars think that the hymns and prayers said in heaven may more or less closely resemble those used in John's community.

Two passages in the Apostolic Fathers deal explicitly with Sunday worship, the first from *Didache* and the second from Ignatius:

---

[8]For extensive argumentation for this understanding of the text (Sunday rather than Saturday evening, and the eucharistic meal), see M. Max B. Turner, "The Sabbath, Sunday, and the Law in Luke/Acts," in *From Sabbath to Lord's Day: A Biblical, Historical, and Theological Investigation*, ed. D. A. Carson (Grand Rapids, Mich.: Academie Books/Zondervan, 1982), pp. 99-157, esp. pp. 128-33; and Roger T. Beckwith, "The Day: Its Divisions and Its Limits in Biblical Times," in *Calendar and Chronology, Jewish and Christian: Biblical, Intertestamental and Patristic Studies*, Arbeiten zur Geschichte des antiken Judentums und des Urchristentums 33 (Leiden: E. J. Brill, 1996), pp. 1-9. Beckwith here demonstrates that the later Jewish custom of reckoning the day from sunset till sunset was not yet firmly established in the first century A.D., and that the alternative reckoning of a day from sunrise to sunrise was as common, and that one and the same (Jewish) author could use both, e.g., Josephus.

On "the Lord's [Day]" of the Lord [Greek, *kata kyriakēn de kyriou*] come together, break bread and hold eucharist, after confessing your transgressions that your offering may be pure; but let none who has a quarrel with his fellow join in your meeting until they be reconciled, that your sacrifice be not defiled. (*Didache* 14.1-2)[9]

Very likely, this service took place in the evening. In *Didache* 10.1 it says about the Eucharist: "After you are satisfied with food," which indicates that the eucharistic meal was the main meal of the day; hence the evening meal. (Some other aspects of this passage will be discussed later.)

If then they who walked in ancient customs came to a new hope, no longer living for the Sabbath, but for the Lord's Day, on which also our life sprang up through Him and His death . . . and by this mystery we received faith. (Ignatius, *To the Magnesians* 9.1)[10]

This passage from Ignatius establishes the reason for this day: Christ's resurrection. And if the celebration of Christ's resurrection was the main purpose of the Sunday assembly, should we not expect it to take place Sunday morning?

Our next witness to the Sunday worship is an outsider, in fact a Roman officer interrogating apostate Christians about their "secret" meetings. In A.D. 112 the emperor's envoy to Bithynia, Pliny, got the following information concerning Sunday worship:

[Those who had been Christians but were so no longer, under interrogation] asserted that . . . their custom had been to gather *before dawn* on a fixed day and to sing a hymn antiphonally to Christ as to a God, and to bind themselves by an oath, not for any crime, but to abstain from theft, robbery, adultery, breach of faith, and not to deny a deposit when demanded. When this was done, it had been their custom to separate, and to *meet again to take food*, but ordinary, harmless food.[11]

One cannot exclude the possibility that Pliny misunderstood some of what he was told; on the other hand there is no need to assume he did, provided we can make sense of his information. The main point is clear: Christians met twice on Sunday, first early in the morning, then some time later. The first meeting was apparently without Eucharist. In the second meeting the meal—presumably the Eucharist—was the main point.

---

[9]Kirsopp Lake 1:331, translation modified.
[10]Ibid., p. 205.
[11]Pliny the Younger, *Epistle* 10.96, my translation and italics.

The information on the morning assembly has confused historians of liturgy: Singing hymns is no surprise, but what about taking an oath about not stealing etc.? This is not mentioned in any other early report on the Sunday liturgy, whereas we know that candidates for baptism had to commit themselves to lead a life according to the commandments. Accordingly, Hans Lietzmann suggested that what is at stake here is the preparation of baptismal candidates for baptism, and that this is why the community leaves before the Eucharist: they go to the nearest river to baptize, and then return for the Eucharist, together with the newly baptized.[12]

One of the problems with this solution is that it makes the entire Sunday morning service very long. We have to keep in mind that Sunday was—in the entire pre-Constantinian epoch—a normal day of work. This means that on Sunday the only time available for worship gatherings was early in the morning, before work began, and in the evening, after work was finished. Unlike the Jews (who could sometimes spend the whole day in the synagogue on the sabbath), Christian believers—Jews or Gentiles—had their work to worry about on their day of worship.[13]

There is, however, another possibility of explaining Pliny's report, suggested by experts on Jewish liturgy. It is known from the Mishnah that in the synagogues of the first century—and in the temple—the recital of the *Shema* was introduced by, among other things, a recital of the Ten Commandments. Later this was dropped, according to the Talmuds, "because of the insinuations of the heretics," namely, that only the Ten Commandments were God's revealed law, or only they were still valid.[14] Considering the central position of the *Shema* in Jewish worship, especially the sabbath services, it would be no surprise if Christians took over the recital of the full *Shema* in their weekly morning service. This would include the recital of the Decalogue; hence Pliny's information that they pledged not to steal, commit

---

[12]Hans Lietzmann, "Die liturgischen Angaben des Plinius," and "Carmen = Taufsymbol," in *Kleine Schriften 3: Studien zur Liturgie- und Symbolgeschichte, zur Wissenschaftsgeschichte,* Texte und Untersuchungen 74 (Berlin: Akademie-Verlag, 1962), pp. 48-53, 54-55. The same point of view is also argued by D. H. Tripp, "Pliny and the Liturgy—Yet again," in *Studia Patristica* 15, no. 1 (1984), pp. 581-85. Tripp thinks that Pliny's question, to which the apostate Christians answered, was something like "how were you initiated into Christianity?" Accordingly they would tell him about the baptismal service. Cf. also F. J. van Beek, "The Worship of Christians in Pliny's Letter," *Studia Liturgica* 18 (1988): 121-31.
[13]The attempts by Beckwith, Stott, and others to prove that Christians from the very beginning not only worshiped on Sunday, but also tried to abstain from work on Sunday, are in my view unsuccessful. For criticism, see Bauckham, "Sabbath and Sunday," pp. 280-84.
[14]*TJ Berakhot* 1:4; *TB Berakhot* 12a.

adultery, etc.[15] This must, of course, remain a hypothesis, but we shall see an additional argument for it later. If correct, it would definitely support the interpretation that Pliny was told about a worship service without Eucharist Sunday morning, then a Eucharist celebration in the evening.

We now turn to the first extensive description of the Sunday service, found in Justin, writing in Rome ca. A.D. 150:

> On the day called Sunday all [believers] who live in cities or in the countryside gather together at one place, and the memoirs of the Apostles or the writings of the Prophets are read, as long as time permits. Then, when the reader has finished, the president of the assembly in a speech admonishes and invites all to imitate such examples of virtue. Then we all rise together and pray, and . . . when our prayer is ended, bread and wine and water are brought, and the president likewise offers up prayers and thanksgivings, to the best of his ability, and the people express their approval by saying "Amen." Then there is a distribution to each and a consumption of that over which thanks were given, and to those who are absent a portion is sent by the deacons. The wealthy, if they wish, contribute whatever they desire, and the collected means are placed in the custody of the president, who cares for orphans and widows and those who are in need because of sickness or any other reason, and the captives and strangers in our midst. In short, he takes care of all those in need. Sunday is the day on which we all hold our common assembly, because it is the first day on which God, having transformed the darkness and matter, created the world. And Jesus Christ our Saviour on the same day rose from the dead. (*First Apology* 67.3-7)[16]

In this description, we may already recognize the structure that was to be kept in all later forms of Christian Sunday worship:

* Scripture reading
* Expository sermon
* Common prayer

---

* Bringing forward bread and wine
* Eucharistic prayer
* Partaking of bread and wine
* Bringing donations for the poor

---

[15]See the argument for this theory in Roger T. Beckwith, *Daily and Weekly Worship: From Jewish to Christian*, Alcuin/GROW Liturgical Study 1 (Bramcote, Nottingham: Grove Books, 1987), pp. 34-35.
[16]*ANF* 1:186.

This service clearly has two parts, which historians of liturgy often call (1) "the service of the word" and (2) "the eucharistic service." As we have seen in Pliny and the other evidence, these two parts were originally—at least in some places—independent of each other and celebrated at different times on Sunday: the service of the word early in the morning, the Eucharist at ordinary mealtime in the evening. What has happened in Justin's community is that the Eucharist has been transported from the evening meal into the service of the word in the morning.

This no doubt did something significant to the Eucharist: it was no longer embedded in a real meal. We shall pursue this in the next chapter. Here we shall add more comments on the first element in Justin's description.

The Service of the Word

The Scripture reading of the ancient synagogue was twofold: (a) a reading from the Torah, either in a three to three-and-a-half year cycle (land of Israel) or a one-year cycle (Babylon, probably from the second century A.D., and present practice); and (b) a suitable reading from the Prophets to supplement the Torah reading, the *haftarah*, "the supplement, completion" (in the first century A.D. these readings were probably not yet fixed, but could be chosen from time to time, cf. Lk 4:17).[17] Many scholars believe that from the beginning, the Gospels were read in Christian worship very much like the Torah in Jewish; that is, the Gospels were read in continuous order, the readers taking up next Sunday where they left off the Sunday before. When Justin says that the reading is continued each Sunday "as long as time permits," this would indicate such a continuous reading. To this Gospel reading an appropriate *haftarah* from the Prophets would then be added.[18]

Later—the date of this change is not known—this continuous reading of

---

[17]On the reading from the Bible and the cycles of reading in the ancient synagogue, see C. Perrot, "The Reading of the Bible in the Ancient Synagogue," in *Compendia 2:1:* 137-59; Lawrence H. Schiffman, "The Early History of Public Reading of the Torah," in *Jews, Christians, and Polytheists in the Ancient Synagogue: Cultural Interaction During the Greco-Roman Period*, ed. Steven Fine, Baltimore Studies in the History of Judaism (London and New York: Routledge, 1999), pp. 44-56; Lee E. Levine, *The Ancient Synagogue: The First Thousand Years* (New Haven, Conn./London: Yale University Press, 2000), pp. 506-10. These authors emphasize the very great fluidity and variety in the cycles followed, in the first as well as the second century A.D., and in different places. Even after the Mishnah was published early in the third century not everything was settled.

[18]Provided the *or* in Justin's report is not meant as an absolute alternative, in which case the reading would be either from the Gospels or the Prophets. But it could well mean "and/or also."

the Gospels was abrogated and instead one began to read fixed portions, not in the Gospel sequence, for each Sunday. It seems that this occurred when the Christian year gained importance, which happened early in the first half of the fourth century. (The festival days had their own fixed readings for the occasion, and with an increasing number of festival days, the continuous reading would be too frequently interrupted.)[19] At the same time the reading from the Prophets was suppressed, and instead came a reading from the New Testament epistles (or Acts or Revelation), the so-called "epistle." In this way the medieval and modern practice developed: a set series of readings, called "gospel" and "epistle." This set of fixed passages, *pericopae*, was finally settled in the western church by the sixth century, but its roots are certainly older.[20]

The sermon is described like this by Justin: "When the reader has finished, the president of the assembly in a speech exhorts and invites all to imitate such examples of virtue." In the synagogue tradition the sermon was also often called "a word of exhortation," as in Acts 13:15. This exhortatory character of the sermon corresponds to the character of early Christian sermons that have come down to us in writing, for example, the so-called *Second Epistle of Clement* (ca. A.D. 125-150).[21]

It seems that only on special occasions, such as Easter or in the instruction of candidates for baptism, were the central themes of salvation through the cross and resurrection of Jesus made the main focus of the sermon. A typical example of this is Melito of Sardis's paschal homily (ca. A.D. 175) on Christ as the true paschal lamb.[22]

---

[19]It is interesting to notice Mishnaic (and other rabbinic) evidence indicating that the Jews had the same problem, see M *Megillah* 3:4 and comments in Levine, *Synagogue*, pp. 507.

[20]In parts of the Eastern Church, the Old Testament reading was retained alongside the two from the New Testament, resulting in a threefold Scripture reading. For further information on the Scripture readings in the early church period, see Josef Jungmann, *Missarum Sollemnia*, pp. 501-90; A. Chavasse, "Les plus anciens types du lectionnaire et de l'antiphonaire romains de la messe," *Revue bénédictine* 62 (1952): 3-94; J. A. Lamb, "The Place of the Bible in the Liturgy," in *The Cambridge History of the Bible*, ed. P. R. Ackroyd and C. F. Evans (Cambridge: Cambridge University Press, 1970), 1:563-86.

[21]On this writing, see Karl P. Donfried, and Ernst Baasland, "Der 2. Klemensbrief und frühchristliche Rhetorik: 'Die erste christliche Predigt' im Lichte der neueren Forschung," in Haase, *Aufstieg* 2 27.1:78-157. Generally on early Christian sermons, D. G. Hunter, ed., *Preaching in the Patristic Age: Studies in Honor of Walter J. Burghardt, S.J.* (New York: Paulist, 1989).

[22]Since the sensational discovery of this text in 1936, a lot has been written about it. A very good point to start is the most recent full-scale study of Melito's sermon, which also contains extensive bibliography: Alistair Stewart-Sykes, *The Lamb's High Feast: Melito, Peri Pascha and the Quartodeciman Paschal Liturgy at Sardis*, Supplements to Vigiliae Christianae 42 (Leiden: Brill, 1998).

A prayer of praise and intercession followed the sermon and in some cases possibly also introduced the service. Justin gives some interesting hints concerning the themes of these prayers, and may also give us some clues as to their forms.

1. Justin reports on the *intercessory* prayers made for the newly baptized, apparently at the beginning of the service:

> We offer hearty prayers in common for ourselves and for the baptized person, and for all others in every place, that we may be accounted worthy, now that we have learned the truth, by our works also to be found good citizens and keepers of the commandments, so that we may be saved with an everlasting salvation. Having ended the prayers, we salute one another with a kiss. (*First Apology* 65.1-2).[23]

We notice here the prayer "to be found keepers of the commandments" would accord well with the hypothesis that a recital of the *Shema*, including the Decalogue, was part of the morning service.[24]

2. The element of *praise* comes through in another passage: "For all things wherewith we are supplied, we bless the Maker of all through His Son Jesus Christ, and through the Holy Spirit" (*First Apology* 67.2).[25] Maybe Justin is here referring to the blessing at meals rather than during Sunday worship. In any case, we have here a clear indication that Christians continued to use the Jewish "blessing" (Hebrew, *berakah*) format in their prayers of thanksgiving for food, drink and other gifts from God the creator (on this, see more below, pp. 407-8).

The Christian Day and Week

As was mentioned earlier, prayer was daily—three times a day—in Judaism at the time of Jesus, based on biblical precedent (Dan 6:10,13; Ps 55:17). This determined the ordinary frequency of private prayer on weekdays, and communal prayer on Sabbaths, the normal form of prayer being that which, maybe somewhat later, was stereotyped as the fixed *Tefillah* (or *Amidah* or *Eighteen [Blessings]*).

Apart from this, the Jewish week used Mondays and Thursdays as days for gathering of the rabbinical courts, and also for fasting. Fasting was not obligatory or regular on these days, but if for any special occasion fasting seemed required, these were the days preferred. In Luke 18:12, the Pharisee

---

[23]*ANF* 1:185.
[24]See above, pp. 383-84.
[25]Ibid., pp. 185-86.

obviously took pride in his regular fasting "twice a week," as being something more than normal.

In the *Didache* we meet this Jewish practice of prayer and fasting in the following modification:

> Let not your fasts be with the hypocrites, for they fast on Mondays and Thursdays, but do you fast on Wednesdays and Fridays.
>
> And do not pray as the hypocrites, but as the Lord commanded in his Gospel, pray thus:
>
> > Our Father, who are in heaven,
> > hallowed be your name,
> > your kingdom come,
> > your will be done, as in heaven, so also upon earth;
> > give us today our daily bread,
> > and forgive us our debt as we forgive our debtors,
> > and lead us not into trial,
> > but deliver us from the Evil One,
> > for yours is the power and the glory for ever.
>
> Pray like this three times a day. (*Didache* 8.1-3)

In short, the "Our Father" has taken the place of the *Tefillah;* Wednesday and Friday have taken the place of Monday and Thursday. *Didache* will make us believe that these days were chosen as fasting days in conscious opposition against Pharisaic/rabbinic practice. That may be true, but it is not difficult to imagine that the choice of *Friday* had a much less anti-Pharisaic reason: it was by no means unnatural that if Sunday was the day for believers to rejoice, Friday was the day to fast. But why Wednesday? It seems that Wednesday as well as Friday were days of special importance in the Essene calendar of the Qumran scrolls. Maybe *Didache*'s two days of fasting are closer to Judaism than the author would make us think.[26]

The Christian Year

The only festivals of the Jewish calendar that coincided with fundamental events in the life of Jesus and the first community of disciples were Passover and Weeks (Shavuot, Pentecost).[27] These, accordingly, underwent a reinter-

---

[26]More on this in Talley, *Liturgical Year* (full ref. in Suggestions), pp. 27-31; and Wilson, *Strangers*, pp. 224-25. See also the quite recent discussion of this issue in J. A. Draper, "Ritual Process and Ritual Symbol in *Didache* 7-10," *Vigiliae Christianae* 54 (2000): 121-58.

[27]The best general study from recent years is probably still Talley, *Liturgical Year*.

pretation and modification and were observed by all believers, whether they be Jewish or Gentile. The other festivals of the Jewish calendar were certainly observed by the Jewish believers, but as national, not Jesus-centered festivals, and therefore not by Gentile believers. In this way the Christian year originated, having one festive season, and one only: the time from Passover to Weeks. As in Judaism, this entire period seems to have been regarded as one festive season rather than two festivals separated by an "empty" period of time.

Passover (Pesach) and Easter

First, some remarks on the date of Passover. According to Exodus 12:6-8, the paschal lamb was to be slaughtered and eaten on the evening of the 14th of Nisan. There is a discrepancy between John and the Synoptics concerning the date of the death of Jesus. According to the Synoptics, Jesus ate the Passover meal with his disciples the evening before his crucifixion on Friday, which means that Thursday must have been the 14th of Nisan, Good Friday the 15th. According to John, Jesus died on the same day as the high priest and his fellows were to eat the paschal lamb (Jn 18:28), which means that according to John Good Friday was the 14th of Nisan, and that Jesus died on the cross at the same time as the paschal lambs were slaughtered in the temple (cf. Jn 19:14; 19:36).

Various attempts have been made to harmonize this apparent contradiction—most of them assuming that different calendars were used in the time of Jesus; John following one, the Synoptics another.[28] No solution has so far succeeded in gaining general acceptance.

Now, on which day should Christians celebrate their Passover? Should they synchronize their celebration with the Jewish feast, and if so, should they follow the Synoptic chronology or that of John? Or perhaps they should do neither, but give preference to the fact that Jesus rose from the dead on a Sunday? These questions gave rise to prolonged and heated debates.

In Asia Minor some thought it right to celebrate Passover on the same night as the Jews. They kept a fast on the eve of the 14th of Nisan and cele-

---

[28]There is a wealth of literature on this issue, also treated in most Gospel commentaries. For a classic discussion, assuming discrepancy between a Pharisaic and a Sadducean calendar, see Strack/Billerbeck 2:812-53. In recent years, the theory of a discrepancy between the Essene calendar and the "official" one has been proposed; Jesus and his disciples following the Essene, the representatives of the Sanhedrin (Jn 18:28) following the "official." Cf. for this theory Annie Jaubert, *The Date of the Last Supper* (Staten Island, N.Y.: Alba House, 1965). It is followed, among others, by Bargil Pixner.

brated the resurrection of Jesus at daybreak on the 15th of Nisan, irrespective of what weekday the 15th of Nisan might be. These so-called *quartodecimans* ("fourteeners") apparently did not view their paschal eve and night as a commemoration of Jesus' last meal with his disciples, but as a remembrance of Jesus' death.[29] In other words, they may have followed John's chronology, for their joyous celebration of his resurrection on the morning of the 15th of Nisan would hardly be compatible with the Synoptic chronology, according to which Jesus was nailed to the cross that day.

The alternative to the quartodeciman position was to give priority to Sunday as the day of the resurrection, which meant that the Paschal fast and vigil would always begin on Saturday evening. One could then choose the first Sunday after the 15th of Nisan (Synoptic chronology, followed in Rome) or after the 14th of Nisan (Johannine chronology, followed in Alexandria) as Easter Day.[30]

The debate between these two positions commenced about the middle of the second century A.D. and lasted for some decades. The fact that this controversy took place at all, is by itself a strong testimony to the close links that still existed between Jewish Passover and Christian Easter. But one could also argue that the fact that the quartodeciman position did not prevail indicated the beginning of an alienation on the Christian side—at least it made it necessary for Jewish believers in Jesus to choose whether they would celebrate Passover on the same evening(s) as their compatriots or on Saturday evening together with other Christians. A glimpse of the strikingly "Jewish" quartodeciman celebration is provided in the Passover homily by Melito of Sardis

---

[29]Bernhard Lohse, *Das Passafest der Quartadecimaner*, Beiträge zur Förderung christlicher Theologie, 2. Reihe, 54 (Gütersloh: Bertelsmann, 1953) has expounded the theory that the quartodeciman Passover was totally dominated by the expectation of Christ's return. Lohse interprets the fast as a vicarious fasting for the unbelieving Jews. His interpretation has been criticized by Wolfgang Huber, *Passa und Ostern: Untersuchungen zur Osterfeier der alten Kirche* Beihefte zur Zeitschrift für die neutestamentliche Wissenschaft 35 (Berlin: Alfred Töpelmann, 1969) and others, rightly so. There is no solid evidence that the *contents* of the quartodeciman Passover were different from elsewhere in the church. The entire debate was a debate on date, not contents. Cf. also the excellent discussion of the issue in Josef Blank, *Meliton von Sardes: Vom Passa*, Sophia, Quellen östlicher Theologie 3 (Freiburg im Breisgau: Lambertus-Verlag, 1963), 26-42; and Alistair Stewart-Sykes, *The Lamb's High Feast: Melito, Peri Pascha and the Quartodeciman Paschal Liturgy at Sardis*, Supplements to Vigiliae Christianae 42 (Leiden: Brill, 1998).

[30]It is not explicitly stated in the ancient sources that the difference between Rome and Alexandria should be explained from Synoptic or Johannine chronology; but it seems a reasonable proposal. There is a useful discussion of the issue in Huber, *Passa und Ostern*, pp. 53-55 with notes (and with a conclusion different from mine).

(ca. A.D. 175).[31] He developed a Christian Passover Haggadah from Exodus 12. The dominant motif is Jesus as the true paschal lamb. Melito's homily may be described as anticipated in 1 Corinthian 5:7: "For our paschal lamb, Christ, has been sacrificed."

The Sunday option carried the day, however, and quartodeciman practice seems to have dwindled towards the end of the second century. But an important legacy of the Jewish celebration lived on in the church, irrespective of the question of date: the celebration of the entire Passover event within the time-span of one night and morning. It is only when we come to the Constantinian era that we see a development away from this "Jewish" way of focusing on the one single Passover night (cf. below, chapter twenty-one).

When we turn to the content, the ideas associated with Passover, we also find many interconnections between the Jewish festival and early Christian theology of Easter. Many paschal motifs were taken up by the earliest fathers. Justin Martyr says:

> The mystery of the (paschal) sheep . . . was a type of Christ, with whose blood they who believe on Him anoint their own houses, namely themselves, corresponding to their faith in Him. (*Dialogue with Trypho* 40.1)

> They that were saved in Egypt, when the first-born of the Egyptians perished, were rescued by the blood of the Passover, which was smeared on either side of the posts and the upper lintel. For Christ was the passover, who was sacrificed later, as also Isaiah said: "He was led as a sheep to slaughter.". . . But as the blood of the Passover saved them that were in Egypt, so also will the blood of Christ rescue them that have believed. (*Dialogue with Trypho* 111.4)

Note especially the close connection between the paschal motif and Christian baptism.[32] Sometime during the second century A.D. Easter day emerged as the preferred day for baptism. Many paschal motifs have baptismal connotations.

In the Passover Haggadah the liberation from Egypt is described in terms that transcend the physical delivery as such. They are reminiscent of the terminology used to describe the transition experienced by converts to

---

[31]The current edition is Stuart G. Hall, *Melito of Sardis: On Pascha and Fragments*, Oxford Early Christian Texts (Oxford: Oxford University Press, 1979). Huber's argument to the effect that Melito was not a quartodeciman does not carry conviction. The ancient sources say that he was; cf. Blank, op. cit.; Hall, pp. xxiv-xxv; and Stewart-Sykes, *The Lamb's High Feast*.

[32]The concept of anointing is clearly baptismal. There are other baptismal motifs in the context of both passages. See the more extensive discussion of this theme in Justin in Skarsaune, *The Proof from Prophecy*, pp. 299-303.

Judaism (cf. chapter eighteen above):

> Therefore we are bound to thank, praise, laud, glorify, extol, honour, bless, exalt,
> and reverence Him, . . . for He brought us forth
>> from bondage to freedom,
>> from sorrow to joy,
>> from mourning to holydays,
>> from darkness to great light,
>> and from servitude to redemption.[33]

A similar concept is echoed in several New Testament passages, but the closest is found in Melito's paschal homily. The following passage really reads like a Christianized version of the Passover Haggadah:

> For, Himself [Christ] led as a lamb, and slain as a sheep, He ransomed us from
> the world's service as from the Land of Egypt, and freed us from the devil's sla-
> very as from the hand of Pharaoh. . . . It is He who delivered us
>> from slavery to liberty,
>> from darkness to light,
>> from death to life,
>> from tyranny to eternal royalty,
> and made us a new priesthood.[34]

One final point: In the Passover Haggadah, the gift of the land and entry into the land play a dominant role. Keeping in mind that baptism was often associated with the paschal event, one is not surprised to find that in a baptismal midrash *Barnabas* uses Exodus 33:1, 3 ("Lo, thus says the Lord God, enter into the good land, . . . a land flowing with milk and honey") as a major baptismal text (*Barnabas* 6.8-19). He says that, through baptism, people enter the land of milk and honey.[35] According to the first extensive description of the baptismal liturgy written by Hippolytus at the beginning of the third century, milk and honey were given to the newly baptized at

---

[33] Roth, *The Haggadah: A New Edition* (London: Soncino, 1959) pp. 36-37.
[34] Melito, *On Pascha* 67-68; cf. Stuart G. Hall, "Melito in the Light of the Passover Haggadah," *Journal of Theological Studies*, n.s., 22 (1971): 29-46; David Flusser, "Some Notes on Easter and the Passover Haggadah," *Immanuel* 6 (1976): 52-60; Stewart-Sykes, *The Lamb's High Feast*, esp. pp. 31-54; and Karl Gerlach, *The Antenicene Pascha: A Rhetorical History*, Liturgia condenda 7 (Leuven: Peeters, 1998), pp. 61-78.
[35] Two excellent commentaries on this passage of Barnabas are Nils A. Dahl, "La terre où coulent le lait et le miel selon Barnabé 6,8-19," *Aux sources de la tradition chrétienne: Mélanges offerts à M. Maurice Goguel*. Bibliothèque théologique (Neuchâtel: Delachaux & Niestlé, 1950), pp. 62-70; and Leslie W. Barnard, "A Note on Barnabas 6,8-17," *Studia Patristica* 4.2, Texte und Untersuchungen 79 (Berlin: Akademie-Verlag, 1961), pp. 263-67.

their first Eucharist—a symbol of their entry into the promised land (cf. above, chapter eighteen).

The Jewish Festival of Weeks (Shavuot) and Christian Pentecost
Many scholars think that the links between Jewish Shavuot and Christian Pentecost are feeble, maybe nonexistent. An excellent introduction to our discussion may be found in the following succinct summary of current scholarly opinion concerning the Jewish festival:

> Like the Passover, the Feast of Weeks was eventually related to the history of salvation, but this connexion was made at a far later date. Ex 19:1 says that the Israelites reached Sinai in the third month after they had left Egypt; and since they had left Egypt in the middle of the first month, the Feast of Weeks became the feast commemorating the Covenant at Sinai. 2 Chron 15:10 mentions that under Asa, a religious feast was held in the third month to renew the covenant, but it does not expressly state that this was the Feast of Weeks. The first time the connexion is openly mentioned is in the *Book of Jubilees,* which puts all the covenants it can discover in the Old Testament (from Noah to Sinai) on the day of the Feast of Weeks. The Qumran sect, too, which called itself the community of the New Covenant, celebrated the renewal of the Covenant on the Feast of Weeks, and this was the most important feast in its calendar. Among orthodox Jews, however, the Feast of Weeks always remained of secondary importance. It is omitted from the calendar of Ezek 45:18-25, and (apart from liturgical texts) it is mentioned only in late books of the Old Testament, and only in connexion with something else (2 Macc 12:31f. and Tob 2:1). The Mishnah gives a complete treatise to all the annual feasts except this one, and the idea that it commemorated the day on which the Law was given on Sinai was not accepted by the Rabbis until the second century of our era. The Christian feast of Pentecost had, from the first, a different meaning. According to Acts 2, it was marked by the gift of the Holy Spirit and by the calling of all nations into the new church. The fact that it coincides with a Jewish feast shows that the old system of worship has passed away, and that the promises which that system foreshadowed are now fulfilled. But there is no connexion between the Christian Feast of Pentecost and the Feast of Weeks as understood by the Qumran community or, in later days, by orthodox Judaism. The story in Acts contains no allusion to the Sinaitic Covenant nor to the New Covenant of which Christ is the mediator.[36]

The latter part of this summary, especially the last clause, has been successfully challenged by Georg Kretschmar in an important article on early Chris-

---

[36]Roland de Vaux, *Ancient Israel,* vol. 2: *Religious Institutions* (New York/Toronto: McGraw-Hill Books, 1965), pp. 494-95.

tian Pentecost. Following Kretschmar, we shall review the early Christian material once more, looking for traces of Jewish Shavuot.[37]

First, we should notice that before the fourth century A.D. there was no separate festival of the Ascension of Christ on the 40th day after Easter. Ascension was celebrated at Pentecost and was often more central to this festival than the effusion of the Spirit as recounted in Acts 2. This must mean that in the pre-Constantinian church the Christian festal calendar around Pentecost was not quite simply derived from Acts.

Second, we should notice the following quote from Tertullian:

> The Passover affords the most solemn day for baptism, for on that day the passion of our Lord, in which we are baptized, was fulfilled. . . . After that, Pentecost is a most joyous time for conferring baptisms. During this time the resurrection of the Lord was frequently repeated among the disciples, the grace of the Holy Spirit was given, and the hope of the advent of the Lord indicated in so far as the angels at that time, when he had been received back into the heavens, told the apostles that "He would so come, as He had ascended into the heavens," namely at Pentecost. And, moreover, when Jeremiah says, "And I will gather them together from the extremities of the land in the feast day" (Jer 31:8), he signifies the day of Passover and [besides] Pentecost, which is really one great feast day (Tertullian, *On Baptism* 19).[38]

The decisive point to notice here is that "Pentecost" primarily refers to the whole fifty-day interval following Easter. During this Pentecost period the resurrection, ascension, and giving of the Spirit are celebrated as one single event. When Tertullian says that even the resurrection was "frequently repeated," he probably has in mind the repeated appearances of Jesus.

Such an attitude toward, and such a celebration of, the fifty days following Passover is unlikely to have derived directly from Acts. Where, then, is the background to such a practice?

We turn to the Jewish calendar as found in the Mishnah. On the day following the first day of Passover (i.e., on the 16th of Nisan), the first sheaf of barley was solemnly reaped outside Jerusalem and carried to the temple, there to be waved before the Lord as the first fruit of the year's barley har-

---

[37]Georg Kretschmar, "Himmelfahrt und Pfingsten," *Zeitschrift für Kirchengeschichte* 66 (1954/ 1955): 209-53. Kretschmar's study is taken a step further in Jürgen Boeckh, "Die Entwicklung der altkirchlichen Pentekoste," *Jahrbuch für Liturgik und Hymnologie* 5 (1960): 1-45. In what follows, I am deeply indebted to these two studies.

[38] Translation modified from ANF, 3:678.

vest.[39] The ceremony marked the official beginning of the harvest season, whence the fifty days leading to Shavuot were counted. The Festival of Weeks marked the end of the wheat harvest, signified by the waving of two loaves of leavened bread baked from newly-harvested grain. These loaves are probably to be seen as complements as well as contrasts to the unleavened loaves that were eaten during Passover/Festival of Unleavened Bread *(Mazzot)*. The fiftieth day's festival marked the final end of Passover as well as of the grain harvest. The rabbis noted this feature by calling the festival of Weeks "the Closing of the Passover."

One would expect such a period to be one of joy, but rabbinic literature does not treat it as such. It is rather a time for sorrow and mourning, a fact which probably reflects the post-70 A.D. situation, following the destruction of the temple and the cessation of the offering of first fruits. Jewish tradition explains the sorrow of these days by referring to a plague that killed many of Rabbi Akiba's disciples. Very likely, this season in the pre-70 situation was a time of joy, dominated by the idea of the first fruits being gathered from the fields.

Against this background let us review some New Testament passages: "Very truly, I tell you, unless a grain of wheat falls into the earth and dies, it remains just a single grain; but if it dies, it bears much fruit" (Jn 12:24). "Christ has been raised from the dead, the first fruits of those who have died" (1 Cor 15:20). In passing, let us also note that, according to John's chronology, Jesus was resurrected on the 16th of Nisan, the very day of the offering of barley first fruits in the temple! A third passage from the New Testament applies the concept of first fruits to the Spirit: "We know that the whole creation has been groaning in labor pains until now; and not only the creation, but we ourselves, who have the first fruits of the Spirit, groan inwardly while we wait for adoption" (Rom 8:22-23).

None of these passages makes explicit reference to the festal cycle of the church, but the first two are related to the time of Passover. They may indicate motifs present in the Jewish calendar, which could easily be reinterpreted and given a profound Christian significance. Is this not the kind of Christian adaptation we meet in Tertullian? Christ's resurrection and the gift of the Spirit are both conceived as first fruits, celebrated during the fifty days of first fruits of grain in the Jewish calendar. That seems to make very good sense.

---

[39]The reader is strongly advised to look up the vivid description of the reaping scene in *M Menahot* 10:2-4 (Danby, pp. 505-6).

There is more, however, to be said of the fiftieth day itself, Shavuot strictly speaking. Ephesians 4:8 informs us that Christ gave the church charismatic ministries. The text does so while referring to an Old Testament proof text, Psalm 68:18: "When he ascended on high . . . he gave gifts to his people" (Eph 4:8). The Old Testament text is thus taken as a pentecostal text. It closely relates Christ's ascension with the gift of the Spirit (or charisms): Christ ascended and gave the Spirit. In rabbinic sources we find this text from Psalms applied to Moses: He ascended Mount Sinai and came back with a gift, the gift of the Torah. It thus seems that Paul has used a rabbinic proof text concerning the giving of the law at Sinai and made it speak of the giving of the Spirit. Why would he do that?

If we take a closer look at Acts 2, two features claim our attention: First, the tongues "as of fire" (Acts 2:3); second, that the proclamation of the gospel is "split up" into several languages, so that it may be understood by all present. Turning to rabbinic interpretations of Exodus 19 (Moses ascending Sinai and God giving the Torah), we note that in the Hebrew text of verse 16 the theophany of God is accompanied by "thunders," or, more literally, "voices" (Hebrew, *qoloth*). The rabbis fastened on this word. They said that at Sinai God's voice "split up" into several voices. They further combined this notion with the poem concerning God's voice in Psalm 29. Verse 7 of this psalm reads, "the voice of the LORD flashes forth flames of fire." From this they concluded that at Sinai God's voice split up into seven voices which appeared as flames of fire. Later exegesis further elaborated on this. The seven voices became seventy languages (tongues), so that all the seventy peoples of the earth, assembled at Sinai, could understand God's voice.[40]

It is therefore hardly correct to state that "the story in Acts contains no allusion to the Sinaitic Covenant" (R. de Vaux, quoted above). True, the rabbinic texts are comparatively late (no quoted rabbi is earlier than the second century A.D.). But the fact that the New Testament seems to contain such indisputable echoes of rabbinic ideas is, in itself, a strong argument for an early date for the rabbinic concepts, and the consistent application of these ideas to the Pentecost season in the New Testament is an argument that Sinai and Shavuot were already combined in mainstream Judaism in New Testament times. In that case, the sectarian emphasis on Shavuot in *Jubilees* and in Qumran could be seen as early stages in the development of the idea, not iso-

---

[40]The rabbinic material is collected in Kretschmar's article (see note 37).

lated occurrences totally unrelated to the theology of the rabbis.[41] Thus we may conclude that, although the sources partly fail us, there is every reason to think that, below the surface, there are many subtle lines of connection between Jewish Shavuot and Christian Pentecost. In several Scripture reading cycles of the post-Constantinian church, Exodus 19 crops up as the reading for the Sunday of Pentecost. This is hardly directly derived from the New Testament, and it testifies to continued points of contact between Jews and Christians.

Suggestions for Further Reading
An excellent single-volume survey of the theme of this chapter is Paul F. Bradshaw, *Early Christian Worship: A Basic Introduction to Ideas and Practice* (London: SPCK, 1996). Cf. also the more extensive study by the same author: *The Search for the Origins of Christian Worship: Sources and Methods for the Study of Early Liturgy* (London: SPCK, 1992).

A short but instructive booklet on our theme is Roger T. Beckwith, *Daily and Weekly Worship: From Jewish to Christian*, Alcuin/GROW Liturgical Studies 1 (Bramcote, Nottingham: Grove Books, 1987).

A collection of articles focusing on Jewish roots is Eugene J. Fisher, ed., *The Jewish Roots of Christian Liturgy* (New York/Mahwah: Paulist, 1990). Cf. also Paul F. Bradshaw and Lawrence A. Hoffman, *The Making of Jewish and Christian Worship*, Two Liturgical Traditions 1 (Notre Dame, Ind./London: University of Notre Dame Press, 1991).

Other comprehensive surveys:
The classic on all aspects of the development of what became the Mass (Sunday morning service), is Josef Andreas Jungmann, *Missarum Sollemnia: Eine genetische Erklärung der römischen Messe*, 2 vols. (Vienna: Verlag Herder, 1952). Cf. also the same author's briefer survey: *The Early Liturgy to the Time of Gregory the Great* (Notre Dame, Ind.: University of Notre Dame Press, 1959; reprint London: Darton, Longman & Todd, 1960, and later); Cheslyn Jones, Geoffrey Wainwright and Edward Yarnold, eds., *The Study of Liturgy* (London: SPCK, 1978 and reprints); Jean Daniélou, *The Bible and the Liturgy* (Notre Dame, Ind.: University of Notre Dame Press, 1956; paperback ed. 1966).

On Sabbath and Sunday:
A useful collection of sources in translation: Willy Rordorf, *Sabbat und Sonntag in der Alten Kirche*, Traditio Christiana 2 (Zürich: TVZ-Verlag, 1972). French ed.: *Sabbat et dimanche dans l'Église ancienne*, Traditio Christiana 2 (Paris/Neuchâtel: Delachaux et Niestlé, 1972).

---

[41]For an extensive argument for an early (pre-Christian) date of Shavuot as commemoration of the giving of the law at Sinai, cf. Moshe Weinfeld, "Pentecost as Festival of the Giving of the Law," *Immanuel* 8 (1978): 7-18. Weinfeld argues that Ps 50 and 81 and also 2 Chron 15:10-15 refer to the Festival of Weeks.

Important studies include Willy Rordorf, *Der Sonntag: Geschichte des Ruhe- und Gottesdiensttages im ältesten Christentum,* Abhandlungen zur Theologie des Alten und Neuen Testaments 43 (Zürich: Zwingli-Verlag, 1962); English trans.: *Sunday: The History of the Day of Rest and Worship in the Earliest Centuries of the Christian Church* (London: SCM Press/New York: Westminster Press, 1968).

Roger T. Beckwith and Wilfrid Stott, *This Is The Day: The Biblical Doctrine of the Christian Sunday in Its Jewish and Early Church Setting* (London: Marshall, Morgan & Scott, 1978). Beckwith's contribution to this book ("The Sabbath and Sunday," pp. 2-47) is reprinted with some revisions in idem, *Calendar and Chronology, Jewish and Christian: Biblical, Intertestamental and Patristic Studies,* Arbeiten zur Geschichte des antiken Judentums und des Urchristentums 33 (Leiden: E. J. Brill, 1996), pp. 10-50.

R. Goldenberg, "The Jewish Sabbath in the Roman World up to the Time of Constantine the Great," in Haase, *Aufstieg 2* 19.1:414-47.

D. A. Carson, ed., *From Sabbath to Lord's Day: A Biblical, Historical and Theological Investigation* (Grand Rapids, Mich.: Academie Books/Zondervan, 1982), esp. chaps. 8, "The Lord's Day," and 9, "Sabbath and Sunday in the Post-Apostolic Church," by Richard J. Bauckham, pp. 221-98.

On Passover/Easter/Pentecost:

An excellent collection of source texts is Raniero Cantalamessa, *Ostern in der Alten Kirche,* Traditio Christiana 4 (Bern: Peter Lang, 1981), English trans.: *Easter in the Early Church* (Collegeville, Minn.: Liturgical Press, 1993).

Important studies include the following: Georg Kretschmar, "Himmelfahrt und Pfingsten," *Zeitschrift für Kirchengeschichte* 66 (1954/1955): 209-53.

Annie Jaubert, *La date de la cène: Calendrier biblique et liturgie chrétienne* (Paris: Gabalda, 1957). English trans.: *The Date of the Last Supper* (New York, 1965).

Willy Rordorf, "Zum Ursprung des Osterfestes am Sonntag," *Theologische Zeitschrift* 18 (1962): 167-89.

Wolfgang Huber, *Passa und Ostern: Untersuchungen zur Osterfeier der alten Kirche,* Beiheft zur Zeitschrift für die neutestamentliche Wissenschaft 35 (Berlin: Alfred Töpelmann, 1969)

Stuart G. Hall, "Melito in the Light of the Passover Haggadah," *Journal of Theological Studies,* n.s., 22 (1971): 29-46.

Anthony J. Saldarini, *Jesus and Passover* (New York: Paulist Press, 1984).

Thomas J. Talley, *The Origins of the Liturgical Year* (New York: Pueblo, 1986).

William L. Petersen, "Eusebius and the Paschal Controversy," in *Eusebius, Christianity and Judaism,* ed. Harold W. Attridge and Gohei Hata, Studia Post-Biblica 42 (Leiden/New York/Cologne: E. J. Brill, 1992), pp. 311-25.

Roger T. Beckwith, "Easter and Whitsun: The Origin of the Church's Earliest Annual Festivals," in *Calendar and Chronology, Jewish and Christian: Biblical, Intertestamental and Patristic Studies,* Arbeiten zur Geschichte des antiken Judentums und des Urchristentums 33 (Leiden: E. J. Brill, 1996), pp. 51-70.

20

PASSOVER & EUCHARIST

*W*hat modern Christians commonly call Holy Communion, the early church called Eucharist. It is a Jewish name, insofar as it derives from the Jewish name for meal prayers. Before and after meals, Jews would thank their God in a rather special prayer format, which they found prescribed in Deuteronomy 8:10: "When you have eaten your fill, you shall bless the Lord your God." Accordingly, the Jewish meal prayer begins, "Blessed are you who provides us with . . ." Such a prayer was called "a blessing [of the Lord]," and blessing in this sense is in Greek either eulogia or eucharistia. This at once gives us a first pointer to the original context of the Eucharist: the Jewish meal.

But we can be more specific: we should look to the Jewish Passover meal. It is by no means universally agreed, however, that Christian Eucharist should be seen as rooted in Jewish Passover. Some scholars think that something celebrated once a week cannot stem from a festival celebrated once a year. We have already seen Hans Lietzmann claim that the oldest "Lord's meal" was a resumption, after Jesus' resurrection, of the meal fellowship that the disciples had with him before Passover, and that it contained no reference at all to Passover and did not recall in any special way Jesus' last Passover meal.

Even so, the present chapter—with the majority of scholars—takes for granted that the early Eucharist should be seen against a Passover meal background. Not only *is this deeply embedded in the Synoptic Gospel narratives (and that of Paul, 1 Cor 11:23-26) about Jesus' last meal, it is also recommended, I believe, by the light this approach sheds on the origin and early development of the liturgy of the Eucharist.*

The Eucharist: Lines of Development

Let us begin with recalling the main elements in Justin's description of the eucharistic service: (1) bringing forward of bread and wine; (2) eucharistic prayer; and (3) partaking of bread and wine. Comparing this with typical Protestant practice in our own day, many would miss in this description something which they consider constitutive to holy communion: a recital of the "words of institution," the story Paul tells in 1 Corinthians 11:23-25. Many historians of liturgy would assure us, however, that this recital is really included in Justin's description, because the words of institution are part of the eucharistic prayer.

Seventy years later than Justin we find Hippolytus's eucharistic prayer, in which the words of institution occur. On the other hand—and this has worried many—we do not find the words of institution in the eucharistic prayers of the *Didache* (chaps. 9—10).[1] It seems clear that in this respect a development or change has taken place between the *Didache* (ca. A.D. 100) and Hippolytus (ca. A.D. 210). If so, is Justin closer to *Didache* or to Hippolytus?

In order to unravel the origin and early history of the eucharistic liturgy of the church, the Jewish background should be studied in some detail. Jesus' last meal together with his disciples was a Passover meal, a *Sederabend*, to use the terminology of a much later time.[2] This setting was certainly not soon forgotten or ignored by the first believers, who were Jews themselves. It would be strange if this setting should not give us more than one clue to the early history of the eucharistic service.[3]

---

[1] This observation was part of the argument behind Lietzmann's theory referred to above, pp. 379-80.

[2] This is the unambiguous statement of the Synoptic Gospels; even John, who seems to claim that Jesus died on Passover Eve, by more than one token testifies to the Passover character of Jesus' last meal. The most extensive defense of the Passover meal as the authentic setting of Jesus' last meal is found in Joachim Jeremias, *The Eucharistic Words of Jesus*, 2nd ed. (London: SCM Press, 1966). He has convinced most scholars, but by no means all. On the question of how to reconcile this with John's chronology, see above, p. 389.

[3] In what follows, I am much indebted to two studies in particular: Karl Christian Felmy, "'Was unterscheidet diese Nacht von allen anderen Nächten?' Die Funktion des Einsetzungsberichtes in der urchristlichen Eucharistiefeier nach Didache 9f. und dem Zeugnis Justins," *Jahrbuch für Liturgik und Hymnologie* 27 (1983): 1-15; and Enrico Mazza, *The Origins*

Exactly how the Passover meal was celebrated in A.D. 30 is not known to us; the Passover Haggadah (the order of the things to be said and done during the Passover meal) in present use contains elements old and more recent, and it is very difficult to ascertain with full certainty which elements are pre-70 and which are later.[4] One also has to reckon with the possibility that in the pre-70 situation, prayer texts and formularies may have been less stable and fixed than they became later.[5] Even so, there is hardly reason to doubt that the main structure of the order for the Passover meal was quite stable in the days of Jesus. The allusions to it in the New Testament and other Jewish writings from the period seem to presuppose an order not totally different from the one known to us.[6]

Broadly speaking, the liturgy of the Passover meal comprises the following main elements:

* Opening sanctification of the *first cup of wine.*
* Words of explanation over *the bread:* "This is the bread of affliction."
* Question: Why is this night different?

   * The question triggers the haggadah proper, the story of the first Passover.

   * Renewed questions and answers about Pesach lamb; unleavened bread, bitter herbs.
   * First part of Hallel: Pss 113-114.

* Sanctification of the *second cup of wine and of the bread,* of unleavened bread and bitter herbs.

---

of the Eucharistic Prayer (Collegeville, Minn.: The Liturgical Press, 1995). Cf. also Eugene LaVerdiere, *The Eucharist in the New Testament and the Early Church* (Collegeville, Minn.: Liturgical Press, 1996), esp. chap. 2: "Telling What Happened: The Genesis of a Liturgical Narrative" (pp. 12-28).

[4]Cf. the historical comments on all elements in the present Haggadah by Cecil Roth in his modern edition: *The Haggadah: A New Edition* (London: Soncino, 1959); and the very sophisticated study by Baruch M. Bokser, *The Origins of the Seder: The Passover Rite and Early Rabbinic Judaism* (Berkeley/Los Angeles/London: University of California Press, 1984). *Mishnah Pesahim* 10 gives us a pretty clear idea of how the Passover Haggadah looked around A.D. 200; Josephus, the New Testament, Philo, and some earlier Jewish texts (e.g., *Jubilees*) give us glimpses and indications of earlier stages still. The material is conveniently assembled in Bokser, pp. 19-28. There are also clues to be found by internal historical criteria in the different elements of the Haggadah itself.

[5]Cf. the most recent discussion of this in Stefan C. Reif, *Judaism and Hebrew Prayer: New Perspectives on Jewish Liturgical History* (Cambridge: Cambridge University Press, 1993), chaps. 2-5 passim, esp. pp. 60, 128-29.

[6]The main difference, of course, has to do with the elimination of the Passover lamb after A.D. 70. This was the central focus of the pre-70 meal, as clearly shown by Bokser, op. cit. He has a very perceptive analysis of how the Mishnah tries to present the necessary changes and novelties in the post-70 situation as if they were timeless or old.

    * *The meal.*

* The blessing for the meal, *birkat ha-mazon,* including a blessing of the *third cup of wine.*

    * Second part of Hallel: Ps 115-18.

    * Concluding praise (Ps 136) and prayer.

If we break down this rather complex sequence to its bare essentials, we are left with two basic elements:

1. *The meal,* with an introductory sanctification *(qiddush)* of wine and bread (in this sequence!), and a concluding blessing *(berakah)* for the meal (including a blessing for the wine), the *birkat ha-mazon* ("blessing for the food"). Regarding bread and wine, this gives the following sequence: cup, bread, meal, cup.

2. The *question* of why things are different in this meal, which triggers the *explanatory story,* the *haggadah.* This intrudes into the introductory *qiddush,* resulting in a double *qiddush,* before and after the *haggadah.*

Concerning the food and drink, we notice that the paschal lamb, bread and bitter herbs receive an explanation as to their specific significance, and the bread in particular—but not the wine. One could say that the wine is still waiting for an interpretation, since none is contained in the Old Testament. (In fact, the wine itself is not prescribed in the Old Testament.) With this in mind, let us read the story of Jesus' last Passover meal in Luke 22:14-20:

> When the hour came, Jesus and his apostles reclined at the table. And he said to them, "I have eagerly desired to eat this Passover with you before I suffer. For I tell you, I will not eat it again until it finds fulfillment in the kingdom of God."
>
> * After taking *the cup,* he gave thanks [said the *berakah* for the cup] and said, "Take this and divide it among you. For I tell you that I will not drink again of the fruit of the vine until the kingdom of God comes."
>
> * And he took *bread,* gave thanks [said the *berakah* for the bread] and broke it, and gave it to them,
>
> > * saying, "This is my body given for you; do this in remembrance of me."
> >
> > * In the same way, after *the supper*
>
> * he took *the cup,*
>
> > * saying, "This cup is the new covenant in my blood, which is poured out for you."[7]

─────────────────────────────────

[7]NIV with paragraph divisions and italics added to bring out the structure of the ritual more clearly.

There are several features of this text that call for comment.[8] Let us first of all notice the sequence: cup, bread, meal, cup—exactly as in the Passover meal. The introductory two *berakot* for cup and bread are the *qiddush* before the meal, the final cup after the meal is the cup included in the blessing after the meal (the *birkat ha-mazon*). Before the meal, only the bread (not the cup) receives words of explanation: "This is . . ." Only after the meal does the (second or third) cup "in the same way" receive words of explanation: "This is . . ."

Luke's rendering of the last meal provides us not only with an obviously authentic imbedding of Jesus' words and actions in the Passover meal; it also provides us with the means for explaining the main lines in the further development of the Christian Eucharist. Let us consider first the sequence of cup, *bread*, meal, *cup*. The italicized elements are explained or interpreted as the body of Jesus and the new covenant in his blood (so Luke and Paul; Mark and Matthew: his blood of the new covenant). We would expect that the one cup without interpretation would soon be felt superfluous and would be combined with the other, so that only the one cup and the bread remained. This would result in either cup and bread together before the meal (= cup-bread sequence) or bread before the meal and cup after (= bread-cup sequence). We find both variants in early Christian references to the Eucharist:

Cup-bread sequence:	**Bread-cup sequence:**
1 Corinthians 10:16-17	Mark 14:22-24/Matthew 26:26-28
Didache 9	1 Corinthians 11:23-25

---

[8]There is a textual problem involved: some western manuscripts omit the latter part of v. 19 and all of v. 20. Some scholars think that this omitted part is a later interpolation into Luke's account, stemming from 1 Cor 11:24-25 (so, e.g., David Flusser, "The Last Supper and the Essenes," in Flusser, *Judaism*, pp. 202-6; esp. 203). There can hardly be any doubt, however, that the "long" text in Luke is original. The decisive argument for this is the simple fact that the long text in Luke is the only one that does *not* conform to any known liturgical practice in the later church. It therefore cannot be explained as an attempt to streamline the account of the last supper into conformity with later liturgical practice, whereas the short version of Luke's text makes it agree with the liturgy of *Didache* 9. If Luke 22:19-20 were a literary interpolation from 1 Cor 11, we would have the strange situation that a purely literary operation resulted in a text which makes excellent sense within the sequence of the Passover meal! For a discussion of the textual problem, and a review of recent discussion and literature, see I. Howard Marshall, *The Gospel of Luke: A Commentary on the Greek Text*, The New International Greek Testament Commentary (Exeter: Paternoster, 1978), pp. 792-807. Among the many extensive discussions of the "historicity" of Luke 22:14-20., I would especially recommend Hermann Patsch, *Abendmahl und historischer Jesus*, Calwer Theologische Monographien, Reihe A, 1 (Stuttgart: Calwer Verlag, 1972), 95-102.

As one can easily see from the relative "weight" of these texts, the bread-cup sequence was to become the winner.[9] This tendency to fuse the two cups into one would of course gain momentum when the Eucharist was made independent of the evening meal, as had happened already in Justin (ca. A.D. 150). He described a eucharistic service that has been incorporated in the early morning service and in which no real meal takes place. The meal between the eucharistic bread and the eucharistic cup has disappeared, and it seems that already as early as in Justin the eucharistic prayers over bread and wine (originally two, one before, one after the meal) have become one. In terms of the history of the development of the eucharistic prayer(s), we should expect this change in setting to have rather far-reaching consequences for the format and structure of the prayer. (Scholars of liturgical history sometimes seem to overlook this.)

Some further consequences can also be drawn from this Passover setting of the eucharistic service. We clearly have to distinguish, in this service, between the *meal prayers (qiddush and birkat ha-mazon)* on the one hand, and the *explanatory story*, the haggadah, on the other. The prayers contain thanks for the wine, the bread, the food. The haggadah contains the story that answers the questions, Why do we do this? What does it mean? Turning to the Christian eucharistic service, we find the same two elements, and in the beginning they seem to have been kept apart, as they were in the Jewish Passover liturgy: (1) Eucharistic prayer *without* Christian haggadah (*Didache* 9—10). (2) The Christian haggadah as a separate element, not part of the prayer: the "words of institution," answering the why question.[10]

This structure may still be clearly discerned in Justin's report:

> Bread and a cup containing wine mixed with water are brought forward to the one presiding over the brethren.

─────────────────────────────────

[9] I think this explanation (put forward by Mazza, *Origins*, pp. 30-34, 66-97) is simpler and more convincing than the one proposed by Flusser in the quoted article above, note 8. According to Flusser, the cup-bread sequence of Luke's short text, 1 Cor 10 and *Didache* 9 reflect "normal" Jewish practice and the practice of Jesus at the last supper, whereas the (later) bread-cup sequence betrays Essene influence on early Christianity.

[10] For this and the following analysis, cf. esp. Karl Christian Felmy, "'Was unterscheidet diese Nacht von allen anderen Nächten?' Die Funktion des Stiftungsberichtes in der urchristlichen Eucharistiefeier nach Didache 9f. und dem Zeugnis Justins," *Jahrbuch für Liturgik und Hymnologie* 27 (1983): 1-15; C. Giraudo, "Le recit de l'institution dans la priere eucharistique a-t-il des antecedants?" *Nouvelle Revue Theologique* 106 (1984): 404-20: LaVerdiere, *The Eucharist*, pp. 12-28.

* He takes them and offers praise and glory to the Father of all, through the name of the Son and of the Holy Spirit, and he says lengthy prayers of thanksgiving [eucharistia] to God in the name of those to whom He granted these favors. At the end of these prayers and thanksgiving, all those present approve by saying "Amen." . . .

Combined *qiddush* before the meal and *birkat ha-mazon* after. Early Christian version: *Didache* 9—10.

* When he who presides has said the *eucharistia* and all the people have responded, they who are called deacons permit each one present to partake of the bread that has been blessed, and the wine and the water, and they also carry them to those not present.

Partaking of bread and wine.

* We call this food *eucharistia*. We partake of it not as ordinary bread nor as ordinary drink,

Christian haggadah, (1) explaining why the eucharistic food is different from ordinary food, and

but just as, through the word of God, our Savior Jesus Christ became incarnate and took upon himself flesh and blood for our salvation,

so, we have been taught,

the food which has been blessed by the prayer according to his word, and which nourishes our flesh and blood by assimilation, *is the flesh and blood of that Jesus who was made flesh.*

The Apostles in their memoirs, which are called Gospels, have handed down what Jesus ordered them to do:

(2) rendering the foundational story behind the celebration.

he took bread, gave thanks, and said: "Do this in remembrance of me; this is my body."

In the same way, he took also the cup, gave thanks, and said: "This is my blood;" and he gave it only to them.

It is difficult to know when this haggadah in Justin made its way into the eucharistic prayer itself, and if this had already happened prior to Justin (we shall see indications below that it probably had). It may not have happened at the same time everywhere, either. But there is no doubt that this happened, as we can see in the eucharistic prayer of Hippolytus, in which Justin's haggadah has been incorporated more or less wholesale (see below, pp. 414-15).

It is tempting to suggest the following scenario for this development: As long as the Eucharist was part of a real meal, there was a natural occasion for a haggadah in story format, told as an independent part of the meal "liturgy," answering the question why this meal was special and not an ordinary meal. When the meal disappeared, the haggadah lost its natural setting, while the *berakah* (eucharistic prayer) over the bread and wine was kept intact. Therefore the haggadah was incorporated into the remaining element from the old meal setting, the eucharistic prayer.

After this overview of some main lines of development in the eucharistic service, we shall turn to a more detailed study of the eucharistic prayer, to see if our thesis of a Jewish Passover background for this prayer stands up to scrutiny.

The Eucharistic Prayer and the Passover Meal

The Eucharistic Prayers in Didache 9—10

We take as a working hypothesis that the prayers in *Didache* 9 and 10 really are eucharistic prayers and not simply ordinary meal prayers.[11] These two prayers, as the context shows, are intended as model prayers for the prayers to be said before and after the eucharistic meal. At this early time (ca. A.D. 100) the eucharistic meal was obviously still a real meal, very likely the main meal of the day, which means that it was in the evening, as in Acts 20:7-12 and 1 Cor 11:20-33. Indications in 1 Corinthians that this was an evening meal include that fact that wine was drunk and that this was the meal to still one's hunger.

This pattern of one prayer *before the meal*, sanctifying cup and bread (in this sequence!), and one *after the meal*, praising God for his gift of nourishment, is entirely Jewish. It was followed in the Sabbath evening meal and also at the Passover meal. The opening prayer over wine and bread is called a "sanctifi-cation," in Hebrew, a *qiddush*. The closing prayer is called "the blessing for the nourishment," *birkat ha-mazon*. In the *Didache*, the prayers in chapter 9 seem

---

[11]For a full survey of the discussion of this issue, see Niederwimmer, *Didache*, pp. 176-80.

to represent the *qiddush* pattern, while the longer prayer in chapter 10 is the closing *birkat ha-mazon*, after the meal. We shall study this in some detail in a moment.

First, however, let us pay attention to a matter of form in Jewish prayers. All of the relevant Jewish meal-prayers (and many others, too) have the form of a so-called blessing (Hebrew *berakah*, plural *berakot*). They all begin with the words "Blessed are you, O Lord, our God." One of the reasons for the choice of this particular format is an important biblical injunction in Deuteronomy 8:10: "When you have eaten and are satisfied, *bless* the Lord Your God" (author's translation). In Greek, the equivalent of the verb *bless (berek)* is *eulogein* or *eucharistein;* the corresponding nouns are *eulogia* and *eucharistia*. This means that the most common name for holy communion in the early church, *eucharistia*, is derived from what was regarded as the most fundamental characteristic of the whole event: the saying of the *prayer* over bread and wine.

Now the blessing format was usually not used much in early Christian prayers, and it is not represented in the *Didache* prayers. Does this indicate distance from Jewish practice? Not necessarily. In rabbinic literature and in the synagogue service the *berakah* was no doubt the most usual form of thanksgiving: "Blessed are you, Lord, who . . ." It seems, however, that in the time of Jesus this format of thanksgiving had no monopoly, and in the Qumran scrolls we find it side by side with the form used often by Jesus himself and in the *Didache*: "I/We thank you (Father, God)." The fact that this formula is chosen in the *Didache* is thus no sign of distance from Judaism; it is rather an indicator of the early date of these prayers.[12]

One more note on form, also of relevance to the question of date: Joseph Heinemann in his study of *Prayer in the Talmud* has noticed that concluding a prayer with a doxology like "Blessed be the name of the glory of his kingdom for ever and ever" was typical of the temple liturgy, not of the synagogal prayers.[13] Could it be that the repeated doxology—"yours is the glory [and

---

[12]Later, in the church of Syria, the *berakah* format was much used, and even a Christianized version of the *Tefillah*, the Eighteen Benedictions of the synagogue service, is documented (in the so-called *Apostolic Constitutions* from the fourth century A.D.). Cf. on this David A. Fiensy, *Prayers Alleged to be Jewish: An Examination of the Constitutiones Apostolorum*, Brown Judaic Studies 65 (Chico, Calif.: Scholars Press, 1985). On prayer in the Qumran Scrolls, cf. Bilhah Nitzan, *Qumran Prayer and Religious Poetry*, Studies on the Texts of the Desert of Judah 12 (Leiden/New York/Cologne: E. J. Brill, 1994), esp. pp. 72-80. and 323-24. On the *berakah* pattern being only one among others in early Jewish prayers, cf. Joseph Heinemann, *Prayer in the Talmud*, Studia Judaica 9 (Berlin/New York: Walter de Gruyter, 1977), pp. 39-40; Fiensy, p. 225.
[13]Heinemann, *Prayer in the Talmud*, pp. 134-38.

the power] for ever"—in the *Didache* prayers is reminiscent of those early days when the first believers would "meet together in the temple courts" (Acts 2:46)?

After these preliminaries, let us take a closer look at the eucharistic prayers in *Didache* 9, the ones which are parallel to the *qiddush* of the Passover meal:

Didache 9	**Passover meal**
Concerning the eucharist, hold eucharist thus:	
(A) First concerning the cup:	
We give thanks to you, our Father,	Blessed are You, O Lord, our God, King of the Universe,
for the holy vine of David your servant which you made known to us through Jesus your servant —yours is the glory for ever.	Creator of the fruit of the vine.
(B) And for the broken bread:	
We give thanks to you, our Father,	Blessed are You, O Lord, our God, King of the Universe,
(1) for the life and knowledge which you did make known to us through Jesus your servant —yours is the glory for ever.	the bringer forth of bread out of the earth.

(2) As this broken bread was scattered upon the mountains, but was brought together and became one, so let your Church be gathered together from the ends of the earth into your kingdom
—for yours is the glory and the power through Jesus Christ for ever.

But let none eat or drink of your eucharist except those who have been baptised in the Lord's Name. For concerning this also the Lord said, "Give not that which is holy to the dogs."

We shall not at once comment on all the interesting features of these prayers, because some of them are most easily explained as "imports" into the *qiddush* pattern from the prayer following the meal, in *Didache* 10. It is easy, however, to see the main principle according to which the Jewish *berakot* for wine and bread have been modified in *Didache* 9. The Jewish prayers thank God for the physical drink and nourishment enjoyed by the body through wine and bread; the *Didache* prayers thank God for *spiritual* gifts conveyed through the cup and the bread. These spiritual gifts, however, are described in such a way as to keep the reference to wine and bread intact: the "fruit of the vine" becomes "the holy vine of David," and "bread out of the earth" becomes "life and knowledge." The basic idea behind this is well stated by Justin Martyr, some fifty years later than the *Didache*, in his comments on the bread and wine of the Eucharist: "Not as ordinary bread or as ordinary drink do we partake of them" (*First Apology* 66.2).

We shall comment briefly on some details. "The holy vine of David" is, strictly speaking, not a biblical expression, nor has it been found in Jewish literature of the period. The vine, however, was a traditional metaphor for the salvation and blessing of the messianic kingdom.[14] And the promises of a messianic kingdom—and the Messiah himself—were often, in Jewish prayer language, associated with David's name. In the traditional Passover prayers we find the following: "Have mercy, O Lord, our God . . . upon the *kingdom of the house of David*, your anointed." "Our God, and God of our Fathers! May there ascend, and come, and arrive, and be seen, and accepted, and heard, and visited, and remembered . . . the remembrance of the Messiah, *son of David your servant*." These two prayers are included in the expanded *birkat ha-mazon* after the Passover meal, and the "David, your servant" theme could easily spill over into the opening *qiddush* for the "fruit of the vine."

"The holy vine of David, your servant" therefore probably refers to the gifts of salvation associated with the messianic kingdom promised to David (2 Sam 7:10-17; 2 Sam 23:5; Is 55:3 etc.); the closest New Testament parallels being Luke 1:50-55 and 1:68-79. In terms of Christology, "your servant" seems to be primarily a royal, messianic title, applied to David as well as Jesus—very likely in a sense similar to the messianic "Son of God."

"Life and knowledge" are the gifts associated with the bread. In Jewish parlance, life and knowledge are considered gifts of salvation imparted by God's Wisdom, normally identified with the Torah. As this theme recurs in the *birkat ha-mazon* of *Didache* 10, we shall be content to point out in this context the very close parallel to this motive in John 6. Jesus said, "I am the *bread of life*" (Jn 6:35-50), meaning the bread that gives eternal life. This seems to echo Wisdom Christology: in Proverbs 9:1-4 Wisdom invites to a meal of

---

[14]Cf. esp. Willy Rordorf, "La vigne et le vin dans la tradition juive et chrétienne," in *Liturgie, foi et vie des premiers chrétiens: Études patristiques*, Théologie historique 75 (Paris: Beauchesne, 1989), pp. 493-508.

wine and food, which must mean that eating is a metaphor for gaining knowledge from Wisdom, and this knowledge imparts life.[15]

The theme of the final petition in the prayer is the future ingathering of the church from the ends of the earth; this motif is tied to the eucharistic bread through the parable of the scattered grains being united in one bread. This is best explained from the *birkat ha-mazon* in *Didache* 10, to which we now turn.

But after you are satisfied with food, thus give thanks:

(1) We give thanks to you, O Holy Father,

(A) for your Holy Name which you made tabernacle in our hearts,

(B) and for the knowledge and faith and immortality which you made known to us through Jesus your servant—yours is the glory for ever.

(2) You, Lord Almighty, did create all things for the sake of your Name, and gave food and drink to men for their enjoyment, so that they might thank you. But us you have blessed with spiritual food and drink and eternal light through your servant.

Above all we give thanks to you because you are mighty—yours is the glory for ever.

(3) Remember, Lord, your Church, to deliver it from all evil and to make it perfect in your love, and gather it together from the four winds, sanctified, to your kingdom which you have prepared for it—yours is the power and the glory for ever.

Let grace come and let this world pass away.

Hosannah to the God of David.

If any man be holy, let him come!

If any man be not, let him repent!

Maran atha, Amen.[16]

---

[15]On the Wisdom background of John 6:35-50, cf. esp. Raymond E. Brown, *The Gospel According to John (i-xii)*, Anchor Bible 29 (Garden City, N.Y.: Doubleday, 1966), pp. 272-75. Very likely we have a close parallel to this part of the eucharistic prayer in 1 *Clement* 36:2, where also Wisdom Christology and eucharistic context seem evident: "Jesus Christ, the High Priest *of our offerings* . . . through Him the eyes of our *hearts* were opened, through Him our foolish and darkened understanding blossoms toward the *light*, through Him the Master willed that we should *taste immortal knowledge*." On Wisdom inviting to her meal in Jewish literature of the period, see Karl-Gustav Sandelin, *Wisdom as Nourisher: A Study of an Old Testament Theme, Its Development Within Early Judaism and Its Impact on Early Christianity*, Acta Academiae Aboensis Ser. A Humaniora 64.3 (Åbo: Åbo Akademi, 1986). On Prov 9:1-6, see Sandelin, pp. 19-26; on John 6, see ibid., pp. 177-85. Interestingly, Sandelin proposes that "vine of David" might also have Wisdom connotations; see his analysis of *Didache* 9—10 on pp. 186-228.

[16]Paragraph divisions and enumeration added to bring out the structure.

In the first century A.D. the Jewish grace after meals, the *birkat ha-mazon,* was probably not yet fully fixed in its wording, but seems to have had a three-fold structure and a set of permanent motifs in each of its three parts. In a now classic study, Louis Finkelstein reconstructed what he took to be the basic version of the prayer.[17] It ran somewhat like this:

> 1. Blessed are you, O Lord, our God, King of the universe, who feeds the whole world with goodness, with grace and with mercy.
> 2. We thank you, O Lord, our God, that you have caused us to inherit a good and pleasant land.
> 3. Have mercy, O Lord, our God, on Israel, your people, and on Jerusalem, your city, and upon Zion, the dwelling place of your glory, and upon your altar and upon your temple. Blessed are you, who build Jerusalem.

As one can see, the first two prayers are thanksgivings, the third is a petition. Finkelstein made use of the prayer in *Didache* 10 in his reconstruction of the first-century *birkat ha-mazon* because he found it had the same tripartite structure. The only points he found that differed between the Jewish and Christian prayer was that the two first elements had changed places in the *Didache* version, and that the third had been somewhat spiritualized. In a more recent analysis, Enrico Mazza has questioned this conclusion and proposed an alternative analysis.[18] According to Mazza, the sequence between the three elements is basically the same in the Jewish and the *Didache* versions, but the Christian version has *spiritualized* the Jewish prayers, very much on the same principle as in the *qiddush* prayers studied above. Continuing Mazza's line of investigation while keeping in mind the valid insights of Finkelstein, I would like to suggest the following analysis of *Didache* 10 as a Christian *birkat ha-mazon* in a Passover setting.

The first two blessings in the *birkat ha-mazon* are based on Deuteronomy 8:10: "When you have eaten and are satisfied, bless *(berakhta)* the Lord your God for the good land he has given you."[19] This was understood as a biblical command to praise God after meals with a prayer in the *berakah* format. In the *birkat ha-mazon* it is the second thanksgiving which most directly takes up Deuteronomy 8:10. The *berakah* version used in the Passover meal makes explicit this reference to Deuteronomy 8:10 as a biblical injunction:

[17]Finkelstein, "The Birkat ha-mazon," *The Jewish Quarterly Review,* n.s., 19 (1928-1929): 211-62.
[18]Mazza, *Origin,* pp. 16-30.
[19]My own translation.

Blessed be your name in the mouth of all that lives, continually and for ever-more: as it is written, "When you have eaten and *are satisfied*, bless *[berakhta]* the Lord your God for the good land he has given you" [Deut 8:10]. Blessed are you, O Lord, for the land and for the nourishment *[ha-mazon]*.[20]

Nevertheless, the first thanksgiving for nourishment given by the Creator is no doubt also seen as a fulfillment of the injunction in Deuteronomy 8:10.

The third element in the *birkat ha-mazon,* the petition, is based on a text found in one of the Apocrypha, Sirach 36:10-23:

Sirach	Birkat ha-mazon
	Didache 10:
Gather all the tribes of Jacob	Gather the Church together from the four winds,
and give them their inheritance, as at the beginning.	to your kingdom which you have prepared for it.
	Jewish Passover:
Have mercy, O Lord,	Have mercy, O Lord, our God
on the people called by your name,	upon Israel your people,
on Israel, whom you have named your firstborn.	
Have pity upon the city of your sanctuary,	and upon
Jerusalem, the place of your dwelling.	Jerusalem, your city, and upon Zion the abiding-place
Fill Zion with your majesty, and your temple with your glory.	of your glory . . . and upon the great and holy House which is called by your Name.

As one can see, *Didache* as well as the *birkat ha-mazon* of the Passover meal both depend on the same text in Sirach, only picking up different parts of it. This probably means that the prayer in *Didache* 10 goes back to a period when the Jewish *birkat ha-mazon* was still in its formative period, not yet having a fixed wording.

Behind the *Didache* prayers we discerned (above) Wisdom Christology. The following Wisdom passages contain some of the main catchwords of the *Didache* prayers: Wisdom says, "Come, eat my food and drink the wine I have

---

[20]C. Roth, *The Haggadah,* p. 47, italics added.

mixed. Leave your simple ways and you will live; walk in the way of understanding" (Prov 9:5-6 NIV). "[Wisdom] will feed him [the God-fearing person] with the bread of learning and give him the water of wisdom to drink" (Sirach 15:3).[21]

With this, we have presented some of the material that points to the conclusion that the eucharistic prayers in the *Didache* are christological adaptations of the Jewish *qiddush* and *birkat ha-mazon* prayers, especially in the form these had in the Passover meal. These prayers had probably not yet attained a fixed form in this early period, so we are not claiming any simple literary dependence on the prayers of the later Passover Haggadah. All we have basis for claiming is that the *Didache* prayers evidence structural and thematic relationships to the main prayers of the Passover meal, stemming from a period of flexibility in the wording of these prayers.

The Eucharistic Prayer in Justin and Polycarp
We now turn to our next witness to the text and contents of the eucharistic prayer: Justin (ca. A.D.150-160).[22] Above we have quoted one of his main renderings of the eucharistic service, which gave us first intimations of the content of the eucharistic prayer as he knew it. Here we shall add some other indications:

> For Jesus our Lord ordered us to do this in remembrance of the suffering which he suffered on behalf of those who are being purged . . . in order that we should at the same time give thanks to God
> * for having created the world with all that is in it for man's sake,
> * and also for having set us free from the evil in which we had been,
> * and for having destroyed the powers and the authorities with a complete destruction by means of Him who underwent suffering according to His will. (*Dialogue with Trypho* 41.1)[23]

This passage from Justin's *Dialogue with Trypho* gives several hints as to the wording of the eucharistic prayer, although Justin never quotes it in full. We

---

[21]For an extensive treatment of the "meal of Wisdom" motif in *Didache* and the Jewish texts, see the study by Sandelin, referred to in note 15 above.

[22]On the Eucharist in Justin, see H. Boone Porter, "The Eucharistic Piety of Justin Martyr," *The Anglican Theological Review* 39 (1957): 24-33; E. C. Ratcliff, "The Eucharistic Institution Narrative of Justin Martyr's First *Apology*," *Journal of Ecclesiastical History* 22 (1971): 97-102; J. D. B. Hamilton, "Justin's *Apology*, 66. A Review of Scholarship and a Suggested Synthesis," *Ephemerides Theologicae Lovanienses* 48 (1972): 554-60; LaVerdiere, *Eucharist*, pp. 167-84 (chap. 11: "The Food Called Eucharist: The Eucharist in the Writings of Justin Martyr").

[23]Lukyn Williams, pp. 81-82, with bullets to show structure added.

easily recognize the meal *berakah:* "having created the world and all that is in it." In the two following sayings about salvation through Christ, we recognize the Passover terminology: salvation is the *setting free* from slavery, made real through destruction of opposing forces (as with Egypt's power).

There are other scattered hints in Justin's writings that can be pieced together. What results is strikingly close to something resembling the full text of the eucharistic prayer given by Hippolytus 60-70 years later. We shall study that in a moment, but first we shall take a brief look at another prayer approximately contemporary with Justin. It is not a eucharistic prayer according to its setting; in fact, it is the prayer of the bishop of Smyrna, Polycarp, as he was bound to the stake to be burned as a martyr. But if we subtract the elements that clearly refer to his impending martyrdom, we are left with a prayer (in italics below) that seems clearly eucharistic, suggesting that the narrative makes the old bishop—in these his last words—paraphrase a prayer most familiar to him: the prayer he said every Sunday during holy communion:

> O Lord God Almighty, Father of your beloved and blessed Child, Jesus Christ, *through Whom we have received full knowledge of you,* the God of Angels and powers, and *of all creation,* and of the whole family of the righteous, who live before you. *I bless you,* that you have granted me this day and hour, *that I may share,* among the number of the martyrs, *in the cup of your Christ,* for the resurrection to everlasting life, both of soul and body in the immortality of the Holy Spirit. And may I, today, be received among them before you, as a rich and acceptable sacrifice, as you, the God who never lies and is truth, has prepared beforehand, and shown forth, and fulfilled. For this reason *I also praise you for all things, I bless you, I glorify you through the everlasting and heavenly high Priest, Jesus Christ, your beloved Child, through whom be glory to you with him and the Holy Spirit, both now and for ages that are to come, Amen (Martyrdom of Polycarp* 14.1-3).[24]

It is not difficult to recognize in this prayer some themes shared with the prayers in the *Didache,* and also those we can discern in Justin.

The Eucharistic Prayer in Hippolytus

We turn now to the last and final text in this survey, the full text of the eucharistic prayer prescribed by Hippolytus:

> (1) Bishop: The Lord be with you.
> People: And with your spirit.

[24]For an extensive analysis of Polycarp's prayer, see Mazza, *Origins,* pp. 154-56.

Bishop: Lift up your hearts!
People: We have them with the Lord.
Bishop: Let us give thanks unto the Lord.
People: It is meet and right.

(2) Bishop: We render thanks unto you, O God, through your beloved Servant Jesus Christ,

(A) Whom in the last times you sent to us as Saviour and Redeemer and Angel of your counsel,
Who is your Word unseparable from you, through Whom you made all things and in Whom you were well pleased;
Whom you sent from heaven into the Virgin's womb and who, conceived within her, was made flesh and demonstrated to be your Son being born of the Holy Spirit and a Virgin;
Who fulfilling your will and preparing for you a holy people stretched forth his hands for suffering that He might release from sufferings those who have believed in you;

(B) Who—when He was betrayed to voluntary suffering that He might abolish death and rend the bonds of the devil and tread down hell and enlighten the righteous and establish the limit and demonstrate the resurrection—taking bread and giving thanks to you said:
Take, eat; this is My Body which is broken for you.
Likewise also the cup, saying:
This is My Blood which is shed for you. When you do this, do it in remembrance of me.

(C) Therefore, remembering His death and resurrection, we offer you the bread and the cup, thanking you because you have made us worthy to stand before you and serve you as priests.

(D) And we pray you that you will send your Holy Spirit upon the oblation of your holy Church and that you will grant to all who partake to be united, that they may be fulfilled with the Holy Spirit for the confirmation of faith in truth—so that we may praise and glorify you through your Servant Jesus Christ through whom glory and honour be unto you with the Holy Spirit in your Holy Church now and for ever and eternally. Amen. (*Apostolic Tradition* 4.3-13)[25]

---

[25]Dix/Chadwick, pp. 7-9, paragraph divisions and enumeration added.

Some brief comments on passages 1 and 2A-D:

(1) This introductory dialogue between people and bishop became one of the most permanent elements in later eucharistic liturgies and is still used in all traditionally liturgical churches. Its traditional name is the *Preface*. It could be a great deal older than Hippolytus's time, because the original meaning of the exhortation "lift up your hearts" is probably that people who are drowsy from much food should wake up and concentrate on prayer and Eucharist. In other words, the exhortation originates from a practice where the Eucharist was still part of a full meal.

(2A) The opening words of the Bishop's prayer still recall the *birkat ha-mazon*, but the prayer soon turns to a christological haggadah which reminds us of the one we studied in Justin Martyr. At the end of the second part of the haggadah (B), the words of institution are rendered as part of the telling of the passion story. Enrico Mazza has studied this whole haggadah in great detail and claims that its terminology is strikingly parallel to the *paschal sermons* we have from Melito of Sardis (ca. A.D. 175) and others.[26] In these sermons, the saving act of Christ is described in the terminology and the imagery of the Passover-exodus event, and this spills over into Hippolytus's haggadah.

(2C) This short element is something entirely new, compared with the prayers in *Didache* 9—10. When thanking God for his gift of food (bread and cup) to us, it is not very natural at the same time to bring God the bread and cup as a sacrifice. This element can therefore hardly have originated within the eucharistic prayer context and must have another background. We are going to study this more closely in the next section, and reserve further comment until then.

(2D) This element is traditionally called the "calling upon (or invocation of) [the Spirit]"; Greek *epiklēsis*. This element *does* have a background in motifs internal to the eucharistic prayer: Justin says "not as ordinary bread or as ordinary drink" do we consider the eucharistic elements, but they are "the flesh and blood of that Jesus who was made flesh" (*First Apology* 66.2) *after the prayer has been said over them*. *Didache* supplements the positive side of "not ordinary": "You have blessed us with *spiritual* food and drink" (*Didache* 10:3).

In later times, the Eastern Church considered this *epiklesis* the constitutive

---

[26]Mazza, *Origin*, pp. 98-128. Not everyone is convinced by this part of Mazza's argument. Cf. a paper read at the 13th International Conference on Patristic Studies in Oxford (August 16-21, 1999) by Paul F. Bradshaw, "A Paschal Root to the Anaphora of the Apostolic Tradition?"

moment of the whole celebration: through the coming down of the Spirit upon the bread and wine they "became" or were transformed into the body and blood of Christ. The Western (Latin) church took instead the recital of the explanatory words of Jesus ("this is the . . .") to be the constitutive moment. Hippolytus's liturgy probably does not yet contain any reflection upon this question; it is rather the whole liturgical action as such which constitutes the bread and wine as spiritual carriers of Christ's flesh and blood.

We shall now turn to an interesting and in modern times hotly debated issue: the ideas about the Eucharist as *sacrifice* in the early church.

The Eucharist as Sacrifice

When Justin said that bread, wine and water (to be mixed with the wine according to Jewish custom) "are brought [forward]," he was not using neutral terminology, but rather words that reminded all his readers of "bringing forward (to an altar) as sacrifice."[27]

Let us repeat *Didache's* prescriptions for the Eucharist:

> On the Lord's day of the Lord come together, break bread and hold eucharist, after confessing your transgressions, *that your offering may be pure.* But let no one who has a quarrel with his fellow join in your meeting until they be reconciled, *that your sacrifice be not defiled.* For this is that which was spoken by the Lord, "In every place and time *offer me a pure sacrifice,* for I am a great king," says the Lord, "and my name is wonderful among the heathen" [Mal 1:11]. (*Didache* 14:1-3)

What is meant here when the Eucharist is called a sacrifice (Greek *thysia*)? A passage in *Didache* 13:3-7 may help us:

> Therefore thou shalt take the firstfruits [Greek, *aparchē*] of the produce of the winepress and of the threshingfloor and of oxen and sheep, and shalt give them as the firstfruits to the prophets, for they are your high priests. But if you have not a prophet, give to the poor. *If thou makest bread, take the firstfruits, and give it according to the commandment.* Likewise when thou openest a *jar of wine or oil, give the firstfruits to the prophets.* Of money also and clothes, and of all your possessions, take the firstfruits, as it seems best to you, and give according to the commandment.[28]

This is an injunction to provide visiting prophets or teachers with food, drink and other commodities, and is seen as a fulfillment of the Torah's com-

---

[27]For the following, see esp. Richard P. C. Hanson, *Eucharistic Offering in the Early Church,* Grove Liturgical Study 19 (Bramcote: Grove Books, 1979).
[28]Kirsopp Lake 1:329.

mandment to offer first fruits, *bikkurim*. First fruits clearly belong to the category of *offering of thanksgiving*. Very likely, this concept was also applied to the bringing forward of bread and wine, and the prayer being said over them in the Eucharist.[29]

With this concept of thanksgiving and offering of *bikkurim* in our minds, we return to the passage quoted from *Didache* 14. The biblical text quoted is Malachi 1:11 in a very free version—perhaps because it was used liturgically already in this period (ca. A.D. 100). Later this text is quoted again and again by many church fathers. Justin says:

> The offering of fine flour . . . which was ordered to be offered on behalf of those who were cleansed from leprosy [Lev 14:10], was a [prophetic] type of the bread of the eucharist. For Jesus our Lord ordered us to do this in remembrance of the suffering which he suffered on behalf of those who are being purged . . . in order that we should at the same time give thanks to God
>
> * for having created the world with all that is in it for man's sake,
> * and also for having set us free from the evil in which we had been,
> * and for having destroyed the powers and the authorities with a complete destruction by means of Him who underwent suffering according to His will. . . .
>
> [Here follows an extensive quotation of Mal 1:10-12].
>
> He speaks at that time, so long beforehand, concerning the sacrifices that are being offered to Him in every place by us Gentiles, that is to say, the bread of the eucharist and likewise the cup of the eucharist. (*Dialogue with Trypho* 41.1-3)

We have already quoted and commented upon the eucharistic prayer hinted at in this passage. Here we shall concentrate upon the sayings about sacrifice. Justin expressly identifies the offering foretold by Malachi as the eucharistic bread and wine. How should we understand this—and is there any connection with the content of the eucharistic prayer? Let us look at another passage from Justin:

> God therefore has long since borne witness that all sacrifices offered in His name—which Jesus the Messiah enjoined, namely at the thanksgiving over the bread and the cup, which are offered in every place on the earth by the Christians—are well pleasing to Him. . . . [A new quotation of Mal 1:10-12 follows.] . . . Now, that both prayers and thanksgivings, when made by worthy people, are the only perfect and acceptable sacrifices to God, I also myself affirm. For

---

[29] In chapter nineteen above we saw how dominating the theme of first fruits was precisely in the Passover-Pentecost season, pp. 394-95.

these alone were Christians taught to make, even at the remembrance of their food, both dry and liquid, in which also the suffering which the Son of God has suffered for their sake is brought to mind. (*Dialogue with Trypho* 117.1-3)

Apparently the eucharistic prayer itself—possibly together with other, ordinary meal prayers—is here seen as the acceptable sacrifice spoken of by Malachi.

Can we synthesize these different concepts into a coherent picture? The following is proposed as a working hypothesis: Bread and wine, precisely in their capacity as bread and wine, first fruits from the field, are offered as a sacrifice of thanksgiving to the Creator, as *bikkurim*. But this is not a sacrifice in the strict, technical meaning. The wine is not poured out on the altar, and there is no burning of cereals, no smoke. Justin perhaps would have said, oh yes, there is smoke, rising to God, carrying our offering before him, a smoke acceptable to him, and that smoke is the prayers of the believers, rising from their lips.

In fact, in Revelation 5:8 we meet exactly this concept: the prayers of the saints are described as the smoke of incense. Interpreted in this way, Justin's two passages on Malachi 1:10-12 go nicely together: we offer bread and wine as an offering of thanksgiving from the first fruits of God's creation, commemorating his creation and his new creation in the saving act of Christ, and then there arises to God the pleasant and acceptable smoke of the prayers of the saints.

For a test of this hypothetical interpretation, let us turn to Irenaeus (ca. A.D. 190).

The Lord gave directions to his disciples to offer first-fruits to God from God's own creatures, not as if God stood in need of them, but that they themselves may be neither unfruitful nor ungrateful. Thus, he took the bread, which comes from creation, and he gave thanks, saying: "This is my body." He did likewise with the cup, which is part of the creation to which we ourselves belong, declaring it to be his blood, and (so) he taught the new offering of the new covenant. This is the offering which the Church received from the Apostles and which it offers throughout the world, to God who provides us with nourishments, the first-fruits of divine gifts in this new covenant.[30] Of this offering, among the prophets, Malachi had spoken beforehand . . . [another quotation of Mal 1:10-11 follows. After a while Irenaeus comments on the "incense" in the prophet's saying:] Now John, in Revelation, declares that the "incense" is "the prayers of the

---

[30]Notice how Irenaeus here spiritualizes the concept of first fruits, very much along the same lines as the *Didache* prayers spiritualized the wine and bread.

saints." The oblation of the Church, therefore, which the Lord gave instructions to be offered throughout the world, is accounted with God a pure sacrifice, and is acceptable to him. . . . For by the gift both honour and affection are shown towards the King; and the Lord, wishing us to offer it in all simplicity and innocence, did express himself thus: "When you offer your gift on the altar, and remember that your brother has anything against you . . . [Mt 5:23-24 as in *Didache* 14:2]. We are bound, therefore, to offer to God the firstfruits of his creation, as Moses also says, "You shall not appear emptyhanded in the presence of the Lord your God." (*Against Heresies* 4.17.5—18.1)

This text fully confirms our provisional interpretation of Justin's fragmentary remarks; it is also a nice completion of *Didache* 14.

It would seem that all this implies a fundamental distinction made by the early church with regard to the Old Testament sacrifices—a distinction, roughly speaking, between sacrifices of thanksgiving on the one hand and sacrifices of atonement on the other hand. The early church shared the conviction of Hebrews that the *atoning* sacrifices had once and for all been replaced by Jesus' death on the cross. There is therefore no continuation of any atoning sacrifice in Christian worship. But the early church took a different position concerning the sacrifices of praise and thanksgiving. These sacrifices continue, not only as a sacrifice of the lips, but even as a sacrifice of bread and wine, first fruits of God's creation.

What happened later—we may perhaps observe its beginnings in Hippolytus[31]—was a shift in the Christian understanding of the nature of the eucharisic sacrifice. More and more, it *was* understood as an atoning sacrifice, and the object of the sacrifice was then no longer understood to be bread and wine, but the body and blood of Christ. At that point, we have arrived at the classic Catholic concept of "the sacrifice of the Mass"; but as we have shown above, this was not how the Eucharist was understood from the beginning.

So, to link back to what we saw in Irenaeus above, we could perhaps sum up by saying that we offer bread and wine on the altar as a sacrifice of thanksgiving, a sacrifice of first fruits "of the first creation," and we carry these offerings before God's heavenly throne through the eucharistic prayer. Then, after the prayer is finished, we receive them back, no longer as bread and wine only, but as the body and blood of Christ, the first fruits "of the new creation."

---

[31]Not in the eucharistic prayer, but in the prayer for the consecration of a bishop.

Postscript

To my mind there is a remarkable continuity in the development of the eucharistic service, which we have traced from Luke 22, via *Didache,* Justin and Irenaeus. The Passover setting and the Passover connotations are most clearly seen in the beginning, but are never lost sight of. This confirms the proposition made in chapter nineteen: each Eucharist is a small, weekly Passover celebration, even when the meal was eliminated and the Eucharist itself transposed to Sunday morning rather than evening. It is not difficult to understand how this dislocation weakened the Passover connection. It is all the more remarkable that it was not entirely lost.

Temple Square

The Jewish Passover celebration on the 14th of Nisan had two focal points: first the father of the family brought his lamb for Passover into the temple courtyard and slaughtered it there as a sacrifice. In so doing, he acted in a *priestly* role, and the sacrifice could only take place in the temple. Secondly, he brought the sacrificed lamb home, and shared it with his household as the main dish during the Passover meal. This meal was not a temple event, and nobody in particular was acting as priest there. (One could say, perhaps, that in feasting on sacrificial meat, everyone present acted as priests).

In the early Christian Eucharist, the act in the temple clearly corresponded to Jesus' sacrificial death on the cross. The new temple is Calvary. The eucharistic meal, on the other hand, corresponds to that which does not take place in the temple, but in the homes afterwards: the Passover meal.

This is how it was in the beginning. But beginning with Hippolytus and gaining momentum in Cyprian (ca. A.D. 250), a new understanding came to the fore: *even the sacrificial act of Jesus is repeated* (in some sense) during the eucharistic service of the church. Then the leader of the Eucharist becomes a priest, offering sacrifice like the priests of the old temple. And the people are no longer priests bringing their offering of praise and thanksgiving, but become a non-priestly people receiving the sacrificial food offered by the priest. The old temple comes back and transforms the new.

Suggestions for Further Reading

Many of the general studies listed for chapter nineteen contain relevant material on the Eucharist and its development. In addition, note the following more specialized studies (listed in chronological order):

Hans Lietzmann, *Messe und Herrenmahl: Eine Studie zur Geschichte der Liturgie,* Arbeiten zur Kirchengeschichte 8 (Bonn: Marcus und Weber, 1926; 3rd ed. Berlin: Walter de Gruyter, 1955); English edition: *Mass and Lord's Supper,* with additional material by R. D. Richardson (Leiden: E. J. Brill, 1953; new ed. 1979).

Willy Rordorf et al., *The Eucharist of the Early Christians* (New York: Pueblo, 1978).

R. P. C. Hanson, *Eucharistic Offering in the Early Church,* Grove Liturgical Study 19 (Bramcote: Grove, 1979).

Gillian Feeley-Harnik, *The Lord's Table: Eucharist and Passover in Early Christianity*

(Philadelphia: University of Pennsylvania Press, 1981).

Enrico Mazza, *The Origins of the Eucharistic Prayer* (Collegeville, Minn.: Liturgical Press, 1995).

Eugene LaVerdiere, *The Eucharist in the New Testament and the Early Church* (Collegeville, Minn.: Liturgical Press, 1996).

PART 4

EPILOGUE

21

THE CHURCH FACING
A NEW ERA

*D*uring *the twenty preceding chapters, we have been studying different aspects of the life and faith of the pre-Constantinian church—though somewhat selectively. The purpose of this epilogue is not to tie up loose ends and supplement what has been left out in the preceding chapters, but rather to focus on the significant event that marked the end of the period we have been studying and opened an entirely new era of church history—the event commonly known as "the Constantinian revolution." It is not my purpose to give anything like a comprehensive coverage of this event and its consequences. Rather, I think it appropriate to focus on those aspects that have been our guidelines all the way: What effect did this event have on the Christian-Jewish relation and on Christianity's relationship to its Jewish roots?*

The Great Roman Crisis and Restitution

In the greater part of the third century the Roman Empire staggered from one crisis to another, on the external frontiers as well as with regard to internal struggles for power. Along the western and eastern frontiers foreign armies succeeded repeatedly in overrunning the Roman legions, sometimes on many borders simultaneously. Internally, the empire was weakened in its very center of power: there was an apparently endless series of coups by rivaling caesars and of mutiny from below. The impressive building of the empire was cracking in its walls as well as in its foundations.

Two emperors in particular should be credited with mending the walls and rebuilding the foundations—so successfully, in fact, that the main part of the empire (the Eastern) was to last for another thousand years (until the Turkish conquest of Constantinople, "New Rome," in A.D. 1453). They are Diocletian (284-305) and Constantine (306-337). (They had an important precursor in Aurelian, 270-275.) These two names belong together as far as the political and military, internal and external restructuring of the empire is concerned. At the same time, these two names encapsulate the dramatic change that took place with regard to the religious and ideological basis of the empire: Diocletian initiated the most large-scale attempt to eradicate the church and Christianity, trying to reestablish traditional Roman religion as the basis of the empire; Constantine made Christianity part of the very foundation of the empire and made the church his ally.

The Great Persecution
It was only toward the end of his reign that Diocletian paid much attention to the Christians. The forty-plus years since the last great persecutions under Decius (250-251) and Valerian (257-260) had been a tranquil and prosperous period for the church, and especially during the last quarter of the third century converts to Christianity were received in large numbers. It is very likely that the sheer numerical strength of the church worried the emperor a great deal. In addition to this, the church displayed a solid yet flexible organization, a high degree of internal discipline and loyalty, and a remarkable cohesion and unity despite the fact that communities were scattered all over the empire's territory. One has to call to mind that Christians all along had refused to comply with a duty incumbent on all Roman citizens: to pay homage to the Roman national gods, so as to ensure their benevolent protection of the empire. The Jews were the only people who were granted an exemption from this duty; the church never was. Strictly speaking, Christians had, therefore, been illegally neglecting one important aspect of their duties as citizens of the empire. For emperors who took traditional religion seriously, Christians were, by their very existence, a threat to stability: they might provoke the gods to anger. This seems to have been the driving force behind the first large-scale persecutions under Decius and Valerian; it probably also motivated Diocletian, and especially his fellow emperor and eventual successor

(after Diocletian's abdication in 305), Galerius. The Christians at this time may still have been "a small group, but they succeeded in becoming a big problem."[1]

It seems that Diocletian wanted to crush the church by harassing and compromising its leaders, rather than by producing martyrs in great numbers. No blood was to be shed, he said, but in February 303 he issued an edict that ordered the demolition of all buildings used as churches and the burning of the Christians' sacred books, to be handed over by their leaders. This last measure was perhaps calculated to discredit bishops and presbyters as traitors—a tactic that succeeded in some cases. Christians in high offices were also to be deposed. These measures were clearly intended to make church-life nonfunctional: the leaders and the most influential members were to be discredited and humiliated, church buildings and the Scriptures to be destroyed.

Apparently this policy met with only moderate success, because in the summer of 303 the first edict was followed by yet another. This time the imperial order was that bishops and other heads of Christian communities should be arrested and forced to sacrifice to the Roman gods. This, in fact, created a problem with over-crowded prisons; veteran criminal inmates had to be thrown out to make room for bishops and presbyters! Therefore a third edict the same year ordered the church leaders to sacrifice in a hurry and then be released. Some yielded, but not many.

During 304, Diocletian's fellow emperor Galerius took over as managing director of the persecution, and he soon escalated the campaign to an all-out war on Christians. A fourth edict early in 304 ordered every Christian to sacrifice or suffer torture and death.[2] This policy was actually executed in the eastern part of the empire, under Galerius's jurisdiction, and continued intermittently until 311. It was the longest and most terrible persecution the church had to suffer from the Roman Empire. In the West, little was done to enforce any of the decrees, and after 305 all persecutions ceased.

"The Constantinian Revolution"

It was, actually, from the westernmost and northernmost part of the empire that a new imperial leader and a completely new policy came. In 306 the Caesar of the West, Constantius Chlorus, died, and his son Constantine was proclaimed *Augustus* (supreme emperor) by the Roman legion in York in

---

[1]Peter R. Brown, *The World of Late Antiquity: From Marcus Aurelius to Muhammad* (London: Thames & Hudson, 1976), p. 65.
[2]The whole series of edicts is found in Frend, *New Eusebius*, pp. 273-75.

England.[3] From this point of departure, Constantine systematically worked his way eastward and southward, expanding his political and military powerbase all the time. In 312 he had come as far as Rome, and in a famous battle by the Milvian Bridge immediately north of Rome he defeated the then reigning Caesar of the West, Maxentius. Two Christian historians have told the story of this battle, Lactantius and Eusebius, and both claim that Constantine had a vision before the battle: he saw a cross of light and perceived the words "by this, conquer!" *(in hoc vinces)*. Accordingly, Constantine had all his soldiers wear cross-marked shields.[4]

This event is usually called "the conversion of Constantine," and although its exact meaning is controversial among scholars, there is no doubt that from then on Constantine constantly favored the Christians and increasingly talked about "the supreme God" or even "Christ" as the deity that had called him and guided him to restore the Roman Empire and bring peace and order.

In the meantime, Galerius in the East—on his deathbed early in 311—had recalled the edicts ordering the persecutions. His somewhat strained explanation for ending the persecutions tells much about the frame of mind among the last pagan emperors: He had ordered the persecution, in the first place, to protect the welfare of the state because Christians offensively had abandoned the religious practices of their (pagan) fathers. But this, he said, had the unfortunate consequence that Christians not only continued not to pray to the gods of Rome, but even stopped conducting worship to their own God (the very aim of the measures of the persecution!). The edict concludes: "Wherefore, in accordance with this our indulgence it will be their duty to pray their god for our good estate, and that of the state, and their own, that the commonwealth may endure on every side unharmed, and they may be able to live securely in their habitations."[5] It was, of course, a veiled admission that Galerius was beaten, that his policies had failed and had to be completely reversed.

His successor in the East, Maximin, tried to reverse the policy once more and resumed a brief but intense persecution. Constantine, however, had

---

[3]The quarters of this legion were found by accident under reconstruction works on the foundations of the York Minster (the Gothic cathedral) in the 1960s, and are presently to be seen in the new crypt under the cathedral.

[4]Lactantius, *On the Deaths of the Persecutors* 44:3-6; and Eusebius, *Life of Constantine* 1:26-29; English translation of both texts in *New Eusebius*, pp. 283-84. According to Lactantius, a Latin X "with its top bent over" was marked on the shields, "thus he marked Christ." This could indicate that the Latin X was modified to form the Greek XP monogram, the first two letters in the Greek title Christ [XPICTOC].

[5] Frend, *New Eusebius*, p. 280, where Galerius's edict of toleration is given in full (Lactantius *On the Death of the Persecutors* 34).

found a new ally in the East, Licinius, who beat Maximin in battle in 313. In June of the same year, Constantine and Licinius published an edict later known as "the Edict of Milan" as valid law for all the empire. It became the Magna Carta of Christian victory over the persecutors. Formally, it put Christian faith and all other faiths on equal footing—and the decree almost sounds modern in its propagation of full freedom of conscience and personal choice in religious matters. But it can escape no reader of the edict that it singled out Christianity as the only religion named and that the whole purpose of the edict was to favor Christianity and give full restitution to the church after the persecutions.

Licinius later changed his mind, acted against the spirit of the decree and also established himself as Constantine's rival and enemy in the East. But that became his own destruction; Constantine went after him in 324, routed him out of his stronghold in Byzantium (present day Istanbul) and had him captured and put in jail on September 18, 324. Constantine became the one and only ruler of all the empire; he abolished the fragile sharing of power between four elected caesars instituted by Diocletian and in practice established a dynastic pattern instead. From now on the empire was to be ruled by the emperor's sons, plain and simple.

Bishop Eusebius of Caesarea, who had lived through the great persecution in the East and had probably started work on his monumental *Ecclesiastical History* before the persecution, had postponed its publication in order to be able to include "the end of the story." Now, finally, in the aftermath of Constantine's defeat of Licinius, he could put the final stroke to his master work and conclude it with the following exuberant finale:

> Constantine, the most mighty victor, resplendent with every virtue that godliness bestows, together with his son Crispus, an emperor most dear to God and in all respects resembling his father, recovered the East that belonged to them, and formed the Roman Empire, as in the days of old, into a single united whole, bringing under their peaceful rule all of it, from the rising sun . . . even to the uttermost limits of the declining day. So then, there was taken away from men all fear of those who formerly oppressed them; they celebrated brilliant festivals; all things were filled with light, and men, formerly downcast, looked at each other with smiling faces and beaming eyes; with dancing and hymns in city and country alike they gave honour first of all to God the universal King, for this they had been instructed to do, and then to the pious emperor with his sons beloved of God. Old ills were forgotten and oblivion cast on every deed of impiety. Present good things were enjoyed, with the further hope of those which were yet to come. In short, there were promulgated in every place ordinances of

the victorious emperor full of love for humanity, and laws that betokened munificence and true piety. Thus truly, when all tyranny had been purged away, the kingdom that belonged to them was preserved steadfast and undisputed for Constantine and his sons alone: who, when they had made it their very first action to cleanse the world from the hatred of God, conscious of the good things that he had bestowed upon them, displayed their love of virtue and of God, their piety and gratitude towards the Deity, by their manifest deeds in the sight of all men. (*Ecclesiastical History* 10.9.6-9)[6]

For believers who had experienced the great persecution of 303-313, the events under Constantine between 313 and 324 must have been amazing, indeed wonderful, and Eusebius may be excused for thinking—as indeed he seems to have done—that this heralded the establishment of the kingdom of God on earth. The majority of believers no doubt saw the embrace of Christianity by their former persecutors as an obvious sign of God's merciful governance of history, and as the beginning of an entirely new epoch in the history of the church.

What Has the Emperor to Do with the Church?

It soon appeared that the Roman emperor in many ways was a problematic ally, especially when he insisted upon being not only in some sense the supreme ruler of the church, at least in its external affairs, but also the one whose responsibility it was to secure unity and peace within the church. The first ones to experience this side of the Christian Roman Empire were believers in North Africa. A church schism occurred there in 311-312; soon the breakaway faction was named after its supreme leader, Bishop Donatus. Even before becoming ruler in the East, Constantine tried to set matters straight in North Africa by coercing the Donatists back into line (from 313 onward). He did not succeed, but many Christians learned the lesson that an emperor meddling in church affairs might be a worse persecutor than a pagan one. "For Donatus and his followers the empire was still Babylon and the emperor had no call to meddle in Church affairs."[7]

It is not easy in just a few words to describe the new challenges that now faced Christians in the East and West. Here we must be content with the following brief descriptions.

---

[6]Lawlor/Oulton 1:324-25.
[7]Frend, *Martyrdom and Persecution*, p. 554. Frend's last chapter in this book, "What Has the Emperor to Do with the Church? 312-361," pp. 536-68, is highly relevant to our present theme.

Renouncing the World in a "Christian" Empire

Christians had been used to considering themselves a small elect group, surrounded by a hostile majority, "the world." They had been the "called ones," the few elected from the masses of a lost world. Now, all of a sudden, "the world" was supposed to belong to the church. Ideally all Roman citizens were supposed to be or become Christians; under Emperor Theodosius, A.D. 380, orthodox Christianity was by law made the only legal religion in the empire. The repercussions, of course, were many and long-lasting.

How were Christians in these new circumstances to "renounce the world"? How were they to continue the proud martyr tradition of the pre-Constantinian church? How realize the old conception of the church as the chosen minority in a hostile world? The answer was found in a new movement that originated in the same years that Constantine swept from West to East to Christianize the empire. The answer was found in a literal exodus from the wealthy, affluent society in the city into the desert. The answer came in a new form of Christian life: that of the hermit and monk, the ascetic, celibate follower of Christ's command: Sell everything, follow me! The answer was found in the monastery. From the early fourth century, two types of Christian life existed side by side in the church and were to continue as two distinct models right up to our own days in the Orthodox and Catholic Churches. Some chose to live as a Christian "in the world," involved in civil life through family, job and eventually some public office. Others chose the "apostolic," or even "heavenly" life of the ascetic who has made an exodus from the world and in living apart from the world has already anticipated the heavenly life.

"The Sanctification of Time"

Substantive changes took place in the worship and community life of the church. Soon after 320, Constantine began constructing several large church buildings, then and later known as *basilicas*,[8] that could hold large crowds of people. But since all the world was now supposed to attend service in the church, the barrier between the crowd in the church and the holiness of the service at the altar had to be emphasized in a new way. Thus the service became something done by the consecrated priests, "the chosen ones" (Greek, *kleros*), with the crowd, "the people," watching from a distance.

---

[8]The name means "royal (halls)"; the exact background and meaning of applying this name to the Constantinian and post-Constantinian church buildings is not known. Possibly the idea was that the churches were images of the heavenly royal hall in which Christ sat on his royal throne. In this they would be somewhat functionally parallel to the Jerusalem temple.

Ceremonies from the imperial court were introduced into worship, such as carrying candles and censers in front of the bishop (or priests). The fact that these paralleled ceremonies described in the Bible for the tabernacle or temple was not by accident: the ceremonies of the temple to a great extent had the same background in ceremonies of the Oriental royal court. Accordingly, the net result of this development as regards liturgy was that Christian worship, from being modeled mainly on the simple pattern of the synagogue worship—the worship of the priestly people—became more like the Old Testament temple worship with the high priest (bishop), priests (presbyters) and Levites (deacons) conducting the service, with the laypeople attending.[9]

In the pre-Constantinian period the worship had been oriented toward the future coming of the kingdom. There had been no complete "ecclesiastical year"; the only festive season was the period from Pesach to Shavuot, during which time Jesus as the risen one had visited his disciples—and now met them during worship. The dramatic events of Jesus' Passover were celebrated within one single night and day (cf. above, chapter nineteen). This orientation toward the future and Christ's second coming was deeply modified and weakened during the Constantinian period. Instead of looking forward to being released from the world, Christians began to think that they were to *stay* in the world and Christianize it, conquer it. Worship developed a different orientation; instead of being mainly future-oriented, it began looking back to the decisive events of salvation history, it became "historicized." In the weekly services of Sunday morning the whole of biblical history was retold and liturgically reenacted, especially the story of Christ, but gradually also the entire biblical history from creation to new Jerusalem.

The Christian year was also restructured according to the same principle: during the whole year, the story of Jesus was followed through its main events. This meant that the Passover-Shavuot season had to be restructured. It was now conceived of as a day-by-day reenactment of Jesus' final week in Jerusalem, followed by Ascension on the fortieth day and Pentecost on the fiftieth day after Easter Sunday. The whole Easter season was preceded by the community's time of preparation through prayer, exorcisms and fasting: Lent.

But this principle, "with Jesus through the year," made clear that some

---

[9]On the new Constantinian and post-Constantinian elements in the liturgy, see Jungmann, *The Early Liturgy* (Suggestions chapter nineteen), pp. 122-52.

vital events in the life of Jesus had no corresponding festivals and were not celebrated: for example, his birth, his circumcision, his baptism by John. The reason these events had no festivals during the entire pre-Constantinian period is probably the simple fact that they did not synchronize with any Jewish festivals in the New Testament story. (Indirectly, this is a strong testimony to the Jewish character of early Christian worship!) And even in the fourth century only the *birth* of Jesus acquired a separate festival: Christmas on December 25th. In this way, the Christian year got the same two foci of attention as the creed itself: it passed directly from Christ's birth (Christmas) to his passion/resurrection/ascension (Easter/Pentecost). This basic fourth-century structure still determines the ecclesiastical year, although minor celebrations of the other gospel events (circumcision and baptism of Jesus, his transfiguration, the announcement to Mary, John's nativity etc.) were added later, mostly in the early medieval period.

The new festival of Christmas had, as we said, no Jewish background and was accordingly fixed on the basis of the Roman (Julian) calendar, not the Jewish. Easter, too, was moved away from Judaism with regard to calendar. We have seen that the first move in this direction occurred already in the second century, with the choice of the nearest Sunday as the day of the resurrection rather than Passover Eve on the fourteenth of Nisan. But this still kept Christian Easter roughly simultaneous with the Jewish Passover. The Council of Nicaea (325) took a new step: it was branded as "Judaizing" when Eastern Christians synchronized their calendar (not necessarily their Easter) with the Jewish calendar.

> We ought not have anything in common with the Jews, for the Saviour has shown us another way; our worship follows a more legitimate and more convenient course. Consequently, . . . we desire, dearest brethren, to separate ourselves from the detestable company of the Jews, for it is truly shameful for us to hear them boast that without their direction [concerning calendar] we could not keep this festival.[10]

Accordingly, from now on the Jewish and Christian year drifted further apart.

The Sanctification of Places: The Idea of the Holy Land

If in respect to calendar (the dimension of time) the church distanced itself

---

[10]Encyclical letter of the Nicene council, quoted by Eusebius in *Life of Constantine* 3.17-20; the quotation here is from 3.18, *NPNF* 2nd ser. 1:524.

from its Jewish roots, there was to some extent an opposite tendency with regard to its attitude toward the geographical roots of Christianity.[11] The land of Israel was now part of a Christian Roman Empire, and the first project Constantine undertook in the land of Israel was quite literally to dig. And his archaeologists and architects were not digging at random.

In the aftermath of the Bar Kokhba war, the Roman Emperor Hadrian had more or less razed Jerusalem and built it anew as *Aelia Capitolina* according to a different plan altogether. As a part of this project he built a huge temple platform on the place where Golgotha and the tomb of Jesus had been, and a Venus temple on top of it, so that these places became inaccessible, physically as well as morally, to Christians. It seems Hadrian did the same to the cave in Bethlehem that was regarded by believers as the room in which Jesus was born. According to Jerome, who lived for many years in Bethlehem (at the end of the fourth century) and should be well informed, a sacred grove dedicated to Tammuz/Adonis had been on top of the cave, and in the cave itself Adonis had been worshipped. Hadrian had all Jews expelled from Bethlehem, and may have consecrated the cave to Adonis as a deliberate profanation of the place which he knew was sacred to Jewish believers.

Constantine's mother Helena came to the land of Israel with the emperor's architects and master builders, and they immediately began three great building projects. In Bethlehem the cave of birth was cleaned and decorated, and above it an enormous basilica raised. In Jerusalem the temple of Hadrian on top of Golgotha was demolished, and they started digging away the temple platform beneath it. On the slopes of the Mount of Olives a third church building was raised; the church commemorating the ascension of Jesus and his return. As John Wilkinson has well observed, these three Constantinian churches in the land of Israel correspond to the main events in the second article of the creed:[12]

[11]For the following, cf. W. Telfer, "Constantine's Holy Land Plan," *Studia Patristica*, vol. 1, Texte und Untersuchungen 63 (Berlin: Akademieverlag, 1955), pp. 696-700; Peter W. L. Walker, *Holy City, Holy Places? Christian Attitudes to Jerusalem and the Holy Land in the Fourth Century*, Oxford Early Christian Studies (Oxford: Clarendon, 1990); Robert L. Wilken, *The Land Called Holy: Palestine in Christian History and Thought* (New Haven and London: Yale University Press, 1992); cf. also Wilken's briefer survey in "Byzantine Palestine. A Christian Holy Land," *Biblical Archaeologist* 51 (1988): 214-37; E. D. Hunt, "Constantine and Jerusalem," *Journal of Ecclesiastical History* 48 (1997): 405-24.
[12]Wilkinson, *Jerusalem*, p. 178.

* Born of Mary:
* Crucified under Pontius Pilate
  Buried, risen the third day
* Ascended to heaven,
  Shall return.

* Church of Nativity in Bethlehem
* Church of the Holy Sepulchre
  (Golgotha, tomb of Jesus)
* Eleona Church (now in ruins,
  Mount of Olives)

The most dramatic of these projects was the one on the site of Golgotha and the tomb of Jesus. Eusebius wrote an eyewitness report of what happened:

> The emperor [after having demolished Hadrian's temple] directed that the ground itself should be dug up to a considerable depth, and the soil which had been polluted by the foul impurities of demon worship transported to a far distant place. This also was accomplished without delay. But as soon as the original surface of the ground, beneath the covering of earth, appeared, immediately, and contrary to all expectation, the venerable and hallowed monument of our Saviour's resurrection [the tomb] was discovered. Then indeed did this most holy cave present a faithful similitude of His return to life, in that, after lying buried in darkness, it again emerged to light, and afforded to all who came to witness the sight, a clear and visible proof of the wonders of which that spot had once been the scene, a testimony to the resurrection of the Saviour clearer than any voice could give. (*Life of Constantine* 3.28)[13]

In the years following Constantine's reign, other large basilicas were erected, one after the other, on all the important scenes of the gospel stories, and even on many important Old Testament sites. Just as the worship service was formed to celebrate the entire history of salvation, so the land of Israel became the living illustrated Bible, containing the scenes and locations of sacred history—first and foremost the scenes of the Word-become-flesh. At a time when theology emphasized the divine nature of Christ, this living Bible was there to remind theologians as well as other pious visitors that the Word had really become flesh; that there was a physical concreteness to all salvation history that should never be forgotten. Thus originated the Christian-Byzantine concept of "the Holy Land"; the fourth- and fifth-century basilicas enshrining this idea are still with us, ruined or still standing.[14]

---

[13]*NPNF* 2nd ser. 1:527-28. For extensive comment on this passage, and on the difficult question of why Eusebius is apparently silent concerning the cliff of Golgotha, see esp. Stephan Borgehammar, *How the Holy Cross was Found: From Event to Medieval Legend*, Bibliotheca Theologiae Practicae, Kyrkovetenskapliga Studier 47 (Stockholm: Almquist & Wiksell, 1991), pp. 93-122.
[14]The two books by Walker and Wilken listed in note 11 trace the development of the Holy Land concept in great detail.

This search for the geographical roots of Christianity was not accompanied by any corresponding appreciation of the Jewish people and Judaism as the legitimate owners of these places and this land. Rather, the most sacred place for all Jews, the temple area, was neither renovated nor adorned by any Byzantine building (except possibly the sixth- or seventh-century building of the Golden Gate). It was left in its miserable ruined condition, as a sign of Judaism's defeat.

Christian Philo-Semitism: A Grassroots Movement

"Anti-Semitism" is an established term in our days, used for almost every type of enmity towards Judaism and the Jewish people. It is more difficult to find a good term for the opposite attitude: sympathy for Jews and Judaism. "To love" in Greek is *philein*, to be a philo-sopher is to love wisdom *(sophia)*. Accordingly, some scholars have coined the term "philo-Semitism" to describe a positive attitude toward Judaism. For convenience, we shall use this term here.

From what we have seen above, it would be reasonable to conclude that the Constantinian era heralded an increase in anti-Semitic attitudes among Christians, rather than the opposite. And if we stick to utterances by church leadership, councils and imperial legislation, that is no doubt true. Almost all preserved literary and documentary sources represent the above-mentioned authorities and their points of view, and there is no doubt that we have a very pronounced anti-Judaism in these sources.[15]

But—and this is often overlooked—these same sources often indirectly testify to quite different attitudes among those to whom they are directed. When bishops warned their flock not to socialize with Jews, this must mean that at least some Christians socialized with Jews. When church councils passed canons forbidding Christians to visit synagogues or take part in Jewish festivals, it probably meant that at least some Christians did so. The very existence of these anti-Jewish measures, and the need to repeat them and even sharpen them all through antiquity and during the early Middle Ages, is eloquent testimony to the untold and unwritten story of Christian philo-Semitism. It seems to have been very much a Christian grassroots phenomenon.

One of the literary sources that allows us an extraordinaryily good and broad look at this phenomenon is a series of sermons that usually play a great role in every story of Christian anti-Semitism. In A.D. 386-387 John Chrysos-

---

[15]For a nearly complete survey of anti-Jewish documents and utterances of all kinds and categories, see Heinz Schreckenberg, *Die christlichen Adversus-Judaeos-Texte und ihr literarisches und historisches Umfeld (1.-11.Jh.)*, Europäische Hochschulschriften Reihe 23 Theologie 172 (Frankfurt am Main/Bern: Peter Lang, 1982).

tom, newly ordained presbyter, preached eight sermons in the great basilica at Antioch in Syria.[16] His stated purpose in these sermons was to win back to the church some Christians who had begun visiting the local synagogue. They themselves did not consider this a break with the church nor an apostasy from their Christian faith. But that was the way Chrysostom viewed the matter, and his eight sermons—traditionally called *Against the Jews*—are not really addressed to the Jews, but to these *Christian* "Judaizers."

Chrysostom provided us with some rather specific information concerning these people. First of all, let us notice something he did *not* say. He did not accuse them of any doctrinal error. He did not say there is something wrong with their Christology or their ethics. The Judaizers were not blamed for something they believed or taught or said, but for something they did.

First, he said they "go to watch the [Jewish] festivals, and others will join the Jews in keeping their feasts and observing their fasts."[17] This means that these Christians took part in the Jewish festival celebrations in the synagogue. Chrysostom specified this: they took part in the fast from New Year *(Rosh Hashanah)* to Yom Kippur, and then joined the celebration of Tabernacles *(Disc. 1,* 1.5, p. 3-4); they also celebrated the Passover according to the Jewish calendar and the Jewish ritual *(Disc. 3,* passim, pp. 47-70), and seem to have been invited to share the Passover meal with their Jewish friends. "You observe with them [the Jews] the fellowship of the festivals, you go to their profane places, enter their unclean doors, and share in the table of demons" *(Disc.1,* 7.5, p. 28). "How can we blame the Jews for waiting for you in their houses when it is you who go running to them?" *(Disc.3,* 6.10, p. 69). In general, the Judaizers held the Jewish festivals and the Jewish way of life to be something venerable and holy: "Many, I know, respect the Jews and think their present way of life is a venerable one" *(Disc.1,* 3.1, p. 10). The Judaizers admired the Jewish ceremonies, they thought they were "venerable and great" *(Disc. 1,* 6.5, pp. 23-24); and that the Jewish festivals had "something solemn and great about them" *(Disc. 1,* 7.1, p. 26).

The Judaizers also visited the synagogue. "What is it that you are rushing to see in the synagogue?" Chrysostom asked *(Disc. 4,* 7.4, p. 92). In his own

---

[16]Greek text in Migne, *Patrologia graeca,* vol. 48, cols. 843-942; English trans.: Paul W. Harkins, *Saint John Chrysostom: Discourses against Judaizing Christians,* The Fathers of the Church: A New Translation 68 (Washington, D.C.: The Catholic University of America Press, 1979). In the following, references are given to Discourse number, chapter, and passage; and page reference to Harkins's translation.

[17]*Discourse 1,* 1.5; p. 4. Cf. *Disc. 1,* 4.7, p. 16; 5.1, p. 18; 6.5, pp. 23-24; 7.5, p. 28; 8.1, p. 32; *Disc. 2,* 3.8, p. 45; *Disc. 3,* 2.5-6, pp. 53-54; *Disc. 4,* 3.4-5, pp. 77-78; 3.8-9, p. 80; 4.1, pp. 80-81; 7.4, p. 92.

polemics, he gave some indications of the real answers of the Judaizers to this question. "Many are now . . . destroying us and exalting the Jews. These men consider the Jews as more trustworthy teachers than their own Fathers" (*Disc. 3*, 6.6, p. 68). The Judaizers seem to have held the local rabbi in high regard. Not only did they attend the synagogue service, they also preferred the rabbi as a mitigator in their lawsuits. Chrysostom tells us about a Christian husband who took his wife to the synagogue "to swear there an oath about some matters under dispute with him" (*Disc. 1*, 3.4, p. 12). Chrysostom tried to prevent this, and "asked him why he rejected the church and dragged the woman to the place where the Hebrews assembled. He answered that many people had told him that oaths sworn there were more to be feared" (*Disc. 1*, 3:5, p. 12). Chrysostom also tells us that the synagogue building itself was regarded with great reverence by the Judaizers, partly because the Torah rolls kept in the synagogue were regarded holy. "Since there are some who think of the synagogue as a holy place, I must say a few words to them. Why do you reverence that place? . . . They answer that the Law and the books of the prophets are kept there" (*Disc. 1*, 5.2, p. 19).

The Judaizers also had a high regard for the Jews as intercessors and physicians in case of illness. "You profess you are a Christian, but you rush off to their synagogues and beg them to help you" (*Disc. 8*, 8.9, p. 238). The Judaizers were reported as saying, "They (the Jews) promise to make me well, and so I go to them" (*Disc. 8*, 5.6, p. 222).

In all of this, the Judaizers did not convert to Judaism, did not circumcise, and only kept *some* ritual laws (*Disc. 2*, 2, pp. 38-42). The very fact that Jews were willing to receive them at their tables and have meal fellowship with them is indirect proof that the Judaizers at least obeyed the apostolic decree of Acts 15 concerning blood and strangled animals. It is possible that they avoided pork and tried, in general, to respect the rules of *kashrut* when eating together with Jews.

Chrysostom tells us two things more about the Judaizers. First, they seem to have been simple people; they were unable to give satisfactory theological, theoretical reasons for their behavior.

> If I were to ask them, you would then clearly know how untimely the contentiousness of these men is. They cannot explain what they do. But they refuse to ask anybody, just as if they were wiser than anybody else. . . . They do not have the answers themselves, but they refuse to follow those who have been appointed to lead them. They have simply risked all they have on this silly practice. (*Disc. 3*, 2.6, p. 54)

In other words, this was a grassroots phenomenon, much disliked by appointed teachers such as Chrysostom.

Second, the majority of the Judaizers were women. Chrysostom exhorted the husbands to take authority over their Judaizing wives (*Disc. 2*, 3.2-5, pp. 43-45); it seems that a Judaizing wife rather than husband was the typical situation.

Finally, how many of these philo-Semites were there in the Christian community of Antioch? Chrysostom hints: far too many, so many that one should rather not speak about it.

> Let us not go around saying: "How many kept the [Jewish] fast? . . . Rather, let us show our concern for them. Even if those who observed the fast are many, you, my beloved, must not make a show and a parade of this calamity in the church; you must cure it. If someone tells you that many have observed the fast, stop him from talking so that the rumor may not get around and become public knowledge. (*Disc. 8*, 4.5, p. 218)

These glimpses from Chrysostom in the last decades of the fourth century have considerable exemplary value and should not be regarded as unique exceptions.[18] But how are we to explain this phenomenon in a church whose leadership was against it all the time? If we think of the effect of countless sermons and lectures given in the churches, the existence of Christian anti-Jewish attitudes needs no explanation. But the existence of philo-Semitism does.

Let us reflect a while on its characteristics. The Judaizers were not a sect in the classical meaning of that term; that is, they were not followers of any particular leader. One cannot name any sect founder; even the old sources do not.[19] It was not an organized movement. It had no leadership structure of its own. Even the old sources do not speak of the Judaizers as a distinctive group or party. They had no distinctive doctrines, heretical or otherwise.

It seems Marcel Simon has captured well the situation when he says that the phenomenon of Judaizers does not represent a sect on the fringes of the church, but simply a tendency within the church; a certain direction that

---

[18]As was said earlier, the story of Christian philo-Semitism is mostly untold and unwritten. Some preliminary sketches are given in Oskar Skarsaune, "The Neglected Story of Christian Philo-Semitism in Antiquity and the Early Middle Ages," *Mishkan* 21, no. 2 (1994), 40-51; for a somewhat fuller treatment of Chrysostom's evidence, see Wolfram Kinzig, "'Non-Separation': Closeness and Co-Operation Between Jews and Christians in the Fourth Century," *Vigiliae Christianae* 45 (1991): 27-53.

[19]In general, the heresiologists of the early church had a tendency to invent "founders" where none existed, as with the famous "Ebion" in Tertullian: fictive founder of the Ebionites (*Prescription Against Heretics*, 10:8; 32:3-5; 33:11).

mainstream Christianity took in certain milieus.[20] One could add that the Judaizing tendency seems to have had few adherents among the clergy; it was a lay phenomenon. And many women were involved.

So how do we explain this phenomenon? Simon points, quite simply, to the social contact with neighbor Jews. The Judaizing movement seems to have been strongest in areas with strong Jewish colonies, especially where these colonies were known to have been well-integrated into social life and not isolated.[21]

But still, this would explain social contact, it would explain a general friendliness, but why the active participation in Jewish festivals? Why the partial observance of ritual laws, far beyond what was necessary for social contact? And, perhaps the most puzzling question: How do we explain that these Christians seem to have been received in such a friendly manner by the Jews?

At this point I suggest we take a step beyond Simon and propose an explanation based on the theory of early Christian mission that has been propounded in this book. Briefly summarized, the theory is this: The most important target group for early Christian mission among the Gentiles was the so-called God-fearing Gentiles, that is, the Gentiles who were attracted to Judaism, visited the synagogue, were familiar with the Scriptures (the Septuagint), believed in the God of Israel, and tried to conduct their lives according to the moral commandments of the Old Testament and some of the ritual commandments, too. (Primarily one would think of the laws of ritual purity.) Very likely they took part in the main festivals of the synagogue community.[22]

---

[20]"C'est là un phénomène beaucoup plus nuancé encore et plus complexe que le judéo-christianisme vulgaire; plus diffus aussi et moins défini, puisqu'il représente, non pas une secte en marge de l'Église, mais simplement une tendance dans l'Église, une direction imprimée au christianisme ecclésiastique par certains milieux" (*Verus Israel*, p. 357).

[21]The quote in the former note continues: "Sa répartition géographique suffrait à établir, comme sa cause essentielle, le contact direct de la Synagogue." Cf. his precisions of this thesis on pp. 382-88.

[22]A lot has been written in recent years concerning the so-called God-fearers; some of it has been referred to in the early chapters of this book. For the reader's convenience, I repeat some of the entries here: B. Lifshitz, "Du Nouveau sur les 'Sympathisants," *Journal for the Study of Judaism* 1 (1970): 77-84; Folker Siegert, "Gottesfürchtige und Sympathisanten," *Journal for the Study of Judaism* 4 (1973): 109-64; M. Wilcox, "The 'God-Fearers' in Acts: A Reconsideration," *Journal for the Study of the New Testament* 13 (1981): 102-22; T. M. Finn, "The God-Fearers Reconsidered," *The Catholic Biblical Quarterly* 47 (1985): 74-85; Louis H. Feldman, "The Omnipresence of the God-Fearers," *Biblical Archaeology Review* 12, no. 5 (1986): 58-69; J. G. Gager, "Jews, Gentiles, and Synagogues in the Book of Acts," *Harvard Theological Review* 79 (1986): 91-99; Shaye J. D. Cohen, "Respect for Judaism by Gentiles According to Josephus," *Harvard Theological Review* 80 (1987): 409-30; J. A. Overman, "The God-Fearers: Some Neglected Features," *Journal for the Study of the New Testament* 32 (1988):

What would these Gentiles be called by their pagan neighbors? One obvious way of describing them would be to say that they were *ioudaizontes*, Judaizers, philo-Semites.[23]

Now if Christian mission was particularly successful among such people, these converts to Christianity would have been philo-Semites before they became Christians. Would their conversion to Christianity suddenly make them anti-Semites? Well, if our sources do not misrepresent the situation too much, their local Christian leader would do his best to turn them away from Judaism and their Jewish friends, but would he always succeed? From Ignatius to Chrysostom we have a cloud of witnesses saying no.[24]

This would explain the grassroots character of this movement and the female majority (which was characteristic of the God-fearer group).[25] This would explain the active involvement with Jewish festivals, Jewish calendar, *kashrut* regulations, trust in the rabbinical courts, etc. In short, the explanation we propose for the phenomenon of Christian Judaizers is not that some Christians became Judaizers but that many Judaizers became Christians.[26]

17-26; Shaye J. D. Cohen, "Crossing the Boundary and Becoming a Jew," *Harvard Theological Review* 82 (1989): 13-33. Cf. also the two following notes.

[23]See esp. Stephen G. Wilson, "Gentile Judaizers," *New Testament Studies* 38 (1992): 605-16.

[24]The evidence on Jewish/Christian contact which I mentioned at the end of chapter eleven above—following Daniel Boyarin—would indicate that this grassroots sympathy and socializing was indeed mutual, and this clearly follows from Chrysostom's evidence as well. For a striking archaeological confirmation of this from the Byzantine period in Sardis, see J. S. Crawford, "Multiculturalism at Sardis," *Biblical Archaeology Review* 22, no. 5 (1996): 38-47. Jewish and Christian shopkeepers in the long shopping mall outside the wall of the great synagogue in Sardis seem to have been on remarkably friendly terms and to have made a common front against pagan shopkeepers. The evidence Boyarin adduces to prove the near identity of the two groups is, in my view, better understandable against the background outlined here. I think Boyarin has weakened his case by overstating it. (See his article "Martyrdom and the Making of Christianity and Judaism," *Journal of Early Christian Studies* 6 [1998]: 577-627).

[25]Cf. B. J. Brooten, *Women Leaders in the Ancient Synagogue: Inscriptional Evidence and Background Issues*, Brown Judaic Studies 36 (Chico, Calif.: Scholars Press, 1982); and many other studies.

[26]See the same point of view in Gager, op. cit., p. 112: "it is safe to assume that many Gentile converts (to Christianity) were drawn from those already attracted in some fashion to Judaism. . . . We must reckon with the possibility that the widespread tendency toward Judaizing in early Christian communities arose not only as the result of (Jewish) missionary activity within the Christian movement but also from the experience of Gentile converts whose familiarity with Judaizing predated their acceptance of Christianity." The same point is also made by Stephen G. Wilson with regard to the Judaizers in Ignatius (*To the Philadelphians* and *To the Magnesians*): "Who then would these [Christian Judaizers] have been? Most obviously they would have been former godfearers or sympathizers, who had been attached to the synagogue, had now joined the Church, and had brought

In conclusion, we should notice the date of Chrysostom's evidence for this lively Christian-Jewish contact: the late 380s, sixty years after the anti-Jewish measures of Nicaea in the Passover/Easter question; sixty years after Constantine's embrace of Christianity and the beginning of anti-Jewish legislation by the Christian empire. Obviously this must mean that on the grassroots level there was no absolute break and total separation or isolation between Christians and Jews even in the post-Constantinian era. In an important study on the fifth-century bishop Cyril of Alexandria, Robert L. Wilken has made the important point that Jewish-Christian contact, debate and dialogue never really ceased, but continued to take place, and also continued to occupy the minds of church leaders, perhaps more than they cared to admit.[27] As late as in Cyril, Wilken discovers a genuine controversy with Judaism as a living community of faith.

Postscript: No End

The Constantinian/post-Constantinian era presents an intriguing ambiguity with regard to the Jewish-Christian relationship and Christianity's awareness of its "Jewish connection." We see an ecclesiastical and a political leadership bent on keeping things apart, separating Christians from Jews in a clear-cut way—and there are indications that leaders among the Jews were very much concerned with the same thing. We should not, I believe, take this to mean that on a grassroots level there was no distinction between Jews and Christians, and that this distinction was more or less an ideological construct created or maintained by the respective leadership on each side. No ecclesiastical writer, to my knowledge, blames fellow Christians for allowing Jews to take part in Christian worship, not to speak of the Eucharist. So it probably did not happen, which means that there were, in practice, some clear boundaries.

What we do find clearly attested in the sources available to us is a surprisingly high degree of mutual socializing and a mutual attitude of sympathy and friendliness among part of the grassroots constituency in both communities. I think we should not put it stronger than this; we have no proof positive that these attitudes were at any period the majority position among Christians, nor among Jews.

---

with them the predilections of their former existence. Their judaizing was not therefore something new but merely an extension of their past practice" ("Gentile Judaizers," pp. 608-9).

[27]Wilken, *Judaism;* see esp. the introductory essay, "Jewish-Christian Relations in the Roman Empire," pp. 9-38.

What about the continuation of the story? In ninth-century France, we find the strongly anti-Jewish bishop Agobard of Lyons. In his writings we get the feeling he saw himself as almost isolated with his attitudes, in a sea of Christian philo-Semitism, extending all the way up to the royal house and court.[28] In the early and high Middle Ages we encounter Christian scholars who were in close scholarly dialogue with Jewish scholars.[29] One of the greatest interpreters of Scripture among the medieval scholastics, Andrew of St. Victor (+ 1175), spent much time in studying and conversing with Jewish exegetes—so much that the marked Jewishness of his exegesis surprised his contemporaries as well as modern scholars.[30] Examples like this do not diminish during the Renaissance and later. Rather they multiply.[31]

The sad story of Christian anti-Judaism is well known and well documented. But there was, at many times and often in unexpected places, an undercurrent flowing in the opposite direction. Again, we should not exaggerate its strength. But we should not underestimate it, either.

For Christians who, at the beginning of the twenty-first century, feel excitement and fascination at rediscovering the Jewish roots of their own faith and practice, it should be of some significance that they are not the first Christians to do so. There were precursors. Let us hope there will also be successors.

Suggestions for Further Reading

The primary sources for the Diocletian persecution and the Constantinian revolution are to be found in Eusebius and Lactantius: Eusebius, *Ecclesiastical History*, books 8-10; *Life of Constantine* with the *Oration* (the latter two in English translation in *NPNF* 2nd ser. 1:481-610). Lactantius, *On the Death of the Persecutors* (English translation in *ANF* 7:301-22). A very full selection of sources in German translation is contained in V. Keil, *Quellensammlung zur Religionspolitik Konstantins des Grossen*, Texte zur Forschung 54 (Darmstadt: Wissenschaftliche Buchgesellschaft, 1989). Cf. also the translated sources in Frend, *New Eusebius*, pp. 269-89, 297-372.

---

[28]Cf. Rengstorf/Kortzfleisch, *Kirche und Synagoge*, pp. 109-11; Schreckenberg 1:491-99.

[29]Cf. as an example Marianne Awerbuch, *Christlich-jüdische Begegnung im Zeitalter der Frühscholastik*, Abhandlungen zum christlich-jüdischen Dialog 8 (Munich: Chr. Kaiser Verlag, 1980).

[30]Cf. Beryl Smalley, *The Study of the Bible in the Middle Ages* (Notre Dame, Ind.: University of Notre Dame Press, 1964), pp. 112-85; Rainer Berndt, "Andrew of St. Victor," in *Hebrew Bible/Old Testament: The History of Its Interpretation*, ed. Magne Sæbø, vol. 1: *From the Beginnings to the Middle Ages (Until 1300)*, part 2: *The Middle Ages* (Göttingen: Vandenhoeck & Ruprecht, 2000), pp. 479-84.

[31]For a general survey, see Alan Edelstein, *An Unacknowledged Harmony: Philo-Semitism and the Survival of European Jewry*, Contributions in Ethnic Studies 4 (Westport, Conn./London: Greenwood, 1982).

One of the best surveys of the persecution and the Constantinian revolution from a perspective close to the one adopted in this book is Frend, *Martyrdom and Persecution,* pp. 477-568.

Other important studies:

A. H. M. Jones, *Constantine and the Conversion of Europe* (Harmondsworth: Pelican Books, 1972 [or reprints]).

Gerhard Ruhbach, ed., *Die Kirche angesichts der konstantinischen Wende,* Wege der Forschung 306 (Darmstadt: Wissenschaftliche Buchgesellschaft, 1976).

Alistair Kee, *Constantine Versus Christ: The Triumph of Ideology* (London: SCM Press, 1982).

Specifically on the consequences of the Constantinian revolution for Jewish/Christian relations, see Parkes, *Conflict,* pp. 157-60; and Simon, *Verus Israel,* pp. 155-62.

See also A. M. Rabello, "The Legal Conditions of the Jews in the Roman Empire," in Haase, *Aufstieg* 2 13 (1980), pp. 662-762.

On Christian-Jewish relations in the Constantinian era and on Christian philo-Semitism, see Wolfram Kinzig, "'Non-Separation': Closeness and Co-Operation between Jews and Christians in the Fourth Century," *Vigiliae Christianae* 45 (1991): 27-53; idem, "Philosemitismus. Teil 1: Zur Geschichte des Begriffs," and "Philosemitismus. Teil 2: Zur historiographischen Verwendung des Begriffs," *Zeitschrift für Kirchengeschichte* 105 (1994): 202-28, 361-83. Of a more general nature are the following: Wilken, *Judaism* (1971); Wayne A. Meeks and Robert L. Wilken, *Jews and Christians in Antioch in the First Four Centuries of the Common Era,* Society of Biblical Literature: Sources for Biblical Study 13 (Ann Arbor, Mich.: Scholars Press, 1978), pp. 25-52; Oskar Skarsaune, "The Neglected Story of Christian Philo-Semitism in Antiquity and the Early Middle Ages," *Mishkan* Issue 21, no. 2 (1994): 40-51.

Professor Oskar Skarsaune, the author of this book, is leading a major ongoing research project called The History of Jewish Believers in Jesus from Antiquity to the Present. As part of the project's research on the modern era, there is interest in coming in contact with church members who have a Jewish background, whether or not they identify themselves as Jews.

For more information please contact:

Caspari Research Project
P.O. Box 280
Cross Plains, TN 37049
USA
Phone/fax: 615.654.4682
Toll-free (in USA): 877.876.2580
E-mail: *research@casparicenter.org*
Website: www.casparicenter.org

Index of Modern Authors

Index of Subjects

Index of Ancient Writings